Writing for Change

A Community Reader

WRITING
FOR
CHANGE

A Community Reader

Ann Watters
Stanford University

Marjorie Ford
Stanford University

McGRAW-HILL, INC.

New York   St. Louis   San Francisco   Auckland   Bogotá   Caracas
Lisbon   London   Madrid   Mexico City   Milan   Montreal
New Delhi   San Juan   Singapore   Sydney   Tokyo   Toronto

This book was set in Palatino by ComCom, Inc.
The editors were Tim Julet and Scott Amerman;
the production supervisor was Paula Keller.
The cover was designed by Rafael Hernandez.
R. R. Donnelley & Sons Company was printer and binder.

Cover photo: America Hurrah, NYC

WRITING FOR CHANGE
A Community Reader

Acknowledgments appear on pages 452–454, and on this page by reference.

This book is printed on acid-free paper.

2 3 4 5 6 7 8 9 0 DOC DOC 9 0 9 8 7 6 5

ISBN 0-07-068615-7

Library of Congress Cataloging-in-Publication Data

Watters, Ann.
    Writing for change: a community reader / Ann Watters, Marjorie Ford.
        p.   cm.
    ISBN 0-07-068615-7
    1. College readers.   2. Community life—Problems, exercises, etc.
3. English language—Rhetoric.   4. Readers—Social sciences.
5. Readers—Community life.   I. Ford, Marjorie (Marjorie A.)
II. Title.
PE1417.W29   1995
808'.0427—dc20   94-22116

About the Authors

ANN WATTERS is a lecturer in English at Stanford University. She has directed the Program in Writing and Critical Thinking at Stanford and co-developed and co-directed the Community Service Writing Project. She has co-authored *Coming from Home* (1993) with Marjorie and Jon Ford and *Creating America: Reading and Writing Arguments* (1995) with Joyce Penn Moser. She also authored a forthcoming interactive CD-Rom multimedia program for teaching rhetoric.

MARJORIE FORD is a lecturer in English at Stanford University where she teaches in the Program in Writing and Critical Thinking and edits the program's newsletter, *Notes in the Margins.* With Jon Ford she has written and edited *Dreams and Inward Journeys* (1990 and 1994), *Writing as Revelation* (1992), and *Imagining Worlds* (1995). With Jon Ford and Ann Watters she has written and edited *Coming from Home* (1993).

Writing for Change: A Community Reader and *Guide for Change: Resources for Implementing Community Service Writing* were developed out of their experiences working in the Community Service Writing Project which is jointly run by the Writing and Critical Thinking Program and the Haas Center for Public Service at Stanford University.

Contents

3   Education and Community   139

4   Social and Economic Struggles in the Community   206

5 Health and Community   303

6 Nature and Community   379

Preface for Instructors

We all live in communities. As citizens we have an interest in addressing those social problems that undermine the well-being of our communities: homelessness, health care, family policy, educational reform, and environmental protection. As a nation, and as individual citizens, we need to inform ourselves and to think critically about these issues. In our families, our schools, in the work place—at political forums, social groups, religious congregations— we make decisions that help to shape and define our lives. *Writing for Change: A Community Reader* has been designed to inform students and to help them reflect on the issues that they face as members of their communities.

Writing for Change: A Community Reader is appropriate for first-year and advanced courses in composition. Instructors can use this text as an issues-oriented reader that provides thoughtful readings on community. Chapter themes include "Family and Community", "The Individual and the Community", "Education and Community", "Social and Economic Struggles in the Community", "Health and Community", and "Nature and Community." *Writing for Change* offers both traditional and innovative writing assignments. Each chapter includes a range of choices, from reflective, personal essays, to argumentative essays, to research projects that take students to the library and off campus into their communities.

These assignments enable students to develop their skills by writing not only for classroom audiences, but also for communities beyond the classroom. Such writing assignments might include letters to the editor of the school newspaper, articles and informational brochures, grant proposals, interviews, press releases, or fact sheets for local community groups or schools. *Writing for Change: A Community Reader* can be used in a number of different ways. The book can serve as an issues-oriented reader. Instructors may ask students to write expository or argumentative essays on social issues or to develop journal entries that connect the readings with situations in their own lives or their communities. For those students already engaged in community work, asking them to keep a writing journal will provide them with a place to reflect on the connections between their community experiences and their readings for the course. Instructors who want to develop a course with more emphasis on community-based work or community service writing may want to look at the companion text, *A Guide for Change.* This text provides worksheets that outline the practical and pedagogical issues that will arise as students complete community service writing projects. Examples of community service writing projects produced collaboratively by students are also included.

COMMUNITIES OF WRITERS

Writing about community issues in nonacademic as well as academic contexts is radical in the true sense of the word: students are returning to the roots of the discipline and to the practical concerns of Aristotle and Quintilian. Like the classical rhetoricians, students undertake writing to effect change, writing to move, writing to carry on in day to day living—if not in the courtroom and the political arena, then in modern public forums for discussing local and global concerns of contemporary society. Our approach emphasizes the role of the writer working in the context of the community, trying to convey information and viewpoints not only clearly and concisely but also responsibly.

In the academic world students take courses in different disciplinary communities: for example, in physics class, they learn the language of physicists and the issues important to physicists; in sociology courses, they learn the concerns, the approaches, and the language of social scientists. One of our goals in designing *Writing for Change: A Community Reader* was to extend the Writing across the Curriculum approach to the next logical step: enabling students to write well for diverse communities not only within, but also beyond the academy.

PREPARATION FOR OTHER ACADEMIC SUBJECTS

A key concern in integrating writing for community audiences is the degree to which it prepares students for writing in other academic subjects. Many instructors, students, and administrators see the first-year composition course as one that primarily trains students to write academic papers. Yet, as many have observed, college is short, and life is long. Students need to learn strategies that will serve them in both in the academic and nonacademic worlds. And surely there is little conflict of interest; "real-world" writing assignments require the use of processes, modes, and strategies of writing that are fundamental in academic papers and traditional composition classrooms: observing, gathering information, interviewing, summarizing, reporting, narrating, analyzing, explaining, and arguing to persuade. In contrast to the classroom research assignment that often relies primarily on library research, community service writing projects frequently involve reflection, analysis, and integration of information from diverse sources, including interviews from professional speakers and average citizens as well as library sources. *Writing for Change: A Community Reader* encourages students to increase their awareness of context, audience, and research to a greater degree than many traditional academic essay assignments require.

ACKNOWLEDGMENTS

In shaping and developing a book that takes an innovative approach to writing and writing instruction, we relied on the insight and support of dedicated friends and colleagues. They include our associates at the Haas Center for Public Service at Stanford University, Tim Stanton and Janet Luce, whose energy and vision sparked the Community Service Writing Project. Numerous other Haas Center staff members also provided support for the project from its inception to its completion. Deans Tom Wasow and Al Camarillo have supported us with words and deeds, as have our chair and directors, Ron Rebholz, Charles Fifer, and Kenneth Fields.

Faculty and other friends of the project who gave us encouragement and excellent advice include Shirley Brice Heath, Edward Zlotkowski, Kay Butler-Nalin, Steven Pensinger, and Keith Morton. We also thank those who provided excellent materials or suggestions that have been incorporated into the texts: Jeremy Cohen, Joyce Speiller-Morris, Patricia O'Connor, Susan Wyle, Richard Holeton, Jon Ford, Carolyn Ross, Carolyn Keen, Nadinne Cruz, David Londow and Fleda Mask Jackson. At McGraw-Hill Lesley Denton, Scott Amerman, Phil Butcher, and Tim Julet made important contributions to the project to help see it through to publication.

We thank colleagues at the Conference on College Composition and Communication (CCCC), the National Society for Experiential Education (NSEE), the University of California at Berkeley (Donald McQuade, Lauren Muller), San Jose State University (Hans Guth and Gabrielle Rico), and the University of Miami for enabling us to present papers on community service writing at their conferences or campuses. Our thanks also go to Campus Compact, Campus Outreach Opportunity League, the Invisible College, and the Johnson Foundation for their guidance and leadership in service learning.

Our reviewers gave us thorough and useful feedback throughout the project; we want to thank Liz Buckley, East Texas State University; Robin Calitri, Merced College; Walter Cannon, Central College; Lynn Coddington, University of California–Berkeley; Kirk Combe, Denison University; Virginia Heringer, Pasadena City College; Joyce Speiller Morris, University of Miami; Kay Butler Nalin, University of Northern Iowa; Sarah Hope Parameter; Madeleine

Picciotto, Spellman College; Alan Powers, Bristol Community College; Jeff Sommers, Miami University; and Edward Zlotkowski, Bentley College.

Special thanks go to our students who learned with us and helped us to shape and develop both the text and the community service writing project. Much of their work is included in this book; many more outstanding pieces of writing continue to inform and enlighten the students' academic and neighborhood communities.

Finally we thank our friends and families who formed a sustaining community with us and around us as we wrote and rewrote, shaped and edited, the many drafts of *Writing for Change: A Community Reader.*

Ann Watters
Marjorie Ford

Introduction for Students

YOUR ROLE: WRITING FOR CHANGE

As a writer you have a double identity, a dual role: you write for yourself and you write for an audience. This double identity is at the core of many writing issues. Writing begins as a personal act. Because we think about what we are writing, because we try to express our observations, thoughts, and feelings through our words, we feel closely connected to what we write. At the same time, we strive to communicate clearly to our readers, to our audience. *Writing for Change* is designed to help you write for academic and public communities. Through writing, individuals can share and argue for what they believe in and can involve others in the issues that are important to them, both as private individuals and as members of a community.

Writing for Change encourages you to understand your thoughts and feelings through class discussion, through writing about the readings, and through sharing what you have written with your classmates. Your writing process may begin with an inner struggle to express what you feel and think. Then you will need to work on revising, clarifying, and shaping your ideas, selecting the most accurate and expressive words, composing clear sentences, developing paragraphs with clear examples, and using effective organizational strategies to communicate and to persuade. Relying on your friends and classmates for feedback will become an essential part of your writing process. As you share your writing and develop dialogues with the other students in your class, a community of writers will begin to form. You will find that the feedback from your peers and your instructor helps you to shape, clarify, and refine your ideas. You will begin to understand more fully the importance of expressing your ideas in a way that reflects an awareness of your audience's interests and background knowledge of your topic.

Your writing may touch only a handful of your friends or those in your classroom. Your words may speak to members of your community, or they may move many people to make serious changes in their values and their attitudes towards others. The words of Martin Luther King, Jr.'s "I Have A Dream" speech, delivered in 1963 at the Lincoln Memorial in Washington, DC, to an audience of 250,000 people, changed the world irrevocably:

> [N]ow is the time to make real the promises of democracy; now is the time to rise from the dark and desolate valley of segregation to the sunlit path of racial injustice to the solid rock of brotherhood; now is the time to make justice a reality for all of God's children.

Expressing your thoughts and feelings clearly, communicating your point of view to your audience, will bring you many rewards. You will begin to feel a sense of connection or community with those to whom you write, and to realize that your words can make a difference. Writing that asks others to listen and offers meaningful information, an intelligent analysis, or a practical solution can effect real change. Writing for change will empower you and have an impact on the community for whom you write. Words can be tokens, messengers, calls to action, or battle cries; they can be special gifts or songs.

THE THEMES THAT BIND: A COMMUNITY READER

A community can be thought of as a group of people with something in common, something that binds them together: a common history, culture, interest, activity, need, or goal. As you are forming a writer's community in your classroom through sharing your writing, the thematic structure of this text will help you to develop a better understanding of the relationships you have as an individual with the many communities to which you belong. At its best, a community can provide you with the motivation to change and to grow, and the support to rethink your plans and goals when they don't work as well as you had hoped. It is also important to develop a sense of allegiance to your community and work to help the community maintain itself and prosper.

Because we cannot always rely solely on ourselves or on our families for support, we need to turn to a variety of groups and communities. Family, neighborhood, workplace, college classes, social groups, special interest groups, political groups, religious groups—all of these communities help you to shape your identity. Each of the six chapters in *Writing For Change: A Community Reader* explores a different aspect of your relationship as an individual with the larger communities to which you belong. The chapters may also introduce you to new issues of community. The selections in Chapter 1, "Family and Community," present different ways that individuals come to define themselves and their needs as individuals and as members of their first communities, their families. Chapter 2, "The Individual and the Community," provides historical, theoretical, and personal perspectives on the reasons why individuals form, benefit from, and help to sustain their communities as they shape their self-concepts and goals. The chapter presents definitions of democracy, community, and altruism, as well as personal responses to these definitions. The selections in "Education and Community," Chapter 3, explore the challenges that today's educators must face and overcome if they are to shape educational curricula that address the changing needs and interests of today's students and their communities. While some of the chapter selections advocate programs that educate individuals through integrating theoretical knowledge and practical experience—through observing, studying, understanding, and serving their communities—other selections call for a return to a standardized academic curriculum.

Chapter 4, "Economic and Social Struggles in the Community," examines issues that less privileged groups of individuals—working-class people, women, ethnic and religious minorities—struggle with in the hopes of making better lives for themselves within their communities. The selections in "Health and Community," Chapter 5, present a range of health issues that are influenced by community values, including the decentralization of health care, changing medical ethics, the role that community support plays in the healing process, and the AIDS crisis. Finally, Chapter 6, "Nature and Community," looks at the natural world as an extension of our human community. From a variety of perspectives—political, social, personal and ethical—the writers selected for this chapter come to similar conclusions: if we can observe, reflect upon, and respect the integrity of our natural world, our human communities will function in a healthier and saner way.

THE RANGE OF READINGS

Each of the chapters includes both professional and student writing. While the majority of the selections are essays, stories and poems were also chosen. Many of you will discover that your essay writing will improve through reading a variety of texts; you may want to use a particular essay as a model or you may think that the readings are interesting because of the issues, feelings, and even paradoxes that they present. Our students frequently find themselves identifying with the characters and emotions expressed in stories and poems; we hope that the literature selected will speak to you.

The student writing included in *Writing for Change* takes the form of essays, poetry, and research papers. In addition, each of the chapters features a community service writing project that was completed by students who worked with one another and with a supervisor at a nonprofit community agency. The included projects provide you with examples of types of writing that can be completed for agencies in your community: brochures, newsletters, public service announcements, fact sheets, and researched reports. Many of our students have shared their enthusiasm about working on these projects. Jeremy Taylor, whose essay appears in Chapter 3, has explained why his project became a meaningful learning experience: "This project introduced me to people, to ideas, and to situations that I would not have experienced in the classroom. It illustrated that I am able to reach out to people through my writing." As Taylor suggests, a community service writing project can create a bridge between two communities: the academic world and the "real world."

THE RANGE OF THINKING AND WRITING ASSIGNMENTS

Journal Topics

Each reading is introduced by a journal topic. Approach these topics with an open mind; write down what you think; try to capture your thought process as you write. Don't censor what you write, worry about your spelling, or force yourself to write in a particular form—just write down what comes into your mind as you respond immediately to the topic. If you write in your journal on a regular schedule, your writing will improve. Writing without the anxiety of thinking that your teacher will be reading and grading what you have written may help you to better understand yourself and your unique way of expressing ideas.

Questions for Discussion

Following each selection are six questions for discussion. We suggest that you think about these questions right after you have finished reading the selection. Jot down any answers that come to your mind and skim the selection to see if that helps you to formulate answers. If you are stumped by some of the questions, don't worry; you will get a chance to discuss these selections with the other students in your class. Also remember to write down questions that you have about the selection. Take these questions to share with your discussion group. The more questions you ask yourself about any selection that you read, the more likely you are to become engaged in understanding what you are reading. Our questions were designed to help you think about thematic issues, organizational strategies, and ways that the writer was conscious of engaging his or her audience. Some of the questions encourage you to think about how the selection you are reading is related to another selection in the chapter.

Ideas for Writing

These topics offer a variety of writing assignments for short and more developed papers. Some ask you to respond personally or creatively, while others ask you to write an analysis or a comparison. You will also find argumentative topics, and other subjects that will involve you in library research or in interviews with members of your community.

Chapter Writing Projects

These assignments provide you with ideas for connecting the subthemes that are interwoven into each chapter and encourage you to do library research, to write book or movie reviews, or to do field research or writing for a community agency. Further writing suggestions and specific information on how to complete community service writing projects are included in *A Guide for Change,* which we have developed to accompany this text.

We hope that as you read and write your way through *Writing for Change,* you will come to understand that writers can help to bring about significant change in their communities. Writing for change is a realistic form of social action that involves research, reflection, and personal commitment. We encourage you to give yourself a chance to write and to let your voice be heard.

Ann Watters
Marjorie Ford

Writing for Change

A Community Reader

CHAPTER 1

Family and Community

It takes a village to raise a child.

—African Proverb

So it was decided that Ultima should come and live with us. I knew that my father and mother did good by providing a home for Ultima. It was the custom to provide for the old and the sick. There was always room in the safety and warmth of la familia for one more person, be that person a stranger or a friend.

—Rudolfo A. Anaya, from *Bless Me, Ultima*

The legacies that parents and church and teachers left to my generation of Black children were priceless but not material: a living faith reflected in daily service, the discipline of hard work and stick-to-it-ness, and a capacity to struggle in the face of adversity.

—Marian Wright Edelman, "A Family Legacy"

The bridge between the self and the other, the family, first protects us from and then connects us to the outside world. Many different types of families and family structures have existed over time and continue to flourish as each culture values family and community in unique ways. Early Native American communities revolved around kinship patterns and tribal or clan associations; some still do, from Hawaiian and Inuit or Eskimo groups to American Indians who strive to recapture their traditions, to immigrant families with multi-generational homes and businesses.

While we traditionally define family through genetic heritage, many contemporary families are recreated through divorce and remarriage or through domestic partnerships. In addition, sometimes we create other kinds of families through organizations, friends, through neighborhoods, schools, residence halls, the workplace. We seek to be nurtured, sustained, and supported through our biological or created families.

Traditional extended clans and contemporary American families have banded together not only for companionship, but for survival. Survival today is often cast in economic struggles, with multiple members of a family working to contribute to the common good. In spite of their best efforts, families confronting economic and social pressures may need the support of the greater community's resources. In some cases the community can provide for its families, sometimes to the point of serving as advocate for its most vulnerable citizens, children, in disputes within families. While the lessening and sometimes complete breakdown of family connections puts increasing stress on the community, when families and individual members work together for common goals the community can grow stronger and more effective. With this belief, members of communities wrestle with the issues and problems of family welfare, trying to represent the state's interest in supporting individuals without undermining the family as a social unit.

This chapter explores both the values sustained by families and the public's interest in the family; the readings look at the family as a resource for communities and the community as a resource for family. While the readings discuss some different ways in which the family and society can provide mutual support, the chapter focuses on a fundamental question: To what degree can, or should, the community serve as a type of clan or extended family? The proverb that begins the chapter presents the tradition of an extended community and its role in helping children to develop and grow. In the quote from Rudolfo Anaya's story, the young narrator asserts the values about family and community he has learned at home and among his people. Marian Wright Edelman notes, as well, the role of the extended family of the community to foster values and beliefs. While such an extended community network may seem more like an idea than an actuality, social scientists, such as Judith Wallerstein, and our own observations, tell us that current economic, social, and other changes take an enormous toll, particularly on children, as we try to find our way as families and communities. They tell us that we need to build stronger families and stronger communities, that the strength of one can bring strength to the other, that our very survival depends on helping one another in communities that provide support—economic, social, and spiritual.

Some social problems might be alleviated, if not resolved, with an increased effort to create or maintain small clans or communities of nuclear and extended families, neighborhood groups, and active citizenry in the local community. The expression "Think globally, act locally" may best be observed by starting small and gradually expanding out to the larger society. We are nurtured in families as children; society at large can begin by supporting those among us who are doing the rewarding yet exhausting and trying job of rearing young children. As the Erdrich story illustrates, this can be a complex task. We can support, as a society, the most vulnerable members until they can care for themselves. We can argue for and support public policies on school, day care, welfare, and other issues that directly affect children. And, on a personal level, we can reflect on our own membership in family systems and do our best to create supportive families and peer groups through which we sustain each other.

In the first selection, "American Horse," Louise Erdrich's rich narrative sketches a family in distress: we see a Native American woman, her son, and her uncle fighting off the police and the social worker who want to take her son away; social workers can be society's watchdogs or guardian angels, depending on one's point of view. Children of the economically well off don't go unscathed either, and Robert Coles's narrative, "Problem Child," shows that wealthy children can be neglected, isolated, and in need of support. Susan, the lonely, poorly parented child of an ambitious father and a drinking mother, does not find the police at the door but finds that she needs psychiatric support and the kinship of other children who are also in therapy.

Marian Wright Edelman's narrative, "A Family Legacy," offers a strong contrast to Susan's isolation. Edelman praises the ethics, the values, with which not only her family, but also her church, school, and local community instill in the community's young people, captured in the phrase, "Service is the rent we pay for living." Rudolfo Anaya's fictional narrative, the first chapter of his novel *Bless Me, Ultima*, describes the family's role, in turn, in supporting other members of the community, stranger or friend. Some community efforts to support young people of the community, especially those in difficult social circumstances, are discussed in Shirley Brice Heath's and Milbrey McLaughlin's article "Community Organizations as Family." The two educators studied successful and unsuccessful community programs designed to support young people; they offer several conclusions about developing sound programs that can provide positive activities for young people, such as the popular "midnight basketball" programs being developed in a number of cities.

The next two selections weave together different vignettes to create an image of community. In "Silent Dancing," Judith Ortiz Cofer writes of the enclave of her childhood and of the conflicts inherent in her family's assimilation into mainstream American culture. Nora Cain's cluster of poems, "A Treasury of Quilts," creates stories within quilts and within poems. Cain's poems bring to mind some of the created social communities of the past as well. Quilting and other home crafts not only filled vital needs for the family; they were often an important social activity for rural women; like the barn-raising, quilting bees were communal efforts; like the AIDS memorial quilt today, quilting brings together a rich variety of materials and many hands to form the whole work.

We then turn to a recent look at family issues in James Q. Wilson's essay, "The Family Values Debate." Wilson provides a conservative view and questions the arguments of those who suggest that alternatives to the two-parent family are as good as, or perhaps even have more to offer than, the traditional nuclear family. Students will find it useful to examine both Wilson's claims and those of the scholars and politicians whom he cites.

Another call for community support comes from student writer Richard Stolz, who explores ways that violence in the home can be decreased in his essay "Domestic Violence: Confronting Myths of Masculinity." Stolz looks not only at issues within the family, but also at the ways in which society contributes to this problem and can help to provide solutions. Our last Chapter 1 selection is a collaborative project by three students, Sue Becker, Bonnie Kimmel, and Alaine Murdock. Working for an organization called WATCH, Women and Their Children's Housing, the students brainstormed together and then crafted a series of public service announcements for radio. The announcements were written to inform the public about the extent of domestic violence and opportunities for support services.

In this chapter and in those that follow, we invite you to use these readings to begin discussions of the issues and to reach beyond the texts to make connections with other readers and writers both within your college community and into the "real-world" communities that define your neighborhoods and political lives. As families link the individual and the greater community, so should these readings connect readers with ideas, with issues, with reflections on family and the community.

American Horse

Louise Erdrich

Louise Erdrich (b. 1954), contemporary novelist and poet, part Lakota Indian, is the author of *Love Medicine* (1986), *The Beet Queen* (1986), and *Tracks* (1988), three best-selling novels, as well as two collections of poetry, *Jacklight* (1984) and *Baptism of Desire* (1990). Her most recent work, *The Crown of Columbus* (1991), was written with her husband, Michael Dorris. The following story, first published in 1983, weaves threads of Native American lore about children being spirited away and bewitched with contemporary social struggles in family life.

Journal

In what circumstances do you think children should be removed from their homes? Who should make this decision?

The woman sleeping on the cot in the woodshed was Albertine American Horse. The name was left over from her mother's short marriage. The boy was the son of the man she had loved and let go. Buddy was on the cot too, sitting on the edge because he'd been awake three hours watching out for his mother and besides, she took up the whole cot. Her feet hung over the edge, limp and brown as two trout. Her long arms reached out and slapped at things she saw in her dreams.

Buddy had been knocked awake out of hiding in a washing machine while 2 herds of policemen with dogs searched through a large building with many tiny rooms. When the arm came down, Buddy screamed because it had a blue cuff and sharp silver buttons. "Tss," his mother mumbled, half awake, "wasn't nothing." But Buddy sat up after her breathing went deep again, and he watched.

There was something coming and he knew it.   3

It was coming from very far off but he had a picture of it in his mind. It 4 was a large thing made of metal with many barbed hooks, points, and drag chains on it, something like a giant potato peeler that rolled out of the sky, scraping clouds down with it and jabbing or crushing everything that lay in its path on the ground.

Buddy watched his mother. If he woke her up, she would know what to 5 do about the thing, but he thought he'd wait until he saw it for sure before he shook her. She was pretty, sleeping, and he liked knowing he could look at her as long and close up as he wanted. He took a strand of her hair and held it in his hands as if it was the rein to a delicate beast. She was strong enough and could pull him along like the horse their name was.

Buddy had his mother's and his grandmother's name because his father 6 had been a big mistake.

"They're all mistakes, even your father. But *you* are the best thing that ever 7 happened to me."

8   That was what she said when he asked.

9   Even Kadie, the boyfriend crippled from being in a car wreck, was not as good a thing that had happened to his mother as Buddy was. "He was a medium-sized mistake," she said. "He's hurt and I shouldn't even say that, but it's the truth." At the moment, Buddy knew that being the best thing in his mother's life, he was also the reason they were hiding from the cops.

10   He wanted to touch the satin roses sewed on her pink T-shirt, but he knew he shouldn't do that even in her sleep. If she woke up and found him touching the roses, she would say, "Quit that, Buddy." Sometimes she told him to stop hugging her like a gorilla. She never said that in the mean voice she used when he oppressed her, but when she said that he loosened up anyway.

11   There were times he felt like hugging her so hard and in such a special way that she would say to him, "Let's get married." There were also times he closed his eyes and wished that she would die, only a few times, but still it haunted him that his wish might come true. He and Uncle Lawrence would be left alone. Buddy wasn't worried, though, about his mother getting married to somebody else. She had said to her friend, Madonna, "All men suck," when she thought Buddy wasn't listening. He had made an uncertain sound, and when they heard him they took him in their arms.

12   "Except for you, Buddy," his mother said. "All except for you and maybe Uncle Lawrence, although he's pushing it."

13   "The cops suck the worst, though," Buddy whispered to his mother's sleeping face, "because they're after us." He felt tired again, slumped down, and put his legs beneath the blanket. He closed his eyes and got the feeling that the cot was lifting up beneath him, that it was arching its canvas back and then traveling, traveling very fast and in the wrong direction for when he looked up he saw the three of them were advancing to meet the great metal thing with hooks and barbs and all sorts of sharp equipment to catch their bodies and draw their blood. He heard its insides as it rushed toward them, purring softly like a powerful motor and then they were right in its shadow. He pulled the reins as hard as he could and the beast reared, lifting him. His mother clapped her hand across his mouth.

14   "Okay," she said. "Lay low. They're outside and they're gonna hunt."

15   She touched his shoulder and Buddy leaned over with her to look through a crack in the boards.

16 They were out there all right, Albertine saw them. Two officers and that social worker woman. Vicki Koob. There had been no whistle, no dream, no voice to warn her that they were coming. There was only the crunching sound of cinders in the yard, the engine purring, the dust sifting off their car in a fine light brownish cloud and settling around them.

17   The three people came to a halt in their husk of metal—the car emblazoned with the North Dakota State Highway Patrol emblem which is the glowing profile of the Sioux policeman, Red Tomahawk, the one who killed Sitting Bull. Albertine gave Buddy the blanket and told him that he might have to wrap it around him and hide underneath the cot.

"We're gonna wait and see what they do." She took him in her lap and 18
hunched her arms around him. "Don't you worry," she whispered against his
ear. "Lawrence knows how to fool them."

Buddy didn't want to look at the car and the people. He felt his mother's 19
heart beating beneath his ear so fast it seemed to push the satin roses in and
out. He put his face to them carefully and breathed the deep, soft powdery
woman smell of her. That smell was also in her little face cream bottles, in her
brushes, and around the washbowl after she used it. The satin felt so unbear-
ably smooth against his cheek that he had to press closer. She didn't push him
away, like he expected, but hugged him still tighter until he felt as close as he
had ever been to back inside her again where she said he came from. Within
the smells of her things, her soft skin, and the satin of her roses, he closed his
eyes then, and took his breaths softly and quickly with her heart.

They were out there, but they didn't dare get out of the car yet because of 20
Lawrence's big, ragged dogs. Three of these dogs had loped up the dirt driveway with the car. They were rangy, alert, and bounced up and down on their
cushioned paws like wolves. They didn't waste their energy barking, but posi-
tioned themselves quietly, one at either car door and the third in front of the
bellied-out screen door to Uncle Lawrence's house. It was six in the morning
but the wind was up already, blowing dust, ruffling their short moth-eaten
coats. The big brown one on Vicki Koob's side had unusual black and white
markings, stripes almost, like a hyena and he grinned at her, tongue out and
teeth showing.

"Shoo!" Miss Koob opened her door with a quick jerk. 21

The brown dog sidestepped the door and jumped before her, tiptoeing. Its 22
dirty white muzzle curled and its eyes crossed suddenly as if it was zeroing
its cross-hair sights in on the exact place it would bite her. She ducked back
and slammed the door.

"It's mean," she told Officer Brackett. He was printing out some type of 23
form. The other officer, Harmony, a slow man, had not yet reacted to the car's
halt. He had been sitting quietly in the back seat, but now he rolled down his
window and with no change in expression unsnapped his holster and drew
his pistol out and pointed it at the dog on his side. The dog smacked down
on its belly, wiggled under the car and was out and around the back of the
house before Harmony drew his gun back. The other dogs vanished with him.
From wherever they had disappeared to they began to yap and howl, and the
door to the low shoebox-style house fell open.

"Heya, what's going on?" 24

Uncle Lawrence put his head out the door and opened wide the one eye 25
he had in working order. The eye bulged impossibly wider in outrage when
he saw the police car. But the eyes of the two officers and Miss Vicki Koob
were wide open too because they had never seen Uncle Lawrence in his sleeping get-up or, indeed, witnessed anything like it. For his ribs, which were
cracked from a bad fall and still mending, Uncle Lawrence wore a thick white
corset laced up the front with a striped sneakers' lace. His glass eye and his

set of dentures were still out for the night so his face puckered here and there, around its absences and scars, like a damaged but fierce little cake. Although he had a few gray streaks now, Uncle Lawrence's hair was still thick, and because he wore a special contraption of elastic straps around his head every night, two oiled waves always crested on either side of his middle part. All of this would have been sufficient to astonish, even without the most striking part of his outfit—the smoking jacket. It was made of black satin and hung open around his corset, dragging a tasseled belt. Gold thread dragons struggled up the lapels and blasted their furry red breath around his neck. As Lawrence walked down the steps, he put his arms up in surrender and the gold tassels in the inner seams of his sleeves dropped into view.

26   "My heavens, what a sight." Vicki Koob was impressed.

27   "A character," apologized Officer Harmony.

28   As a tribal police officer who could be counted on to help out the State Patrol, Harmony thought he always had to explain about Indians or get twice as tough to show he did not favor them. He was slow-moving and shy but two jumps ahead of other people all the same, and now, as he watched Uncle Lawrence's splendid approach, he gazed speculatively at the torn and bulging pocket of the smoking jacket. Harmony had been inside Uncle Lawrence's house before and knew that above his draped orange-crate shelf of war medals a blue-black German luger was hung carefully in a net of flat-headed nails and fishing line. Thinking of this deadly exhibition, he got out of the car and shambled toward Lawrence with a dreamy little smile of welcome on his face. But when he searched Lawrence, he found that the bulging pocket held only the lonesome-looking dentures from Lawrence's empty jaw. They were still dripping denture polish.

29   "I had been cleaning them when you arrived," Uncle Lawrence explained with acid dignity.

30   He took the toothbrush from his other pocket and aimed it like a rifle.

31   "Quit that, you old idiot." Harmony tossed the toothbrush away. "For once you ain't done nothing. We came for your nephew."

32   Lawrence looked at Harmony with a faint air of puzzlement.

33   "Ma Frere, listen," threatened Harmony amiably, "those two white people in the car came to get him for the welfare. They got papers on your nephew that give them the right to take him."

34   "Papers?" Uncle Lawrence puffed out his deeply pitted cheeks. "Let me see them papers."

35   The two of them walked over to Vicki's side of the car and she pulled a copy of the court order from her purse. Lawrence put his teeth back in and adjusted them with busy workings of his jaw.

36   "Just a minute," he reached into his breast pocket as he bent close to Miss Vicki Koob. "I can't read these without I have in my eye."

37   He took the eye from his breast pocket delicately, and as he popped it into his face the social worker's mouth fell open in a consternated O.

38   "What is this," she cried in a little voice.

39   Uncle Lawrence looked at her mildly. The white glass of the eye was cold as lard. The black iris was strangely charged and menacing.

"He's nuts," Bracket huffed along the side of Vicki's neck. "Never mind 40 him."

Vicki's hair had sweated down her nape in tiny corkscrews and some of 41 the hairs were so long and dangly now that they disappeared into the zippered back of her dress. Brackett noticed this as he spoke into her ear. His face grew red and the backs of his hands prickled. He slid under the steering wheel and got out of the car. He walked around the hood to stand with Leo Harmony.

"We could take you in too," said Brackett roughly. Lawrence eyed the offi- 42 cers in what was taken as defiance. "If you don't cooperate, we'll get out the handcuffs," they warned.

One of Lawrence's arms was stiff and would not move until he'd rubbed 43 it with witch hazel in the morning. His other arm worked fine though, and he stuck it out in front of Brackett.

"Get them handcuffs," he urged them. "Put me in a welfare home."   44

Brackett snapped one side of the handcuffs on Lawrence's good arm and 45 the other to the handle of the police car.

"That's to hold you," he said. "We're wasting our time. Harmony, you 46 search that little shed over by the tall grass and Miss Koob and myself will search the house."

"My rights is violated!" Lawrence shrieked suddenly. They ignored him. 47 He tugged at the handcuff and thought of the good heavy file he kept in his tool box and the German luger oiled and ready but never loaded, because of Buddy, over his shelf. He should have used it on these bad ones, even Harmony in his big-time white man job. He wouldn't last long in that job anyway before somebody gave him what for.

"It's a damn scheme," said Uncle Lawrence, rattling his chains against the 48 car. He looked over at the shed and thought maybe Albertine and Buddy had sneaked away before the car pulled into the yard. But he sagged, seeing Albertine move like a shadow within the boards. "Oh, it's all a damn scheme," he muttered again.

"I want to find that boy and salvage him," Vicki Koob explained to Officer 49 Brackett as they walked into the house. "Look at his family life—the old man crazy as a bedbug, the mother intoxicated somewhere."

Brackett nodded, energetic, eager. He was a short hopeful redhead who 50 failed consistently to win the hearts of women. Vicki Koob intrigued him. Now, as he watched, she pulled a tiny pen out of an ornamental clip on her blouse. It was attached to a retractable line that would suck the pen back, like a child eating one strand of spaghetti. Something about the pen on its line excited Brackett to the point of discomfort. His hand shook as he opened the screendoor and stepped in, beckoning Miss Koob to follow.

They could see the house was empty at first glance. It was only one rec- 51 tangular room with whitewashed walls and a little gas stove in the middle. They had already come through the cooking lean-to with the other stove and washstand and rusty old refrigerator. That refrigerator had nothing in it but some wrinkled potatoes and a package of turkey necks. Vicki Koob noted that in her perfect-bound notebook. The beds along the walls of the big room were covered with quilts that Albertine's mother, Sophie, had made from bits of old wool coats and pants that the Sisters sold in bundles at the mission. There was no one hiding beneath the beds. No one was under the little aluminum dinette table covered with a green oilcloth, or the soft brown wood chairs tucked up to it. One wall of the big room was filled with neatly stacked crates of things— old tools and springs and small half-dismantled appliances. Five or six television sets were stacked against the wall. Their control panels spewed colored wires and at least one was cracked all the way across. Only the topmost set, with coathanger antenna angled sensitively to catch the bounding signals around Little Shell, looked like it could possibly work.

52   Not one thing escaped Vicki Koob's trained and cataloguing gaze. She made note of the cupboard that held only commodity flour and coffee. The unsanitary tin oil drum beneath the kitchen window, full of empty surplus pork cans and beer bottles, caught her eye as did Uncle Lawrence's physical and mental deteriorations. She quickly described these "benchmarks of alcoholic dependency within the extended family of Woodrow (Buddy) American Horse" as she walked around the room with the little notebook open, pushed against her belly to steady it. Although Vicki had been there before, Albertine's presence had always made it difficult for her to take notes.

53   "Twice the maximum allowable space between door and threshold," she wrote now. "Probably no insulation. Two three-inch cracks in walls inadequately sealed with whitewashed mud." She made a mental note but could see no point in describing Lawrence's stuffed reclining chair that only reclined, the shadeless lamp with its plastic orchid in the bubble glass base, or the three-dimensional picture of Jesus that Lawrence had once demonstrated to her. When plugged in, lights rolled behind the water the Lord stood on so that he seemed to be strolling although he never actually went forward, of course, but only pushed the glowing waves behind him forever like a poor tame rat in a treadmill.

54   Brackett cleared his throat with a nervous rasp and touched Vicki's shoulder.

55   "What are you writing?"

56   She moved away and continued to scribble as if thoroughly absorbed in her work. "Officer Brackett displays an undue amount of interest in my person," she wrote. "Perhaps?"

57   He snatched playfully at the book, but she hugged it to her chest and moved off smiling. More curls had fallen, wetted to the base of her neck. Looking out the window, she sighed long and loud.

58   "All night on brush rollers for this. What a joke."

59   Brackett shoved his hands in his pockets. His mouth opened slightly, then shut with a small throttled cluck.

60 When Albertine saw Harmony ambling across the yard with his big brown thumbs in his belt, his placid smile, and his tiny black eyes moving back and forth, she put Buddy under the cot. Harmony stopped at the shed and stood quietly. He spread his arms to show her he hadn't drawn his big police gun.

"Ma Cousin," he said in the Michif dialect that people used if they were 61 relatives or sometimes if they needed gas or a couple of dollars, "why don't you come out here and stop this foolishness?"

"I ain't your cousin," Albertine said. Anger boiled up in her suddenly. "I 62 ain't related to no pigs."

She bit her lip and watched him through the cracks, circling, a big tan 63 punching dummy with his boots full of sand so he never stayed down once he fell. He was empty inside, all stale air. But he knew how to get to her so much better than a white cop could. And now he was circling because he wasn't sure she didn't have a weapon, maybe a knife or the German luger that was the only thing that her father, Albert American Horse, had left his wife and daughter besides his name. Harmony knew that Albertine was a tall strong woman who took two big men to subdue when she didn't want to go in the drunk tank. She had hard hips, broad shoulders, and stood tall like her Sioux father, the American Horse who was killed threshing in Belle Prairie.

"I feel bad to have to do this," Harmony said to Albertine. "But for god- 64 sakes, let's nobody get hurt. Come on out with the boy, why don't you? I know you got him in there."

Albertine did not give herself away this time. She let him wonder. Slowly 65 and quietly she pulled her belt through its loops and wrapped it around and around her hand until only the big oval buckle with turquoise chunks shaped into a butterfly stuck out over her knuckles. Harmony was talking but she wasn't listening to what he said. She was listening to the pitch of his voice, the tone of it that would tighten or tremble at a certain moment when he decided to rush the shed. He kept talking slowly and reasonably, flexing the dialect from time to time, even mentioning her father.

"He was a damn good man. I don't care what they say, Albertine, I knew 66 him."

Albertine looked at the stone butterfly that spread its wings across her fist. 67 The wings looked light and cool, not heavy. It almost looked like it was ready to fly. Harmony wanted to get to Albertine through her father but she would not think about American Horse. She concentrated on the sky blue stone.

Yet the shape of the stone, the color, betrayed her. 68

She saw her father suddenly, bending at the grille of their old gray car. 69 She was small then. The memory came from so long ago it seemed like a dream—narrowly focused, snapshot-clear. He was bending by the grille in the sun. It was hot summer. Wings of sweat, dark blue, spread across the back of his work shirt. He always wore soft blue shirts, the color of shade cloudier than this stone. His stiff hair had grown out of its short haircut and flopped over his forehead. When he stood up and turned away from the car, Albertine saw that he had a butterfly.

"It's dead," he told her. "Broke its wings and died on the grille." 70

She must have been five, maybe six, wearing one of the boy's T-shirts 71 Mama bleached in Hilex-water. American Horse took the butterfly, a black and yellow one, and rubbed it on Albertine's collarbone and chest and arms until the color and the powder of it were blended into her skin.

"For grace," he said. 72

73   And Albertine had felt a strange lightening in her arms, in her chest, when he did this and said, "For grace." The way he said it, grace meant everything the butterfly was. The sharp delicate wings. The way it floated over grass. The way its wings seemed to breathe fanning in the sun. The wisdom of the way it blended into flowers or changed into a leaf. In herself she felt the same kind of possibilities and closed her eyes almost in shock or pain, she felt so light and powerful at that moment.

74   Then her father had caught her and thrown her high into the air. She could not remember landing in his arms or landing at all. She only remembered the sun filling her eyes and the world tipping crazily behind her, out of sight.

75   "He was a damn good man," Harmony said again.

76   Albertine heard his starched uniform gathering before his boots hit the ground. Once, twice, three times. It took him four solid jumps to get right where she wanted him. She kicked the plank door open when he reached for the handle and the corner caught him on the jaw. He faltered, and Albertine hit him flat on the chin with the butterfly. She hit him so hard the shock of it went up her arm like a string pulled taut. Her fist opened, numb, and she let the belt unloop before she closed her hand on the tip end of it and sent the stone butterfly swooping out in a wide circle around her as if it was on the end of a leash. Harmony reeled backward as she walked toward him swinging the belt. She expected him to fall but he just stumbled. And then he took the gun from his hip.

77   Albertine let the belt go limp. She and Harmony stood within feet of each other, breathing. Each heard the human sound of air going in and out of the other person's lungs. Each read the face of the other as if deciphering letters carved into softly eroding veins of stone. Albertine saw the pattern of tiny arteries that age, drink, and hard living had blown to the surface of the man's face. She saw the spoked wheels of his iris and the arteries like tangled threads that sewed him up. She saw the living net of springs and tissue that held him together, and trapped him. She saw the random, intimate plan of his person.

78   She took a quick shallow breath and her face went strange and tight. She saw the black veins in the wings of the butterfly, roads burnt into a map, and then she was located somewhere in the net of veins and sinew that was the tragic complexity of the world so she did not see Officer Brackett and Vicki Koob rushing toward her, but felt them instead like flies caught in the same web, rocking it.

79   "Albertine!" Vicki Koob had stopped in the grass. Her voice was shrill and tight. "It's better this way, Albertine. We're going to help you."

80   Albertine straightened, threw her shoulders back. Her father's hand was on her chest and shoulders lightening her wonderfully. Then on wings of her father's hands, on dead butterfly wings, Albertine lifted into the air and flew toward the others. The light powerful feeling swept her up the way she had floated higher, seeing the grass below. It was her father throwing her up into the air and out of danger. Her arms opened for bullets but no bullets came. Harmony did not shoot. Instead, he raised his fist and brought it down hard on her head.

Albertine did not fall immediately, but stood in his arms a moment. Per- 81 haps she gazed still farther back behind the covering of his face. Perhaps she was completely stunned and did not think as she sagged and fell. Her face rolled forward and hair covered her features, so it was impossible for Harmony to see with just what particular expression she gazed into the head-splitting wheel of light, or blackness, that overcame her.

Harmony turned the vehicle onto the gravel road that led back to town. 82 He had convinced the other two that Albertine was more trouble than she was worth, and so they left her behind, and Lawrence too. He stood swearing in his cinder driveway as the car rolled out of sight. Buddy sat between the social worker and Officer Brackett. Vicki tried to hold Buddy fast and keep her arm down at the same time, for the words she'd screamed at Albertine had broken the seal of antiperspirant beneath her arms. She was sweating now as though she'd stored up an ocean inside of her. Sweat rolled down her back in a shallow river and pooled at her waist and between her breasts. A thin sheen of water came out on her forearms, her face. Vicki gave an irritated moan but Brackett seemed not to take notice, or take offense at least. Air-conditioned breezes were sweeping over the seat anyway, and very soon they would be comfortable. She smiled at Brackett over Buddy's head. The man grinned back. Buddy stirred. Vicki remembered the emergency chocolate bar she kept in her purse, fished it out, and offered it to Buddy. He did not react, so she closed his fingers over the package and peeled the paper off one end.

The car accelerated. Buddy felt the road and wheels pummeling each other 83 and the rush of the heavy motor purring in high gear. Buddy knew that what he'd seen in his mind that morning, the thing coming out of the sky with barbs and chains, had hooked him. Somehow he was caught and held in the sour tin smell of the pale woman's armpit. Somehow he was pinned between their pounds of breathless flesh. He looked at the chocolate in his hand. He was squeezing the bar so hard that a thin brown trickle had melted down his arm. Automatically he put the bar in his mouth.

As he bit down he saw his mother very clearly, just as she had been when 84 she carried him from the shed. She was stretched flat on the ground, on her stomach, and her arms were curled around her head as if in sleep. One leg was drawn up and it looked for all the world like she was running full tilt into the ground, as though she had been trying to pass into the earth, to bury herself, but at the last moment something had stopped her.

There was no blood on Albertine, but Buddy tasted blood now at the sight 85 of her, for he bit down hard and cut his own lip. He ate the chocolate, every bit of it, tasting his mother's blood. And when he had the chocolate down inside him and all licked off his hands, he opened his mouth to say thank you to the woman as his mother had taught him. But instead of a thank you coming out he was astonished to hear a great rattling scream, and then another, rip out of him like pieces of his own body and whirl onto the sharp things all around him.

Questions for Discussion

1. What meanings do the images in the opening scene and in Buddy's dream hold for you? In what ways do they shape your perceptions of what is to follow?
2. Study the dialogues. What are Albertine's attitudes toward her family? Toward men? Toward the police? What does Buddy think about her beliefs?
3. As a whole class or in small groups, have different people in the class role-play each character in the story, arguing his or her point of view verbally or in a written dialogue. Then, as time allows, have people switch roles. Do you gain any insights from the experience? Do you view the conflicts in the story any differently?
4. What conflicts between biological community and the larger social communities does the story present? Do you think that there are alternatives to the social worker's approach? Discuss your response.
5. What cultural conflicts does the story suggest? What conflicts about the role of family and its relationship to the community does the story suggest?
6. What future do you foresee for Buddy? For Albertine? For Harmony?

Ideas for Writing

1. "I want to find that boy and salvage him," says the social worker, Vicki Koob. How do you think she envisions Buddy's future? In what ways might her vision reflect a lack of cultural awareness or sensitivity? Why does she feel she must intervene? Explain why you are sympathetic or opposed to her point of view.
2. Assume the role of a case worker and write up a report on Buddy. Include your recommendations for an upcoming custody hearing.
3. In what ways can fiction make a point in a way that case histories or factual accounts may not? For example, analyze the style and tone of the story; consider the multiple points of view within the story as well—the social worker's observation notes compared to other points of view in the story. What does the contrast between fiction and case history suggest about how family problems within the community might be defined and solved?

Privileged Ones: Problem Child

Robert Coles

Robert Martin Coles, writer, educator, psychiatrist, was born in 1929 in Boston, Massachusetts, and was educated at Harvard University (B.A.) and Columbia University (M.D.). He is currently a professor of psychiatry and medical humanities at Harvard University. Winner of many awards, including the Pulitzer Prize and a MacArthur Foundation Fellowship, Coles wrote the landmark multivolume work, *Children of Crisis,* published between 1967 and 1978. Coles is best known for his work exploring the inner, spiritual, and moral world of children. He published *The Political Life of Children* and *The Moral Life of Children* in 1986. Coles currently teaches, among other courses, "The Literature of Social Reflection." His most recent book, *The Call of Service* (1993), was an immediate success.

Journal

What kinds of problems do you imagine children of wealthy families have? If you are well off, what kinds of problems have you had that may not be apparent to others?

Maids brought up the girl from the beginning. Her mother was a mere drinker when pregnant, but a few months after her daughter was born her husband began to use the phrase "heavy drinker" about his wife. The girl's father is himself rather knowing about alcohol. He has slowly worked his way up in corporate management. He started with a Cincinnati department store, moved to a Chicago insurance company, then to Cincinnati again, with Procter & Gamble, then to an Illinois steel company, then out to California, then back East to Virginia, and finally to a New England electronics firm. He is one of a number of vice-presidents—a man who knows how to manage employees, arrange for advertising, keep an eye on all sorts of budgets, conclude arrangements, deal with various contractors, and, not least, get along with other executives like himself. During twelve years of marriage he and his wife have lived in seven cities—the Midwest, the far West, the upper South, and finally, New England. All the while his alcoholic intake has steadily increased. All the while his wife pretended to be abstemious; at times she claimed to be a teetotaler. She never drank in front of him. When she became dizzy, unstable, slurred of speech, he was likely to be away from home. If he was at home, she took to her bed, worried out loud that she had "a strange neurological disease." He said she ought to go see a doctor. But for periods of a week, even a month, she became suddenly better. Then she urged *him* to see a doctor; he drank too much. Yes, he agreed; but he was getting more and more influential, and so had to face constant pressure. One day, he might well get to be president of a company; then he would have to take no one's orders, and would be quite at ease with himself—and so, uninterested in whiskey, gin, beer, wine, brandy. Meanwhile, he drank them all.

His wife drank only vodka, had been doing so most of their marriage— 2 heavily, and most often alone. No one had ever found one of her empty bottles. She prided herself on her control, her guile, her circumspection, her resourcefulness. She was so smart that she even fooled herself; she would drink a lot, complain of severe headaches and unsteadiness, wonder out loud whether she ought call a doctor, suggest to the maid or her husband that she be taken to a hospital for "tests," then mysteriously lose all her symptoms. The pattern, the cycle, the addiction and apparent remission from addiction lasted for years. Meanwhile there were two children who needed a mother and a father—the older child a boy, the younger a girl. The latter was born when the mother's secret drinking was accelerating; was born in the midst of yet another family move; was born on the way to a strange hospital.

When the girl was eight she was able to describe the experience as if she 3 were a grown-up witness to it, rather than an extremely young participant: "We have moved a lot. We have never lived in the same place more than two years. Daddy is going to be the boss in a business one day, but it takes time. He has to go where there's a good job. Each time we move, he gets a better job. I remember the friends I had in California. I don't remember being born, but my mother has told me how it happened. And our maid has heard the story, and if I forget something, she reminds me. Daddy got a better job, so we had to move to Chicago. I wasn't supposed to be born when they were moving. I came early. My mother and father and brother were driving to Chicago. They said good-bye to our house. Halfway to Chicago my mother began to have pain. My father kept telling her she needed to eat, and that was why she had the pain. She doesn't eat very much. The maid will cook us supper, and Mommy says she's not hungry. Then she tells us to eat. A lot of the time I don't feel like eating, either. The doctor gave me pills to take, so I'll grow. He says I may not be getting all the vitamins I need.

4   "When my mother kept saying she hurt in the tummy, my father stopped at a Howard Johnson's. He told my mother she had to eat. My mother ordered fried clams, but she didn't touch them. Then she went to the bathroom. When she came out, she told my father she was in real trouble. He went to find out where the nearest hospital was. She was in pain, and she ordered a drink. Daddy says it was one of the few times he's seen Mommy drink out in the open. They took her to the hospital, and that's when I was born, on the way. That's why I have to say I was born in Indiana, even though my parents never lived there. My mother had to stay in the hospital with me; my father left her and drove to Chicago with my brother. He was only two then; my grandmother came to take care of him, but she was sick, and she had to go into a hospital in Chicago a few days after she got there. Daddy hired a maid. He's the one who usually hires the new maid, if we lose our old one. Mommy says she doesn't want any maid around. But we need one. Without a maid, there would be trouble."

5   The girl is called Susie by her mother, but insists on being addressed as Susan by the maid. When she was seven the maid's name was also Susan; they agreed that young Susan would call the maid Sue. That particular maid was "the best one," according to the girl. On her bureau she has kept a picture of the two of them, taken by the child's father. The maid stayed with the family for a year and a half, and was sorely missed by the girl. When she was nine she remembered that maid fondly: "I liked her the best. She's the only one I liked. We used to take walks. I liked living in that house. I wish we were still there. But we rented it; Daddy doesn't want to buy a house until he knows he'll be staying with the same company for a long time. My mother was sick when Sue was with us, but we didn't know what the illness was. The doctors aren't sure now, either. But they are giving her tests. My brother says it's a mysterious disease. We've heard Mommy and Daddy fight; Daddy blames Mommy for being sick. He says it's her fault. Mommy says that if she is sick, she shouldn't be blamed.

6   "I feel sick a lot. My old maid, Sue, used to hold me on her lap, and she'd make an ice cream soda, and when I had it I'd feel better. My favorite was strawberry. I wish she was back with us. She was going to move with us, but

my mother didn't want her to come, because then she'd be part of the family. It's too bad she didn't. The new maid has a whole suite for her own. She has a bedroom, a sitting room, a little kitchen and a bathroom, and a hall. She has her own steps going upstairs. This is the biggest house we've ever lived in. We own it. We have sixteen rooms, I think. We have nine acres of land. A lot of it is just trees; but Daddy wants to cut some of them down and build a tennis court and a swimming pool. If Sue was with us, she could go swimming next summer. That's when we're going to build our pool, just before it gets hot, so we can swim all during July and August. Sue would have liked our house."

The girl worried her parents when she was four and five; she spent hours 7 with her dolls and their dollhouse, and had scant interest in other children. Her nursery school teachers observed that she had no interest at all in the dolls or dollhouses at school. When the family moved yet again—she was six—Susie abandoned her dolls completely. She went through what her mother described as "a change of personality." The girl, who had been shy, withdrawn, seemingly uninterested in others, became a willful person who was especially interested in outdoor activities. She loved to swing, to run about, and, at seven, to ice-skate. She announced to her mother that she would, one day, become a well-known skater—would make money doing exhibition skating. She had seen a documentary on ice-skating, had dedicated herself to becoming as proficient as possible. She drew a picture, when eight, of herself skating. She was tall, upright, nicely balanced. Her arms were outstretched. She wore a red jacket, a blue hat. Though she usually skated on a pond near her house, or an indoor rink of a private school, she showed herself skating on what looked like a river or highway of ice, lined by fir trees, all under a blazing sun hanging low in a clear, deep blue sky.

She was indulging in a bit of fantasy, as she made clear: "I told my mother 8 this morning that I'd like to skate so fast that people would think I have a motor in each skate, and I'm being pushed by the two engines. I woke up and I was a little scared during the night. I must have been crying, I guess, because my mother came to my room and she asked me what was the matter. I'd had this dream. In the dream I was skating so fast I passed all the automobiles. It was real weird. I was on a road, I think. Maybe it was the Charles River. (My mother said it must have been!) But I was passing all these cars, so I think it could have been a road, and it was icy, and that's how I was able to skate on the road. I remember seeing a church, and some stores, and then all of a sudden I saw our old house, the one we lived in before we moved here, and I think that was when I woke up, and I remember being scared, because just when I saw our old house, the ice melted, I think, and I was afraid I was going to fall in the water and drown. I'm glad I woke up. Dreams can be real funny."

She was an exceptionally active dreamer when seven, eight, nine—to the 9 point that her parents were often unnerved by her accounts of what she had seen and heard and said to herself or others while asleep. They consulted a pediatrician: ought the child be dreaming so much, and be so willing to talk about her dreams, and if not, what was to be done? The doctor reassured them:

some children do indeed have frequent, vivid dreams, and are not shy about remembering them out loud. When Susan was nine she woke up screaming one night. Her father was away on business. Her mother was in a stuporous sleep, and did not hear the child. The maid came, and tried to comfort the sobbing, frightened girl. In the morning the maid told the mother what had happened, but the mother could not, for a long while, convince her daughter to talk about the nightmare. Finally, the mother did learn what had been dreamed, and so did the maid and the father and even some of the dreamer's friends. In a picture done with paints the girl tried to show what she had seen that night. With brown paint she constructed a rather deep hole; then she built a fence around part of the hole; then she placed herself near the fence. That was all there was to the dream—a child climbing up a hole, trying to get out, but not able to do so because a fence blocked her way.

10   With no one's help the girl had figured out what had happened, and why she had been terrified: "I knew that a tornado had just taken place. Once when we were moving, we almost got killed by a tornado. We could see it coming, and my Daddy stopped the car, and we got out and went into a ditch and just lay there and prayed. My father asked God to spare us. My mother said she'd be a better mother if only we'd be spared. My father said he wouldn't make us move ever again. And we were saved! The tornado hopped, skipped, and jumped all over, but it didn't touch us. Then we got in the car and we kept going. My father said we sure were lucky. We passed a lot of houses that had been picked up—just picked up!—by the tornado and dumped someplace else. You could see the cellars of the houses. I think that's what I was remembering in my nightmare. I was in a ditch or something, maybe the cellar of our house, and trying to get out, but there was this big fence, and I couldn't find a way to get through it. And I could hear my mother and father; they were someplace, but I didn't know where, and I couldn't see them. I think my mother was in the ditch too, and she was telling me that it's best to 'stay put'— those are the words she uses a lot, when she wants me to stop being 'antsy.' And my father was someplace else, on the other side of the fence, and he was telling me to hurry up (like he always says) and get out, and climb the fence and come with him. It was confusing. And I was scared, I guess. Then I woke up, and our maid was asking me if I wanted some warm milk, and I said no."

11   In her painting she had neglected to show any of the debris scattered by the tornado, but she had made the sky black, and for years she described that sky to friends. When the family moved one more time (she was ten) her first question was about tornadoes: would there be any "there"? Her next question was about skating rinks: were any nearby? In her fanciful moments she wondered whether she might win prizes as a skater, or get caught, fatefully, on a frozen pond when a tornado struck. Would she be able to skate faster than the tornado? She had been told that tornadoes don't come in the middle of the winter or, for that matter, don't come at all where she now lived. Still, she could not forget them, even as she placed great and continuing store in her ability to skate "as fast as lightning." And when her father boasted of her achievements he too emphasized speed as well as canniness: "Daddy says I

should learn to skate so fast that people will say I'm gone before I start! He says you've got to stay ahead of all the other people, or you'll be in trouble. There's always someone who wants to win the race! Daddy gets up early and he goes to bed late. He says if he doesn't stay ahead, he'll fall way behind, and then we'll all be in trouble. If you keep your eyes open and watch what everyone else is going to do, then you can get yourself all set, and try as hard as you can, and whiz ahead and stay ahead. Daddy says that if you keep yourself ahead, you win."

She was extremely competitive in school. She would cry, in the second and 12 third grades, when she learned that she had made a mistake or two on a paper, whereas classmates she knew had not. In the fourth grade she stated how assertive she felt obliged to be: "My hope is to have a good Christmas. I would like to win the ice-skating contest at the rink. My mother would like me to win, and my father would. He is almost a president of a company. We will not move, if Daddy becomes president. I would like to be a president of a company later, when I'm big. Daddy says I will, if I keep my eye on the ball."

That expression has always been a favorite of her father's and has become 13 one of hers. In the fifth grade—she was ten—Susan tried to explain to a teacher what she meant when she talked about keeping her eyes on the ball; she meant "knowing what's important." She meant "trying not to lose, never forgetting that if you lose, you'll have no friends, but if you win, everyone will want to be nice to you." At about that time she became aware that her mother was "sick" and that her father was not sorry for his wife or compassionate, but rather, quite angry and self-pitying. She began to tell her friends that her mother would stumble, would speak incoherently, would cry inexplicably, would have wild suspicions or come forth with sordid accusations. She began to tell her friends that her father was thinking of sending her mother away to a hospital—though all his wife had to do was "behave herself," the girl pointed out.

When the girl's teachers heard about her "family problems," they decided 14 to intervene, tactfully. One teacher called Susan aside, asked her what was wrong. She said nothing, but immediately contradicted herself, told everything she knew—a tale of a well-to-do family's "troubles." Susan used that word. A week after her eleventh birthday she drew a picture of a house she wanted—for herself and her cat, Lilly, and her books and her beloved skates, and her clock-radio, which she declared her single most important possession. The house was small, rather quaint; it had plants and flowers on a front lawn and on the window sills; it had a thick brown roof, with hay on top—a thatched roof; it had warmth—smoke curling out of the chimney; a storybook house. Nearby was a pond—frozen over, for skating. The sun was large, kindly in its smiling nearness to the land. The trees bent gently toward the house, protectingly. The artist made no effort later to deny the debt she owed to picture books she used to read: "I remember seeing little cottages that belonged to farmers. I think my mother once gave me a book called *The Farm Girl*, and it was the best present I've ever got, because I loved reading about the nice people and their nice little house. For a while I read the book every day! Then my mother wanted to take it away and throw it out, but I wouldn't let her. I hid the book from her! She forgot about it.

15   "She has a lot of troubles. I don't know what's the matter with her. I wish I did. Daddy won't tell me what her troubles are. He says he would like to go away for a week and just be by himself. He's always going on trips, but that's business, and he has to go to a lot of meetings. If I had a place like this house I've just drawn, I'd go there on weekends, after school is over, on Friday. One of our teachers goes away every weekend to a home she has in New Hampshire. I wish I had a home I could go to—besides the one we have here. Daddy says that even if we didn't have to move anymore, he still wouldn't want to stay in this house for the rest of his life. We have the maid, and we have a woman who comes and helps the maid, because the maid can't do everything by herself, and my mother is in bed a lot, or she goes to the doctor, or she has to have a 'rest.' She goes to a 'rest place,' and then she comes back and she promises us that everything will be different, and we're starting a new slate. But then she gets sick again.

16   "If I had a little house like this one in the picture, I would watch my favorite programs and make myself sandwiches, and then I'd go skating, and I'd ride my bike. Maybe I'd make friends; maybe there would be a girl not too far away, and I could skate with her, or ride on my bike with her. But if there wasn't anyone, I wouldn't mind. A lot of days, I leave the house and go on a hike, all by myself. The maid jokes with me; she says that I spend too much time with myself, and I should give other people a chance to be my friends. I have some friends, but we get into fights a lot. One of my friends says she wishes she could skate the way I do. Another friend is good in school, but I got better grades than she did last time. She beat me the time before. We went to camp together last summer. I hated the place. I won't go there again. Daddy said I had to go, because he was going to be away a lot, and my mother has all her troubles. I said I'd go if I could be with my brother, but Daddy said no, we had to be in different camps. So, we went to different camps, and we both had a rotten time.

17   "I cried a lot. When I didn't stop crying, after a week, I guess it was, they called up home. Daddy was away and my mother was in the hospital. I *had* to stay, they told me at camp. I couldn't go home to an empty house. But the maid was there! They let *me* call her up. She said it was all right with her if I came home. But they wouldn't let me, even so. I got up one morning, and I hated everyone in my cabin, and those stupid counselors, and the idiot who ran the camp. That's why I ran away. I decided to leave. The breakfast was awful—more Rice Krispies and hard toast! I just walked to the town, and then I put out my thumb, and a truck driver picked me up. He wanted to know where I was going. I said back toward Boston. He took me as far as Plymouth and let me off. Then I started hitching again; but the state police spotted me, and I was in trouble. They wanted to know where I lived. I told them. They called up, and the maid wasn't home. They took me to a jail. They didn't put me in, though! Finally the maid got home, and they spoke with her, and I guess she told them I was supposed to be in camp. They took me back. I never spoke

to that maid again. I finally convinced my mother, after I got home from camp, to fire her."

That summer was a turning point for Susan. When she came home she 18 was fidgety; she ate less and complained of headaches. She turned twelve in the autumn, and talked openly of running away from home—perhaps to an aunt in Jacksonville, Florida. The girl had always liked her, and had learned to imitate her Southern accent rather well. But Susan did not run away to Florida; she ran into the woods near her parents' home, and camped out there for a day, a night, another day. Her mother and father called the police, of course. Everyone looked everywhere—except in the woods in back of the house. At the beginning of the second night she decided to return home, and did—for an hour or so. She almost went unobserved. The maid saw her as she was leaving for the woods again with a supply of provisions. The girl's parents were, of course, glad to see her; but in no time their thankfulness turned to bitterness and anger. Why had she gone? What is the matter with children like her, who have been given "everything" and who still are not "happy," and who keep acting "as if they are kings and queens"?

Susan had no answers. Her grim and persistent silence only prompted 19 more questions from her mother, her father, and eventually the family doctor, who suggested (when he too was met with unrelenting silence) that a child psychiatrist be consulted. The parents were as alarmed and angered by that suggestion as they were by their daughter's behavior and her subsequent moody withdrawal. They did, however, ask the girl whether she would consent to go "talk with someone." The girl asked who. The parents replied directly and briefly: a doctor. The girl asked (right to the point) what kind of a doctor. The mother had no answer. The father began to describe the doctor as "someone who understands children." The girl made his circumlocutions utterly unnecessary: "You mean a psychiatrist." The parents pulled back, asked their daughter if she wouldn't promise to "behave," in which case they would certainly not urge any visits with a psychiatrist. But Susan, in fact, wanted to go talk with a doctor—about her parents. And did. She approached her seventh-grade teacher and asked if she might speak to the school psychologist. She poured out her story to him, pleaded with him not to tell her parents that she had gone to see him. But he did tell them; so did the school's principal. When the girl learned that her parents had been told, she again ran away, this time on her bike.

She filled her knapsack with nuts, fruit, chewing gum, and some Life 20 Savers. She tied her skates on the bike's handlebars, and pedaled away south, toward Connecticut. She almost got there before she was spotted by the police. She cleverly used local roads rather than highways. She had a map and used it quite intelligently. But she had not reckoned on a flat tire. As she stood by the side of a road, wondering what to do next, a state police car pulled up. The girl protested hard, screamed, cried, begged to be let go. But of course she was taken home. Shortly afterward she and her parents jointly took themselves to a child psychiatrist for a "consultation," and shortly after that the girl began seeing the doctor, and her parents began seeing, together, another psychiatrist.

21   After six months of "talks" with "a nice woman," Susan spoke quite grate-
fully and reflectively: "I thought at first that I must be nuts. I knew I wanted
to go see someone, but I didn't know what I'd say, once I got there. I was sure
I was the only one I knew twelve years old who was seeing a psychiatrist. But
I've found out that there are a lot of kids who go. The lady, the doctor, told
me that she sees kids *all day*—and some of them are a lot younger than me. I
asked her how old the youngest is, and she said he's a boy, and he's only four
years old. And she said she once treated a kid who was younger than that. I
can't figure out what we do in her office, except talk. And I don't know why
I feel better after I've left the office, but I do. I guess it's because with the doctor
I try to say what's on my mind. With my mother, I can't; she's got her troubles.
With my father, I can't; he's always working. With my brother, I can't; he's too
young, and he gets scared when I ask him questions about what he thinks of
our parents. Like the doctor says, he doesn't want to tell me what's on his
mind. I don't blame him, either.

22   "I don't want to tell a lot that's on my mind to anyone. The doctor said
I'm lonely, and I told her I don't mind being lonely! But now that I've met
some kids who go to psychiatrists, I don't feel peculiar any more. I met one of
the kids from school coming out of the building where the doctor's office is;
and we said hello. The next day she came up to me during a recess, and she
asked me who I was seeing. I was surprised. I didn't know what to say. She
said they're all psychiatrists in that building, so she knew I'd been to see one,
but not to worry, because she sees one, and so do a lot of kids. Then she started
pointing out some of the kids, right then and there. I was upset. I thought it
wasn't fair. But later I realized that the kids didn't mind; it was *me* who
minded. I found that out when I met another kid from my school coming out
of the doctor's office, a couple of weeks later, and she was like the first girl—
she came right up to me and said I could join the 'club.' Well, there really isn't
a club; but in a way, I guess, there is one.

23   "After you've talked with a psychiatrist for a while you begin to realize
that it's like talking to someone older, who's nice and is trying to help you.
My mother started crying the other day, after I'd come out of the doctor's office
and while we were driving home. She said that if she'd been a better mother
and if my father had been a better father, then I wouldn't be going to a doctor to talk. But I told her not to worry, and not to feel bad, because I don't
mind going to a doctor. She's a nice doctor, anyway. She reminds me of the
nice maid Sue we once had. My mother said my father had told her that there
are times when he wonders if it's all worth it—the struggle he's had to get on
top. Now they are on top, but he feels as if he's wading his way through a big,
squishy swamp, and any minute he'll fall, or he'll step into some quicksand,
and he'll sink. He asked my mother if she'd be willing to settle for ten thousand a year and him home all the time. She said yes, she would. So would I.
But he said it wouldn't be so nice to be poor; and he's probably right. I like
my room, and I like my skating lessons, and I like the woods we have, and
our swimming pool."

24   She also liked going to talk with the doctor. But after six months of doing

so the news came that her father would at last be the president of a substantial company, at a high salary (well over a hundred thousand dollars a year); but he would have to move yet again, this time to Westport, Connecticut. His wife was upset; she had begun attending Alcoholics Anonymous meetings, a move she made several months after her daughter started seeing a psychiatrist. His son was upset; he had two good friends, and he did not want to lose them. Nor did he want to go to school elsewhere. Nor did he want to give up his room, his wall covered with pictures of animals, hockey players, the Six Million Dollar Man, and Batman. As for Susan, she was quiet, resigned, compliant at first. She pointed out—to herself, to her mother and brother, to her doctor, to her teacher—that there wasn't anything she could do about the projected move, anyway. It was best to go along, try to look at the brighter side, try to emphasize their good prospects—an even larger home, a summer home, perhaps in Massachusetts (Cape Cod), and vacations all over the world. (She had dreamed for years of foreign travel.)

But a week or two before moving time the girl became sad, teary, lethar- 25 gic, moody, unable to sleep well, and without appetite. The pediatrician pronounced her well physically. The child psychiatrist, saying good-bye, said Susan still had "problems," but was more aware of them than she once had been. The mother rallied around the girl as never before. The mother was determined to be sober, to make amends for her past errors of omission or commission. And the father came into the girl's room one day, sat down, and candidly acknowledged how "rotten" he felt, how much "to blame" he was for the girl's state of mind, and how hard he would work, in Connecticut, to give her everything, *everything* she might want—including an ice rink, if she wanted one, in which she could practice and practice, right at home. After that talk, everyone noted the girl's spirits seemed to pick up a bit, though no one was exactly sure why, including the girl. She was quite impressed with her father's generosity, even moved by it. But she told him no, she didn't want such a gift. She would be embarrassed by having it. And she wondered out loud whether he was promising her the stars, in order to tide her over a bad period, in the hope that she would forget his offer or shy away from it—as she did.

Questions for Discussion

1. What tone does the short opening sentence set? How do the phrases "mere drinker" and "heavy drinker" affect your interpretation of the situation that follows?
2. Through the title and introduction to this selection, the author spends a lot of time establishing the family situation. How does this frame or context prepare the reader for the narrative that follows? How effective is the use of first-person narrative combined with the author's third-person narration? What is gained, or lost, through the first-person accounts?
3. Describe the family situation. Why does Susan feel stressed and unhappy? What are the parents' goals and values? What are the daughter's goals and values? Who is doing most of the parenting?
4. Discuss the statement at the end of paragraph 18, "What is the matter with children like her who have been given 'everything' and are still not 'happy'?"

5. Do you think people of different socioeconomic groups have difficulties understanding and communicating with each other? Why? How can such differences be overcome? Develop your response with reference to this selection and your own observations and experiences.
6. What do you think will happen to Susan and her family? How will Susan's future be similar to and yet different from Buddy's in "American Horse"?

Ideas for Writing

1. As you may have done for the last selection, "American Horse," assume the role of a case worker and write up a report on Susan. You could compare and contrast the two accounts. Are the children and their problems alike and different in expected or unexpected ways?
2. Investigate Al-Anon, the support group for families of alcoholics. Alternatively, research the incidence of alcoholism by class, geography, ethnicity. Summarize your findings and share them with the class or develop your research into a longer essay.
3. Write a story that captures a theme of your own childhood, either in a reflective journal account for yourself or in a form that you can share with your peers. Then, write a short analysis of the process. How did you select material to include? What did you decide to exclude? What was it like to write about yourself? Draw some pictures of yourself at various stages of your life to accompany the journal writing.

A Family Legacy

Marian Wright Edelman

Marian Wright Edelman (b. 1939), attorney and founding president of the Children's Defense Fund, has spent her professional life as an activist for disadvantaged Americans, particularly children. One of five children, she is the daughter of a Baptist minister who was influenced by the self-help philosophy of Booker T. Washington and who expected his children to be educated and to serve their community. As Edelman once said, "Working for the community was as much a part of our existence as eating and sleeping and church." Edelman graduated from Spelman College and Yale University Law School; she was the first black woman to pass the bar in Mississippi. Edelman's life has included many other firsts, numerous awards, and honorary degrees. Her extensive writings include *Children Out of School in America* (1974), *Black and White Children in America* (1980), and *Families in Peril: An Agenda for Social Change* (1987). The following essay is excerpted from her book, *The Measure of Our Success: A Letter to My Children and Yours* (1992).

Journal

What did your family teach you about relationships between the value of work, education, material well being, and community involvement?

South Carolina is my home state and I am the aunt, granddaughter, daughter, and sister of Baptist ministers. Service was as essential a part of my upbringing as eating and sleeping and going to school. The church was a hub of Black children's social existence, and caring Black adults were buffers against the segregated and hostile outside world that told us we weren't important. But our parents said it wasn't so, our teachers said it wasn't so, and our preachers said it wasn't so. The message of my racially segregated childhood was clear: let no man or woman look down on you, and look down on no man or woman.

We couldn't play in public playgrounds or sit at drugstore lunch counters 2 and order a Coke, so Daddy built a playground and canteen behind the church. In fact, whenever he saw a need, he tried to respond. There were no Black homes for the aged in Bennettsville, so he began one across the street for which he and Mama and we children cooked and served and cleaned. And we children learned that it was our responsibility to take care of elderly family members and neighbors, and that everyone was our neighbor. My mother carried on the home after Daddy died, and my brother Julian has carried it on to this day behind our church since our mother's death in 1984.

Finding another child in my room or a pair of my shoes gone was far from 3 unusual, and twelve foster children followed my sister and me and three brothers as we left home.

Child-rearing and parental work were inseparable. I went everywhere 4 with my parents and was under the watchful eye of members of the congregation and community who were my extended parents. They kept me when my parents went out of town, they reported on and chided me when I strayed from the straight and narrow of community expectations, and they basked in and supported my achievements when I did well. Doing well, they made clear, meant high academic achievement, playing piano in Sunday school or singing or participating in other church activities, being helpful to somebody, displaying good manners (which is nothing more than consideration toward others), and reading. My sister Olive reminded me recently that the only time our father would not give us a chore ("Can't you find something constructive to do?" was his most common refrain) was when we were reading. So we all read a lot! We learned early what our parents and extended community "parents" valued. Children were taught—not by sermonizing, but by personal example—that nothing was too lowly to do. I remember a debate my parents had when I was eight or nine as to whether I was too young to go with my older brother, Harry, to help clean the bed and bedsores of a very sick, poor woman. I went and learned just how much the smallest helping hands and kindness can mean to a person in need.

The ugly external voices of my small-town, segregated childhood (as a 5 very young child I remember standing and hearing former South Carolina Senator James Byrnes railing on the local courthouse lawn about how Black children would never go to school with whites) were tempered by the internal voices of parental and community expectation and pride. My father and I waited anxiously for the *Brown v. Board of Education* decision in 1954. We talked about it and what it would mean for my future and for the future of millions of other Black children. He died the week before *Brown* was decided. But I and other children lucky enough to have caring and courageous parents and other adult role models were able, in later years, to walk through the new and heavy doors that *Brown* slowly and painfully opened—doors that some are trying to close again today.

6   The adults in our churches and community made children feel valued and important. They took time and paid attention to us. They struggled to find ways to keep us busy. And while life was often hard and resources scarce, we always knew who we were and that the measure of our worth was inside our heads and hearts, and not outside in our possessions or on our backs. We were told that the world had a lot of problems; that Black people had an extra lot of problems, but that we were able and obligated to struggle and change them; that being poor was no excuse for not achieving; and that extra intellectual and material gifts brought with them the privilege and responsibility of sharing with others less fortunate. In sum, we learned that service is the rent we pay for living. It is the very purpose of life and not something you do in your spare time.

7   When my mother died, an old white man in my hometown of Bennettsville asked me what I do. In a flash I realized that in my work at the Children's Defense Fund I do exactly what my parents did—just on a different scale. My brother preached a wonderful sermon at Mama's funeral, but the best tribute was the presence in the back pew of the town drunk, whom an observer said he could not remember coming to church in many years.

8   The legacies that parents and church and teachers left to my generation of Black children were priceless but not material: a living faith reflected in daily service, the discipline of hard work and stick-to-it-ness, and a capacity to struggle in the face of adversity. Giving up and "burnout" were not part of the language of my elders—you got up every morning and you did what you had to do and you got up every time you fell down and tried as many times as you had to to get it done right. They had grit. They valued family life, family rituals, and tried to be and to expose us to good role models. Role models were of two kinds: those who achieved in the outside world (like Marian Anderson, my namesake) and those who didn't have a whole lot of education or fancy clothes but who taught us by the special grace of their lives the message of Christ and Tolstoy and Gandhi and Heschel and Dorothy Day and Romero and King that the Kingdom of God was within—in what you are, not what you have. I still hope I can be half as good as Black church and community elders like Miz Lucy McQueen, Miz Tee Kelly, and Miz Kate Winston, extraordinary women who were kind and patient and loving with children and others and who, when I went to Spelman College, sent me shoeboxes with chicken and biscuits and greasy dollar bills.

9   It never occurred to any Wright child that we were not going to college or were not expected to share what we learned and earned with the less fortunate. I was forty years old before I figured out, thanks to my brother Harry's

superior insight, that my Daddy often responded to our requests for money by saying he didn't have any change because he *really* didn't have any rather than because he had nothing smaller than a twenty dollar bill.

I was fourteen years old the night my Daddy died. He had holes in his [10] shoes but two children out of college, one in college, another in divinity school, and a vision he was able to convey to me as he lay dying in an ambulance that I, a young Black girl, could be and do anything; that race and gender are shadows; and that character, self-discipline, determination, attitude, and service are the substance of life.

I have always believed that I could help change the world because I have [11] been lucky to have adults around me who did—in small and large ways. Most were people of simple grace who understood what Walker Percy wrote: You can get all As and still flunk life.

Life was not easy back in the 1940s and 1950s in rural South Carolina for [12] many parents and grandparents. We buried children who died from poverty (and I can't stand it that we still do). Little Johnny Harrington, three houses down from my church parsonage, stepped on and died from a nail because his grandmother had no doctor to advise her, nor the money to pay for health care. (Half of all low-income urban children under two are still not fully immunized against preventable childhood diseases like tetanus and polio and measles.) My classmate, Henry Munnerlyn, broke his neck when he jumped off the bridge into the town creek because only white children were allowed in the public swimming pool. I later heard that the creek where Blacks swam and fished was the hospital sewage outlet. (Today thousands of Black children in our cities and rural areas are losing their lives to cocaine and heroin and alcohol and gang violence because they don't have enough constructive outlets.) The migrant family who collided with a truck on the highway near my home and the ambulance driver who refused to take them to the hospital because they were Black still live in my mind every time I hear about babies who die or are handicapped from birth when they are turned away from hospitals in emergencies or their mothers are turned away in labor because they have no health insurance and cannot pay pre-admission deposits to enter a hospital. I and my brothers and sister might have lost hope—as so many young people today have lost hope—except for the stable, caring, attentive adults in our family, school, congregation, civic and political life who struggled with and for us against the obstacles we faced and provided us positive alternatives and the sense of possibility we needed.

At Spelman College in Atlanta, I found my Daddy and Mama's values [13] about taking responsibility for your own learning and growth reinforced in the daily (except Saturday) chapel service. Daily chapel attendance was compulsory and enforced by the threat of points taken off one's earned grade average as a result of truancy. For all my rebellion then, I remember now far more from the chapel speakers who came to talk to us about life and the purpose of education than from any class. And during my tenure as chairwoman of Spelman's board, I advocated reinstitution of some compulsory assemblies (monthly, not daily!) so our young women would have to hear what we adults think is important.

14   Many of my mentors and role models, such as Dr. Benjamin Mays, then president of Morehouse College, Whitney Young, dean of the School of Social Work at Atlanta University and later National Urban League head, M. Carl Holman, a professor at Clark College, later head of the National Urban Coalition, Dr. Howard Thurman, dean of the Chapel at Boston University, and Dr. King, all conveyed the same message as they spoke in Sisters Chapel at Spelman: education is for improving the lives of others and for leaving your community and world better than you found it. Other important influences during my Spelman years—Ella Baker, Septima Clark, Howard Zinn, Charles E. Merrill, Jr., and Samuel Dubois Cook—stretched my vision of the future and of one person's ability to help shape it. I'm still trying to live up to their teachings and to the examples of the extraordinary ordinary people whom I had the privilege to serve and learn from after law school during my civil rights sojourn in Mississippi between 1963 and 1968.

15   Fannie Lou Hamer, Amzie Moore, Winston and Dovie Hudson, Mae Bertha Carter, school desegregation and voting rights pioneers in Mississippi, and Unita Blackwell, who rose from sharecropper to mayor of rural Mayersville, Mississippi—and countless courageous men and women who gave their voices and homes and lives to get the right to vote and to secure for their children a better life than they had—guide and inspire me still. Those largely unknown and usually unlettered people of courage and commitment, along with my parents, remind me each day to keep trying and to let my little light shine, as Mrs. Hamer sang and did through her inspiring life. In a D.C. neighborhood church, I recently saw a banner that reminded me "there is not enough darkness in the world to snuff out the light of even one small candle."

16   I have always felt extraordinarily blessed to live in the times I have. As a child and as an adult—as a Black woman—I have had to struggle to understand the world around me. Most Americans remember Dr. King as a great leader. I do too. But I also remember him as someone able to admit how often he was afraid and unsure about his next step. But faith prevailed over fear and uncertainty and fatigue and depression. It was his human vulnerability and his ability to rise above it that I most remember. In this he was not different from many Black adults whose credo has been to make "a way out of no way."

17   The Children's Defense Fund was conceived in the cauldron of Mississippi's summer project of 1964 and in the Head Start battles of 1965, where both the great need for and limits of local action were apparent. As a private civil rights lawyer, I learned that I could have only limited, albeit important, impact on meeting epidemic family and child needs in that poor state without coherent national policy and investment strategies to complement community empowerment strategies. I also learned that critical civil and political rights would not mean much to a hungry, homeless, illiterate child and family if they lacked the social and economic means to exercise them. And so children—my

own and other people's—became the passion of my personal and professional life. For it is they who are God's presence, promise, and hope for humankind.

It is the responsibility of every adult—especially parents, educators, and religious leaders—to make sure that children hear what we have learned from the lessons of life and to hear over and over that we love them and that they are not alone. Daddy used to say that in school we got our lessons from our teachers first and then got examined on how well we had learned them. In life the consequences often come first and the lessons afterward. In today's era of AIDS and drugs and violence and too-early and unsafe sex, the consequences can be deadly or last a lifetime. So parental communication, guidance, and example are more crucial than ever. **18**

Too many young people—of all colors, and all walks of life—are growing up today unable to handle life in hard places, without hope, without adequate attention, and without steady internal compasses to navigate the morally polluted seas they must face on the journey to adulthood. **19**

As a result, we are on the verge of losing two generations of Black children and youths to drugs, violence, too-early parenthood, poor health and education, unemployment, family disintegration—and to the spiritual and physical poverty that both breeds and is bred by them. Millions of Latino, Native American, and other minority children face similar threats. And millions of white children of all classes, like too many minority children, are drowning in the meaninglessness of a culture that rewards greed and guile and tells them life is about getting rather than giving. **20**

I believe that we have lost our sense of what is important as a people in a world that is reinventing itself at an unprecedented pace both technologically and politically. My generation learned that to accomplish anything, we had to get off the dime. Our children today must learn to get off the paradigm, over and over, and to be flexible, quick, and smart about it. **21**

Children and young adults—all of us—face dazzling international changes and challenges and extraordinary social and economic upheavals. One single decade's profligacy has changed our nation from a lender to debtor. Our aging population and future work force depend on a shrinking pool of young workers, a majority of whom will be female, minority, or both. Our culturally diverse child and worker population confronts increasing racial and gender intolerance fueled by recession and greed. Our education system is drowning in the wake of the new and flexible skills required in a postindustrial economy. The nurturance of children is at risk as extended families disappear, both parents work, and more children rely on a single parent. A cacophony of cultural messages bombard our children about what they must buy and how they must act to be "with it"—with a nearly deafening silence from too many homes and the too-few moral leaders and positive role models in either our private or public lives. Meanwhile, time and economic pressures mount and are unrelieved by extended family networks or family-friendly private sector and public policies. **22**

23   Despite these social and cultural tidal waves, I believe there are some enduring spiritual, family, community, and national values and lessons that we need to rediscover in this last decade of this last century in this millennium. I agree with Archibald MacLeish that "there is only one thing more powerful than learning from experience and that is not learning from experience."

Questions for Discussion

1. A legacy is a tradition of values and attitudes handed down from one generation to the next. Discuss some of the values handed down to Edelman. What might the family legacies be for Buddy and his mother ("American Horse")? For Susan ("Problem Child")?
2. Who is Edelman's family or clan? Her community? How do the two complement each other? How do the roles of adults in your neighborhood, congregation, or community compare to those explored in Edelman's essay?
3. Edelman says, "Service is the rent we pay for living. It is the very purpose of life and not something you do in your spare time." Relate this statement to other points of view presented in this chapter.
4. Discuss the relationship between religious belief and service as discussed in this memoir. Do you think someone who does not practice a religious faith might nevertheless hold some of the ethics and values of Edelman's family?
5. With peers, create a dialogue between Edelman and the parents of Susan in "Problem Child" on the subject of raising children.
6. This selection is from a book entitled, *The Measure of Our Success: A Letter to My Children and Yours.* What do you believe is Edelman's measure of success in raising children? And why does she address this memoir to children?

Ideas for Writing

1. Edelman praises the enduring family work and spiritual values with which she grew up. Do you think the values she writes about are at the center of the current "family values" debates among politicians and journalists? Discuss.
2. Develop your journal into an essay about your family legacy. What have you learned about the relationships between family, work, religion, and education?

from *Bless Me, Ultima*

Rudolfo A. Anaya

Rudolfo A. Anaya (b. 1937) was born in New Mexico and attended public schools in Santa Rosa, New Mexico; he graduated from the University of New Mexico. Anaya is the winner of the Second Annual Premio Quinto Sol national Chicano literary award. First printed in 1972, his novel *Bless Me, Ultima,* is now in its fifth printing. The first chapter of that novel follows.

Journal

Have relatives or other people ever come to live with you? How was your family's situation changed by the individual's presence? In what ways were these changes positive or negative? If you haven't had this experience, how do you think you would react?

Ultima came to stay with us the summer I was almost seven. When she came the beauty of the llano unfolded before my eyes, and the gurgling waters of the river sang to the hum of the turning earth. The magical time of childhood stood still, and the pulse of the living earth pressed its mystery into my living blood. She took my hand, and the silent, magic powers she possessed made beauty from the raw, sun-baked llano, the green river valley, and the blue bowl which was the white sun's home. My bare feet felt the throbbing earth and my body trembled with excitement. Time stood still, and it shared with me all that had been, and all that was to come. . . .

Let me begin at the beginning. I do not mean the beginning that was in 2 my dreams and the stories they whispered to me about my birth, and the people of my father and mother, and my three brothers—but the beginning that came with Ultima.

The attic of our home was partitioned into two small rooms. My sisters, 3 Deborah and Theresa, slept in one and I slept in the small cubicle by the door. The wooden steps creaked down into a small hallway that led into the kitchen. From the top of the stairs I had a vantage point into the heart of our home, my mother's kitchen. From there I was to see the terrified face of Chávez when he brought the terrible news of the murder of the sheriff; I was to see the rebellion of my brothers against my father; and many times late at night I was to see Ultima returning from the llano where she gathered the herbs that can be harvested only in the light of the full moon by the careful hands of a curandera.

That night I lay very quietly in my bed, and I heard my father and mother 4 speak of Ultima.

"Está sola," my father said, "ya no queda gente en el pueblito de Las Pas- 5 turas—"

He spoke in Spanish, and the village he mentioned was his home. My 6 father had been a vaquero all his life, a calling as ancient as the coming of the Spaniard to Nuevo Méjico. Even after the big rancheros and the tejanos came and fenced the beautiful llano, he and those like him continued to work there, I guess because only in that wide expanse of land and sky could they feel the freedom their spirits needed.

"¡Qué lástima," my mother answered, and I knew her nimble fingers 7 worked the pattern on the doily she crocheted for the big chair in the sala.

I heard her sigh, and she must have shuddered too when she thought 8 of Ultima living alone in the loneliness of the wide llano. My mother was not a woman of the llano, she was the daughter of a farmer. She could not see beauty in the llano and she could not understand the coarse men who lived half their lifetimes on horseback. After I was born in Las Pasturas she persuaded my father to leave the llano and bring her family to the town of Guadalupe where she said there would be opportunity and school for us. The move lowered my father in the esteem of his compadres, the other vaqueros of the llano who clung tenaciously to their way of life and freedom. There was no room to keep animals in town so my father had to sell his small herd, but he would not sell his horse so he gave it to a good friend, Benito Campos. But Campos could not keep the animal penned up because somehow the horse was very close to the spirit of the man, and so the horse was allowed to roam free and no vaquero on that llano would throw a lazo on that horse. It was as if someone had died, and they turned their gaze from the spirit that walked the earth.

9   It hurt my father's pride. He saw less and less of his old compadres. He went to work on the highway and on Saturdays after they collected their pay he drank with his crew at the Longhorn, but he was never close to the men of the town. Some weekends the llaneros would come into town for supplies and old amigos like Bonney or Campos or the Gonzales brothers would come by to visit. Then my father's eyes lit up as they drank and talked of the old days and told the old stories. But when the western sun touched the clouds with orange and gold the vaqueros got in their trucks and headed home, and my father was left to drink alone in the long night. Sunday morning he would get up very crudo and complain about having to go to early mass.

10   "—She served the people all her life, and now the people are scattered, driven like tumbleweeds by the winds of war. The war sucks everything dry," my father said solemnly, "it takes the young boys overseas, and their families move to California where there is work—"

11   "Ave María Purísima," my mother made the sign of the cross for my three brothers who were away at war. "Gabriel," she said to my father, "it is not right that la Grande be alone in her old age—"

12   "No," my father agreed.

13   "When I married you and went to the llano to live with you and raise your family, I could not have survived without la Grande's help. Oh, those were hard years—"

14   "Those were good years," my father countered. But my mother would not argue.

15   "There isn't a family she did not help," she continued, "no road was too long for her to walk to its end to snatch somebody from the jaws of death, and not even the blizzards of the llano could keep her from the appointed place where a baby was to be delivered—"

16   "Es verdad," my father nodded.

17   "She tended me at the birth of my sons—" And then I knew her eyes glanced briefly at my father. "Gabriel, we cannot let her live her last days in loneliness—"

18   "No," my father agreed, "it is not the way of our people."

19   "It would be a great honor to provide a home for la Grande," my mother murmured. My mother called Ultima la Grande out of respect. It meant the woman was old and wise.

"I have already sent word with Campos that Ultima is to come and live 20
with us," my father said with some satisfaction. He knew it would please my
mother.

"I am grateful," my mother said tenderly, "perhaps we can repay a little 21
of the kindness la Grande has given to so many."

"And the children?" my father asked. I knew why he expressed concern 22
for me and my sisters. It was because Ultima was a curandera, a woman who
knew the herbs and remedies of the ancients, a miracle-worker who could heal
the sick. And I had heard that Ultima could lift the curses laid by brujas, that
she could exorcise the evil the witches planted in people to make them sick.
And because a curandera had this power she was misunderstood and often
suspected of practicing witchcraft herself.

I shuddered and my heart turned cold at the thought. The cuentos of the 23
people were full of the tales of evil done by brujas.

"She helped bring them into the world, she cannot be but good for the 24
children," my mother answered.

"Está bien," my father yawned, "I will go for her in the morning." 25

So it was decided that Ultima should come and live with us. I knew that 26
my father and mother did good by providing a home for Ultima. It was the
custom to provide for the old and the sick. There was always room in the safety
and warmth of la familia for one more person, be that person stranger or
friend.

It was warm in the attic, and as I lay quietly listening to the sounds of the 27
house falling asleep and repeating a Hail Mary over and over in my thoughts,
I drifted into the time of dreams. Once I had told my mother about my dreams
and she said they were visions from God and she was happy, because her own
dream was that I should grow up and become a priest. After that I did not tell
her about my dreams, and they remained in me forever and ever . . .

In my dream I flew over the rolling hills of the llano. My soul wandered over the 28
dark plain until it came to a cluster of adobe huts. I recognized the village of Las Pas-
turas and my heart grew happy. One mud hut had a lighted window, and the vision
of my dream swept me towards it to be a witness at the birth of a baby.

I could not make out the face of the mother who rested from the pains of birth, 29
but I could see the old woman in black who tended the just-arrived, steaming baby.
She nimbly tied a knot on the cord that had connected the baby to its mother's blood,
then quickly she bent and with her teeth she bit off the loose end. She wrapped the
squirming baby and laid it at the mother's side, then she returned to cleaning the bed.
All linen was swept aside to be washed, but she carefully wrapped the useless cord
and the afterbirth and laid the package at the feet of the Virgin on the small altar. I
sensed that these things were yet to be delivered to someone.

Now the people who had waited patiently in the dark were allowed to come in and 30
speak to the mother and deliver their gifts to the baby. I recognized my mother's broth-
ers, my uncles from El Puerto de los Lunas. They entered ceremoniously. A patient
hope stirred in their dark, brooding eyes.

This one will be a Luna, the old man said, he will be a farmer and keep our cus- 31
toms and traditions. Perhaps God will bless our family and make the baby a priest.

32   *And to show their hope they rubbed the dark earth of the river valley on the baby's forehead, and they surrounded the bed with the fruits of their harvest so the small room smelled of fresh green chile and corn, ripe apples and peaches, pumpkins and green beans.*

33   *Then the silence was shattered with the thunder of hoofbeats; vaqueros surrounded the small house with shouts and gunshots, and when they entered the room they were laughing and singing and drinking.*

34   *Gabriel, they shouted, you have a fine son! He will make a fine vaquero! And they smashed the fruits and vegetables that surrounded the bed and replaced them with a saddle, horse blankets, bottles of whiskey, a new rope, bridles, chapas, and an old guitar. And they rubbed the stain of earth from the baby's forehead because man was not to be tied to the earth but free upon it.*

35   *These were the people of my father, the vaqueros of the llano. They were an exuberant, restless people, wandering across the ocean of the plain.*

36   *We must return to our valley, the old man who led the farmers spoke. We must take with us the blood that comes after the birth. We will bury it in our fields to renew their fertility and to assure that the baby will follow our ways. He nodded for the old woman to deliver the package at the altar.*

37   *No! the llaneros protested, it will stay here! We will burn it and let the winds of the llano scatter the ashes.*

38   *It is blasphemy to scatter a man's blood on unholy ground, the farmers chanted. The new son must fulfill his mother's dream. He must come to El Puerto and rule over the Lunas of the valley. The blood of the Lunas is strong in him.*

39   *He is a Márez, the vaqueros shouted. His forefathers were conquistadores, men as restless as the seas they sailed and as free as the land they conquered. He is his father's blood!*

40   *Curses and threats filled the air, pistols were drawn, and the opposing sides made ready for battle. But the clash was stopped by the old woman who delivered the baby.*

41   *Cease! she cried, and the men were quiet. I pulled this baby into the light of life, so I will bury the afterbirth and the cord that once linked him to eternity. Only I will know his destiny.*

42   The dream began to dissolve. When I opened my eyes I heard my father cranking the truck outside. I wanted to go with him, I wanted to see Las Pasturas, I wanted to see Ultima. I dressed hurriedly, but I was too late. The truck was bouncing down the goat path that led to the bridge and the highway.

43   I turned, as I always did, and looked down the slope of our hill to the green of the river, and I raised my eyes and saw the town of Guadalupe. Towering above the housetops and the trees of the town was the church tower. I made the sign of the cross on my lips. The only other building that rose above the housetops to compete with the church tower was the yellow top of the schoolhouse. This fall I would be going to school.

44   My heart sank. When I thought of leaving my mother and going to school a warm, sick feeling came to my stomach. To get rid of it I ran to the pens we kept by the molino to feed the animals. I had fed the rabbits that night and they had alfalfa and so I only changed their water. I scattered some grain for the hungry chickens and watched their mad scramble as the rooster called

them to peck. I milked the cow and turned her loose. During the day she would forage along the highway where the grass was thick and green, then she would return at nightfall. She was a good cow and there were very few times when I had to run and bring her back in the evening. Then I dreaded it, because she might wander into the hills where the bats flew at dusk and there was only the sound of my heart beating as I ran and it made me sad and frightened to be alone.

I collected three eggs in the chicken house and returned for breakfast. 45

"Antonio," my mother smiled and took the eggs and milk, "come and eat 46 your breakfast."

I sat across the table from Deborah and Theresa and ate my atole and the 47 hot tortilla with butter. I said very little. I usually spoke very little to my two sisters. They were older than I and they were very close. They usually spent the entire day in the attic, playing dolls and giggling. I did not concern myself with those things.

"Your father has gone to Las Pasturas," my mother chattered, "he has gone 48 to bring la Grande." Her hands were white with the flour of the dough. I watched carefully. "—And when he returns, I want you children to show your manners. You must not shame your father or your mother—"

"Isn't her real name Ultima?" Deborah asked. She was like that, always 49 asking grown-up questions.

"You will address her as la Grande," my mother said flatly. I looked at 50 her and wondered if this woman with the black hair and laughing eyes was the woman who gave birth in my dream.

"Grande," Theresa repeated. 51

"Is it true she is a witch?" Deborah asked. Oh, she was in for it. I saw my 52 mother whirl then pause and control herself.

"No!" she scolded. "You must not speak of such things! Oh, I don't know 53 where you learn such ways." Her eyes flooded with tears. She always cried when she thought we were learning the ways of my father, the ways of the Márez. "She is a woman of learning," she went on and I knew she didn't have time to stop and cry, "she has worked hard for all the people of the village. Oh, I would never have survived those hard years if it had not been for her—so show her respect. We are honored that she comes to live with us, understand?"

"Sí, mamá," Deborah said half willingly. 54

"Sí, mamá," Theresa repeated. 55

"Now run and sweep the room at the end of the hall. Eugene's room—" 56 I heard her voice choke. She breathed a prayer and crossed her forehead. The flour left white stains on her, the four points of the cross. I knew it was because my three brothers were at war that she was sad, and Eugene was the youngest.

"Mamá." I wanted to speak to her. I wanted to know who the old woman 57 was who cut the baby's cord.

"Sí." She turned and looked at me. 58

"Was Ultima at my birth?" I asked. 59

"¡Ay Dios mío!" my mother cried. She came to where I sat and ran her 60 hand through my hair. She smelled warm, like bread. "Where do you get such questions, my son. Yes," she smiled, "la Grande was there to help me. She was there to help at the birth of all of my children—"

61   "And my uncles from El Puerto were there?"

62   "Of course," she answered, "my brothers have always been at my side when I needed them. They have always prayed that I would bless them with a—"

63   I did not hear what she said because I was hearing the sounds of the dream, and I was seeing the dream again. The warm cereal in my stomach made me feel sick.

64   "And my father's brother was there, the Márez' and their friends, the vaqueros—"

65   "Ay!" she cried out, "Don't speak to me of those worthless Márez and their friends!"

66   "There was a fight?" I asked.

67   "No," she said, "a silly argument. They wanted to start a fight with my brothers—that is all they are good for. Vaqueros, they call themselves, they are worthless drunks! Thieves! Always on the move, like gypsies, always dragging their families around the country like vagabonds—"

68   As long as I could remember she always raged about the Márez family and their friends. She called the village of Las Pasturas beautiful; she had gotten used to the loneliness, but she had never accepted its people. She was the daughter of farmers.

69   But the dream was true. It was as I had seen it. Ultima knew.

70   "But you will not be like them." She caught her breath and stopped. She kissed my forehead. "You will be like my brothers. You will be a Luna, Antonio. You will be a man of the people, and perhaps a priest." She smiled.

71   A priest, I thought, that was her dream. I was to hold mass on Sundays like father Byrnes did in the church in town. I was to hear the confessions of the silent people of the valley, and I was to administer the holy Sacrament to them.

72   "Perhaps," I said.

73   "Yes," my mother smiled. She held me tenderly. The fragrance of her body was sweet.

74   "But then," I whispered, "who will hear my confession?"

75   "What?"

76   "Nothing," I answered. I felt a cool sweat on my forehead and I knew I had to run, I had to clear my mind of the dream. "I am going to Jasón's house," I said hurriedly and slid past my mother. I ran out the kitchen door, past the animal pens, towards Jasón's house. The white sun and the fresh air cleansed me.

77   On this side of the river there were only three houses. The slope of the hill rose gradually into the hills of juniper and mesquite and cedar clumps. Jasón's house was farther away from the river than our house. On the path that led to the bridge lived huge, fat Fío and his beautiful wife. Fío and my father worked together on the highway. They were good drinking friends.

78   "¡Jasón!" I called at the kitchen door. I had run hard and was panting. His mother appeared at the door.

"Jasón no está aquí," she said. All of the older people spoke only in Span- 79
ish, and I myself understood only Spanish. It was only after one went to school
that one learned English.

"¿Dónde está?" I asked. 80

She pointed towards the river, northwest, past the railroad tracks to the 81
dark hills. The river came through those hills and there were old Indian
grounds there, holy burial grounds Jasón told me. There in an old cave lived
his Indian. At least everybody called him Jasón's Indian. He was the only
Indian of the town, and he talked only to Jasón. Jasón's father had forbidden
Jasón to talk to the Indian, he had beaten him, he had tried in every way to
keep Jasón from the Indian.

But Jasón persisted. Jasón was not a bad boy, he was just Jasón. He was 82
quiet and moody, and sometimes for no reason at all wild, loud sounds came
exploding from his throat and lungs. Sometimes I felt like Jasón, like I wanted
to shout and cry, but I never did.

I looked at his mother's eyes and I saw they were sad. "Thank you," I said, 83
and returned home. While I waited for my father to return with Ultima I
worked in the garden. Every day I had to work in the garden. Every day I
reclaimed from the rocky soil of the hill a few more feet of earth to cultivate.
The land of the llano was not good for farming, the good land was along the
river. But my mother wanted a garden and I worked to make her happy.
Already we had a few chile and tomato plants growing. It was hard work. My
fingers bled from scraping out the rocks and it seemed that a square yard of
ground produced a wheelbarrow full of rocks which I had to push down to
the retaining wall.

The sun was white in the bright blue sky. The shade of the clouds would 84
not come until the afternoon. The sweat was sticky on my brown body. I heard
the truck and turned to see it chugging up the dusty goat path. My father was
returning with Ultima.

"¡Mamá!" I called. My mother came running out, Deborah and Theresa 85
trailed after her.

"I'm afraid," I heard Theresa whimper. 86

"There's nothing to be afraid of," Deborah said confidently. My mother 87
said there was too much Márez blood in Deborah. Her eyes and hair were very
dark, and she was always running. She had been to school two years and she
spoke only English. She was teaching Theresa and half the time I didn't understand what they were saying.

"Madre de Dios, but mind your manners!" my mother scolded. The truck 88
stopped and she ran to greet Ultima. "Buenos días le de Dios, Grande," my
mother cried. She smiled and hugged and kissed the old woman.

"Ay, María Luna," Ultima smiled, "Buenos días te de Dios, a ti y a tu 89
familia." She wrapped the black shawl around her hair and shoulders. Her
face was brown and very wrinkled. When she smiled her teeth were brown. I
remembered the dream.

"Come, come!" my mother urged us forward. It was the custom to greet 90
the old. "Deborah!" my mother urged. Deborah stepped forward and took
Ultima's withered hand.

91   "Buenos días, Grande," she smiled. She even bowed slightly. Then she pulled Theresa forward and told her to greet la Grande. My mother beamed. Deborah's good manners surprised her, but they made her happy, because a family was judged by its manners.

92   "What beautiful daughters you have raised," Ultima nodded to my mother. Nothing could have pleased my mother more. She looked proudly at my father who stood leaning against the truck, watching and judging the introductions.

93   "Antonio," he said simply. I stepped forward and took Ultima's hand. I looked up into her clear brown eyes and shivered. Her face was old and wrinkled, but her eyes were clear and sparkling, like the eyes of a young child.

94   "Antonio," she smiled. She took my hand and I felt the power of a whirlwind sweep around me. Her eyes swept the surrounding hills and through them I saw for the first time the wild beauty of our hills and the magic of the green river. My nostrils quivered as I felt the song of the mockingbirds and the drone of the grasshoppers mingle with the pulse of the earth. The four directions of the llano met in me, and the white sun shone on my soul. The granules of sand at my feet and the sun and sky above me seemed to dissolve into one strange, complete being.

95   A cry came to my throat, and I wanted to shout it and run in the beauty I had found.

96   "Antonio." I felt my mother prod me. Deborah giggled because she had made the right greeting, and I who was to be my mother's hope and joy stood voiceless.

97   "Buenos días le de Dios, Ultima," I muttered. I saw in her eyes my dream. I saw the old woman who had delivered me from my mother's womb. I knew she held the secret of my destiny.

98   "¡Antonio!" My mother was shocked I had used her name instead of calling her Grande. But Ultima held up her hand.

99   "Let it be," she smiled. "This was the last child I pulled from your womb, María. I knew there would be something between us."

100   My mother who had started to mumble apologies was quiet. "As you wish, Grande," she nodded.

101   "I have come to spend the last days of my life here, Antonio," Ultima said to me.

102   "You will never die, Ultima," I answered. "I will take care of you—" She let go of my hand and laughed. Then my father said, "Pase, Grande, pase. Nuestra casa es su casa. It is too hot to stand and visit in the sun—"

103   "Sí, sí," my mother urged. I watched them go in. My father carried on his shoulders the large blue-tin trunk which later I learned contained all of Ultima's earthly possessions, the black dresses and shawls she wore, and the magic of her sweet smelling herbs.

104   As Ultima walked past me I smelled for the first time a trace of the sweet fragrance of herbs that always lingered in her wake. Many years later, long after Ultima was gone and I had grown to be a man, I would awaken some-

times at night and think I caught a scent of her fragrance in the cool-night breeze.

And with Ultima came the owl. I heard it that night for the first time in   105
the juniper tree outside of Ultima's window. I knew it was her owl because the other owls of the llano did not come that near the house. At first it disturbed me, and Deborah and Theresa too. I heard them whispering through the partition. I heard Deborah reassuring Theresa that she would take care of her, and then she took Theresa in her arms and rocked her until they were both asleep.

I waited. I was sure my father would get up and shoot the owl with the   106
old rifle he kept on the kitchen wall. But he didn't, and I accepted his understanding. In many cuentos I had heard the owl was one of the disguises a bruja took, and so it struck a chord of fear in the heart to hear them hooting at night. But not Ultima's owl. Its soft hooting was like a song, and as it grew rhythmic it calmed the moonlit hills and lulled us to sleep. Its song seemed to say that it had come to watch over us.

I dreamed about the owl that night, and my dream was good. La Virgen   107
de Guadalupe was the patron saint of our town. The town was named after her. In my dream I saw Ultima's owl lift la Virgen on her wide wings and fly her to heaven. Then the owl returned and gathered up all the babes of Limbo and flew them up to the clouds of heaven.

The Virgin smiled at the goodness of the owl.   108

Questions for Discussion

1. Discuss the two different communities that the narrator's family comes from. What kinds of conflict do they create for the narrator? Is this an uncommon conflict for young people?
2. What attitudes about caring for members of one's community are conveyed in the narrative? Refer to examples from the text to support your conclusions.
3. Compare and contrast the values you discern in this reading with those in Edelman's essay. What connections do you find?
4. How are people outside the narrator's family, such as Ultima and Benito Campos, connected to the web of family and community life?
5. The language of this selection is full of imagery. Discuss the ways in which such language evokes a mood, or conveys an attitude. Refer to examples from the text to support your view.

Ideas for Writing

1. Discuss the role of older relatives, such as aunts or grandparents, in your own family or in a particular subculture or ethnic group. Develop this topic further by doing library research and presenting your findings in a documented essay.
2. Obtain a copy of the book from which this selection is excerpted, and analyze the narrative. Using your response to question 2 above as a starting point, select a theme or issue brought up in this selection and discuss the ways in which the theme is developed throughout the novel. You could look at the dream sequences, the images of nature, or the conflicts between families as a starting point.

Community Organizations as Family

Shirley Brice Heath and Milbrey McLaughlin

Shirley Brice Heath, professor, lecturer, writer, was born in Winston-Salem, North Carolina. She holds a B.A. in English and Spanish, an M.A. in comparative education and linguistics, and a Ph.D. in anthropology from Columbia University. Heath is currently a professor of English and linguistics at Stanford University and has received many prestigious awards including the MacArthur, Guggenheim, and National Endowment for the Humanities Fellowships. She has conducted extensive ethnographic fieldwork, some of which culminated in the landmark work, *Ways with Words: Language, Life, and Work in Communities and Classrooms* (1983). With Shelby Wolf, she wrote *The Braid of Literature: Creativity, Connections, and Criticism* (1993). Heath has sponsored and directed Humanities and Arts Fellowships enabling college students to teach their art to children in the local communities.

Milbrey McLaughlin graduated from Connecticut College and earned an Ed.M. and Ed.D. in education and social policy at Harvard University. Director of the Center for Research on the Context of Secondary School Teaching since 1987, she is also a professor of education at Stanford University; her areas of specialization include school context, workplace, and policy analysis and implementation. As part of her extensive research background, McLaughlin served as coprincipal investigator with Shirley Brice Heath of a multiyear project, "Language, Socialization, and Neighborhood-Based Organizations," examining the extent to which voluntary organizations at several inner-city sites affect language uses, attitudes, and future goals of high school youth. The article that follows first appeared in *Phi Delta Kappan* in 1992.

Journal

Community members and leaders frequently call for programs that keep young people "off the streets" and engaged in productive activities. What kinds of activities and programs do you think would be successful? Or write about an organization in which you've been involved.

Bruce, a.k.a. Superman, squints in concentration, measuring the distance to the trampolette placed in front of the tumbling mats. Nineteen of his red-and-white-clad teammates position themselves in a tight row, forming a human bridge and a challenge to Bruce's strength and tumbling skills. Nicknamed for another man of flight, Bruce is the finale for the night's show. He takes a deep breath, sprints down the gym floor, springs from the trampolette, and flies over the backs of his teammates. He lands with arms raised, gold chains glinting, and a smile that lights the room.

*   *   *

"Come on, Eric. What are you waiting on? What you waiting on? C'mon, 2 c'mon. Move it. Move it. Give it up. Right there. There you go. There you go."

These shouts from Coach Beam echo against the empty stands of the gym- 3 nasium where the local YMCA boys' basketball team is practicing for a game against their arch rivals from the next town. The YMCA is located in a neighborhood of project housing that is being torn down to make room for a new freeway. The boys on the court, known as "Beam's boys," are 12- to 14-year-old African-Americans who spend an average of 15 hours a week at practice and doing homework under the watchful eye of the coach.

*   *   *

The director of a local youth organization tells a visiting political leader: 4 "You should know about Darlene—and, oh yes, her brother, Tyrone, too. But we call him Toot around here. Mother died of AIDS six months ago. Father left them and two younger girls. Darlene brings the youngest ones to the Girls Club at 7 each morning, and we send them off to school and then keep them occupied while she's at work after school. Toot works all day and picks the girls up at 7 each night, after he leaves the Boys Club, where he boxes. He feeds the girls and gets them to bed before Darlene gets home. Each day it's the same."

*   *   *

These three vignettes are drawn from our ongoing research.[1] They depict 5 adolescents' lively and voluntary involvement in constructive, positive alternatives to the counterproductive teenage ventures that fill the morning newspapers, most particularly drug-related activities and gang violence.

Bruce is a young African-American, born and reared in one of the nation's 6 toughest housing projects; he navigates through a neighborhood known nationally for violence and gang dominance. His "gang" is a tumbling team. Eric and the other basketball players hang out at the Y in their spare time to keep out of harm's way—off the streets. They have found a protected niche of developmentally appropriate, adult-monitored activities. For Darlene and Toot, the neighborhood organizations are not just places to spend pleasant times with their peers, but institutions that support them in their early assumptions of responsibility.

[1]With the support of the Spencer Foundation, we are involved in a multi-year research project that examines the resources and programs available to youths, especially adolescents, in diverse urban settings. In identifying the organizations that young people find supportive and relevant, we depended on community informants—youths and adults—rather than on official organizational lists or rosters. Consequently, we observed youths participating in a broad variety of activities and supported by diverse sponsors—the spectrum included everything from small endeavors created and sustained by the energy of a single individual to neighborhood "branches" of national organizations.

7   Unlike Toot, Darlene is still in school, although her family responsibilities may soon force her to quit and take a full-time job. Both youths essentially left school several years ago; piles of cuts and tardies planted them firmly in school administrators' minds as early dropouts. For several years, they have served as caregivers and heads of their household. For all the teenagers described above, nonschool organizations provide multiple services that sustain them in their family roles and give them broad support for their identities as teenagers.

8   Policy makers and practitioners concerned with American youth acknowledge the special and critical contribution of community organizations as resources that extend beyond family and schools. Their view recognizes the limitations of today's schools and families. Schools as social institutions are inadequate because they are built on outmoded assumptions about family and community. Too many families simply lack the emotional, financial, experiential, or cognitive supports that a developing youngster requires.[2] Policy makers and practitioners no longer need to be convinced of the importance of positive local alternatives to a family- and school-based system of support.

9   Most adolescents, however, are not involved in any community-based activities on a regular basis. For some young people, especially those growing up in stressed inner-city or rural communities, this lack of participation reflects lack of opportunity; there simply are few organizations or undertakings available to them. As a school superintendent in a large eastern city grumbled, the only "youth-serving" agents in the city are the police. A city official in another urban area said that his community's youth policy was "parks and police"— parks to provide a place for youths to gather outside their neighborhoods and police to monitor their behavior once gathered there.

10   But lack of opportunity is not the whole (or even the most important) reason why young people generally are not involved in organized, constructive activities during out-of-school hours. Effective strategies for enabling such local organizations to attract youths are not well-understood and are the exceptions rather than the rule. Practitioners from diverse youth-serving organizations—churches, sports organizations, youth clubs, schools, social clubs—say that a major problem they confront is *attracting and sustaining the involvement of young people*, especially teenagers. Well-equipped gymnasiums in the inner city too often sit empty; computer labs that are the fruits of prodigious fundraising efforts serve a handful rather than a roomful of students after school; pony leagues fold for lack of players; church workers give up on planning social activities for youngsters past the age of 12.

11   What kinds of activities constructively engage adolescents? What kinds of programs effectively address the developmental needs of youngsters as they move from childhood to adulthood in high-risk environments? What kinds of youth-serving organizations do adolescents choose to join? We have waited in

[2]We develop this point in more detail in Shirley Brice Heath and Milbrey Wallin McLaughlin, "A Child Resource Policy: Moving Beyond Dependence on School and Family," *Phi Delta Kappan*, April 1987, pp. 576–80.

many empty gyms for the students to come by for after-school theater class; we have made small talk with adult sponsors of tutoring centers as the hoped-for clients failed to materialize. But we have also observed adolescents cheerfully and fully engaged in activities located in their communities, activities that keep them off the streets and provide them with the tutoring help needed to keep them in school. These organizations, through their form and flexibility in activities, have fortified these youths during their difficult adolescent years.

What makes the enterprises that succeed different from those that fail to attract and hold the interest of teenagers? Activities and sponsoring organizations such as those in our opening vignettes are not of a single type. What they have in common is their diversity and their insistence that members feel that they belong to an intimate group. The integration of members into the life of the group depends on differentiation within the group: varied activities, varied rhythms of work and play, and the valuing of differing talents, ages, and approaches. 12

Successful organizations adopt an approach that is both firm and flexible; they empower rather than infantilize youths; they are clear about their goals and their rules of membership. Dance troupes, basketball teams, tumbling groups, and theater groups boom and buzz with the energy of adolescents. The focus of any local youth organization that effectively serves youths in the 1990s has less to do with what it is than with how it is defined and operated. 13

Not surprisingly, these out-of-school settings—whether they be grassroots youth organizations, local chapters of national groups (such as Boys Clubs, Future Farmers of America, and so on), local religious organizations, or parks and recreation centers—share many of the features that in earlier eras characterized family life. 14

These organizations provide a strong sense of membership with numerous marks of identification. Their approach to youths is highly personalized. In one of Tyrone's early visits to the Boys Club, he became "Toot" when he picked up a saxophone left lying around by one of the older boys. The sound he made as he attempted to play the instrument won him a nickname that stuck, even when he became one of the club's best boxers and an instructor for the younger boys, who insisted on calling him "Tootie." For Toot and others like him, the Boys Club is a fortress against the outside world. Within the walls of the club, he can be teased, called by a silly diminutive, teach younger boys, horse around with friends who also like to box, and enter, if only briefly, the stable life of an ordinary teenager. 15

The club offers a range of activities that are developmentally appropriate for all the boys who come there; some work in the art room, others in sculpture, others on dramatic productions that they write, direct, and produce. Still others make up the swim team and the boxing club, and all have access to the study room, where older members help the younger ones with homework, and adults—volunteer and paid—are also available to provide assistance. The "something for everyone" menu of activities includes youngsters from ages 9 16 to 19 in a range of designated events and spaces. More important, the norm at the club is that everyone helps out to keep the place going. Nonswimmers count laps for the 500-yard free-style, and nonactors clear the mats from the gym floor in preparation for a play rehearsal.

17   Out-of-school organizations to which youths like Bruce, Toot and Darlene, and Beam's boys find their way envelop teens firmly in a socializing community that holds them responsible for their own actions. In addition, the members are held accountable for the institution's well-being and for the actions of others within the protected walls of the organization. Membership brings with it acceptance of "minimal rules with maximal impact." The central rules of these organizations are simple and broad: no hanging out with gang members; no smoking dope; leave this area just like you'd want to find it; put up or shut up; don't forget you represent us—all of us—and if you blow it, you'll have all of us to answer to; and no "doing the dozens."

18   Of course, within such broad rules are numerous others that have to do with appropriate language and dress, management of specific activities, and the security and cleanliness of the building. Breaking one of these minor rules brings an immediate reminder of the higher rules of membership and calls into question the individual's right to belong to the group.

19   The consistent and reliable adults—from directors to custodians—who operate these youth organizations not only enforce the rules for the members but also make it evident that *everyone* is equally responsible for monitoring the behavior of those who come to the organization. Rules are clear, and enforcement is certain; it is "tough love." Flexibility comes not in mitigated punishments, but in the willingness to help youths plan, reform, reshape, and assess events within the organization. Adults do not plan without their clients; any performance, special event, or extra activity requires the involvement of the young people themselves.

20   These features are reminiscent of the concepts of family pride, shared responsibility for maintaining a household, and the "golden rule" of communal living. Moreover, like family life, these organizations do not move from the peak of one planned "special event" to the next. Instead, their pace is seasonal and moves constantly through practice toward performances, all of which are somewhat graduated in level of importance. For example, swim meets, run-throughs of plays, play-offs to prepare for tournaments, within-group rounds of boxing competitions, and in-house judging of artworks to choose a few pieces for county or state competition are peak moments of judgment and reassessment in preparation for actual competition or performance. The final public performance of a season may begin a transitional period of "down time," during which some youths explore other activities (another sport, a different dramatic production, and so on) or try just "being around" with one another.

21   The push toward performance and the ongoing emphasis on collaborating in activities support the habit of talking through what is going on and how mistakes and successes happen. Interpreting events in which all have participated bonds members to one another, often through extensive teasing, special

terms to refer to "bloopers," and an abundance of evidence that members do "mind each other's business." This mutual responsibility for monitoring behavior fits well with the norms of an idealized family or communal support group. The members "look out for each other." Newcomers and younger members often "belong" for a while to those who have been around longer or are older.

In out-of-school organizations that successfully attract youngsters, adults and youngsters alike talk about the need for the institution to value differences. Newcomers are scouted for their talents: "Can you play center?" "You ever been in a play before?" "You know anything about us? Why'd you come here?" Members of these organizations make it clear that they value differences—among themselves, in their activities, and in strategies and approaches. Such valuing of differences does not, however, extend to radical extremes; to do so would be to break the central rules of the organization that ensure its survival. Thus the mission of the organization and its teams must be the clear focus driving any member's radical ideas for changing things.

Youth-serving organizations that successfully attract young people invariably have some links to education—but rarely to schools. Many include homework sessions and tutoring opportunities, and all let members talk openly about problems and successes in school. The ethos of these organizations encourages members to stay in school, keep up attendance, and try harder with schoolwork. Many provide youths with "natural learning activities" that call for skills that are also presumably useful in school (e.g., keeping the books for a dance ensemble, reading plays to get ideas for creative skits, studying old playbills to learn how to prepare a program for a production). Often, helping teens stay in school requires the assistance and support of organizations that are as little like their neighborhood schools as possible.

These family-like organizations and activities differ in at least six crucial elements of design and orientation from those youth-serving institutions that are less successful in attracting and engaging adolescents.

1. These organizations share a common conception of young people as resources to be developed, rather than as problems to be managed. This conception of young people generates program activities that respect the views and abilities youths bring with them, that are attuned to their developmental needs and cultural differences, and that strive to provide support that meshes with their unmet needs. Activities consistent with this conception of youths embrace the whole person—not just single issues, such as pregnancy, substance abuse, or school success. While a single focus, such as basketball or tumbling, may define the organization, it also embraces the full emotional, social, educational, and economic needs of participating adolescents.

2. Activities that young people elect to join most often yield a recognizable "product"—a performance, a team record, a newspaper, an edited volume. Adolescent youths living in stressed urban environments generally spurn the purely "recreational" activities that middle-class parents assume their teenagers want. These adolescents are product-oriented. They want to create

something that signals accomplishment. Contrary to the assumptions of many program planners, youths (especially those from at-risk environments) seem to recognize that they cannot really afford to spend much time and energy on "just plain fun." It has to amount to something.

27   3. Activities driven by a conception of youths as resources to be developed also invest a significant measure of responsibility for that development in the young people themselves. Entrusting important activities to them plays a critical role in the development of young people from an early age. The successful activities we have observed suggest that ownership and trust are essential for adolescents. A program attractive to teenagers is a program that is "theirs," not an activity organized and planned in a way that reminds them of a controlling parent or stern teacher. What's "good stuff" from the perspective of an adult, teenagers tell us clearly, is not always good—or even appropriate—stuff in their view.

28   4. Neighborhood investment is also important. For example, the director of a neighborhood Boys Club tells of the debilitating decline in the number of community volunteers and board members when the club's financial authority was centralized "downtown" and local residents no longer had a sense that the money they raised went to *their* club. Youth-serving organizations that are vital and effective from the community's perspective have their roots deep in the community, and they can draw on the local environment for political, financial, and instrumental support. Thus the local organization is not a stranger; it is a recognized and legitimate member of the community family because the community members have helped to develop, shape, and reform the programs that "fit" the community's youths.

29   5. Community organizations that attract youngsters are responsive to the "local ecology," the untapped resources and unmet needs of those who become their members. Generic program models or standardized service menus, especially those created at some remove, risk being redundant or irrelevant. Not all neighborhoods have the same configuration of schools, recreational activities, social services, family coherence, political clout, or cultural opportunities. Not all youth programs need to offer the same sports, education, social supports, or training. Efforts that have effectively engaged and sustained the participation of young people define their emphases and offerings in terms of the communities they serve.

30   6. As youth-serving organizations listen to and respond to community needs, they must also change to meet shifts in the ecology of the neighborhood. As neighborhoods move up or down the socioeconomic ladder, as their ethnic makeup shifts, and as other youth-serving institutions (such as schools) are perceived as responding or not responding to the needs of local youngsters, community organizations must move quickly to realign their activities, hours, administrative style, and sources of financial support to the new realities of the community. Community organizations that serve youths must simultaneously understand and change themselves. Thus effective youth-serving organizations are not often found in the "organizational yellow pages," either because they escape the notice of official institutional census takers or

because the form, identification, and even location of the organization change as the group responds to local circumstances.

In the current enthusiasm for looking at learning as situated or socially 31 constructed knowledge,[3] the features of community youth-serving organizations outlined here are examples of theory put into practice. The resources of each organization include the collective memory of the group's members, as well as the dynamics of current social relationships and seasonal activities that provide a full cycle to fulfillment through the completion of an individual task or performance or of a seasonal activity (e.g., basketball). The activities of these organizations, like the idealized family life whose features they reflect, structure fields for action, reflection, and constructive social interaction.

Questions for Discussion

1. Do you find the anecdotal introduction effective? Why? How do these stories involve you in the issues? Would an anecdotal example be suitable for the kinds of essays you write in your courses? Explain your response.
2. According to the authors, what are the main reasons that many youths are not involved in community activities? Why do some organizations succeed and others fail? What are the key features of successful organizations for youths?
3. The authors assert that "schools as social organizations are inadequate because they are built on outmoded assumptions about family and community." What are some of those assumptions, from your own observations and as discussed in this essay?
4. What is youth "empowerment"? How do some organizations empower youths? What are the benefits of doing so? In what ways can schools foster or undermine empowerment?
5. According to Heath and McLaughlin, in what ways do the organizations function as family? What do you think Edelman's response would be to community organizations stepping into this role?

Ideas for Writing

1. Using your own experience or observations, write an essay supporting or refuting the thesis of this article. Be sure to refer to relevant examples to support your point of view.
2. Write an essay arguing for local resources (college service center, city, county, recreation centers) to be used to support a program in your community such as the authors describe. Assume an audience not only of instructor and peers, but also of administrators of the center who should provide the resources. Think about how you will appeal to the specific audience and what benefits you will point out. After listening to feedback from your class, revise the essay and submit it as a letter to the appropriate authority.

[3]See, for example, Jean Lave, *Cognition in Practice* (Cambridge: Cambridge University Press, 1988); Lauren B. Resnick, "Learning in School and Out," *Educational Researcher*, December 1987, pp. 13–20; and James G. Greeno, "Understanding Procedural Knowledge in Mathematics Instruction," *Educational Psychologist*, vol. 12, 1978, pp. 262–83.

Silent Dancing

Judith Ortiz Cofer

Judith Ortiz Cofer (b. 1952) is the daughter of a teenage mother and a career Navy father. As a child she traveled between the mainland United States and Puerto Rico where she was born. She married in college, had a daughter, did graduate work in English at Oxford, and now resides in Florida where she teaches and writes poetry about the experiences of living in more than one culture. Her collections include *Reaching for the Mainland* (1987) and *Terms of Survival* (1988), and she has also written a novel, *The Line of the Sun* (1989), and a memoir, *Silent Dancing* (1990), from which the following selection is excerpted. In her memoir, Cofer vividly describes the communities of her childhood and youth and the conflicts she experienced living in a multicultural society.

Journal

Reflect on the different people in your community, whether at school or in your hometown. How do people from different backgrounds get along? Alternatively, write about what goes through your mind when you look at old snapshots, videos, or home movies from your past.

We have a home movie of this party. Several times my mother and I have watched it together, and I have asked questions about the silent revelers coming in and out of focus. It is grainy and of short duration, but it's a great visual aid to my memory of life at that time. And it is in color—the only complete scene in color I can recall from those years.

2   We lived in Puerto Rico until my brother was born in 1954. Soon after, because of economic pressures on our growing family, my father joined the United States Navy. He was assigned to duty on a ship in Brooklyn Yard— a place of cement and steel that was to be his home base in the States until his retirement more than twenty years later. He left the Island first, alone, going to New York City and tracking down his uncle who lived with his family across the Hudson River in Paterson, New Jersey. There my father found a tiny apartment in a huge tenement that had once housed Jewish families but was just being taken over and transformed by Puerto Ricans, overflowing from New York City. In 1955 he sent for us. My mother was only twenty years old, I was not quite three, and my brother was a toddler when we arrived at *El Building*, as the place had been christened by its newest residents.

3   My memories of life in Paterson during those first few years are all in shades of gray. Maybe I was too young to absorb vivid colors and details, or to discriminate between the slate blue of the winter sky and the darker hues of the snow-bearing clouds, but that single color washes over the whole period.

The building we lived in was gray, as were the streets, filled with slush the first few months of my life there. The coat my father had bought for me was similar in color and too big; it sat heavily on my thin frame.

I do remember the way the heater pipes banged and rattled, startling all 4 of us out of sleep until we got so used to the sound that we automatically shut it out or raised our voices above the racket. The hiss from the valve punctuated my sleep (which has always been fitful) like a nonhuman presence in the room—a dragon sleeping at the entrance of my childhood. But the pipes were also a connection to all the other lives being lived around us. Having come from a house designed for a single family back in Puerto Rico—my mother's extended-family home—it was curious to know that strangers lived under our floor and above our heads, and that the heater pipe went through everyone's apartments. (My first spanking in Paterson came as a result of playing tunes on the pipes in my room to see if there would be an answer.) My mother was as new to this concept of beehive life as I was, but she had been given strict orders by my father to keep the doors locked, the noise down, ourselves to ourselves.

It seems that Father had learned some painful lessons about prejudice 5 while searching for an apartment in Paterson. Not until years later did I hear how much resistance he had encountered with landlords who were panicking at the influx of Latinos into a neighborhood that had been Jewish for a couple of generations. It made no difference that it was the American phenomenon of ethnic turnover which was changing the urban core of Paterson, and that the human flood could not be held back with an accusing finger.

"You Cuban?" one man had asked my father, pointing at his name tag on 6 the Navy uniform—even though my father had the fair skin and light-brown hair of his northern Spanish background, and the name Ortiz is as common in Puerto Rico as Johnson is in the United States.

"No," my father had answered, looking past the finger into his adversary's 7 angry eyes. "I'm Puerto Rican."

"Same shit." And the door closed.   8

My father could have passed as European, but we couldn't. My brother 9 and I both have our mother's black hair and olive skin, and so we lived in El Building and visited our great-uncle and his fair children on the next block. It was their private joke that they were the German branch of the family. Not many years later that area too would be mainly Puerto Rican. It was as if the heart of the city map were being gradually colored brown—*café con leche* brown. Our color.

The movie opens with a sweep of the living room. It is "typical" immigrant Puerto 10 *Rican decor for the time: The sofa and chairs are square and hardlooking, upholstered in bright colors (blue and yellow in this instance), and covered with the transparent plastic that furniture salesmen then were so adept at convincing women to buy. The linoleum on the floor is light blue; if it had been subjected to spike heels (as it was in most places), there were dime-sized indentations all over it that cannot be seen in this movie. The room is full of people dressed up: dark suits for the men, red dresses for the women. When I have asked my mother why most of the women are in red that night, she has shrugged, "I don't remember. Just a coincidence." She doesn't have my obsession for assigning symbolism to everything.*

11   *The three women in red sitting on the couch are my mother, my eighteen-year-old cousin, and her brother's girlfriend. The* novia *is just up from the Island, which is apparent in her body language. She sits up formally, her dress pulled over her knees. She is a pretty girl, but her posture makes her look insecure, lost in her full-skirted dress, which she has carefully tucked around her to make room for my gorgeous cousin, her future sister-in-law. My cousin has grown up in Paterson and is in her last year of high school. She doesn't have a trace of what Puerto Ricans call* la mancha *(literally, the stain: the mark of the new immigrant—something about the posture, the voice, or the humble demeanor that makes it obvious to everyone the person has just arrived on the mainland). My cousin is wearing a tight, sequined, cocktail dress. Her brown hair has been lightened with peroxide around the bangs, and she is holding a cigarette expertly between her fingers, bringing it up to her mouth in a sensuous arc of her arm as she talks animatedly. My mother, who has come up to sit between the two women, both only a few years younger than herself, is somewhere between the poles they represent in our culture.*

12   It became my father's obsession to get out of the barrio, and thus we were never permitted to form bonds with the place or with the people who lived there. Yet El Building was a comfort to my mother, who never got over yearning for *la isla.* She felt surrounded by her language: The walls were thin, and voices speaking and arguing in Spanish could be heard all day. *Salsas* blasted out of radios, turned on early in the morning and left on for company. Women seemed to cook rice and beans perpetually—the strong aroma of boiling red kidney beans permeated the hallways.

13   Though Father preferred that we do our grocery shopping at the supermarket when he came home on weekend leaves, my mother insisted that she could cook only with products whose labels she could read. Consequently, during the week I accompanied her and my little brother to *La Bodega*—a hole-in-the-wall grocery store across the street from El Building. There we squeezed down three narrow aisles jammed with various products. Goya's and Libby's—those were the trademarks that were trusted by *her mamá,* so my mother bought many cans of Goya beans, soups, and condiments, as well as little cans of Libby's fruit juices for us. And she also bought Colgate toothpaste and Palmolive soap. (The final *e* is pronounced in both these products in Spanish, so for many years I believed that they were manufactured on the Island. I remember my surprise at first hearing a commercial on television in which Colgate rhymed with "ate.") We always lingered at La Bodega, for it was there that Mother breathed best, taking in the familiar aromas of the foods she knew from Mamá's kitchen. It was also there that she got to speak to the other women of El Building without violating outright Father's dictates against fraternizing with our neighbors.

Yet Father did his best to make our "assimilation" painless. I can still see 14 him carrying a real Christmas tree up several flights of stairs to our apartment, leaving a trail of aromatic pine. He carried it formally, as if it were a flag in a parade. We were the only ones in El Building that I knew of who got presents on both Christmas day AND *día de Reyes*, the day when the Three Kings brought gifts to Christ and to Hispanic children.

Our supreme luxury in El Building was having our own television set. It 15 must have been a result of Father's guilt feelings over the isolation he had imposed on us, but we were among the first in the barrio to have one. My brother quickly became an avid watcher of Captain Kangaroo and Jungle Jim, while I loved all the series showing families. By the time I started first grade, I could have drawn a map of Middle America as exemplified by the lives of characters in "Father Knows Best," "The Donna Reed Show," "Leave It to Beaver," "My Three Sons," and (my favorite) "Bachelor Father," where John Forsythe treated his adopted teenage daughter like a princess because he was rich and had a Chinese houseboy to do everything for him. In truth, compared to our neighbors in El Building, *we* were rich. My father's Navy check provided us with financial security and a standard of life that the factory workers envied. The only thing his money could not buy us was a place to live away from the barrio—his greatest wish, Mother's greatest fear.

In the home movie the men are shown next, sitting around a card table set up in 16 *one corner of the living room, playing dominoes. The clack of the ivory pieces was a familiar sound. I heard it in many houses on the Island and in many apartments in Paterson. In "Leave It to Beaver," the Cleavers played bridge in every other episode; in my childhood, the men started* every *social occasion with a hotly debated round of dominoes. The women would sit around and watch, but they never participated in the games.*

Here and there you can see a small child. Children were always brought to par- 17 *ties and, whenever they got sleepy, were put to bed in the host's bedroom. Babysitting was a concept unrecognized by the Puerto Rican women I knew: A responsible mother did not leave her children with any stranger. And in a culture where children are not considered intrusive, there was no need to leave the children at home. We went where our mother went.*

Of my preschool years I have only impressions: the sharp bite of the wind 18 in December as we walked with our parents towards the brightly lit stores downtown; how I felt like a stuffed doll in my heavy coat, boots, and mittens; how good it was to walk into the five-and-dime and sit at the counter drinking hot chocolate. On Saturdays our whole family would walk downtown to shop at the big department stores on Broadway. Mother bought all our clothes at Penney's and Sears, and she liked to buy her dresses at the women's specialty shops like Lerner's and Diana's. At some point we'd go into Woolworth's and sit at the soda fountain to eat.

We never ran into other Latinos at these stores or when eating out, and it 19 became clear to me only years later that the women from El Building shopped mainly in other places—stores owned by other Puerto Ricans or by Jewish merchants who had philosophically accepted our presence in the city and decided to make us their good customers, if not real neighbors and friends. These establishments were located not downtown but in the blocks around our street, and they were referred to generically as *La Tienda, El Bazar, La Bodega, La Botánica.* Everyone knew what was meant. These were the stores where your face did not turn a clerk to stone, where your money was as green as anyone else's.

20   One New Year's Eve we were dressed up like child models in the Sears catalogue: my brother in a miniature man's suit and bow tie, and I in black patent-leather shoes and a frilly dress with several layers of crinoline underneath. My mother wore a bright red dress that night, I remember, and spike heels; her long black hair hung to her waist. Father, who usually wore his Navy uniform during his short visits home, had put on a dark civilian suit for the occasion: We had been invited to his uncle's house for a big celebration. Everyone was excited because my mother's brother Hernan—a bachelor who could indulge himself with luxuries—had bought a home movie camera, which he would be trying out that night.

21   Even the home movie cannot fill in the sensory details such a gathering left imprinted in a child's brain. The thick sweetness of women's perfumes mixing with the ever-present smells of food cooking in the kitchen: meat and plantain *pasteles,* as well as the ubiquitous rice dish made special with pigeon peas—*gandules*—and seasoned with precious *sofrito* sent up from the Island by somebody's mother or smuggled in by a recent traveler. *Sofrito* was one of the items that women hoarded, since it was hardly ever in stock at La Bodega. It was the flavor of Puerto Rico.

22   The men drank Palo Viejo rum, and some of the younger ones got weepy. The first time I saw a grown man cry was at a New Year's Eve party: He had been reminded of his mother by the smells in the kitchen. But what I remember most were the boiled *pasteles*—plantain or yucca rectangles stuffed with corned beef or other meats, olives, and many other savory ingredients, all wrapped in banana leaves. Everybody had to fish one out with a fork. There was always a "trick" pastel—one without stuffing—and whoever got that one was the "New Year's Fool."

23   There was also the music. Long-playing albums were treated like precious china in these homes. Mexican recordings were popular, but the songs that brought tears to my mother's eyes were sung by the melancholy Daniel Santos, whose life as a drug addict was the stuff of legend. Felipe Rodríguez was a particular favorite of couples, since he sang about faithless women and brokenhearted men. There is a snatch of one lyric that has stuck in my mind like a needle on a worn groove: *De piedra ha de ser mi cama, de piedra la cabezera . . . la mujer que a mi me quiera . . . ha de quererme de veras. Ay, Ay, Ay, corazón, porque no amas.*[1] . . . I must have heard it a thousand times since the idea of a bed

---

[1]My bed must be stone, my pillow, stone . . . the woman who loves me must truly love me. Ay, ay, ay, heart, why don't you love. [Ed.]

made of stone, and its connection to love, first troubled me with its disturbing images.

The five-minute home movie ends with people dancing in a circle—the 24 creative filmmaker must have set it up, so that all of them could file past him. It is both comical and sad to watch silent dancing. Since there is no justification for the absurd movements that music provides for some of us, people appear frantic, their faces embarrassingly intense. It's as if you were watching sex. Yet for years I've had dreams in the form of this home movie. In a recurring scene, familiar faces push themselves forward into my mind's eye, plastering their features into distorted close-ups. And I'm asking them: "Who is *she?* Who is the old woman I don't recognize? Is she an aunt? Somebody's wife? Tell me who she is."

> "See the beauty mark on her cheek as big as a hill on the lunar landscape of 25 her face—well, that runs in the family. The women on your father's side of the family wrinkle early; it's the price they pay for that fair skin. The young girl with the green stain on her wedding dress is *La Novia*—just up from the Island. See, she lowers her eyes when she approaches the camera, as she's supposed to. Decent girls never look at you directly in the face. *Humilde,* humble, a girl should express humility in all her actions. She will make a good wife for your cousin. He should consider himself lucky to have met her only weeks after she arrived here. If he marries her quickly, she will make him a good Puerto Rican–style wife; but if he waits too long, she will be corrupted by the city—just like your cousin there."

> "She means me. I do what I want. This is not some primitive island I live 26 on. Do they expect me to wear a black mantilla on my head and go to mass every day? Not me. I'm an American woman, and I will do as I please. I can type faster than anyone in my senior class at Central High, and I'm going to be a secretary to a lawyer when I graduate. I can pass for an American girl anywhere—I've tried it. At least for Italian, anyway—I never speak Spanish in public. I hate these parties, but I wanted the dress. I look better than any of these *humildes* here. My life is going to be different. I have an American boyfriend. He is older and has a car. My parents don't know it, but I sneak out of the house late at night sometimes to be with him. If I marry him, even my name will be American. I hate rice and beans—that's what makes these women fat."

> "Your *prima* is pregnant by that man she's been sneaking around with. 27 Would I lie to you? I'm your *Tiá Política,* your great-uncle's common-law wife—the one he abandoned on the Island to go marry your cousin's mother. *I* was not invited to this party, of course, but I came anyway. I came to tell you that story about your cousin that you've always wanted to hear. Do you remember the comment your mother made to a neighbor that has always haunted you? The only thing you heard was your cousin's name, and then you saw your mother pick up your doll from the couch and say: 'It was as big as this doll when they flushed it down the toilet.' This image has bothered you for years, hasn't it? You had nightmares about babies being flushed down the toilet, and you wondered why anyone would do such a horrible thing. You didn't dare ask your mother about it. She would only tell you that you

had not heard her right, and yell at you for listening to adult conversations. But later, when you were old enough to know about abortions, you suspected.

28   "I am here to tell you that you were right. Your cousin was growing an *Americanito* in her belly when this movie was made. Soon after she put something long and pointy into her pretty self, thinking maybe she could get rid of the problem before breakfast and still make it to her first class at the high school. Well, *Niña*, her screams could be heard downtown. Your aunt, her mamá, who had been a midwife on the Island, managed to pull the little thing out. Yes, they probably flushed it down the toilet. What else could they do with it—give it a Christian burial in a little white casket with blue bows and ribbons? Nobody wanted that baby—least of all the father, a teacher at her school with a house in West Paterson that he was filling with real children, and a wife who was a natural blonde.

29   "Girl, the scandal sent your uncle back to the bottle. And guess where your cousin ended up? Irony of ironies. She was sent to a village in Puerto Rico to live with a relative on her mother's side: a place so far away from civilization that you have to ride a mule to reach it. A real change in scenery. She found a man there—women like that cannot live without male company—but believe me, the men in Puerto Rico know how to put a saddle on a woman like her. *La Gringa*, they call her. Ha, ha, ha. *La Gringa* is what she always wanted to be. . . ."

30 The old woman's mouth becomes a cavernous black hole I fall into. And as I fall, I can feel the reverberations of her laughter. I hear the echoes of her last mocking words: *La Gringa, La Gringa!* And the conga line keeps moving silently past me. There is no music in my dream for the dancers.

31   When Odysseus visits Hades to see the spirit of his mother, he makes an offering of sacrificial blood, but since all the souls crave an audience with the living, he has to listen to many of them before he can ask questions. I, too, have to hear the dead and the forgotten speak in my dream. Those who are still part of my life remain silent, going around and around in their dance. The others keep pressing their faces forward to say things about the past.

32   My father's uncle is last in line. He is dying of alcoholism, shrunken and shriveled like a monkey, his face a mass of wrinkles and broken arteries. As he comes closer I realize that in his features I can see my whole family. If you were to stretch that rubbery flesh, you could find my father's face, and deep within *that* face—my own. I don't want to look into those eyes ringed in purple. In a few years he will retreat into silence, and take a long, long time to die. *Move back, Tío,* I tell him. *I don't want to hear what you have to say. Give the dancers room to move. Soon it will be midnight. Who is the New Year's Fool this time?*

Questions for Discussion

1. What are the author's parents' attitudes toward assimilation? How does her father view the barrio? What are her mother's feelings about maintaining a sense of cultural connectedness in Paterson? How might her father's workplace, and her mother's work in the home, have contributed to their attitudes?

2. Contrast what Cofer and her brother learn from American television with her attitudes toward the home movie. How does the author seem to feel about her assimilation?

3. Study the narrative technique in the selection. How does the author weave together the two cultures? the past and present? Is her technique effective?

4. Why do you think the selection is entitled "Silent Dancing"? What meaning does Cofer see in the silent dancing in the home movie? What meaning do you see in the image?

5. Analyze the image of the beehive and its significance to the memoir. What does *El Building* represent to the members of the author's family? to the community?

6. Discuss the gender roles implied and explicitly discussed in the selection. Consider the expectations for a "Puerto Rican–style" wife as opposed to one who has erased *la mancha*, the "stain" of the recent immigrant.

Ideas for Writing

1. Discuss the ways in which families from diverse backgrounds could or should act as they come together in a community. How can families preserve their own ethnic heritage and culture and yet be a part of mainstream American society? Or should they even try?

2. Write your own memoir. If possible, include an imaginary "home movie" or description of an actual video you have seen. Focus your memoir on a specific aspect of your past life, much as Cofer focuses on the connections between assimilation and family rather than biographical information. As does Cofer, do your best to weave together the textual narrative and video narrative, bringing the elements together to form a thematic point.

A Treasury of Quilts

Nora Cain

Nora Cain (b. 1952) was born in Brooklyn but has spent much of her adult life in California, where she now resides with her husband, a poet, and their two daughters. Cain was awarded a Stegner Fellowship at Stanford University in 1978 where she studied and wrote poetry. Her poems have appeared in *Gramercy Review* and *Sequoya;* Cain drew from her interest in quilting for the suite of poems, "A Treasury of Quilts," which was published in 1982 in *Sequoya.*

Journal

Are there any handmade crafts or heirlooms in your family? Have you seen any fiber arts or crafts represented in museums? What do they tell us about American cultures? Alternatively, if you haven't seen any handmade crafts, why do you suppose such arts are not commonly represented in many art museums?

Darting Minnows

The minnows are actually small diamonds that run across the quilt in an open cross-hatch design. Tossed on a bed, or over a sleeping person, the pattern seems to move like small fish.

Sleep children, and dream of the rain,
the steep whisper of the run-off,
the heavy loam settling in the fields,
and the unquenchable green of spring wheat
5   filling the land.

Sleep, and forget the rasp
of the thistle on the screen, the
hopeless chant of the cricket rising
above the scalded earth.

10   Sleep, and I'll spread over you this dream of water;
the quilt's shifting patterns
slide like the slow moving river,
and in the darkest blue,
under the shadow of the willow, where you hang your feet,
15   the tiny diamonds, now white,
now silver, flash like the minnows,
and you feel their curious kisses
before they move upstream.

Wandering Foot

A jagged triangle fills a corner of each Wandering Foot block. Four blocks are arranged so that the points of the triangles meet, and the jagged edges of the "foot" point out toward the corners of the quilt. Folk myth held that the Wandering Foot induced wanderlust in those who slept under it.

As powerful as wolfsbane, mandrake
and nightshade, the charm of the jagged
foot, set in the corner of the simple block,
works its way into the dreaming sleeper.

5   Under the warmth of its spell,
the boundaries of his world chafe,
and he turns, restless
and uneasy in his sleep, eager
to follow the song of the unknown bird
10   weaving through the icy night.

Where four blocks meet, the tracks
point outward like the markings on a compass,
and his heart pivots freely now, seeking
another direction, a truer north. He hears
15   the winds from the four corners of the earth,

and from his boots rises the sharp smell
of fresh earth and broken vines.
When you rise, he will be gone.

Be canny with this magic, protect
what's dear—husband and children—   20
and lay this spell gently
over those who should be moving on,
the unwelcome or tiresome visitor.

Indian Hatchet

*The block is merely a square divided by a diagonal stripe. It gains its effect when four blocks
are sewn together with the diagonals facing the same direction, and the eye is able to make out
the "hatchet" blade. Indian Hatchet was a popular beginner's pattern.*

The bright slash of red splitting
the white block three times on the diagonal
seemed the most of the story
she could remember: "We was all of us working
in the field, even the little ones, trying   5
to bring in the last of the corn, when we heard them call.
They's pretty calls, Indian calls,
like the meadowlarks, and when I heard it the second time
I could hear the raspy sound of the grass
moving where there wasn't a soul, and Tom,   10
your grandaddy, dropped his sack, waving his arms
at me to run, and already they were upon him.
I snatched up the baby and ran through the corn
to the woods. When I couldn't run anymore
I hid us under some bushes, pulling the leaves   15
over me to bury my dress. The baby never cried.
We lay there all night and I could see for
a little while the glow of fire over the woods—
I knew that was the house.
At dawn I crept back and found them all   20
lying in the burned fields—the three children
were scalped, fallen together, but Tom's head
was split clean open, he'd died that moment
he heard the second call."

She fitted the blocks slash   25
leading to slash in the center, the blows
moving out in four directions, surrounding
everything—the woods, the fields,
her grandmother's small cabin
and the family going about its chores inside—   30
surrounding everything, even a young girl

like herself seated by the fire
piecing a simple quilt.

Grief Quilt

This is not a particular pattern but a genre in which the quilt serves as an expression of the seamstress' grief. No two grief quilts are alike but it was popular to applique fences along the quilt's borders, creating a cemetery in the center. Coffins and gravestones were cut from the garments of loved ones who had died.

Against this stark ground of white,
the iron fence, webbing of bushes,
and bare trees reach out from the
meticulous order of death.
5   I keep them here—husband, children, friends—
away from the distractions of summer;
the rank confusion of daylillies, ubiquitous
weeds and wildflowers, cloying honeysuckle.

Nothing grows above the stones, losses
10   are never blurred or worn from the heart,
and with these stitches I make
a kind of hybrid life, more stable and kind
than any I have known.

At night my hands trace over the border of coffins
15   and I read once more the stories of my days:
the soft batiste of the baby's gown,
a daughter's party dress crackles under my touch,
and from my husband's best suit,
the fragrance of his pipe.

20   Under the weight of my grief,
I turn in the dark
honing my losses like the scythe
that will carry me, dreamless and vigilant,
into their midst.

Questions for Discussion

1. Many quilts, both in life and in these poems, are pieced together from different cloths to make one coherent design. In what ways might this process be a metaphor for community?
2. Which quilt pattern seems the most vivid to you, based on its description? Which poem seems most vivid? Which poem represents loss and remembrance of loved ones? What contemporary quilting project is reminiscent of that type of quilt?
3. Read each poem carefully, slowly. What notions and images of family life do you infer from the poems? What do you think each quilt represented to its maker?
4. What is the situation conveyed in "Indian Hatchet"? Who is speaking? Who is lis-

tening? What does the quilt represent to the listeners and the speaker? What social and historical connections are being made?

5. Discuss the genre of poetry, as opposed to fiction, memoir, essay, or photography and painting, as a means of storytelling.

Ideas for Writing

1. Write an essay that contrasts poetry and quiltmaking or another art or craft as creative expressions of one's experience and feelings.

2. Research the Names Project (headquartered in San Francisco), the organization coordinating the quilt squares remembering AIDS victims. Write a history of the project to inform your peers. Consider sending it to your college paper or a local paper. Alternatively, work with a peer group to design a square for a member of your community who has died of AIDS. Write a reflective essay about the process of designing the square. How were you able to turn your feelings and ideas into a specific design?

3. Research social activities available to nineteenth century American women, especially in rural areas. Consider the role of the quilting bee or some other communal activity. In addition to library research, you could interview an older craftswoman in the community. You might get leads from local fabric or crafts shops, or perhaps through church groups. Perhaps you could observe such a gathering and write about the kind of community it reflects.

The Family Values Debate

James Q. Wilson

James Q. Wilson (b. 1931) graduated from the University of Chicago in 1957 and has spent his life writing about crime and the urban condition. He has participated in numerous antidrug and anticrime task forces; currently he is Collins Professor of Management and Public Policy at UCLA. His books include a collection of essays entitled *On Character*, and *The Moral Sense*. Wilson has been called a "neoconservative social theorist." Essays like "The Family Values Debate" demonstrate his concern for issues that address mainstream American values.

Journal

"Family values" was one of the catch phrases of the 1992 presidential campaign. What does the expression mean to you?

There are two views about the contemporary American family, one held by the public and the other by policy elites. In his presidential campaign, Bill Clinton appeared to endorse the public's view. It remains to be seen which view President Clinton will support.

   The public's view is this: the family is the place in which the most basic 2 values are instilled in children. In recent years, however, these values have become less secure, in part because the family has become weaker and in part because rivals for its influence—notably television and movies—have gotten stronger. One way the family has become weaker is that more and more children are being raised in one-parent families, and often that one parent is a teenage girl. Another way is that parents, whether in one- or two-parent families, are spending less time with their children and are providing poorer discipline. Because family values are so important, political candidates should talk about them, though it is not clear that the government can do much about them. Overwhelmingly, Americans think that it is better for children if one parent stays home and does not work, even if that means having less money.[1]

3   No such consensus is found among scholars or policy-makers. That in itself is revealing. Beliefs about families that most people regard as virtually self-evident are hotly disputed among people whose job it is to study or support families.

4   A good example of the elite argument began last fall on the front page of the *Washington Post,* where a reporter quoted certain social scientists as saying that the conventional two-parent family was not as important for the healthy development of children as was once supposed. This prompted David Popenoe, a professor at Rutgers who has written extensively on family issues, to publish in *The New York Times* an op-ed piece challenging the scholars cited in the *Post.* Popenoe asserted that "dozens" of studies had come to the opposite conclusion, and that the weight of the evidence "decisively" supported the view that two-parent families are better than single-parent families.

5   Decisively to him, perhaps, but not to others. Judith Stacey, another professor of sociology, responded in a letter to the *Times* that the value of a two-parent family was merely a "widely shared prejudice" not confirmed by empirical studies; Popenoe, she said, was trying to convert "misguided nostalgia for 'Ozzie-and-Harriet'-land into social-scientific truth." Arlene and Jerome Skolnick, two more professors, acknowledged that although Popenoe might be correct, saying so publicly would "needlessly stigmatize children raised in families that don't meet the 'Ozzie-and-Harriet' model." After all, the Skolnicks observed, a man raised outside that model had just been elected President of the United States.

6 The views of Stacey and the Skolnicks are by no means unrepresentative of academic thinking on this subject. Barbara Dafoe Whitehead recently surveyed the most prominent textbooks on marriage and the family. Here is my paraphrase of her summary of what she found:

7   The life course is full of exciting options. These include living in a commune, having a group marriage, being a single parent, or living together. Marriage is one life-style choice, but before choosing it people weigh its costs and benefits against other options. Divorce is a part of the normal family cycle and is neither deviant nor tragic. Rather, it can serve as a foundation for individual

[1]Evidence for these beliefs can be found in the poll data gathered in the *American Enterprise,* September-October 1992, pp. 85–86.

renewal and new beginnings. Marriage itself should not be regarded as a special, privileged institution; on the contrary, it must catch up with the diverse, pluralistic society in which we live. For example, same-sex marriages often involve more sharing and equality than do heterosexual relationships. But even in the conventional family, the relationships between husband and wife need to be defined after carefully negotiating agreements that protect each person's separate interests and rights.[2]

Many politicians and reporters echo these sentiments and carry the argu- 8 ment one step further. Not only do poor Ozzie and Harriet (surely the most maligned figures in the history of television) stand for nostalgic prejudice and stigmatizing error, they represent a kind of family that in fact scarcely exists. Congresswoman Pat Schroeder has been quoted as saying that only about 7 percent of all American families fit the Ozzie-and-Harriet model. Our daily newspapers frequently assert that most children will not grow up in a two-parent family. The message is clear: not only is the two-parent family not especially good for children, but fortunately it is also fast disappearing.

Yet whether or not the two-parent family is good for children, it is plainly 9 false that this kind of family has become a historical relic. For while there has been a dramatic increase in the proportion of children, especially black children, who will spend some or even most of their youth in single-parent families, the vast majority of children—nationally, about 73 percent—live in a home with married parents. Today, the mothers in those families are more likely to work than once was the case, though most do not work full time. (I am old enough to remember that even Harriet worked, at least in real life. She was a singer.)

The proponents of the relic theory fail to use statistics accurately. The way 10 they arrive at the discovery that only 7 percent of all families fit the Ozzie-and-Harriet model is by calculating what proportion of all families consists *exactly* of a father, mother, and two (not three or four) children and in which the mother never works, not even for two weeks during the year helping out with the Christmas rush at the post office.

The language in which the debate over two-parent families is carried on sug- 11 gests that something more than scholarly uncertainty is at stake. If all we cared about were the effects of one- versus two-parent families on the lives of children, there would still be a debate, but it would not be conducted on op-ed pages in tones of barely controlled anger. Nor would it be couched in slogans about television characters or supported by misleading statistics.

What is at stake, of course, is the role of women. To defend the two-par- 12 ent family is to defend, the critics worry, an institution in which the woman is subordinated to her husband, confined to domestic chores with no opportunity to pursue a career, and taught to indoctrinate her children with a belief

[2]Paraphrased from Barbara Dafoe Whitehead, *The Expert's Story of Marriage*, Institute for American Values, Publication No. WP14 (August 1992), pp. 11–12. Whitehead supplies references to the texts she summarizes. She does not endorse—just the opposite!—the views she has compiled.

in the rightness of this arrangement. To some critics, the woman here is not simply constrained, she is abused. The traditional family, in this view, is an arena in which men are free to hit, rape, and exploit women. To defend the traditional family is to defend sexism. And since single-parent families are disproportionately headed by black women, criticizing such families is not only sexist but racist.

13 Perhaps the most influential book on this subject to appear during the 1970's was *The Future of Marriage* by Jessie Bernard, a distinguished scholar. Widely reviewed, its central message was that the first order of business for marriage must be "mitigating its hazards for women."

14 Unlike more radical writers, Bernard thought that the future of marriage was assured, but this would be the case only because marriage would now take many forms. Traditional marriages would persist but other forms would gain (indeed, had already gained) favor—communes, group marriages, the *ménage à trois,* marital "swinging," unmarried cohabitation, and limited-commitment marriages. (She did not discuss mother-only families as one of these "options." Nor did she discuss race.) In principle, no one form was better than another because "there is nothing in human nature that favors one kind of marriage over another." In practice, the forms that were best were those that were best for the woman. What might be best for children was not discussed. Children, it would seem, were incidental to marriage, except insofar as their care imposed strains on their parents, especially their mothers.

15 The main theme of much of the writing about marriage and families during the 1970's and 1980's was that of individual rights. Just as politics were only legitimate when they respected individual rights, so also marriages were worthy of respect only when they were based on a recognition of rights.

16 This view impressed itself on many who were not scholars, as is evident from an essay published in 1973 in the *Harvard Educational Review.* It urged that the "legal status of infancy . . . be abolished" so that a child would be endowed with all the rights of an adult. Even more, any law that classified people as children and treated them differently from adults "should be considered suspect." As a result, the state "would no longer be able to assume the rationality of regulations based on age." The author of this essay was Hillary Rodham.

17 A rights-based, individualistic view of marriage is questionable in its own terms, but these theoretical questions would become insuperable objections if it could be shown that children are harmed by growing up in mother-only, or communal, or swinging, or divorced households. The academic study of families during the 1970's, however, did not produce an unchallenged body of evidence demonstrating that this was the case. There were several studies that attempted to measure the impact of mother-only families on their children's school attainment, job success, and personal conduct, but many discovered either no effects or ones that were ambiguous or equivocal.

18 I first became aware of this in the early 1980's when Richard J. Herrnstein

and I were writing *Crime and Human Nature.* One of my tasks was to prepare the first draft of the chapter on the effects on crime rates of what were then called broken homes. I fully expected to find a raft of studies showing that growing up in a mother-only home put the child, especially the boy, at risk for criminality.

I did not find what I had expected to find. To be sure, I ran across the 19 familiar fact that men in prison tended disproportionately to come from broken homes, but men in prison also tended to have parents who were themselves criminal and to come from poor, minority backgrounds. Since these factors—class, race, parental criminality, and family status—tended to co-vary, it was not clear that family background had any effect independent of temperament or circumstance. Similarly, Elizabeth Herzog and Cecelia Sudia reviewed eighteen studies of female-headed families carried out between 1950 and 1970. They found that in seven there was more delinquency in father-absent homes, in four there was less, and in seven the results were mixed. Some studies showed boys in father-absent homes failing to develop an appropriate masculine identity and others uncovered no such effect. (There was—and is—ample evidence that children from cold, discordant homes are likely to have plenty of problems, but there are lots of cold, discordant *two*-parent families.)

Since I wrote that chapter, though, the evidence that single-parent fami- 20 lies are bad for children has mounted. There will never be anything like conclusive proof of this proposition unless we randomly assign babies at birth to single- and two-parent families of various economic and ethnic circumstances and then watch them grow up. Happily the laws and customs of this country make such an experiment unlikely. Short of that, the best evidence comes from longitudinal studies that follow children as they grow up in whatever kind of family nature has provided.

One example: when the 5,000 children born in the United Kingdom dur- 21 ing the first week of March 1946 were followed for three decades, those raised in families broken by divorce or desertion were more likely than those living in two-parent families to become delinquent.[3]

A second example: for many years, Sheppard Kellam and his colleagues 22 at Johns Hopkins University followed several hundred poor, black, first-grade children in a depressed neighborhood in Chicago. Each child lived in one of several different family types, depending on how many and what kinds of adults were present. In about one-third of families the mother was the only adult present; in another third there was both a mother and a father. (Only a tiny fraction was headed by a father with no mother present.) The remainder was made up of various combinations of mothers, grandparents, uncles, aunts, adult brothers and sisters, and various unrelated adults. By the time the children entered the third grade, those who lived with their mothers alone were the worst off in terms of their socialization. After ten years, the boys who had grown up in mother-only families (which by then made up about half the total)

[3]M.E.J. Wadsworth, *Roots of Delinquency*, Barnes & Noble (1979).

reported more delinquencies, regardless of family income, than those who had grown up in families with multiple adults, especially a father.[4]

23   By 1986, when Rolf and Magda Loeber of the University of Pittsburgh reviewed 23 studies assessing the relationship of parental absence (usually, father absence) to juvenile delinquency, they found an effect, though smaller than the one caused by discord within a two-parent family.[5] One problem with their overall conclusion was that they lumped together families where the biological father had never been present with those in which he left, as a result of separation, divorce, or death, while the child was growing up. Inspecting their data suggests that if the latter cases are omitted, the connection between family status and criminality is strengthened a bit: fathers never present create greater hazards than fathers who depart (owing to death or divorce) later in the child's life. The greatest hazard of all is found in families where the parents have the greatest number of problems—they are absent, discordant, rejecting, incompetent, and criminal.

24   The most recent important study of family structure was done in 1988 by the Department of Health and Human Services. It surveyed the family arrangements of more than 60,000 children living in households all over the country. Interviews were conducted in order to identify any childhood problems in health, schoolwork, and personal conduct. These results were tabulated according to the age, sex, and ethnicity of the child and the income and marital status of the parents.

25   The results were striking. At every income level save the very highest (over $50,000 per year), for both sexes and for whites, blacks, and Hispanics alike, children living with a never-married or a divorced mother were substantially worse off than those living in two-parent families. Compared to children living with both biological parents, children in single-parent families were twice as likely to have been expelled or suspended from school, to display emotional or behavioral problems, and to have problems with their peers; they were also much more likely to engage in antisocial behavior. These differences were about as wide in households earning over $35,000 a year as they were in those making less than $10,000.[6]

26   Charles Murray of the American Enterprise Institute has been looking at

[4]Sheppard Kellam et al., "The Long-Term Evolution of the Family Structure of Teenage and Older Mothers," *Journal of Marriage and the Family*, vol. 44 (1982), pp. 539–554; Kellam *et al.*, "Family Structure and the Mental Health of Children," *Archives of General Psychiatry*, vol. 34 (1977), pp. 1012–1022; Margaret Ensminger *et al.*, "School and Family Origins of Delinquency: Comparisons By Sex," in Katharine T. Van Dusen and Sarnoff A. Mednick, eds., *Prospective Studies of Crime and Delinquency*, Kluwer-Nijhoff (1983).
[5]"Family Factors as Correlates and Predictors of Juvenile Conduct Problems and Delinquency," in Michael Tonry and Norval Morris, eds., *Crime and Justice: An Annual Review of Research*, University of Chicago Press (1986), pp. 29–149.
[6]Deborah A. Dawson, "Family Structure and Children's Health: United States, 1988," *Vital and Health Statistics*, Series 10, No. 178 (June 1991).

the people whose lives have been followed by the National Longitudinal Study of Youth (NLSY) since they were in high school (they are now in their late twenties or early thirties). The NLSY not only keeps careful records of the schooling, jobs, and income of these young adults, it also looks at the home environment in which they are raising any children they may have. These home observations rate emotional quality, parental involvement in child care, style of discipline, and the like. The homes, thus observed, can be ranked from best to worst.

Murray has compared the home environments with the economic status 27 of the parents and the legal status of the child. The odds of the children living in the worst home environments were powerfully affected by two things: whether the parents were married when they had the baby and whether they were regular welfare recipients. The child of an unmarried woman who was a chronic welfare recipient had one chance in six of growing up in the worst— that is, emotionally the worst—environment. The child of a married woman who never went on welfare had only one chance in 42.[7]

Being poor hurts children. Living in a rotten neighborhood hurts them. 28 Having cold or neglectful parents certainly hurts them. But so also does being illegitimate and living on welfare. This is generally true for whites as well as blacks.

And so also does being a teenage mother. For many years, Frank Fursten- 29 berg of the University of Pennsylvania and his colleagues have been following 300 teenage mothers living in Baltimore. What they have found supports the public's view. Teenage girls who have babies fare much worse than ones who postpone child-bearing, and this is true even among girls of the same socioeconomic background and academic aptitude. They are more likely to go on welfare, and less likely to enter into a stable marriage. The children of teenage mothers, compared with those of older ones, tend to have more trouble in school, to be more aggressive, and to have less self-control. This is especially true of boys.[8]

We have always had teenage mothers, and in some less-developed soci- 30 eties that is the norm. What is new and troubling about the present situation is the vast increase in the number of teenage mothers and their concentration in the same neighborhoods. A girl with a baby presents one kind of problem when she is either a rarity or is embedded in an extended family that provides guidance and assistance from older women living with her. She presents a very different and much more serious problem when she is one of thousands of similarly situated youngsters living in the same neighborhood or public-housing project, trying to maintain an independent household on welfare.

---

[7]"Reducing Poverty and Reducing the Underclass: Different Problems, Different Solutions," paper presented to the Conference on Reducing Poverty in America, January 15, 1993, at the Anderson Graduate School of Management, UCLA.

[8]Frank F. Furstenberg, Jr., Jeanne Brooks-Gunn, and Lindsay Chase-Lansdale, "Teenage Pregnancy and Childbearing," *American Psychologist*, vol. 44 (1989), pp. 313–329.

31   A lot more light will be shed on these issues when Sara McLanahan at Princeton and Gary Sandefur at the University of Wisconsin publish their careful analysis of the best available longitudinal data bases.[9] There are at least four of these files—the already-mentioned National Longitudinal Study of Youth; the Panel Study of Income Dynamics; the High School and Beyond Study; and the National Survey of Families and Households. McLanahan and Sandefur are looking at the effect of family structure, after controlling for income, race, and education, on such things as a child's chances of graduating from high school, a girl's chances of becoming a teenage mother, and a boy's chances of being idle (that is, neither working nor in school). Their results so far suggest that children who grow up in single-parent families do less well than those who grow up in intact families, and that this is true whether they are white or black, rich or poor, boys or girls. These other factors make a difference—it is better to be white than black, rich than poor—but so does family status.

32 I think that the American people are right in their view of families. When they look at the dramatic increase in divorce, single-parent families, and illegitimate children that has taken place over the last 30 years, they see families in decline. They do not need studies to tell them that these outcomes are generally bad, because they have had these outcomes happen to them or to people they know. Divorce may sometimes be the right and necessary remedy for fundamentally flawed marriages and for the conditions created by an abusive or neglectful spouse, but in general divorce makes people worse off: the woman becomes poorer and the children more distressed. Properly raising a child is an enormous responsibility that often taxes the efforts and energies of two parents; one parent is likely to be overwhelmed. Children born out of wedlock are in the great majority of cases children born into poverty. Millions of people are living testimony to these bleak facts. If scholars say that the evidence is not conclusive, so much the worse for scholars. But now, I believe, scholars are starting to find hard facts to support popular impressions.

33   The debate over the effects of family structure continues, albeit with some prospect of a consensus emerging some time in the near future. But there is not even a glimmer of such an accord with respect to the other hot topic in family studies—day care. The dominant view among child psychologists is that day care is not harmful. For a long time Professor Jay Belsky of Pennsylvania State University shared that view. When he changed his mind, he was excoriated. He is now of the opinion that day care, especially in the first year of life, is harmful in some respects to some children.

34   In a widely-reported 1988 article, Belsky reviewed all the studies measuring the effect of nonmaternal care on attachment and social development and concluded that, subject to many caveats,

[9]*Uncertain Childhood, Uncertain Future,* Harvard University Press (forthcoming).

entry into [day] care in the first year of life for twenty hours or more per week is a "risk factor" for the development of insecure attachment in infancy and heightened aggressiveness, noncompliance, and withdrawal in the preschool and early school years.[10]

By "risk factor" Belsky meant that the child in day care was somewhat more likely to experience these adverse outcomes than would a similar child under parental care, especially if the day care was not of high quality.

Some critics argued with Belsky on scientific grounds, saying that the evi- 35 dence was less clearcut than he suggested, that the measure of emotional well-being he used (observing how a child reacts after it is separated from its mother) was flawed, that children turn out well in cultures where nonparental care is commonplace, and that whatever ill effects exist, (if any) do not last.

But many attacked him politically, and even the scholarly critiques had a 36 sharp edge to them. As with family structure, what is at stake in this controversy are not just facts and interpretations but philosophy and policy: if day care has bad effects, then women ought to care for their children in their own homes. And that is a politically-incorrect conclusion. Many scholars feel, I believe, that to support the claim of family decline is to give aid and comfort to conservative politicians and religious leaders who bemoan that decline and call for the reassertion of "traditional values." In short, what is at stake is Murphy Brown.

THE CHANGING CULTURE

Both teenage pregnancies and single-parent families have increased dramati- 37 cally since the 1950's. Changes in the economy and in the provision of welfare benefits explain some of this growth but not all or even most of it. There are no doubt some features peculiar to American society that explain some of it, but since the decline of the family—that is, in lasting marriages and legitimate births—has happened in many nations, it cannot be entirely the result of American policies or peculiarities.

We are witnessing a profound, worldwide, long-term change in the fam- 38 ily that is likely to continue for a long time. The causes of that change are not entirely understood, but probably involve two main forces: a shift in the family's economic function and a shift in the culture in which it is embedded. The family no longer is the unit that manages economic production, as it was when agriculture was the dominant form of production, nor is it any longer the principal provider of support for the elderly or education for the young.

At the same time, the family no longer exercises as much control over its 39 members as it once did, and broader kinship groupings (clans, tribes, and extended families) no longer exercise as much control over nuclear families.

---

[10]"The Effects of Infant Day Care Reconsidered," *Early Childhood Research Quarterly*, vol. 3 (1988), pp. 235–272. For a response, see Tiffany Field, *Infancy*, Harvard University Press (1990), pp. 90–93.

Since the Enlightenment, the dominant tendency in legal and philosophical thought has been to emancipate the individual from all forms of tutelage—the state, revealed religion, ancient custom—including the tutelage of kin. This emancipation has proceeded episodically and unevenly, but relentlessly. Liberal political theory has celebrated the individual and constrained the state, but it has been silent about the family.

40   What is remarkable is how well the family has survived this process. Were the family the mere social convention that some scholars imagine, it would long since have gone the way of cottage industries and the owner-occupied farm, the inevitable victim of the individualizing and rationalizing tendencies of modern life. But, of course, the family is not a human contrivance invented to accomplish some goal and capable of being reinvented or reformulated to achieve different goals.

41   Family—and kinship generally—are the fundamental organizing facts of all human societies, primitive or advanced, and have been such for tens of thousands of years. The family is the product of evolutionary processes that have selected against people who are inclined to abandon their offspring and for people who are prepared to care for them, and to provide this caring within kinship systems defined primarily along genetic lines. If kinship were a cultural artifact, we could as easily define it on the basis of height, athletic skill, or political status, and children would be raised in all manner of collectives, ranging from state-run orphanages to market-supplied foster homes. Orphanages and foster homes do of course exist, but only as matters of last resort designed (with great public anxiety) to provide care when the biological family does not exist or cannot function.

42   If the family were merely a convenience and if it responded entirely to economic circumstances, the current debate over family policy would be far less rancorous than it is. Liberals would urge that we professionalize child-rearing through day care; conservatives would urge that we subsidize it through earned-income tax credits. Liberals would define the welfare problem as entirely a matter of poverty and recommend more generous benefits as the solution; conservatives would define it as entirely a matter of dependency and recommend slashing benefits as the solution. Liberals would assume that the problem is that families have too little money, conservatives that families get such money as they have from the state. There would still be a battle, but in the end it would come down to some negotiated compromise involving tradeoffs among benefit levels, eligibility rules, and the public-private mix of child-care providers.

43   But once one conceives of the family problem as involving to a significant degree the conflict between a universal feature of human society and a profound cultural challenge to the power of that institution, the issue takes on a different character. To the extent that one believes in the cultural challenge—that is, in individual emancipation and individual choice—one tends to question the legitimacy and influence of the family. To the extent that one believes in the family, one is led to question some or all parts of the cultural challenge.

That is why the debate over "family values" has been so strident. On 44 both sides people feel that it is the central battle in the culture war that now grips Americans (or at least American elites). They are absolutely right. To many liberals, family values means a reassertion of male authority, a reduction in the hard-earned rights of women, and a license for abusive or neglectful parents to mistreat their children free of prompt and decisive social intervention. For some liberals, family values means something even more troubling: that human nature is less malleable than is implied by the doctrine of environmental determinism and cultural relativism—that it is to some significant degree fixed, immutable. To many conservatives, family values is the main line of resistance against homosexual marriages, bureaucratized child care, and compulsory sex education in the schools. For some conservatives, the family means a defense against the very idea of a planned society.

Now, reasonable people—say, the typical mother or father—will take a less 45 stark view of the alternatives. They will agree with conservatives that the family is the central institution of society, incapable of being replaced or even much modified without disastrous consequences. They will be troubled by same-sex marriages, upset by teenage girls becoming mothers, angered by public subsidies for illegitimate births, and outraged by the distribution of condoms and explicit sex-education manuals to elementary-school children. But they will agree with many liberals that we ought not to confine women to domestic roles or make them subservient to male power and that we ought to recognize and cope with the financial hardships that young couples have today when they try to live on one income in a big city.

On one issue most parents will squarely identify with the conservative 46 side, and it is, in my view, the central issue. They will want our leaders, the media, television programs, and motion pictures to take their side in the war over what the family is. It is not one of several alternative life-styles; it is not an arena in which rights are negotiated; it is not an old-fashioned and reactionary barrier to a promiscuous sex life; it is not a set of cost-benefit calculations. *It is a commitment.*

It is a commitment required for child-rearing and thus for any realistic 47 prospect of human happiness. It is a commitment that may be entered into after romantic experimentation and with some misgivings about lost freedoms, but once entered into it is a commitment that persists for richer or for poorer, in sickness and in health, for better or for worse. It is a commitment for which there is no feasible substitute, and hence no child ought lightly to be brought into a world where that commitment—from both parents—is absent. It is a commitment that often is joyfully enlivened by mutual love and deepening friendship, but it is a commitment even when these things are absent.

There is no way to prepare for the commitment other than to make it. The 48 idea that a man and a woman can live together without a commitment in order to see if they would like each other after they make the commitment is preposterous. Living together may inform you as to whether your partner snores or is an alcoholic or sleeps late; it may be fun and exciting; it may even be the best you can manage in an imperfect world. But it is not a way of finding out how married life will be, because married life is shaped by the fact that the couple has made a solemn vow before their family and friends that this is for keeps and that any children will be their joint and permanent responsibility. It changes everything.

49   Despite high divorce rates and a good deal of sleeping around, most people understand this. Certainly women understand it, since one of their most common complaints about the men they know is that they will not make a commitment. You bet they won't, not if they can get sex, cooking, and companionship on a trial basis, all the while keeping their eyes peeled for a better opportunity elsewhere. Marriage is in large measure a device for reining in the predatory sexuality of males. It works quite imperfectly, as is evident from the fact that men are more likely than women to have extramarital affairs and to abandon their spouses because a younger or more exciting possibility has presented herself. But it works better than anything else mankind has been able to invent.

50   Because most people understand this, the pressures, economic and cultural, on the modern family have not destroyed it. And this is remarkable, considering the spread of no-fault divorce laws. The legal system has, in effect, said, "Marriage is not a commitment; it is a convenience. If you feel yours is inconvenient, we will make it easy for you to get out of it." This radical transformation of family law occurred, as Mary Ann Glendon of the Harvard Law School has shown, in many industrialized countries at about the same time. It may or may not have caused the rise in the divorce rate, but it certainly did nothing to slow it down.

51   The legal system has also altered child-custody rules so that, instead of being automatically assigned to the father (as was the case in the 19th century, when the father was thought to "own" all the family's property including the child), the child is now assigned by the judge on the basis of its "best interests." In the vast majority of cases, that means with the mother. I sometimes wonder what would happen to family stability if every father knew for certain that, should the marriage end, he would have to take custody of the children. My guess is: more committed fathers.

52   These cultural and legal changes, all aimed at individualizing and empowering family members, have had an effect. In 1951, 51 percent of all Americans agreed with the statement that "parents who don't get along should not stay together because there are children in the family." By 1985, 86 percent agreed.[11] Still, these changes have not devastated modern families. The shopping malls, baseball stadiums, and movie theaters are filled with them doing what families have always done. That fact is a measure of the innate power of the family bond.

[11]David Popenoe, "The Family Condition of America," paper prepared for a Brookings Institution seminar on values and public policy (March 1992), citing a study by Norval Glenn.

Yet the capacity for resisting these changes is unequally distributed in soci- 53
ety. Christopher Jencks of Northwestern University puts it this way:

> Now that the mass media, the schools, and even the churches have begun to
> treat single parenthood as a regrettable but inescapable part of modern life,
> we can hardly expect the respectable poor to carry on the struggle against ille-
> gitimacy and desertion with their old fervor. They still deplore such behavior,
> but they cannot make it morally taboo. Once the two-parent norm loses its
> moral sanctity, the selfish considerations that always pulled poor parents apart
> often become overwhelming.[12]

CULTURE AND POLITICS

The central issue in family policy is whether or not it will be animated entirely 54
by an economic view of family functions and consist entirely of economic solutions to family needs. The principal source of domestic social-policy advice to
Bill Clinton during his presidential campaign was the Progressive Policy Institute (PPI), and in particular Elaine Kamarck and William Galston. "The best
antipoverty program for children is a stable, intact family," they wrote in their
report, *Mandate for Change.* Though not neglecting economic measures, such as
a tax credit for each child and an earned-income tax credit to supplement the
wages of the working poor, the PPI urged that the divorce laws be changed
to protect children better, that efforts be intensified to promote parental
responsibility for child care, that pregnant women who use drugs be required
to undergo periodic drug testing, and that the earnings of absent parents be
taxed to pay for their children. And the report called for the President to use
his bully pulpit to reinforce the importance of intact and caring families.

As of this writing, only Galston of all those connected with the PPI has 55
been appointed to even a moderately significant position in the Clinton administration (he joined the White House domestic-policy staff). Clinton's Secretary
of Health and Human Services, Donna Shalala, had virtually nothing to say
about these matters in her confirmation hearing before the Senate Finance
Committee. There will in time be a debate on welfare policy; Clinton has
promised to appoint a task force to make recommendations. Perhaps something will happen, though the history of past efforts at welfare reform suggests that few in Congress have the stomach for it and few scholars expect that
such reforms as pass will make much of a difference.

The truth of the matter is that the most important features of family life 56
are beyond the reach of policy. The recently passed family-leave bill in large
measure merely ratifies opportunities that large firms have been granting to
their employees for some time; it will make things a bit easier for middle-class
mothers but will do little for poor, teenage ones. The far more contentious issue
of welfare reform will not be so easily resolved, but it is hard to imagine any
feasible change in the existing rules that will make much of a difference in the

---

[12]"Deadly Neighborhoods," *New Republic,* June 13, 1988, pp. 23–32.

chances of a child being born out of wedlock. Expanding the earned-income tax credit may help poor working parents, but do we really want single mothers of two-year-old children to work? Tightening the divorce laws may be a good idea, but it will not make much difference to parents who never got married in the first place. Improving the system for collecting child-support payments is a good idea, but many fathers who desert their children have little money to be collected and, in any event, this is not likely to convert uncommitted impregnators into committed fathers.

57   I suspect that the culture of the family will have to be rebuilt from the bottom up. Certainly Robert Woodson, head of the National Center for Neighborhood Enterprise, thinks so. He and his associates have been energetically pursuing this goal by supporting local church-related groups that try to encourage men to take responsibility for their children. There are many other local efforts to get men to marry their pregnant lovers and to sign the birth certificates of their children.

58   But these efforts proceed against the cultural grain, or at least against the grain of the high culture. When the people who deliver mocking attacks on "traditional family values" are the same ones who endorse condom distribution among elementary-school children, the average parent is led to wonder whether he or she is being a sucker for trying to stay together and raise the kids. Most Americans, I would guess, understand very clearly the difference between a traditional family and an oppressive one; they want the former but not the latter. Most women, I would guess, can distinguish very easily between the rights they have won and the obligations they retain; they cherish both and see no fundamental conflict between them, except the inescapable problem that there is not enough time for everything and so everyone must make choices.

59   It is extraordinary how well most husbands and wives have held up in the face of constant taunts comparing them to Ozzie and Harriet. The family life that most Americans want is regarded by the eminences of the media and the academy as a cartoon life, fit only for ridicule and rejection. When the history of our times is written, this raging cultural war will deserve careful attention, for it is far more consequential than any of the other cleavages that divide us.

60   Many Americans hope that President Clinton will stand up for "traditional family values," by which they mean, not male supremacy, spouse abuse, or docile wives, but the overriding importance of two-parent families that make child care their central responsibility. Clinton wants to stay in touch with the people at town meetings; fine, but let him say at those meetings that nobody should conceive a child that he and she are not emotionally ready to care for. The best, albeit an imperfect, sign of that readiness is the marriage vow. Let him say that it is wrong—not just imprudent, but wrong—to bear children out of wedlock. Let him meet with local ministers and neighborhood groups that are trying to encourage marriage and discourage predatory male sexuality. Such statements may earn Clinton dismayed groans from sitcom producers and ideological accusations from sociology professors, but at least the people would know that he is on their side.

Questions for Discussion

1. Examine the evidence on both sides of the single-parent versus two-parent family issue. Which side's evidence seems more persuasive? Does Wilson's critique of the so-called "elite" position seem accurate?
2. Is the core issue, as Wilson suggests, the role of women? Do you agree that "to defend the traditional family is to defend sexism"? Or that "what is at stake is Murphy Brown"?
3. Does Wilson ever satisfactorily address the concern that women will be subordinated and kept at home if the research shows that children are worse off in single-parent homes?
4. Wilson focuses on the research about children from one- and two-parent homes. What is the connection to what he believes most Americans think? Is he arguing for politicians to recognize what society thinks? To do something about it? Is he suggesting a role or proposing some course of action for Americans? Discuss.
5. Is Wilson's argument consistent with what you perceived the family values debate to be about? Is it really a debate between two clear positions, or is there room for a number of different views?

Ideas for Writing

1. How do you envision maintaining your own individuality while sharing your life with another in a long-term relationship? How will you negotiate roles, allowing for individual and family needs? If you intend to have children, how will you arrange for their care and upbringing? If you are already in a long-term relationship, write about an incident in which individual and partnership needs conflicted; discuss how you resolved that conflict.
2. What should society's role and concern be in the rearing of children? What is the state's interest in the upbringing of children? To what degree should it supersede individual or even family wishes? What is society's role in "encouraging" two-parent families or "discouraging" one-parent families? Discuss.
3. Investigate services commonly available to single-parent families in your area. Do such services coincide with the events and trends that Wilson outlines? Were they formed to respond to certain needs? Consider not only welfare or entitlement programs, but also educational opportunities, programs in the schools, child care, and the like. Write up a summary and submit both to your instructor and to an interested agency in your area.

Domestic Violence: Confronting Myths of Masculinity

Richard Stolz

Richard Stolz (b. 1974) was born in Seoul, South Korea. At age three, he moved to the San Francisco Bay Area with his parents. In high school Stolz worked as a news editor for his school paper and was captain of the debate team. He is a member of the service fraternity Alpha Phi Omega, a group affiliated with his campus's public service center. Stolz is majoring in American studies and plans to develop a career in public service. He decided to research the topic of domestic violence to gain a deeper understanding of an issue that undermines many of today's families.

Journal

What messages does society send boys and men, or girls and women, about what it means to be masculine?

In 1985, the second National Family Violence Survey revealed the following statistics:

- An assault occurred in 8.7 million American couples.
- Violence occurred in one out of every six couples.
- Injury occurred in 3.4 million of these instances.
- Three out of 100 women were severely beaten by their mates.
- Thirty-four out of 1000 wives were severely beaten by their husbands.
- One out of eight husbands attacked his wife (Gelles et al., 47).

These statistics illustrate the often violent nature of the relationship between the sexes. As startling as these statistics are, most would consider these as a large number of distinct incidents perpetrated by violently deviant individual males against their mates. But the sheer number of incidents suggests another explanation. Though it may be a simple task to view these numbers from a seemingly safe distance, avoiding societal introspection, the violence exhibited here is only a symptom of a broader issue. The concept of social constructionism, a theory that evaluates psychological deviancy in the context of an imperfect society, suggests that violence does not exist because male-kind is inherently evil, but because society teaches men to behave in a certain manner. The male batterer is a symptom of such societal pressures called gender role expectations which are further intensified within the unique institution of marriage.

2   The widespread scope of domestic violence is staggering, but the National Family Violence Survey suggests that these statistics are *under*estimates. Other surveys indicate that one out of every two marriages will have at least one incident of domestic violence. And as many as one in five marriages will experience ongoing violence (Martin et al., 2). A study performed by the Federal Bureau of Investigation estimated that in America, a woman is battered by her mate every 18 seconds (Patai, 92).

3   The existence of these statistics can be considered keeping in mind the gender stratification perpetuated throughout society. Inherent in typical gender roles is aggressiveness which is encouraged in the male and discouraged in the female. This "socialization" as named by some, is a direct result of expectations imposed on boys and girls as they mature in the context of a male-dominated society. It indicates that, despite the strides made by women to achieve parity, society still predominantly views women as the meeker sex and

consequently subordinate. Gelles and Straus assert, "Wife beating is most common in a context where women's status in economic, educational, legal and political institutions is relatively high but where prevailing norms favor their subordination within marriage" (Gelles et al., 398).

Contributing to this weighted hierarchy, there may be no other influence 4 as powerful in society as the media. Several prominent sociologists argue that, "[The media teaches] us that women are victims in the same existential sense that grass is green" (Martin et al., 19). The Music Television (MTV) Network highlights their concern. In a study concerning the programming of MTV, it was discovered that 59.7% of the videos portrayed sex when and where the male wanted it, only 56.5% showcased dancing, and 53.2% portrayed violence, often gratuitous (Thorne-Finch, 69). In almost all cases, the male instigated the violence against women. These statistics imply that it is acceptable for men to be violent, aggressive and dominating, especially when venting these emotions against women. What the media perpetrates is a sort of subtle pornography objectifying women and enforcing societal prescriptions of a non-communitative, demanding and dominating male. "[The point is that] pornography (especially as it is legitimized in mainstream TV shows, ads, fashion lay outs, etc.) socializes men into thinking that the maltreatment of women is erotic, sexually desirable, desired by the woman and a necessary proof of virility" (Patai, 96). In a broader analysis, however, the media does not exist in a vacuum; it reflects the stereotypical expectations and desires of mainstream America. Violence exists in the media because it exists in the real world. And gender related roles of dominance and submission exist in the media because they exist in society.

Only a century and a half ago, Blackstone's *Common Law in America* 5 employed "the rule of thumb." Society at the time considered the wife to be equivalent in position to a child as her husband's property. In other words, a husband was free to chastise his wife in any manner he saw fit so long as the stick he used was no thicker than his thumb.

While much has changed since then, the fundamental way in which soci- 6 ety views marriage has not. For the majority of couples in America, a marriage is likened to monarchy where the house is the kingdom, the husband is king and the wife is servant. It is this social prescription that creates an environment where domestic violence is possible. But while the discrimination women find in the world outside the family is well documented, a woman's subordination within the home is not seen as a problem. Tradition asks that the wife take her husband's name and place herself on a lower tier in the family hierarchy. Men are expected to hold a level of authority within the household. Five years ago, when the Senate attempted to address the widespread occurrence of domestic violence, it was possible for a Senator to argue effectively that intervention in any manner was "social engineering," eliminating the husband as the head of the household.

Furthermore, the nature of the institution precludes intervention. Whether 7 it is a fear of "social engineering" or simply an inherent respect for privacy, the family is usually viewed as an entity distinct from society. Parents set the rules in the household and the nature of this micro-community is intrinsically private, and has been throughout history. Therefore, if the male head of the household chooses to use violence to get his way, there are few obstacles in his path. As a matter of fact, what a male cannot get away with in society at large, he can easily do within the marriage. Incredibly, it has been estimated that the home can be as much as 200 times more violent than the world outside (Straus, 18).

8   In order to discover the extent to which the need for violence to assert dominance may be an issue, Stuart and Gelles, prominent researchers in the field, studied egalitarian, wife-dominant and male-dominant marriages. Husbands had assaulted wives in 3.7% of the egalitarian couples surveyed, in 7.1% of wife-dominant couples and in 10.7% of male-dominated couples (Gelles et al., 394). A viable explanation of these numbers stems from the nature of each type of relationship. These numbers may appear to contradict the spirit of the thesis. According to logic, the egalitarian and wife-dominated couples should be the most violent because it is the male who, out of feelings of inadequacy, will attempt to take control of the relationship through violence. But a closer discussion defeats this supposition. Violence is a tool of power. Where it is used provides insight into why it is used.

9   When a husband beats his wife, he is trying to establish, in no small terms, his domination of the relationship. As Stuart and Gelles explain, "Erratic, unpredictable, uncontrollable violence induces helplessness, passivity and despair" (Gelles et al., 485). It also induces acceptance. Dominated individuals feel helpless and acted upon. Unable to end the violence they often try to pacify their spouse's aggressiveness through submission and appeasement. "In order to compensate for deep feelings of inadequacy (she feels as a result of being attacked) she overcompensates by highlighting the culturally valued feminine characteristic of passive acceptance, hoping this will make her worthy [of her husband]" (Morgan, 55). Interpreting these statistics, Thorne-Finch suggests emphatically, "Thus women's safety continues to be viewed as a disposable commodity, something that can be ignored in order to perpetuate the nature of masculinity which is the foundation of the existing social, political, and economic order" (Thorne-Finch, 190).

10   In a society which expects males to be the dominant partner in marriage, husbands feeling inadequate in a wife-dominated marriage may resort to violence to reject female dominance. "It is postulated that when husbands feel entitled to dominate yet lack the resources to do so 'legitimately' they will turn to violence as the ultimate resource" (Gelles et al., 387). In a male-dominated relationship men may resort to violence to maintain a level of authority once they have it. A discussion of the batterer's psyche is necessary to truly understand continuing violence, where the influence of society on individual male becomes violent.

11   Martin, Sonkin and Walker universalize the dilemma of the male batterer when they address the underlying causes of violence. "All men to one degree or another share the problems of the male batterer when they are unable to communicate their feelings, when they do not struggle toward equality in their

relationships with women, when they devalue the feminine aspect of themselves or devalue the women around them" (Martin et al., 5). Society teaches men to repress their feminine characteristics and to be aggressive. This oppressive programming can lead to problems within male-female relationships. "When men devalue all that is feminine in themselves, they will ultimately devalue the female figures in their lives, objectify them, and eventually relegate them to a status of limited utility, such as sex objects, violent objects, or servants" (Martin et al., 185). Combining to perpetuate this are societal expectations of dominance within marriage and the media's tendency to objectify women, creating an environment in which they can be devalued. Gelles takes this analysis further by concluding that "men who assault their wives are actually living up to cultural prescriptions that are cherished in Western Society— aggressiveness, male dominance, and female subordination . . ." (Gelles et al., 385). This social constructionist's argument is compelling. Domestic violence is not a matter of an individual's pathology or deviance, but a symptom of a fundamental problem within society.

In 1977, several researchers attempted to distinguish between several types 12 of violent relationships. One study divided battering marriages into four distinct categories. The first is dominated by the controller male, who responds to internal anxieties by physically abusing his wife. The second is the defender who will abuse his wife out of some fear of emotional harm that she will inflict on him, a preemptive strike. The third is the approval seeker who cannot be challenged without being insulted and turning violently angry. The final is the incorporator who needs affirmation through his wife, becoming so dependent on her that he must ensure her subordination and submission through violence (Morgan, 67). The common feature is a conflict within the male: the desire to be in control and the fear of losing his spouse and family.

This fear takes on the form of dependence, a critical issue in violent mar- 13 riages. It is a master-slave relationship in which the master retains his authority only so long as the slave believes he has the power to maintain it. Within the relationship, "Men who batter are usually very dependent on their partners as [their] sole source of love, support, intimacy and problem solving" (Martin et al., 43). Furthermore, the male often recognizes this fact and will resort to violence as a form of control. He batters his wife until he is certain that she will not be independent enough to leave him. Since he lacks self esteem, he can never be certain of it; violence continues whenever he feels the dominance he has established is threatened.

Another manifestation of the conflict between actual male and societal 14 expectation of male is a sense of isolation which also contributes to a batterer's dependence on the relationship. He often isolates the family from the outside world, limiting his wife's dealings with potential rivals for his affection or her attention toward him. This holds implications for the male's ability to function in society without the relationship. As Martin indicates, "When someone leaves, it is most often the woman who does so. Once separated, women tend to function better, given similar support systems, than the men. Many men tend to have a great deal of difficulty living on their own" (Martin et al.,

113). Women married to abusive husbands often find themselves responsible for a very large, violent child.

15   This immaturity, isolation and dependence are indicative of other emotional problems experienced by battering husbands trying to deal with a fear of failure, of not fulfilling their role as household lord and provider. Despite their violent tendencies, they have difficulty asserting themselves. Violence is a last recourse for an individual who has failed to communicate his needs in a non-threatening way and in like manner, batterers usually suffer from low self esteem. For a husband who does not achieve the respect in the world outside of his marriage it is necessary for him to ensure that he gets respect within it. Violence is an outlet for the anger such men have repressed within themselves, anger directed at themselves and their inability to meet the model of the dominant, successful male.

16   An explanation for these concurring emotions, anger, low self esteem, failure, dependence, lies in a theory developed in the 1940's called neurotic pride. "[It] refers to a person's self image [and] substitutes for the real self confidence the person lacks, and serves to reduce anxiety while providing an acceptable identity" (Morgan, 28). Batterers find it necessary to aggressively defend their masculinity using any method, including violence. Neurotic pride drives them to isolate their families and physically bully their wives into submission. Hence, wife abuse could hypothetically be considered a psychological disorder.

17   The belief that domestic violence is a social and psychological problem lends credence to the supposition that it can be treated. Males facing problems of dependence and neurotic pride can deal with them. Often the male seeks help because he has been given an ultimatum from his wife, or the criminal justice system has referred him to corrective programs. An example of an effective method of treatment is the peer group, often called a men's collective. "The group provides a place where a batterer can decrease his isolation and his dependency on the victim. In the group, he learns to make connections with his peers and to develop the interpersonal skills necessary in order to meet his own needs constructively. He has instant peer role models as well as the opportunity to be a positive role model for others. Groups are more successful in confronting denial, as well as giving support, once changes in behavior begin" (National Institute of Justice, 109). Groups allow men the opportunity to explore the restrictions society places on their behavior with others facing similar struggles and to determine new ways in which they can be confident in their individual identities and masculinity.

18   The success of any potential treatment rests on the ability of a program to address the following issues: decrease isolation and provide support systems, force the male to take responsibility for his actions, develop an awareness of violence in society at large, educate him about sex-role behavior, increase his assertiveness, improve his ability to communicate, increase self esteem and personal control, teach him methods of stress management, and encourage the male to provide a model for others. Only then can therapy succeed in ending all battering behavior. The process can be difficult and time consuming. Sometimes even a year of group therapy will not be enough to redirect the feelings

of failure and frustration experienced by the male batterer and his reliance on violence to maintain dominance because of these feelings.

But no matter how willing an individual is to change, it requires a community response to ensure that change will occur. Emerge, one of the first men's collectives in America, "considers a strong community education program to be equally as important as counseling men in the work of stopping the abuse of women" (Adams and McCormick, 171). It is absolutely necessary for battering men to realize that alternative models of behavior exist that do not require men to be dominant, aggressive and successful. The community must provide this to the individual, even as the group raises the level of acceptance an individual has to these alternative models. The only solution is a shift of view throughout the community that encourages egalitarianism between the sexes.

It is important that the abusers be treated and not simply incarcerated. Batterers are indeed committing crimes, but in many ways these crimes have been sanctioned by society. The nature of the family, the problem of recidivism, and the fact that it is better to rehabilitate than destroy relationships, encourage a humane approach to treating and punishing the male batterer. Unfortunately, contemporary legislation has required police officers on the scene of a battering case to arrest the abuser immediately, but even though arrest is an effective deterrent to abuse, it is not the *most* effective way of ending domestic violence. Often police do not want to get involved in domestic disputes, even if violence has been used. "Even in states with mandatory arrest laws, there is as little as 40% compliance" (Gondolf and McFerron, 435). And there are unexpected results as well. Mandatory arrest laws have resulted in more dual arrests in which both the husband and wife are arrested, because the officer believes they have both been violent, the wife often in response to the male. Such a response is not an incentive for the woman to report abuse to the police.

In light of the failure of the mandatory arrest law, promising alternatives to the current trend of law enforcement do exist. The dual police role of law enforcement and community service has been recognized and strengthened in a new method called the crisis teams approach. Police are taught basic counseling and mediation skills and they are teamed with professional social workers. The team can determine the extent of the problem and abuse on the scene and professionally decide the most effective course of action. "Eighty-three percent of families (approached in this way) felt they had been treated in a humane manner, and 92% indicated they would call the teams directly if problems arose in the future" (Carr, 226).

In order to end domestic violence, men must be made to understand that they need not be ideal images of masculinity, and that partnerships do not require dominance, but sharing. The only way to successfully remove the sterile concept of female submission and male domination is therapy on an individual basis for batterers and on a societal level for all people. The relationships between individual men and women today are affected to a large degree by images of gender roles provided by the media, families and mainstream society. Though women have attempted to change the manner in which they are viewed by society, men find themselves still beholden to societal preconceptions and expectations of dominance and aggressiveness. The effects these expectations have on the male psyche, and consequently on the male-female relationship, have important repercussions for male-female relationships in general. It is the male who must take the first step; law enforcement who must encourage him; and the community who must establish new, productive models to emulate.

Works Cited

Adams, David C., and Andrew J. McCormick. "Men Unlearning Violence: A Group Approach Based on the Collective Model." *The Abusive Partner: An Analysis of Domestic Battering.* Ed. Maria Roy. New York: Van Nostrand Reinhold Company, 1982. 170–197.

Carr, John J. "Treating Family Abuse Using a Police Crisis Team Approach." *The Abusive Partner: An Analysis of Domestic Battering.* Ed. Maria Roy. New York: Van Nostrand Reinhold Company, 1982. 216–228.

Gelles, Richard J., et al. *Physical Violence in American Families.* New Brunswick: Transaction Publishers, 1990.

Gondolf, Edward W., and J. Richard McFerron. "Handling Battering Men: Police Action in Wife Abuse Cases." *Criminal Justice and Behavior,* Dec. 1989: 429–439.

Martin, Dell, Daniel Jay Sonkin, Ph.D., and Lenore E. A. Walker, Ed.D. *The Male Batterer: A Treatment Approach.* New York: Springer Publishing Company, 1985.

Morgan, Steven M. *Conjugal Terrorism: A Psychological and Community Treatment Model of Wife Abuse.* Palo Alto: R & E Research and Associates, 1982.

National Institute of Justice. *Confronting Domestic Violence: A Guide for Criminal Justice Agencies.* Washington DC: Department of Justice, 1986.

Patai, Frances. "Pornography and Woman Battering: Dynamic Similarities." *The Abusive Partner: An Analysis of Domestic Battering.* Ed. Maria Roy. New York: Van Nostrand Reinhold Company, 1982. 91–99.

Straus, Murray A. "Physical Violence in American Families: Incidence Rates, Causes, and Trends." *Abused and Battered.* Eds. Dean D. Knudsen and JoAnn L. Miller. New York: Aldine de Gruyter, 1991. 17–34.

Thorne-Finch, Ron. *Ending the Silence: The Origins and Treatment of Male Violence against Women.* Toronto: University of Toronto Press, 1992.

Questions for Discussion

1. Analyze the essay rhetorically. How effective is the lead-in? What is the thesis? Is it well supported with convincing evidence? Is the evidence appropriately documented?
2. Stolz writes of the theory of social constructionism. Explain this theory in your own words. In what ways does it account for domestic violence?
3. Discuss the "gender-designated roles" Stolz mentions in paragraph 3. According to Stolz, what are these roles and where do they come from? How do they contribute to domestic violence?
4. According to Stolz, in what ways does society contribute to domestic violence? How can society help reduce the incidence of domestic violence? What contributions toward solving the problem of domestic violence can both small groups and the larger society make?

Ideas for Writing

1. Write an essay discussing the ways in which extended families and community net-works discussed in other chapter readings can work to reduce domestic violence.
2. Argue that what goes on in a family is, or is not, the community's "business."

WATCH (Women and Their Children's Housing): Public Service Announcements

Sue Becker, Bonnie Kimmel, and Alaine Murdock

WATCH is a second-step transitional housing program for victims of domestic violence and their children. The goal of the program is to break the cycle of violence by providing subsidized housing and comprehensive support services to enable the families to become economically self-sufficient and emotionally stable. WATCH housing is available to nineteen families for up to two years.

A group of first-year students, Sue Becker, Bonnie Kimmel, and Alaine Murdock, worked together to research and assemble an annual report, a newsletter, and several public service announcements (PSAs) for radio for WATCH. The PSAs they wrote collaboratively for the radio announcements broadcast in Santa Clara County in California make up this reading.

Journal

Think about the public service announcements you hear on the radio from time to time. Are they memorable? Have they ever alerted you to services you didn't know existed? Write about what the producers of such announcements could do to make them more effective and what they do correctly. How do radio announcements capture your attention?

10 SECOND

October is domestic violence awareness month. Help women help themselves. Support WATCH.

Every twelve seconds in America a woman is beaten. Help victims help themselves. Support WATCH.

6,000 people die annually as a result of domestic violence. Help stop the cycle of domestic violence. Support WATCH.

20 SECOND

Each year, 3 to 4 million women are battered by their husbands or partners. 3.3 million children are victims or witnesses of domestic violence. October is domestic violence awareness month. Help these victims help themselves. Support WATCH.

Each year 3 to 4 million women are battered by their husbands or partners. WATCH helps victims of domestic violence break the cycle of abuse. It's the only long-term transitional housing service for women and their children in Santa Clara County. Get involved.

20% of all hospital room emergency cases involve domestic violence. WATCH provides the only safe long-term alternative for victims in Santa Clara County. As one WATCH mother said, "The program works. It definitely works. It was the safest and best two years of my life." Help victims help themselves. Get involved with WATCH.

30 SECOND

October is domestic violence awareness month. Domestic violence occurs among all races, social, and economic groups; it is not just a problem of the poor and minorities. Each year 3 to 4 million women are battered by their husbands or partners. This accounts for 20% of all hospital emergency room cases and 6,000 deaths annually. WATCH needs your support.

One, two, three, by the time this sentence is finished, four, five, six, another life will be shattered, seven, eight, nine, an innocent victim in a vicious cycle, ten, eleven, twelve (SMACK). Every twelve seconds in America a woman is beaten. We need your help to stop the cycle of domestic violence.

Every year 3 to 4 million women are battered by their husbands or partners. WATCH, Women and Their Children's Housing, provides second-step transitional housing for battered women and their children. It is the only long-term safe alternative for victims of domestic violence in Santa Clara County. As one WATCH mother said, "The program works. It definitely works. It was the safest and best two years of my life." Help victims help themselves. Support WATCH.

60 SECONDS

One, two, three, by the time this sentence is finished, four, five, six, another life will be shattered, seven, eight, nine, an innocent victim in a vicious cycle, ten, eleven, twelve (SMACK). Every twelve seconds in America a woman is beaten. We need your help to stop the cycle of domestic violence. WATCH, Women and Their Children's Housing, is a non-profit organization that provides second-step transition housing and support services for battered women and their children. WATCH helps women rebuild their lives by teaching them to be economically and emotionally self-sufficient.

October is domestic violence awareness month. Three to five billion dollars are lost per year because of abuse-related absenteeism. WATCH, Women and Their Children's Housing, provides safe alternatives for victims of domestic violence. WATCH helps battered women attain a non-violent lifestyle in order to break the cycle of abuse. Women gain economic and emotional independence through the many programs provided. Services include subsidized housing, job development, family counseling, and support groups for mothers and children. As a non-profit organization, WATCH needs your support.

3.3 million children are victims or witnesses of domestic violence. Physical and mental abuse leaves children traumatized, and leads to high risk of drug and alcohol abuse and juvenile delinquency. WATCH, Women and Their Children's Housing, helps victims of domestic violence break the cycle of abuse. It's the only long-term transitional housing service for women and their children in Santa Clara County. WATCH provides counseling groups which teach children how to express themselves and resolve problems non-violently. This is crucial in overcoming the behavioral patterns of an abusive parent. As a non-profit organization, WATCH needs your support to help these children survive domestic violence.

Questions for Discussion

1. In groups or as a class, discuss the strategies the writers used to gain listener attention. Which strategy did you find most effective?
2. Did the writers effectively evoke images with concrete, sensory, or specific details? Give examples of the most effective ones.
3. Compare the announcements of different lengths and analyze the information that was included in the longer radio spots and excluded from the shorter ones. Would you have made the same decisions about what to include and what to leave out in the ten-second spots? Discuss.

Ideas for Writing

1. Many local area radio stations will air public service announcements that serve the public interest, as will local television stations through their editorial department. As a community service writing project, speak out on an issue of community concern by writing an editorial on the subject for local broadcast.
2. Alternatively, offer your services, perhaps in a small peer group, to a local service organization in your area to help write public service announcements or press releases.

CHAPTER WRITING PROJECTS

1. Drawing on the different points of view presented in this chapter as needed, write an essay discussing the ways in which communities should, or should not, serve as extended families in supporting both young and old.

2. Research kinship and extended families in American ethnic communities. In what ways have they contributed to the strength and support of their members? You could compare and contrast two systems, or you may want to focus on one ethnic group and research it thoroughly.

3. If you are in a military community, investigate the kinds of resources available for families of service members. You might pay special attention to services designed to help service people who lose their jobs or are encouraged to leave the service due to downsizing of the military: job placement and retraining services, for example. You could interview service members and families to try to understand how they cope with the stresses of military life and to determine what kinds of needs are going unmet. Write up your findings for the appropriate local support organizations.

4. Using your campus volunteer office or community volunteer bureau as a resource, if either is available, or doing first-hand field research if not, investigate the needs and current resources for families in your community. (Working in peer groups or as a class will help divide the labor and can make the experience more enjoyable.) Such needs may range from developing support services for older people to teaming up with younger students for afterschool arts and theatrical projects. Innovative projects might include coaching sports, teaching math, or reading and telling stories; collecting ethnic folk tales and helping students and families to put them together in small publications; or working with adult literacy projects. Keep a log during your experiences; work collaboratively if possible. Develop your interest in this work by writing your term paper on the subject of your work (immigration policy if you work with an immigrant group, for example). Try to link your library and research work with your field work so that each experience will illuminate and build on the other.

5. Get involved in a community program that does outreach to local families. Offer to do basic research, field research (data collection, summarizing reports, reading and reporting on pending legislation). Write about your experiences in a journal or in an essay analyzing your experience.

6. Investigate organizations and clubs for youths in your area. Select one in particular, review it in depth, and analyze it in view of Heath and McLaughlin's suggestions for effective youth organizations. You may want to interview administrators and clients.

7. Conduct library research on health and social issues in Native American communities. In what ways are they similar to and different from other communities or cultural groups? Alternatively, research policies in your community or state about foster care intervention. Summarize your findings for your class and any other interested group.

8. With peers in a school, church, or social group, design and put together a crib quilt to donate to a local nonprofit group for a child in need. Work with a local craft shop for help. During the project, keep a notebook on the project; then write an analytical or reflective essay, dialogue, poem, or story describing this community experience.

9. Did your family relocate during your childhood? How did you cope with the changes? How did you go about establishing ties in your new community: finding new resources, developing friendships, coming to feel at home in your new neighborhood? Write either a reflective essay about the experience or a how-to essay with advice for other young people who have to relocate.

10. Analyze the role of the family in preserving the greater clan or community, or the role of the community in preserving the family.

11. With peers from your class or dorm, attend one of the following or other movies on the subject of family and community. Films to consider include *Mississippi Massala, Volunteers, Fifth of July, Eating, Avalon, Dim Sum, I Know Why the Caged Bird Sings, Driving Miss Daisy,* and *The Joy Luck Club.* Develop a discussion afterward or write a critique for your class.

CHAPTER 2

The Individual and the Community

Service is the rent we pay for living.

—Marian Wright Edelman

The energy, the faith, the devotion which we bring to this endeavor will light our country and all who serve it—and the glow from that fire can truly light the world. And so, my fellow Americans: ask not what your country can do for you—ask what you can do for your country.

—John F. Kennedy

Individuals grow up in the small communities of their nuclear and extended families and then make their way in increasingly larger academic, professional, and social groups or communities. Sometimes individual needs coincide with those of their communities; sometimes they conflict. These conflicts raise fundamental questions about the individual's role in and responsibility to the greater community: What are our obligations to others in our communities? In what ways are our pasts and futures intertwined? In this chapter, we examine a number of different views, from national leaders, scientists, writers, and fellow citizens, about the role of individuals in creating and supporting communities.

While self-interest and community support can conflict, they can also reinforce each other and create stronger personal satisfaction, community ties, and support systems. While weaknesses in family systems can cause problems for individuals, strong family bonds can help family members to grow and develop as members of the greater community. Just as increasing community involvement can improve neighborhoods, raise standards of living, and reach out to the struggling members of society, so can such involvement increase the individual's personal satisfaction and emotional and spiritual connections with others. Thomas Jefferson and other early founders and observers of the United States such as French political scientist Alexis de Tocqueville noted the important connections between active, informed citizens and a strong democracy, and our own contemporary educators and leaders such as John Gardner, Ben Barber, and Frances Moore Lappé have called for a renewed citizen involvement and service for the common good.

Children's advocate Marian Wright Edelman, quoted above, argues that service to our community is integral to our responsibilities; calling service "rent for living," she casts service to others in terms of obligations—we get, and we give back in return. For Edelman, service is a logical and necessary return on what we have already received; it is part of a web of connections among all members of a society, with each individual participating and exchanging with other members of the collective. In the readings that follow, the writers present different approaches to and views on the cooperation and conflict inherent in the struggle of individuals to combine forces for the greater benefit of all.

We begin the chapter with John F. Kennedy's "Inaugural Address," a speech that called a generation to public involvement and service for the betterment of their communities and of society as a whole. Kennedy's speech sought to unite audiences both within and outside of America; it proposed an agenda for a decade drawing on the reservoir of energy, hope, and spirit in the American people. The next selection by Jacqueline Rouse, "A New First Lady," focuses on the actions of an individual rather than of a generation. This reading is excerpted from a biography of social reformer Lugenia Burns Hope; it chronicles Hope's life and work as the wife of the president of a historically black college and the ways in which she not only continued her lifelong neighborhood organizing efforts but also encouraged connections between the students' course work and the needs in the local community.

In a personal reflection on one's role in the community, P. W. Alexander's memoir, "Christmas at Home," shares her family tradition of community work. Student writer Bess Kennedy, as well, writes of community work in a newly established national program, the Summer of Service. Kennedy's essay, "Summer of Success," chronicles her experience in this pilot summer project. Following Alexander's and Kennedy's accounts is Desmond Morris's essay "Altruistic Behavior," in which he challenges the view that altruism is anything but self-serving; Morris argues that altruistic behavior is a kind of genetic self-preservation, wherein saving our children, or our tribe/kinspeople, is in fact saving ourselves.

We then turn to an historical account of voluntary associations in America. "Public Associations and Civil Life," is excerpted from *Democracy in America*, by Alexis de Tocqueville, French political scientist and observer of American institutions and customs. As Tocqueville's account makes clear, voluntary associations have extensive roots in Colonial era America. Tocqueville's well-known work provides a wider context in which to study contemporary communities and public involvement.

The role of political, grass roots organizing is a key issue in Toni Cade Bambara's story, "My Man Bovanne." This story presents an African-American community that comes together for grass roots organizing to discover they have quite different agendas and concerns. The narrator, Miss Hazel, decides that building community involves not only political agendas, but more importantly, reaching out to neighbors one person at a time. Robert Frost's "Mending Wall," too, looks at the ways in which we connect with, or set up boundaries between, ourselves and others, not on a policy level or through volunteer efforts, but by reaching out to our neighbors.

Stepping beyond the neighborhood and the purely voluntary nature of public involvement, in "A Call to Arms," William F. Buckley draws up an outline for a national service policy focusing on college-age people. Buckley, noted conservative commentator, argues for universal community service which, through a carrot and stick reward and sanction system, strongly encourages community service for everyone.

After looking at community and public involvement in neighborhoods, colleges, communities, and society at large, we turn to Abraham Lincoln's powerful "Address at Gettysburg." Citing neither the specifics of the battle nor the divisive issue of slavery, Lincoln, honors the war dead and their gift of "the last full measure of devotion," their lives. Lincoln then exhorts the living to give their fullest as well to preserve the nation and its principles. He interprets the meaning and obligations of community in the broadest ethical and political sense.

The chapter closes with a student-produced document written collaboratively for SPOON, a campus-based food program that delivers surplus food to homeless shelters. Demonstrating that students can contribute practically and substantially to their community, the "Community Service Writing Student Project: SPOON (Stanford Project on Nutrition) Informational Flyer" offers a good example of the kinds of informative and persuasive writing students can do for their writing courses. Such writing can teach students to write for audiences beyond the classroom while contributing to the common good.

While these readings do not represent all of the ways of looking at an individual's role in society, they do invite readers to embark on a process of reflection: to consider their own communities and the ways in which they relate to and communicate within their communities. We offer these readings and chapter assignments not to finish the discussion, but to begin it.

Inaugural Address

John F. Kennedy

John Fitzgerald Kennedy (1917–1963) was born in Brookline, Massachusetts, and graduated from Harvard University. Kennedy served as a torpedo boat commander in the Pacific during World War II and received both the Navy Medal and the Purple Heart. Kennedy won the Pulitzer Prize for his book *Profiles in Courage.* After a career in Congress, he became the youngest person ever elected U.S. president. Kennedy was an ardent supporter of civil rights legislation and demonstrated resolve in the Cuban Missile Crisis, but his administration was cut tragically short when rifle fire from an assassin ended his life in 1963. Kennedy's "Inaugural Address" exemplifies the youth and vitality he has come to represent.

Journal

What have you learned about John F. Kennedy's contributions as President?

We observe today not a victory of party but a celebration of freedom—symbolizing an end as well as a beginning—signifying renewal as well as change. For I have sworn before you and Almighty God the same solemn oath our forebears prescribed nearly a century and three-quarters ago.

The world is very different now. For man holds in his mortal hands the 2 power to abolish all forms of human poverty and all forms of human life. And yet the same revolutionary beliefs for which our forebears fought are still at issue around the globe—the belief that the rights of man come not from the generosity of the state but from the hand of God.

We dare not forget today that we are the heirs of that first revolution. Let 3 the word go forth from this time and place, to friend and foe alike, that the torch has been passed to a new generation of Americans—born in this century, tempered by war, disciplined by a hard and bitter peace, proud of our ancient heritage—and unwilling to witness or permit the slow undoing of those human rights to which this nation has always been committed, and to which we are committed today at home and around the world.

Let every nation know, whether it wishes us well or ill, that we shall pay 4 any price, bear any burden, meet any hardship, support any friend, oppose any foe to assure the survival and the success of liberty.

This much we pledge—and more. 5

To those old allies whose cultural and spiritual origins we share, we 6 pledge the loyalty of faithful friends. United, there is little we cannot do in a host of co-operative ventures. Divided, there is little we can do—for we dare not meet a powerful challenge at odds and split asunder.

To those new states whom we welcome to the ranks of the free, we pledge 7 our word that one form of colonial control shall not have passed away merely to be replaced by a far more iron tyranny. We shall not always expect to find them supporting our view. But we shall always hope to find them strongly supporting their own freedom—and to remember that, in the past, those who foolishly sought power by riding the back of the tiger ended up inside.

8   To those people in the huts and villages of half the globe struggling to break the bonds of mass misery, we pledge our best efforts to help them help themselves, for whatever period is required—not because the Communists may be doing it, not because we seek their votes, but because it is right. If a free society cannot help the many who are poor, it cannot save the few who are rich.

9   To our sister republics south of the border, we offer a special pledge—to convert our good words into good deeds—in a new alliance for progress—to assist free men and free governments in casting off the chains of poverty. But this peaceful revolution of hope cannot become the prey of hostile powers. Let all our neighbors know that we shall join with them to oppose aggression or subversion anywhere in the Americas. And let every other power know that this hemisphere intends to remain the master of its own house.

10   To that world assembly of sovereign states, the United Nations, our last best hope in an age where the instruments of war have far outpaced the instruments of peace, we renew our pledge of support—to prevent it from becoming merely a forum for invective—to strengthen its shield of the new and the weak—and to enlarge the area in which its writ may run.

11   Finally, to those nations who would make themselves our adversary, we offer not a pledge but a request: that both sides begin anew the quest for peace, before the dark powers of destruction unleashed by science engulf all humanity in planned or accidental self-destruction.

12   We dare not tempt them with weakness. For only when our arms are sufficient beyond doubt can we be certain beyond doubt that they will never be employed.

13   But neither can two great and powerful groups of nations take comfort from our present course—both sides overburdened by the cost of modern weapons, both rightly alarmed by the steady spread of the deadly atom, yet both racing to alter that uncertain balance of terror that stays the hand of mankind's final war.

14   So let us begin anew—remembering on both sides that civility is not a sign of weakness, and sincerity is always subject to proof. Let us never negotiate out of fear. But let us never fear to negotiate.

15   Let both sides explore what problems unite us instead of belaboring those problems which divide us.

16   Let both sides, for the first time, formulate serious and precise proposals for the inspection and control of arms—and bring the absolute power to destroy other nations under the absolute control of all nations.

17   Let both sides seek to invoke the wonders of science instead of its terrors. Together let us explore the stars, conquer the deserts, eradicate disease, tap the ocean depths, and encourage the arts and commerce.

18   Let both sides unite to heed in all corners of the earth the command of Isaiah—to "undo the heavy burdens . . . [and] let the oppressed go free."

19   And if a beachhead of co-operation may push back the jungle of suspicion, let both sides join in creating a new endeavor, not a new balance of power,

but a new world of law, where the strong are just and the weak secure and the peace preserved.

All this will not be finished in the first one hundred days. Nor will it be 20 finished in the first one thousand days, nor in the life of this administration, nor even perhaps in our lifetime on this planet. But let us begin.

In your hands, my fellow citizens, more than mine, will rest the final suc- 21 cess or failure of our course. Since this country was founded, each generation of Americans has been summoned to give testimony to its national loyalty. The graves of young Americans who answered the call to service surround the globe.

Now the trumpet summons us again—not as a call to bear arms, though 22 arms we need—not as a call to battle, though embattled we are—but a call to bear the burden of a long twilight struggle, year in and year out, "rejoicing in hope, patient in tribulation"—a struggle against the common enemies of man: tyranny, poverty, disease, and war itself.

Can we forge against these enemies a grand and global alliance, North and 23 South, East and West, that can assure a more fruitful life for all mankind? Will you join in that historic effort?

In the long history of the world, only a few generations have been granted 24 the role of defending freedom in its hour of maximum danger. I do not shrink from this responsibility—I welcome it. I do not believe that any of us would exchange places with any other people or any other generation. The energy, the faith, the devotion which we bring to this endeavor will light our country and all who serve it—and the glow from that fire can truly light the world.

And so, my fellow Americans: ask not what your country can do for you— 25 ask what you can do for your country.

My fellow citizens of the world: ask not what America will do for you, but 26 what together we can do for the freedom of man.

Finally, whether you are citizens of America or citizens of the world, ask 27 of us here the same high standards of strength and sacrifice which we ask of you. With a good conscience our only sure reward, with history the final judge of our deeds, let us go forth to lead the land we love, asking His bless- ing and His help, but knowing that here on earth God's work must truly be our own.

Questions for Discussion

1. Kennedy's "Inaugural Address" was hailed as the call to action for a generation of Americans. Identify the appeals he uses to convey this message: ethos, or appeals to common values and beliefs; pathos, or appeals to empathy and emotion; and logos, or appeals through the form and logic of the argument.
2. What themes and images does Kennedy draw upon to unite his audience in a com- mon purpose? What rhetorical strategies does he use—for example, repetition, bal- anced sentences, parallelism?
3. Kennedy speaks to a number of different communities or audiences. Identify sev- eral of them, and then discuss the message he transmits to each audience.
4. Discuss the use of style and syntax in the speech and the ways in which they reflect the world political situation of the times and the East-West, USSR–U.S. conflict. For

example, consider his repeated use of "Let both sides" as a strategy for coherence and organization.

5. What can you infer from this text about Kennedy's human rights platform?
6. To what extent is Kennedy's address applicable today? Despite a radically different international political climate, do parts of the speech still speak to you? To the nation? To the world?

Ideas for Writing

1. Read the address out loud, or listen to a video or audio recording. Write an essay analyzing the themes, the ways in which Kennedy reaches out to his audiences, and the stylistic strategies that make the speech effective.
2. Interview someone who remembers the 1960 election and ask him or her about the Richard Nixon-John F. Kennedy debates on television or about the campaign generally. Taking the interviewee's political affiliation into account, ask him or her about the persuasiveness of the debates and about the ways in which each candidate represented himself to fellow Americans. Discuss, in your essay and if possible with peers, the extent to which television and Kennedy's rhetorical and personal style may have swayed audiences to support him.
3. Find out about the Peace Corps, VISTA, and other volunteer corps that evolved during or after the Kennedy administration, or investigate the new "teacher corps" movement active in a number of communities. How did they come about? To what extent are such organizations still active today? Do they recruit on your campus? Write up a report and share it with your classmates and perhaps your student newspaper. This topic could be developed into a research project.

A New First Lady

Jacqueline Rouse

Jacqueline Anne Rouse (b. 1950) is associate professor of history at Morehouse College. She has co-edited *Women in the Civil Rights Movement: Trailblazers and Torchbearers*, 1941–1965 (1990). Her biography *Lugenia Burns Hope, Black Southern Reformer* (1989), from which the following selection was excerpted, chronicles Hope's life and public service.

Journal

Discuss the ways in which students at your school responded to a period of social unrest such as the Persian Gulf War or the Rodney King trials. Alternatively, what do you know about historically black colleges or about women's or men's colleges? Do you feel that such specialized academic institutions can be effective, or do you hold a different view?

In 1906 Atlanta was the scene of the South's most sensational race riot. For months the city had been whipped into a fury of race hatred by efforts to disfranchise Blacks and by irresponsible journalism.

For over a year the leading gubernatorial candidates, Hoke Smith and 2
Clark Howell, had centered their campaigns on the disfranchisement of Blacks.
Smith, a cabinet member under former president Grover Cleveland, conducted
a rabidly anti-Black campaign that had the support of white supremacist and
ex-Populist Tom Watson. Denouncing Blacks as inferior beings and guaranteeing that suffrage would be completely denied them were he elected, Smith
made inflammatory statements like "We will control the Negro peacefully if
we can, but with guns if we must." He advocated enacting a constitutional
amendment to control Black voting, as other southern states had done, for such
an action would free elections of the "corrupt, ignorant vote of the Negro, but
not deny suffrage to the illiterate whites."

Clark Howell, editor of the Atlanta *Constitution,* condemned Smith's cam- 3
paign as an attempt to use racism to support his own cause. He pointed out
that the Fifteenth Amendment made disfranchisement unconstitutional and
that in fact the party primaries, begun in 1877, had accomplished a de facto
disfranchisement anyway. Smith nonetheless won an overwhelming victory.

The radical and racial nature of the gubernatorial campaign continued to 4
be a catalyst that sold newspapers even after the political contest was over. A
survival struggle ensued, in which each of the evening papers, the Atlanta
Georgian, the Atlanta *Journal,* and the Atlanta *News,* tried to outdo the others
by exploiting sensational news and publishing numerous extras.

Extreme measures were instituted to attract readers. The best strategy for 5
results proved to be the abuse of Blacks. John Temple Graves, in particular,
reported Black violence in vivid detail in the *News.* Walter White, a native
Atlantan, recalled later that such stories were standard and familiar and frequently ran as "eight column streamers instead of the two or four column
ones." Front-page headlines like "Insulting Negro Badly Beaten at Terminal
Station," "Bold Negro Kisses Girl's Hand," "Empty Gun Saves Her," "Negro
Grabs Girl as She Steps Out on Back Porch" appeared daily. Emphatic calls
and pleas were made to southern white men to "protect" their women: "To
think of the awful crimes being committed against our women is alarming. It
seems that men are justified in adopting the most radical punishment for the
perpetrations of such deeds that can be devised this side of the region of fire
and brimstone. Then to Arms! Men of Georgia." Sensational pieces of this sort
were common, and unproved charges of assault upon white women by Black
men were enough to incite mobs, giving them license to attack and in some
cases murder innocent and unsuspecting Blacks.

Such was the situation on Saturday, September 22. In rough notes written 6
years later, Lugenia recalled the tensions in the city and the events surrounding the riot:

> Negroes [were] leaving the country and small towns for northern cities to   7
> escape [the] terrorizing effect of the campaign of hate.
>> Negroes [were] not able to buy fire arms for months before the Riot.   8
>> Negroes were quite unsuspecting that their white friends had planned to   9
> destroy them. The Negro[es] will never forget or forgive the shock of realiz-
> ing that their white friends had betrayed them. They should have protected
> their servants at least. When the storm broke it was Sat. night when Negroes

were doing their marketing for Sun. They were at the market with their whole family. Out of a clear sky the white people began kicking—beating. They would stop the street cars, pull the Negroes out to beat them—Some times the conductor would at the point of a revolver dare the mobsters to get on his car. This [kept] up until midnight. It had gotten out of control of the police.

10 She continued, describing the situation as it affected the campus, where John had recently been installed as president:

11   Sunday night John Hope patrolled the campus—the rioters threatened to burn all of the Negro colleges. . . . [T]he responsibility [for] Morehouse [fell to] John Hope. Finally a man[,] U.S. Army on furlough[,] came over and gave Mr. Hope a gun & cartridge belt. Another teacher joined the two. They patrolled all night taking shifts. The militia came and camped at the corner and another camped at Spelman. We were not happy until we learned . . . martial law was declared. The gangsters were camping at our gates . . . and the city fathers had to send to other cities for militia and it was an out of town group at our gate. Monday we had received fire arms for protection. Friends had sent out of town for fire arms. We had enough to feel secure or rather so. It was said they came in the city in coffins. However, we had the fire arms and even though the city was under martial law, the Negroes succeeded in getting the fire arms to the people who needed them. Some were carried in soiled laundry.

12   The Mayor gave [an] order to have Negro homes searched for fire arms. The Negroes hid their arms and also those of their neighbors who were not at home. When this order came thru, the Negroes telephoned the Governor, "take our arms and we will fire the city." That stopped the house to house inspection.

13   The section called Darktown prepared for the mob—when the Gov. said every part of the city would be protected. The Darktown people sent word to the Gov. "Don't send the militia but send the mob." They had smothered the lights and when the mob . . . looked at those black streets, [they] were afraid and left and went off to South Atlanta where the Negroes were expecting them and there would have been blood shed—But knowing what would happen the mayor had a gatling gun hauled over the RR track and dared the mob to cross. Then he had the men in the black community arrested and of course took their arms away. We did not get the Sunday *Constitution* until about eleven o'clock. One of the department heads brought the paper and explained why he had to bring it. Told us all about the happenings of the night before. Seemed very much ashamed of the whole affair. The city streets were terrible.

14   John Hope got in touch with Miss Giles, Pres. of Spelman—called the Governor, asked for protection of the property of Spelman and the women on the campus. The gangsters started up to Morehouse but some of the group refused to come—They knew that [it was] a school for Negro men—& the cowards were afraid to come. Toward evening streams of women and children came up the walks. The men in the community sent the women and children to have the protection of those brick buildings while they stayed home.

15   In my neighborhood all of the white children were put in one of the white public schools and soldiers patrolled the school grounds. Homes were nailed up . . . —fear. These white people knew how they had treated the Negro all the while, now they feared retribution. The Negro man went home, sat in the

door with his gun across his knees and was prepared to die protecting his home and family. Not until then did the good Christian white people care what happened to the Negro. But when they saw the Negro in sheer desperation decided to protect himself or die—did the churches open their doors— Fear.

No one person could have brought those people [Black Atlantans] to terms. They felt they had stood as much as any man could—They were prepared for every eventuality. So a committee was called of both races . . . with representation of [the] Negro race. They discussed [issues] man to man. The white man learned . . . in this riot . . . to get along together [with Blacks,] that there must be cooperation. 16

Though her active local community participation extended back to her first arrival in Atlanta, the riot heightened Lugenia's civic consciousness. The plight of Black Atlanta became a stark reality to her. Race-baiting culminating in mob rule forced Black racial unity as a means of survival. Places and people associated with leadership were sought out for protection, so the college campuses became havens for people, especially women and children, seeking shelter. A woman named Mrs. Banks brought her son to the Hopes to ensure his safety while she stayed with the white family she worked for. The security of the "brick buildings" at Spelman and Atlanta Baptist colleges was reinforced not only by the presence of an armed militia made up mainly of out-of-town soldiers but moreover by the presence of armed Black men of the community— the husbands, brothers, and fathers of the families seeking safety. Lugenia recalled their strong stand on racial solidarity in their community. 17

Lugenia saw herself as accountable to her own West Fair neighborhood both as a community activist and as the wife of a powerful Black man. In 1906 John Hope was inaugurated as Atlanta Baptist College's first Black president, and Lugenia became the first lady of this all-male campus. In her transition from the wife of a professor to the wife of the president, her influence and prestige accelerated, but so did her duties and obligations. This new position would provide her with a different avenue to address difficult issues, but it would also bring more issues and problems to address. It would mean that those in need would expect her, Mrs. John Hope, to have immediate access to resources that would produce immediate results. People would expect her success rate to be high and her endurance long-suffering. In addition, she was to be a role model and mother figure for the student body of the college, a mother to Edward and later also to John II, and a promoter and official hostess for the school as she stood by her husband in all of his endeavors. She was to care for his home, his sons, his guests, the live-in students, and the female faculty, and she was expected to continue and expand her social activism—though the college would be her first loyalty. 18

Lugenia, the first lady, also inherited power. Being the president's wife would open doors previously closed or only cracked. It was a status that would bring her audiences with municipal officials who could promise, and even implement, changes in the Black community. It would bring influential memberships and leadership on a national and international basis. It would grant her a wider platform from which to continue the social reform work she 19 had begun as Lugenia Burns. Yet there was some question whether being the first lady of Atlanta Baptist College, with all of the rights and privileges and responsibilities pertaining thereto, would stifle Lugenia Burns's spirit of independence.

20   As Lugenia assumed her new role on campus, her first concern was the students. Several former students remembered her as, in the words of one of them, "charming, seldom ruffled, firm, gentle, a careful thinker, and a very soft and cultured woman." Another student spoke of her as being "not the aggressive type" but "soft-spoken, a home-type person though very active in community activities." Another remembered that she would "stand on the porch, stop the students passing by, and invite them to listen to the radio, especially if something important such as a presidential address was being broadcasted." Other students felt that she "cultivated in them certain habits in dress and mannerism and set a cultural and moral tone for them." As her son Edward put it, "Dignity and self respect were fundamental aspects of her character. Money, while not to be ignored, was less important than a life of service to one's own downtrodden people. . . . Through out the College students were taught that morality, dignity, and self respect were more valuable than money or any earthly thing." Still another student recalled the "warmth in her face that invited the young men of the college to come to her to relax and tell her their problems."

21   During the thirty-three years that Lugenia lived on the campus of Atlanta Baptist College, later Morehouse College, she tried to impart to the young men her sensitivity toward the needs of the community and the necessity of alleviating them. She encouraged students to become involved, to acquaint themselves with the low-income families nearby, and to collect toys, fruit, and food for those families at Thanksgiving, Christmas, and other holidays. Some sociology classes—those of Professors Gary Moore, Walter Chivers, and John B. Watson, for example—conducted surveys of the needs in the adjoining community for the Neighborhood Union. Once ascertained, the results were organized into a plan of action. Atlanta Baptist College and Atlanta University students joined the union in mounting special projects for the community's children. Students tutored classes in school subjects for the young children. Some conducted such industrial arts classes as woodworking and cabinet-making. Others supervised playground activities, and still others taught Vacation Bible School during the summers and participated in intercollegiate track meets that served as fund-raisers for the union. Some of these students also worked with Lugenia in making door-to-door surveys to encourage voter registration.

22   Officially, Lugenia was for many years the dormitory mother of Graves Hall. A former student and later academic dean, Brailsford Brazeal, remembered her daily room inspections: "We knew that she would be coming about nine or nine-thirty every morning. Many of us would have our doors open waiting for her." In his eulogy of Lugenia at Morehouse's memorial service in 1947, Ira de A. Reid of Atlanta University reiterated that her early days at the college were "seldom glamorous ones for she was called upon to super-

vise the cleaning of buildings and grounds; to keep the college accounts; and to make men out of the students." As noted, Lugenia also taught sculpture classes in her attic to those students of Atlanta Baptist and Spelman colleges whom she saw as gifted. During the summers she usually offered a millinery class at Spelman.

Because her own experiences had persuaded her of the value of the under- 23 taking, Lugenia sought to establish training classes in social work, to be offered through the Neighborhood Union. In 1918 the union organized a Social Service Institute at Morehouse—a workshop of lectures on prenatal and infant care, juvenile delinquency, malnutrition, and the value of social service. Lugenia aided Professor Moore's class in organizing the three-day workshop and served as one of its faculty members. Out of this institute grew the Atlanta School of Social Work, which in 1920 became affiliated with Atlanta University. Many social work students got their field experience by working with Lugenia in the union. Some served as matrons or assistants at the settlement centers; others worked in various clinics of the union; others organized recreational programs for the young children.

Lugenia was one of the founders of the still extant Morehouse Auxiliary. 24 Organized in 1923, the auxiliary consisted of the wives of faculty and staff members united in order to enhance social life on the campus and to raise funds for the school. As a charter member, Lugenia took part in various auxiliary-sponsored functions: plays, campus-life discussions, parties, and other social affairs. The auxiliary assisted in many fund-raising campaigns by operating a snack shop in the basement of Graves Hall and holding bazaars, baby contests, and other activities that enabled it to establish scholarships and to donate a thousand dollars toward the construction of the school's first gymnasium.

Lugenia's involvement with Morehouse was not limited even to this wide 25 range of activities. Her husband is credited with organizing the first football team on campus. The team had winning seasons, and Lugenia was a team supporter. Edward recalled:

> In the days before athletic scholarships, before glorified professional athletes, 26
> when the old line college sports were center stage and the little colleges such
> as ABC in the Negro world were just getting started, mother was in the foreground in promoting athletics. A few young players went out for the fun of
> it, but generally among the older students who were necessary to fill out the
> team since they predominated in the student body, one played football for the
> honor and glory of the college or not at all. I have a feeling that mother especially in the very early days helped convert some of these old timers into solid
> reliable football players.

She undoubtedly contributed to the collegiate atmosphere of the cheering sec- 27 tion:

> The school was a very drab, serious, hardworking place. . . . The fans, stu- 28
> dents and their guests went to the games gaily with colorful arm bands, waving bright colored pennants. So mother began making maroon and white

colored pennants, cutting and sewing the letters on by hand. I doubt that mother had any financial aid but the satisfaction was in seeing the sidelines become a mass of alumni, friends, and students gaily and loyally displaying their colors.

29   In 1929 John Hope again made history: he was inaugurated the first Black president of Atlanta University. In addition to his duties as president of Morehouse College, John now assumed the awesome task of building the first Black graduate school in the South. Atlanta University, begun in the Reconstruction era as an undergraduate institution, was now being converted to a graduate school and relocated to its current site. Former Atlanta University undergraduate students were transferred to Spelman or Morehouse colleges; after graduation, some of these students would enroll in graduate courses at Atlanta University. John at once began his drive to consolidate the organization of the Atlanta University Consortium—Morehouse College, Spelman College, and Atlanta University. He also worked to affiliate Morris Brown College, Clark University (now Clark College), and Gammon Theological Seminary. He proposed that these institutions share faculty, resources, and a library; in return, he expected these schools to improve their faculty salaries in order to attract quality teachers. Since the teachers were to be shared, he wanted all of them eligible to teach at Spelman and Morehouse. He wished to relocate Clark University, located in South Atlanta, closer to the budding intellectual center—a goal accomplished in 1942.

30   In 1931, convinced that he had secured Morehouse's endowment, John resigned as Morehouse's leader and began to build Atlanta University. He traveled extensively to raise the necessary funds to erect a physical plant, a business administration building, a library, and the president's house.

31   While John was building and traveling for Atlanta University, Lugenia still lived in the president's house on the Morehouse campus. She continued to serve as first lady of the school, but she was involved little or not at all in the administration of Morehouse and the building of Atlanta University. Though she had encouraged her husband to take the university job, her participation was limited to organizing the family's move into the newly completed president's house in 1932 and planning the decoration of the house. Her community work dominated the years of John's administration at Atlanta University, as her career concentrated on the settlement projects of the Neighborhood Union. She did seek to incorporate graduate social work students into the union's community organizing and building. Just as she had secured sociology students from Morehouse over the years to assist the union's work, she now developed an alliance between the School of Social Work at the university and the union. Graduate social work majors could use the union's programs and projects to complete their required volunteer and practical works. Lugenia worked with the School of Social Work in organizing programs to bring the school and the neighborhood of West Fair closer together. For example, Atlanta University social work students assisted the union with its unem-

ployment program in the West Fair area during the depression. Soup kitchens, clothing drives, and temporary shelters were provided as relief for needy families. Lugenia also worked for slum clearance in the Beaver Slide area. She and her husband, and other members of the union, agreed to sell the union's property on West Fair Street when the federal government promised to build public housing for the Black community. Thus University Homes became one of the earliest public housing projects for Blacks in the country. In these ways Mrs. First Lady of Atlanta University continued her public life, extending it even more deeply into the community around her than she had done during her Morehouse years.

Questions for Discussion

1. Politicians often make ethos appeals, or appeals to the beliefs and values of their audiences, and pathos appeals, or appeals that engage their emotions. Discuss the kinds of appeals used during the gubernatorial campaign and quoted in the newspaper accounts in the beginning of this selection. Examine as well the rhetoric of the newspaper headlines. To what ethos or emotions are the papers appealing? Toward what purpose? How do such appeals unite some parts of the community and divide others?
2. The author writes, "Race-bating culminating in mob rule forced Black racial unity as a means of survival." How might a threat to members of a group help to develop a sense of community within the group?
3. Paragraph 21 discusses Lugenia Burns Hope's efforts to involve students in adjoining communities through conducting neighborhood surveys, tutoring, teaching, and supervising activities, as well as collecting holiday toys and food and participating in fundraisers. Do you believe colleges should be involved in helping local communities? In what ways? Should community activities be relevant to their course work (i.e., neighborhood needs assessments by sociology students)? Or are direct services such as toy drives equally important?
4. What sort of person is Hope? Would you like to meet her? Have you known people like her? Does she seem typical of someone you would characterize as a community activist? Explain your response.
5. The author notes that during the riots, "places and people associated with leadership were sought out for protection, so the college campuses became havens for people." Do you think that colleges today help to develop strong leaders? What other institutions have an impact on the development of leaders in society?

Ideas for Writing

1. It has been said that one person can make a huge difference. Write an essay discussing not only immediate, but also long term effects of Hope's efforts or of another leader who has made a significant difference in his or her community.
2. Critics of women's colleges sometimes charge them with reverse discrimination, while supporters argue that such learning environments can nurture and empower women, and that white male students are already sufficiently empowered in our society. Argue for or against colleges that support one gender or one ethnic or religious group.

Christmas at Home

P. W. Alexander

P. W. Alexander (b. 1951), who grew up in South Florida, is a teacher and a writer; she is one of ten children from a Mexican-American family. Alexander was educated at San Francisco State University and the University of California, San Diego. Currently an advanced graduate student in educational psychology at Stanford University, Alexander is dedicated to community service and has taught or served as a consultant at a wide range of schools, particularly inner city schools. Her commitment to public service has been lifelong; her involvement ranges from working with Cesar Chavez and farm workers to teaching in prisons and elementary schools. In the following memoir, Alexander reflects on her family's tradition of community involvement.

Journal

As a young person were you encouraged to do volunteer work or to donate money or goods to a charitable cause? If so, write about such an experience. If not, would you consider doing so? Alternatively, do you belong to a religious congregation that encourages service work? Discuss.

"It must have been fun growing up in a big family. I bet the holidays were great."

I look into the face of the woman standing before me. Her expression is some combination of curiosity, affirmation, and hope. It is a question I hear from time to time and not one as easily answered as asked. I can say, "Oh it was wonderful. We had a house full of people. We laughed, we cried, we fought and we made up. I had lots of sisters to love and to tease and to tell my darkest secrets." It is the second question, I bet the holidays were great, that causes me to hesitate, to look at the asker and wonder how much she really wants to hear.

2   As a child I did not look forward to the holidays. We have an expectation for holidays here in America. It is family time. We have a Norman Rockwell picture of the clan gathered around a long table, in the center of a comfortably furnished dining room, draped in freshly pressed linen and festooned with candles and flowers. At the center of attention is the huge bird, glistening, beckoning us to overeat. People are smiling. Children are neat, Sunday-best-dressed. It is a hopeful image, and I admit, I too am taken by it. It is a holiday scene that would have fit our family well. We had the well-furnished dining room. We had a long cherrywood table that could seat fourteen, three more chairs than our family needed. We had the yards of lace and linen and the wreaths, candles, centerpieces and china. My parents, however, had some other vision of how the holidays should be spent.

3   As a young child I simply accepted our family observance of holidays; I knew nothing else. It began with Halloween. In the morning we went to church and in the evening we collected for UNICEF. At first I thought little of

the cup of money I brought home that was poured into a large glass jar and eventually spirited away somewhere. As I got older and greedier I began to dislike those nameless, faceless children in countries with odd names pointed out to me on the globe in the library. I wanted to take just one of those dimes and buy a full-size Snickers bar. I was glad when I became "too big" to go out trick or treating.

Thanksgiving and Christmas were equally painful. My mother would sign 4 us all up to work at the soup kitchen. While other families watched televised parades, chased cousins under the piano and yelled at grandma because she had left her hearing aid home, we stood in line and served people from the fringe. We chopped and washed and sliced in the church kitchen. We wore old clothes because the work was messy and we didn't want to "show off." My brother and I were fascinated with the size of the ovens and the number of turkeys that they contained. We carried stacks of plates and bowls and dragged crates of vegetables across the concrete floors. My older brother had the most annoying habit of whistling or humming as he went about his kitchen chores. He was never a part of our kitchen shenanigans. We had games we played between ourselves—who could wash the most forks in one minute, how many cups of coffee could we carry on one tray without spilling. We stuck our fingers in pumpkin pies and covered the damage with whipped cream from a can.

One particularly cold Thanksgiving we were in West Virginia for the 5 school holidays. My father found a place for us to serve. It was snowing hard. People came in long before the meal was ready. I remember them warming their hands on hot cups of coffee. I shivered in the warm church basement. They brought the icy wind inside with them. It was in their thin coats and wet shoes. The image of that red, cracked skin on their hands and faces stayed with me for a long time. I remember how much people would eat, and how quickly. I was scandalized at their table manners. Napkins were often left untouched at the side of their plates. My younger brother, Carlos, relished these meals. He delighted in the piles of food and lack of rules. He announced once on the way home, "I ate mashed potatoes—with my fingers!" I had seen people surreptitiously stuffing unwrapped food into their pockets. They never left anything on the plate, not even a polite pea or a genteel stalk of asparagus.

As I got older, I began to ask more questions. Why don't they have homes? 6 Why don't they have food? Why don't they work? And I always asked, WHY do WE have to do this? My mother's response was always the same. The same five words in the same calm, even voice. It was as if she had some perverse tape running inside her head that spewed out the same tired message time after time: "Because we have so much."

The year I was thirteen I thought we would all be saved the embarrass- 7 ment, the humiliation, the torture of the slave galley. Grandmother was coming from Boston. Grandmother was a lady who always wore gloves. White gloves with little pearl buttons and lacy fingers. Grandmother would never ladle murky soup into plastic bowls or slice great slabs of turkey into scratched beige plates with little compartments. But Grandmother did. She did it with grace and humility. She hugged unwashed people with matted hair and open sores. She shook hands with their red, raw claws and she blessed them. She asked them to pray for her. She wrapped turkey legs in newspaper and openly invited people to take them home. She sat down next to a scruffy little girl and introduced herself as grandma. People smiled at her and showed her all the teeth they didn't have.

8   That night, my sister Josefina and I snuggled close together in my top bunk and talked long into the night. She often crept up from her bed so we could whisper together after "lights out." We had never spoken much about our service. It was a dreaded event, something to complain about, one more reason to stand by our resolve never to sell our children into indentured servitude. But that night, that Thanksgiving that Grandmother came and took off her white lacy gloves and served gravy to poor people, that night we talked of other things.

9   We talked about how hard it was not to stare. We knew staring was impolite. These people were so dirty, so poor, and so ugly. If they caught you looking at them they turned away quickly. There was something haunting in their eyes, something of pain and of shame and of sadness. They looked at the floor, at the plate of food heaped before them, at the crucifix on the wall over the table. "They have no dad." My sister Isabel cried out in the darkness from her bed on the other side of the room. "Grandmother washed those two boys' hands in the kitchen sink and she sat by them and they told her they had no dad." I squeezed Josefina's hand. *No Dad.* Who took them to the beach, who gave them quarters for the movie, who told them stories at bedtime so they wouldn't have bad dreams?

10   A month later, at Christmas, Josefina and I gave away our two favorite books to the gift drive our church held. My older brother donated his bicycle and his skates. We didn't put up a tree that year but we did buy one and give it to some people we had read about in the newspaper. Their house and all their presents burned up in a fire.

11   I work at the homeless shelter and I stand in the serving line and ladle soup and gravy. I shake hands with people who don't bathe and I have on occasion hugged people with dried vomit on their clothing. Three years ago I came home on Thanksgiving with head lice. It is a small part of the job. It is a very small part of the experience. I am in service to my fellow human beings. I do this not out of any sense of duty or obligation; I do it because it is my family tradition. It would not be Thanksgiving or Christmas if I did not stand for a brief moment in front of my closet, gaze at my favorite party frock and feel a slight twinge of regret. It passes very quickly and then I put on my work clothes and I go to the church kitchen to do my service. I see the same hard, lined faces, the same out-of-fashion ragged clothes. I smell the same street dirt and sour alcohol. I hear the same stories of injustice and pain. The people whose eyes I avoided as a child I now seek. I search their faces for some harbinger of hope, some sign of change. If you ask me why I do it, I can only say, because I have so much.

Questions for Discussion

1. Describe Alexander's family tradition. How does her mother justify their holiday observance? What is Alexander's attitude toward it? In what ways does her attitude change?
2. How do you think Alexander and her family would define community? How do her actions support this definition?
3. Do you think the family's commitment represents altruistic behavior? How might Alexander respond to Desmond Morris's arguments? (This selection appears later in this chapter.) Do you believe holiday time service is important? Do you think service should only be for long-term commitments? Discuss.
4. Do you believe it is right, or appropriate, or wise, for Alexander's parents to force her and her siblings to perform public service?
5. What is the tone of this essay? Do you sense sadness, regret, happiness, satisfaction? Discuss the specific language or examples that convey this tone.
6. How effective do you think personal writing is in articulating a philosophy of community and service? Do you find it more, or less, effective than other readings in the chapter that present an argument for community involvement? Discuss.

Ideas for Writing

1. Write a personal essay that responds to and reflects on Alexander's experience.
2. Write your own memoir about a family tradition. In what ways does the tradition help to bind you and your family to the larger community?

Summer of Success

Bess Kennedy

Bess Kennedy (b. 1975), originally from Palo Alto, California, enjoys hiking, working with youngsters, and meeting new people. In her essay "Summer of Success," written during her first year of college, Kennedy reflects on some of the emotions and setbacks she encountered while participating in the Summer of Service program. She plans to major in international relations and hopes to continue with her community service work.

Journal

Would you consider spending your summer working on community projects, if you had the opportunity and modest financial support? Discuss.

A bright yellow sun peeking out over a red and white banner adorned the t-shirts of the 1,500 youths gathered at Treasure Island, San Francisco. With almost tangible enthusiasm, this group of young people from across the country gathered together for one week of training to inaugurate the much awaited national service program, Summer of Service. The logo reflected the youth service pioneers' high hopes and spirits; their energy and dedication foreshadowed the future success of Summer of Service. To understand the promise of Summer of Service, one must look beyond the limited scope of this first summer and consider the experiences that participants will remember for the rest of their lives. As Summer of Service expands in coming years, these experiences, not hard facts, will be the most important measure of the program's success.

2   With talk of a national service network starting during the presidential campaign, many were skeptical of ever seeing a plan put into action. People wondered whether Clinton would follow through on his promise to create a national service organization and still others questioned the effectiveness of such a program. But here stood 1,500 young people, ages 17–25, embarking on a nine-week service commitment that began as one of Bill Clinton's campaign promises. Having been involved in service for the majority of my life, I was pleased that a president who was ready to make community service a priority had been elected. Although unable to vote, I had followed the presidential campaign earnestly, intrigued by many of Clinton's new ideas for service. Once elected, Clinton was quick to act on his word. In a speech on March 1, 1993, Clinton stated, "I . . . ask all of you to join me in creating a new system of voluntary national service—something that I believe in the next few years will change America forever and for the better" (Summer of Service). Three months later, I filled out an application for Summer of Service, a pilot program for Clinton's Corporation for National and Community Service.

3   Much of the program was designed after the Commission on National and Community Service, established with bipartisan support by Congress in 1990. The founding principles of these two organizations were to be similar: small-scale programs, matching grants, local sponsorship, entrepreneurial ideas, committed community volunteers. Summer of Service was administered by the Commission on National and Community Service to "renew the American ethic of service and civic responsibility" (White House Office). Four-hundred-and-thirty project proposals were submitted by agencies from across the U.S., all eager to be a part of this pioneering group. Of these, 16 were selected to employ the 1,500 youth participants. According to Catherine Milton, Executive Director of the Commission on National and Community Service, Summer of Service program winners were selected for their "quality, their clearly defined and measurable effects on children at-risk, and for their potential to develop service leaders for the future" (White House Office). Milton added, "These programs will serve as a foundation for an effective, high quality network of national service" (White House Office). Choosing participants was an equally selective task. Thousands of youths applied for the 1,500 jobs. Those with strong service backgrounds were favored while bilingual skills were also an important factor. Creating a diverse group was also a priority for the Commission and as a result, 75% of participants were minorities. On a national level, Summer of Service was seen as a stepping stone toward a national service network. More specifically, as outlined by Eli Segal, director of the White House Office of National Service, Summer of Service was to demonstrate three

positive aspects of community service: "the potential of national service to provide tangible and measurable community benefits; to develop national service leaders, and to unleash the talents and energies of young Americans eager to make a difference in their communities" (White House Office). For participants, the goals were more personal: to have a child write his name for the first time, to teach a mother how to care for her infant, to show the children that someone was making a commitment to them. Reflecting on personal stories of both participants and those in the communities served, the pilot program was successful in demonstrating each of these benefits of community service.

As a participant in Summer of Service, I was able to witness first hand the 4 successes of the program on a personal level. I was a member of the largest program funded by Summer of Service, that of the East Bay Conservation Corps. The E.B.C.C. had 250 participants engaged in over fifteen projects in the San Francisco Bay Area. My twenty-four member team worked at a nearby city school district summer school. Each Summer of Service participant worked in a classroom from 8:30–1:00, assisting the teacher in everything from Xeroxing papers to working in small groups or one-on-one with those who needed extra attention. From 1:00–3:00, the Summer of Service team ran an after school program which included sports, arts and crafts, and academic tutoring.

Every morning at 8:00 I'd leave my suburban world and travel across the 5 freeway to a city where poverty and violence prevail, bullet holes pock the store fronts and drug dealers and prostitutes roam the streets. Once at school, it was not uncommon to hear the kids whispering about Mike, who had been shot the night before, or Rachel, who, at age fourteen, was having her second child. The challenges these children faced daily were so different from those I faced in my life. I empathized with them but at the same time I was impressed by their determination. Many of them would be the first in their families to finish high school, or to learn to read and to write. While I was being asked which college I planned to attend, these kids were hoping they'd live to be twenty-five. This was the world I entered every morning, a world so distant and separate from my own.

These differences became even more apparent when I walked into the 6 adult English as a Second Language classroom I worked in. Aside from the teacher, I was the only Caucasian person there. Most of the students had recently immigrated from Mexico and were struggling to survive in their new homes. Mothers, unable to afford a babysitter, brought their children, and people were always arriving late or leaving early, trying to balance jobs and classes.

Although I enjoyed working with this class, my true challenge didn't begin 7 until 1:00 every afternoon, when I tutored Junior. Junior was thirteen years old and big for his age. He was enrolled in the summer school in hopes that he would not have to repeat fifth grade for the third time. At an age where most kids are writing book reports and learning geometry, Junior was struggling with his multiplication tables and his A, B, C's. Like many kids at his school, Junior had managed to get to the fifth grade without knowing how to read or write. Sadly enough, as with many of these illiterate children, the teachers had given up hope of Junior ever learning to read or write. Already four years older than his classmates, Junior had only three years left before he was required by the district to attend high school. This meant that if he didn't pass fifth grade this time, he'd have to skip either sixth, seventh, or eighth grade. But rather than focus on his illiteracy, I was told to teach him his multiplication tables; after all, that was only memorizing and anyone could do that. Unfortunately, this was the fate for many of the students. With class sizes upwards of thirty, many teachers were forced to make choices. Should they focus on Maria, who had a chance of attending college and came from a supportive family, or should they give Francisco the extra help he needed to learn addition? Usually, Maria would win the teacher's attention and Francisco would become another drop-out statistic. I was here to give Junior that extra attention, that help he didn't receive in class, in hopes that he too would not fall through the cracks.

8   I didn't truly realize how much work lay ahead of me until my first meeting with Junior when I tried to get some estimate of where to begin. "Okay, what's seven times one?" I asked him. Junior pondered the question for a moment and finally answered, "Forty-one." I tried not to let him know how shocked I was, how discouraged I felt that he did not even have a grasp of the basics. My determination to teach Junior his multiplication tables was mixed with a tinge of anxiety. After all, what did I know about teaching? Of course I'd spent twelve years in the educational system but I was always the student, not the teacher. Despite my lack of experience, I felt responsible for Junior's education: if he didn't succeed, then I was a failure. I went home that night and tried to remember all my teachers had told me about multiplication. I checked out books from the library and asked my friends' younger siblings for advice. I arrived for our tutoring session the next day full of ideas and with a bulging bag of M&M's, to be used for counting and later as rewards.

9   Every afternoon for the next few weeks we worked on times tables. One day Junior would understand perfectly and the next day he would have forgotten everything. I was so proud of him when he finally mastered the twos times tables, only to discover that he didn't even realize that two times five was the same thing as five times two. Setbacks like this occurred daily. Sometimes Junior wouldn't show up for our tutoring sessions and I'd find out the next day that he had to go home and take care of his younger brothers and sisters. We worked around these setbacks and slowly, Junior began making progress. He made flash cards and practiced them at home. As time went by, I found myself frequenting the store more often for those treasured bags of M&M's.

10   Just as we were beginning the seven times tables, something happened that brought our tutoring sessions to an abrupt halt. After school one day, another kid who was not involved in the summer school but was often hanging around the campus pulled a knife on Junior. It just so happened that

Junior's mother, who had recently finished serving a seven year prison sentence, was on campus at that same time. She began chasing after the kid with the knife and threatening him. Undaunted, the kid yelled back that he was going to go to their house that night with a gun. Junior's mother responded by pulling her son out of the summer school. The shock I experienced following this incident was not due to the violent act of the teenager. I had grown accustomed to violence as a means of survival for these kids. Rather, my shock came from the ensuing conversation I had with Junior's mother as we were walking to her car. She seemed doubtful when I told her that Junior was a hard worker and was doing quite well. "He's retarded you know," she blurted out as we approached her vehicle. I stopped, stunned by what she had just said. Junior may have been slower than most of the kids his age but he was not retarded. For years, however, Junior's mother had been telling him that he was mentally handicapped. I later learned from Junior's teacher that his mother would come in to class and announce that her son was retarded to Junior's classmates, ostensibly to spare him any teasing about his slowness. Junior's so called "retardation" became an excuse for him not to perform well. Any hopes he had of achieving success were immediately squelched by his mother's reminder.

I didn't see Junior after that day. His mother refused to allow him to come 11 even to the tutoring sessions. I was discouraged; we hadn't achieved our goal and come fall, Junior would return to the fifth grade. But our work together wasn't a complete failure. What I learned to do more and more that summer was to find success on a smaller level. So maybe Junior never did learn the seven times tables, but at least he knew someone out there cared, and probably for the first time in his life, someone believed in him and his ability to succeed.

For the majority of Summer of Service participants, the summer program 12 was neither a beginning nor an end to community service in their lives. Rather, their participation reflected life long commitments to service. Although it remains to be seen whether or not these participants will become national service leaders, many are continuing to serve their communities. Deborah Kim, a Summer of Service worker who spent her summer at the Golden Gate Child Development Center, noted that although her summer of service was over, her "commitment to helping urban school children" (Akizuki) was not. As Clinton's pilot program officially ended, "Kim was planning to volunteer once a week in the same center where she worked for the past eight weeks" (Akizuki).

Works Cited

Akizuki, Dennis. "Youth Program Workers Catch Spirit of Service." *San Jose Mercury News* 21 August 1993.
Summer of Service. Press brief. East Bay Conservation Corps, 1993.
White House Office of National and Community Service and the Commission on National and Community Service. 6 May 1993.

Questions for Discussion

1. Kennedy cites the Commission on National and Community Service's imperative to "renew the American ethic of service and civic responsibility." How would you describe the "American ethic of service"? Do you think the experience described by Kennedy supports the commission's goal?
2. In what ways did Kennedy's students, such as Junior, help her to learn about teaching? About difference? About values?
3. Do you think Kennedy's experience is typical of many participants in the Summer of Service? If so, in what ways? If not, how might it differ?
4. Kennedy's essay integrates both outside sources and her own observation and experience. Do you find both types of evidence equally convincing and compelling? Discuss.
5. The selection process for the Summer of Service gave preference to students who had prior service experience. Do you think organizers should favor those who have a history of service, or should they try to get students who have never before done community or public service to participate? Discuss the pros and cons of each approach.

Ideas for Writing:

1. Bess Kennedy cites Clinton's campaigning and the Commission on National and Public Service; others may cite the Points of Light Foundation, associated more with the Bush administration. Some critics charge that community service, particularly on college campuses and in the college curriculum, promotes a liberal political agenda. Do you feel that community service has become the political "property" of one political party or the other? If so, how does it reflect a particular party's platform? If not, how can people from opposing sides of the political spectrum find common ground in community involvement and service? Discuss.
2. The Summer of Service comes some thirty years after John F. Kennedy's "Inaugural Address." In what ways do you think the project or its founding commission fulfill some of the goals articulated in John Kennedy's speech?
3. Would you be interested in spending a summer participating in community-oriented projects? Write an essay that outlines the reasons for your interest and the goals you would hope to pursue. You may be able to submit the essay as a personal statement should you decide to apply.

Altruistic Behavior

Desmond Morris

Desmond Morris (b. 1928) was born in Wiltshire, England, and took a B.Sc. degree at the University of Birmingham and a D. Phil. at Magdalen College, Oxford, in 1954. He worked as a researcher in animal behavior at Oxford and held positions in Granada TV and Film Unit (England) and the Institute of Contemporary Arts, London. He is a scientific fellow of the Zoological Society of London and served as curator of mammals. A full-time writer since 1968, Morris's numerous works include both scientific publications and books for mainstream adult audiences and children. Probably his work most well known to the general public, though at times criticized by anthropologists, is *The Naked Ape* (1967), which presents the study of humans as one variation within the ape family. In the selection below, Morris argues that behavior that might seem selfless is often, in fact, self-serving in fostering the survival of one's own community or tribe.

Journal

Write about a time when you helped someone else, perhaps a stranger, a child, a fellow student whom you did not know. What do you think motivated you? Alternatively, if you avoided responding actively in a situation where a person needed help, why do you think you did so?

Altruism is the performance of an unselfish act. As a pattern of behavior this act must have two properties: it must benefit someone else, and it must do so to the disadvantage of the benefactor. It is not merely a matter of being helpful, it is helpfulness at a cost to yourself.

This simple definition conceals a difficult biological problem. If I harm 2 myself to help you, then I am increasing your chances of success relative to mine. In broad evolutionary terms, if I do this, your offspring (or potential offspring) will have better prospects than mine. Because I have been altruistic, your genetic line will stand a better chance of survival than mine. Over a period of time, my unselfish line will die out and your selfish line will survive. So altruism will not be a viable proposition in evolutionary terms.

Since human beings are animals whose ancestors have won the long strug- 3 gle for survival during their evolutionary history, they cannot be genetically programmed to display true altruism. Evolution theory suggests that they must, like all other animals, be entirely selfish in their actions, even when they appear to be at their most self-sacrificing and philanthropic.

This is the biological, evolutionary argument and it is completely con- 4 vincing as far as it goes, but it does not seem to explain many of mankind's "finer moments." If a man sees a burning house and inside it his small daughter, an old friend, a complete stranger, or even a screaming kitten, he may, without pausing to think, rush headlong into the building and be badly burned in a desperate attempt to save a life. How can actions of this sort be described as selfish? The fact is that they can, but it requires a special definition of the term "self."

When you think of your "self," you probably think of your living body, 5 complete, as it is at this moment. But biologically it is more correct to think of yourself as merely a temporary housing, a disposable container, for your genes. Your genes—the genetic material that you inherited from your parents and which you will pass on to your children—are in a sense immortal. Our bodies are merely the carriers which they use to transport themselves from one generation to the next. It is they, not we, who are the basic units of evolution.

We are only their guardians, protecting them from destruction as best we can, for the brief span of our lives.

6   Religion pictures man as having an immortal soul which leaves his body at death and floats off to heaven (or hell, as the case may be), but the more useful image is to visualize a man's immortal soul as sperm-shaped and a woman's as egg-shaped, and to think of them as leaving the body during the breeding process rather than at death. Following this line of thought through, there is, of course, an afterlife, but it is not in some mysterious "other world"; it is right here in the heaven (or hell) of the nursery and the playground, where our genes continue their immortal journey down the tunnel of time, re-housed now in the brand-new flesh-containers we call children.

7   So, genetically speaking, our children are us—or, rather, half of us, since our mate has a half share of the genes of each child. This makes our devoted and apparently selfless parental care nothing more than *genetic self-care*. The man who risks death to save his small daughter from a fire is in reality saving his own genes in their new body-package. And in saving his genes, his act becomes biologically selfish, rather than altruistic.

8   But supposing the man leaping into the fire is trying to save, not his daughter, but an old friend? How can this be selfish? The answer here lies in the ancient history of mankind. For more than a million years, man was a simple tribal being, living in small groups where everyone knew everyone else and everyone was closely genetically related to everyone else. Despite a certain amount of out-breeding, the chances were that every member of your own tribe was a relative of some kind, even if a rather remote one. A certain degree of altruism was therefore appropriate where all the other members of your tribe were concerned. You would be helping copies of your own genes, and although you might not respond so intensely to their calls for help as you would do with your own children, you would nevertheless give them a degree of help, again on a basis of genetic selfishness.

9   This is not, of course, a calculated process. It operates unconsciously and is based on an emotion we call "love." Our love for our children is what we say we are obeying when we act "selflessly" for them, and our love of our fellow-men is what we feel when we come to the aid of our friends. These are inborn tendencies and when we are faced with calls for help we feel ourselves obeying these deep-seated urges unquestioningly and unanalytically. It is only because we see ourselves as "persons" rather than as "gene machines" that we think of these acts of love as unselfish rather than selfish.

10   So far, so good, but what about the man who rushes headlong into the fire to save a complete stranger? The stranger is probably *not* genetically related to the man who helps him, so this act must surely be truly unselfish and altruistic? The answer is Yes, but only by accident. The accident is caused by the rapid growth of human populations in the last few thousand years. Previously, for millions of years, man was tribal and any inborn urge to help his fellow-men would have meant automatically that he was helping gene-sharing relatives, even if only remote ones. There was no need for this urge to be selective, because there were no strangers around to create problems. But with the urban explosion, man rapidly found himself in huge communities, surrounded

by strangers, and with no time for his genetic constitution to alter to fit the startingly new circumstances. So his altruism inevitably spread to include all his new fellow-citizens, even though many of them may have been genetically quite unrelated to him.

Politicians, exploiting this ancient urge were easily able to spread the aid- 11 system even further, to a national level called patriotism, so that men would go and die for their country as if it were their ancient tribe or their family.

The man who leaps into the fire to save a small kitten is a special case. To 12 many people, animals are child-substitutes and receive the same care and love as real children. The kitten-saver is explicable as a man who is going to the aid of his symbolic child. This process of symbolizing, of seeing one thing as a metaphorical equivalent of another, is a powerful tendency of the human animal and it accounts for a great deal of the spread of helpfulness across the human environment.

In particular it explains the phenomenon of dying for a cause. This always 13 gives the appearance of the ultimate in altruistic behavior, but a careful examination of the nature of each cause reveals that there is some basic symbolism at work. A nun who gives her life for Christ is already technically a "bride" of Christ and looks upon all people as the "children" of God. Her symbolism has brought the whole of humanity into her "family circle" and her altruism is for her symbolic family, which to her can become as real as other people's natural families.

In this manner it is possible to explain the biological bases for man's seem- 14 ingly altruistic behavior. This is in no way intended to belittle such activities, but merely to point out that the more usual, alternative explanations are not necessary. For example, it is often stated that man is fundamentally wicked and that his kind acts are largely the result of the teachings of moralists, philosophers and priests; that if he is left to his own devices he will become increasingly savage, violent and cruel. The confidence trick involved here is that if we accept this viewpoint we will attribute all society's good qualities to the brilliant work of these great teachers. The biological truth appears to be rather different. Since selfishness is genetic rather than personal, we will have a natural tendency to help our blood-relatives and hence our whole tribe. Since our tribes have swollen into nations, our helpfulness becomes stretched further and further, aided and abetted by our tendency toward accepting symbolic substitutes for the real thing. Altogether this means that we are now, by nature, a remarkably helpful species. If there are break-downs in this helpfulness, they are probably due, not to our "savage nature" reasserting itself, but to the unbearable tensions under which people so often find themselves in the strained and over-crowded world of today.

It would be a mistake, nevertheless, to overstate man's angelic helpfulness. 15 He is also intensely competitive. But under normal circumstances these rival tendencies balance each other out, and this balance accounts for a great deal of human intercourse, in the form of *transactional behavior*. This is behavior of the "I'll-scratch-your-back-if-you'll-scratch-mine" type. We do deals with one another. My actions help you, but they are not altruistic because they also help me at the same time. This co-operative behavior is perhaps the dominant feature of day-to-day social interaction. It is the basis of trade and commerce and it explains why such activities do not become more ruthless. If the competitive element were not tempered by the basic urge to help one another, business practices would rapidly become much more savage and brutal than they are, even today.

16   An important extension of this two-way cooperative behavior is embodied in the phrase: "one good turn now deserves another later." This is delayed, or nonspecific cooperation. I give help to you now, even though you cannot help me in return. I do this daily to many people I meet. One day I will need help and then, as part of a "long-term deal," they will return my help. I do not keep a check on what I am owed or by whom. Indeed, the person who finally helps me may not be one of the ones I have helped. But a whole network of social debts will have built up in a community and, as there is a great division of labor and skills in our species today, such a system will be beneficial to all the members of the society. This has been called "reciprocal altruism." But once again it is not true altruism because sooner or later, one way or another, I will be rewarded for my acts of helpfulness.

17   Anticipation of a delayed reward of this kind is often the hidden motive for a great deal of what is claimed to be purely altruistic behavior. Many countries hand out official awards to their citizens for "service to the community," but frequently these services have been deliberately undertaken in the anticipation that they are award-worthy. Comparatively few public honors ever come as a surprise. And many other "good works" are undertaken with later social (or heavenly) rewards in mind. This does not necessarily make the "works" any less good, of course; it merely explains the motives involved.

18   The following table sums up the relationship between competitiveness and helpfulness, and their intermediates:

1. Self-assertive behavior	Helps me	Harms you	Mild competitiveness to full criminality
2. Self-indulgent behavior	Helps me	No effect on you	The private, non-social pleasure
3. Co-operative behavior	Helps me	Helps you	Transaction, trade, barter and negotiation
4. Courteous behavior	No effect on me	Helps you	Kindness and generosity
5. "Altruistic" behavior	Harms me	Helps you	Loving devotion, philanthropy, self-sacrifice and patriotism

Questions for Discussion

1. State Morris's definition of altruism in your own words. Do you agree with his definition? How do you define altruism?
2. What is Morris's biological definition of the self? Is his definition persuasive? Do you accept the notion that selfless parental care is merely "gene self-care"?

3. Individually or in small groups, construct your own definition of the terms "altruism" and "self." Compare and contrast your definitions with Morris's.
4. According to Morris, what is the connection between "transactional behavior" and altruistic behavior? How does transactional behavior support day-to-day living? Do you find evidence of transactional behavior in academic communities such as your college? Discuss.
5. Identify several examples that Morris uses to develop his points. Do you find them convincing? Can you think of other kinds of support he could have used? Do you find his chart helpful? Is it appropriate for the selection?

Ideas for Writing

1. Review your journal entry for this selection. Write an essay analyzing the incident in view of Morris's argument. Does your example support or refute Morris's claims about altruistic behavior?
2. Discuss the ways in which altruistic behavior serves one's tribe or community. Consider, for example, what role love plays in altruism. How does altruistic behavior relate to patriotism? How does Morris's theory help to explain why people participate in community service and philanthropy?
3. Write a letter of response to Morris, or write a dialogue between Morris and Alexander or between Morris and one of the other authors whose work is included in this chapter or in Chapter 1.

Public Associations and Civil Life

Alexis de Tocqueville

Count Alexis [Charles Henri Maurice Clerel] de Tocqueville (1805–1859) was a French historian known for his observations of and writings on democracy. He held a number of positions in the French government, including deputy and minister under Louis Napoleon, and he once served on a mission to the United States. One of his best known works is *Democracy in America (Democratie en Amerique)* (1835–1839), from which the following excerpt is taken. Tocqueville's work is considered a landmark study of American institutions and is often quoted to this day. Tocqueville's insights into American society make his work invaluable when studying both historical and contemporary aspects of individualism and community.

Journal

Discuss an association, volunteer group, club, or nonprofit organization in your community and the needs it fulfills.

I do not propose to speak of those political associations by the aid of which men endeavor to defend themselves against the despotic action of a majority, or against the aggressions of regal power. That subject I have already treated. If each citizen did not learn, in proportion as he individually becomes more feeble, and consequently more incapable of preserving his freedom single-handed, to combine with his fellow-citizens for the purpose of defending it, it is clear that tyranny would unavoidably increase together with equality.

2   Those associations only which are formed in civil life, without reference to political objects, are here adverted to. The political associations which exist in the United States are only a single feature in the midst of the immense assemblage of associations in that country. Americans of all ages, all conditions, and all dispositions, constantly form associations. They have not only commercial and manufacturing companies, in which all take part, but associations of a thousand other kinds,—religious, moral, serious, futile, general or restricted, enormous or diminutive. The Americans make associations to give entertainments, to found seminaries, to build inns, to construct churches, to diffuse books, to send missionaries to the antipodes; they found in this manner hospitals, prisons, and schools. If it be proposed to inculcate some truth, or to foster some feeling by the encouragement of a great example, they form a society. Wherever, at the head of some new undertaking, you see the government in France, or a man of rank in England, in the United States you will be sure to find an association.

3   I met with several kinds of associations in America of which I confess I had no previous notion; and I have often admired the extreme skill with which the inhabitants of the United States succeed in proposing a common object to the exertions of a great many men, and in inducing them voluntarily to pursue it.

4   I have since traveled over England, whence the Americans have taken some of their laws and many of their customs; and it seemed to me that the principle of association was by no means so constantly or adroitly used in that country. The English often perform great things singly, whereas the Americans form associations for the smallest undertakings. It is evident that the former people consider association as a powerful means of action, but the latter seem to regard it as the only means they have of acting.

5   Thus, the most democratic country on the face of the earth is that in which men have, in our time, carried to the highest perfection the art of pursuing in common the object of their common desires, and have applied this new science to the greatest number of purposes. Is this the result of accident? or is there in reality any necessary connection between the principle of association and that of equality?

6   Aristocratic communities always contain, amongst a multitude of persons who by themselves are powerless, a small number of powerful and wealthy citizens, each of whom can achieve great undertakings single-handed. In aristocratic societies, men do not need to combine in order to act, because they are strongly held together. Every wealthy and powerful citizen constitutes the head of a permanent and compulsory association, composed of all those who are dependent upon him, or whom he makes subservient to the execution of his designs.

7   Amongst democratic nations, on the contrary, all the citizens are independent and feeble; they can do hardly anything by themselves, and none of them can oblige his fellow-men to lend him their assistance. They all, there-

fore, become powerless, if they do not learn voluntarily to help each other. If men living in democratic countries had no right and no inclination to associate for political purposes, their independence would be in great jeopardy; but they might long preserve their wealth and their cultivation: whereas, if they never acquired the habit of forming associations in ordinary life, civilization itself would be endangered. A people amongst whom individuals should lose the power of achieving great things single-handed, without acquiring the means of producing them by united exertions, would soon relapse into barbarism.

Unhappily, the same social condition which renders associations so nec- 8 essary to democratic nations, renders their formation more difficult amongst those nations than amongst all other. When several members of an aristocracy agree to combine, they easily succeed in doing so: as each of them brings great strength to the partnership, the number of its members may be very limited; and when the members of an association are limited in number, they may easily become mutually acquainted, understand each other, and establish fixed regulations. The same opportunities do not occur amongst democratic nations, where the associated members must always be very numerous for their association to have any power.

I am aware that many of my countrymen are not in the least embarrassed 9 by this difficulty. They contend, that, the more enfeebled and incompetent the citizens become, the more able and active the government ought to be rendered, in order that society at large may execute what individuals can no longer accomplish. They believe this answers the whole difficulty, but I think they are mistaken.

A government might perform the part of some of the largest American 10 companies; and several States, members of the Union, have already attempted it; but what political power could ever carry on the vast multitude of lesser undertakings which the American citizens perform every day, with the assistance of the principle of association? It is easy to foresee that the time is drawing near when man will be less and less able to produce, of himself alone, the commonest necessaries of life. The task of the governing power will therefore perpetually increase, and its very efforts will extend it every day. The more it stands in the place of associations, the more will individuals, losing the notion of combining together, require its assistance: these are causes and effects which unceasingly create each other. Will the administration of the country ultimately assume the management of all the manufactures which no single citizen is able to carry on? And if a time at length arrives when, in consequence of the extreme subdivision of landed property, the soil is split into an infinite number of parcels, so that it can only be cultivated by companies of husbandmen, will it be necessary that the head of the government should leave the helm of state to follow the plough? The morals and the intelligence of a democratic people would be as much endangered as its business and manufactures, if the government ever wholly usurped the place of private companies.

Feelings and opinions are recruited, the heart is enlarged, and the human 11 mind is developed, only by the reciprocal influence of men upon each other. I have shown that these influences are almost null in democratic countries;

they must therefore be artificially created, and this can only be accomplished by associations.

12   When the members of an aristocratic community adopt a new opinion, or conceive a new sentiment, they give it a station, as it were, beside themselves, upon the lofty platform where they stand; and opinions or sentiments so conspicuous to the eyes of the multitude are easily introduced into the minds or hearts of all around. In democratic countries, the governing power alone is naturally in a condition to act in this manner; but it is easy to see that its action is always inadequate, and often dangerous. A government can no more be competent to keep alive and to renew the circulation of opinions and feelings amongst a great people, than to manage all the speculations of productive industry. No sooner does a government attempt to go beyond its political sphere, and to enter upon this new track, than it exercises, even unintentionally, an insupportable tyranny; for a government can only dictate strict rules, the opinions which it favors are rigidly enforced, and it is never easy to discriminate between its advice and its commands. Worst still will be the case, if the government really believes itself interested in preventing all circulation of ideas; it will then stand motionless and oppressed by the heaviness of voluntary torpor. Governments, therefore, should not be the only active powers: associations ought, in democratic nations, to stand in lieu of those powerful private individuals whom the equality of conditions has swept away.

13   As soon as several of the inhabitants of the United States have taken up an opinion or a feeling which they wish to promote in the world, they look out for mutual assistance; and as soon as they have found each other out, they combine. From that moment they are no longer isolated men, but a power seen from afar, whose actions serve for an example, and whose language is listened to. The first time I heard in the United States that a hundred thousand men had bound themselves publicly to abstain from spirituous liquors, it appeared to me more like a joke than a serious engagement; and I did not at once perceive why these temperate citizens could not content themselves with drinking water by their own firesides. I at last understood that these hundred thousand Americans, alarmed by the progress of drunkenness around them, had made up their minds to patronize temperance. They acted just in the same way as a man of high rank who should dress very plainly, in order to inspire the humbler orders with a contempt of luxury. It is probable that, if these hundred thousand men had lived in France, each of them would singly have memorialized the government to watch the public houses all over the kingdom.

14   Nothing, in my opinion, is more deserving of our attention than the intellectual and moral associations of America. The political and industrial associations of that country strike us forcibly; but the others elude our observation, or, if we discover them, we understand them imperfectly, because we have hardly ever seen anything of the kind. It must, however, be acknowledged, that they are as necessary to the American people as the former, and perhaps more so. In democratic countries, the science of association is the mother of science; the progress of all the rest depends upon the progress it has made.

Amongst the laws which rule human societies, there is one which seems 15
to be more precise and clear than all others. If men are to remain civilized, or
to become so, the art of associating together must grow and improve in the
same ratio in which the equality of conditions is increased.

Questions for Discussion

1. What are some of the kinds of associations Tocqueville describes? To what kinds of
   individual, family, or community needs do they respond?
2. According to Tocqueville, how are Americans different from Europeans in their
   reliance on voluntary associations? How do the voluntary associations support
   democracy? Why do democratic nations need them more than aristocratic nations?
3. How do voluntary associations balance government control? According to Tocqueville, how does the process of forming organizations empower individuals? In
   answering this question, consider the local organizing efforts during the 1906 riots
   discussed in the Rouse selection (this chapter).
4. Discuss Tocqueville's example in paragraph 13 of abstention from drink and how it
   relates to the use of voluntary associations in America. How is such a temperance
   organization different from the approach that might be taken in France? What does
   this example convey about characteristics of Americans?
5. Are the voluntary associations Tocqueville writes about similar to those that exist in
   your community? Identify some of your community's groups or nonprofit agencies.
   Do such groups seem to be motivated by self-interest, or community interest, or
   some combination?
6. Although this essay has been translated from French, do you perceive a sense of the
   writer's voice and tone? How formal is the language compared to other chapter
   selections? Refer to specific examples to support your view. What does the language
   tell us about the audience for this selection?

Ideas for Writing

1. Why do you think Americans form groups, clubs, cliques, or, in some cases, gangs?
   You might decide to focus on a specific population group such as young people.
   Alternatively, write an essay describing a community group to which you or family members belong. What brought group members together? In what ways are they
   a community?
2. Compare and contrast Tocqueville's and Morris's concepts of self-interest.

My Man Bovanne

Toni Cade Bambara

Toni Cade Bambara (b. 1939), writer, professor, civil rights activist, received her
B.A. from Queens College in 1959 and her M.A. from City College of the City University of New York in 1964, where she also worked as an instructor. Bambara

worked for the New York State Department of Welfare and was founder/director of Pajola Writers Collective from 1976 to 1985. She won the American Book Award for *The Salt Eaters* in 1981. Bambara's subjects most often include African-American families and communities; the following story, included in *Gorilla, My Love* (1970), explores such themes.

Journal

Write about a time when your parents, grandparents, or other relatives embarrassed you. Why do you think you reacted as you did?

Blind people got a hummin jones if you notice. Which is understandable completely once you been around one and notice what no eyes will force you into to see people, and you get past the first time, which seems to come out of nowhere, and it's like you in church again with fat-chest ladies and old gents gruntin a hum low in the throat to whatever the preacher be saying. Shakey Bee bottom lip all swole up with Sweet Peach and me explainin how come the sweetpotato bread was a dollar-quarter this time stead of dollar regular and he say uh hunh he understand, then he break into this *thizzin* kind of hum which is quiet, but fiercesome just the same if you ain't ready for it. Which I wasn't. But I got used to it and the onliest time I had to say somethin bout it was when he was playin checkers on the stoop one time and he commenst to hummin quite churchy seem to me. So I says. "Look here Shakey Bee, I can't beat you and Jesus too." He stop.

2   So that's how come I asked My Man Bovanne to dance. He ain't my man mind you, just a nice ole gent from the block that we all know cause he fixes things and the kids like him. Or used to fore Black Power got hold their minds and mess em around till they can't be civil to ole folks. So we at this benefit for my niece's cousin who's runnin for somethin with this Black party somethin or other behind her. And I press up close to dance with Bovanne who blind and I'm hummin and he hummin, chest to chest like talkin. Not jammin my breasts into the man. Wasn't bout tits. Was bout vibrations. And he dug it and asked me what color dress I had on and how my hair was fixed and how I was doin without a man, not nosy but nice-like, and who was at this affair and was the canapes dainty-stingy or healthy enough to get hold of proper. Comfy and cheery is what I'm trying to get across. Touch talkin like the heel of the hand on the tambourine or on a drum.

3   But right away Joe Lee come up on us and frown for dancin so close to the man. My own son who knows what kind of warm I am about; and don't grown men call me long distance and in the middle of the night for a little Mama comfort? But he frown. Which ain't right since Bovanne can't see and defend himself. Just a nice old man who fixes toasters and busted irons and bicycles and things and changes the lock on my door when my men friends get messy. Nice man. Which is not why they invited him. Grassroots you see. Me and Sister Taylor and the woman who does heads at Mamies and the man from the barber shop, we all there on account of we grassroots. And I

ain't never been souther than Brooklyn Battery and no more country than the window box on my fire escape. And just yesterday my kids tellin me to take them countrified rags off my head and be cool. And now can't get Black enough to suit em. So everybody passin sayin My Man Bovanne. Big deal, keep stepping and don't even stop a minute to get the man a drink or one of them cute sandwiches or tell him what's goin on. And him standin there with a smile ready case someone do speak he want to be ready. So that's how come I pull him on the dance floor and we dance squeezin past the tables and chairs and all them coats and people standin round up in each other face talkin bout this and that but got no use for this blind man who mostly fixed skates and skooters for all these folks when they was just kids. So I'm pressed up close and we touch talkin with the hum. And here come my daughter cuttin her eye at me like she do when she tell me about my "apolitical" self like I got hoof and mouf disease and there ain't no hope at all. And I don't pay her no mind and just look up in Bovanne shadow face and tell him his stomach like a drum and he laugh. Laugh real loud. And here come my youngest, Task, with a tap on my elbow like he the third-grade monitor and I'm cuttin up on the line to assembly.

"I was just talkin on the drums," I explained when they hauled me into   4 the kitchen. I figured drums was my best defense. They can get ready for drums what with all this heritage business. And Bovanne stomach just like that drum Task give me when he come back from Africa. You just touch it and it hum thizzim, thizzim. So I stuck to the drum story. "Just drummin that's all."

"Mama, what are you talkin about?"   5

"She had too much to drink," say Elo to Task cause she don't hardly say   6 nuthin to me direct no more since that ugly argument about my wigs.

"Look here, Mama," say Task, the gentle one. "We just tryin to pull your   7 coat. You were makin a spectacle of yourself out there dancing like that."

"Dancin like what?"   8

Task run a hand over his left ear like his father for the world and his father   9 before that.

"Like a bitch in heat," say Elo.   10

"Well uhh, I was goin to say like one of them sex-starved ladies gettin on   11 in years and not too discriminating. Know what I mean?"

I don't answer cause I'll cry. Terrible thing when your own children talk   12 to you like that. Pullin me out the party and hustlin me into some stranger's kitchen in the back of a bar just like the damn police. And ain't like I'm old old. I can still wear me some sleeveless dresses without the meat hangin off my arm. And I keep up with some thangs through my kids. Who ain't kids no more. To hear them tell it. So I don't say nuthin.

"Dancin with that tom," say Elo to Joe Lee, who leanin on the folks'   13 freezer. "His feet can smell a cracker a mile away and go into their shuffle number post haste. And them eyes. He could be a little considerate and put on some shades. Who wants to look into them blown-out fuses that—"

"Is this what they call the generation gap?" I say.   14

15   "Generation gap," spits Elo, like I suggested castor oil and fricassee possum in the milk shakes or somethin. "That's a white concept for a white phenomenon. There's no generation gap among Black people. We are a col—"

16   "Yeh, well never mind," says Joe Lee. "The point is Mama . . . well, it's pride. You embarrass yourself and us too dancin like that."

17   "I wasn't shame." Then nobody say nuthin. Them standin there in they pretty clothes with drinks in they hands and gangin up on me, and me in the third-degree chair and nary a olive to my name. Felt just like the police got hold to me.

18   "First of all," Task say, holding up his hand and tickin off the offenses, "the dress. Now that dress is too short, Mama, and too low cut for a woman your age. And Tamu's going to make a speech tonight to kick off the campaign and will be introducin you and expecting you to organize the Council of Elders—"

19   "Me? Didn nobody ask me nuthin. You mean Nisi? She change her name?"

20   "Well, Norton was supposed to tell you about it. Nisi wants to introduce you and then encourage the older folks to form a Council of the Elders to act as an advisory—"

21   "And you going to be standing there with your boobs out and that wig on your head and that hem up to your ass. And people'll say, 'Ain't that the horny bitch that was grindin with the blind dude?' "

22   "Elo, be cool a minute," say Task, gettin to the next finger. "And then there's the drinkin. Mama, you know you can't drink cause next thing you know you be laughin loud and carryin on," and he grab another finger for the loudness. "And then there's the dancin. You been tattooed on the man for four records straight and slow draggin even on the fast numbers. How you think that look for a woman your age?"

23   "What's my age?"

24   "What?"

25   "I'm axin you all a simple question. You keep talkin bout what's proper for a woman my age. How old am I anyhow?" And Joe Lee slams his eyes shut and squinches up his face to figure. And Task run a hand over his ear and stare into his glass like the ice cubes goin calculate for him. And Elo just starin at the top of my head like she goin rip the wig off any minute now.

26   "Is your hair braided up under that thing? If so, why don't you take it off? You always did do a neat cornroll."

27   "Uh huh," cause I'm think how she couldn't undo her hair fast enough talking bout cornroll so countrified. None of which was the subject. "How old, I say?"

28   "Sixtee-one or—"

29   "You a damn lie Joe Lee Peoples."

30   "And that's another thing," say Task on the fingers.

31   "You know what you all can kiss," I say, gettin up and brushin the wrinkles out my lap.

"Oh, Mama," Elo say, puttin a hand on my shoulder like she hasn't done 32
since she left home and the hand landin light and not sure it supposed to be
there. Which hurt me to my heart. Cause this was the child in our happiness
fore Mr. Peoples die. And I carried that child strapped to my chest till she was
nearly two. We was close is what I'm tryin to tell you. Cause it was more me
in the child than the others. And even after Task it was the girl-child I covered in the night and wept over for no reason at all less it was she was a chub-
chub like me and not very pretty, but a warm child. And how did things get
to this, that she can't put a sure hand on me and say Mama we love you and
care about you and you entitled to enjoy yourself cause you a good woman?

"And then there's Reverend Trent," say Task, glancin from left to right like 33
they hatchin a plot and just now lettin me in on it. "You were suppose to be
talking with him tonight, Mama, about giving us his basement for campaign
headquarters and—"

"Didn nobody tell me nuthin. If grassroots mean you kept in the dark I 34
can't use it. I really can't. And Reven Trent a fool anyway the way he tore into
the widow man up there on Edgecombe cause he wouldn't take in three of
them foster children and the woman not even comfy in the ground yet and
the man's mind messed up and—"

"Look here," say Task. "What we need is a family conference so we can 35
get all this stuff cleared up and laid out on the table. In the meantime I think
we better get back into the other room and tend to business. And in the meantime, Mama, see if you can't get to Reverend Trent and—"

"You want me to belly rub with the Reven, that it?" 36

"Oh damn," Elo say and go through the swingin door. 37

"We'll talk about all this at dinner. How's tomorrow night, Joe Lee?" 38

While Joe Lee being self-important I'm wonderin who's doin the cookin 39
and how come nobody ax me if I'm free and do I get a corsage and things like
that. Then Joe nod that it's O.K. and he go through the swingin door and just
a little hubbub come through from the other room. Then Task smile his smile,
lookin just like his daddy, and he leave. And it just me in this stranger's
kitchen, which was a mess I wouldn't never let my kitchen look like. Poison
you just to look at the pots. Then the door swing the other way and it's My
Man Bovanne standin there saying Miss Hazel but lookin at the deep fry and
then at the steam table, and most surprised when I come up on him from the
other direction and take him on out of there. Pass the folks pushing up toward
the stage where Nisi and some other people settin and ready to talk, and folks
getting to the last of the sandwiches and the booze fore they settle down in
one spot and listen serious. And I'm thinkin bout tellin Bovanne what a lovely
long dress Nisi got on and the earrings and her hair piled up in a cone and
the people bout to hear how we all gettin screwed and gotta form our own
party and everybody there listenin and lookin. But instead I just haul the man
on out of there, and Joe Lee and his wife look at me like I'm terrible, but they
ain't said boo to the man yet. Cause he blind and old and don't nobody there
need him since they grown up and don't need they skates fixed no more.

40   "Where we goin, Miss Hazel?" Him knowin all the time.

41   "First we gonna buy you some dark sunglasses. Then you comin with me to the supermarket so I can pick up tomorrow's dinner, which is goin to be a grand thing proper and you invited. Then we going to my house."

42   "That be fine. I surely would like to rest my feet." Bein cute, but you got to let men play out they little show, blind or not. So he chat on bout how tired he is and how he appreciate me taking him in hand this way. And I'm thinkin I'll have him change the lock on my door first thing. Then I'll give the man a nice warm bath with jasmine leaves in the water and a little Epsom salt on the sponge to do his back. And then a good rubdown with rosewater and olive oil. Then a cup of lemon tea with a taste in it. And a little talcum, some of that fancy stuff Nisi mother sent over last Christmas. And then a massage, a good face massage round the forehead which is the worryin part. Cause you gots to take care of the older folks. And let them know they still needed to run the mimeo machine and keep the spark plugs clean and fix the mailboxes for folks who might help us get the breakfast program goin, and the school for the little kids and the campaign and all. Cause old folks is the nation. That what Nisi was sayin and I mean to do my part.

43   "I imagine you are a very pretty woman, Miss Hazel."

44   "I surely am," I say just like the hussy my daughter always say I was.

Questions for Discussion

1. What is your sense of the narrator's community? Is her view of community consistent with her children's?
2. What is Bovanne's role in the community? How has his role changed over time? Are his contributions appreciated?
3. Contrast Miss Hazel's children's expectations of her public role in organizing the elders with her private acts of friendship with Bovanne. Does one seem more genuine and supportive than the other? Discuss.
4. This short story gives a fictional look at grass roots organizing. Do you think that it is a realistic presentation of some of the issues that come up as groups try to organize for political purposes? Explain.
5. In what ways do imagery and dialogue help to develop a sense of a community? Do you find that the common language, or vernacular, unifying, or does it distance you from the story? Are you able to appreciate the touches of humor? Refer to examples from the text.
6. Do you see evidence of age discrimination in your school, community, church, or neighborhood? Relate this discrimination to the events in "My Man Bovanne."

Ideas for Writing

1. Interview others in your class about their family traditions and attitudes with respect to the elderly. Try to work with peers from a different cultural background than your own. Write up and share your findings with your class.
2. Compare and contrast the attitudes about community organizing presented in this selection with those discussed in the biographical selection on Lugenia Burns Hope in this chapter.

Mending Wall

Robert Frost

Robert Frost (1875–1963) was born in San Francisco and raised in the mill town of Lawrence, Massachusetts. Attending university off and on, taking odd jobs including some teaching, Frost knew that he was to be a poet. He moved to a farm, spent time in England, and found success upon the publication of his second book of poems, *North of Boston,* in 1914. From that time until his death, Frost became the best known of modern American poets: he received four Pulitzer Prizes and read at John F. Kennedy's inauguration; in doing so, he affirmed the public nature of poetry. His poem "Mending Wall," published in 1914, takes as its subject the manner, and degree, of connections between neighbors.

Journal

You may have heard the expression, "Good fences make good neighbors." Discuss what you think it means.

Something there is that doesn't love a wall,
That sends the frozen-ground-swell under it,
And spills the upper boulders in the sun;
And makes gaps even two can pass abreast.
The work of hunters is another thing: 5
I have come after them and made repair
Where they have left not one stone on a stone,
But they would have the rabbit out of hiding,
To please the yelping dogs. The gaps I mean,
No one has seen them made or heard them made,   10
But at spring mending-time we find them there.
I let my neighbor know beyond the hill;
And on a day we meet to walk the line
And set the wall between us once again.
We keep the wall between us as we go.   15
To each the boulders that have fallen to each.
And some are loaves and some so nearly balls
We have to use a spell to make them balance:
"Stay where you are until our backs are turned!"
We wear our fingers rough with handling them.   20
Oh, just another kind of outdoor game,
One on a side. It comes to little more:
There where it is we do not need the wall:
He is all pine and I am apple orchard.
My apple trees will never get across   25
And eat the cones under his pines, I tell him.

He only says, "Good fences make good neighbors."
Spring is the mischief in me, and I wonder
If I could put a notion in his head:
30 *"Why* do they make good neighbors? Isn't it
Where there are cows? But here there are no cows.
Before I built a wall I'd ask to know
What I was walling in or walling out,
And to whom I was like to give offense.
35 Something there is that doesn't love a wall,
That wants it down." I could say "Elves" to him,
But it's not elves exactly, and I'd rather
He said it for himself. I see him there
Bringing a stone grasped firmly by the top
40 In each hand, like an old-stone savage armed.
He moves in darkness as it seems to me,
Not of woods only and the shade of trees.
He will not go behind his father's saying,
And he likes having thought of it so well
45 He says again, "Good fences make good neighbors."

Questions for Discussion

1. Describe the situation in the poem: the characters, the speaker, and his neighbor. What diction and imagery suggest these characterizations? What touches of humor?
2. What do you think the speaker means by the "something" that "doesn't love a wall"? What does the speaker mean by "walling in" and "walling out"?
3. Examine specific concrete images in the poem, such as the stones. What do they contribute to the theme? How do they work to evoke an image, a reaction in the reader? Examine the pauses and rhythms of the lines and discuss what they contribute to the poem's meaning.
3. What kinds of walls, whether psychological, social, or cultural, do we construct in our society? Why do we do so? Does the poem offer any insight into this issue?
4. The world celebrated the destruction of the Berlin Wall. Discuss the literal and symbolic significance of that wall's collapse, particularly in view of this poem.
5. Frost reflects on community in a poem, rather than an essay or other form. How does the form affect the message? Contrast this selection with another work in this chapter, such as "My Man Bovanne" or "Christmas at Home." Does poetry add some dimension to your understanding? Is the point of the poem as well-developed as the point of the story and memoir?

Ideas for Writing

1. Write a dialogue between yourself and the speaker, or yourself and the neighbor, on the subject of good neighbors. Or write a dialogue between and speaker and the neighbor, over pie and coffee on the front porch, after the fence-mending.
2. Write an essay that analyzes the theme of the poem, with specific references to the text, and then discuss its implications for establishing a community in a particular political, educational, or social situation.

A Call to Arms

William F. Buckley, Jr.

William F. Buckley, Jr. (b. 1925), was born in New York City and took his B.A. at Yale University in 1950. The recipient of a number of honorary degrees, Buckley is generally considered one of the more eloquent and erudite spokespersons for conservative thought; he has hosted the television program *Firing Line* since 1966 and is editor of the magazine *National Review*. His numerous publications include *American Dialogues* (1960) and *American Conservative Thought in the Twentieth Century* (1970). In this selection from his most recent book *Gratitude* (1990), Buckley outlines a specific proposal for national public service.

Journal

What do you think about mandatory public service for young people, a requirement analogous to the military draft?

Let us proceed to describe a plan whose essential design I endorse. Some of my proposals are also endorsed by authors of other models for a national service program.

Richard Danzig and Peter Szanton in their book anatomize four models of ₂ national service programs. The first is a school-based program, in which states would require a certain number of unpaid hours from high school seniors before they became eligible for a high school diploma. The second model is draft-based—a completely civilian national service as an alternative to military service. Model three is voluntary, building on existing philanthropic programs and government programs without significantly increasing existing incentives. The fourth (and final) model identified is universal service, a system in which a year of civil or military service is exacted of every citizen, with sanctions in the form of criminal penalties and tax surcharges. In addition to these four models, some analysts—e.g., James Strock, the Assistant Administrator for Enforcement in the EPA and formerly on the board of directors of Youth Service America—identify what they call "the Buckley model," based on the passage devoted to the subject in my book *Four Reforms*, substantially reproduced in Chapter 9—i.e., a program in which colleges and universities take the initiative by declining to accept applicants who have not served.

I have already submitted to second thoughts the so-called Buckley model. ₃ And I have given reasons for opposing the universal (or conscription-based) national service; the military-draft-based model; and the model that, though voluntary, is unreinforced by rewards and sanctions. The school-based model described by Danzig and Szanton is promising, but only as an element of a fifth model which I proceed to recommend and designate as the Service Franchise model while, along with Gladstone, awaiting a better term for it.

4   The word "franchise," in recent generations, has been restricted to the vote or to the licensing of retail outlets. In fact, the *Oxford English Dictionary* devotes only minor attention to such restrictive meanings. The meaning that most clarifies the use to which I put it: "A privilege or exceptional right, granted by the sovereign power to any person or body of persons."

5   What I propose to call the Service Franchise is the aggregate of privileges and benefits to which a veteran of national service should be entitled. Although I envision a uniform federal service franchise, there is no reason to discourage individual states from augmenting these benefits, even as some of them augmented benefits that came to military veterans after the Second World War.

6   As I conceive it, the essentials of a service franchise model of national service would be the following:

7   1. The objective should be to enroll, by the turn of the century, more than 80 percent of Americans born in 1973 or later. The stress is on those years, but the National Service Franchise Administration (as we shall call it for the moment)—NSFA—should welcome participation by men and women of all ages. Whereas certification as a veteran of the program by the NSFA would be formal in the case of young people, no harm is done, quite the contrary, in an equivalent of honorary certification for those Americans desiring to participate in national service who were born before 1973.

8   In order to achieve such a goal it is, above almost any other consideration, important to lean on what one might call the moral sanctions. Here what is needed is a conscious mobilization of social, philanthropic, and civic enthusiasm for the idea of national service. This is not a point that needs elaboration, given that every reader of these words, on reflection, could probably name a half-dozen persons who engage in civic and philanthropic work on their own initiative but who have never backed, and in some cases are even unaware of the call for, a national service program.

9   A second force that needs to be mobilized in favor of the program is, obviously, government, at both federal and state levels. Different sanctions are appropriate depending on which government we speak of.

10   2. Yes, there needs to be a National Service Franchise Administration. Its primary function should be to gather information for use by the states and indeed by individuals seeking (for instance) a locality that sustains an NSFA program most congenial to their inclination ("Dear Sirs: Where do you go if you are interested in learning how to fight the hoof-and-mouth disease?"). But the NSFA, observing its mandate, should also recommend appropriate legislation to Congress, legislation having primarily to do with federal sanctions. No federal money would be used to finance national service; federal money would be made available only to absorb administrative costs run up by the National Service Franchise Administration—whose directors should be volunteers (*their* national service?), appointed by the President with due concern to broaden the constituency of the program.

11   A vital function of the Administration would be to establish how long a

participant would need to work in order to qualify for his certificate of service. The states decide what are the accrediting activities and which should be given precedence. But only a single agency can reasonably decide what the total contribution, measured in time served, ought to be.

The idea of one year's service appeals, one supposes, primarily because 12 one year has the psychological impact of a life integer, even as one spends four *years* in college, and college students after one *year* go from being freshmen to sophomores and so on to juniors to seniors. One year should be the time span the NSFA should be concerned to institutionalize.

But the Administration would have the authority to permit arrangements 13 other than consecutive, full-time, fifty-week service. What of the young man or woman eager to do national service but wishing to do it concurrently with college work—by, let us say, devoting two thousand hours over four years, or five hundred hours per year; at forty hours per week, the equivalent of three months per year? This accommodation could be done without trespassing on college calendar property: most colleges suspend work for three months during the summer. The alternative should be authorized, always provided that the NSFA was alert to evasions in the making—but here, except in extraordinary circumstances of the kind mentioned above, the state would be the accrediting agent. The NSFA would govern only in that that agency alone could agree to suspend the prohibition against federal student financial aid by the federal government. It would (should), as a matter of course upon receiving the recommendation of the state branch, accommodate students desiring custom-made arrangements. There are students who routinely work many more hours in a week than forty. There are the Stakhanovites who might, in eight weeks rather than twelve, discharge their four-hundred-hour obligation. The NSFA should always remind itself that its function is to assist in the evolution of a national ethos and that it is entirely in the spirit of American individualism to encourage individuated programs, provided they are not primarily evasive in design.

3. Beginning with the promulgation of an NSFA code, all federal financial 14 educational aid would cease for any student who did not have a certificate in hand giving evidence that he was a veteran of national service, or was scheduled to serve soon, even as it ceases today for any student failing to register for the draft.

I have urged above what I deem a refinement in the "rewards" system, as 15 the psychologists use the term. The Nunn bill speaks of ten thousand dollars forwarded to the college of choice of the National Service graduate, tax free. Under the Service Franchise model, on the other hand, National Service graduates should be permitted immunity from the first ten thousand dollars owed to Internal Revenue. Under the Nunn alternative, a National Service graduate needs to do one of two things in order to walk into his reward: go to college, or buy a house. There is no reason to make the reward restrictive. And since anyone who chooses to do anything other than become a Carthusian monk is almost certain to pay taxes, the prospect of relief from ten thousand dollars in taxes is both real and appropriate—real because the sum of money is substantial, appropriate because the government is acknowledging a service done. I foresee, as already mentioned, the objection that the very poor are for all intents and purposes never taxed, especially after the comprehensive relief granted in the 1986 tax reform to the lower brackets. But the number of Americans who go a full lifetime without incurring any federal tax is insignificantly small. Any citizen who failed to engage in productive endeavor through a lifetime probably should not experience "relief" that would anyhow be supererogatory, given that citizens at that level are regular beneficiaries of state welfare payments.

16   For the sake of administrative convenience, the governing body, the NSFA, might stagger the rules here, with the objective in mind of shuffling young volunteers into the program other than in great one-year generational batches. It might be prudent, for instance, to rule that those born in 1973 would need to do their service sometime before beginning junior year, and would be free to apply for conventional federal aid as freshmen and sophomores; while those born in 1974 would need to display their NSFA certificates before matriculating as freshmen.

17   The denial of post-secondary school loans has no force, needless to say, with full-time students who do not seek federal loans (they are about one half of those who go to college), whether it is because they don't need them or because they don't qualify for them. Those students who don't get federal loans but do get loans from their colleges are easily reached by applying sanctions on the colleges themselves—e.g., no college that fails to expedite NSFA performance by its students will qualify as a vehicle for federal grants. Here the administrative machinery of the civil rights acts is relevant. In 1978 students at Grove City College were disqualified by the courts from receiving federal grants on the grounds that the college refused to sign compliance forms for Title IX of the Higher Education Act of 1972 which forbids sex discrimination. What can be done to discourage sex discrimination can be done to discourage civic neglect, apathy, etc. Students who do not need aid of any kind are immune from this particular sanction, even as during the Civil War for a considerable period of time people who could come up with three hundred dollars were immune from the draft. But it is not just the poor who are to be punished. We have mentioned the loss of a driver's license. John Cadwalader Abercrombie III would have a hard time playing the gay blade at school if he needed either a bicycle or a chauffeur. Not much more needs to be said on the point.

18   The financial aid sanction in question, as noted, is of course useless against the 1.6 million young people who will not be going to college in 1991 or 1992. These are less easily reached by the federal government, given that they rely, at that age, so little on government. It would hardly intimidate an eighteen-year-old to be told that his bank accounts will no longer be protected by the Federal Deposit Insurance Corporation. Few eighteen-year-olds, or for that matter twenty-one-year-olds, own and operate their own farms, relying for their economic survival on the government for farm subsidies. And for so long as the minimum wage is lower than the wage one has to pay in order to hire

an hour of a productive eighteen-year-old's working time, tampering with the minimum wage intending to discourage non-volunteers is not an effective device. Moreover, it would be bizarre to use it in situations in which a primary objective is to persuade young people to work for one year at, in most cases, less than the minimum wage. Youth not bound for college would need sanctions exercised by individual states. These could include the denial of a driver's license—in most cases, the ultimate weapon.

4. Although the rights of the individual states to shape their own pro- 19
grams, specifying compensation and the like, should be preserved, the national aspect of the plan would fail if deviations were to become eccentric, particularly so if they were to do that to the point of luring young men and women either to a state that had synthetic national service programs, or away from a state that had only especially disagreeable programs. Having said this, obviously it is desirable that excesses of states be tamed, as to some extent they now are in taxation policies by citizens who register their dissent with their feet, moving their residence elsewhere. A state that moved too heavily in the direction of Sparta would begin to lose its mobile population to Athens.

But if we have in mind a national service program, it needs to be that, as 20
distinguished from bizarre programs that appeal to states responding to bizarre lobbies, publicly desirable programs receive priority—e.g., care for the aged, over teaching children how to swim.

The reason for this is self-evident: The formal satisfaction felt by volun- 21
teers when their service is done should be keen, even as the formal stigma that would attach to those who shirk their duty should be felt keenly. But these experiences are unlikely if there is too great a blur around the kind of services performed. A plausible National Service Franchise Program would bind all the states to cooperation, on a showing of massive support by voters in those states for no-nonsense participation in the program. And the program having been approved by the individual states, its realization would be made possible by the appropriation of state money. And the infrastructure of state programs would be supported by the use of those sanctions of the federal government already discussed.

5. Beyond the question of federal loans proffered or withheld, the selec- 22
tion of appropriate auxiliary sanctions ought to be primarily the business of the individual state, even as, on the question of who should establish the criteria by which national service obligations are discharged, it is the states that should make the decision, within the boundaries established by the federal program. Granted that there will be some flimsy programs, even as in any college there is the "gut," or easy, course. The state is bound to crop up that will want to give credit for, oh, one hundred hours of television watching in order to explore ethnic bias; that sort of thing. The states should exercise workaday authority to license activities as qualifying for NSFA credit, and to assign priorities respecting what needs most to be done. In Florida, perhaps care for the old; in Wyoming, conservation; in Illinois, school tutoring; in the District of Columbia, crime prevention. But probably the NSFA should be given the right, when let us say ten of its twelve members are agreed on the matter, to dis-

qualify for credit any state program that appears to be outrageously circumventive of the whole idea.

23   And, of course, the federal government can put pressure on individual states, even as it applies pressure on the states in other matters—speed limits, drinking ages for minors, highway billboards. Then the national service idea can absorb an element of latitudinarianism, just as a first-rate college can get away with a few gut courses.

24   The National Service Franchise Administration might elect, as the program evolves, to recommend to Congress that it impose sanctions designed to prod the consciences of morally sluggish state legislatures. True, a few years' experience with national service might establish that there is no need for the federal government to goad the states, there being so much good to be done that serves everyone's purposes. But a huge array of incentives and sanctions is there to be used, should it be deemed useful and desirable, against refractory states. Obviously Congress is not going to impose sanctions unless the majority of Americans, expressing themselves through the House of Representatives, and the majority of the states, through the Senate, are determined to universalize the service. In the absence of a national political will, a national service program is fated to founder.

25   In reaching for intensified sanctions, we should rely on individual states to come up with their own.

26   Suppose, say, that the legislature of the State of California came to the conclusion that the time had come to transform the idea of national service from a desirable abstraction into a concrete requirement of effective citizenship. What might the state government routinely do in California to cultivate effective, contributory, creative citizenship?

27   Among other things, California requires attendance at high school, a diploma from which is a valuable credential for many who seek jobs. One sanction might be the denial of a high school diploma except to students who produce the qualifying certificate from the NSFA. This sanction should be examined and applied with care, inasmuch as it would hardly advance the objectives of national service to devise criteria for qualification which permitted boys and girls of exaggeratedly young age to discharge their obligations. Or to discourage anyone from finishing high school. Age sixteen should be the first year at which credits under the NSFA program can begin to be earned.

28   6. What about the 1.3 million eighteen-year-olds who go on to college?

29   While it is desirable that national student service be performed before matriculation, to do national service while still at college is practical. There is already a substantial tradition of taking a junior year elsewhere, often abroad. Year Three could become the time in which the college student does his national service. We are talking now about twenty-year-olds, and their increased maturity and experience would not only make it easier to train them for more specialized work than that expected of eighteen-year-olds, there would be time, during the first two college years, to give special thought to

the nature of national service work done, with the view to wedding it to the profession the student has in mind to pursue—doctor, lawyer, businessman, accountant, government worker, teacher. It could thus be compatible with internships, field work, etc.

There will be the student who, for reasons ranging from plausible to com- 30 pelling, wishes to put off national service but does not want to risk forfeiting the benefits to be received on the strength of a pledge to national service. We are speaking about the student who says: For this reason and that, I am most anxious to continue in college without interruption for the next four years, but I pledge that the year after I graduate will be devoted to national service.

The state's National Service Board having accepted the student's bona 31 fides, that student would continue to receive those benefits otherwise reserved for national service alumni. The question arises, What is to be done in the event of a subsequent default? And how do we reasonably define a default?

At age twenty-two, having graduated from college, student L.A.Z. Evader 32 does not show up for duty, as he had promised to do. (We distinguish between him and the young man or woman who negotiates an extension with the National Service Board.) On the evader, the law would visit all the relevant sanctions. On the procrastinator, attenuated penalties. If by age twenty-five the volunteer has defaulted for three consecutive years, the law will judge him to be a delinquent, and while the sanctions will be ongoing—the same sanctions that would apply to those who had never volunteered for national service— the government will seek a return on those benefits already extended. Here one might study and learn from the history of the federal government's efforts to get from delinquents payments on money owed. We know that 18 percent, as of 1987, had defaulted on student loans. At first the government was indulgent toward the deadbeats, but as the dollar amount of such defaults rose (by 276 percent between 1983 and 1987), attitudes hardened, and it was decided, pursuant to the goals already stipulated in the Debt Collection Act of 1982, to try everything to satisfy delinquent debts: use private collection agencies, report delinquent debtors to commercial credit bureaus, offset federal employees' salaries, and withhold IRS tax refunds.

These and other such details do not engross us and should not distract us. 33 But a moment's thought should be given to whether, and if so how, in later years a delinquent might cure the record. Presumably if, at age thirty-eight, he turned himself over to the national service board and went out to serve for one year, he would extirpate the default. It should be made possible for him to regain his first-class citizenship by doing something less than full-time work, because any demand that exigent on a grown person occupied professionally and probably also as a parent is an inducement to live with the delinquency rather than to effect exculpation. A strictly mathematical formula would require the adult citizen to serve as many hours as the eighteen-year-old did who worked full-time for one year. At forty hours per week, the full-time volunteer did community service for two thousand hours. To give that many hours of service, but over a period of five or ten years, becomes manageable. Over ten years, that comes to two hundred hours per year of community service, or four hours per week, a half day.

34   It might prove desirable—experience will tell—to increase the number of hours owed to national service in proportion as one delays discharging that duty, so that, let us say, at age forty the citizen might owe not two thousand hours, but three thousand hours. Such variations are best experimented with. They too depend substantially for their success on the spirit generated by the entire enterprise. If successful, the citizen would a.) wish to serve, and b.) wish to reintegrate himself with his fellow citizens, born in 1973 or thereafter, measuring his delinquency not merely in terms of lost benefits, but lost self-esteem.

35   7. Is there any formal way in which to recognize what one might think of as further, postgraduate work in national service? Not really. If the program succeeds, then at age twenty-one the veteran, his certificate in his pocket, is not likely to forget that there are old, lonely people out there, families who need day care, illiterates who need coaching, streets that need cleaning, forest fires that need fighting. The last thing one would wish a national service program to promulgate is a regimented society, but it is not regimentation to attempt consciously to universalize a continuing concern for one's fellow men, a felt gratitude for those Americans, dead now, who passed along what we enjoy, in usufruct.

36   The idea of rendering service, we know already, isn't dependent on a national service program. If it were, there would be no civic work going on, as there is at present, when there is no formal service system. The program here proposed is the kernel of a national possibility, nurtured by an ongoing civic disposition, even as college is supposed to be the kernel of an ongoing attitude toward learning. If the idea takes hold, as one hopes that it will, the appetite to contribute to the health and morale of the republic would endure. Far from thinking themselves entirely discharged from showing interest in other people, and in other concerns, they would find their appetite stimulated, as noted, even as the aesthetic appetite is stimulated by early exposure to music and the arts. The satisfaction that comes from the discharge of an obligation gives life to the problem that was faced. If it was a military problem, the veteran understands the purpose of, and even the need for, a military. If one once kept company with a dying old woman, one knows that today another woman, who needs company, is dying. As veterans of national service, these graduates will have earned chevrons and their sense of involvement with the community will run deeper. It is after all only sensible to expect that a sense of solidarity with one's fellow citizens, a sharpened esprit de corps, will survive the initial term of service. Successive experiences would remind our Robert Ely, now a veteran of national service, of his status as a Citizen, First Class, even as a military veteran is from time to time reminded of his status long after the experience of service has been lost to recollection. Not so much in the service itself, then, as in the recall of service, engraved and re-engraved gently but insistently by a dozen burins, decade after decade, lodged in the moral memory.

Such mild but suggestive privileges—society's recognition of his status 37
and of the service with which he has earned a place in his home—are welcome. A greater share of its patrimony would continually reinforce the awareness in the veteran's mind of his connection to the community, of his indebtedness to it, and, little by little, of its indebtedness to him.

Questions for Discussion

1. Buckley's essay is both a plan and an argument. What is the thesis of his argument?
   Where does he anticipate opposing views? Does he respond to them convincingly?
   Cite examples from the text.
2. Buckley writes that NSFA should "assist in the development of a national ethos. . . ."
   If "ethos" refers to the beliefs, values, and ethics of a society, what do you think is
   the "national ethos" that Buckley believes should develop in terms of national service?
3. Buckley is noted for having an elegant style and projecting the persona of a well-
   educated individual. Based on this selection, do you agree? Why or why not? Refer
   to specific passages in the text to support your point of view.
4. Buckley's plan calls for using rewards in instituting the service requirement. Do you
   think that requiring service, and then paying something for it in credits or public
   esteem, or other rewards, undermines the very ethos Buckley seeks to instill? Explain
   your point of view.
5. From what you have read or heard about it (see also Bess Kennedy's essay, this chapter) how does President Clinton's plan for national service reflect Buckley's thinking and also present national service in a different light?
6. Use your journal entry as the basis for a group discussion of national service.

Ideas for Writing

1. Write a response to Buckley, agreeing with him or arguing against his plan or
   some specific aspects of his plan for mandatory public service. Alternatively, write
   an imaginative dialogue between one of the other authors in the chapter and
   Buckley.
2. Investigate the Points of Light Foundation or the Summer of Service. You could start
   with the library's newspaper and magazine indexes to see what has been written
   about the organization or project recently. Has it made any progress along the lines
   that Buckley discusses? Has the Clinton administration refined specific plans for
   national service? Write up your findings in a documented report.

Address at Gettysburg

Abraham Lincoln

Abraham Lincoln (1809–1865) was born in Hodgesville, Kentucky. After working
as a clerk, postmaster, and county surveyor, Lincoln studied law and was elected
to the legislature in 1834. A prominent member of the newly organized Republican Party, Lincoln became president on the eve of the Civil War. In 1862, after the

Union victory at Antietam, Lincoln issued the Emancipation Proclamation—the crowning achievement of an illustrious presidency. Lincoln died by an assassin's bullet in 1865. Lincoln's "Address at the Dedication of the Gettysburg National Cemetery," even more than his "Second Inaugural Address" and his "House Divided" speech, remains one of the most famous American speeches.

Journal

Before you read the "Address at Gettysburg," write down what you know about its significance in history and its significant phrases.

Four score and seven years ago our fathers brought forth on this continent, a new nation, conceived in liberty, and dedicated to the proposition that all men are created equal.

2   Now we are engaged in a great civil war, testing whether that nation or any nation so conceived and so dedicated, can long endure. We are met on a great battle-field of that war. We have come to dedicate a portion of that field, as a final resting place for those who here gave their lives that that nation might live. It is altogether fitting and proper that we should do this.

3   But, in a larger sense, we can not dedicate—we can not consecrate—we can not hallow—this ground. The brave men, living and dead, who struggled here, have consecrated it, far above our poor power to add or detract. The world will little note, nor long remember what we say here, but it can never forget what they did here. It is for us the living, rather, to be dedicated here to the unfinished work which they who fought here have thus far so nobly advanced. It is rather for us to be here dedicated to the great task remaining before us—that from these honored dead we take increased devotion to that cause for which they gave the last full measure of devotion—that we here highly resolve that these dead shall not have died in vain—that this nation, under God, shall have a new birth of freedom—and that government of the people, by the people, for the people, shall not perish from the earth.

Questions for Discussion

1. Though the occasion for his speech was the dedication of a cemetery for those who died in the Battle of Gettysburg, Lincoln used it to unite the nation as well as to honor the dead. Discuss the ways in which Lincoln avoided divisiveness and sought to unite both sides of the conflict.
2. Lincoln's speech at Gettysburg, though extremely brief, has become one of the monuments of American prose. Have someone in the class read the speech aloud. Wait a few moments; write down your emotional and intellectual responses to the speech. Compare notes with classmates. In what ways are your responses similar? What parts of the speech evoke the strongest response? Analyze Lincoln's strategies for appealing to his audiences—both his contemporaries and future generations.
3. Analyze and discuss the themes and motifs of birth and death in the speech. What do they contribute to the speech's overall meaning? How do they support the purpose of his speech?

4. Gary Wills, author of *Lincoln at Gettysburg,* writes, "Lincoln derives a new, transcendental significance from the bloody episode. Both North and South strove to win the battle for *interpreting* Gettysburg as soon as the physical battle ended. Lincoln is after even larger game—he means to "win" the whole Civil War in ideological terms as well as military ones." How do you interpret the Battle of Gettysburg in terms of the "Gettysburg Address"? Is your interpretation consistent with what you may have thought before this reading of the address? Does your interpretation depend on what region of the country or what community you come from? Discuss.
5. Though speaking in broad, national terms, Lincoln cites individual sacrifice—"the last full measure of devotion"—as that which can make possible "a new birth of freedom" for the nation and for all Americans. How does he unite "the living" in a community with those who died at Gettysburg "that the nation might live"?

Ideas for Writing:

1. Individually or in groups, view the film *Gettysburg* or the Public Broadcasting System special series by Ken Burns, *The Civil War.* Does viewing the film or series alter your reading of Lincoln's speech? Does it change your perception of the American Civil War? Discuss.
2. Write an essay analyzing the speech in terms of theme or style. Relate your analysis to the implications that the speech holds for the relationship between the individual and the community.
3. Look up accounts and analyses of Lincoln's speech at Gettysburg published in the newspapers and magazines of his day. Were Lincoln's contemporaries as impressed as twentieth-century audiences? If so, what did they find most appealing? If not, to what do you attribute the modest reception for the speech?

Community Service Writing Student Project: SPOON (Stanford Project on Nutrition) Informational Flyer

The following is an informational page about surplus food in the residence hall dining rooms at Stanford University. The students who developed this message for fellow students had a number of rhetorical considerations to keep in mind in order to write a persuasive message that would interest, inform, and avoid alienating their readers.

Journal

Think about whether or not such a flyer in a campus building, on a bulletin board, in your mailbox, would encourage you to read and reflect on the message. Write down your conclusions.

SOME PEOPLE NEVER COMPLAIN ABOUT FOOD
SERVICE FOOD . . .

Every day unused food from campus eateries, food which otherwise would
have been wasted, is collected by a student organization known as SPOON for
distribution to area shelters for the hungry. Stanford is the largest single food
consumer on the Peninsula, and although some of the uneaten food is recy-
cled and served as leftovers, most of it is thrown away. Last year, Stanford
houses, eating clubs, fraternities, dorms, Tressider, and eateries together
donated over 23,000 pounds of food to Urban Ministry of Palo Alto and St.
Anthony's kitchen in Menlo Park.

Most Food Service employees enthusiastically support SPOON. Ray Hernandez, the head chef at Tressider, says "I'm glad I could put some of the leftovers to good use." Sue Nunan, the manager at Wilbur, said that she thought
that it was a very valuable service. Libby Long, the manager at Kimball, said
"I understand the SPOON system and their worthy cause . . . I believe that the
cause is a good one." Without the support of Food Service employees, a system like SPOON's would not be possible.

Food Service cooks determine which of the food ought to be thrown away and
which can be donated to the shelters. Because students aren't served food
which is re-heated more than once or which has exceeded the code date, there
is a lot of edible food which would otherwise go to waste. SPOON is very careful only to collect food which otherwise would be thrown away to avoid feeding the hungry by increasing University costs.

One thing we can all do is make sure our eyes aren't bigger than our stomachs. Carole Miller, the assistant manager of food service at Lagunita, says that
one of the biggest problems Food Service faces is students who take much
more food then they actually eat. By taking food they don't want and won't
eat, students often increase the cost of the meal in the long-term, as well as
keeping the food from the hungry in the short term.

Questions for Discussion

In small groups or as a class, analyze the audience and purpose of this assignment and
the ways in which the writers did or did not meet the specific needs for the audience and purpose. Do the authors appeal to the audience's logic? Emotions? Values?

Ideas for Writing

1. Whether or not your campus has a formal food-service collection program for local
shelters, you could write a letter, a flyer, or some other form of message to fellow
students to discourage waste of food. Remember rhetorical considerations: get a
clear sense of audience; state the message concisely, with important points at the

beginning and end. Use lively language that is courteous and does not cast blame. Consider the kinds of appeals to values, beliefs, empathy, and logic you will need to make.

2. Write an essay that explores the ways in which Americans waste food and the local or national organizations that help to distribute surplus food.

3. Develop a research paper on food distribution in Third World countries.

CHAPTER WRITING PROJECTS

1. Consider the common themes and the contrasting views about community presented by the readings in this chapter. Select several, or perhaps just two, and discuss them in an essay. Which readings speak to you and your beliefs most directly?

2. Select a film or literary work with a prominent hero or heroine. In view of your readings about community in this chapter, write about the ways in which the film's hero or heroine reflects aspects of devotion to community, or to individual achievement, or some combination of both. Alternatively, in peer groups, select a film with a theme of community, such as *Grand Canyon, Avalon, The Long Walk Home, Volunteers, City of Hope*, or others. Have a discussion session after the film, write up film reviews, and then share them with your group.

3. Trace the history of voluntary associations, or a specific voluntary association or group, in America. You could start by reviewing Tocqueville's *Democracy in America* to develop a clearer understanding of the roots of voluntarism, and then delve into library materials. A number of "shoestring" nonprofit groups might be able to use a comprehensive history of their organization and could provide you with primary materials and interview subjects to get started.

4. Working in peer groups, collect from friends, neighbors, or families different examples of appeals (direct mail, advertising, and the like) from charitable groups. Summarize your findings in a collaboratively written report for the class. Do different types of charities use different types of appeals? For example, do some groups appeal to a donor's sense that he or she is vulnerable to a certain disease? Do funding appeals for education use special tactics to win support from older citizens who presumably have already educated their children?

5. Research communal living arrangements or clan governments among Native American peoples, such as American Indians, Inuits, or Hawaiians; then write a report sharing your findings. Alternatively, research some other types of collectives—religious groups, for example, or 1960s-era communes.

6. Interview people in your community, college, club, or neighborhood to

learn more about the roots of that particular community, with the intention of sharing your write-up with that community.

7. Research specific religion-based American communities, such as the Shakers or the Mormons; alternatively, study the role of the church in various American ethnic communities, such as among African Americans or Polish Catholics. Or investigate the negative effects of the search for community: you could study a religious community gone wrong—the People's Temple or Waco, Texas, cult tragedies, for example.

8. If you belong to a religious faith, write about the role of public service or charity in your faith or congregation. You could discuss theological or Biblical issues or those from other religious texts (*Koran, Book of Mormon,* and the like), or you could focus on a practical social program or example.

9. Why do people join gangs? Why do gangs typically seem to be composed of young people? Write a paper using library research and interviews with community leaders or educators who are informed about the issue.

10. Do library and field research on the subject of community gardens; some possible approaches include garden therapy for the ill or elderly, collaborative gardening in schools, or urban gardening.

11. Attend a city council meeting or another government gathering to observe the process of community groups trying to influence the political process. Write up your observations and analyze your findings.

12. Research voluntary associations in earlier eras in America, such as during Colonial times, during industrialization, in wartime, or during the Great Depression. Consider minority as well as dominant American cultures. What role did volunteer groups serve during the era chosen? You may need to limit your topic to one organization, region, or time frame.

13. How do the writers in this chapter help you to define and understand altruism? Discuss the connections between Morris's assertions in "Altruistic Behavior" and another chapter selection, such as John F. Kennedy's speech, Bess Kennedy's essay, or Jacqueline Rouse's biography of Lugenia Burns Hope.

CHAPTER 3

Education and Community

Anyone who has read a great deal can imagine the new world that opened. Let me tell you something: from then until I left that prison, in every free moment I had, if I was not reading in the library, I was reading on my bunk. . . . In fact, up to then, I never had been so truly free in my life.
—Malcolm X, "On Learning to Read"

Knowing and learning are "communal" acts. They require many eyes and ears, many observations and experiences. They require a continual cycle of discussion, disagreement and consensus over what has been seen and what it all means. This is the essence of the "community of scholars," and it should be the essence of the classroom as well.
—Parker Palmer, "Community, Conflict, and Ways of Knowing"

Educational communities are no longer "ivory towers." While many scholars and scientists develop their theories and inventions in the libraries or laboratories of universities, what they discover is applied to real issues within our communities. Like our scholars and scientists, educational leaders are working to develop college programs that will make a positive and meaningful impact on the lives of today's youth. Our nation's educational values and goals need to acknowledge and integrate the vital issues that students at two- and four-year colleges, at private and public institutions, confront in their families, in their communities, and in popular culture.

We are at an educational crossroads. The realities of poverty, cultural diversity, and gender inequalities can no longer be ignored. An education that incorporates a broader curriculum with collaborative and community-based methods of learning is beginning to be implemented in schools throughout our nation. These new approaches to teaching and learning take into account the rich and varied experiences of immigrants, of minorities, of the disabled, of women—of those whose experiences were not addressed directly in college classes until the late 1970s and 1980s.

The changing nature of education is directly related to issues of community. As citizens, in what ways should we take responsibility for improving the quality of life in our communities? Disparities in income and opportunity affect the well being of the rich, the middle class, the working class, and the poor. In this context, seeing the classroom as a community is fundamental for two reasons. First, the classroom provides a community setting where collaborative learning and democratic education can be practiced and modeled. Second, when the desire to learn is self-motivated, then reading and writing can help individuals to understand themselves better and to learn from other students. In colleges all over the country we are seeing the emergence of classrooms where students take an active role in shaping the content and process of their classes. In these classrooms students work with their instructors and with one another. Their more active participation helps them to get engaged in learning and to find more meaning in their education.

Students are becoming more active members of their classroom communities in other ways. More and more high school and college students are being asked to participate in service learning education by working at nonprofit organizations in their communities to help people whose lives are at risk. From these types of service learning experiences, students can begin to understand more about the lives of people from different cultures, and different social and economic classes. Through educational experiences in their communities, students can develop critical thinking skills as they test their assumptions about social class and social problems in real-life situations. Acknowledging the power of life experiences in the context of academic learning, can begin to transform the quality of students' education.

We have chosen the selections in this chapter to encourage you to think about how you learn, to think critically about how you have been taught that you should learn, and to reflect upon what an education can provide for you as a member of a classroom, a college, a neighborhood community. In the first selection, "Poem for the Creative Writing Class, Spring 1982," Merle Woo defines the power of sharing her writing: "What is language after all/but the touching and uplifting/one to others." In "Mother Tongue," the next selection, Amy Tan also discusses how she developed the courage to speak her own voice and to listen to her heart by rebelling against the "bars" of her high school education, the English achievement tests that predicted her inability to succeed as a writer.

In Grace Paley's short story, "The Loudest Voice," the main character, a young Jewish girl, listens like Tan to the voice within her. In spite of her mother's religious objections, she distinguishes herself in a Christmas pageant because she can project her voice; both father and daughter see education as a way of speaking up and of sharing cultures. In the essay "Graduation," Maya

Angelou also points to the power of finding one's voice and speaking one's mind for oneself and for one's community, especially in the face of racial discrimination and oppression.

The writers of the next two selections are critical of the quality of public education in inner-city schools of large urban areas. In "I Just Wanna Be Average," Mike Rose writes of his own liberation from the bars of education that separated students into college and vocational tracks, and he questions the validity of educational tests in predicting a student's ability to progress in high school and to succeed in applying his or her education after graduation. In "Corla Hawkins," an excerpt from Jonathan Kozol's best-selling expose of urban public schools, *Savage Inequalities,* the intelligence, love, and success of one teacher at an elementary school in inner-city Chicago is presented as a light in "the sinkhole" of public education. Kozol and Rose reveal the serious crisis in public education in America today.

This chapter's final selections present current ideas for educational curricula and programs that will perpetuate the democratic principles of our nation. In the selection "Education-Based Community Service at Rutgers University," taken from his recent book, *An Aristocracy of Everyone,* Benjamin Barber outlines the nine principles that form the foundation of the community service–based model program at Rutgers University. He argues that an education needs to foster "active citizens who see in service not the altruism of charity but the responsibility of citizenship on which liberty ultimately depends." In contrast, in the next selection "Cultural Literacy," E. D. Hirsch, Jr. is skeptical of the academic value of service learning. He proposes a different perspective on the best direction for curriculum development that emphasizes the need for a standard of cultural literacy: "Literate culture is the most democratic culture of our land: it is not usually one's first culture, but it should be every one's second, existing as it does beyond the narrow spheres of family neighborhood, and region." The student essay by Jeremy Taylor, "Service Learning: Education with a Purpose," discusses the educational advantages of teaching civic responsibility through a service learning curriculum.

The chapter closes with articles written for a "Community Service Writing Project: *Reach Out Newsletter,*" a collaborative writing project that was produced by students in a first-year composition class. This selection provides a model of social action writing. Five students worked with a tutoring and support service for first-generation college-bound students from low-income families. The newsletter that they wrote and produced was distributed to students who were just beginning the program and to their families as well as to the five high school districts and educational support organizations in Santa Clara county, in California.

Whether you write to help yourself to reflect on the educational reforms that are needed in your community, or you write for local papers or community agencies to affect social change, thinking about the relationships between educational and community values will be a challenging and rewarding endeavor.

Poem for the Creative Writing Class, Spring 1982

Merle Woo

Merle Woo (b. 1941) is the daughter of Chinese-Korean immigrants. Her essays, stories, and poems have been included in a number of anthologies, such as *This Bridge Called My Back: Writings by Radical Women of Color* (1981), and in her own poetry collection, *Yellow Woman Speaks* (1986). Like many of the writers selected for this text, Woo believes in the importance of combining her work as teacher, activist, and poet: ". . . we poets who are outspoken as Asian Americans, women, lesbians/gays, workers, cannot separate ourselves from the reality in which we live. We are freedom fighters with words as our weapons—on the page or on the picket sign." Reading and reflecting on Woo's poem, we hope, will encourage you to value the community of writers in your classroom and the sense of freedom and self-discovery that writing can bring.

Journal

Write about a classroom that felt like a cage or a prison or about a classroom where you felt you had space to learn and to grow.

The silence in the classroom
of people I've grown to respect—
seems like so much potential here:
men and women
5   brown black yellow jewish white
gay and straight.

Classrooms are ugly,
cages with beautiful birds in them.
scraped, peeling walls
10   empty bookcases
an empty blackboard—
no ideas here.

And one window.
One writer comes in
15   from sitting on the sill,
three stories up.
We all want to fly
and feel the sun on the backs of our wings—

Inhale the breath
20   pulling in the energy of
seventeen people around me

and exhale
putting out my ideas, ideas, ideas.
We all want to fly out that window.
A breeze comes in once in a while,   25
we want to go out with it
to where the birds are.

To take flight
using the words
that give us wings.   30

What is language after all
but the touching and uplifting
one to the others:
scenes
poems   35
dreams
our own natural imagery:
coins
a train to El Salvador
sleeping, pregnant mothers   40
menacing garages/a fist pounding/voices yelling
a yogi
cops being the bowery boys
roller coasters
blood   45
a girl on a swing
roses
water, streams, rivers, oceans
rise. rise.

Who can keep us caged?   50

Questions for Discussion

1. What point does the speaker make in the first stanza? How does the poet link this idea to the image in the second stanza of a classroom as a cage? Does imagining that the stanzas in a poem are similar to the paragraphs in an essay help you to understand this poem better?
2. What two meanings can be read into the image "three stories up"?
3. The speaker suggests that the classroom of writers brings energy to each of their flights with words. Does sharing your writing with your classmates give you energy and motivation to write?
4. The speaker describes her writing process, "Using the words/that give us wings." Have you ever felt that words gave you wings? When?
5. In the poem the speaker claims that language takes the students in the creative writing class into their own natural imagery. Discuss why you agree or disagree with her.

6. How would you answer the speaker's final question: "Who can keep us caged?" What relationship do you see between the community of writers and the sense of individual self discovery that writing can bring? Is a community of writers presented as essential to the creative process in this poem?

Ideas for Writing

1. Write an essay about a class you took whose members began to function as a family or community. What helped to establish positive communication within the class? What did you learn from this group experience?

2. Write a poem or short story beginning with the image of a classroom as a cage or develop your own image of the classroom. Integrate the idea of the classroom as community into your poem or story.

Mother Tongue

Amy Tan

Amy Tan (b. 1952) was born in China and moved with her parents to Oakland, California, when she was two years old. Although her mother wanted her to be a doctor, Tan earned a B.A. and M.A. at San Jose State University in Linguistics. Tan began her career as a technical writer and has said that she turned to fiction as a form of therapy. Her first novel, *The Joy Luck Club* (1989), was an immediate success. *The Kitchen God's Wife* (1991) and her children's book *Moon Lady* (1992) have also been enthusiastically read by critics and the public. Tan's novels explore the conflicts that Chinese-American women experience as they come to understand the importance of their Chinese heritage. In the essay that follows, "Mother Tongue," Tan explains why she believes that her success as a writer was directly related to her determination to capture the legacy of her cultural heritage, especially the experiences and language rhythms of her family.

Journal

Imagine that you are a teacher of a nonnative student whose parents do not speak English in their home. What advice would you give your students to help them improve their writing and speaking skills?

I am not a scholar of English or literature. I cannot give you much more than personal opinions on the English language and its variations in this country or others.

2   I am a writer. And by that definition, I am someone who has always loved language. I am fascinated by language in daily life. I spend a great deal of my time thinking about the power of language—the way it can evoke an emotion, a visual image, a complex idea, or a simple truth. Language is the tool of my trade. And I use them all—all the Englishes I grew up with.

Recently, I was made keenly aware of the different Englishes I do use. I 3 was giving a talk to a large group of people, the same talk I had already given to half a dozen other groups. The nature of the talk was about my writing, my life, and my book, *The Joy Luck Club*. The talk was going along well enough, until I remembered one major difference that made the whole talk sound wrong. My mother was in the room. And it was perhaps the first time she had heard me give a lengthy speech, using the kind of English I have never used with her. I was saying things like, "The intersection of memory upon imagination" and "There is an aspect of my fiction that relates to thus-and-thus"— a speech filled with carefully wrought grammatical phrases, burdened, it suddenly seemed to me, with nominalized forms, past perfect tenses, conditional phrases, all the forms of standard English that I had learned in school and through books, the forms of English I did not use at home with my mother.

Just last week, I was walking down the street with my mother, and I again 4 found myself conscious of the English I was using, the English I do use with her. We were talking about the price of new and used furniture and I heard myself saying this: "Not waste money that way." My husband was with us as well, and he didn't notice any switch in my English. And then I realized why. It's because over the twenty years we've been together I've often used that same kind of English with him, and sometimes he even uses it with me. It has become our language of intimacy, a different sort of English that relates to family talk, the language I grew up with.

So you'll have some idea of what this family talk I heard sounds like, I'll 5 quote what my mother said during a recent conversation which I videotaped and then transcribed. During this conversation, my mother was talking about a political gangster in Shanghai who had the same last name as her family's, Du, and how the gangster in his early years wanted to be adopted by her family, which was rich by comparison. Later, the gangster became more powerful, far richer than my mother's family, and one day showed up at my mother's wedding to pay his respects. Here's what she said in part:

"Du Yusong having business like fruit stand. Like off the street kind. He 6 is Du like Du Zong—but not Tsung-ming Island people. The local people call putong, the river east side, he belong to that side local people. That man want to ask Du Zong father take him in like become own family. Du Zong father wasn't look down on him, but didn't take seriously, until that man big like become a mafia. Now important person, very hard to inviting him. Chinese way, came only to show respect, don't stay for dinner. Respect for making big celebration, he shows up. Mean gives lots of respect. Chinese custom. Chinese social life that way. If too important won't have to stay too long. He come to my wedding. I didn't see, I heard it. I gone to boy's side, they have YMCA dinner. Chinese age I was nineteen."

You should know that my mother's expressive command of English belies 7 how much she actually understands. She reads the *Forbes* report, listens to *Wall Street Week*, converses daily with her stockbroker, reads all of Shirley MacLaine's books with ease—all kinds of things I can't begin to understand. Yet some of my friends tell me they understand 50 percent of what my mother says. Some say they understand 80 to 90 percent. Some say they understand none of it, as if she were speaking pure Chinese. But to me, my mother's English is perfectly clear, perfectly natural. It's my mother tongue. Her language, as I hear it, is vivid, direct, full of observation and imagery. That was the language that helped shape the way I saw things, expressed things, made sense of the world.

8 Lately, I've been giving more thought to the kind of English my mother speaks. Like others, I have described it to people as "broken" or "fractured" English. But I wince when I say that. It has always bothered me that I can think of no way to describe it other than "broken," as if it were damaged and needed to be fixed, as if it lacked a certain wholeness and soundness. I've heard other terms used, "limited English," for example. But they seem just as bad, as if everything is limited, including people's perceptions of the limited English speaker.

9 I know this for a fact, because when I was growing up, my mother's "limited" English limited *my* perception of her. I was ashamed of her English. I believed that her English reflected the quality of what she had to say. That is, because she expressed them imperfectly her thoughts were imperfect. And I had plenty of empirical evidence to support me: the fact that people in department stores, at banks, and at restaurants did not take her seriously, did not give her good service, pretended not to understand her, or even acted as if they did not hear her.

10 My mother has long realized the limitations of her English as well. When I was fifteen, she used to have me call people on the phone to pretend I was she. In this guise, I was forced to ask for information or even to complain and yell at people who had been rude to her. One time it was a call to her stockbroker in New York. She had cashed out her small portfolio and it just so happened we were going to go to New York the next week, our very first trip outside California. I had to get on the phone and say in an adolescent voice that was not very convincing, "This is Mrs. Tan."

11 And my mother was standing in the back whispering loudly, "Why he don't send me check, already two weeks late. So mad he lie to me, losing me money."

12 And then I said in perfect English, "Yes, I'm getting rather concerned. You had agreed to send the check two weeks ago, but it hasn't arrived."

13 Then she began to talk more loudly. "What he want, I come to New York tell him front of his boss, you cheating me?" And I was trying to calm her down, make her be quiet, while telling the stockbroker, "I can't tolerate any more excuses. If I don't receive the check immediately, I am going to have to speak to your manager when I'm in New York next week." And sure enough, the following week there we were in front of this astonished stockbroker, and I was sitting there red-faced and quiet, and my mother, the real Mrs. Tan, was shouting at his boss in her impeccable broken English.

14 We used a similar routine just five days ago, for a situation that was far less humorous. My mother had gone to the hospital for an appointment, to

find out about a benign brain tumor a CAT scan had revealed a month ago. She said she had spoken very good English, her best English, no mistakes. Still, she said, the hospital did not apologize when they said they had lost the CAT scan and she had come for nothing. She said they did not seem to have any sympathy when she told them she was anxious to know the exact diagnosis, since her husband and son had both died of brain tumors. She said they would not give her any more information until the next time and she would have to make another appointment for that. So she said she would not leave until the doctor called her daughter. She wouldn't budge. And when the doctor finally called her daughter, me, who spoke in perfect English—lo and behold—we had assurances the CAT scan would be found, promises that a conference call on Monday would be held, and apologies for any suffering my mother had gone through for a most regrettable mistake.

I think my mother's English almost had an effect on limiting my possibil- 15 ities in life as well. Sociologists and linguists probably will tell you that a person's developing language skills are more influenced by peers. But I do think that the language spoken in the family, especially in immigrant families which are more insular, plays a large role in shaping the language of the child. And I believe that it affected my results on achievement tests, IQ tests, and the SAT. While my English skills were never judged as poor, compared to math, English could not be considered my strong suit. In grade school I did moderately well, getting perhaps B's, sometimes B-pluses, in English and scoring perhaps in the sixtieth or seventieth percentile on achievement tests. But those scores were not good enough to override the opinion that my true abilities lay in math and science, because in those areas I achieved A's and scored in the ninetieth percentile or higher.

This was understandable. Math is precise; there is only one correct answer. 16 Whereas, for me at least, the answers on English tests were always a judgment call, a matter of opinion and personal experience. Those tests were constructed around items like fill-in-the-blank sentence completion, such as, "Even though Tom was _____, Mary thought he was _____." And the correct answer always seemed to be the most bland combinations of thoughts, for example, "Even though Tom was shy, Mary thought he was charming," with the grammatical structure "even though" limiting the correct answer to some sort of semantic opposites, so you wouldn't get answers like, "Even though Tom was foolish, Mary thought he was ridiculous." Well, according to my mother, there were very few limitations as to what Tom could have been and what Mary might have thought of him. So I never did well on tests like that.

The same was true with word analogies, pairs of words in which you were 17 supposed to find some sort of logical, semantic relationship—for example, "*Sunset* is to *nightfall* as _____ is to _____." And here you would be presented with a list of four possible pairs, one of which showed the same kind of relationship: *red* is to *stoplight*, *bus* is to *arrival*, *chills* is to *fever*, *yawn* is to *boring*. Well, I could never think that way. I knew what the tests were asking, but I could not block out of my mind the images already created by the first pair, *"sunset* is to *nightfall"*—and I would see a burst of colors against a darkening sky, the moon rising, the lowering of a curtain of stars. And all the other pairs of words—red, bus, stoplight, boring—just threw up a mass of confusing images, making it impossible for me to sort out something as logical as saying: "A sunset precedes nightfall" is the same as "a chill precedes a fever." The only way I would have gotten that answer right would have been to imagine an associative situation, for example, my being disobedient and staying out past sunset, catching a chill at night, which turns into feverish pneumonia as punishment, which indeed did happen to me.

18 I have been thinking about all this lately, about my mother's English, about achievement tests. Because lately I've been asked, as a writer, why there are not more Asian Americans represented in American literature. Why are there few Asian Americans enrolled in creative writing programs? Why do so many Chinese students go into engineering? Well, these are broad sociological questions I can't begin to answer. But I have noticed in surveys—in fact, just last week—that Asian students, as a whole, always do significantly better on math achievement tests than in English. And this makes me think that there are other Asian-American students whose English spoken in the home might also be described as "broken" or "limited." And perhaps they also have teachers who are steering them away from writing and into math and science, which is what happened to me.

19   Fortunately, I happen to be rebellious in nature and enjoy the challenge of disproving assumptions made about me. I became an English major my first year in college, after being enrolled as pre-med. I started writing nonfiction as a freelancer the week after I was told by my former boss that writing was my worst skill and I should hone my talents toward account management.

20   But it wasn't until 1985 that I finally began to write fiction. And at first I wrote using what I thought to be wittily crafted sentences, sentences that would finally prove I had mastery over the English language. Here's an example from the first draft of a story that later made its way into *The Joy Luck Club,* but without this line: "That was my mental quandary in its nascent state." A terrible line, which I can barely pronounce.

21   Fortunately, for reasons I won't get into today, I later decided I should envision a reader for the stories I would write. And the reader I decided upon was my mother, because these were stories about mothers. So with this reader in mind—and in fact she did read my early drafts—I began to write stories using all the Englishes I grew up with: the English I spoke to my mother, which for lack of a better term might be described as "simple"; the English she used with me, which for lack of a better term might be described as "broken"; my translation of her Chinese, which could certainly be described as "watered down"; and what I imagined to be her translation of her Chinese if she could speak in perfect English, her internal language, and for that I sought to preserve the essence, but neither an English nor a Chinese structure. I wanted to capture what language ability tests can never reveal: her intent, her passion, her imagery, the rhythms of her speech and the nature of her thoughts.

Apart from what any critic had to say about my writing, I knew I had suc- 22
ceeded where it counted when my mother finished reading my book and gave
me her verdict: "So easy to read."

Questions for Discussion

1. Amy Tan writes about how she uses language differently when speaking with particular audiences. Have you been aware of consciously choosing your words in order
   to communicate effectively and expressively with particular audiences? Share an
   example with your class.
2. Tan is critical of the term "limited English." How did this term affect her perception
   of and attitude toward her own mother? What do Tan's examples of speaking for
   her mother reveal about Tan and her mother? Have you ever been in a situation that
   was similar to Tan's?
3. Explain how the title "Mother Tongue" integrates the issues explored in the essay.
4. Amy Tan is critical of the achievement tests she was given in high school. Explain
   why you agree or disagree with her point of view and conclusions.
5. How does Tan explain her success as a writer in spite of the advice given to her by
   her high school teachers and her boss? According to Tan, what is the real test of a
   writer?
6. What communities affected Tan's decisions to become a writer? Why has Tan been
   successful? What advice does Tan offer to the person who aspires to be a successful
   writer?

Ideas for Writing

1. Write an essay about an experience or period in your life when you rebelled against
   the advice of your teachers, proving to them and to yourself that you could make
   sound decisions on your own. How did you change and mature from this experience?
2. Interview several first-generation immigrant parents about the problems that they
   have had learning the language, relating to their children who may be more fluent
   in English, adjusting to life in their community. Write an essay that shares your findings and proposes solutions to the problems that many immigrants face.

The Loudest Voice

Grace Paley

Grace Paley (b. 1922) was the daughter of Russian-Jewish immigrants. She grew
up in the Bronx and studied at Hunter College and New York University. Although
she began writing poetry, Paley is best known for her collections of short stories:
The Little Disturbances of Man (1959), *Enormous Changes at the Last Minute*
(1974), *Later the Same Day* (1985), and her most recent, *Long Walks and Intimate
Talks* (1991). Currently, she teaches at Sarah Lawrence College. Paley's stories
always return to the importance of the Russian, Yiddish culture of her family. She

believes that "the greatest influence you have is the language of your childhood." A long-time political activist as well as teacher and devoted mother, Paley thinks that "art, literature, fiction, poetry whatever it is, makes justice in the world. That's why it almost always has to be on the side of the underdog." In "The Loudest Voice," which was first published in *The Little Disturbances of Man*, Paley shows how a young Jewish girl matures as she integrates two different cultural traditions, one at home and one at school.

Journal

Write about how you would share your favorite religious or cultural ritual or celebration with a friend from a different culture and/or another religion.

There is a certain place where dumb-waiters boom, doors slam, dishes crash; every window is a mother's mouth bidding the street shut up, go skate somewhere else, come home. My voice is the loudest.

2   There, my own mother is still as full of breathing as me and the grocer stands up to speak to her. "Mrs. Abramowitz," he says, "people should not be afraid of their children."

3   "Ah, Mr. Bialik," my mother replies, "if you say to her or her father 'Ssh,' they say, 'In the grave it will be quiet.' "

4   "From Coney Island to the cemetery," says my papa. "It's the same subway; it's the same fare."

5   I am right next to the pickle barrel. My pinky is making tiny whirlpools in the brine. I stop a moment to announce: "Campbell's Tomato Soup. Campbell's Vegetable Beef Soup. Campbell's S-c-otch Broth . . ."

6   "Be quiet," the grocer says, "the labels are coming off."

7   "Please, Shirley, be a little quiet," my mother begs me.

8   In that place the whole street groans: Be quiet! Be quiet! but steals from the happy chorus of my inside self not a tittle or a jot.

9   There, too, but just around the corner, is a red brick building that has been old for many years. Every morning the children stand before it in double lines which must be straight. They are not insulted. They are waiting anyway.

10   I am usually among them. I am, in fact, the first, since I begin with "A."

11   One cold morning the monitor tapped me on the shoulder. "Go to Room 409, Shirley Abramowitz," he said. I did as I was told. I went in a hurry up a down staircase to Room 409, which contained sixth-graders. I had to wait at the desk without wiggling until Mr. Hilton, their teacher, had time to speak.

12   After five minutes he said, "Shirley?"

13   "What?" I whispered.

14   He said, "My! My! Shirley Abramowitz! They told me you had a particularly loud, clear voice and read with lots of expression. Could that be true?"

15   "Oh yes," I whispered.

16   "In that case, don't be silly; I might very well be your teacher someday. Speak up, speak up."

17   "Yes," I shouted.

"More like it," he said. "Now, Shirley, can you put a ribbon in your hair 18
or a bobby pin? It's too messy."

"Yes!" I bawled.   19

"Now, now, calm down." He turned to the class. "Children, not a sound. 20
Open at page 39. Read till 52. When you finish, start again." He looked me
over once more. "Now, Shirley, you know, I suppose, that Christmas is com-
ing. We are preparing a beautiful play. Most of the parts have been given out.
But I still need a child with a strong voice, lots of stamina. Do you know what
stamina is? You do? Smart kid. You know, I heard you read 'The Lord is my
shepherd'[1] in Assembly yesterday. I was very impressed. Wonderful delivery.
Mrs. Jordan, your teacher, speaks highly of you. Now listen to me, Shirley
Abramowitz, if you want to take the part and be in the play, repeat after me,
'I swear to work harder than I ever did before.' "

I looked to heaven and said at once, "Oh, I swear." I kissed my pinky and 21
looked at God.

"That is an actor's life, my dear," he explained: "Like a soldier's, never 22
tardy or disobedient to his general, the director. Everything," he said,
"absolutely everything will depend on you."

That afternoon, all over the building, children scraped and scrubbed the 23
turkeys and the sheaves of corn off the schoolroom windows. Goodbye
Thanksgiving. The next morning a monitor brought red paper and green paper
from the office. We made new shapes and hung them on the walls and glued
them to the doors.

The teachers became happier and happier. Their heads were ringing like 24
the bells of childhood. My best friend Evie was prone to evil, but she did not
get a single demerit for whispering. We learned "Holy Night" without an
error. "How wonderful!" said Miss Glacé, the student teacher. "To think that
some of you don't even speak the language!" We learned "Deck the Halls"
and "Hark! The Herald Angels". . . . They weren't ashamed and we weren't
embarrassed.

Oh, but when my mother heard about it all, she said to my father: "Misha, 25
you don't know what's going on there. Cramer is the head of the Tickets Committee."

"Who?" asked my father. "Cramer? Oh yes, an active woman."   26

"Active? Active has to have a reason. Listen," she said sadly, "I'm sur- 27
prised to see my neighbors making tra-la-la for Christmas."

My father couldn't think of what to say to that. Then he decided: "You're 28
in America! Clara, you wanted to come here. In Palestine the Arabs would be
eating you alive. Europe you had pogroms.[2] Argentina is full of Indians. Here
you got Christmas. . . . Some joke, ha?"

"Very funny, Misha. What is becoming of you? If we came to a new coun- 29
try a long time ago to run away from tyrants, and instead we fall into a creep-

[1]Psalms 23: A Psalm of David.
[2]An organized and often officially encouraged massacre or persecution of a minority group, especially one conducted against the Jews.

ing pogrom, that our children learn a lot of lies, so what's the joke? Ach, Misha, your idealism is going away."

30   "So is your sense of humor."

31   "That I never had, but idealism you had a lot of."

32   "I'm the same Misha Abramovitch, I didn't change an iota. Ask anyone."

33   "Only ask me," says my mama, may she rest in peace. "I got the answer."

34   Meanwhile the neighbors had to think of what to say too.

35   Marty's father said: "You know, he has a very important part, my boy."

36   "Mine also," said Mr. Sauerfeld.

37   "Not my boy!" said Mrs. Klieg. "I said to him no. The answer is no. When I say no! I mean no!"

38   The rabbi's wife said, "It's disgusting!" But no one listened to her. Under the narrow sky of God's great wisdom she wore a strawberry-blond wig.[3]

39   Every day was noisy and full of experience. I was Right-hand Man. Mr. Hilton said: "How could I get along without you, Shirley?"

40   He said: "Your mother and father ought to get down on their knees every night and thank God for giving them a child like you."

41   He also said: "You're absolutely a pleasure to work with, my dear, dear child."

42   Sometimes he said: "For God's sakes, what did I do with the script? Shirley! Shirley! Find it."

43   Then I answered quietly: "Here it is, Mr. Hilton."

44   Once in a while, when he was very tired, he would cry out: "Shirley, I'm just tired of screaming at those kids. Will you tell Ira Pushkov not to come in till Lester points to that star the second time?"

45   Then I roared: "Ira Pushkov, what's the matter with you? Dope! Mr. Hilton told you five times already, don't come in till Lester points to that star the second time."

46   "Ach, Clara," my father asked, "what does she do there till six o'clock she can't even put the plates on the table?"

47   "Christmas," said my mother coldly.

48   "Ho! Ho!" my father said. "Christmas. What's the harm? After all, history teaches everyone. We learn from reading this is a holiday from pagan times also, candles, lights, even Chanukah.[4] So we learn it's not altogether Christian. So if they think it's a private holiday, they're only ignorant, not patriotic. What belongs to history, belongs to all men. You want to go back to the Middle Ages? Is it better to shave your head with a secondhand razor? Does it hurt Shirley to learn to speak up? It does not. So maybe someday she won't live between the kitchen and the shop.[5] She's not a fool."

49   I thank you, Papa, for your kindness. It is true about me to this day. I am foolish but I am not a fool.

---

[3]Wigs are worn by orthodox Jewish women after they marry.
[4]An eight-day Jewish festival celebrated in December or late November, commemorating the Maccabees' victory over the Syrians in 165 B.C. and the rededication of the Temple at Jerusalem.
[5]Jewish immigrant women toiled in sweatshops as well as in kitchens.

That night my father kissed me and said with great interest in my career, 50 "Shirley, tomorrow's your big day. Congrats."

"Save it," my mother said. Then she shut all the windows in order to pre- 51 vent tonsillitis.

In the morning it snowed. On the street corner a tree had been decorated 52 for us by a kind city administration. In order to miss its chilly shadow our neighbors walked three blocks east to buy a loaf of bread. The butcher pulled down black window shades to keep the colored lights from shining on his chickens. Oh, not me. On the way to school, with both my hands I tossed it a kiss of tolerance. Poor thing, it was a stranger in Egypt.[6]

I walked straight into the auditorium past the staring children. "Go ahead, 53 Shirley!" said the monitors. Four boys, big for their age, had already started work as propmen and stagehands.

Mr. Hilton was very nervous. He was not even happy. Whatever he started 54 to say ended in a sideward look of sadness. He sat slumped in the middle of the first row and asked me to help Miss Glacé. I did this, although she thought my voice too resonant and said, "Show-off!"

Parents began to arrive long before we were ready. They wanted to make 55 a good impression. From among the yards of drapes I peeked out at the audience. I saw my embarrassed mother.

Ira, Lester, and Meyer were pasted to their beards by Miss Glacé. She 56 almost forgot to thread the star on its wire, but I reminded her. I coughed a few times to clear my throat. Miss Glacé looked around and saw that everyone was in costume and on line waiting to play his part. She whispered, "All right . . ." Then:

Jackie Sauerfeld, the prettiest boy in first grade, parted the curtains with 57 his skinny elbow and in a high voice sang out:

"Parents dear   58
We are here
To make a Christmas play in time.
It we give
In narrative
And illustrate with pantomime."

He disappeared.   59

My voice burst immediately from the wings to the great shock of Ira, 60 Lester, and Meyer, who were waiting for it but were surprised all the same.

"I remember, I remember, the house where I was born . . ."[7]   61

Miss Glacé yanked the curtain open and there it was, the house—an old 62 hayloft, where Celia Kornbluh lay in the straw with Cindy Lou, her favorite doll. Ira, Lester, and Meyer moved slowly from the wings toward her, sometimes pointing to a moving star and sometimes ahead to Cindy Lou.

---

[6]An allusion to Moses' sojourn in Egypt. See Exodus 2:2. As the persecuted Israelites were out of place in Egypt, so was the Christmas tree in an all-Jewish neighborhood.
[7]A sentimental poem by Thomas Hood (1798–1845).

63   It was a long story and it was a sad story. I carefully pronounced all the words about my lonesome childhood, while little Eddie Braunstein wandered upstage and down with his shepherd's stick, looking for sheep. I brought up lonesomeness again, and not being understood at all except by some women everybody hated. Eddie was too small for that and Marty Groff took his place, wearing his father's prayer shawl. I announced twelve friends, and half the boys in the fourth grade gathered round Marty, who stood on an orange crate while my voice harangued. Sorrowful and loud, I declaimed about love and God and Man, but because of the terrible deceit of Abie Stock we came suddenly to a famous moment. Marty, whose remembering tongue I was, waited at the foot of the cross. He stared desperately at the audience. I groaned, "My God, my God, why hast thou forsaken me?"[8] The soldiers who were sheiks grabbed poor Marty to pin him up to die, but he wrenched free, turned again to the audience, and spread his arms aloft to show despair and the end. I murmured at the top of my voice, "The rest is silence,[9] but as everyone in this room, in this city—in this world—now knows, I shall have life eternal."

64   That night Mrs. Kornbluh visited our kitchen for a glass of tea.

65   "How's the virgin?"[10] asked my father with a look of concern.

66   "For a man with a daughter, you got a fresh mouth, Abramovitch."

67   "Here," said my father kindly, "have some lemon, it'll sweeten your disposition."

68   They debated a little in Yiddish, then fell in a puddle of Russian and Polish. What I understood next was my father, who said, "Still and all, it was certainly a beautiful affair, you have to admit, introducing us to the beliefs of a different culture."

69   "Well, yes," said Mrs. Kornbluh. "The only thing . . . you know Charlie Turner—that cute boy in Celia's class—a couple others? They got very small parts or no part at all. In very bad taste, it seemed to me. After all, it's their religion."

70   "Ach," explained my mother, "what could Mr. Hilton do? They got very small voices; after all, why should they holler? The English language they know from the beginning by heart. They're blond like angels. You think it's so important they should get in the play? Christmas . . . the whole piece of goods . . . they own it."

71   I listened and listened until I couldn't listen any more. Too sleepy, I climbed out of bed and kneeled. I made a little church of my hands and said, "Hear, O Israel[11] . . ." Then I called out in Yiddish, "Please, good night, good night. Ssh." My father said, "Sssh yourself," and slammed the kitchen door.

72   I was happy. I fell asleep at once. I had prayed for everybody: my talking family, cousins far away, passersby, and all the lonesome Christians. I expected to be heard. My voice was certainly the loudest.

---

[8]Psalm 22, A Psalm of David. Also the fourth of the seven last words of Christ on the cross.
[9]*Hamlet,* V, ii.
[10]The virgin Mary portrayed by Mrs. Kornbluth's daughter in the school play.
[11]"Hear, O Israel, the Lord our God, the Lord is One." The most often recited Jewish prayer.

Questions for Discussion

1. Why does Shirley's mother object to her daughter's loud voice? How does Shirley's father feel about his daughter's voice?
2. Why does Mr. Hilton choose Shirley to be in the play? What point does Paley make through contrasting the negative attitude of Shirley's mother to her daughter's loud voice to the positive attitude of Shirley's teachers?
3. Compare and contrast the reactions of Shirley's mother and father to their daughter's participation in the Christmas pageant. Do you find yourself more sympathetic to the point of view of Shirley's mother or father? Why?
4. What does Shirley learn from her experiences in the pageant? Why do Shirley's mother's feelings about her daughter's participation in the pageant change after the performance?
5. How is the Jewish community affected by the presentation of the Christmas pageant? Did similar types of cultural and or religious conflicts occur in your community or at your elementary school?
6. Why is the story's title appropriate? What does Shirley's loud voice come to represent?

Ideas for Writing

1. Write an essay that discusses ways that different cultures maintain their distinctive traditions in your community. In what ways does this cultural diversity have a positive impact on your community?
2. Contact several of the local elementary schools in your community to learn about how they encourage cultural diversity in their holiday and cultural programs. Write a paper that presents the information you have gathered for your class and/or for a community paper. Or, if you have a child in elementary school, discuss the ways that cultural diversity has been presented in your child's classroom. Evaluate the strengths and weaknesses of the school's approach.

Graduation

Maya Angelou

Maya Angelou (b. 1928) spent her childhood in the tiny town of Stamps, Arkansas, as well as in the urban areas of St. Louis, San Francisco, and Los Angeles. Angelou is best known for her autobiographical writing, especially *I Know Why the Caged Bird Sings* (1970); she also writes poetry and plays and has worked as a stage and screen performer and singer. In addition, Angelou has lectured all over the world and has been active in the civil rights movement. Angelou read a long poem, "On The Pulse of Morning," at Bill Clinton's Presidential inauguration. Her most recent work, *Wouldn't Take Nothing for My Journey Now* (1993), became a best-seller upon publication. The following essay, which is excerpted from *I Know Why the Caged Bird Sings,* will give you a good sense of the important role that the African-American community in Stamps, Arkansas, played in Maya Angelou's education.

Journal

Describe your graduation from elementary or secondary school. How did it mark a turning point in your life? Did your community support you as a graduate? In what ways?

The children in Stamps trembled visibly with anticipation. Some adults were excited too, but to be certain the whole young population had come down with graduation epidemic. Large classes were graduating from both the grammar school and the high school. Even those who were years removed from their own day of glorious release were anxious to help with preparations as a kind of dry run. The junior students who were moving into the vacating classes' chairs were tradition-bound to show their talents for leadership and management. They strutted through the school and around the campus exerting pressure on the lower grades. Their authority was so new that occasionally if they pressed a little too hard it had to be overlooked. After all, next term was coming, and it never hurt a sixth grader to have a play sister in the eighth grade, or a tenth-year student to be able to call a twelfth grader Bubba. So all was endured in a spirit of shared understanding. But the graduating classes themselves were the nobility. Like travelers with exotic destinations on their minds, the graduates were remarkably forgetful. They came to school without their books, or tablets, or even pencils. Volunteers fell over themselves to secure replacements for the missing equipment. When accepted, the willing workers might or might not be thanked, and it was of no importance to the pregraduation rites. Even teachers were respectful of the now quiet and aging seniors, and tended to speak to them, if not as equals, as beings only slightly lower than themselves. After tests were returned and grades given, the student body, which acted like an extended family, knew who did well, who excelled, and what piteous ones had failed.

2   Unlike the white school, Lafayette County Training School distinguished itself by having neither lawn, nor hedges, nor tennis court, nor climbing ivy. Its two buildings (main classrooms, the grade school, and home economics) were set on a dirt hill with no fence to limit either its boundaries or those of bordering farms. There was a large expanse to the left of the school which was used alternately as a baseball diamond or a basketball court. Rusty hoops on the swaying poles represented the permanent recreational equipment, although bats and balls could be borrowed from the P.E. teacher if the borrower was qualified and if the diamond wasn't occupied.

3   Over this rocky area relieved by a few shady tall persimmon trees the graduating class walked. The girls often held hands and no longer bothered to speak to the lower students. There was a sadness about them, as if this old world was not their home and they were bound for higher ground. The boys, on the other hand, had become more friendly, more outgoing. A decided change from the closed attitude they projected while studying for finals. Now they seemed not ready to give up the old school, the familiar paths and classrooms. Only a small percentage would be continuing on to college—one of the

South's A & M (agricultural and mechanical) schools, which trained Negro youths to be carpenters, farmers, handymen, masons, maids, cooks, and baby nurses. Their future rode heavily on their shoulders, and blinded them to the collective joy that had pervaded the lives of the boys and girls in the grammar school graduating class.

Parents who could afford it had ordered new shoes and ready-made 4 clothes for themselves from Sears and Roebuck or Montgomery Ward. They also engaged the best seamstresses to make the floating graduating dresses and to cut down secondhand pants which would be pressed to a military slick-ness for the important event.

Oh, it was important, all right. Whitefolks would attend the ceremony, and 5 two or three would speak of God and home, and the Southern way of life, and Mrs. Parsons, the principal's wife, would play the graduation march while the lower-grade graduates paraded down the aisles and took their seats below the platform. The high school seniors would wait in empty classrooms to make their dramatic entrance.

In the Store I was the person of the moment. The birthday girl. The cen- 6 ter. Bailey[1] had graduated the year before, although to do so he had had to forfeit all pleasures to make up for his time lost in Baton Rouge.

My class was wearing butter-yellow piqué dresses, and Momma launched 7 out on mine. She smocked the yoke into tiny crisscrossing puckers, then shirred the rest of the bodice. Her dark fingers ducked in and out of the lemony cloth as she embroidered raised daisies around the hem. Before she considered herself finished she had added a crocheted cuff on the puff sleeves, and a pointy crocheted collar.

I was going to be lovely. A walking model of all the various styles of fine 8 hand sewing and it didn't worry me that I was only twelve years old and merely graduating from the eighth grade. Besides, many teachers in Arkansas Negro schools had only that diploma and were licensed to impart wisdom.

The days had become longer and more noticeable. The faded beige of for- 9 mer times had been replaced with strong and sure colors. I began to see my classmates' clothes, their skin tones, and the dust that waved off pussy wil-lows. Clouds that lazed across the sky were objects of great concern to me. Their shiftier shapes might have held a message that in my new happiness and with a little bit of time I'd soon decipher. During that period I looked at the arch of heaven so religiously my neck kept a steady ache. I had taken to smil-ing more often, and my jaws hurt from the unaccustomed activity. Between the two physical sore spots, I suppose I could have been uncomfortable, but that was not the case. As a member of the winning team (the graduating class of 1940) I had outdistanced unpleasant sensations by miles. I was headed for the freedom of open fields.

Youth and social approval allied themselves with me and we trammeled 10 memories of slights and insults. The wind of our swift passage remodeled my

[1]The author's brother. The children help out in their grandmother's store. [Ed.]

features. Lost tears were pounded to mud and then to dust. Years of with-drawal were brushed aside and left behind, as hanging ropes of parasitic moss.

11   My work alone had awarded me a top place and I was going to be one of the first called in the graduating ceremonies. On the classroom blackboard, as well as on the bulletin board in the auditorium, there were blue stars and white stars and red stars. No absences, no tardinesses, and my academic work was among the best of the year. I could say the preamble to the Constitution even faster than Bailey. We timed ourselves often: "WethepeopleoftheUnited-Statesinordertoformamoreperfectunion . . ." I had memorized the Presidents of the United States from Washington to Roosevelt in chronological as well as alphabetical order.

12   My hair pleased me too. Gradually the black mass had lengthened and thickened, so that it kept at last to its braided pattern, and I didn't have to yank my scalp off when I tried to comb it.

13   Louise and I had rehearsed the exercises until we tired out ourselves. Henry Reed was class valedictorian. He was a small, very black boy with hooded eyes, a long, broad nose, and an oddly shaped head. I had admired him for years because each term he and I vied for the best grades in our class. Most often he bested me, but instead of being disappointed I was pleased that we shared top places between us. Like many Southern Black children, he lived with his grandmother, who was as strict as Momma and as kind as she knew how to be. He was courteous, respectful, and soft-spoken to elders, but on the playground he chose to play the roughest games. I admired him. Anyone, I reckoned, sufficiently afraid or sufficiently dull could be polite. But to be able to operate at a top level with both adults and children was admirable.

14   His valedictory speech was entitled "To Be or Not to Be." The rigid tenth-grade teacher had helped him to write it. He'd been working on the dramatic stresses for months.

15   The weeks until graduation were filled with heady activities. A group of small children were to be presented in a play about buttercups and daisies and bunny rabbits. They could be heard throughout the building practicing their hops and their little songs that sounded like silver bells. The older girls (non-graduates, of course) were assigned the task of making refreshments for the night's festivities. A tangy scent of ginger, cinnamon, nutmeg, and chocolate wafted around the home economics building as the budding cooks made sam-ples for themselves and their teachers.

16   In every corner of the workshop, axes and saws split fresh timber as the woodshop boys made sets and stage scenery. Only the graduates were left out of the general bustle. We were free to sit in the library at the back of the build-ing or look in quite detachedly, naturally, on the measures being taken for our event.

17   Even the minister preached on graduation the Sunday before. His subject was, "Let your light so shine that men will see your good works and praise your Father, Who is in Heaven." Although the sermon was purported to be addressed to us, he used the occasion to speak to backsliders, gamblers, and general ne'er-do-wells. But since he had called our names at the beginning of the service we were mollified.

Among Negroes the tradition was to give presents to children going only 18 from one grade to another. How much more important this was when the person was graduating at the top of the class. Uncle Willie and Momma had sent away for a Mickey Mouse watch like Bailey's. Louise gave me four embroidered handkerchiefs. (I gave her three crocheted doilies.) Mrs. Sneed, the minister's wife, made me an underskirt to wear for graduation, and nearly every customer gave me a nickel or maybe even a dime with the instruction "Keep on moving to higher ground," or some such encouragement.

Amazingly the great day finally dawned and I was out of bed before I 19 knew it. I threw open the back door to see it more clearly, but Momma said, "Sister, come away from that door and put your robe on."

I hoped the memory of that morning would never leave me. Sunlight was 20 itself still young, and the day had none of the insistence maturity would bring it in a few hours. In my robe and barefoot in the backyard, under cover of going to see about my new beans, I gave myself up to the gentle warmth and thanked God that no matter what evil I had done in my life He had allowed me to live to see this day. Somewhere in my fatalism I had expected to die, accidentally, and never have the chance to walk up the stairs in the auditorium and gracefully receive my hard-earned diploma. Out of God's merciful bosom I had won reprieve.

Bailey came out in his robe and gave me a box wrapped in Christmas 21 paper. He said he had saved his money for months to pay for it. It felt like a box of chocolates, but I knew Bailey wouldn't save money to buy candy when we had all we could want under our noses.

He was as proud of the gift as I. It was a soft-leather-bound copy of a col- 22 lection of poems by Edgar Allan Poe, or, as Bailey and I called him, "Eap." I turned to "Annabel Lee" and we walked up and down the garden rows, the cool dirt between our toes, reciting the beautifully sad lines.

Momma made a Sunday breakfast although it was only Friday. After we 23 finished the blessing, I opened my eyes to find the watch on my plate. It was a dream of a day. Everything went smoothly and to my credit. I didn't have to be reminded or scolded for anything. Near evening I was too jittery to attend to chores, so Bailey volunteered to do all before his bath.

Days before, we had made a sign for the Store and as we turned out the 24 lights Momma hung the cardboard over the doorknob. It read clearly: CLOSED. GRADUATION.

My dress fitted perfectly and everyone said that I looked like a sunbeam 25 in it. On the hill, going toward the school, Bailey walked behind with Uncle Willie, who muttered, "Go on, Ju." He wanted him to walk ahead with us because it embarrassed him to have to walk so slowly. Bailey said he'd let the ladies walk together, and the men would bring up the rear. We all laughed, nicely.

Little children dashed by out of the dark like fireflies. Their crepe-paper 26 dresses and butterfly wings were not made for running and we heard more than one rip, dryly, and the regretful "uh uh" that followed.

The school blazed without gaiety. The windows seemed cold and 27 unfriendly from the lower hill. A sense of ill-fated timing crept over me, and if Momma hadn't reached for my hand I would have drifted back to Bailey and Uncle Willie, and possibly beyond. She made a few slow jokes about my feet getting cold, and tugged me along to the now-strange building.

28   Around the front steps, assurance came back. There were my fellow "greats," the graduating class. Hair brushed back, legs oiled, new dresses and pressed pleats, fresh pocket handkerchiefs and little handbags, all homesewn. Oh, we were up to snuff, all right. I joined my comrades and didn't even see my family go in to find seats in the crowded auditorium.

29   The school band struck up a march and all classes filed in as had been rehearsed. We stood in front of our seats, as assigned, and on a signal from the choir director, we sat. No sooner had this been accomplished than the band started to play the national anthem. We rose again and sang the song, after which we recited the pledge of allegiance. We remained standing for a brief minute before the choir director and the principal signaled to us, rather desperately I thought, to take our seats. The command was so unusual that our carefully rehearsed and smooth-running machine was thrown off. For a full minute we fumbled for our chairs and bumped into each other awkwardly. Habits change or solidify under pressure, so in our state of nervous tension we had been ready to follow our usual assembly pattern: the American National Anthem, then the pledge of allegiance, then the song every Black person I knew called the Negro National Anthem. All done in the same key, with the same passion and most often standing on the same foot.

30   Finding my seat at last, I was overcome with a presentiment of worse things to come. Something unrehearsed, unplanned, was going to happen, and we were going to be made to look bad. I distinctly remember being explicit in the choice of pronoun. It was "we," the graduating class, the unit, that concerned me then.

31   The principal welcomed "parents and friends" and asked the Baptist minister to lead us in prayer. His invocation was brief and punchy, and for a second I thought we were getting back on the high road to right action. When the principal came back to the dais, however, his voice had changed. Sounds always affected me profoundly and the principal's voice was one of my favorites. During assembly it melted and lowed weakly into the audience. It had not been in my plan to listen to him, but my curiosity was piqued and I straightened up to give him my attention.

32   He was talking about Booker T. Washington, our "late great leader," who said we can be as close as the fingers on the hand, etc. . . . . Then he said a few vague things about friendship and the friendship of kindly people to those less fortunate than themselves. With that his voice nearly faded, thin, away. Like a river diminishing to a stream and then to a trickle. But he cleared his throat and said, "Our speaker tonight, who is also our friend, came from Texarkana to deliver the commencement address, but due to the irregularity of the train schedule, he's going to, as they say, 'speak and run.' " He said that we understood and wanted the man to know that we were most grateful for the time he was able to give us and then something about how we were willing always to adjust to another's program, and without more ado—"I give you Mr. Edward Donleavy."

Not one but two white men came through the door offstage. The shorter 33
one walked to the speaker's platform, and the tall one moved over to the center seat and sat down. But that was our principal's seat, and already occupied.
The dislodged gentleman bounced around for a long breath or two before the
Baptist minister gave him his chair, then with more dignity than the situation
deserved, the minister walked off the stage.

Donleavy looked at the audience once (on reflection, I'm sure that he 34
wanted only to reassure himself that we were really there), adjusted his
glasses, and began to read from a sheaf of papers.

He was glad "to be here and to see the work going on just as it was in the 35
other schools."

At the first "Amen" from the audience I willed the offender to immediate 36
death by choking on the word. But Amens and Yes, sir's began to fall around
the room like rain through a ragged umbrella.

He told us of the wonderful changes we children in Stamps had in store. 37
The Central School (naturally, the white school was Central) had already been
granted improvements that would be in use in the fall. A well-known artist
was coming from Little Rock to teach art to them. They were going to have
the newest microscopes and chemistry equipment for their laboratory. Mr.
Donleavy didn't leave us long in the dark over who made these improvements
available to Central High. Nor were we to be ignored in the general betterment scheme he had in mind.

He said that he had pointed out to people at a very high level that one of 38
the first-line football tacklers at Arkansas Agricultural and Mechanical College
had graduated from good old Lafayette County Training School. Here fewer
Amen's were heard. Those few that did break through lay dully in the air with
the heaviness of habit.

He went on to praise us. He went on to say how he had bragged that "one 39
of the best basketball players at Fisk sank his first ball right here at Lafayette
County Training School."

The white kids were going to have a chance to become Galileos and 40
Madame Curies and Edisons and Gauguins, and our boys (the girls weren't
even in on it) would try to be Jessie Owenses and Joe Louises.

Owens and the Brown Bomber were great heroes in our world, but what 41
school official in the white-goddom of Little Rock had the right to decide that
those two men must be our only heroes? Who decided that for Henry Reed to
become a scientist he had to work like George Washington Carver, as a boot-
black, to buy a lousy microscope? Bailey was obviously always going to be too
small to be an athlete, so which concrete angel glued to what country seat had
decided that if my brother wanted to become a lawyer he had to first pay
penance for his skin by picking cotton and hocing corn and studying correspondence books at night for twenty years?

The man's dead words fell like bricks around the auditorium and too 42
many settled in my belly. Constrained by hard-learned manners I couldn't look
behind me, but to my left and right the proud graduating class of 1940 had
dropped their heads. Every girl in my row had found something new to do
with her handkerchief. Some folded the tiny squares into love knots, some into

triangles, but most were wadding them, then pressing them flat on their yellow laps.

43   On the dais, the ancient tragedy was being replayed. Professor Parsons sat, a sculptor's reject, rigid. His large, heavy body seemed devoid of will or willingness, and his eyes said he was no longer with us. The other teachers examined the flag (which was draped stage right) or their notes, or the windows which opened on our now-famous playing diamond.

44   Graduation, the hush-hush magic time of frills and gifts and congratulations and diplomas, was finished for me before my name was called. The accomplishment was nothing. The meticulous maps, drawn in three colors of ink, learning and spelling decasyllabic words, memorizing the whole of *The Rape of Lucrece*—it was nothing. Donleavy had exposed us.

45   We were maids and farmers, handymen and washerwomen, and anything higher that we aspired to was farcical and presumptuous. Then I wished that Gabriel Prosser and Nat Turner had killed all whitefolks in their beds and that Abraham Lincoln had been assassinated before the signing of the Emancipation Proclamation, and that Harriet Tubman had been killed by that blow on her head and Christopher Columbus had drowned in the *Santa Maria*.

46   It was awful to be Negro and have no control over my life. It was brutal to be young and already trained to sit quietly and listen to charges brought against my color with no chance of defense. We should all be dead. I thought I should like to see us all dead, one on top of the other. A pyramid of flesh with the whitefolks on the bottom, as the broad base, then the Indians with their silly tomahawks and teepees and wigwams and treaties, the Negroes with their mops and recipes and cotton sacks and spirituals sticking out of their mouths. The Dutch children should all stumble in their wooden shoes and break their necks. The French should choke to death on the Louisiana Purchase (1803) while silkworms ate all the Chinese with their stupid pigtails. As a species, we were an abomination. All of us.

47   Donleavy was running for election, and assured our parents that if he won we could count on having the only colored paved playing field in that part of Arkansas. Also—he never looked up to acknowledge the grunts of acceptance—also, we were bound to get some new equipment for the home economics building and the workshop.

48   He finished, and since there was no need to give any more than the most perfunctory thank-you's, he nodded to the men on the stage, and the tall white man who was never introduced joined him at the door. They left with the attitude that now they were off to something really important. (The graduation ceremonies at Lafayette County Training School had been a mere preliminary.)

49   The ugliness they left was palpable. An uninvited guest who wouldn't leave. The choir was summoned and sang a modern arrangement of "Onward, Christian Soldiers," with new words pertaining to graduates seeking their place in the world. But it didn't work. Elouise, the daughter of the Baptist minister, recited "Invictus," and I could have cried at the impertinence of "I am the master of my fate, I am the captain of my soul."

My name had lost its ring of familiarity and I had to be nudged to go and 50 receive my diploma. All my preparations had fled. I neither marched up to the stage like a conquering Amazon, nor did I look in the audience for Bailey's nod of approval. Marguerite Johnson, I heard the name again, my honors were read, there were noises in the audience of appreciation, and I took my place on the stage as rehearsed.

I thought about colors I hated: ecru, puce, lavender, beige, and black. 51

There was shuffling and rustling around me, then Henry Reed was giving 52 his valedictory address, "To Be or Not to Be." Hadn't he heard the whitefolks? We couldn't *be*, so the question was a waste of time. Henry's voice came out clear and strong. I feared to look at him. Hadn't he got the message? There was no "nobler in the mind" for Negroes because the world didn't think we had minds, and they let us know it. "Outrageous fortune"? Now, that was a joke. When the ceremony was over I had to tell Henry Reed some things. That is, if I still cared. Not "rub," Henry, "erase." "Ah, there's the erase." Us.

Henry had been a good student in elocution. His voice rose on tides of 53 promise and fell on waves of warnings. The English teacher had helped him to create a sermon winging through Hamlet's soliloquy. To be a man, a doer, a builder, a leader, or to be a tool, an unfunny joke, a crusher of funky toadstools. I marveled that Henry could go through the speech as if we had a choice.

I had been listening and silently rebutting each sentence with my eyes 54 closed; then there was a hush, which in an audience warns that something unplanned is happening. I looked up and saw Henry Reed, the conservative, the proper, the A student, turn his back to the audience and turn to us (the proud graduating class of 1940) and sing, nearly speaking,

> Lift ev'ry voice and sing
> Till earth and heaven ring
> Ring with the harmonies of Liberty . . .

It was the poem written by James Weldon Johnson. It was the music composed by J. Rosamond Johnson. It was the Negro National Anthem. Out of habit we were singing it.

Our mothers and fathers stood in the dark hall and joined the hymn of 55 encouragement. A kindergarten teacher led the small children onto the stage and the buttercups and daisies and bunny rabbits marked time and tried to follow:

> Stony the road we trod
> Bitter the chastening rod
> Felt in the days when hope, unborn, had died.
> Yet with a steady beat
> Have not our weary feet
> Come to the place for which our fathers sighed?

Every child I knew had learned that song with his ABCs and along with 56 "Jesus Loves Me This I Know." But I personally had never heard it before.

Never heard the words, despite the thousands of times I had sung them. Never thought they had anything to do with me.

57   On the other hand, the words of Patrick Henry had made such an impression on me that I had been able to stretch myself tall and trembling and say, "I know not what course others may take, but as for me, give me liberty or give me death."

58   And now I heard, really for the first time:

> We have come over a way that with tears has been watered,
> We have come, treading our path through the blood
>   of the slaughtered.

59   While echoes of the song shivered in the air, Henry Reed bowed his head, said "Thank you," and returned to his place in the line. The tears that slipped down many faces were not wiped away in shame.

60   We were on top again. As always, again. We survived. The depths had been icy and dark, but now a bright sun spoke to our souls. I was no longer simply a member of the proud graduating class of 1940; I was a proud member of the wonderful, beautiful Negro race.

61   Oh, Black known and unknown poets, how often have your auctioned pains sustained us? Who will compute the lonely nights made less lonely by your songs, or by the empty pots made less tragic by your tales?

62   If we were a people much given to revealing secrets, we might raise monuments and sacrifice to the memories of our poets, but slavery cured us of that weakness. It may be enough, however, to have it said that we survive in exact relationship to the dedication of our poets (include preachers, musicians, and blues singers).

Questions for Discussion

1. What points does Angelou make by contrasting the neighboring white school and her Negro school, the attitudes of the graduating girls and the graduating boys? Do the gender and ethnic assumptions implied in these contrasts still exist in American culture and in your own community? To what extent have these gender and racial attitudes changed?
2. How does the African-American community in Stamps feel about the graduation and their graduates? How do they support their graduates? What does an education represent to them? Why does Angelou feel proud of herself and of Henry Reed, the class valedictorian?
3. Donleavy's expectations of the graduation class of Lafayette County Training School undermine the spirits of the students and their relatives. Which images does Angelou use to convey a sense of disillusionment and defeat after the speech? Why are the images that she uses effective? Have you ever experienced feelings that were similar to the ones that Angelou had at her graduation?
4. When Henry Reed decides to lead the class in the Negro National Anthem, why does Angelou hear and understand for the first time the meaning behind the words of the song? In what ways have the unknown Negro poets inspired their community to have faith? Do you agree with Angelou when she suggests that Negroes have more spiritual faith than white people?

5. In what ways is Angelou's graduation a passage from innocence to experience? In what ways is Angelou's sense of hope also a triumph of her community?
6. What insights into the role of prejudice and the power of community does this narrative suggest?

Ideas for Writing

1. Write an essay about your graduation as an experience of "initiation and passage." Did your graduation give you faith in your power to succeed in spite of the obstacles that you realized you would have to overcome? Did your graduating class have a sense of community? Did your community support you as a graduating student?
2. Write an essay in which you contrast the social attitudes toward African Americans in education portrayed in Angelou's story with the attitudes toward African Americans in education today. You might draw on your own experiences at elementary and secondary school, as well as what you have learned from reading or from popular culture.

I Just Wanna Be Average

Mike Rose

Mike Rose (b. 1944) grew up in East Los Angeles and taught students for whom an education was a reminder of their marginalized position in society, for whom hope was a possibility only if they were extremely determined and found teachers who supported them. Rose has written college texts as well as articles on language and literacy. He has received awards from the National Academy of Education and the National Council of Teachers. Currently he is an associate director of the University of California at Los Angeles Writing Programs. Mike Rose is best known for *Lives on the Boundary* (1989), his account of the educational underclass in America. The selection from that book which follows explores the injustices that the educational system perpetuates through tracking. Rose's story is a hopeful one: he comes to understand the drawbacks of "being average" as he breaks out of the cycle of poverty and hopelessness that trapped so many of his friends.

Journal

Write about a teacher or a fellow student who was a role model and/or a counselor. How did this individual influence your personal, educational, and career goals?

It took two buses to get to Our Lady of Mercy. The first started deep in South Los Angeles and caught me at midpoint. The second drifted through neighborhoods with trees, parks, big lawns, and lots of flowers. The rides were long but were livened up by a group of South L.A. veterans whose parents also thought that Hope had set up shop in the west end of the country. There was

Christy Biggars, who, at sixteen, was dealing and was, according to rumor, a pimp as well. There were Bill Cobb and Johnny Gonzales, grease-pencil artists extraordinaire, who left Nembutal-enhanced[1] swirls of "Cobb" and "Johnny" on the corrugated walls of the bus. And then there was Tyrrell Wilson. Tyrrell was the coolest kid I knew. He ran the dozens[2] like a metric halfback, laid down a rap that outrhymed and outpointed Cobb, whose rap was good but not great—the curse of a moderately soulful kid trapped in white skin. But it was Cobb who would sneak a radio onto the bus, and thus underwrote his patter with Little Richard, Fats Domino, Chuck Berry, the Coasters,[3] and Ernie K. Doe's mother-in-law, an awful woman who was "sent from down below." And so it was that Christy and Cobb and Johnny G. and Tyrrell and I and assorted others picked up along the way passed our days in the back of the bus, a funny mix brought together by geography and parental desire.

2   Entrance to school brings with it forms and releases and assessments. Mercy relied on a series of tests, mostly the Stanford-Binet,[4] for placement, and somehow the results of my tests got confused with those of another student named Rose. The other Rose apparently didn't do very well, for I was placed in the vocational track, a euphemism for the bottom level. Neither I nor my parents realized what this meant. We had no sense that Business Math, Typing, and English-Level D were dead ends. The current spate of reports on the schools criticizes parents for not involving themselves in the education of their children. But how would someone like Tommy Rose, with his two years of Italian schooling, know what to ask? And what sort of pressure could an exhausted waitress apply? The error went undetected, and I remained in the vocational track for two years. What a place.

3   My homeroom was supervised by Brother Dill, a troubled and unstable man who also taught freshman English. When his class drifted away from him, which was often, his voice would rise in paranoid accusations, and occasionally he would lose control and shake or smack us. I hadn't been there two months when one of his brisk, face-turning slaps had my glasses sliding down the aisle. Physical education was also pretty harsh. Our teacher was a stubby ex-lineman who had played old-time pro ball in the Midwest. He routinely had us grabbing our ankles to receive his stinging paddle across our butts. He did that, he said, to make men of us. "Rose," he bellowed on our first encounter; me standing geeky in line in my baggy shorts. " 'Rose'? What the hell kind of name is that?"

4   "Italian, sir," I squeaked.

5   "Italian! Ho. Rose, do you know the sound a bag of shit makes when it hits the wall?"

6   "No, sir."

7   "Wop!"[5]

---

[1]*Nembutal:* trade name for pentobarbital, a sedative drug.
[2]*the dozens:* a verbal game of African origin in which competitors try to top each other's insults.
[3]*Little Richard, Fats Domino, Chuck Berry, the Coasters:* popular Black musicians of the 1950s.
[4]*Stanford-Binet:* an IQ test.
[5]*Wop:* derogatory term for Italian.

Sophomore English was taught by Mr. Mitropetros. He was a large, bejew- 8
eled man who managed the parking lot at the Shrine Auditorium. He would
crow and preen and list for us the stars he'd brushed against. We'd ask questions and glance knowingly and snicker, and all that fueled the poor guy to
brag some more. Parking cars was his night job. He had little training in English, so his lesson plan for his day work had us reading the district's required
text, *Julius Caesar*, aloud for the semester. We'd finish the play way before the
twenty weeks was up, so he'd have us switch parts again and again and start
again: Dave Snyder, the fastest guy at Mercy, muscling through Caesar to the
breathless squeals of Calpurnia, as interpreted by Steve Fusco, a surfer who
owned the school's most envied paneled wagon. Week ten and Dave and Steve
would take on new roles, as would we all, and render a water-logged Cassius
and a Brutus that are beyond my powers of description.

Spanish I—taken in the second year—fell into the hands of a new recruit. 9
Mr. Montez was a tiny man, slight, five foot six at the most, soft-spoken and
delicate. Spanish was a particularly rowdy class, and Mr. Montez was as prepared for it as a doily maker at a hammer throw. He would tap his pencil to
a room in which Steve Fusco was propelling spitballs from his heavy lips, in
which Mike Dweetz was taunting Billy Hawk, a half-Indian, half-Spanish,
reed-thin, quietly explosive boy. The vocational track at Our Lady of Mercy
mixed kids traveling in from South L.A. with South Bay surfers and a few
Slavs and Chicanos from the harbors of San Pedro. This was a dangerous mis-
cellany: surfers and hodads[6] and South-Central blacks all ablaze to the metro-
nomic tapping of Hector Montez's pencil.

One day Billy lost it. Out of the corner of my eye I saw him strike out with 10
his right arm and catch Dweetz across the neck. Quick as a spasm, Dweetz
was out of his seat, scattering desks, cracking Billy on the side of the head,
right behind the eye. Snyder and Fusco and others broke it up, but the room
felt hot and close and naked. Mr. Montez's tenuous authority was finally
ripped to shreds, and I think everyone felt a little strange about that. The cha-
rade was over, and when it came down to it, I don't think any of the kids really
wanted it to end this way. They had pushed and pushed and bullied their way
into a freedom that both scared and embarrassed them.

Students will float to the mark you set. I and the others in the vocational 11
classes were bobbing in pretty shallow water. Vocational education has aimed
at increasing the economic opportunities of students who do not do well in
our schools. Some serious programs succeed in doing that, and through exceptional teachers—like Mr. Gross in *Horace's Compromise*[7]—students learn to
develop hypotheses and troubleshoot, reason through a problem, and communicate effectively—the true job skills. The vocational track, however, is most
often a place for those who are just not making it, a dumping ground for the
disaffected. There were a few teachers who worked hard at education; young
Brother Slattery, for example, combined a stern voice with weekly quizzes to

---

[6]*hodads:* nonsurfers.
[7]*Horace's Compromise:* a book on American education by Theodore Sizer. See p. 496.

try to pass along to us a skeletal outline of world history. But mostly the teachers had no idea of how to engage the imaginations of us kids who were scuttling along at the bottom of the pond.

12   And the teachers would have needed some inventiveness, for none of us was groomed for the classroom. It wasn't just that I didn't know things—didn't know how to simplify algebraic fractions, couldn't identify different kinds of clauses, bungled Spanish translations—but that I had developed various faulty and inadequate ways of doing algebra and making sense of Spanish. Worse yet, the years of defensive turning out in elementary school had given me a way to escape quickly while seeming at least half alert. During my time in Voc. Ed., I developed further into a mediocre student and a somnambulant problem solver, and that affected the subjects I did have the wherewithal to handle: I detested Shakespeare; I got bored with history. My attention flitted here and there. I fooled around in class and read my books indifferently—the intellectual equivalent of playing with your food. I did what I had to do to get by, and I did it with half a mind.

13   But I did learn things about people and eventually came into my own socially. I liked the guys in Voc. Ed. Growing up where I did, I understood and admired physical prowess, and there was an abundance of muscle here. There was Dave Snyder, a sprinter and halfback of true quality. Dave's ability and his quick wit gave him a natural appeal, and he was welcome in any clique, though he always kept a little independent. He enjoyed acting the fool and could care less about studies, but he possessed a certain maturity and never caused the faculty much trouble. It was a testament to his independence that he included me among his friends—I eventually went out for track, but I was no jock. Owing to the Latin alphabet and a dearth of *R*s and *S*s, Snyder sat behind Rose, and we started exchanging one-liners and became friends.

14   There was Ted Richard, a much-touted Little League pitcher. He was chunky and had a baby face and came to Our Lady of Mercy as a seasoned street fighter. Ted was quick to laugh and he had a loud, jolly laugh, but when he got angry he'd smile a little smile, the kind that simply raises the corner of the mouth a quarter of an inch. For those who knew, it was an eerie signal. Those who didn't found themselves in big trouble, for Ted was very quick. He loved to carry on what we would come to call philosophical discussions: What is courage? Does God exist? He also loved words, enjoyed picking up big ones like *salubrious* and *equivocal* and using them in our conversations—laughing at himself as the word hit a chuckhole rolling off his tongue. Ted didn't do all that well in school—baseball and parties and testing the courage he'd speculated about took up his time. His textbooks were *Argosy* and *Field and Stream*, whatever newspapers he'd find on the bus stop—from the *Daily Worker* to pornography—conversations with uncles or hobos or businessmen he'd meet in a coffee shop, *The Old Man and the Sea*. With hindsight, I can see that Ted was developing into one of those rough-hewn intellectuals whose sources are a mix of the learned and the apocryphal, whose discussions are both assured and sad.

And then there was Ken Harvey. Ken was good-looking in a puffy way 15
and had a full and oily ducktail and was a car enthusiast . . . a hodad. One
day in religion class, he said the sentence that turned out to be one of the most
memorable of the hundreds of thousands I heard in those Voc. Ed. years. We
were talking about the parable of the talents, about achievement, working
hard, doing the best you can do, blah-blah-blah, when the teacher called on
the restive Ken Harvey for an opinion. Ken thought about it, but just for a second, and said (with studied, minimal affect), "I just wanna be average." That
woke me up. Average? Who wants to be average? Then the athletes chimed
in with the clichés that make you want to laryngectomize them, and the
exchange became a platitudinous melee. At the time, I thought Ken's assertion
was stupid, and I wrote him off. But his sentence has stayed with me all these
years, and I think I am finally coming to understand it.

Ken Harvey was grasping for air. School can be a tremendously disori- 16
enting place. No matter how bad the school, you're going to encounter notions
that don't fit with the assumptions and beliefs that you grew up with—maybe
you'll hear these dissonant notions from teachers, maybe from the other students, and maybe you'll read them. You'll also be thrown in with all kinds
of kids from all kinds of backgrounds, and that can be unsettling—this is
especially true in places of rich ethnic and linguistic mix, like the L.A. basin.
You'll see a handful of students far excel you in courses that sound exotic and
that are only in the curriculum of the elite: French, physics, trigonometry. And
all this is happening while you're trying to shape an identity, your body is
changing, and your emotions are running wild. If you're a working-class kid
in the vocational track, the options you'll have to deal with this will be constrained in certain ways: you're defined by your school as "slow": you're
placed in a curriculum that isn't designed to liberate you but to occupy
you, or, if you're lucky, train you, though the training is for work the society
does not esteem; other students are picking up the cues from your school
and your curriculum and interacting with you in particular ways. If you're a
kid like Ted Richard, you turn your back on all this and let your mind roam
where it may. But youngsters like Ted are rare. What Ken and so many
others do is protect themselves from such suffocating madness by taking on
with a vengeance the identity implied in the vocational track. Reject the confusion and frustration by openly defining yourself as the Common Joe. Cham-
pion the average. Rely on your own good sense. Fuck this bullshit. Bullshit, of
course, is everything you—and the others—fear is beyond you: books, essays,
tests, academic scrambling, complexity, scientific reasoning, philosophical
inquiry.

The tragedy is that you have to twist the knife in your own gray matter 17
to make this defense work. You'll have to shut down, have to reject intellectual stimuli or diffuse them with sarcasm, have to cultivate stupidity, have to
convert boredom from a malady into a way of confronting the world. Keep
your vocabulary simple, act stoned when you're not or act more stoned than
you are, flaunt ignorance, materialize your dreams. It is a powerful and effective defense—it neutralizes the insult and the frustration of being a vocational

kid and, when perfected, it drives teachers up the wall, a delightful secondary effect. But like all strong magic, it exacts a price.

18   My own deliverance from the Voc. Ed. world began with sophomore biology. Every student, college prep to vocational, had to take biology, and unlike the other courses, the same person taught all sections. When teaching the vocational group, Brother Clint probably slowed down a bit or omitted a little of the fundamental biochemistry, but he used the same book and more or less the same syllabus across the board. If one class got tough, he could get tougher. He was young and powerful and very handsome, and looks and physical strength were high currency. No one gave him any trouble.

19   I was pretty bad at the dissecting table, but the lectures and the textbook were interesting: plastic overlays that, with each turned page, peeled away skin, then veins and muscle, then organs, down to the very bones that Brother Clint, pointer in hand, would tap out on our hanging skeleton. Dave Snyder was in big trouble, for the study of life—versus the living of it—was sticking in his craw. We worked out a code for our multiple-choice exams. He'd poke me in the back: once for the answer under *A*, twice for *B*, and so on; and when he'd hit the right one, I'd look up to the ceiling as though I were lost in thought. Poke: cytoplasm. Poke, poke: methane. Poke, poke, poke: William Harvey. Poke, poke, poke, poke: islets of Langerhans. This didn't work out perfectly, but Dave passed the course, and I mastered the dreamy look of a guy on a record jacket. And something else happened. Brother Clint puzzled over this Voc. Ed. kid who was racking up 98s and 99s on his tests. He checked the school's records and discovered the error. He recommended that I begin my junior year in the College Prep program. According to all I've read since, such a shift, as one report put it, is virtually impossible. Kids at that level rarely cross tracks. The telling thing is how chancy both my placement into and exit from Voc. Ed. was; neither I nor my parents had anything to do with it. I lived in one world during spring semester, and when I came back to school in the fall, I was living in another.

20   Switching to College Prep was a mixed blessing. I was an erratic student. I was undisciplined. And I hadn't caught onto the rules of the game: why work hard in a class that didn't grab my fancy? I was also hopelessly behind in math. Chemistry was hard; toying with my chemistry set years before hadn't prepared me for the chemist's equations. Fortunately, the priest who taught both chemistry and second-year algebra was also the school's athletic director. Membership on the track team covered me; I knew I wouldn't get lower than a C. U.S. history was taught pretty well, and I did okay. But civics was taken over by a football coach who had trouble reading the textbook aloud—and reading aloud was the centerpiece of his pedagogy. College Prep at Mercy was certainly an improvement over the vocational program—at least it carried some status—but the social science curriculum was weak, and the mathematics and physical sciences were simply beyond me. I had a miserable quantitative background and ended up copying some assignments and finessing the rest as best I could. Let me try to explain how it feels to see again and again material you should once have learned but didn't.

You are given a problem. It requires you to simplify algebraic fractions or 21
to multiply expressions containing square roots. You know this is pretty basic
material because you've seen it for years. Once a teacher took some time with
you, and you learned how to carry out these operations. Simple versions, anyway. But that was a year or two or more in the past, and these are more complex versions, and now you're not sure. And this, you keep telling yourself, is
ninth- or even eighth-grade stuff.

Next it's a word problem. This is also old hat. The basic elements are as 22
familiar as story characters: trains speeding so many miles per hour or shadows of buildings angling so many degrees. Maybe you know enough, have sat
through enough explanations, to be able to begin setting up the problem: "If
one train is going this fast . . ." or "This shadow is really one line of a triangle . . ." Then: "Let's see . . ." "How did Jones do this?" "Hmmmm." "No."
"No, that won't work." Your attention wavers. You wonder about other things:
a football game, a dance, that cute new checker at the market. You try to focus
on the problem again. You scribble on paper for a while, but the tension wins
out and your attention flits elsewhere. You crumple the paper and begin day-
dreaming to ease the frustration.

The particulars will vary, but in essence this is what a number of students 23
go through, especially those in so-called remedial classes. They open their textbooks and see once again the familiar and impenetrable formulas and dia-
grams and terms that have stumped them for years. There is no excitement
here. *No* excitement. Regardless of what the teacher says, this is not a new challenge. There is, rather, embarrassment and frustration and, not surprisingly,
some anger in being reminded once again of long-standing inadequacies. No
wonder so many students finally attribute their difficulties to something
inborn, organic: "That part of my brain just doesn't work." Given the troubling
histories many of these students have, it's miraculous that any of them can lift
the shroud of hopelessness sufficiently to make deliverance from these classes
possible.

Through this entire period, my father's health was deteriorating with cruel 24
momentum. His arteriosclerosis progressed to the point where a simple nick
on his shin wouldn't heal. Eventually it ulcerated and widened. Lou Minton
would come by daily to change the dressing. We tried renting an oscillating
bed—which we placed in the front room—to force blood through the con-
stricted arteries in my father's legs. The bed hummed through the night, moving in place to ward off the inevitable. The ulcer continued to spread, and the
doctors finally had to amputate. My grandfather had lost his leg in a stock-
yard accident. Now my father too was crippled. His convalescence was slow
but steady, and the doctors placed him in the Santa Monica Rehabilitation Center, a sun-bleached building that opened out onto the warm spray of the
Pacific. The place gave him some strength and some color and some training
in walking with an artificial leg. He did pretty well for a year or so until he
slipped and broke his hip. He was confined to a wheelchair after that, and the
confinement contributed to the diminishing of his body and spirit.

I am holding a picture of him. He is sitting in his wheelchair and smiling 25 at the camera. The smile appears forced, unsteady, seems to quaver, though it is frozen in silver nitrate. He is in his mid-sixties and looks eighty. Late in my junior year, he had a stroke and never came out of the resulting coma. After that, I would see him only in dreams, and to this day that is how I join him. Sometimes the dreams are sad and grisly and primal: my father lying in a bed soaked with his suppuration,[8] holding me, rocking me. But sometimes the dreams bring him back to me healthy: him talking to me on an empty street, or buying some pictures to decorate our old house, or transformed somehow into someone strong and adept with tools and the physical.

26   Jack MacFarland couldn't have come into my life at a better time. My father was dead, and I had logged up too many years of scholastic indifference. Mr. MacFarland had a master's degree from Columbia and decided, at twenty-six, to find a little school and teach his heart out. He never took any credentialing courses, couldn't bear to, he said, so he had to find employment in a private system. He ended up at Our Lady of Mercy teaching five sections of senior English. He was a beatnik who was born too late. His teeth were stained, he tucked his sorry tie in between the third and fourth buttons of his shirt, and his pants were chronically wrinkled. At first, we couldn't believe this guy, thought he slept in his car. But within no time, he had us so startled with work that we didn't much worry about where he slept or if he slept at all. We wrote three or four essays a month. We read a book every two to three weeks, starting with the *Iliad* and ending up with Hemingway. He gave us a quiz on the reading every other day. He brought a prep school curriculum to Mercy High.

27   MacFarland's lectures were crafted, and as he delivered them he would pace the room jiggling a piece of chalk in his cupped hand, using it to scribble on the board the names of all the writers and philosophers and plays and novels he was weaving into his discussion. He asked questions often, raised everything from Zeno's paradox to the repeated last line of Frost's "Stopping by Woods on a Snowy Evening." He slowly and carefully built up our knowledge of Western intellectual history—with facts, with connections, with speculations. We learned about Greek philosophy, about Dante, the Elizabethan world view, the Age of Reason, existentialism. He analyzed poems with us, had us reading sections from John Ciardi's *How Does a Poem Mean?*, making a potentially difficult book accessible with his own explanations. We gave oral reports on poems Ciardi didn't cover. We imitated the styles of Conrad, Hemingway, and *Time* magazine. We wrote and talked, wrote and talked. The man immersed us in language.

28   Even MacFarland's barbs were literary. If Jim Fitzsimmons, hung over and irritable, tried to smart-ass him, he'd rejoin with a flourish that would spark the indomitable Skip Madison—who'd lost his front teeth in a hapless tackle—to flick his tongue through the gap and opine, "good chop," drawing out the single "o" in stinging indictment. Jack MacFarland, this tobacco-stained intellectual, brandished linguistic weapons of a kind I hadn't encountered before.

---

[8]*suppuration:* discharge from wounds.

Here was this *egghead*, for God's sake, keeping some pretty difficult people in line. And from what I heard, Mike Dweetz and Steve Fusco and all the notorious Voc. Ed. crowd settled down as well when MacFarland took the podium. Though a lot of guys groused in the schoolyard, it just seemed that giving trouble to this particular teacher was a silly thing to do. Tomfoolery, not to mention assault, had no place in the world he was trying to create for us, and instinctively everyone knew that. If nothing else, we all recognized MacFarland's considerable intelligence and respected the hours he put into his work. It came to this: the troublemaker would look foolish rather than daring. Even Jim Fitzsimmons was reading *On the Road* and turning his incipient alcoholism to literary ends.

There were some lives that were already beyond Jack MacFarland's min- 29
istrations, but mine was not. I started reading again as I hadn't since elementary school. I would go into our gloomy little bedroom or sit at the dinner table while, on the television, Danny McShane was paralyzing Mr. Moto with the atomic drop, and work slowly back through *Heart of Darkness*, trying to catch the words in Conrad's sentences. I certainly was not MacFarland's best student; most of the other guys in College Prep, even my fellow slackers, had better backgrounds than I did. But I worked very hard, for MacFarland had hooked me. He tapped my old interest in reading and creating stories. He gave me a way to feel special by using my mind. And he provided a role model that wasn't shaped on physical prowess alone, and something inside me that I wasn't quite aware of responded to that. Jack MacFarland established a literacy club, to borrow a phrase of Frank Smith's, and invited me—invited all of us—to join.

There's been a good deal of research and speculation suggesting that the 30
acknowledgment of school performance with extrinsic rewards—smiling faces, stars, numbers, grades—diminishes the intrinsic satisfaction children experience by engaging in reading or writing or problem solving. While it's certainly true that we've created an educational system that encourages our best and brightest to become cynical grade collectors and, in general, have developed an obsession with evaluation and assessment, I must tell you that venal though it may have been, I loved getting good grades from MacFarland. I now know how subjective grades can be, but then they came tucked in the back of essays like bits of scientific data, some sort of spectroscopic readout that said, objectively and publicly, that I had made something of value. I suppose I'd been mediocre for too long and enjoyed a public redefinition. And I suppose the workings of my mind, such as they were, had been private for too long. My linguistic play moved into the world; . . . these papers with their circled, red B-pluses and A-minuses linked my mind to something outside it. I carried them around like a club emblem.

One day in the December of my senior year, Mr. MacFarland asked me 31
where I was going to go to college. I hadn't thought much about it. Many of the students I teach today spent their last year in high school with a physics text in one hand and the Stanford catalog in the other, but I wasn't even aware of what "entrance requirements" were. My folks would say that they wanted

me to go to college and be a doctor, but I don't know how seriously I ever took that; it seemed a sweet thing to say, a bit of supportive family chatter, like telling a gangly daughter she's graceful. The reality of higher education wasn't in my scheme of things: no one in the family had gone to college; only two of my uncles had completed high school. I figured I'd get a night job and go to the local junior college because I knew that Snyder and Company were going there to play ball. But I hadn't even prepared for that. When I finally said, "I don't know," MacFarland looked down at me—I was seated in his office—and said, "Listen, you can write."

32   My grades stank. I had A's in biology and a handful of B's in a few English and social science classes. All the rest were C's—or worse. MacFarland said I would do well in his class and laid down the law about doing well in the others. Still, the record for my first three years wouldn't have been acceptable to any four-year school. To nobody's surprise, I was turned down flat by USC and UCLA. But Jack MacFarland was on the case. He had received his bachelor's degree from Loyola University, so he made calls to old professors and talked to somebody in admissions and wrote me a strong letter. Loyola finally accepted me as a probationary student. I would be on trial for the first year, and if I did okay, I would be granted regular status. MacFarland also intervened to get me a loan, for I could never have afforded a private college without it. Four more years of religion classes and four more years of boys at one school, girls at another. But at least I was going to college. Amazing.

33   In my last year of high school, I elected a special English course fashioned by Mr. MacFarland, and it was through this elective that there arose at Mercy a fledgling literati. Art Mitz, the editor of the school newspaper and a very smart guy, was the kingpin. He was joined by me and by Mark Dever, a quiet boy who wrote beautifully and who would die before he was forty. MacFarland occasionally invited us to his apartment, and those visits became the high point of our apprenticeship: we'd clamp on our training wheels and drive to his salon.

34   He lived in a cramped and cluttered place near the airport, tucked away in the kind of building that architectural critic Reyner Banham calls a *dingbat*. Books were all over: stacked, piled, tossed, and crated, underlined and dog eared, well worn and new. Cigarette ashes crusted with coffee in saucers or spilled over the sides of motel ashtrays. The little bedroom had, along two of its walls, bricks and boards loaded with notes, magazines, and oversized books. The kitchen joined the living room, and there was a stack of German newspapers under the sink. I had never seen anything like it: a great flophouse of language furnished by City Lights and Café le Metro. I read every title. I flipped through paperbacks and scanned jackets and memorized names: Gogol, *Finnegans Wake*, Djuna Barnes, Jackson Pollock, *A Coney Island of the Mind*, F. O. Matthiessen's *American Renaissance*, all sorts of Freud, *Troubled Sleep*, Man Ray, *The Education of Henry Adams*, Richard Wright, *Film as Art*, William Butler Yeats, Marguerite Duras, *Redburn*, *A Season in Hell*, *Kapital*. On the cover of Alain-Fournier's *The Wanderer* was an Edward Gorey drawing of a young man on a road winding into dark trees. By the hotplate sat a strange

Kafka novel called *Amerika,* in which an adolescent hero crosses the Atlantic to find the Nature Theater of Oklahoma. Art and Mark would be talking about a movie or the school newspaper, and I would be consuming my English teacher's library. It was heady stuff. I felt like a Pop Warner[9] athlete on steroids.

Art, Mark, and I would buy stogies and triangulate from MacFarland's apartment to the Cinema, which now shows X-rated films but was then L.A.'s premier art theater, and then to the musty Cherokee Bookstore in Hollywood to hobnob with beatnik homosexuals—smoking, drinking bourbon and coffee, and trying out awkward phrases we'd gleaned from our mentor's bookshelves. I was happy and precocious and a little scared as well, for Hollywood Boulevard was thick with a kind of decadence that was foreign to the South Side. After the Cherokee, we would head back to the security of MacFarland's apartment, slaphappy with hipness.

Let me be the first to admit that there was a good deal of adolescent passion in this embrace of the avant-garde: self-absorption, sexually charged pedantry, an elevation of the odd and abandoned. Still it was a time during which I absorbed an awful lot of information: long lists of titles, images from expressionist paintings, new wave shibboleths,[10] snippets of philosophy, and names that read like Steve Fusco's misspellings—Goethe, Nietzsche, Kierkegaard. Now this is hardly the stuff of deep understanding. But it was an introduction, a phrase book, a Baedeker[11] to a vocabulary of ideas, and it felt good at the time to know all these words. With hindsight I realize how layered and important that knowledge was.

It enabled me to do things in the world. I could browse bohemian bookstores in far-off, mysterious Hollywood; I could go to the Cinema and see events through the lenses of European directors; and, most of all, I could share an evening, talk that talk, with Jack MacFarland, the man I most admired at the time. Knowledge was becoming a bonding agent. Within a year or two, the persona of the disaffected hipster would prove too cynical, too alienated to last. But for a time it was new and exciting: it provided a critical perspective on society, and it allowed me to act as though I were living beyond the limiting boundaries of South Vermont.[12]

Questions for Discussion

1. How does Rose's opening description of his friends on the bus set the scene for the experiences and the ideas that he develops in the selection? Why is his opening effective?

2. Why is Rose placed in the vocational education track? Why does he stay there for two years? How does Rose feel about the quality of the teachers in the vocational education track? What do you think Rose learns from being in this track?

---

[9]*Pop Warner:* a nationwide youth athletics organization.
[10]*new wave shibboleths:* trendy phrases or jargon.
[11]*Baedeker:* travel guide.
[12]*South Vermont:* a street in an economically depressed area of Los Angeles.

3. How does Ken Harvey's assertion, "I just wanna be average," help to explain his behavior in the vocational track? How does Harvey's statement have a long-term impact on Rose's educational choices? How do you feel about tracking?
4. How does Rose get switched into the college prep track? Why is the switch a "mixed blessing"? Why is Rose confused about his educational goals?
5. How does Jack MacFarland help Rose to get accepted to college? Do you think Rose was just lucky to be placed in Jack MacFarland's class or do you think that Rose's native intelligence helped him to find a positive role model?
6. How accurate do you think Rose's story about vocational tracking and the effects of poverty on a student's chance to get a decent education is in comparison to experiences you have had or information you have been exposed to through books and popular culture?
7. From reading Rose's article, what role do you think he feels the community should assume in relationship to students who come from poor or dysfunctional families that do not provide a stable home life and the encouragement to do well in school? What role do you think the community should take?

Ideas for Writing

1. Write an essay in which you discuss the struggles of a high school friend who lived "on the boundary" as Rose describes it in his essay. What happened to this person? In your final paragraphs develop some conclusions about what you think are the most serious disadvantages that a person who lives on the boundary must overcome. Consider also the advantages a person who lives on the boundary might have.
2. Write an essay in which you explain why you think that some students achieve their educational potential in spite of the discrimination that they must overcome while others do not. Refer to examples from your junior and high school experiences to support your point of view.
3. Interview a guidance counselor at your college or high school who works with students whose parents did not attend college. Try to learn more about the lives of these students and what helps them to succeed in college. Write an article that discusses what you have discovered for your class and/or a campus paper.

Corla Hawkins

Jonathan Kozol

Jonathan Kozol (b. 1936) has worked as a writer and social critic all of his life. He is best known for his nonfiction that reveals the corruption in the public school systems where poor children are not given a fair chance to get an education. Kozol won the National Book Award in 1967 for *Death at an Early Age*. Other of his works include: *Prisoner of Silence: Breaking the Bonds of Adult Illiteracy in the United States* (1980), *Alternative Schools: A Guide for Educators and Parents* (1982), and *Rachel and Her Children: Homeless Families in America* (1988). The selection we have included, "Corla Hawkins," is excerpted from his newest book *Savage Inequalities* (1992), which exposes the failure of public education in inner-city schools: "Looking around some of these inner-city schools, where filth and disrepair were worse than anything I'd ever seen in 1964, I often wondered why we would agree to let our children go to school in places where no politician, school board president, or business CEO would dream of working."

Journal

Describe the elementary or junior high school teacher from whom you learned the most. What did his or her classroom look like? How did you learn in this class?

Even in the most unhappy schools there are certain classes that stand out like little islands of excitement, energy and hope. One of these classes is a combination fifth and sixth grade at Bethune, taught by a woman, maybe 40 years of age, named Corla Hawkins.

The classroom is full of lively voices when I enter. The children are at 2 work, surrounded by a clutter of big dictionaries, picture books and gadgets, science games and plants and colorful milk cartons, which the teacher purchased out of her own salary. An oversized Van Gogh collection, open to a print of a sunflower, is balanced on a table-ledge next to a fish tank and a turtle tank. Next to the table is a rocking chair. Handwritten signs are on all sides: "Getting to know you," "Keeping you safe," and, over a wall that holds some artwork by the children, "Mrs. Hawkins's Academy of Fine Arts." Near the windows, the oversized leaves of several wild-looking plants partially cover rows of novels, math books, and a new World Book Encyclopedia. In the opposite corner is a "Science Learning Board" that holds small packets which contain bulb sockets, bulbs and wires, lenses, magnets, balance scales and pliers. In front of the learning board is a microscope. Several rugs are thrown around the floor. On another table are a dozen soda bottles sealed with glue and lying sideways, filled with colored water.

The room looks like a cheerful circus tent. In the center of it all, within the 3 rocking chair, and cradling a newborn in her arms, is Mrs. Hawkins.

The 30 children in the class are seated in groups of six at five of what she 4 calls "departments." Each department is composed of six desks pushed together to create a table. One of the groups is doing math, another something that they call "math strategy." A third is doing reading. Of the other two groups, one is doing something they describe as "mathematics art"—painting composites of geometric shapes—and the other is studying "careers," which on this morning is a writing exercise about successful business leaders who began their lives in poverty. Near the science learning board a young-looking woman is preparing a new lesson that involves a lot of gadgets she has taken from a closet.

"This woman," Mrs. Hawkins tells me, "is a parent. She wanted to help 5 me. So I told her, 'If you don't have somebody to keep your baby, bring the baby here. I'll be the mother. I can do it.'"

As we talk, a boy who wears big glasses brings his book to her and asks 6 her what the word *salvation* means. She shows him how to sound it out, then tells him, "Use your dictionary if you don't know what it means." When a boy at the reading table argues with the boy beside him, she yells out, "You ought to be ashamed. You woke my baby."

7   After 15 minutes she calls out that it is time to change their tables. The children get up and move to new departments. As each group gets up to move to the next table, one child stays behind to introduce the next group to the lesson.

8   "This is the point of it," she says. "I'm teaching them three things. Number one: self-motivation. Number two: self-esteem. Number three: you help your sister and your brother. I tell them they're responsible for one another. I give no grades in the first marking period because I do not want them to be too competitive. Second marking period, you get your grade on what you've taught your neighbors at your table. Third marking period, I team them two-and-two. You get the same grade as your partner. Fourth marking period, I tell them, 'Every fish swims on its own.' But I wait a while for that. The most important thing for me is that they teach each other. . . .

9   "All this stuff"—she gestures at the clutter in the room—"I bought myself because it never works to order things through the school system. I bought the VCR. I bought the rocking chair at a flea market. I got these books here for ten cents apiece at a flea market. I bought that encyclopedia"—she points at the row of World Books—"so that they can do their research right here in this room."

10   I ask her if the class reads well enough to handle these materials. "Most of them can read some of these books. What they cannot read, another child can read to them," she says.

11   "I tell the parents, 'Any time your child says, "I don't have no homework," call me up. Call me at home.' Because I give them homework every night and weekends too. Holidays I give them extra. Every child in this classroom has my phone."

12   Cradling the infant in her lap, she says, "I got to buy a playpen."

13   The bottles of colored water, she explains, are called "wave bottles." The children make them out of plastic soda bottles which they clean and fill with water and food coloring and seal with glue. She takes one in her hand and rolls it slowly to and fro. "It shows them how waves form," she says. "I let them keep them at their desks. Some of them hold them in their hands while they're at work. It seems to calm them: seeing the water cloud up like a storm and then grow clear. . . .

14   "I take them outside every day during my teacher-break. On Saturdays we go to places like the art museum. Tuesdays, after school, I coach the drill team. Friday afternoons I tutor parents for their GED [high school equivalency exam]. If you're here this afternoon, I do the gospel choir."

15   When I ask about her own upbringing, she replies, "I went to school here in Chicago. My mother believed I was a 'gifted' child, but the system did not challenge me and I was bored at school. Fortunately one of my mother's neighbors was a teacher and she used to talk to me and help me after school. If it were not for her I doubt that I'd have thought that I could go to college. I promised myself I would return that favor."

At the end of class I go downstairs to see the principal, and then return to 16 a second-floor room to see the gospel choir in rehearsal. When I arrive, they've already begun. Thirty-five children, ten of whom are boys, are standing in rows before a piano player. Next to the piano, Mrs. Hawkins stands and leads them through the words. The children range in age from sixth and seventh graders to three second graders and three tiny children, one of whom is Mrs. Hawkins's daughter, who are kindergarten pupils in the school.

They sing a number of gospel songs with Mrs. Hawkins pointing to each 17 group—soprano, alto, bass—when it is their turn to join in. When they sing, "I love you, Lord," their voices lack the energy she wants. She interrupts and shouts at them, "Do you love Him? Do you?" They sing louder. The children look as if they're riveted to her directions.

"This next song," she says, "I dreamed about this. This song is my 18 favorite."

The piano begins. The children start to clap their hands. When she gives 19 the signal they begin to sing:

Clap your hands! 20
Stamp your feet!
Get on up
Out of your seats!
Help me
Lift 'em up, Lord!
Help me
Lift 'em up!

When a child she calls "Reverend Joe" does not come in at the right note, 21 Mrs. Hawkins stops and says to him: "I thought you told me you were saved!"

The children smile. The boy called "Reverend Joe" stands up a little 22 straighter. Then the piano starts again. The sound of children clapping and then stamping with the music fills the room. Mrs. Hawkins waves her arms. Then, as the children start, she also starts to sing.

Help me lift 'em up, Lord! 23
Help me lift 'em up!

There are wonderful teachers such as Corla Hawkins almost everywhere 24 in urban schools, and sometimes a number of such teachers in a single school. It is tempting to focus on these teachers and, by doing this, to paint a hopeful portrait of the good things that go on under adverse conditions. There is, indeed, a growing body of such writing; and these books are sometimes very popular, because they are consoling.

The rationale behind much of this writing is that pedagogic problems in 25 our cities are not chiefly matters of injustice, inequality or segregation, but of insufficient information about teaching strategies: If we could simply learn "what works" in Corla Hawkins's room, we'd then be in a position to repeat this all over Chicago and in every other system.

But what is unique in Mrs. Hawkins's classroom is not what she does but 26 who she is. Warmth and humor and contagious energy cannot be replicated and cannot be written into any standardized curriculum. If they could, it would have happened long ago; for wonderful teachers have been heroized in books and movies for at least three decades. And the problems of Chicago are, in any case, not those of insufficient information. If Mrs. Hawkins's fellow fifth grade teachers simply needed information, they could get it easily by walking 20 steps across the hall and visiting her room. The problems are systemic: The number of teachers over 60 years of age in the Chicago system is twice that of the teachers under 30. The salary scale, too low to keep exciting, youthful teachers in the system, leads the city to rely on low-paid subs, who represent more than a quarter of Chicago's teaching force. "We have teachers," Mrs. Hawkins says, "who only bother to come in three days a week. One of these teachers comes in usually around nine-thirty. You ask her how she can expect the kids to care about their education if the teacher doesn't even come until nine-thirty. She answers you, 'It makes no difference. Kids like these aren't going anywhere.' The school board thinks it's saving money on the subs. I tell them, 'Pay now or pay later.' "

27   But even substitute teachers in Chicago are quite frequently in short supply. On an average morning in Chicago, 5,700 children in 190 classrooms come to school to find they have no teacher. The number of children who have no teachers on a given morning in Chicago's public schools is nearly twice the student population of New Trier High School in nearby Winnetka.

28   "We have been in this class a whole semester," says a 15-year-old at Du Sable High, one of Chicago's poorest secondary schools, "and they still can't find us a teacher."

29   A student in auto mechanics at Du Sable says he'd been in class for 16 weeks before he learned to change a tire. His first teacher quit at the beginning of the year. Another teacher slept through most of the semester. He would come in, the student says, and tell the students, "You can talk. Just keep it down." Soon he would be asleep.

30   "Let's be real," the student says. "Most of us ain't going to college. . . . We could have used a class like this."

31   The shortage of teachers finds its parallel in a shortage of supplies. A chemistry teacher at the school reports that he does not have beakers, water, bunsen burners. He uses a popcorn popper as a substitute for a bunsen burner, and he cuts down plastic soda bottles to make laboratory dishes.

32   Many of these schools make little effort to instruct their failing students. "If a kid comes in not reading," says an English teacher at Chicago's South Shore High, "he goes out not reading."

33   Another teacher at the school, where only 170 of 800 freshmen graduate with their class, indicates that the dropout rate makes teaching easier. "We lose all the dregs by the second year," he says.

34   "We're a general high school," says the head of counseling at Chicago's Calumet High School. "We have second- and third-grade readers. . . . We hope to do better, but we won't die if we don't."

35   At Bowen High School, on the South Side of Chicago, students have two or three "study halls" a day, in part to save the cost of teachers. "Not much

studying goes on in study hall," a supervising teacher says. "I let the students play cards. . . . I figure they might get some math skills out of it."

At the Lathrop Elementary School, a short walk from the corner lot where 36 Dr. King resided in North Lawndale, there are no hoops on the basketball court and no swings in the playground. For 21 years, according to the *Chicago Tribune*, the school has been without a library. Library books, which have been piled and abandoned in the lunch room of the school, have "sprouted mold," the paper says. Some years ago the school received the standard reading textbooks out of sequence: The second workbook in the reading program came to the school before the first. The principal, uncertain what to do with the wrong workbook, was told by school officials it was "all right to work backwards. . . ."

This degree of equanimity in failure, critics note, has led most affluent par- 37 ents in Chicago to avoid the public system altogether. The school board president in 1989, although a teacher and administrator in the system for three decades, did not send his children to the public schools. Nor does Mayor Richard Daley, Jr., nor did any of the previous four mayors who had school-age children.

"Nobody in his right mind," says one of the city's aldermen, "would send 38 [his] kids to public school."

Many suburban legislators representing affluent school districts use terms 39 such as "sinkhole" when opposing funding for Chicago's children. "We can't keep throwing money," said Governor Thompson in 1988, "into a black hole."

The *Chicago Tribune* notes that, when this phrase is used, people hasten to 40 explain that it is not intended as a slur against the race of many of Chicago's children. "But race," says the *Tribune*, "never is far from the surface. . . ."

Questions for Discussion

1. Explain why you agree or disagree with Hawkins' assertion: "The most important thing for me is that they teach each other." How does Hawkins create a sense of community in her classroom? How do the students learn in her classroom?
2. Why is Corla Hawkins' devoted to her students? Have you had teachers like Corla Hawkins? Did you learn more in their classes? Explain your answer.
3. Do you think Corla Hawkins is a gifted teacher? What is your definition of a gifted teacher?
4. Why does Kozol think that having other teachers use Mrs. Hawkins' approach to teaching would not necessarily improve the quality of education in the poor neighborhoods of Chicago or in other urban neighborhoods in large cities? Explain why you agree or disagree with Kozol.
5. What problems in the educational systems in poor urban neighborhoods make learning at school impossible? Did Kozol's statistics on the high rate of failure in the Chicago schools shock you? What do you think could be done to reverse this frightening reality in urban public schools?
6. Kozol points out that the affluent parents and even the mayor of the city send their children to private schools. How does their lack of support for the public schools affect the quality of public education? What do you think about their decision?

Ideas For Writing

1. Write an essay in which you discuss the quality of the public education in your community's schools. What impact has the quality of public schools had on your family? What solutions have been proposed in your community to improve the quality of public education?

2. After reading this short excerpt from *Savage Inequalities,* what hope do you think Kozol has for the future of public education? What solutions do you think are implied in his argument? What hope do you have for the future of public education? What changes would you implement to improve the quality of education in your community?

3. Research model and alternative schools. Write an essay that profiles several of these types of schools and then discuss ways that the educational concepts applied in these model or alternative schools could be used to improve the quality of education at schools in your community.

Education-Based Community Service at Rutgers University

Benjamin Barber

Benjamin Barber (b. 1939) earned his Certificate in 1959 at the London School of Economics, a B.A. from Grinnell College in 1960, and his Ph.D. from Harvard in 1966. Barber is the Director of the Walt Whitman Center of Political Science for the Culture and Politics of Democracy at Rutgers University. He writes regularly for many publications such as *Harper's, The New York Times,* and *The Atlantic.* His recent books include *Strong Democracy: Participatory Politics for a New Age* (1984) and *The Conquest of Politics* (1988). The following selection, which outlines a service learning curriculum at Rutgers University, is excerpted from Barber's newest book, *An Aristocracy of Everyone: The Politics of Education and the Future of America* (1992).

Journal

Write about an experience doing volunteer work for an agency at your school or in your community. Alternatively, discuss a film or television movie that featured characters involved in volunteer work.

In the spring of 1988, President Edward Bloustein of Rütgers University gave a commencement address in the form of a meditation on the sad state into which America's large universities had fallen—the pathologies of community and the classroom that had created a sense of crisis in the nation at large. Remembering his own wartime experience in a proto-multicultural army, he proposed a mandatory program of citizen education and community service as a graduation requirement for all students at the State University of New Jersey. When President Bloustein asked me to chair the committee charged with exploring the idea of service in the academy, and trying to develop a program through which it could be realized, I had no idea how far service learning might take the university. In the course of the next three years, with the support of Bloustein's successor, Francis L. Lawrence, as well as many faculty and students, Rutgers pioneered an extended pilot program in which classroom civic education and practical community service were united in a number of bold new courses and a residence hall devoted to service learning. The Rutgers experience offers a model of how service learning can redefine what it means to teach liberty.

The Rutgers program was premised on nine governing principles, which ₂ were hammered out in a year of discussion among faculty, students, and administrators. The principles, listed below, are remarkable in how they fold notions of community, democracy, and citizenship into pedagogy in an attempt to redress the pathologies of modern education.

1. That to teach the art of citizenship and responsibility is to practice it: so ₃ that teaching in this domain must be about acting and doing as well as about listening and learning, but must also afford an opportunity for reflecting on and discussing what is being done. In practical terms, this means that community service can only be an instrument of education when it is connected to an academic learning experience in a classroom setting. But the corollary is also true, that civic education can only be effective when it encompasses experiential learning of the kind offered by community service or other similar forms of group activity.

2. That the crucial democratic relationship between rights and responsi- ₄ bilities, which have too often been divorced in our society, can only be made visible in a setting of experiential learning where academic discussion is linked to practical activity. In other words, learning about the relationship between civic responsibility and civic rights means exercising the rights and duties of membership in an actual community, whether that community is a classroom, a group project or community service team, or the university/college community at large.

3. That antisocial, discriminatory and other forms of selfish and abusive ₅ or addictive behavior are often a symptom of the breakdown of civic community—both local and societal. This suggests that to remedy many of the problems of alienation and disaffection of the young requires the reconstruction of the civic community, something that a program of civic education based on experiential learning and community service may therefore be better able to accomplish than problem-by-problem piecemeal solutions pursued in isolation from underlying causes.

4. That respect for the full diversity and plurality of American life is pos- ₆ sible only when students have an opportunity to interact outside of the classroom in ways that are, however, the subject of scrutiny and open discussion in the classroom. An experiential learning process that includes both classroom

learning and group work outside the classroom has the greatest likelihood of impacting on student ignorance, intolerance, and prejudice.

7   5. That membership in a community entails responsibilities and duties which are likely to be felt as binding only to the degree individuals feel empowered in the community. As a consequence, empowerment ought to be a significant dimension of education for civic responsibility—particularly in the planning process to establish civic education and community service programs.

8   6. That civic education as experiential learning and community service must not discriminate among economic or other classes of Americans. If equal respect and equal rights are two keys to citizenship in a democracy, then a civic education program must assure that no one is forced to participate merely because they are economically disadvantaged, and no one is exempted from service merely because they are economically privileged.

9   7. That civic education should be communal as well as community-based. If citizen education and experiential learning of the kind offered by community service are to be a lesson in community, the ideal learning unit is not the individual but the small team, where people work together and learn together, experiencing what it means to become a small community together. Civic education programs thus should be built around teams (of say 5 or 10 or 20) rather than around individuals.

10   8. That the point of any community service element of civic education must be to teach citizenship, not charity. If education is aimed at creating citizens, then it will be important to let the young see that service is not just about altruism or charity; or a matter of those who are well-off helping those who are not. It is serving the public interest, which is the same thing as serving enlightened self-interest. Young people serve themselves as members of the community by serving a public good that is also their own. The responsible citizen finally serves liberty.

11   9. That civic education needs to be regarded as an integral part of liberal education and thus should both be mandatory and should receive academic credit. Because citizenship is an acquired art, and because those least likely to be spirited citizens or volunteers in their local or national community are most in need of civic training, an adequate program of citizen training with an opportunity for service needs to be mandatory. There are certain things a democracy simply must teach, employing its full authority to do so: citizenship is first among them.

12   The program Rutgers developed on the foundation of these principles, endorsed by representatives of the student body and by the board of governors and currently being reviewed by duly constituted faculty bodies, calls for

13   **A Mandatory Civic Education Course** organized around (though not limited to) a classroom course with an academic syllabus, but also including a strong and innovative experiential learning focus utilizing group projects. A primary vehicle for these projects will be community service, as one of a number of experiential learning options; while the course will be mandatory, students

will be free to choose community service or nonservice projects as their experiential learning group project. The required course will be buttressed by a program of incentives encouraging students to continue to participate in community service throughout their academic careers at Rutgers.

Course Content will be broad and varied, but should guarantee some coverage of vital civic issues and questions, including the following: 14

1. The nature of the social or civic bond; social contract, legitimacy,   15
authority, freedom, constitutionalism—the key concepts of a political community;
2. The meaning of citizenship—representation versus participation, pas   16
sive versus active forms of civic life; citizenship and service;
3. The university community; its structure and governance; the role of   17
students, faculty, and administrators; questions of empowerment;
4. The place of ethnicity, religion, race, class, gender, and sexual orienta   18
tion in a community: Does equality mean abolishing differences? Or learning to respect and celebrate diversity and inclusiveness? How does a community deal with differences of the kind represented by the disequalizing effects of power and wealth?
5. The nature of service: differences between charity and social responsi   19
bility; between rights and needs or desires. What is the relationship between community service and citizenship? Can service be mandatory? Does a state have the right to mandate the training of citizens or does this violate freedom?
6. The nature of leadership in a democracy: Are there special features to   20
democratic leadership? Do strong leaders create weak followers? What is the relationship between leadership and equality?
7. Cooperation and competition, models of community interaction: How   21
do private and public interests relate in a community?
8. The character of civic communities, educational, local, regional, and   22
national. What is the difference between society and the state? Is America a "community"? Is Rutgers a community? Do its several campuses (Camden, Newark, New Brunswick) constitute a community? What is the relationship between them and the communities in which they are located? What are the real issues of these communities—issues such as sexual harassment, suicide, date rape, homophobia, racism, and distrust of authority?

Variations on the Basic Model will be encouraged within the basic course design,   23
with ample room for significant variations. Individual colleges, schools, and departments will be encouraged to develop their own versions of the course to suit the particular needs of their students and the civic issues particular to their disciplines or areas. Thus, the Engineering School might wish to develop a program around "the responsibilities of scientists," the Mason Gross School for the Performing Arts might wish to pioneer community service options focusing on students performing in and bringing arts education to schools and senior centers in the community, or Douglass College might want to capitalize on its long-standing commitment to encourage women to become active leaders by developing its own appropriate course variations.

Experiential Learning is crucial to the program, for the key difference between   24
the program offered here and traditional civic education approaches is the focus on learning outside the classroom, integrated into the classroom. Stu-

dents will utilize group projects in community service and in other extraseminar group activities as the basis for reading and reflecting on course material. Experiential learning permits students to apply classroom learning to the real world, and to subject real world experience to classroom examination. To plan adequately for an experiential learning focus and to assure that projects are pedagogically sound and responsible to the communities they may engage, particular attention will be given to its design in the planning phase.

25 *The Team Approach* is a special feature of the Rutgers proposal. All experiential learning projects will be group projects where individuals learn in concert with others; where they experience community in part by practicing community during the learning process. We urge special attention be given to the role of groups or teams in the design both of the classroom format and the experiential learning component of the basic course.

26 *Community Service* is only one among the several options for experiential learning, but it will clearly be the choice of a majority of students, and is in fact the centerpiece of the Rutgers program. We believe that community service, when related to citizenship and social responsibility in a disciplined pedagogical setting, is the most powerful form of experiential learning. As such, it is central to our conception of the civic education process.

27 *An Incentive Program for Continuing Service* is built into the Rutgers project, because our objective is to instill in students a spirit of citizenship that is enduring. It is thus vital that the program, though it is centered on the freshman-year course, not be limited to that initial experience, and that there be opportunities for ongoing service and participation throughout the four years of college.

28 The Rutgers pilot program—at this stage it is still experimental and voluntary—is only one among many new efforts at a number of different schools and universities aimed at incorporating service learning into academic curricula. Service learning, in turn, is only one example of a number of approaches that, without abandoning the intellectual integrity of autonomous educational institutions, attempt to give practical meaning to the philosophy which places teaching liberty at the center of liberal education.

29 In a vigorous democracy capable of withstanding the challenges of a complex, often undemocratic, interdependent world, creating new generations of citizens is not a discretionary activity. Freedom is a hothouse plant that flourishes only when it is carefully tended. Without active citizens who see in service not the altruism of charity but the responsibility of citizenship on which liberty ultimately depends, no democracy can function properly or, in the long run, even survive. Without education that treats women and men as whole, as beings who belong to communities of knowledge, there may be no stopping place on the slippery road from dogmatism to nihilism. Without schools that take responsibility for what goes on beyond as well as in the classroom, and work to remove the walls that separate the two worlds, students will continue to bracket off all that they learn from life and keep their lives at arm's length from what they learn. Without teachers who are left alone to teach, students

will fall prey to the suasion of an illiterate society all too willing to make its dollars their tutors.

National service is not merely a good idea; or, as William Buckley has sug- 30 gested, a way to repay the debt owed our "patrimony." It is an indispensable prerequisite of citizenship and thus a condition for democracy's preservation. Democracy does not just "deserve" our gratitude; it demands our participation as a price of survival. The Rutgers program and others like it offer a model that integrates liberal teaching, experiential learning, community service, and citizen education. It also suggests a legislative strategy for establishing a national service requirement without raising up still one more elephantine national bureaucracy. Require service of all Americans through federal guidelines; but permit the requirement to be implemented through service-learning programs housed in schools, universities, and, for those not in the school system, other local institutions, such as the YMCA or the Chamber of Commerce. Employing the nation's schools and colleges as laboratories of citizenship and service might at once offer an attractive way to develop civic service opportunities for all Americans and help educate the young to the obligations of the democratic citizen. This would not only serve democracy, it could restore to our educational institutions a sense of mission they have long lacked.

Questions for Discussion

1. In 1988 President Edward Bloustein of Rutgers University proposed a mandatory program of citizen education and community service. Why did Bloustein think that such a program would help to solve the crisis in modern education? Do you agree or disagree with him?
2. Of the nine principles that form the foundation of the program, discuss the two or three that seem most important. Why did you choose these particular principles?
3. Which of the issues in the course proposed by the Rutgers planning committee would you be most interested in learning more about? Explain your response.
4. Why does the Rutgers model emphasize a group approach to the community service projects? Do you think this collaborative approach would work in your classes? Why or why not?
5. What is the most important difference between the Rutgers program and traditional civic education? Would you prefer to be enrolled in a traditional curriculum or one built on the principles of the Rutgers model? Explain your choice.
6. Barber asserts: "Without active citizens who see in service not the altruism of charity but the responsibility of citizenship on which liberty ultimately depends, no democracy can function properly or, in the long run, even survive." Do you agree or disagree with Barber? Present evidence to support your point of view.

Ideas for Writing

1. Discuss how the Rutgers model could be adapted to work at your college. In shaping your point of view you might want to refer to selections in this chapter to support your proposal.
2. Develop discussion question 5 or 6 into an essay.
3. Develop your journal into an essay.

Cultural Literacy

E. D. Hirsch, Jr.

E. D. Hirsch, Jr. (b. 1928) was born in Tennessee. He earned his B.A. at Cornell University in 1950 and completed his Ph.D. at Yale in 1957. Hirsh has been awarded many distinguished fellowships, including the Guggenheim and the Fulbright. A professor of English at the University of Virginia, Hirsch published a number of articles on cultural literacy in *The New York Times Education Supplement*, *The American Scholar*, and *American Educator*, before his controversial book, *Cultural Literacy: What Every American Needs to Know* (1987), from which the following selection is excerpted, became a national best seller. Hirsch believes that good teaching will only be possible when students share a common body of information. He is a founding member of the federally sponsored Foundation of Literacy Project.

Journal

How were you taught cultural values in junior high school and high school? What is the approach to teaching cultural values at the college or university that you currently attend?

During the period of 1970–1985, the amount of shared knowledge that we have been able to take for granted in communicating with our fellow citizens has also been declining. More and more of our young people don't know things we used to assume they knew.

2   A side effect of the diminution in shared information has been a noticeable increase in the number of articles in such publications as *Newsweek* and the *Wall Street Journal* about the surprising ignorance of the young. My son John, who recently taught Latin in high school and eighth grade, often told me of experiences which indicate that these articles are not exaggerated. In one of his classes he mentioned to his students that Latin, the language they were studying, is a dead language that is no longer spoken. After his pupils had struggled for several weeks with Latin grammar and vocabulary, this news was hard for some of them to accept. One girl raised her hand to challenge my son's claim. "What do they speak in Latin America?" she demanded.

3   At least she had heard of Latin America. Another day my son asked his Latin class if they knew the name of an epic poem by Homer. One pupil shot up his hand and eagerly said, "The Alamo!" Was it just a slip for *The Iliad?* No, he didn't know what the Alamo was, either. To judge from other stories about information gaps in the young, many American schoolchildren are less well informed than this pupil. The following, by Benjamin J. Stein, is an excerpt from one of the most evocative recent accounts of youthful ignorance.

4   I spend a lot of time with teenagers. Besides employing three of them part-time, I frequently conduct focus groups at Los Angeles area high schools to learn about teenagers' attitudes towards movies or television shows or nuclear arms or politicians. . . .

I have not yet found one single student in Los Angeles, in either college 5
or high school, who could tell me the years when World War II was fought.
Nor have I found one who could tell me the years when World War I was
fought. Nor have I found one who knew when the American Civil War was
fought. . . .

A few have known how many U.S. senators California has, but none has 6
known how many Nevada or Oregon has. ("Really? Even though they're so
small?") . . . Only two could tell me where Chicago is, even in the vaguest
terms. (My particular favorite geography lesson was the junior at the University of California at Los Angeles who thought that Toronto must be in Italy.
My second-favorite geography lesson is the junior at USC, a pre-law student,
who thought that Washington, D.C. was in Washington State.) . . .

Only two could even approximately identify Thomas Jefferson. Only one 7
could place the date of the Declaration of Independence. None could name
even one of the first ten amendments to the Constitution or connect them with
the Bill of Rights. . . .

On and on it went. On and on it goes. I have mixed up episodes of igno- 8
rance of facts with ignorance of concepts because it seems to me that there is
a connection. . . . The kids I saw (and there may be lots of others who are different) are not mentally prepared to continue the society because they basically do not understand the society well enough to value it.

My son assures me that his pupils are not ignorant. They know a great 9
deal. Like every other human group they share a tremendous amount of
knowledge among themselves, much of it learned in school. The trouble is that,
from the standpoint of their literacy and their ability to communicate with others in our culture, what they know is ephemeral and narrowly confined to their
own generation. Many young people strikingly lack the information that writers of American books and newspapers have traditionally taken for granted
among their readers from all generations. For reasons explained in this book,
our children's lack of intergenerational information is a serious problem for
the nation. The decline of literacy and the decline of shared knowledge are
closely related, interdependent facts.

The evidence for the decline of shared knowledge is not just anecdotal. In 10
1978 NAEP [National Assessment of Educational Progress] issued a report
which analyzed a large quantity of data showing that our children's knowledge of American civics had dropped significantly between 1969 and 1976. The
performance of thirteen-year-olds had dropped an alarming 11 percentage
points. That the drop has continued since 1976 was confirmed by preliminary
results from a NAEP study conducted in late 1985. It was undertaken both
because of concern about declining knowledge and because of the growing
evidence of a causal connection between the drop in shared information and
in literacy. The Foundations of Literacy project is measuring some of the specific information about history and literature that American seventeen-year-
olds possess.

Although the full report will not be published until 1987, the preliminary 11
field tests are disturbing. If these samplings hold up, and there is no reason to
think they will not, then the results we will be reading in 1987 will show that
two thirds of our seventeen-year-olds do not know that the Civil War occurred

between 1850 and 1900. Three quarters do not know what *reconstruction* means. Half do not know the meaning of the *Brown decision* and cannot identify either Stalin or Churchill. Three quarters are unfamiliar with the names of standard American and British authors. Moreover, our seventeen-year-olds have little sense of geography or the relative chronology of major events. Reports of youthful ignorance can no longer be considered merely impressionistic.

12   My encounter in the seventies with this widening knowledge gap first caused me to recognize the connection between specific background knowledge and mature literacy. The research I was doing on the reading and writing abilities of college students made me realize two things. First, we cannot assume that young people today know things that were known in the past by almost every literate person in the culture. For instance, in one experiment conducted in Richmond, Virginia, our seventeen- and eighteen-year-old subjects did not know who Grant and Lee were. Second, our results caused me to realize that we cannot treat reading and writing as empty skills, independent of specific knowledge. The reading skill of a person may vary greatly from task to task. The level of literacy exhibited in each task depends on the relevant background information that the person possesses.

THE DECLINE OF TEACHING CULTURAL LITERACY

13   Why have our schools failed to fulfill their fundamental acculturative responsibility? In view of the immense importance of cultural literacy for speaking, listening, reading, and writing, why has the need for a definite, shared body of information been so rarely mentioned in discussions of education? In the educational writings of the past decade, I find almost nothing on this topic, which is not arcane. People who are introduced to the subject quickly understand why oral or written communication requires a lot of shared background knowledge. It's not the difficulty or novelty of the idea that has caused it to receive so little attention.

14   Let me hazard a guess about one reason for our neglect of the subject. We have ignored cultural literacy in thinking about education—certainly I as a researcher also ignored it until recently—precisely because it was something we have been able to take for granted. We ignore the air we breathe until it is thin or foul. Cultural literacy is the oxygen of social intercourse. Only when we run into cultural illiteracy are we shocked into recognizing the importance of the information that we had unconsciously assumed.

15   To be sure, a minimal level of information is possessed by any normal person who lives in the United States and speaks elementary English. Almost everybody knows what is meant by *dollar* and that cars must travel on the right-hand side of the road. But this elementary level of information is not sufficient for a modern democracy. It isn't sufficient to allow us to read newspapers (a sin against Jeffersonian democracy), and it isn't sufficient to achieve economic fairness and high productivity. Cultural literacy lies *above* the everyday levels of knowledge that everyone possesses and *below* the expert level

known only to specialists. It is that middle ground of cultural knowledge possessed by the "common reader." It includes information that we have traditionally expected our children to receive in school, but which they no longer do.

During recent decades Americans have hesitated to make a decision about 16 the specific knowledge that children need to learn in school. Our elementary schools are not only dominated by the content-neutral ideas of Rousseau and Dewey, they are also governed by approximately sixteen thousand independent school districts. We have viewed this dispersion of educational authority as an insurmountable obstacle to altering the fragmentation of the school curriculum even when we have questioned that fragmentation. We have permitted school policies that have shrunk the body of information that Americans share, and these policies have caused our national literacy to decline.

At the same time we have searched with some eagerness for causes such 17 as television that lie outside the schools. But we should direct our attention undeviatingly toward what the schools teach rather than toward family structure, social class, or TV programming. No doubt, reforms outside the schools are important, but they are harder to accomplish. Moreover, we have accumulated a great deal of evidence that faulty policy in the schools is the chief cause of deficient literacy. Researchers who have studied the factors influencing educational outcomes have found that the school curriculum is the most important controllable influence on what our children know and don't know about our literate culture.

It will not do to blame television for the state of our literacy. Television 18 watching does reduce reading and often encroaches on homework. Much of it is admittedly the intellectual equivalent of junk food. But in some respects, such as its use of standard written English, television watching is acculturative. Moreover, as Herbert Walberg points out, the schools themselves must be held partly responsible for excessive television watching, because they have not firmly insisted that students complete significant amounts of homework, an obvious way to increase time spent on reading and writing. Nor should our schools be excused by an appeal to the effects of the decline of the family or the vicious circle of poverty, important as these factors are. Schools have, or should have, children for six or seven hours a day, five days a week, nine months a year, for thirteen years or more. To assert that they are powerless to make a significant impact on what their students learn would be to make a claim about American education that few parents, teachers, or students would find it easy to accept.

Just how fragmented the American public school curriculum has become 19 is described in *The Shopping Mall High School*, a report on five years of first-hand study inside public and private secondary schools. The authors report that our high schools offer courses of so many kinds that "the word 'curriculum' does not do justice to this astonishing variety." The offerings include not only academic courses of great diversity, but also courses in sports and hobbies and a "services curriculum" addressing emotional or social problems. All these courses are deemed "educationally valid" and carry course credit. Moreover, among academic offerings are numerous versions of each subject, corresponding to different levels of student interest and ability. Needless to say, the material covered in these "content area" courses is highly varied.

20   Cafeteria-style education, combined with the unwillingness of our schools to place demands on students, has resulted in a steady diminishment of commonly shared information between generations and between young people themselves. Those who graduate from the same school have often studied different subjects, and those who graduate from different schools have often studied different material even when their courses have carried the same titles. The inevitable consequence of the shopping mall high school is a lack of shared knowledge across and within schools. It would be hard to invent a more effective recipe for cultural fragmentation.

21   The formalistic educational theory behind the shopping mall school (the theory that any suitable content will inculcate reading, writing, and thinking skills) has had certain political advantages for school administrators. It has allowed them to stay scrupulously neutral with regard to content. Educational formalism enables them to regard the indiscriminate variety of school offerings as a positive virtue, on the grounds that such variety can accommodate the different interests and abilities of different students. Educational formalism has also conveniently allowed school administrators to meet objections to the traditional literate materials that used to be taught in the schools. Objectors have said that traditional materials are class-bound, white, Anglo-Saxon, and Protestant, not to mention racist, sexist, and excessively Western. Our schools have tried to offer enough diversity to meet these objections from liberals and enough Shakespeare to satisfy conservatives. Caught between ideological parties, the schools have been attracted irresistibly to a quantitative and formal approach to curriculum making rather than one based on sound judgments about what should be taught.

22   Some have objected that teaching the traditional literate culture means teaching conservative material. Orlando Patterson answered that objection when he pointed out that mainstream culture is not the province of any single social group and is constantly changing by assimilating new elements and expelling old ones. Although mainstream culture is tied to the written word and may therefore seem more formal and elitist than other elements of culture, that is an illusion. Literate culture is the most democratic culture in our land: it excludes nobody; it cuts across generations and social groups and classes; it is not usually one's first culture, but it should be everyone's second, existing as it does beyond the narrow spheres of family, neighborhood, and region.

23   As the universal second culture, literate culture has become the common currency for social and economic exchange in our democracy, and the only available ticket to full citizenship. Getting one's membership card is not tied to class or race. Membership is automatic if one learns the background information and the linguistic conventions that are needed to read, write, and speak effectively. Although everyone is literate in some local, regional, or ethnic culture, the connection between mainstream culture and the national written language justifies calling mainstream culture *the* basic culture of the nation.

Questions for Discussion

1. What evidence does Hirsch present to support his claim that our shared cultural knowledge declined in the years between 1970 and 1985? Is his evidence convincing?
2. How does Hirsch define cultural literacy?
3. According to Hirsch why has there been a decline in the shared cultural knowledge in America? Do you agree with Hirsch's point of view, or do you think that the decline in cultural literacy can be attributed to other causes, perhaps some of the causes that Hirsch dismisses?
4. Hirsch is critical of the "shopping mall high school" and "cafeteria style education." Define these two concepts.
5. Discuss why you agree or disagree with Hirsch when he is critical of the fragmentation of high school education, particularly of offerings that "include not only academic courses of great diversity, but also courses in sports and hobbies and a 'services curriculum' addressing emotional or social problems."
6. Hirsch presents an objection to his point of view, acknowledging that some feel that "teaching traditional literate culture means teaching conservative material." Do you agree with Hirsch or with his opponents?

Ideas for Writing

1. Write an essay that argues in favor of or against Hirsch's conclusion to this selection: "Literate culture is the most democratic culture of our land . . . it is not usually one's first culture, but it should be everyone's second, existing as it does beyond the narrow spheres of family, neighborhood, and region." Refer to selections in this chapter and in your own experiences to support your point of view.
2. Write an essay that expresses your opinion on the highly debated issue of the importance of a uniform standard of cultural literacy. You may have to do some research to understand the positions; then write a personal opinion paper or a longer research paper.

Service Learning: Education with a Purpose

Jeremy Taylor

Jeremy Taylor (b. 1974) grew up in Willows, a rural community in northern California. His interests include sports, traveling, and spending time with his friends and family, especially his twin brother. His academic interests are quite diverse, but he is currently taking premedical courses. His first year at college introduced him to many new people and ideas, both in and out of the classroom. Taylor participated in a community service writing project as a part of his "Writing and Critical Thinking" course. He had never experienced community service as part of the academic curriculum and this project sparked his interest in the subject. He decided to write his research paper on the topic of service learning. In the essay that follows Jeremy Taylor combines his own experiences with his research to present an argument for the integration of service learning into the classroom.

Journal

Write about an experience you had tutoring a younger child or helping a friend with his or her school work. Alternatively, write about a film or television program that interested you about a young person who was working as a volunteer, teacher, or tutor.

> We need in education a transformation as far reaching as the one which has America's vanquished enemies in World War II into its most dependable allies.
>
> —Benjamin Barber

The call to revamp and reform our nation's educational system has been sounded. Test scores of American high school students are dropping rapidly while those of Asian and European high school students are improving. Our high school dropout rate is increasing, as is teenage drug abuse and pregnancy. Today's educators are exploring a variety of alternative learning approaches. The introduction of community service into the classroom is a potential solution that is gaining momentum across the country. The successful integration of a service learning curriculum demonstrates that civic responsibility is fundamental to the advancement of society. Through participation in community service learning projects, students can begin to better understand their role in their community and their responsibility to others. The introduction of community service into the classroom can be a vital part of the restructuring of our nation's educational goals as well as a valuable tool in teaching social responsibility.

2   By combining classroom work with community projects, students are able to see the applications of their knowledge. Students learn through this method because they are involved personally with the outcome; they do not have to feel like passive bystanders. This approach brings a sense of purpose back to education. Presently, classrooms are filled with students asking questions such as "Why do I need to learn this?" and "When am I ever going to use that?" Participating in service learning experiences in the "real world" helps students to begin to find some answers to these challenging questions. As students realize that knowledge gained through regular course work and classroom learning can be applied outside the classroom, students' educational experiences are enhanced.

3   Application of community service as a way to revitalize the learning process is supported at many levels. After the passage of the landmark Community Service Act of 1990, Senator Edward Kennedy explained why he supports service learning:

4   Service learning should be a central component of current efforts to reform education. There are few better ways to inspire a child's interest in science

> than by allowing him or her to analyze and clean a polluted stream. There are few better ways to help a student's grammar than by having him or her tutor a recent immigrant learning to speak and write English. (Kennedy 772)

Along with Senator Kennedy, students, administrators, and teachers all over the country are realizing the value of service learning. When students see their knowledge promoting the growth of the community, their degree of knowledge retention is increased. A sixteen-year-old member of an ambulance crew says:

> In school you learn chemistry and biology and stuff and then forget it as soon as the test is over. Here you've got to remember it because somebody's life depends on it. (Conrad and Hedin 745)

In addition to increasing learning retention, studies also show that students who participate in community service learning experiences develop a more positive attitude toward others as well as a higher sense of self esteem; they also have fewer disciplinary problems (Conrad and Hedin 747). Most importantly, working with others on community service projects can increase students' motivation to learn. Teacher Don Zwach of Waseca, Minnesota, who incorporates community service into his curriculum, points to the significant impact that community service projects have had on his students' motivation:

> This is the most enthusiastic class I've had in thirty years. You hear a lot of other teacher's report that their academic goals are much more easily accomplished when students apply their knowledge to situations outside of the classroom. For example, after tutoring third and fourth graders seventeen year old Quinn Hammond said, "This taught me to have more patience and gave me a real good feeling. Volunteering gave me a new sense of respect for teachers" (Kilsmeier and Nathan 741).

Opponents of civic learning hold to the belief that the purpose of an educational system is to educate, not to teach civic responsibility. They claim that an academic institution has no right to coerce students into a service behavior. Benjamin Barber captures the limitation of such "academic purism" in his new book *An Aristocracy for Everyone* when he says that these educators believe in learning "not for career, not for life, not for democracy, not for money; for neither power nor happiness, neither career nor quality of life, but for its own pure sake" (Barber 203).

While the debate on whether to include community service in the academic curriculum grows more intense, this method of education through service is not new. When America's first colleges were established, service was one of their fundamental values and goals; they structured curricula to support their belief in service to the church, service to the local community, and service to the emerging nation. In fact, Rutgers University was chartered in 1766 to promote "learning for the benefit of the community" (Barber 246).

From 1766 to the present many approaches and opinions have been offered on the subject of education through community service. Today's proponents work with ideas that are similar to those of John Dewey. In *Experience and Edu-*

cation, published in 1913, Dewey developed the idea of stimulating academic achievement through actions directed towards others. Dewey spent much of his life trying to bring education and experience together in order to promote democracy as a "way of life and not just a political system" (Barber 247). When Woodrow Wilson assumed the office of President, he encouraged a renewed interest in civic responsibility and service learning:

12   . . . as a nation we are becoming civically illiterate. Unless we find better ways
             to educate ourselves as citizens, we run the risk of drifting into a new kind of
             Dark Age. (qtd. in Barber 247)

13   In the 1950s, after the "Dark Age" of education during the World War II, a new approach to civic education, the Citizenship Education Project, was developed by teachers from Columbia University. This program urged community involvement and participation and also introduced the famous "Brown Box" with hundreds of ideas for community interaction (Conrad and Hedin 744). The 1970s brought another new wave of reports condemning the passivity of our school systems. The National Committee on Secondary Education, the Panel on Youth of the President's Science Advisory Committee, and the National Panel on High School and Adolescent Education all supported the integration of education into the community (Conrad and Hedin 744). By the mid 1980s, several pilot programs had been initiated, and community service programs were implemented in classrooms throughout the nation.

14   These historical facts provide a background for the educational innovations of the 1990s, and perhaps the most important step in the integration of public service into the classroom. The National and Community Service Act of 1990 passed by the Congress of the United States will provide funding for community service programs from kindergarten through college; it is the most thorough community service bill ever passed. The legislation provided federal appropriations of $62 million in 1991, $95.5 million in 1992, and $105 million in 1993 for community service programs. A major goal of this program is to inspire the interest in community service at a young age. Senator Edward Kennedy hopes that "by teaching young children to help others, we will also be encouraging the values that will help keep America strong for the next generation" (Kennedy 772).

15   Academic communities all over the country are beginning to realize the value of community service, and more programs are being introduced at the high school and college levels. For example, service programs have been developed in Washington and Vermont. One program in particular, PennSERVE, first introduced in Pennsylvania, is achieving incredible success. PennSERVE emphasizes the link between the classroom and community service. Because of PennSERVE, the number of schools offering academic credit for service has doubled in two years and community service has become a common topic of debate (Briscoe 760). PennSERVE is just one of the many programs that have grown and flourished since the passage of the Community Service Act of 1990.

16   I was introduced to service learning through another type of program, a

Community Service Writing Project; my experiences have been both memorable and beneficial. I chose to be placed in a freshman English class with a community service writing option because I had become bored with "regular" English, which I characterize as writing solely to please my teacher and receive a good grade. I looked forward to an English class with a bit of a twist, one that would expose me to community service in my first year of college. Through my English class, I decided to work at a public service organization that helped disadvantaged youths from nearby high schools prepare for college.

17 Along with four other students, I met with the organization's leader and learned how our skills were to be utilized. Our group was to be responsible for developing a newsletter for prospective students and their parents. The newsletter was to include articles highlighting various aspects of the organization, so each person in our group wrote on a different topic. I chose to interview a new staff member, a classmate interviewed students who were involved with the program, and another group member researched the organization's incentive program to learn about how it rewarded students for their academic achievement.

18 While my finished product was less than a full page of text, the "behind the scenes" work was immeasurable and invaluable. I learned "real life" skills while completing this project. First, I had to research the organization to prepare for my interview. It was then necessary to formulate questions for the interview and decide what my focus was going to be. During the interview I discovered how interviewing is an art and realized the difficulty of "staying on track" and directing the conversation towards key points. After the interview, it was necessary to review my notes, determine the focus of my article, and decide what information to include and what to leave out. Finishing this process, I wrote a draft and turned it into the organization. In an English class, after one turns in a paper the process is ended; this was not the case with my interview. The leader of the organization requested that I write another draft with a slightly different focus. While this was a new situation for me, I approached it as a challenge. Complying with the leader's suggestions, I wrote a revised article which addressed the issues she saw as important. This draft received approval to be placed in the newsletter and brought my writing project to a conclusion.

19 Although this project was lengthy and, at times, frustrating, it was an invaluable experience. I was refreshed by writing with a purpose other than to receive an "A" while knowing that my writing would be read by someone other than a professor. I felt a strong sense of responsibility to my organization, and I wanted to produce something of which I would be proud. But the writing was just a minimal part of the overall experience; this project introduced me to people, to ideas, and to situations that I would not have experienced in the classroom. It gave me a sense of pride, and illustrated that I am able to reach out to people in different ways and through different mediums. I would not trade my "real life" experiences while working on this project for any other kind of essay assignment. Through my interaction with the organi-

zation and its members, I feel that in a subtle way this project has prepared me to participate more effectively in society.

20   In the early 1980s, Ernest Boyer and Fred Hechinger asked that: "a new generation of Americans . . . be educated for life in an increasingly complex world . . . through civic education [that] prepares students of all ages to participate more effectively in our social institutions" (Barber 248). Today we stand at a crucial juncture; we can initiate plans to forge ahead into the future, or we can continue to be satisfied with the status quo. Just as the world is changing around us, our educational system must change to meet the needs of today's students. The integration of civic education is an important part of that change. Community service, by showing us that we all have the means to contribute, can be the critical step in producing citizen graduates, graduates who realize their social responsibility and who will participate more effectively in our social institutions. Times have changed, yet our academic institutions have remained the same. The call for change has been sounded. It won't fade away, it will only grow louder.

Works Cited

Barber, Benjamin R. *An Aristocracy of Everyone: The Politics of Education and the Future of America*. New York: Ballantine Books, 1992.

Briscoe, John. "PennSERVE: The Governor's Office of Citizen Service." *Phi Delta Kappan* June 1991: 758–760.

Conrad, Dan, and Diane Hedin. "School Based Community Service: What We Know from Research and Theory." *Phi Delta Kappan* June 1991: 743–749.

Kennedy, Edward M. "National Service and Education for Citizenship." *Phi Delta Kappan* June 1991: 771–773.

Kielsmeier, Jim, and Joe Nathan. "The Sleeping Giant of School Reform." *Phi Delta Kappan* June 1991: 739–742.

Questions for Discussion

1. What reasons does Jeremy Taylor present to support his assertion that community service learning is an effective way to teach social responsibility? Is his point of view persuasive?

2. Does Taylor's use of evidence and authorities adequately support his argument? Identify one example that you feel is effective and one that needs to be more fully developed.

3. Taylor states, "Opponents of civic learning hold to the belief that the purpose of an educational system is to educate, not to teach civic responsibility." Do you agree with Taylor or with the "opponents"? Explain.

4. Do you think that Taylor does a thorough enough job of explaining and refuting the opponent's point of view?

5. Why does Taylor include his own experiences working on a community service project? Do you think this is an effective strategy? Did Taylor's experiences working on a community service project help to convince you that you too could learn from a similar type of service experience?

6. Would you like to see the English Department at your college integrate a service learning project into the first year writing curriculum? Explain your position.

Ideas for Writing

1. Do library research on the National and Community Service Act of 1990. Write a paper that discusses what you think have been the most important effects of this act. Or write a research paper or opinion piece on Clinton's national service programs.

2. Write about an experience that you had working as a volunteer at a community organization. After discussing what you did, reflect on what you learned from the experience and if it changed your values.

Community Service Writing Student Project: *Newsletter**

Kwan Ping Chua and Kathleen Chandler

Six students in their first year composition course collaborated to write and help produce a newsletter for a federally funded tutoring and support service for first-generation college-bound students from low-income families. The newsletter is distributed to the fifty students who are just beginning the program and to their families as well as to the five high school districts and educational support organizations in Santa Clara county, California. The program director met with the group and gave the students choices for their writing topics. After writing their articles individually, the students worked together to produce the newsletter. Included below are two of the student articles that appeared in the newsletter: Kwan Ping Chua's "Bounding through Academic Year Programs" and Kathleen Chandler's "Senior Profiles."

Journal

What do you think would be the most difficult challenges facing high school students who were going to be the first in their families to attend college? What advantages would these students have?

BOUNDING THROUGH ACADEMIC YEAR PROGRAMS

Hey you! Now that I have your attention, do you know why high school students come to Stanford on Saturdays? Is it to watch the football game between the Cardinal and the Nerds from UC Berkeley or is it to catch the Stanford Women's Volleyball team in action? Of course not! They come to Stanford to participate in our program, Reach Out.

Reach Out is an academic program targeted at high school students who ₂

---

*Names of the organization and the students interviewed have been changed to protect their privacy.

are the first in their families to attend college or who come from low income families. The program's goal is to help these high school students academically and to prepare them for college. Seventy students are currently participating in the program and more than 90% of these students will eventually enter college.

3   Reach Out achieves its aim by organizing and coordinating various academic and counseling programs. The most important one is the Academic Year Program that has an intensive academic focus all year round. This program is designed to assess the individual student's academic needs, to assist the student's progress in class, and to provide the student with necessary information concerning the college application processes.

4   The program is divided into different sections to meet the specific needs of different classes of students. Freshmen are enrolled in the Study Skills class while Sophomores are enrolled in the College Exploration class. The purpose of the Study Skills class is to help 9th graders make the transition into high school. The purpose of the College Exploration class is to expose Sophomores to the many different college systems and to help them to select high school classes on the basis of college requirements for admission. Juniors are enrolled in an intensive SAT preparation class which emphasizes verbal drills, as many of the students are not native speakers of English. A typical lesson includes doing comprehension exercises and learning new words to help expand the students' vocabulary.

5   In their senior year, Reach Out students have many opportunities to talk with the project director about their thoughts of going to college and any other questions or concerns they might have concerning college life, which usually includes sharing their apprehension about going away from home to college, as well as selecting colleges and majors. Seniors also receive help in completing the cumbersome college applications, financial aid applications and housing forms. A crash course in writing is also organized for the Seniors to help prepare them for college application essays. Furthermore, Seniors are counseled about what colleges to attend after they have received responses from the various admissions offices.

6   Another way Reach Out assists the students academically is to conduct tutoring sessions every Saturday from 12 P.M. to 3 P.M. Each student has an individual tutor to help him/her with the subjects in which he/she needs help. The tutors are college students who volunteer 3 hours every Saturday for an entire academic year. The tutors also serve as mentors and counselors to the students. In addition, exciting field trips to various college campuses and places of social, cultural, and recreational value are planned for the students regularly.

7   Rosa, a senior at a nearby high school, has been with the program since her freshman year in high school when her brother introduced her to the program. She is receiving tutoring in English and Math which she finds "very useful." The tutoring sessions also help her "not to get behind in class." As a senior in high school, she finds the SAT Prep Class especially beneficial as it

provides her with practice tests and testing strategies. Rosa believes that the program is "worthwhile" and she is "very glad to join it."

Reach Out has helped hundreds of first generation college bound high 8 school students perform better academically and thus has increased their chances to enter college. If you are also a first generation college bound student in need of advice about college and help with school work, get an application now and complete it today.

(Stanford Freshman Community Service Writer: Kwan Ping Chua)

SENIOR PROFILES

One Saturday, I had the opportunity to meet some of the high school seniors in the Reach Out program. When I arrived at the center, they were writing essays for college applications; when I left a few hours later, they were just on their way to individual three hour study sessions with their tutors.

For three to five years these high school seniors have been spending their 2 Saturdays and summers doing school work. Sound crazy? No. They're smart. Focused. Dedicated. Hard working. Determined . . . and totally inspirational.

Heather is a young woman with a plan for her future. She explained that 3 she plans to be an elementary or junior high school counselor and eventually open her own practice. Currently, she is one of the Vice Principal's student assistants, and she works as a peer counselor to help kids at her school keep on track and stay in school by talking to them, calling them daily, and making sure they go to class and do their homework. In talking with Heather, it is clear that her gentle but commanding voice would make her a good counselor. Heather has been in the program since the summer of her eighth grade year and says that it has "helped me out tremendously." She says that it is like an alternative to school, where you know all the kids and have counselors whenever you need them.

Dana goes to Woodside High School now, but she and her family have 4 lived in many parts of the world. She was born in what is now Ho Chi Minh City, Vietnam. When she was four years old, she and her family moved to Indonesia, and one year later, they came to the United States. She has a great talent for languages and can speak Vietnamese, Chinese, and English, and she is learning Spanish in school. Dana wants to major in Business Administration in college. She wants a job where she can travel to other places and meet different people. Reach Out has helped Dana a lot, even though at times she says she's been exhausted from all the work. "They keep nagging you!" Now as she looks forward to college, Dana's happy she had the emotional and academic support from Reach Out. "I feel really comfortable with these people."

Alberto found out about Reach Out when a representative came to his 5 junior high school. Meeting new people is one of the great things about this program for Alberto. And, like nearly all of the people I interviewed, his favorite part of being in the program has been the Stanford summer school program. Every year since he was accepted into Reach Out, he has lived with his fellow students in Stanford University dorms for six weeks during the summer. He has taken a variety of classes ranging from math to ethnic studies. But Alberto's real love is music. One day he'd like to work as a DJ or technician or "just anything" at a radio station.

6   Rosa wants to be a civil engineer. In eighth grade her class went on a tour of the city and talked to the mayor, maintenance workers, and a civil engineer. The engineer told them about a housing project that was about to be built on an old dump site. The project was eventually built, but Rosa says that even though it looks nice, she wouldn't like to live there. Now she's determined to do better. At her school, she takes part in a group called Math, Engineering, and Science Achievement (MESA). She has been in Reach Out for four years and says, "It's really good to come every Saturday and see the friends I haven't seen all week.

7   When I asked *Patty* if she was glad to have been involved in Reach Out for the past five years, she replied with a definite, "Oh yeah." She was soft spoken and friendly, and said that the program has helped her get good grades in high school. Tutors and counselors have answered her many questions, academic and beyond, about high school, college, and job opportunities. Patty speaks Spanish and English, studies French in high school and is thinking about continuing her French studies in college. However, like most high school seniors and college freshman, she hasn't decided in which field she might like to major in college.

8   "Reach Out is a great program" according to Jane, and she would recommend it to any high school student wanting to go to college. Jane goes to Kennedy High School and insists that she wouldn't be thinking about college if she hadn't gotten involved in the program, although she adds that her mom has helped her a lot as well because she "pushes me all the time." Today, women in the police force are still not all that common, but Jane plans to beat the statistics. Her life-long goal is to become a police officer.

9   Pilár is a high energy young woman who is very involved in her high school and her church. She goes to a private school where she is one of only seven Latinos. As a co-founder of her high school's Multi Cultural Awareness club, she is part of a support group for minority students and their parents. The group provides tutoring and counseling, and helps recruit minority students to the school. She is also part of a church group that goes on retreats with high school kids who are having problems at home or in school. Pilár plans to work hard and take advantage of the opportunities that a college can offer by majoring in Human Biology or Pre Med. She also wants to try something new and take a Mexican Dance class (Ballet Folklorico).

10   These are only a few of the students of the 1992 Reach Out senior class.

With just this small taste of the character of the students involved, I was taken by the energy and determination these high school students have. With the amount of time and energy these students put into their high school studies, it's no wonder so many succeed.

Stanford Freshman Community Service Writer: Kathleen B. Chandler

Questions for Discussion

1. In what ways do you think that working on a newsletter project would help you to improve your writing?
2. Have you ever helped to produce a newsletter? What did you learn from that writing project that you have applied to your academic writing assignments?
3. Identify the organizational and analytical strategies used in each of the articles. Which of the articles did you think was more successful?
4. The students working on this project needed to write for a new and particular audience. In what ways would the audience for the newsletter be different from a writing instructor? What evidence in the newsletter's style and content do you see of the students' understanding of their audience?
5. What do you think would be the challenges of working on a group writing project?
6. How would you feel if it were the agency director of your project asking you to revise what you wrote rather than your instructor? Would you revise differently for the agency than for your instructor?

Ideas for Writing

1. With a group of your peers in your writing class volunteer to produce a newsletter for an organization on your campus or in your community. After completing the project, write an evaluation of what you learned about your agency, your topic, and your writing process.
2. Do some research on your campus, at your local high school, and in your college library about summer or year-round programs that help students to make the transition between high school and college. Write an essay that shares what you have learned for your class and/or for a local high school in your community.

CHAPTER WRITING PROJECTS

1. Each of the selections in this chapter argues for educational change. Develop your own perspective on the need for changes in your community's educational programs. Write a research paper that supports your point of view. Or imagine that you could go back to high school and implement curriculum changes to improve the quality of education at your high school. Discuss the advantages of your proposal. Refer to selections in this chapter to develop and support your main ideas and point of view.

2. Write an essay in which you discuss what you think are the most serious national problems with college education. Consider the various points of view raised in this chapter as you shape your response.

3. Interview classmates from different cultures about the value of education and the role of the student in the classroom. Do some library research into how cultural diversity is affecting the way that students learn in classrooms. Write a paper that presents your point of view on how you think differing cultural perspectives and the new emphasis on collaborative learning are changing the way classes today are being conducted and taught.

4. Begin by thinking about your best and worst teachers. Then do some research at the education library on your campus into ways that teachers are taught to assume responsibility in the classroom. Or read about the lives of some well-respected teachers. Drawing on your own experiences and/or the research you have done, write a portrait of an ideal teacher. Consider referring to the selections by Kozol and Rose.

5. Write about your most successful collaborative learning experiences; interpret and evaluate them in light of some of the educational perspectives on collaborative learning and community that have been presented by Woo, Angelou, Rose, Taylor, and Barber.

6. What role do you think the community should assume in relationship to students who come from poor or dysfunctional families that do not provide a stable home life and the encouragement to do well in school? Do library research and/or contact agencies, organizations or schools in your community that help people who did not earn a high school diploma to get a higher education or develop technical skills. Write a paper that discusses the information you have found and your point of view.

7. Research the resources that your community provides for adults who need to learn to write and speak English better. Visit several of these classes and interview the teachers and students. Write an essay for your class and also one for a local or campus paper that is informative and evaluative.

8. Write an argument either for or against the inclusion of public service learning into the academic curriculum. You might want to refer to the selections by Barber, Hirsch, and Taylor.

9. Volunteer to work in a program for disadvantaged children at an elementary or high school in your community. Discuss the strengths and weaknesses of the program that you worked in: your role in the program, what you have learned, and what you'd like to do to help the children and their program in the future. If you do not have an opportunity to work in a program for disadvantaged children, write a research paper on this topic.

10. As a small group project help the children in a local elementary school produce a newsletter or a book that explores a number of cultural traditions. You might want to help the children write stories from their family legacies and then collect them together in a book.

11. As a small group project, or as a class, see a movie that explores the ways that children, adolescents, and adults with special needs and special

strengths are educated. You might consider such films as *Stand and Deliver, To Sir With Love, Little Man Tate, Stanley and Iris, Children of a Lesser God.* As a group or individually write an essay that interprets the film's perspective on the relationship between education and community. Refer to writers in this chapter when relevant to develop your interpretation and critique of the film. In what ways does the film add new insights into the ways that an educational setting can become a positive community?

CHAPTER 4

Social and Economic Struggles in the Community

What we see on the streets of our cities are two dramas, both of which cut to the troubled heart of the culture and demand from us a response we may not be able to make. There is the drama of those struggling to survive by regaining their place in the social order. And there is the drama of those struggling to survive outside of it.
—Peter Marin, "Helping and Hating the Homeless"

I cannot sit idly by in Atlanta and not be concerned about what happens in Birmingham. Injustice anywhere is a threat to justice everywhere. We are caught in an inescapable network of mutuality, tied in a single garment of destiny. Whatever affects one directly, affects all indirectly.
—Martin Luther King, Jr., "Letter from Birmingham Jail"

People create and maintain communities for fellowship and companionship, for protection, for collective economic gain—for many reasons. Sometimes groups are able to work effectively for the common good, and most of the community prospers. Even in prosperous communities, and too often in many communities that are less fortunate, some members of the community remain struggling, disenfranchised, unable to benefit from the strengths of the collective society. The web of community that brings us together is shaken when some members are not able to attain basic social or economic equality. This chapter brings together some of their stories, either directly, through first-hand accounts, or indirectly, through the work of writers who study and inform us about such issues. Through every reading we are reminded of our connections to others in our communities. Martin Luther King, Jr. makes the point eloquently when he writes, "Injustice anywhere is a threat to justice everywhere."

206

Whatever our memberships or affiliations, whatever our political leanings, whether right, left, or center, we are all affected by injustice, by oppression, by poverty and strife in our communities; consequently, we are all, as community members, charged with facing issues of social and economic justice. As college students, as writers and thinkers, you are in a position to reflect on such issues as you take courses that will help you to be and to become productive members of society. The following readings will, we hope, help to stimulate your interest in some of the kinds of issues you will face as students, as workers, as parents, as neighbors, as voters, as participants in citizen democracy.

The chapter readings discuss a range of issues, focusing on struggles for humane conditions and equal rights in the work place, in people's neighborhoods, and in society. The first three readings demonstrate in the context of individual struggles the concepts of alienated labor and economic struggles that are written about in numerous political essays. Studs Terkel's collection of oral histories, *Working*, brings to us the voices of workers from a wide range of occupations. In "Mike LeFevre: Who Built the Pyramids?" a laborer talks about the physically demanding work he performs daily and the insufferable young supervisor wearing a coat and tie—the emblems of success LeFevre wants for his son. In "Cannery Town in August," poet Lorna Dee Cervantes speaks of the alienating and dehumanizing experience of those in the mass labor force, and in Martin Espada's poem "Jorge the Church Janitor Finally Quits," Jorge works for church employers who don't even know his name or where he's from.

Professor Ronald Takaki's essay "Broken Promises: Community of Memory," from his book *Strangers from a Different Shore,* focuses on the experiences of diverse Asian ethnic populations making their way to America, some to find some success, and much struggle, in striving for the "American dream." Student writer Hien Tran, drawing on his own experience and that of other young Vietnamese in America, as well as on research, wrote the essay "Coming to America: Difficulties of Vietnamese Youth" for his first-year college writing course.

As Takaki writes, and as Tran's evidence suggests, the model minority myth hides tremendous suffering on the part of many Asian Americans: some have not achieved basic equality in the work place and society, while others have had great technical success but have met a "glass ceiling" in the managerial ranks. Susan Faludi, author of the essay "Blame it on Feminism" from her recent book *Backlash*, argues as well that even the small gains women have made toward social or economic equality are overstated and unsupported.

Riots and civil strife in our cities have confronted all of us with the continued struggle for justice for all Americans, through the courts as well as in the community. Conflicts between ethnic groups, and between middle class and poor as well as rich and poor, continue to ravage our cities and towns. This type of conflict is illustrated in James Alan McPherson's short story "A Loaf of Bread," when a shopkeeper convinced he is playing by the rules and trying to stay alive economically is challenged by the local community. To liberate himself and his family from his seemingly unsolvable problem, the shop-keeper must revise his own beliefs about work and money, about family and community. In the next selection, "What is Poverty?", Jo Goodwin Parker writes that the poor are part of our community, not some "others" from another time and place. Parker reminds us that "others like me are all around you," challenging us to rethink our stereotypes about the poor and to truly understand their situations.

Striving to understand and to do what we feel is right in regard to people different from ourselves is difficult for many of us. Our ambivalence about the homeless in our communities, for example, is discussed at length by Peter Marin and is captured in the title of his essay "Helping and Hating the Homeless: The Struggle at the Margins of America." Part of our problem is ignorance, part of it fear, part of it simply forgetting that community means "us" and not "them." Citizen involvement in many parts of the community can help bridge the diversity in our communities, and student Julian Castro's "Politics . . . maybe?" provides a portrait of one individual who has spent her life working for the social and economic good of her community.

Martin Luther King, Jr., in "Letter from Birmingham Jail," the next selection, offers the classic argument on behalf of involvement in community action for the benefit of the whole society. King traces the history and broadens the implications of the action in Birmingham by citing precedents from the Bible, from St. Aquinas, from Gandhi's tradition of nonviolence. King reminds us that injustice to anyone threatens the whole society, that by working to liberate the oppressed those in power liberate themselves as well.

Society's efforts to rectify civil injustice have resulted in policies that establish community service programs; whether or not national projects succeed, many local, grass roots organizations continue. One such is the subject of the final selection in this chapter, Tamara Watt's Community Service Writing Student Project: "Urban Ministry," an informational brochure describing the volunteer opportunities in one community for people wanting to help the homeless and others in need.

The readings in this chapter provide, we hope, a range of voices that explore social and economic struggles in their communities; some readings are in direct disagreement with others, some echo core themes. As you read, try to listen to what each writer has to say, but also write down questions, conflicts, contradictions, and ideas about your own ethics and beliefs about work, equality, and justice.

Mike LeFevre: Who Built the Pyramids?

Studs Terkel

Studs Terkel (b. 1912), noted American oral historian, has brought together the stories of working people from all kinds of jobs—from copy editing to streetwalking, from farming to masonry. Terkel's technique, recreating the individual's story in his or her first-person point of view, richly conveys his subjects' voices and stories. In addition to his collection *Working,* from which the following selection is excerpted, Terkel has published *Division Street: America* (1967), *Hard Times* (1970), *American Dreams, Lost and Found* (1980), *The Good War* (1984), *Chicago* (1986), *The Great Divide* (1988), and most recently, *Race: How Blacks and Whites Think and Feel about the American Obsession* (1992).

Journal

Freewrite a response to the following question: Who built the pyramids? Who built the World Trade Center? What do the two peoples or groups have in common?

> Who built the seven towers of Thebes?
> The books are filled with the names of kings.
> Was it kings who hauled the craggy blocks of stone? . . .
> In the evening when the Chinese wall was finished
> Where did the masons go? . . .
>
> —Bertolt Brecht

It is a two-flat dwelling, somewhere in Cicero, on the outskirts of Chicago. He is thirty-seven. He works in a steel mill. On occasion, his wife Carol works as a waitress in a neighborhood restaurant; otherwise, she is at home, caring for their two small children, a girl and a boy.

At the time of my first visit, a sculpted statuette of Mother and Child was on the floor, head severed from body. He laughed softly as he indicated his three-year-old daughter: "She Doctor Spock'd it."

I'm a dying breed. A laborer. Strictly muscle work . . . pick it up, put it down, 2 pick it up, put it down. We handle between forty and fifty thousand pounds of steel a day. (Laughs) I know this is hard to believe—from four hundred pounds to three- and four-pound pieces. It's dying.

You can't take pride any more. You remember when a guy could point to 3 a house he built, how many logs he stacked. He built it and he was proud of it. I don't really think I could be proud if a contractor built a home for me. I would be tempted to get in there and kick the carpenter in the ass (laughs), and take the saw away from him. 'Cause I would have to be part of it, you know.

4   It's hard to take pride in a bridge you're never gonna cross, in a door you're never gonna open. You're mass-producing things and you never see the end result of it. (Muses) I worked for a trucker one time. And I got this tiny satisfaction when I loaded a truck. At least I could see the truck depart loaded. In a steel mill, forget it. You don't see where nothing goes.

5   I got chewed out by my foreman once. He said, "Mike, you're a good worker but you have a bad attitude." My attitude is that I don't get excited about my job. I do my work but I don't say whoopee-doo. The day I get excited about my job is the day I go to a head shrinker. How are you gonna get excited about pullin' steel? How are you gonna get excited when you're tired and want to sit down?

6   It's not just the work. Somebody built the pyramids. Somebody's going to build something. Pyramids, Empire State Building—these things just don't happen. There's hard work behind it. I would like to see a building, say, the Empire State, I would like to see on one side of it a foot-wide strip from top to bottom with the name of every bricklayer, the name of every electrician, with all the names. So when a guy walked by, he could take his son and say, "See, that's me over there on the forty-fifth floor. I put the steel beam in." Picasso can point to a painting. What can I point to? A writer can point to a book. Everybody should have something to point to.

7   It's the not-recognition by other people. To say a woman is *just* a house-wife is degrading, right? Okay. *Just* a housewife. It's also degrading to say *just* a laborer. The difference is that a man goes out and maybe gets smashed.

8   When I was single, I could quit, just split. I wandered all over the coun-try. You worked just enough to get a poke, money in your pocket. Now I'm married and I got two kids . . . (trails off). I worked on a truck dock one time and I was single. The foreman came over and he grabbed my shoulder, kind of gave me a shove. I punched him and knocked him off the dock. I said, "Leave me alone. I'm doing my work, just stay away from me, just don't give me the with-the-hands business."

9   Hell, if you whip a damn mule he might kick you. Stay out of my way, that's all. Working is bad enough, don't bug me. I would rather work my ass off for eight hours a day with nobody watching me than five minutes with a guy watching me. Who you gonna sock? You can't sock General Motors, you can't sock anybody in Washington, you can't sock a system.

10   A mule, an old mule, that's the way I feel. Oh yeah. See. (Shows black and blue marks on arms and legs, burns.) You know what I heard from more than one guy at work? "If my kid wants to work in a factory, I am going to kick the hell out of him." I want my kid to be an effete snob. Yeah, mm-hmm. (Laughs.) I want him to be able to quote Walt Whitman, to be proud of it.

11   If you can't improve yourself, you improve your posterity. Otherwise life isn't worth nothing. You might as well go back to the cave and stay there. I'm sure the first caveman who went over the hill to see what was on the other side—I don't think he went there wholly out of curiosity. He went there because he wanted to get his son out of the cave. Just the same way I want to send my kid to college.

I work so damn hard and want to come home and sit down and lay 12 around. *But I gotta get it out.* I want to be able to turn around to somebody and say, "Hey, fuck you." You know? (Laughs.) The guy sitting next to me on the bus too. 'Cause all day I wanted to tell my foreman to go fuck himself, but I can't.

So I find a guy in a tavern. To tell him that. And he tells me too. I've been 13 in brawls. He's punching me and I'm punching him, because we actually want to punch somebody else. The most that'll happen is the bartender will bar us from the tavern. But at work, you lose your job.

This one foreman I've got, he's a kid. He's a college graduate. He thinks 14 he's better than everybody else. He was chewing me out and I was saying, "Yeah, yeah, yeah." He said, "What do you mean, yeah, yeah, yeah. Yes, *sir*." I told him, "Who the hell are you, Hitler? What is this *"Yes, sir"* bullshit? I came here to work, I didn't come here to crawl. There's a fuckin' difference." One word led to another and I lost.

I got broke down to a lower grade and lost twenty-five cents an hour, 15 which is a hell of a lot. It amounts to about ten dollars a week. He came over— after breaking me down. The guy comes over and smiles at me. I blew up. He didn't know it, but he was about two seconds and two feet away from a hospital. I said, "Stay the fuck away from me." He was just about to say something and was pointing his finger. I just reached my hand up and just grabbed his finger and I just put it back in his pocket. He walked away. I grabbed his finger because I'm married. If I'd a been single, I'd a grabbed his head. That's the difference.

You're doing this manual labor and you know that technology can do it. 16 (Laughs.) Let's face it, a machine can do the work of a man; otherwise they wouldn't have space probes. Why can we send a rocket ship that's unmanned and yet send a man in a steel mill to do a mule's work?

Automation? Depends how it's applied. It frightens me if it puts me out 17 on the street. It doesn't frighten me if it shortens my work week. You read that little thing: what are you going to do when this computer replaces you? Blow up computers. (Laughs.) Really. Blow up computers. I'll be goddamned if a computer is gonna eat before I do! I want milk for my kids and beer for me. Machines can either liberate man or enslave 'im, because they're pretty neutral. It's man who has the bias to put the thing one place or another.

If I had a twenty-hour workweek, I'd get to know my kids better, my wife 18 better. Some kid invited me to go on a college campus. On a Saturday. It was summertime. Hell, if I have a choice of taking my wife and kids to a picnic or going to a college campus, it's gonna be the picnic. But if I worked a twenty-hour week. I could go do both. Don't you think with that extra twenty hours people could really expand? Who's to say? There are some people in factories just by force of circumstance. I'm just like the colored people. Potential Einsteins don't have to be white. They could be in cotton fields, they could be in factories.

The twenty-hour week is a possibility today. The intellectuals, they always 19 say there are potential Lord Byrons, Walt Whitmans, Roosevelts, Picassos working in construction or steel mills or factories. But I don't think they believe it. I think what they're afraid of is the potential Hitlers and Stalins that are there too. The people in power fear the leisure man. Not just the United States. Russia's the same way.

20   What do you think would happen in this country if, for one year, they experimented and gave everybody a twenty-hour week? How do they know that the guy who digs Wallace today doesn't try to resurrect Hitler tomorrow? Or the guy who is mildly disturbed at pollution doesn't decide to go to General Motors and shit on the guy's desk? You can become a fanatic if you had the time. The whole thing is time. That is, I think, one reason rich kids tend to be fanatic about politics: they have time. Time, that's the important thing.

21   It isn't that the average working guy is dumb. He's tired, that's all. I picked up a book on chess one time. That thing laid in the drawer for two or three weeks, you're too tired. During the weekends you want to take your kids out. You don't want to sit there and the kid comes up: "Daddy, can I go to the park?" You got your nose in a book? Forget it.

22   I know a guy fifty-seven years old. Know what he tells me? "Mike, I'm old and tired *all* the time." The first thing happens at work: when the arms start moving, the brain stops. I punch in about ten minutes to seven in the morning. I say hello to a couple of guys I like, I kid around with them. One guy says good morning to you and you say good morning. To another guy you say fuck you. The guy you say fuck you to is your friend.

23   I put on my hard hat, change into my safety shoes, put on my safety glasses, go to the bonderizer. It's the thing I work on. They rake the metal, they wash it, they dip it in a paint solution, and we take it off. Put it on, take it off, put it on, take it off, put it on, take it off . . .

24   I say hello to everybody but my boss. At seven it starts. My arms get tired about the first half-hour. After that, they don't get tired any more until maybe the last half-hour at the end of the day. I work from seven to three thirty. My arms are tired at seven thirty and they're tired at three o'clock. I hope to God I never get broke in, because I always want my arms to be tired at seven thirty and three o'clock. (Laughs.) 'Cause that's when I know that there's a beginning and there's an end. That I'm not brainwashed. In between, I don't even try to think.

25   If I were to put you in front of a dock and I pulled up a skid in front of you with fifty hundred-pound sacks of potatoes and there are fifty more skids just like it, and this is what you're gonna do all day, what would you think about—potatoes? Unless a guy's a nut, he never thinks about work or talks about it. Maybe about baseball or about getting drunk the other night or he got laid or he didn't get laid. I'd say one out of a hundred will actually get excited about work.

26   Why is it that the communists always say they're for the workingman, and as soon as they set up a country, you got guys singing to tractors? They're singing about how they love the factory. That's where I couldn't buy communism. It's the intellectuals' utopia, not mine. I cannot picture myself singing to a tractor, I just can't. (Laughs.) Or singing to steel. (Singsongs.) Oh whoop-

dee-doo, I'm at the bonderizer, oh how I love this heavy steel. No thanks. Never hoppen.

Oh yeah, I daydream. I fantasize about a sexy blonde in Miami who's got 27 my union dues. (Laughs.) I think of the head of the union the way I think of the head of my company. Living it up. I think of February in Miami. Warm weather, a place to lay in. When I hear a college kid say, "I'm oppressed," I don't believe him. You know what I'd like to do for one year? Live like a college kid. Just for one year. I'd love to. Wow! (Whispers) Wow! Sports car! Marijuana! (Laughs.) Wild, sexy broads. I'd love that, hell yes, I would.

Somebody has to do this work. If my kid ever goes to college, I just want 28 him to have a little respect, to realize that his dad is one of those somebodies. This is why even on—(muses) yeah, I guess, sure—on the black thing . . . (Sighs heavily.) I can't really hate the colored fella that's working with me all day. The black intellectual I got no respect for. The white intellectual I got no use for. I got no use for the black militant who's gonna scream three hundred years of slavery to me while I'm busting my ass. You know what I mean? (Laughs.) I have one answer for that guy: go see Rockefeller. See Harriman. Don't bother me. We're in the same cotton field. So just don't bug me. (Laughs.)

After work I usually stop off at a tavern. Cold beer. Cold beer right away. 29 When I was single, I used to go into hillbilly bars, get in a lot of brawls. Just to explode. I got a thing on my arm here (indicates scar). I got slapped with a bicycle chain. Oh, wow! (Softly) Mmm. I'm getting older. (Laughs.) I don't explode as much. You might say I'm broken in. (Quickly) No, I'll never be broken in. (Sighs.) When you get a little older, you exchange the words. When you're younger, you exchange the blows.

When I get home, I argue with my wife a little bit. Turn on TV, get mad 30 at the news. (Laughs.) I don't even watch the news that much. I watch Jackie Gleason. I look for any alternative to the ten o'clock news. I don't want to go to bed angry. Don't hit a man with anything heavy at five o'clock. He just can't be bothered. This is his time to relax. The heaviest thing he wants is what his wife has to tell him.

When I come home, know what I do for the first twenty minutes? Fake it. 31 I put on a smile. I got a kid three years old. Sometimes she says, "Daddy, where've you been?" I say, "Work." I could have told her I'd been in Disneyland. What's work to a three-year-old kid? If I feel bad, I can't take it out on the kids. Kids are born innocent of everything but birth. You can't take it out on your wife either. This is why you go to a tavern. You want to release it there rather than do it at home. What does an actor do when he's got a bad movie? I got a bad movie every day.

I don't even need the alarm clock to get up in the morning. I can go out 32 drinking all night, fall asleep at four, and bam! I'm up at six—no matter what I do. (Laughs.) It's a pseudo-death, more or less. Your whole system is paralyzed and you give all the appearance of death. It's an ingrown clock. It's a thing you just get used to. The hours differ. It depends. Sometimes my wife wants to do something crazy like play five hundred rummy or put a puzzle together. It could be midnight, could be ten o'clock, could be nine thirty.

33 *What do you do weekends?*

34   Drink beer, read a book. See that one? *Violence in America.* It's one of them studies from Washington. One of them committees they're always appointing. A thing like that I read on a weekend. But during the weekdays, gee . . . I just thought about it. I don't do that much reading from Monday through Friday. Unless it's a horny book. I'll read it at work and go home and do my homework. (Laughs.) That's what the guys at the plant call it—homework. (Laughs.) Sometimes my wife works on Saturday and I drink beer at the tavern.

35   I went out drinking with one guy, oh, a long time ago. A college boy. He was working where I work now. Always preaching to me about how you need violence to change the system and all that garbage. We went into a hillbilly joint. Some guy there, I didn't know him from Adam, he said, "You think you're smart." I said, "What's your pleasure?" (Laughs.) He said, "My pleasure's to kick your ass." I told him I really can't be bothered. He said, "What're you, chicken?" I said, "No, I just don't want to be bothered." He came over and said something to me again. I said, "I don't beat women, drunks, or fools. Now leave me alone."

36   The guy called his brother over. This college boy that was with me, he came nudging my arm, "Mike, let's get out of here." I said, "What are you worried about?" (Laughs.) This isn't unusual. People will bug you. You fend it off as much as you can with your mouth and when you can't, you punch the guy out.

37   It was close to closing time and we stayed. We could have left, but when you go into a place to have a beer and a guy challenges you—if you expect to go in that place again, you don't leave. If you have to fight the guy, you fight.

38   I got just outside the door and one of these guys jumped on me and grabbed me around the neck. I grabbed his arm and flung him against the wall. I grabbed him here (indicates throat), and jiggled his head against the wall quite a few times. He kind of slid down a little bit. This guy who said he was his brother took a swing at me with a garrison belt. He just missed and hit the wall. I'm looking around for my junior Stalin (laughs), who loves violence and everything. He's gone. Split. (Laughs.) Next day I see him at work. I couldn't get mad at him, he's a baby.

39   He saw a book in my back pocket one time and he was amazed. He walked up to me and he said, "You read?" I said, "What do you mean, I read?" He said, "All these dummies read the sports pages around here. What are you doing with a book?" I got pissed off at the kid right away. I said, "What do you mean, all these dummies? Don't knock a man who's paying somebody else's way through college." He was a nineteen-year-old effete snob.

40 *Yet you want your kid to be an effete snob?*

41   Yes. I want my kid to look at me and say, "Dad, you're a nice guy, but you're a fuckin' dummy." Hell yes, I want my kid to tell me that he's not gonna be like me . . .

If I were hiring people to work, I'd try naturally to pay them a decent 42 wage. I'd try to find out their first names, their last names, keep the company as small as possible, so I could personalize the whole thing. All I would ask a man is a handshake, see you in the morning. No applications, nothing. I wouldn't be interested in the guy's past. Nobody ever checks the pedigree on a mule, do they? But they do on a man. Can you picture walking up to a mule and saying, "I'd like to know who his granddaddy was?"

I'd like to run a combination bookstore and tavern. (Laughs.) I would like 43 to have a place where college kids came and a steelworker could sit down and talk. Where a workingman could not be ashamed of Walt Whitman and where a college professor could not be ashamed that he painted his house over the weekend.

If a carpenter built a cabin for poets, I think the least the poets owe the 44 carpenter is just three or four one-liners on the wall. A little plaque: Though we labor with our minds, this place we can relax in was built by someone who can work with his hands. And his work is as noble as ours. I think the poet owes something to the guy who builds the cabin for him.

I don't think of Monday. You know what I'm thinking about on Sunday 45 night? Next Sunday. If you work real hard, you think of a perpetual vacation. Not perpetual sleep . . . What do I think of on a Sunday night? Lord. I wish the fuck I could do something else for a living.

I don't know who the guy is who said there is nothing sweeter than an 46 unfinished symphony. Like an unfinished painting and an unfinished poem. If he creates this thing one day—let's say, Michelangelo's Sistine Chapel. It took him a long time to do this, this beautiful work of art. But what if he had to create this Sistine Chapel a thousand times a year? Don't you think that would even dull Michelangelo's mind? Or if da Vinci had to draw his anatomical charts thirty, forty, fifty, sixty, eighty, ninety, a hundred times a day? Don't you think that would even bore da Vinci?

Way back, you spoke of the guys who built the pyramids, not the pharaohs, the 47 *unknowns. You put yourself in their category?*

Yes. I want my signature on 'em, too. Sometimes, out of pure meanness, 48 when I make something, I put a little dent in it. I like to do something to make it really unique. Hit it with a hammer. I deliberately fuck it up to see if it'll get by, just so I can say I did it. It could be anything. Let me put it this way: I think God invented the dodo bird so when we get up there we could tell Him, "Don't you ever make mistakes?" and He'd say, "Sure, look." (Laughs.) I'd like to make my imprint. My dodo bird. A mistake, *mine.* Let's say the whole building is nothing but red bricks. I'd like to have just the black one or the white one or the purple one. Deliberately fuck up.

This is gonna sound square, but my kid is my imprint. He's my freedom. 49 There's a line in one of Hemingway's books. I think it's from *For Whom the Bell Tolls.* They're behind the enemy lines, somewhere in Spain, and she's pregnant. She wants to stay with him. He tells her no. He says, "if you die, I die," knowing he's gonna die. But if you go, I go. Know what I mean? The mystics call it the brass bowl. Continuum. You know what I mean? This is why I work. Every time I see a young guy walk by with a shirt and tie and dressed up real sharp, I'm lookin' at my kid, you know? That's it.

Questions for Discussion

1. Reread the selection, keeping a continuous journal entry about how you react to the different statements LeFevre makes. Use these responses as a starting point for discussion.
2. This narrative is presented in the first person. What sort of person does the speaker seem to be? What is your sense of his voice in the prose? What stylistic signals or cues tell you that this passage is oral speech rather than written prose?
3. How does Mike LeFevre feel about his job? His bosses? His coworkers? What does he find distressing about his work?
4. What are LeFevre's goals for himself? His family? How does LeFevre want to make his mark, his signature, on the world?
5. What are his attitudes toward books and reading? Toward "intellectuals"? Toward race relations? Toward communism? Cite quotes and examples to support your point of view.
6. How does LeFevre's work support the community at large? What do you think Desmond Morris (Chapter 2) might say about LeFevre's contribution to society? About LeFevre's goals for his son?

Ideas for Writing

1. Write an essay in which you explore LeFevre's goals for his son in view of the conflict between laborers and the "college kids" he talks about. In what ways are his goals part of the traditional "American dream"? In what ways are his goals a social or economic struggle?
2. Interview a working person—someone at school, at your workplace, in the community—about his or her work. Write up your account in first or third person. If possible, peer groups could interview people from different occupations on campus or in the local community. Share and discuss the similarities and differences in approaches to and attitudes about work.

Cannery Town in August

Lorna Dee Cervantes

Lorna Dee Cervantes (b. 1954), born of Chicano ancestry in northern California, received a B.A. at San Jose State College (now University) and has also studied at the University of California, Santa Cruz. Her first book of poems, *Emplumada*, was published in 1981. Cervantes has also founded her own press and poetry magazine, *Mango.* In "Cannery Town in August," published in 1981, Cervantes vividly conveys the mood and impression of a town and the dehumanizing life of those cannery workers.

Journal

What images does the expression "cannery town" evoke?

> All night it humps the air.
> Speechless, the steam rises
> from the cannery columns. I hear
> the night bird rave about work
> or lunch, or sing the swing shift   5
> home. I listen, while bodyless
> uniforms and spinach specked shoes
> drift in monochrome down the dark
> moon-possessed streets. Women
> who smell of whiskey and tomatoes,   10
> peach fuzz reddening their lips and eyes—
> I imagine them not speaking, dumbed
> by the can's clamor and drop
> to the trucks that wait, grunting
> in their headlights below.   15
> They spotlight those who walk
> like a dream, with no one
> waiting in the shadows
> to palm them back to living.

Questions for Discussion

1. What mood and scene does the poem suggest? Refer to images that create this mood.
2. Why does the speaker mention "bodyless uniforms" and "spinach specked shoes"? What mood, what feelings about labor do they suggest?
3. What happens to the workers? What effect does their work have on them?

Ideas for Writing

1. Develop your journal entry into an essay that conveys your own impressions of a cannery town or of factory labor. You could develop the theme suggested by Cervantes' poem or offer a different view, but in either case strive to create a mood, to suggest an atmosphere, through precise words, images, and sentences.
2. Compare and contrast this poem with the Parker selection later in the chapter. You could discuss tone, images, language, theme, genre, or some other aspect of the selections.
3. If you live near any factories, canneries, or industrial areas, write a prose description of the place and of the people who work there. Then write a version in poetry.

Jorge the Church Janitor
Finally Quits

Martin Espada

Martin Espada (b. 1957) was born in Brooklyn and currently works as a tenant lawyer in Boston. He has worked at many different jobs such as a radio journalist in Nicaragua, a mental patient advocate, an attendant in a primary nursery, and a bouncer in a bar. His writing reflects the diversity of his experience; his publications include the collections *The Immigrant Iceboy's Bolero* (1986) and *Rebellion Is the Circle of a Lover's Hands* (1990).

Journal

How would you expect a church or religious group to treat working people?

> No one asks
> where I am from,
> I must be
> from the country of janitors,
5 | > I have always mopped this floor.
> Honduras, you are a squatter's camp
> outside the city
> of their understanding.
>
> No one can speak
10 | > my name,
> I host the *fiesta*
> of the bathroom,
> stirring the toilet
> like a punchbowl.
15 | > The Spanish music of my name
> is lost
> when the guests complain
> about toilet paper.
>
> What they say
20 | > must be true:
> I am smart,
> but I have a bad attitude.
>
> No one knows
> that I quit tonight,
25 | > maybe the mop
> will push on without me,
> sniffing along the floor

like a crazy squid
with stringy gray tentacles.
They will call it Jorge.   30

Questions for Discussion

1. Examine the stanza openers: "No one asks," "No one can speak," "No one knows." What point do these phrases make about the employers' perceptions of Jorge?
2. What does the opening stanza suggest about Jorge's identity? What does the speaker mean by "country of janitors"? Relate this point to the "Cannery Town in August."
3. Drawing on your journal entry for discussion, consider the ways in which it is ironic that Jorge's employers belong to a church.
4. Select an image, such as that of the mop, and discuss what that image contributes to the tone and mood of the poem and to the voice of the speaker.

Ideas for Writing

1. Assume the persona of Jorge's boss; then write a response to his resignation.
2. Compare this poem and the previous selection and what they suggest about the work place and work. How are the work places and type of work similar? How are they different? Cite evidence from the poems to support your view.
3. Research laws and statutes pertaining to protecting illegal immigrants from exploitation, such as minimum wage laws. In view of recent revelations about illegal child care workers and others analyze your findings and argue that the relevant laws are appropriate, necessary, not enforceable, or whatever else you may determine. You could report your findings to an appropriate local support group for immigrant workers.

Breaking Silences: Community of Memory

Ronald Takaki

Ronald Takaki is the grandson of immigrant plantation laborers from Japan. He graduated from the College of Wooster in Ohio and holds a Ph.D. from the University of California at Berkeley, where he is the graduate advisor of the Ethnic Studies Program. Takaki's awards include Berkeley's Distinguished Teaching Award and Cornell's Goldwin Smith University Lectureship. His books include *Iron Cages: Race and Culture in Nineteenth-Century America*. The following selection is excerpted from the final chapter of *Strangers from a Different Shore* (1989).

Journal

How did your family come to live where you grew up? Did they come for work, or to build a better life, or to follow other relatives? Discuss.

Like Georg Simmel's "stranger," the early Asian immigrants found themselves viewed and treated as outsiders. As newcomers, they lacked organic and traditional ties to American society. But so did Irish, Jewish, Italian, and other European immigrants. All of them were members of a transnational "industrial reserve army." Coming from lands across the Pacific, however, Asians were "strangers from a different shore." They were "pushed," for "poverty hurt." They were also "pulled" here to meet the labor needs of America's railroads, plantations, mines, farms, and factories. Powered by "necessities" of the "modern world-system," the international labor migrations from Asia to the United States took place, to use Cheng and Bonacich's apt phrase, "under capitalism." But there was in addition "extravagance"—the desire for freedom, and the realization of potentials, for what Carlos Bulosan described as the "building of a new life with untried materials."[1]

2   America seemed to offer a unique place for such a pursuit, for society in this "fresh green breast of the new world" was still an unfinished one. The land was liminal. The "riverbanks" of centuries of customs and strictures had not yet been formed, inviting initiative and the exercise of imagination. "The country is open, go forward," they exclaimed. Their dreams inspired many to break from old patterns and to cross a wide ocean. But here the Asian newcomers encountered a prevailing vision of America as essentially a place where European immigrants would establish a homogeneous white society and where nonwhites would have to remain "strangers." Their distinguishing physical features became what Robert E. Park termed "racial uniforms," and they were placed in a racially stratified labor structure. In order to discipline labor and keep wages low, planters in Hawaii pitted workers of different Asian nationalities against each other, and employers on the mainland promoted "ethnic antagonism" between Asian and white workers.[2]

3   But the Asian immigrants chose not to let the course of their lives be determined completely by the "necessity" of race and class in America. While tensions did develop among the Asian groups in the islands, a remarkable degree of interethnic community emerged among them as they lived together in the camps, spoke the common language of pidgin English, and went out on strike together in 1920 and 1946. On the mainland, the various Asian groups were comparatively isolated from each other and struggled separately against racism and competition from a hostile white working class. Isolated as "strangers," first-wave Chinese and Japanese immigrants developed their own economic enclaves, which in turn provided an economic basis for ethnic solidarity. The early Korean, Asian Indian, and Filipino immigrants did not develop their own colonies. The post-1965 groups have also charted different directions for themselves: the Koreans, Chinese, and Vietnamese have concentrated their economic resources in their own ethnic communities, while the Asian Indians and Filipinos have tended to integrate themselves into American society.

4   Throughout their history in this country, Asians have been struggling in different ways to help America accept and appreciate its diversity. Gradually, through events like World War II as well as through struggles such as the labor

strikes and the Civil Rights Movement, American society has been moving toward a racially inclusive countervision of democracy—the possible pluralistic America depicted by Walt Whitman and Carlos Bulosan. Today Asian Americans live in a very different America from the one the earlier immigrants entered. They are no longer the targets of anti-miscegenation laws: in California in 1980, the rate of marriages to whites for Japanese was 32 percent, Filipinos 24 percent, Asian Indians 23 percent, Koreans 19 percent, Vietnamese 15 percent, and Chinese 14 percent. Asian Americans are no longer victimized by legislation denying them naturalized citizenship and landownership. They have begun to exercise their political voices and have representatives in both houses of Congress as well as in state legislatures and on city councils. They enjoy much of the protection of civil rights laws that outlaw racial discrimination in employment as well as housing and that provide for affirmative action for racial minorities. They have greater freedom than did the earlier immigrants to embrace their own "diversity"—their own cultures as well as their own distinctive physical characteristics, such as their complexion and the shape of their eyes. Many Asian-American children have access to bilingual education and ESL programs, and in universities across the country, from Berkeley to Brown, students find curricula offering courses on Asian-American history. Previously the targets of exclusionist laws, Asian Americans are currently able to maintain the vitality of their communities by the continuing influx of new Asian immigrants. But in many painful ways, they still find themselves unjustly viewed and treated as "strangers from a different shore."

THE MYTH OF THE "MODEL MINORITY"

Today Asian Americans are celebrated as America's "model minority." In 5 1986, NBC Nightly News and the McNeil/Lehrer Report aired special news segments on Asian Americans and their success, and a year later, CBS's 60 Minutes presented a glowing report on their stunning achievements in the academy. "Why are Asian Americans doing so exceptionally well in school?" Mike Wallace asked, and quickly added, "They must be doing something right. Let's bottle it." Meanwhile, U.S. News & World Report featured Asian-American advances in a cover story, and Time devoted an entire section on this meteoric minority in its special immigrants issue, "The Changing Face of America." Not to be outdone by its competitors, Newsweek titled the cover story of its college-campus magazine "Asian-Americans: The Drive to Excel" and a lead article of its weekly edition "Asian Americans: A 'Model Minority.' " Fortune went even further, applauding them as "America's Super Minority," and the New Republic extolled "The Triumph of Asian-Americans" as "America's greatest success story."[3]

The celebration of Asian-American achievements in the press has been 6 echoed in the political realm. Congratulations have come even from the White House. In a speech presented to Asian and Pacific Americans in the chief executive's mansion in 1984, President Ronald Reagan explained the significance of their success. America has a rich and diverse heritage, Reagan declared, and Americans are all descendants of immigrants in search of the "American dream." He praised Asian and Pacific Americans for helping to "preserve that dream by living up to the bedrock values" of America—the principles of "the sacred worth of human life, religious faith, community spirit and the responsibility of parents and schools to be teachers of tolerance, hard work, fiscal responsibility, cooperation, and love." "It's no wonder," Reagan emphatically noted, "that the median incomes of Asian and Pacific-American families are much higher than the total American average." Hailing Asian and Pacific Americans as an example for all Americans, Reagan conveyed his gratitude to them: we need "your values, your hard work" expressed within "our political system."[4]

7   But in their celebration of this "model minority," the pundits and the politicians have exaggerated Asian-American "success" and have created a new myth. Their comparisons of incomes between Asians and whites fail to recognize the regional location of the Asian-American population. Concentrated in California, Hawaii, and New York, Asian Americans reside largely in states with higher incomes but also higher costs of living than the national average: 59 percent of all Asian Americans lived in these three states in 1980, compared to only 19 percent of the general population. The use of "family incomes" by Reagan and others has been very misleading, for Asian-American families have more persons working per family than white families. In 1980, white nuclear families in California had only 1.6 workers per family, compared to 2.1 for Japanese, 2.0 for immigrant Chinese, 2.2 for immigrant Filipino, and 1.8 for immigrant Korean (this last figure is actually higher, for many Korean women are unpaid family workers). Thus the family incomes of Asian Americans indicate the presence of more workers in each family, rather than higher incomes.[5]

8   Actually, in terms of personal incomes, Asian Americans have not reached equality. In 1980 the mean personal income for white men in California was $23,400. While Japanese men earned a comparable income, they did so only by acquiring more education (17.7 years compared to 16.8 years for white men twenty-five to forty-four years old) and by working more hours (2,160 hours compared to 2,120 hours for white men in the same age category). In reality, then, Japanese men were still behind Caucasian men. Income inequalities for other men were more evident: Korean men earned only $19,200, or 82 percent of the income of white men, Chinese men only $15,900 or 68 percent, and Filipino men only $14,500 or 62 percent. In New York the mean personal income for white men was $21,600, compared to only $18,900 or 88 percent for Korean men, $16,500 or 76 percent for Filipino men, and only $11,200 or 52 percent for Chinese men. In the San Francisco Bay Area, Chinese-immigrant men earned only 72 percent of what their white counterparts earned, Filipino-immigrant men 68 percent, Korean-immigrant men 69 percent, and Vietnamese-immigrant men 52 percent. The incomes of Asian-American men were close to and sometimes even below those of black men (68 percent) and Mexican-American men (71 percent).[6]

The patterns of income inequality for Asian men reflect a structural problem: Asians tend to be located in the labor market's secondary sector, where wages are low and promotional prospects minimal. Asian men are clustered as janitors, machinists, postal clerks, technicians, waiters, cooks, gardeners, and computer programmers; they can also be found in the primary sector, but here they are found mostly in the lower-tier levels as architects, engineers, computer-systems analysts, pharmacists, and schoolteachers, rather than in the upper-tier levels of management and decision making. "Labor market segmentation and restricted mobility between sectors," observed social scientists Amado Cabezas and Gary Kawaguchi, "help promote the economic interest and privilege of those with capital or those in the primary sector, who mostly are white men."[7]

This pattern of Asian absence from the higher levels of administration is characterized as "a glass ceiling"—a barrier through which top management positions can only be seen, but not reached, by Asian Americans. While they are increasing in numbers on university campuses as students, they are virtually nonexistent as administrators: at Berkeley's University of California campus where 25 percent of the students were Asian in 1987, only one out of 102 top-level administrators was an Asian. In the United States as a whole, only 8 percent of Asian Americans in 1988 were "officials" and "managers," as compared to 12 percent for all groups. Asian Americans are even more scarce in the upper strata of the corporate hierarchy: they constituted less than half of one percent of the 29,000 officers and directors of the nation's thousand largest companies. Though they are highly educated, Asian Americans are generally not present in positions of executive leadership and decision making. "Many Asian Americans hoping to climb the corporate ladder face an arduous ascent," the *Wall Street Journal* observed. "Ironically, the same companies that pursue them for technical jobs often shun them when filling managerial and executive positions."[8]

Asian Americans complain that they are often stereotyped as passive and told they lack the aggressiveness required in administration. The problem is not whether their culture encourages a reserved manner, they argue, but whether they have opportunities for social activities that have traditionally been the exclusive preserve of elite white men. "How do you get invited to the cocktail party and talk to the chairman?" asked Landy Eng, a former assistant vice president of Citibank. "It's a lot easier if your father or your uncle or his friend puts his arm around you at the party and says, 'Landy, let me introduce you to Walt.' " Excluded from the "old boy" network, Asian Americans are also told they are inarticulate and have an accent. Edwin Wong, a junior manager at Acurex, said: "I was given the equivalent of an ultimatum: 'Either you improve your accent or your future in getting promoted to senior management is in jeopardy.' " The accent was a perceived problem at work. "I felt that just because I had an accent a lot of Caucasians thought I was stupid." But whites with German, French, or English accents do not seem to be similarly handicapped. Asian Americans are frequently viewed as technicians rather than administrators. Thomas Campbell, a general manager at Westinghouse Electric Corp., said that Asian Americans would be happier staying in technical fields and that few of them are adept at sorting through the complexities of large-scale business. This very image can produce a reinforcing pattern: Asian-American professionals often find they "top out," reaching a promotional ceiling early in their careers. "The only jobs we could get were based on merit," explained Kumar Patel, head of the material science division at AT&T. "That is why you find most [Asian-Indian] professionals in technical rather than administrative or managerial positions." Similarly an Asian-Indian engineer who had worked for Kaiser for some twenty years told a friend: "They [management] never ever give you [Asian Indians] an executive position in the company. You can only go up so high and no more."[9]

12   Asian-American "success" has emerged as the new stereotype for this ethnic minority. While this image has led many teachers and employers to view Asians as intelligent and hardworking and has opened some opportunities, it has also been harmful. Asian Americans find their diversity as individuals denied: many feel forced to conform to the "model minority" mold and want more freedom to be their individual selves, to be "extravagant." Asian university students are concentrated in the sciences and technical fields, but many of them wish they had greater opportunities to major in the social sciences and humanities. "We are educating a generation of Asian technicians," observed an Asian-American professor at Berkeley, "but the communities also need their historians and poets." Asian Americans find themselves all lumped together and their diversity as groups overlooked. Groups that are not doing well, such as the unemployed Hmong, the Downtown Chinese, the elderly Japanese, the old Filipino farm laborers, and others, have been rendered invisible. To be out of sight is also to be without social services. Thinking Asian Americans have succeeded, government officials have sometimes denied funding for social service programs designed to help Asian Americans learn English and find employment. Failing to realize that there are poor Asian families, college administrators have sometimes excluded Asian-American students from Educational Opportunity Programs (EOP), which are intended for *all* students from low-income families. Asian Americans also find themselves pitted against and resented by other racial minorities and even whites. If Asian Americans can make it on their own, pundits are asking, why can't poor blacks and whites on welfare? Even middle-class whites, who are experiencing economic difficulties because of plant closures in a deindustrializing America and the expansion of low-wage service employment, have been urged to emulate the Asian-American "model minority" and to work harder.[10]

13   Indeed, the story of the Asian-American triumph offers ideological affirmation of the American Dream in an era anxiously witnessing the decline of the United States in the international economy (due to its trade imbalance and its transformation from a creditor to a debtor nation), the emergence of a new black underclass (the percentage of black female-headed families having almost doubled from 22 percent in 1960 to 40 percent in 1980), and a collapsing white middle class (the percentage of households earning a "middle-class" income falling from 28.7 percent in 1967 to 23.2 percent in 1983). Intellectually,

it has been used to explain "losing ground"—why the situation of the poor has deteriorated during the last two decades of expanded government social services. According to this view, advanced by pundits like Charles Murray, the interventionist federal state, operating on the "misguided wisdom" of the 1960s, made matters worse: it created a web of welfare dependency. But this analysis has overlooked the structural problems in society and our economy, and it has led to easy cultural explanations and quick-fix prescriptions. Our difficulties, we are sternly told, stem from our waywardness: Americans have strayed from the Puritan "errand into the wilderness." They have abandoned the old American "habits of the heart." Praise for Asian-American success is America's most recent jeremiad—a renewed commitment to make America number one again and a call for a rededication to the bedrock values of hard work, thrift, and industry. Like many congratulations, this one may veil a spirit of competition, even jealousy.[11]

Significantly, Asian-American "success" has been accompanied by the rise 14 of a new wave of anti-Asian sentiment. On college campuses, racial slurs have surfaced in conversations on the quad: "Look out for the Asian Invasion." "M.I.T. means Made in Taiwan." "U.C.L.A. stands for University of Caucasians Living among Asians." Nasty anti-Asian graffiti have suddenly appeared on the walls of college dormitories and in the elevators of classroom buildings: "Chink, chink, cheating chink!" "Stop the Yellow Hordes." "Stop the Chinese before they flunk you out." Ugly racial incidents have broken out on college campuses. At the University of Connecticut, for example, eight Asian-American students experienced a nightmare of abuse in 1987. Four couples had boarded a college bus to attend a dance. "The dance was a formal and so we were wearing gowns," said Marta Ho, recalling the horrible evening with tears. "The bus was packed, and there was a rowdy bunch of white guys in the back of the bus. Suddenly I felt this warm sticky stuff on my hair. They were spitting on us! My friend was sitting sidewise and got hit on her face and she started screaming. Our boy friends turned around, and one of the white guys, a football player, shouted: 'You want to make something out of this, you Oriental faggots!'"[12]

Asian-American students at the University of Connecticut and other col- 15 leges are angry, arguing that there should be no place for racism on campus and that they have as much right as anyone else to be in the university. Many of them are children of recent immigrants who had been college-educated professionals in Asia. They see how their parents had to become greengrocers, restaurant operators, and storekeepers in America, and they want to have greater career choices for themselves. Hopeful a college education can help them overcome racial obstacles, they realize the need to be serious about their studies. But white college students complain: "Asian students are nerds." This very stereotype betrays nervousness—fears that Asian-American students are raising class grade curves. White parents, especially alumni, express concern about how Asian-American students are taking away "their" slots—admission places that should have gone to their children. "Legacy" admission slots reserved for children of alumni have come to function as a kind of invisible affirmative-action program for whites. A college education has always represented a valuable economic resource, credentialing individuals for high income and status employment, and the university has recently become a contested terrain of competition between whites and Asians. In paneled offices, university administrators meet to discuss the "problem" of Asian-American "over-representation" in enrollments.

16   Paralleling the complaint about the rising numbers of Asian-American students in the university is a growing worry that there are also "too many" immigrants coming from Asia. Recent efforts to "reform" the 1965 Immigration Act seem reminiscent of the nativism prevalent in the 1880s and the 1920s. Senator Alan K. Simpson of Wyoming, for example, noted how the great majority of the new immigrants were from Latin America and Asia, and how "a substantial portion" of them did not "integrate fully" into American society. "If language and cultural separatism rise above a certain level," he warned, "the unity and political stability of the Nation will—in time—be seriously eroded. Pluralism within a united American nation has been our greatest strength. The unity comes from a common language and a core public culture of certain shared values, beliefs, and customs, which make us distinctly 'Americans.' " In the view of many supporters of immigration reform, the post-1965 immigration from Asia and Latin America threatens the traditional unity and identity of the American people. "The immigration from the turn of the century was largely a continuation of immigration from previous years in that the European stock of Americans was being maintained," explained Steve Rosen, a member of an organization lobbying for changes in the current law. "Now, we are having a large influx of third-world people, which could be potentially disruptive of our whole Judeo-Christian heritage." Significantly, in March 1988, the Senate passed a bill that would limit the entry of family members and that would provide 55,000 new visas to be awarded to "independent immigrants" on the basis of education, work experience, occupations, and "English language skills."[13]

17   Political concerns usually have cultural representations. The entertainment media have begun marketing Asian stereotypes again: where Hollywood had earlier portrayed Asians as Charlie Chan displaying his wit and wisdom in his fortune cookie Confucian quotes and as the evil Fu Manchu threatening white women, the film industry has recently been presenting images of comic Asians (in *Sixteen Candles*) and criminal Asian aliens (in *Year of the Dragon*). Hollywood has entered the realm of foreign affairs. *The Deer Hunter* explained why the United States lost the war in Vietnam. In this story, young American men are sent to fight in Vietnam, but they are not psychologically prepared for the utter cruelty of physically disfigured Viet Cong clad in black pajamas. Shocked and disoriented, they collapse morally into a world of corruption, drugs, gambling, and Russian roulette. There seems to be something sinister in Asia and the people there that is beyond the capability of civilized Americans to comprehend. Upset after seeing this movie, refugee Thu-Thuy Truong exclaimed: "We didn't play Russian roulette games in Saigon! The whole thing was made up." Similarly *Apocalypse Now* portrayed lost innocence: Americans enter the

heart of darkness in Vietnam and become possessed by madness (in the persona played by Marlon Brando) but are saved in the end by their own technology and violence (represented by Martin Sheen). Finally, in movies celebrating the exploits of Rambo, Hollywood has allowed Americans to win in fantasy the Vietnam War they had lost in reality. "Do we get to win this time?" snarls Rambo, our modern Natty Bumppo, a hero of limited conversation and immense patriotic rage.[14]

Meanwhile, anti-Asian feelings and misunderstandings have been exploding violently in communities across the country, from Philadelphia, Boston, and New York to Denver and Galveston, Seattle, Portland, Monterey, and San Francisco. In Jersey City, the home of 15,000 Asian Indians, a hate letter published in a local newspaper warned: "We will go to any extreme to get Indians to move out of Jersey City. If I'm walking down the street and I see a Hindu and the setting is right, I will just hit him or her. We plan some of our more extreme attacks such as breaking windows, breaking car windows and crashing family parties. We use the phone book and look up the name Patel. Have you seen how many there are?" The letter was reportedly written by the "Dotbusters," a cruel reference to the *bindi* some Indian women wear as a sign of sanctity. Actual attacks have taken place, ranging from verbal harassments and egg throwing to serious beatings. Outside a Hoboken restaurant on September 27, 1987, a gang of youths chanting "Hindu, Hindu" beat Navroz Mody to death. A grand jury has indicted four teenagers for the murder.[15]

Five years earlier a similarly brutal incident occurred in Detroit. There, in June, Vincent Chin, a young Chinese American, and two friends went to a bar in the late afternoon to celebrate his upcoming wedding. Two white autoworkers, Ronald Ebens and Michael Nitz, called Chin a "Jap" and cursed: "It's because of you motherfuckers that we're out of work." A fistfight broke out, and Chin then quickly left the bar. But Ebens and Nitz took out a baseball bat from the trunk of their car and chased Chin through the streets. They finally cornered him in front of a McDonald's restaurant. Nitz held Chin while Ebens swung the bat across the victim's shins and then bludgeoned Chin to death by shattering his skull. Allowed to plead guilty to manslaughter, Ebens and Nitz were sentenced to three years' probation and fined $3,780 each. But they have not spent a single night in jail for their bloody deed. "Three thousand dollars can't even buy a good used car these days," snapped a Chinese American, "and this was the price of a life." "What kind of law is this? What kind of justice?" cried Mrs. Lily Chin, the slain man's mother. "This happened because my son is Chinese. If two Chinese killed a white person, they must go to jail, maybe for their whole lives. . . . Something is wrong with this country."[16]

Vincent Chin was the only son of Lily and Hing Chin. Lily's great-grandfather had been an immigrant railroad laborer in the nineteenth century, and she remembers his tales about racial persecution. Hing Chin had arrived in the United States in 1922 at the age of seventeen and had served in the U.S. Army during World War II. After the war, both Lily and Hing Chin worked in a laundry, and Mrs. Chin became an assembly-plant worker after her husband died of a kidney disease in 1980. Their son had high hopes for a career. "When he was a child," Lily Chin recalled, "he wanted to be a writer. I said, 'Vincent, you can't make money at that.' Then he wanted to be a lawyer because he liked to talk. 'Ma, I want to be a lawyer.' 'Oh, you're Chinese, nobody'd believe you,' I said. Then he wanted to be a veterinarian. 'Oh, Vincent, you can't do that. You can't open up the animals, you're scared of blood.'" Vincent graduated from Oak Park High School and studied architecture at the Lawrence Institute of Technology. In the summer of 1982, he was working as a draftsman for Efficient Engineering when he was brutally murdered. "I don't understand how this could happen in America," Mrs. Chin cried out bitterly. "My husband fought for this country. We always paid our taxes and worked hard. Before I really loved America, but now this has made me very angry."[17]

21   The murder of Vincent Chin has aroused the anger and concern of Asian Americans across the country. They know he was killed because of his racial membership: Ebens and Nitz perceived Chin as a "stranger," a foreigner, for he did not look like an American. But why was Chin viewed as an alien? Asian Americans blame the educational system for not including their history in the curricula and for not teaching about U.S. society in all of its racial and cultural diversity. Why are the courses and books on American history so Eurocentric? they have asked teachers and scholars accusingly.

22   Asian Americans and supporters of justice for Vincent Chin have charged that the corporate executives of the auto industry must also be held accountable for Chin's death: the auto manufacturers should have been designing and building fuel-efficient cars twenty years ago, and now they are blaming Japan for Detroit's massive unemployment. "Unemployment is not caused by foreign competition," argued Newton Kamakane of UAW Local 1364 in Fremont, California. "It's the result of mistakes and poor planning of the multinational corporations—and General Motors is one of the biggest of them." Unfortunately, unemployment might not have been entirely the consequence of "mistakes and poor planning." American auto companies have been deliberately locating much of their production outside of the United States. They have assembly plants in places like Ciudad Juarez, Mexico, which has come to be called "Little Detroit." They have even invested in the Japanese auto companies themselves: General Motors owns 34 percent of Isuzu (which builds the Buick Opel), Ford 25 percent of Mazda (which makes transmissions for the Escort), and Chrysler 15 percent of Mitsubishi (which produces the Colt and Charger). In their television commercials and their promotional campaigns to "buy American," the automakers have contributed to the anti-Japan hysteria pervasive among American workers and to the proliferation of bumper stickers that scream "Unemployment—Made in Japan" and "Toyota-Datsun-Honda-and-Pearl Harbor."[18]

23   In their protests, Asian Americans recount a long, unhappy history: "The killing of Vincent Chin happened in 1982, not 1882—the year of the Chinese Exclusion Act!" They see a parallel between then and now. "What disturbs me," explained George Wong of the Asian American Federation of Union Membership, "is that the two men who brutally clubbed Vincent Chin to death in Detroit in 1982 were thinking the same thoughts as the lynch mob in San Francisco Chinatown one hundred years ago: 'Kill the foreigners to save our

jobs! The Chinese must go!' When corporate heads tell frustrated workers that foreign imports are taking their jobs, then they are acting like an agitator of a lynch mob."[19]

The murder of Vincent Chin has underscored the need for Asian Americans to break silences. "For a long time we have not fought back," declared George Suey of San Francisco. "But this time we will stand up and fight for our rights." Indeed all Asian Americans—Chinese, Japanese, Koreans, Filipinos, Asian Indians, and Southeast Asians—are standing up this time. They realize what happened to Vincent Chin could happen to them—to anyone with Asian features. "My blood boiled when I first learned that Vincent Chin was deliberately attacked and murdered as an act of racial hatred," growled Harold Fond of the Chinese-American Citizens Alliance. "When the word 'Jap' gets painted on a door or a man is murdered," declared Congressman Norman Mineta of San Jose, "we ought to let the whole world know." Though they represent diverse communities, Asian Americans have come together and joined their voices in protest. Dr. Marisa Chuang of the newly formed American Citizens for Justice stated: "This is an historical moment for Asian Americans because for the first time we are all united."[20] . . .

> All the dreams of youth
> Shipped in emigration boats
> To reach this far shore.

In America, Asian immigrants and their offspring have been actors in history— the first Chinese working on the plantations of Hawaii and in the gold fields of California, the early Japanese immigrants transforming the brown San Joaquin Valley into verdant farmlands, the Korean immigrants struggling to free their homeland from Japanese colonialism, the Filipino farm workers and busboys seeking the America in their hearts, the Asian-Indian immigrants picking fruit and erecting Sikh temples in the West, the American-born Asians like Jean Park and Jade Snow Wong and Monica Sone trying to find an identity for themselves as Asian Americans, the second-wave Asian immigrants bringing their skills and creating new communities as well as revitalizing old communities with culture and enterprise, and the refugees from the war-torn countries of Southeast Asia trying to put their shattered lives together and becoming our newest Asian Americans. Their dreams and hopes unfurled here before the wind, all of them—from the first Chinese miners sailing through the Golden Gate to the last Vietnamese boat people flying into Los Angeles International Airport—have been making history in America. And they have been telling us about it all along.[21]

Works Cited

1. Georg Simmel, "Der Fremde" or "The Stranger," in Simmel, *On Individuality and Social Forms,* edited by Donald N. Levine (Chicago, 1971), pp. 143–149; Karl Marx, *Capital: A Critique of Political Economy* (New York, 1906), pp. 689–703; Immanuel Wallerstein, *The Modern World-System* (New York, 1974); Lucie Cheng and Edna Bonacich (eds.), *Labor Immigration Under Capitalism: Asian Workers in the United States before World War II* (Berkeley, 1984); Robert E. Park, "Human Migration and the

Marginal Man," *American Journal of Sociology*, vol. 33, no. 6 (May 1928), p. 890; Carlos Bulosan, *America Is in the Heart: A Personal History* (rpt. Seattle, 1981, originally published in 1946), p. 104.

2. F. Scott Fitzgerald, *The Great Gatsby* (rpt. New York, 1953), p. 182; Victor Turner, *Dramas, Fields, and Metaphors: Symbolic Action in Human Society* (Ithaca, N.Y., 1974), pp. 232, 237; Wayne K. Patterson, "The Korean Frontier in America: Immigration to Hawaii, 1896–1910," unpublished Ph.D. thesis, University of Pennsylvania, 1977, p. 252; Maxine Hong Kingston, *The Woman Warrior: Memoirs of a Girlhood Among Ghosts* (New York, 1976), p. 6; Robert E. Park, "Racial Assimilation in Secondary Groups with Particular Reference to the Negro," *Papers and Proceedings, Eighth Annual Meeting of the American Sociological Society, 1913*, vol. 8 (Chicago, 1914), p. 71; Edna Bonacich, "A Theory of Ethnic Antagonism: The Split Labor Market," *American Sociological Review*, vol. 37, no. 5 (October 1972), pp. 547–559.

3. CBS, *60 Minutes*, "The Model Minority," February 1, 1987; "Asian-Americans: Are They Making the Grade?" *U.S. News & World Report*, April 2, 1984, pp. 41–47; "The Changing Face of America," Special Immigrants Issue, *Time*, July 8, 1985, pp. 24–101; "Asian-Americans: The Drive to Excel," *Newsweek on Campus*, April 1984, pp. 4–15; "Asian-Americans: A 'Model Minority,'" *Newsweek*, December 6, 1982, pp. 40–51; "America's Super Minority," *Fortune*, November 26, 1986; David A. Bell, "The Triumph of Asian-Americans: America's Greatest Success Story," *New Republic*, July 15 and 22, 1985, pp. 24–31.

4. President Ronald Reagan, speech to a group of Asian and Pacific Americans in the White House, February 23, 1984, reprinted in *Asian Week*, March 2, 1984.

5. Ronald Takaki, "Have Asian Americans Made It?" *San Francisco Examiner*, January 10, 1984; Ronald Takaki, "Comparisons between Blacks and Asian Americans Unfair," *Seattle Post-Intelligencer*, March 21, 1985.

6. Amado Cabezas and Gary Kawaguchi, "Empirical Evidence for Continuing Asian American Income Inequality: The Human Capital Model and Labor Market Segmentation," in Gary Y. Okihiro et al. (eds.), *Reflections on Shattered Windows: Promises and Prospects for Asian American Studies* (Pullman, Wash., 1988), pp. 148, 154; Amado Cabezas, "The Asian American Today as an Economic Success Model: Some Myths and Realities," paper presented at "Break the Silence: A Conference on Anti-Asian Violence, Examining the Growth and Nature of the Problem and Finding Solutions," May 10, 1986, University of California, Berkeley, pp. 6, 8, 9; Amado Cabezas, Larry Hajime Shinagawa, and Gary Kawaguchi, "A Study of Income Differentials Among Asian Americans, Blacks, and Whites in the SMSAs of San Francisco–Oakland–San Jose and Los Angeles–Long Beach in 1980," paper presented at the "All-UC Invitational Conference on the Comparative Study of Race, Ethnicity, Gender, and Class," May 30 and 31, 1986, University of California, Santa Cruz, pp. 9, 10.

7. Cabezas and Kawaguchi, "Empirical Evidence for Continuing Asian American Income Inequality," pp. 156–157.

8. U.S. Equal Employment Opportunity Commission, report, summary in Laird Harrison, "U.S. Study Finds Few Asians in Management," *Asian Week*, May 13, 1988; Winfred Yu, "Asian-Americans Charge Prejudice Slows Climb to Management Ranks," *Wall Street Journal*, September 11, 1985; editorial, *East/West*, June 30, 1988.

9. L. A. Chung and Michael McCabe, "Bay Area Asians Counting on Economic Success, Poll Says," *San Francisco Chronicle*, July 26, 1988; L. A. Chung, "Shedding an Accent to Attain Success," ibid.; John Schwartz, "A 'Superminority' Tops Out," *Newsweek*, May 11, 1987, pp. 48–49; Aprajita Sikri, "Latent Prejudice, Envy Now,"

India Abroad, December 25, 1987; Hamida Chopra, interview with author, September 12, 1988.

10. Ronald Takaki, "Asian Americans in the University," *San Francisco Examiner,* April 16, 1984; William Raspberry, "Beyond Racism (Cont'd.)," *Washington Post,* November 19, 1984; Barry Bluestone and Bennett Harrison, *The Deindustrialization of America* (New York, 1982).

11. Peter Schmeisser, "Is America in Decline?" *The New York Times Magazine,* April 17, 1988; Paul Kennedy, *The Rise and Fall of the Great Powers* (New York, 1987); William Julius Wilson, *The Truly Disadvantaged: The Inner City, the Underclass, and Public Policy* (Chicago, 1987), p. 65; Chris Tilly, "U-Turn on Equality: The Puzzle of Middle Class Decline," *Dollars & Sense,* May 1986, p. 11 ("middle-class" income is defined as between 75 percent and 125 percent of median household income); Bob Kuttner, "The Declining Middle," *The Atlantic Monthly,* July 1983, pp. 60–72; Barbara Ehrenreich, "Is the Middle Class Doomed?" *The New York Times Magazine,* September 7, 1986, pp. 44, 50, 62; Tom Wicker, "Let 'Em Eat Swiss Cheese," *The New York Times,* September 2, 1988; Don Wycliff, "Why the Underclass Is Still Under," *The New York Times,* November 16, 1987; Charles Murray, *Losing Ground: American Social Policy, 1950–1980* (New York, 1984), pp. 32, 146, 220, 227; Ronald Takaki, "Poverty Is Thriving Under Reagan," *The New York Times,* March 3, 1986.

12. Marta Ho, interview with author, November 5, 1988.

13. Tom Surh, "U.S. Policy on Asian Immigration," *East Wind,* vol. 1, no. 2 (Fall/Winter 1982), pp. 27–28; Zita Arocha, " '80s Immigration Matching the Record 1901–10 Flood," Honolulu *Star-Bulletin and Advertiser,* July 24, 1988; Susan Rasky, "Senate, 88 to 4, Passes Bill Setting Immigration Limits," *The New York Times,* March 16, 1988.

14. Thu-Thuy Truong, panel discussion, Asian American Studies 20A, Spring 1980, University of California, Berkeley; *Rambo: First Blood Part II* (HBO video, New York, 1985).

15. Jean Daskais, "Jersey City Indians Battle Hate," *India West,* October 16, 1987; Savyasaachi Jain, "Threats of Racial Violence Alarm Indians in Jersey City," *India Abroad,* October 2, 1987; "Irregularities Reported in Jersey Asian Slaying Trial," *Asian Week,* September 23, 1988.

16. Ronald Takaki, "Who Really Killed Vincent Chin?" *San Francisco Examiner,* September 21, 1983.

17. Takaki, "Who Really Killed Vincent Chin?"

18. David Smollar, "U.S. Asians Feel Trade Backlash," *Los Angeles Times,* September 14, 1983; Robert Christopher, "Don't Blame the Japanese," *The New York Times Magazine,* October 19, 1986; Ronald Takaki, "I am not a 'Jap'; I am a man," *In These Times,* October 19–25, 1983; Gordon Martin, "Links Between Detroit, Japan?" *San Francisco Chronicle,* September 8, 1983; John Holusha, "The Disappearing 'U.S. Car,' " *The New York Times,* August 10, 1985.

19. Takaki, "Who Really Killed Vincent Chin?"

20. Takaki, "Who Really Killed Vincent Chin?"; Smollar, "U.S. Asians Feel Trade Backlash."

21. Poem by Shigeko, in Kazuo Ito, *Issei,* p. 40.

Questions for Discussion

1. According to Takaki, in what ways are Asian American successes linked to the "American dream"? How does praise for such success relate to a "Puritan work ethic"?

2. What is the evidence that Asian Americans are successful? What evidence does

Takaki offer that such success creates a myth? Why does the myth cause so many problems for Asians? Give specific examples from the reading and, if appropriate, from your own experience.

3. Aside from dealing with the myth, what struggles have Asian Americans had historically? Why was it so much more difficult for Asians to adjust to life in the mainland United States than in Hawaii?

4. What is lost, and what is gained, if anything, in the "model minority" myth?

Ideas for Writing

1. Are there myths about your culture, ethnicity, or gender? Describe such a myth in detail in an essay, or write a narrative that illustrates the concept of that myth.

2. Investigate and analyze the history of a particular ethnic group in America—the ethos, or system of values and beliefs, and the immigration history, if known. Alternatively, look at the history of a particular ethnic group in a specific geographical area—Hawaii, the "dustbowl" states, border states, American Indian reservations, for example.

3. What facilities or support networks are available in your area for immigrant laborers or low-income workers? For newcomers from other countries? You could look into pending legislation that may affect such people or attend town meetings on such issues run by your local government leaders. Write up a summary of the documents for agencies working with new or displaced workers.

Coming to America: Difficulties of Vietnamese Youth

Hien Tran

Hien Tran (b. 1976) is a college student in California who came to America from Vietnam as a youngster, settling in southern California. He has a number of relatives and friends who came to America from Vietnam at different stages of their lives, and he draws upon some of their experiences in this essay. Tran is planning to study medicine.

Journal

Write about your first day at a new school, in a new home, in a new town. How did you feel? How did you learn to adjust?

Between 1964 and 1975, the United States played an important role in assisting Vietnamese resistance to the Communist movement. Yet South Vietnam's government failed on April 30, 1975, with the war ending in Communist takeover. At this point, President Ford ordered the withdrawal of all American troops from Vietnam. Since then, the country has remained under Communist rule, and many Vietnamese have emigrated from Vietnam. From 1975 to the present day, an enormous number of Vietnamese refugees have resettled in the United States. For the many Vietnamese who came to the United States, it was a new beginning in their lives; for others, it was a transplantation of the lives that they already had. A third group, however, the group of youths, could not really start over and did not already have a life to continue. For these youths, the adjustment process is a difficult journey that they never complete, leaving them culturally stranded in a nation that is foreign to them.

In researching this topic, I interviewed by telephone several Vietnamese 2 people from my community who came to the United States during their teen years. Two of these people, Ngoc Tuan Le and Huy Le, are my relatives; the third, Quy Nguyen, is a friend whom I've known since high school. These three youths are all Vietnamese males who have either adjusted into the American culture, are in the process of adjusting, or have adjusted in a negative way. Ngoc came to the United States in 1984 as an unaccompanied minor and stayed with my family. Huy came over just recently, in 1991, when he was 15, and also stayed with my family. Quy, on the other hand, came over as an unaccompanied minor and was placed in a foster home when he was 13 years old.

To start each interview, I asked each person how he came over to the 3 United States and how he felt when he arrived in the United States. I then asked each interviewee questions that pertained to his situation. (Huy's interview was conducted in Vietnamese because he cannot speak English fluently. I later translated his responses into English.) In all three interviews I attempted to reach into the psyche of each and draw out his emotions in the interview. In the end, I realized that these three people demonstrated the difficulty of adjusting at an age when life was just beginning to happen.

Vietnamese youths between the age of thirteen and eighteen face tremen- 4 dous difficulties adjusting to American society. Education is one of the biggest problems encountered by these youths, especially those who do not have the proper educational background from Vietnam. Learning how to speak English is especially hard for older kids who have spoken Vietnamese all their lives. Huy, for example, still speaks in Vietnamese and finds it difficult to speak English. The social aspect is another obstacle Vietnamese youths face in this adjustment process. These youths often find themselves unable to cope with other American people due to their limited English and their different way of life. Not only are these newly arrived youths separated from other Americans, but they are also separated from the Americanized Vietnamese. There is such a big gap between these two groups in the ways they dress and act that they don't even socialize with each other. With all these hurdles, the adjustment of Vietnamese youths to American culture is a long and strenuous task, and it is even more difficult for those who come here unaccompanied. Most youths who come here by themselves often suffer from numerous psychological problems due to their estrangement in a foreign society without the support of friends or families.

Education in the United States plays an extremely crucial role in the 5 process of adjustment for Vietnamese youths. Vietnamese children who arrive at a young age tend to adopt the English language and educational conditions more readily than those in their teen years. This is especially true in my own case. I came over when I was three years old, and learning the English language was not very difficult. I had already learned to speak my own native tongue of Vietnamese, but my ability to speak it was still in its infantile stage. The fact that all languages were new to me made it easier for me to learn any language that I was exposed to. Since I was exposed to English on the television, on the playground, and later in school, I naturally picked up and accepted the language. However, for older kids who are recent immigrants, the process of learning a new language is quite difficult. Older children have grown accustomed to the Vietnamese language and dialect and now must learn a new language. One Vietnamese refugee states, "It was hard to listen and understand English. It was hard to pronounce polysyllabic words . . . I watched television to improve my listening skills" (Tran A30). This Vietnamese youth, like many others, has had difficulties adjusting to the English language because he is used to the simplicity of the Vietnamese language with its strictly monosyllabic words and short sentences.

6   Not only do differences in the language structure affect these youths' rate of adjustment, but their educational background in Vietnam affects it as well. Loi Truong, a Vietnamese outreach counselor in Orange County, states, "Those with an educational background, they progress real fast. . . . Those without a background, they face difficulty" (qtd. in "La Quinta" A30). Those youths who had little schooling in Vietnam tend to perform poorly in American schools and eventually give up trying to obtain a proper education, while those, like Ngoc, who had a solid education tend to perform quite well and use their education as a means of adjusting. Ngoc states, "I did pretty well, mostly A's and B's but occasionally, some C's. I think it's because of my schooling in Vietnam. Back there, I learned advanced math and a bit of English, so I had a little leadway when I got here." With Ngoc's strong educational background, his determination to succeed, and the support of my family, he was later able to attend Rancho Santiago College. Now at the age of twenty-four, Ngoc is a real estate agent. He is able to speak English quite fluently, interact well with both his Vietnamese and American clients, and adapt to the American culture quite well (Ngoc Le interview).

7   On the other hand, most Vietnamese newcomers come from farm communities where education is not stressed. Huy, for example, spent most of his time helping out on the family farm back in Vietnam and spent little time in school. Therefore, he didn't have a strong educational background and could not adjust to the American educational demands. "I feel real stupid . . . it's so hard to keep up with other kids. Sometimes I just don't care anymore," Huy states with dismay (Huy Le interview). Obviously, his desire and ambition for a good education have diminished. Huy's case is not unique but similar to that of many other youths who face the same problem which leads to the failure or slowdown in their adjustment. With a limited education, these Vietnamese youths will find it difficult to integrate into a competitive society that requires basic communication and literacy skills.

Besides learning to deal with education in American schools, Vietnamese 8 youths also face social difficulties in relating to their American peers. Older Vietnamese youths tend to have a tougher time being accepted among their peers than younger Vietnamese refugees. Younger children tend to be more ignorant of the differences between themselves and others. To them, a friend can be anyone; they are unaware of social cliques. Yet at the age of thirteen and older, self-identity, self-awareness, and social acceptance are greatly stressed among American youths. Teenage youths tend to separate themselves according to the way they speak, the way they act, and the way they dress. These categories, therefore, make it more difficult for older Vietnamese youths to blend in and be accepted by other American students.

For Ngoc this was especially true. Ngoc found it extremely difficult at first 9 to adapt to his high school. He felt like "such an outsider in the wrong place . . . real awkward and uncomfortable." He did not feel socially accepted by any of the groups on campus. His sense of identity, defined by belonging and blending in with his peers, was nonexistent. When asked about his self-esteem, he responds, "I didn't have very much of one. I was really intimidated, and I felt inferior to the other American kids. They had everything and I had nothing" (Ngoc Le interview). This statement shows that Ngoc, like many other Vietnamese youths, developed a sense of low self-esteem and loss of identity and confidence due to his new surroundings and his difficulty in adjusting to them.

Not only is there a social gap between the Vietnamese newcomers and 10 American students, but this gap also exists among the newcomers and the Americanized Vietnamese students. One of the major sources of the social gap is the economic background of these newcomers. While Americanized Vietnamese youths often dress in the latest Gap trends, newcomers wear outdated or donated clothing. This separation of the two groups can be seen at lunchtime at La Quinta High School where the "Americanized [Vietnamese] youths hang out in the quad while the newly arrived hang out in the grassy parts of the schoolyard. The former [group] converses in English, the latter in Vietnamese" ("La Quinta" A29). Newly arrived Vietnamese youths also suffer from verbal and sometimes physical abuse by other students. One American-born Vietnamese student at La Quinta says, "It's like making fun of geeks and nerds. We make fun of FOBs [fresh off the boats]. It's no big deal" (qtd. in "La Quinta" A29). Remarks like this trap these newly arrived Vietnamese youths in their own group, their "FOB" group, and separate them from their American peers. Huy's friends, for example, are all Vietnamese newcomers like him. He does not want to associate with other Vietnamese who are already Americanized. He referred to them as "stuck up, and they think they are above others who are not like them. Most of the time I can't understand them because they don't even speak a single word of Vietnamese" (Huy Le interview). This division between the "FOBs" and the Americanized Vietnamese illustrates the clash that occurs when one group has already assimilated and the other has not. The Americanized Vietnamese invoke this division almost as if they are trying to cast away the symbol of their past. They seem to see in these Vietnamese newcomers the image of their own origins, realizing that either they were once in the same social predicament as these newcomers or their parents were. Thus, this separation makes it more difficult for Vietnamese youths to make a smooth transition into American society. After two years of being in the United States, Huy still converses almost exclusively in Vietnamese, has only Vietnamese friends, and has not improved in his academic performance. By isolating himself with the things that he is familiar with, he is not able to make any progress in assimilating into the new American society (Huy Le interview).

11   Among all the Vietnamese refugees, unaccompanied Vietnamese youths suffer the most. These youths "experience a tremendous sense of loss, confusion over their sense of identity and self-worth, and an overwhelming sense of bewilderment at the new world and its demands" (Mortland and Egan 240). Case studies done on unaccompanied minors indicate a high level of depression and anxiety. Nguyen, a seventeen-year-old unaccompanied minor who was waiting resettlement from Camp Pendleton, scored relatively low on a self-esteem test, and other tests showed that he was depressed and disturbed (Felsman et al. 1254). Nguyen is just one example of many unaccompanied Vietnamese minors who are in the United States, for the first time, separated from their families, friends, and any adult guidance. Therefore, Vietnamese youths such as Nguyen feel lost and out of place. The overall results of the case study "suggest that these refugees, especially the young adults and unaccompanied minors, may be at-risk for mental health problems" (Felsman et al. 1255).

12   To make matters worse, some of these unaccompanied minors, the "free cases," are placed into Caucasian foster homes after their resettlement to the United States. These "free cases" are the ones who have no family or friends in America. According to Carol Mortland and Maura Egan, who researched Vietnamese youths in foster care, "unaccompanied refugee minors in foster care in the United States have enormous adjustment difficulties" (Mortland and Egan 240). These youths are separated from other Vietnamese families and the people they traveled with to be placed in the homes of American families. They often have difficulty accepting their new parental figures and frequently experience loneliness, distress and anger (Mortland and Egan 240). Another reason that these youths seem to be unable to adjust in their foster homes is the fact that they come from a society which has different customs and expectations. An example of the conflict between the customs is the roles of the sexes. In Vietnam women do all the household chores and cook meals to the taste of the men; however, in America the chores are shared and the meals are cooked to the taste of the chef, usually the foster mom.

13   Of the three people I interviewed, Quy's case best illustrates the problems of adjustment that the "free cases" face. When Quy came to the United States, he was placed in a Caucasian foster family because he was considered to be a "free case." After being separated from his big family of nine in Vietnam, he was quite reluctant and uncomfortable in accepting new parental figures, especially ones from a different nationality. When asked about his feelings toward them, he says, "They weren't my parents. They were just people I lived with. I didn't really care for them, and I don't think they cared for me either" (Nguyen interview). Quy also states that because of the cultural differences

between him and his foster parents, they could not relate and understand one another's situations (Nguyen interview). Quy's remarks demonstrate an obvious cultural and emotional gap between him and his foster parents. At an age when emotional support and a sense of belonging are necessary, Quy found neither; as a result, he suffered loneliness and low self-esteem.

At the age of fifteen, Quy turned to gangs in search of a sense of acceptance and emotional support. "They're like family. They understand how hard it was for me. A lot of them are like me; they just don't get along with their parents," Quy states (Nguyen interview). Now at the age of seventeen, Quy lives and shares his life with other gang members. He continues to attend high school yet could not care less for his education or his future. He feels that the only good thing that happened to him since his arrival was joining the gang (Nguyen interview). The problems that these unaccompanied minors face are many, and these problems are compounded for those "free cases" who are placed in foster homes, where the cultural divisions make it even more difficult for them to adjust. 14

The story of these "free cases" is also one of unrealistic expectations and goals that are difficult for both them and their foster parents to fulfill. For instance, they expect America to be the land of enormous and easily obtainable wealth. Therefore, these youths strive for monetary and materialistic gain quickly to achieve their main purpose in coming to America—to help their families back home. Their false expectations and assumptions make it harder for them to relate and deal with their foster families and with their new culture. 15

The three youths that I interviewed reveal the emotional and the psychological traumas that most Vietnamese teenagers experience when they first encounter their new society. They are caught in the middle of nowhere. They are too old to make a fresh, clean start like younger Vietnamese children. On the other hand, they are not old enough to have their own lives, their own niches, like adults do. They are at an age when it is hard for their tongue to start practicing a new language, when it is hard to be socially accepted, and when it is hard to develop self-identity. These youths are at an age when they are old enough to remember where their home is and realize that they may never see it again. They are at an age when it is most difficult to adjust to a new environment, a new family, and a new culture. 16

Works Cited

Felsman, J. Kirk, Frederick T. L. Leong, Mark C. Johnson, and Irene Crabtree Felsman. "Estimates of Psychological Distress among Vietnamese Refugees: Adolescents, Unaccompanied Minors and Young Adults." *Social Science and Medicine*, Vol. 31, No. 11 (1990): 1251–1256.

"La Quinta: Big Transition." *Los Angeles Times*, 20 Dec. 1992, Orange County ed.: A1 and pages following.

Le, Huy. Telephone interview. 27 Nov. 1993.

Le, Ngoc Tuan. Telephone interview. 27 Nov. 1993.

Mortland, Carol A., and Maura G. Egan. "Vietnamese Youth in American Foster Care." *Social Work*, Vol. 32, No. 3 (1987): 240–245.

Nguyen, Quy. Telephone interview. 27 Nov. 1993.
Tran, De. "A Story of Assimilation Told in Perfect English." *Los Angeles Times,* 20 Dec.
1992, Orange County ed.: A30.

Questions for Discussion

1. What conclusions about issues for young people coming to America from Vietnam does Tran draw upon his research?
2. How does the issue of language reflect the varying degrees of difficulty for the different groups immigrating?
3. Is Tran's description of high school cliques consistent with your experience?
4. What common themes do you find in this essay and Takaki's (this chapter)?
5. Tran's essay integrates written research with interviews and personal accounts. Do you find the evidence convincing? Discuss.
6. What suggestions would you offer Tran if he were to revise this essay?

Ideas for Writing

1. Develop question 3 above into an essay. Illustrate your thesis with observations or narratives based on your high school experience.
2. Investigate issues of Vietnamese immigration in the United States, perhaps focusing on patterns of immigration, unaccompanied youths or "free cases" as Tran describes, interracial foster care, Vietnamese American churches, gangs, cultural events, and the like. Alternatively, look into the situation of Amerasian children who live in Asian countries such as Vietnam. Write up your findings in a documented essay. Include interviews as well as library materials.

Blame It on Feminism

Susan Faludi

Susan Faludi (b. 1959) was born in New York, the daughter of a photographer and an editor. She earned her B.A. at Harvard in 1981 and now resides in San Francisco, California. Faludi has worked as a reporter for the *Miami Herald,* the *Atlanta Constitution,* the *Mercury News* in San Jose, California, and the *Wall Street Journal.* She received the Pulitzer Prize in 1991 for a *Wall Street Journal* article on the leveraged buyout of Safeway, and the National Book Critics Circle Award, 1991, for *Backlash: The Undeclared War against American Women.* In *Backlash,* from which the following selection is excerpted, the author investigates the attacks she observed on women's social, economic, and political progress in the 1980s.

Journal

Can you think of specific gains or losses that the women's movement has brought to women, or to men, in the past few years? You could consider the work place, and educational, political, social, or personal issues.

To be a woman in America at the close of the 20th century—what good fortune. That's what we keep hearing, anyway. The barricades have fallen, politicians assure us. Women have "made it," Madison Avenue cheers. Women's fight for equality has "largely been won," *Time* magazine announces. Enroll at any university, join any law firm, apply for credit at any bank. Women have so many opportunities now, corporate leaders say, that we don't really need equal opportunity policies. Women are so equal now, lawmakers say, that we no longer need an Equal Rights Amendment. Women have "so much," former President Ronald Reagan says, that the White House no longer needs to appoint them to higher office. Even American Express ads are saluting a woman's freedom to charge it. At last, women have received their full citizenship papers.

And yet . . .   2

Behind this celebration of the American woman's victory, behind the news,   3
cheerfully and endlessly repeated, that the struggle for women's rights is won, another message flashes. You may be free and equal now, it says to women, but you have never been more miserable.

This bulletin of despair is posted everywhere—at the newsstand, on the   4
TV set, at the movies, in advertisements and doctors' offices and academic journals. Professional women are suffering "burnout" and succumbing to an "infertility epidemic." Single women are grieving from a "man shortage." *The New York Times* reports: Childless women are "depressed and confused" and their ranks are swelling. *Newsweek* says: Unwed women are "hysterical" and crumbling under a "profound crisis of confidence." The health advice manuals inform: High-powered career women are stricken with unprecedented outbreaks of "stress-induced disorders," hair loss, bad nerves, alcoholism, and even heart attacks. The psychology books advise: Independent women's loneliness represents "a major mental health problem today." Even founding feminist Betty Friedan has been spreading the word: she warns that women now suffer from a new identity crisis and "new 'problems that have no name.' "

How can American women be in so much trouble at the same time that   5
they are supposed to be so blessed? If the status of women has never been higher, why is their emotional state so low? If women got what they asked for, what could possibly be the matter now?

The prevailing wisdom of the past decade has supported one, and only   6
one, answer to this riddle: it must be all that equality that's causing all that pain. Women are unhappy precisely *because* they are free. Women are enslaved by their own liberation. They have grabbed at the gold ring of independence, only to miss the one ring that really matters. They have gained control of their fertility, only to destroy it. They have pursued their own professional dreams—and lost out on the greatest female adventure. The women's movement, as we are told time and again, has proved women's own worst enemy.

"In dispensing its spoils, women's liberation has given my generation high   7
incomes, our own cigarette, the option of single parenthood, rape crisis centers, personal lines of credit, free love, and female gynecologists," Mona Charen, a young law student, writes in the *National Review,* in an article titled

"The Feminist Mistake." "In return it has effectively robbed us of one thing upon which the happiness of most women rests—men." The *National Review* is a conservative publication, but such charges against the women's movement are not confined to its pages. "Our generation was the human sacrifice" to the women's movement, *Los Angeles Times* feature writer Elizabeth Mehren contends in a *Time* cover story. Baby-boom women like her, she says, have been duped by feminism: "We believed the rhetoric." In *Newsweek,* writer Kay Ebeling dubs feminism "the Great Experiment That Failed" and asserts "women in my generation, its perpetrators, are the casualties." Even the beauty magazines are saying it: *Harper's Bazaar* accuses the women's movement of having "lost us [women] ground instead of gaining it."

8   In the last decade, publications from *The New York Times* to *Vanity Fair* to *The Nation* have issued a steady stream of indictments against the women's movement, with such headlines as WHEN FEMINISM FAILED or THE AWFUL TRUTH ABOUT WOMEN'S LIB. They hold the campaign for women's equality responsible for nearly every woe besetting women, from mental depression to meager savings accounts, from teenage suicides to eating disorders to bad complexions. The "Today" show says women's liberation is to blame for bag ladies. A guest columnist in the *Baltimore Sun* even proposes that feminists produced the rise in slasher movies. By making the "violence" of abortion more acceptable, the author reasons, women's rights activists made it all right to show graphic murders on screen.

9   At the same time, other outlets of popular culture have been forging the same connection: in Hollywood films, of which *Fatal Attraction* is only the most famous, emancipated women with condominiums of their own slink wild-eyed between bare walls, paying for their liberty with an empty bed, a barren womb. "My biological clock is ticking so loud it keeps me awake at night," Sally Field cries in the film *Surrender,* as, in an all too common transformation in the cinema of the '80s, an actress who once played scrappy working heroines is now showcased groveling for a groom. In prime-time television shows, from "thirtysomething" to "Family Man," single, professional, and feminist women are humiliated, turned into harpies, or hit by nervous breakdowns; the wise ones recant their independent ways by the closing sequence. In popular novels, from Gail Parent's *A Sign of the Eighties* to Stephen King's *Misery,* unwed women shrink to sniveling spinsters or inflate to fire-breathing she-devils; renouncing all aspirations but marriage, they beg for wedding bands from strangers or swing axes at reluctant bachelors. We "blew it by waiting," a typically remorseful careerist sobs in Freda Bright's *Singular Women;* she and her sister professionals are "condemned to be childless forever." Even Erica Jong's high-flying independent heroine literally crashes by the end of the decade, as the author supplants *Fear of Flying*'s saucy Isadora Wing, a symbol of female sexual emancipation in the '70s, with an embittered careerist-turned-recovering-"co-dependent" in *Any Woman's Blues*—a book that is intended, as the narrator bluntly states, "to demonstrate what a deadend the so-called sexual revolution had become, and how desperate so-called free women were in the last few years of our decadent epoch."

Popular psychology manuals peddle the same diagnosis for contemporary 10
female distress. "Feminism, having promised her a stronger sense of her own
identity, has given her little more than an identity *crisis*," the best-selling
advice manual *Being a Woman* asserts. The authors of the era's self-help classic *Smart Women/Foolish Choices* proclaim that women's distress was "an unfortunate consequence of feminism," because "it created a myth among women
that the apex of self-realization could be achieved only through autonomy,
independence, and career."

In the Reagan and Bush years, government officials have needed no 11
prompting to endorse this thesis. Reagan spokeswoman Faith Whittlesey
declared feminism a "straitjacket" for women, in the White House's only policy speech on the status of the American female population—entitled "Radical Feminism in Retreat." Law enforcement officers and judges, too, have
pointed a damning finger at feminism, claiming that they can chart a path from
rising female independence to rising female pathology. As a California sheriff
explained it to the press, "Women are enjoying a lot more freedom now, and
as a result, they are committing more crimes." The U.S. Attorney General's
Commission on Pornography even proposed that women's professional
advancement might be responsible for rising rape rates. With more women in
college and at work now, the commission members reasoned in their report,
women just have more opportunities to be raped.

Some academics have signed on to the consensus, too—and they are the 12
"experts" who have enjoyed the highest profiles on the media circuit. On network news and talk shows, they have advised millions of women that feminism has condemned them to "a lesser life." Legal scholars have railed against
"the equality trap." Sociologists have claimed that "feminist-inspired" legislative reforms have stripped women of special "protections." Economists have
argued that well-paid working women have created "a less stable American
family." And demographers, with greatest fanfare, have legitimated the prevailing wisdom with so-called neutral data on sex ratios and fertility trends;
they say they actually have the numbers to prove that equality doesn't mix
with marriage and motherhood.

Finally, some "liberated" women themselves have joined the lamentations. 13
In confessional accounts, works that invariably receive a hearty greeting from
the publishing industry, "recovering Superwomen" tell all. In *The Cost of Loving: Women and the New Fear of Intimacy*, Megan Marshall, a Harvard-pedigreed
writer, asserts that the feminist "Myth of Independence" has turned her generation into unloved and unhappy fast-trackers, "dehumanized" by careers
and "uncertain of their gender identity." Other diaries of mad Superwomen
charge that "the hard-core feminist viewpoint," as one of them puts it, has relegated educated executive achievers to solitary nights of frozen dinners and
closet drinking. The triumph of equality, they report, has merely given women
hives, stomach cramps, eye-twitching disorders, even comas.

But what "equality" are all these authorities talking about?   14

If American women are so equal, why do they represent two-thirds of all 15
poor adults? Why are more than 80 percent of full-time working women mak-

ing less than $20,000 a year, nearly double the male rate? Why are they still far more likely than men to live in poor housing and receive no health insurance, and twice as likely to draw no pension? Why does the average working woman's salary still lag as far behind the average man's as it did twenty years ago? Why does the average female college graduate today earn less than a man with no more than a high school diploma (just as she did in the '50s)—and why does the average female high school graduate today earn less than a male high school dropout? Why do American women, in fact, face the worst gender-based pay gap in the developed world?

16   If women have "made it," then why are nearly 80 percent of working women still stuck in traditional "female" jobs—as secretaries, administrative "support" workers and salesclerks? And, conversely, why are they less than 8 percent of all federal and state judges, less than 6 percent of all law partners, and less than one half of 1 percent of top corporate managers? Why are there only three female state governors, two female U.S. senators, and two Fortune 500 chief executives? Why are only nineteen of the four thousand corporate officers and directors women—and why do more than half the boards of Fortune companies still lack even one female member?

17   If women "have it all," then why don't they have the most basic requirements to achieve equality in the work force? Unlike virtually all other industrialized nations, the U.S. government still has no family-leave and child care programs—and more than 99 percent of American private employers don't offer child care either. Though business leaders say they are aware of and deplore sex discrimination, corporate America has yet to make an honest effort toward eradicating it. In a 1990 national poll of chief executives at Fortune 1000 companies, more than 80 percent acknowledged that discrimination impedes female employees' progress—yet, less than 1 percent of these same companies regarded *remedying* sex discrimination as a goal that their personnel departments should pursue. In fact, when the companies' human resource officers were asked to rate their department's priorities, women's advancement ranked last.

18   If women are so "free," why are their reproductive freedoms in greater jeopardy today than a decade earlier? Why do women who want to postpone childbearing now have fewer options than ten years ago? The availability of different forms of contraception has declined, research for new birth control has virtually halted, new laws restricting abortion—or even *information* about abortion—for young and poor women have been passed, and the U.S. Supreme Court has shown little ardor in defending the right it granted in 1973.

19   Nor is women's struggle for equal education over; as a 1989 study found, three-fourths of all high schools still violate the federal law banning sex discrimination in education. In colleges, undergraduate women receive only 70 percent of the aid undergraduate men get in grants and work-study jobs—and women's sports programs receive a pittance compared with men's. A review of state equal-education laws in the late '80s found that only thirteen states had adopted the minimum provisions required by the federal Title IX law—and only seven states had anti-discrimination regulations that covered all education levels.

Nor do women enjoy equality in their own homes, where they still shoul- 20
der 70 percent of the household duties—and the only major change in the last
fifteen years is that now middle-class men *think* they do more around the
house. (In fact, a national poll finds the ranks of women saying their husbands
share equally in child care shrunk to 31 percent in 1987 from 40 percent three
years earlier.) Furthermore, in thirty states, it is still generally legal for husbands to rape their wives; and only ten states have laws mandating arrest for
domestic violence—even though battering was the leading cause of injury of
women in the late '80s. Women who have no other option but to flee find that
isn't much of an alternative either. Federal funding for battered women's shelters has been withheld and one-third of the 1 million battered women who
seek emergency shelter each year can find none. Blows from men contributed
far more to the rising numbers of "bag ladies" than the ill effects of feminism.
In the '80s, almost half of all homeless women (the fastest growing segment
of the homeless) were refugees of domestic violence.

The word may be that women have been "liberated," but women them- 21
selves seem to feel otherwise. Repeatedly in national surveys, majorities of
women say they are still far from equality. Nearly 70 percent of women polled
by *The New York Times* in 1989 said the movement for women's rights had only
just begun. Most women in the 1990 Virginia Slims opinion poll agreed with
the statement that conditions for their sex in American society had improved
"a little, not a lot." In poll after poll in the decade, overwhelming majorities
of women said they needed equal pay and equal job opportunities, they
needed an Equal Rights Amendment, they needed the right to an abortion
without government interference, they needed a federal law guaranteeing
maternity leave, they needed decent child care services. They have none of
these. So how exactly have we "won" the war for women's rights?

Seen against this background, the much ballyhooed claim that feminism 22
is responsible for making women miserable becomes absurd—and irrelevant.
As we shall see in the chapters to follow, the afflictions ascribed to feminism
are all myths. From "the man shortage" to "the infertility epidemic" to "female
burnout" to "toxic day care," these so-called female crises have had their origins not in the actual conditions of women's lives but rather in a closed system that starts and ends in the media, popular culture, and advertising—an
endless feedback loop that perpetuates and exaggerates its own false images
of womanhood.

Women themselves don't single out the women's movement as the source 23
of their misery. To the contrary, in national surveys 75 to 95 percent of women
credit the feminist campaign with *improving* their lives, and a similar proportion say that the women's movement should keep pushing for change. Less
than 8 percent think the women's movement might have actually made their
lot worse.

*   *   *

What actually is troubling the American female population, then? If the 24
many ponderers of the Woman Question really wanted to know, they might
have asked their subjects. In public opinion surveys, women consistently rank

their own *inequality,* at work and at home, among their most urgent concerns. Over and over, women complain to pollsters about a lack of economic, not marital, opportunities; they protest that working men, not working women, fail to spend time in the nursery and the kitchen. The Roper Organization's survey analysts find that men's opposition to equality is "a major cause of resentment and stress" and "a major irritant for most women today." It is justice for their gender, not wedding rings and bassinets, that women believe to be in desperately short supply. When *The New York Times* polled women in 1989 about "the most important problem facing women today," job discrimination was the overwhelming winner; none of the crises the media and popular culture had so assiduously promoted even made the charts. In the 1990 Virginia Slims poll, women were most upset by their lack of money, followed by the refusal of their men to shoulder child care and domestic duties. By contrast, when the women were asked where the quest for a husband or the desire to hold a "less pressured" job or to stay at home ranked on their list of concerns, they placed them at the bottom.

25   As the last decade ran its course, women's unhappiness with inequality only mounted. In national polls, the ranks of women protesting discriminatory treatment in business, political, and personal life climbed sharply. The proportion of women complaining of unequal employment opportunities jumped more than ten points from the '70s, and the number of women complaining of unequal barriers to job advancement climbed even higher. By the end of the decade, 80 percent to 95 percent of women said they suffered from job discrimination and unequal pay. Sex discrimination charges filed with the Equal Employment Opportunity Commission rose nearly 25 percent in the Reagan years, and charges of general harassment directed at working women climbed 208 percent. In the decade, complaints of sexual harassment jumped 70 percent. At home, a much increased proportion of women complained to pollsters of male mistreatment, unequal relationships, and male efforts to, in the words of the Virginia Slims poll, "keep women down." The share of women in the Roper surveys who agreed that men were "basically kind, gentle, and thoughtful" fell from almost 70 percent in 1970 to 50 percent by 1990. And outside their homes, women felt more threatened, too: in the 1990 Virginia Slims poll, 72 percent of women said they felt "more afraid and uneasy on the streets today" than they did a few years ago. Lest this be attributed only to a general rise in criminal activity, by contrast only 49 percent of men felt this way.

26   While the women's movement has certainly made women more cognizant of their own inequality, the rising chorus of female protest shouldn't be written off as feminist-induced "oversensitivity." The monitors that serve to track slippage in women's status have been working overtime since the early '80s. Government and private surveys are showing that women's already vast representation in the lowliest occupations is rising, their tiny presence in higher-paying trade and craft jobs stalled or backsliding, their minuscule representation in upper management posts stagnant or falling, and their pay dropping in the very occupations where they have made the most "progress." The status of women lowest on the income ladder has plunged most perilously; gov-

ernment budget cuts in the first four years of the Reagan administration alone pushed nearly 2 million female-headed families and nearly 5 million women below the poverty line. And the prime target of government rollbacks has been one sex only: one-third of the Reagan budget cuts, for example, came out of programs that predominantly serve women—even more extraordinary when one considers that all these programs combined represent only 10 percent of the federal budget.

The alarms aren't just going off in the work force. In national politics, the already small numbers of women in both elective posts and political appointments fell during the '80s. In private life, the average amount that a divorced man paid in child support fell by about 25 percent from the late '70s to the mid-'80s (to a mere $140 a month). Domestic-violence shelters recorded a more than 100 percent increase in the numbers of women taking refuge in their quarters between 1983 and 1987. And government records chronicled a spectacular rise in sexual violence against women. Reported rapes more than doubled from the early '70s—at nearly twice the rate of all other violent crimes and four times the overall crime rate in the United States. While the homicide rate declined, sex-related murders rose 160 percent between 1976 and 1984. And these murders weren't simply the random, impersonal by-product of a violent society; at least one-third of the women were killed by their husbands or boyfriends, and the majority of that group were murdered just after declaring their independence in the most intimate manner—by filing for divorce and leaving home. 27

By the end of the decade, women were starting to tell pollsters that they feared their sex's social status was once again beginning to slip. They believed they were facing an "erosion of respect," as the 1990 Virginia Slims poll summed up the sentiment. After years in which an increasing percentage of women had said their status had improved from a decade earlier, the proportion suddenly shrunk by 5 percent in the last half of the '80s, the Roper Organization reported. And it fell most sharply among women in their thirties—the age group most targeted by the media and advertisers—dropping about ten percentage points between 1985 and 1990. 28

Some women began to piece the picture together. In the 1989 *New York Times* poll, more than half of black women and one-fourth of white women put it into words. They told pollsters they believed men were now trying to retract the gains women had made in the last twenty years. "I wanted more autonomy," was how one woman, a thirty-seven-year-old nurse, put it. And her estranged husband "wanted to take it away." 29

The truth is that the last decade has seen a powerful counterassault on women's rights, a backlash, an attempt to retract the handful of small and hard-won victories that the feminist movement did manage to win for women. This counterassault is largely insidious: in a kind of pop-culture version of the Big Lie, it stands the truth boldly on its head and proclaims that the very steps that have elevated women's position have actually led to their downfall. 30

The backlash is at once sophisticated and banal, deceptively "progressive" and proudly backward. It deploys both the "new" findings of "scientific 31 research" and the dime-store moralism of yesteryear; it turns into media sound bites both the glib pronouncements of pop-psych trend-watchers and the frenzied rhetoric of New Right preachers. The backlash has succeeded in framing virtually the whole issue of women's rights in its own language. Just as Reaganism shifted political discourse far to the right and demonized liberalism, so the backlash convinced the public that women's "liberation" was the true contemporary American scourge—the source of an endless laundry list of personal, social, and economic problems.

32   But what has made women unhappy in the last decade is not their "equality"—which they don't yet have—but the rising pressure to halt, and even reverse, women's quest for that equality. The "man shortage" and the "infertility epidemic" are not the price of liberation; in fact, they do not even exist. But these chimeras are the chisels of a society-wide backlash. They are part of a relentless whittling-down process—much of it amounting to outright propaganda—that has served to stir women's private anxieties and break their political wills. Identifying feminism as women's enemy only furthers the ends of a backlash against women's equality, simultaneously deflecting attention from the backlash's central role and recruiting women to attack their own cause.

33   Some social observers may well ask whether the current pressures on women actually constitute a backlash—or just a continuation of American society's long-standing resistance to women's rights. Certainly hostility to female independence has always been with us. But if fear and loathing of feminism is a sort of perpetual viral condition in our culture, it is not always in an acute stage; its symptoms subside and resurface periodically. And it is these episodes of resurgence, such as the one we face now, that can accurately be termed "backlashes" to women's advancement. If we trace these occurrences in American history (as we will do in a later chapter), we find such flare-ups are hardly random; they have always been triggered by the perception—accurate or not—that women are making great strides. These outbreaks are backlashes because they have always arisen in reaction to women's "progress," caused not simply by a bedrock of misogyny but by the specific efforts of contemporary women to improve their status, efforts that have been interpreted time and again by men—especially men grappling with real threats to their economic and social well-being on other fronts—as spelling their own masculine doom.

34   The most recent round of backlash first surfaced in the late '70s on the fringes, among the evangelical right. By the early '80s, the fundamentalist ideology had shouldered its way into the White House. By the mid-'80s, as resistance to women's rights acquired political and social acceptability, it passed into the popular culture. And in every case, the timing coincided with signs that women were believed to be on the verge of breakthrough.

35   Just when women's quest for equal rights seemed closest to achieving its objectives, the backlash struck it down. Just when a "gender gap" at the voting booth surfaced in 1980, and women in politics began to talk of capitalizing on it, the Republican party elevated Ronald Reagan and both political parties began to shunt women's rights off their platforms. Just when support for

feminism and the Equal Rights Amendment reached a record high in 1981, the amendment was defeated the following year. Just when women were starting to mobilize against battering and sexual assaults, the federal government stalled funding for battered-women's programs, defeated bills to fund shelters, and shut down its Office of Domestic Violence—only two years after opening it in 1979. Just when record numbers of younger women were supporting feminist goals in the mid-'80s (more of them, in fact, than older women) and a majority of all women were calling themselves feminists, the media declared the advent of a younger "postfeminist generation" that supposedly reviled the women's movement. Just when women racked up their largest percentage ever supporting the right to abortion, the U.S. Supreme Court moved toward reconsidering it.

In other words, the antifeminist backlash has been set off not by women's 36 achievement of full equality but by the increased possibility that they might win it. It is a preemptive strike that stops women long before they reach the finish line. "A backlash may be an indication that women really have had an effect," feminist psychiatrist Dr. Jean Baker Miller has written, "but backlashes occur when advances have been small, before changes are sufficient to help many people. . . . It is almost as if the leaders of backlashes use the fear of change as a threat before major change has occurred." In the last decade, some women did make substantial advances before the backlash hit, but millions of others were left behind, stranded. Some women now enjoy the right to legal abortion—but not the 44 million women, from the indigent to the military work force, who depend on the federal government for their medical care. Some women can now walk into high-paying professional careers—but not the more than 19 million still in the typing pools or behind the department store sales counters. (Contrary to popular myth about the "have-it-all" baby-boom women, the largest percentage of women in this generation remain typists and clerks.)

As the backlash has gathered force, it has cut off the few from the many— 37 and the few women who have advanced seek to prove, as a social survival tactic, that they aren't so interested in advancement after all. Some of them parade their defection from the women's movement, while their working-class peers founder and cling to the splintered remains of the feminist cause. While a very few affluent and celebrity women who are showcased in news articles boast about having "found my niche as Mrs. Andy Mill" and going home to "bake bread," the many working-class women appeal for their economic rights— flocking to unions in record numbers, striking on their own for pay equity and establishing their own fledgling groups for working women's rights. In 1986, while 41 percent of upper-income women were claiming in the Gallup poll that they were not feminists, only 26 percent of low-income women were making the same claim.

*   *   *

Women's advances and retreats are generally described in military terms: 38 battles won, battles lost, points and territory gained and surrendered. The metaphor of combat is not without its merits in this context and, clearly, the same sort of martial accounting and vocabulary is already surfacing here. But by imagining the conflict as two battalions neatly arrayed on either side of the line, we miss the entangled nature, the locked embrace, of a "war" between women and the male culture they inhabit. We miss the reactive nature of a backlash, which, by definition, can exist only in response to another force.

39   In times when feminism is at a low ebb, women assume the reactive role—privately and most often covertly struggling to assert themselves against the dominant cultural tide. But when feminism itself becomes the tide, the opposition doesn't simply go along with the reversal: it digs in its heels, brandishes its fists, builds walls and dams. And its resistance creates countercurrents and treacherous undertows.

40   The force and furor of the backlash churn beneath the surface, largely invisible to the public eye. On occasion in the last decade, they have burst into view. We have seen New Right politicians condemn women's independence, antiabortion protesters firebomb women's clinics, fundamentalist preachers damn feminists as "whores" and "witches." Other signs of the backlash's wrath, by their sheer brutality, can push their way into public consciousness for a time—the sharp increase in rape, for example, or the rise in pornography that depicts extreme violence against women.

41   More subtle indicators in popular culture may receive momentary, and often bemused, media notice, then quickly slip from social awareness: a report, for instance, that the image of women on prime-time TV shows has suddenly degenerated. A survey of mystery fiction finding the numbers of female characters tortured and mutilated mysteriously multiplying. The puzzling news that, as one commentator put it, "So many hit songs have the B-word [bitch] to refer to women that some rap music seems to be veering toward rape music." The ascendancy of virulently misogynist comics like Andrew Dice Clay—who called women "pigs" and "sluts" and strutted in films in which women were beaten, tortured, and blown up—or radio hosts like Rush Limbaugh, whose broadsides against "femi-Nazi" feminists made his syndicated program the most popular radio talk show in the nation. Or word that in 1987, the American Women in Radio & Television couldn't award its annual prize for ads that feature women positively: it could find no ad that qualified.

42   These phenomena are all related, but that doesn't mean they are somehow coordinated. The backlash is not a conspiracy, with a council dispatching agents from some central control room, nor are the people who serve its ends often aware of their role: some even consider themselves feminists. For the most part, its workings are encoded and internalized, diffuse and chameleonic. Not all of the manifestations of the backlash are of equal weight or significance either; some are mere ephemera, generated by a culture machine that is always scrounging for a "fresh" angle. Taken as a whole, however, these codes and cajolings, these whispers and threats and myths, move overwhelmingly in one direction: they try to push women back into their "acceptable" roles—whether as Daddy's girl or fluttery romantic, active nester or passive love object.

Although the backlash is not an organized movement, that doesn't make 43 it any less destructive. In fact, the lack of orchestration, the absence of a single string-puller, only makes it harder to see—and perhaps more effective. A backlash against women's rights succeeds to the degree that it appears *not* to be political, that it appears not to be a struggle at all. It is most powerful when it goes private, when it lodges inside a woman's mind and turns her vision inward, until she imagines the pressure is all in her head, until she begins to enforce the backlash, too—on herself.

In the last decade, the backlash has moved through the culture's secret 44 chambers, traveling through passageways of flattery and fear. Along the way, it has adopted disguises: a mask of mild derision or the painted face of deep "concern." Its lips profess pity for any woman who won't fit the mold, while it tries to clamp the mold around her ears. It pursues a divide-and-conquer strategy: single versus married women, working women versus homemakers, middle- versus working-class. It manipulates a system of rewards and punishments, elevating women who follow its rules, isolating those who don't. The backlash remarkets old myths about women as new facts and ignores all appeals to reason. Cornered, it denies its own existence, points an accusatory finger at feminism, and burrows deeper underground.

Backlash happens to be the title of a 1947 Hollywood movie in which a man 45 frames his wife for a murder he's committed. The backlash against women's rights works in much the same way: its rhetoric charges feminists with all the crimes it perpetrates. The backlash line blames the women's movement for the "feminization of poverty"—while the backlash's own instigators in Washington pushed through the budget cuts that helped impoverish millions of women, fought pay equity proposals, and undermined equal opportunity laws. The backlash line claims the women's movement cares nothing for children's rights—while its own representatives in the capital and state legislatures have blocked one bill after another to improve child care, slashed billions of dollars in federal aid for children, and relaxed state licensing standards for day care centers. The backlash line accuses the women's movement of creating a generation of unhappy single and childless women—but its purveyors in the media are the ones guilty of making single and childless women feel like circus freaks.

To blame feminism for women's "lesser life" is to miss entirely the point 46 of feminism, which is to win women a wider range of experience. Feminism remains a pretty simple concept, despite repeated—and enormously effective—efforts to dress it up in greasepaint and turn its proponents into gargoyles. As Rebecca West wrote sardonically in 1913, "I myself have never been able to find out precisely what feminism is: I only know that people call me a feminist whenever I express sentiments that differentiate me from a doormat."

The meaning of the word "feminist" has not really changed since it first 47 appeared in a book review in the *Athenaeum* of April 27, 1895, describing a woman who "has in her the capacity of fighting her way back to independence." It is the basic proposition that, as Nora put it in Ibsen's *A Doll's House* a century ago, "Before everything else I'm a human being." It is the simply worded sign hoisted by a little girl in the 1970 Women's Strike for Equality: I AM NOT A BARBIE DOLL. Feminism asks the world to recognize at long last that women aren't decorative ornaments, worthy vessels, members of a "special-interest group." They are half (in fact, now more than half) of the national population, and just as deserving of rights and opportunities, just as capable of participating in the world's events, as the other half. Feminism's agenda is basic: It asks that women not be forced to "choose" between public justice and private happiness. It asks that women be free to define themselves—instead of having their identity defined for them, time and again, by their culture and their men.

48   The fact that these are still such incendiary notions should tell us that American women have a way to go before they enter the promised land of equality.

Questions for Discussion

1. What do women rank as their greatest concern? What do others (in the media, in business and academia, and so forth) claim that women's goals are? How do you account for the difference?
2. What evidence suggests that women have not really "made it" economically? Politically? Socially?
3. To what does Faludi attribute the backlash? How can the backlash hurt women? Can it hurt men and children as well?
4. What tone does the author establish in this essay? Analyze her prose style. What kinds of writing strategies help to establish her tone?
5. How does the author present the views of the opposition? Do you think she represents both sides fairly? Discuss.
6. Study Faludi's counterarguments to the assertions that women's presumed equality has made them equal, in paragraphs 5 through 20. How effective are her assertions? How convincing is the evidence?
7. In view of Faludi's arguments, and in your own opinion, why should society be concerned about equal rights and opportunities for women and men?

Ideas for Writing

1. Reflect on the opportunities women do or don't have in your community. Compare them to those for men. You could also consider the question in terms of race, class, or age—in other words, what restrictions are there on the advancement of other members of your community? You could focus the question by looking at the situation at your own school. As a starting point, you could investigate percentages of women and ethnic groups in your campus's student body, faculty, and staff (the Registrar's and human resources offices could help). Analyze your findings with the goal of confirming, or disputing, Faludi's assertions as they apply to your campus.
2. Opponents of the women's movement claim that equality has brought women unhappiness. The author argues, however, that in fact the lack of equality is the problem. What is your view?

A Loaf of Bread

James Alan McPherson

James Alan McPherson (b. 1943) was born and raised in Georgia; he attended college in Atlanta and then went to Harvard Law School. McPherson worked as a journalist and a college teacher; he has published two collections of short stories, *Hue and Cry* (1977) and *Elbow Room* (1977), in which "A Loaf of Bread" was published. This story conveys individuals and a community in conflict; readers may recognize some of the tensions portrayed in the story as related to some of the current issues of conflict in their community.

Journal

What kinds of community tensions were evident in the film *Do the Right Thing?* If you haven't seen the film, write about reactions in your community to the Rodney King case.

It was one of those obscene situations, pedestrian to most people, but invested with meaning for a few poor folk whose lives are usually spent outside the imaginations of their fellow citizens. A grocer named Harold Green was caught red-handed selling to one group of people the very same goods he sold at lower prices at similar outlets in better neighborhoods. He had been doing this for many years, and at first he could not understand the outrage heaped upon him. He acted only from habit, he insisted, and had nothing personal against the people whom he served. They were his neighbors. Many of them he had carried on the cuff during hard times. Yet, through some mysterious access to a television station, the poor folk were now empowered to make grand denunciations of the grocer. Green's children now saw their father's business being picketed on the Monday evening news.

No one could question the fact that the grocer had been overcharging the 2 people. On the news even the reporter grimaced distastefully while reading the statistics. His expression said, "It is my job to report the news, but sometimes even I must disassociate myself from it to protect my honor." This, at least, was the impression the grocer's children seemed to bring away from the television. Their father's name had not been mentioned, but there was a close-up of his store with angry black people, and a few outraged whites, marching in groups of three in front of it. There was also a close-up of his name. After seeing this, they were in no mood to watch cartoons. At the dinner table, disturbed by his children's silence, Harold Green felt compelled to say, "I am not a dishonest man." Then he felt ashamed. The children, a boy and his older sister, immediately left the table, leaving Green alone with his wife. "Ruth. I am not dishonest," he repeated to her.

Ruth Green did not say anything. She knew, and her husband did not, that 3 the outraged people had also picketed the school attended by their children.

They had threatened to return each day until Green lowered his prices. When they called her at home to report this, she had promised she would talk with him. Since she could not tell him this, she waited for an opening. She looked at her husband across the table.

4   "I did not make the world," Green began, recognizing at once the seriousness in her stare. "My father came to this country with nothing but his shirt. He was exploited for as long as he couldn't help himself. He did not protest or picket. He put himself in a position to play by the rules he had learned." He waited for his wife to answer, and when she did not, he tried again. "I did not make this world," he repeated. "I only make my way in it. Such people as these, they do not know enough to not be exploited. If not me, there would be a Greek, a Chinaman, maybe an Arab or a smart one of their own kind. Believe me, I deal with them. There is something in their style that lacks the patience to run a concern such as mine. If I closed down, take my word on it, someone else would do what has to be done."

5   But Ruth Green was not thinking of his leaving. Her mind was on other matters. Her children had cried when they came home early from school. She had no special feeling for the people who picketed, but she did not like to see her children cry. She had kissed them generously, then sworn them to silence. "One day this week," she told her husband, "you will give free, for eight hours, anything your customers come in to buy. There will be no publicity, except what they spread by word of mouth. No matter what they say to you, no matter what they take, you will remain silent." She stared deeply into him for what she knew was there. "If you refuse, you have seen the last of your children and myself."

6   Her husband grunted. Then he leaned toward her. "I will not knuckle under," he said. "I will *not* give!"

7   "We shall see," his wife told him.

8   The black pickets, for the most part, had at first been frightened by the audacity of their undertaking. They were peasants whose minds had long before become resigned to their fate as victims. None of them, before now, had thought to challenge this. But now, when they watched themselves on television, they hardly recognized the faces they saw beneath the hoisted banners and placards. Instead of reflecting the meekness they all felt, the faces looked angry. The close-ups looked especially intimidating. Several of the first pickets, maids who worked in the suburbs, reported that their employers, seeing the activity on the afternoon news, had begun treating them with new respect. One woman, midway through the weather report, called around the neighborhood to disclose that her employer had that very day given her a new china plate for her meals. The paper plates, on which all previous meals had been served, had been thrown into the wastebasket. One recipient of this call, a middle-aged woman known for her bashfulness and humility, rejoined that her husband, a sheet-metal worker, had only a few hours before been called "Mister" by his supervisor, a white man with a passionate hatred of color. She added the tale of a neighbor down the street, a widow-woman named Murphy, who had at first been reluctant to join the picket; this woman now

was insisting it should be made a daily event. Such talk as this circulated among the people who had been instrumental in raising the issue. As news of their victory leaked into the ears of others who had not participated, they received all through the night calls from strangers requesting verification, offering advice, and vowing support. Such strangers listened, and then volunteered stories about indignities inflicted on them by city officials, policemen, other grocers. In this way, over a period of hours, the community became even more incensed and restless than it had been at the time of the initial picket.

Soon, the man who had set events in motion found himself a hero. His 9 name was Nelson Reed, and all his adult life he had been employed as an assembly-line worker. He was a steady husband, the father of three children, and a deacon in the Baptist church. All his life he had trusted in God and gotten along. But now something in him capitulated to the reality that came suddenly into focus. "I was wrong," he told people who called him. "The onliest thing that matters in this world is *money*. And when was the last time you seen a picture of Jesus on a dollar bill?" This line, which he repeated over and over, caused a few callers to laugh nervously, but not without some affirmation that this was indeed the way things were. Many said they had known it all along. Others argued that although it was certainly true, it was one thing to live without money and quite another to live without faith. But still most callers laughed and said. "You right. You *know* I know you right. Ain't it the truth, though?" Only a few people, among them Nelson Reed's wife, said nothing and looked very sad.

Why they looked sad, however, they would not communicate. And any- 10 one observing their troubled faces would have to trust his own intuition. It is known that Reed's wife, Betty, measured all events against the fullness of her own experience. She was skeptical of everything. Brought to the church after a number of years of living openly with a jazz musician, she had embraced religion when she married Nelson Reed. But though she no longer believed completely in the world, she nonetheless had not fully embraced God. There was something in the nature of Christ's swift rise that had always bothered her, and something in the blood and vengeance of the Old Testament that was mellowing and refreshing. But she had never communicated these thoughts to anyone, especially her husband. Instead, she smiled vacantly while others professed leaps of faith, remained silent when friends spoke fiercely of their convictions. The presence of this vacuum in her contributed to her personal mystery; people said she was beautiful, although she was not outwardly so. Perhaps it was because she wished to protect this inner beauty that she did not smile now, and looked extremely sad, listening to her husband on the telephone.

Nelson Reed had no reason to be sad. He seemed to grow more energized 11 and talkative as the days passed. He was invited by an alderman, on the Tuesday after the initial picket, to tell his story on a local television talk show. He sweated heavily under the hot white lights and attempted to be philosophical. "I notice," the host said to him, "that you are not angry at this exploitative treatment. What, Mr. Reed, is the source of your calm?" The assembly-line worker looked unabashedly into the camera and said, "I have always believed in *Justice* with a capital *J*. I was raised up from a baby believin' that God ain't gonna let nobody go *too* far. See, in *my* mind God is in charge of *all* the capital letters in the alphabet of this world. It say in the Scripture He is Alpha and Omega, the first and the last. He is just about the *onliest* capitalizer they is." Both Reed and the alderman laughed. "Now, when *men* start to capitalize, they gets *greedy*. They put a little *j* in *joy* and a littler one in *justice*. They raise up a big *G* in *Greed* and a big *E* in *Evil*. Well, soon as they commence to put a little *g* in *God*, you can expect some kind of reaction. The Savior will just raise up the *H* in *Hell* and go on from there. And that's just what I'm doin', giving these sharpies *HELL* with a big *H*." The talk show host laughed along with Nelson Reed and the alderman. After the taping they drank coffee in the back room of the studio and talked about the sad shape of the world.

12   Three days before he was to comply with his wife's request, Green, the grocer, saw this talk show on television while at home. The words of Nelson Reed sent a chill through him. Though Reed had attempted to be philosophical, Green did not perceive the statement in this light. Instead, he saw a vindictive-looking black man seated between an ambitious alderman and a smug talk-show host. He saw them chatting comfortably about the nature of evil. The cameraman had shot mostly close-ups, and Green could see the set in Nelson reed's jaw. The color of Reed's face was maddening. When his children came into the den, the grocer was in a sweat. Before he could think, he had shouted at them and struck the button turning off the set. The two children rushed from the room screaming. Ruth Green ran in from the kitchen. She knew why he was upset because she had received a call about the show, but she said nothing and pretended ignorance. Her children's school had been picketed that day, as it had the day before. But both children were still forbidden to speak of this to their father.

13   "Where do they get so much power?" Green said to his wife. "Two days ago, nobody would have cared. Now, everywhere, even in my home, I am condemned as a rascal. And what do I own? An airline? A multinational? Half of South America? *No!* I own three stores, one of which happens to be in a certain neighborhood inhabited by people who cost me money to run it." He sighed and sat upright on the sofa, his chubby legs spread wide. "A cab driver has a meter that clicks as he goes along. I pay extra for insurance, iron bars, pilfering by customers and employees. Nothing clicks. But when I add a little overhead to my prices, suddenly everything clicks. But for someone else. When was there last such a world?" He pressed the palms of both hands to his temples, suggesting a bombardment of brain-stinging sounds.

14   This gesture evoked no response from Ruth Green. She remained standing by the door, looking steadily at him. She said, "To protect yourself, I would not stock any more fresh cuts of meat in the store until after the giveaway on Saturday. Also, I would not tell it to the employees until after the first customer of the day has begun to check out. But I would urge you to hire several security guards to close the door promptly at seven-thirty, as is usual." She

wanted to say much more than this, but did not. Instead, she watched him. He was looking at the blank gray television screen, his palms still pressed against his ears. "In case you need to hear again," she continued in a weighty tone of voice. "I said two days ago, and I say again now, that if you fail to do this you will not see your children again for many years."

He twisted his head and looked up at her. "What is the color of these peo- 15 ple?" he asked.

"Black," his wife said.   16

"And what is the name of my children?"   17

"Green."   18

The grocer smiled. "There is your answer," he told his wife. "Green is the 19 only color I am interested in."

His wife did not smile. "Insufficient," she said.   20

"The world is mad!" he moaned. "But it is a point of sanity with me to 21 not bend. I will not bend." He crossed his legs and pressed one hand firmly atop his knee. *"I will not bend,"* he said.

"We will see," his wife said.   22

Nelson Reed, after the television interview, became the acknowledged 23 leader of the disgruntled neighbors. At first a number of them met in the kitchen at his house; then, as space was lacking for curious newcomers, a mass meeting was held on Thursday in an abandoned theater. His wife and three children sat in the front row. Behind them sat the widow Murphy, Lloyd Dukes, Tyrone Brown, Les Jones—those who had joined him on the first picket line. Behind these sat people who bought occasionally at the store, people who lived on the fringes of the neighborhood, people from other neighborhoods come to investigate the problem, and the merely curious. The middle rows were occupied by a few people from the suburbs, those who had seen the talk show and whose outrage at the grocer proved much more powerful than their fear of black people. In the rear of the theater crowded aging, old-style leftists, somber students, cynical young black men with angry grudges to explain with inarticulate gestures. Leaning against the walls, and huddled near the doors at the rear, tape-recorder-bearing social scientists looked as detached and serene as bookies at the track. Here and there, in this diverse crowd, a politi- cian stationed himself, pumping hands vigorously and pressing his palms gen- tly against the shoulders of elderly people. Other visitors passed out leaflets, buttons, glossy color prints of men who promoted causes, the familiar and obscure. There was a hubbub of voices, a blend of the strident and the play- ful, the outraged and the reverent, lending an undercurrent of ominous energy to the assembly.

Nelson Reed spoke from a platform on the stage, standing before a yel- 24 lowed, shredded screen that had once reflected the images of matinee idols. "I don't mind sayin' that I have always been a sucker," he told the crowd. "All my life I have been a sucker for the words of Jesus. Being a natural-born fool, I just ain't never had the *sense* to learn no better. Even right today, while the whole world is sayin' wrong is right and up is down, I'm so dumb I'm *still* steady believin' what is wrote in the Good Book. . . ."

25   From the audience, especially the front rows, came a chorus singing, "Preach!"

26   "I have no doubt," he continued in a low baritone, "that it's true what is writ in the Good Book: 'The last shall be first and the first shall be last.' I don't know about y'all, but I have *always* been the last. I never wanted to be the first, but sometimes it look like the world get so bad that them that's holdin' onto the tree of life is the onliest ones left when God commence to blowin' dead leafs off the branches."

27   "Now you preaching," someone said.

28   In the rear of the theater a white student shouted an awkward "Amen."

29   Nelson Reed began walking across the stage to occupy the major part of his nervous energy. But to those in the audience, who now hung on his every word, it looked as though he strutted. "All my life," he said, "I have claimed to be a man without earnin' the right to call myself that. You know, the *average* man ain't really a man. The average man is a *boot-licker*. In fact, the *average* man would *run away* if he found hisself standing alone facin' down a adversary. I have done that *too many a time* in my life! But *not no more*. Better to be *once* was than *never* was a man. I will tell you tonight, there is somethin' *wrong* in being average. *I intend to stand up!* Now, if your average man that ain't really a man stand up, two things gonna happen: *One,* he g'on bust through all the weights that been place on his head, and *two,* he g'on feel a lot of pain. But that same hurt is what make things fall in place. That, and gettin' your hands on one of these slick four-flushers tight enough so's you can squeeze him and say, *'No more!'* You do that, you g'on hurt some, but *you won't be average no more*. . . ."

30   "No *more!*" a few people in the front rows repeated.

31   "I say *no more!*" Nelson Reed shouted.

32   *"No more! No more! No more!"* The chant rustled through the crowd like the rhythm of an autumn wind against a shedding tree.

33   Then people laughed and chattered in celebration.

34   As for the grocer, from the evening of the television interview he had begun to make plans. Unknown to his wife, he cloistered himself several times with his brother-in-law, an insurance salesman, and plotted a course. He had no intention of tossing steaks to the crowd. "And why should I, Tommy?" he asked his wife's brother, a lean, bald-headed man named Thomas. "I don't cheat anyone. I have never cheated anyone. The businesses I run are always on the up-and-up. So why should I pay?"

35   "Quite so," the brother-in-law said, chewing an unlit cigarillo. "The world has gone crazy. Next they will say that people in my business are responsible for prolonging life. I have found that people who refuse to believe in death refuse also to believe in the harshness of life. I sell well by saying that death is a long happiness. I show people the realities of life and compare this to a funeral with dignity, *and* the promise of a bundle for every loved one salted away. When they look around hard at life, they usually buy."

36   "So?" asked Green. Thomas was a college graduate with a penchant for philosophy.

"So," Thomas answered. "You must fight to show these people the reality ₃₇ of both your situation and theirs. How would it be if you visited one of their meetings and chalked out, on a blackboard, the dollars and cents of your operation? Explain your overhead, your security fees, all the additional expenses. If you treat them with respect, they might understand."

Green frowned. "That I would never do," he said. "It would be admission ₃₈ of a certain guilt."

The brother-in-law smiled, but only with one corner of his mouth. "Then ₃₉ you have something to feel guilty about?" he asked.

The grocer frowned at him. *"Nothing!"* he said with great emphasis.   ₄₀

"So?" Thomas said.   ₄₁

This first meeting between the grocer and his brother-in-law took place on ₄₂ Thursday, in a crowded barroom.

At the second meeting, in a luncheonette, it was agreed that the grocer ₄₃ should speak privately with the leader of the group, Nelson Reed. The meeting at which this was agreed took place on Friday afternoon. After accepting this advice from Thomas, the grocer resigned himself to explain to Reed, in as finite detail as possible, the economic structure of his operation. He vowed to suppress no information. He would explain everything: inventories, markups, sale items, inflation, balance sheets, specialty items, overhead, and that mysterious item called profit. This last item, promising to be the most difficult to explain. Green and his brother-in-law debated over for several hours. They agreed first of all that a man should not work for free, then they agreed that it was unethical to ruthlessly exploit. From these parameters, they staked out an area between fifteen and forty percent, and agreed that someplace between these two borders lay an amount of return that could be called fair. This was easy, but then Thomas introduced the factor of circumstance. He questioned whether the fact that one serviced a risky area justified the earning of profits closer to the forty-percent edge of the scale. Green was unsure. Thomas smiled. "Here is a case that will point out an analogy," he said, licking a cigarillo. "I read in the papers that a family wants to sell an electric stove. I call the home and the man says fifty dollars. I ask to come out and inspect the merchandise. When I arrive I see they are poor, have already bought a new stove that is connected, and are selling the old one for fifty dollars because they want it out of the place. The electric stove is in good condition, worth much more than fifty. But because I see what I see I offer forty-five."

Green, for some reason, wrote down this figure on the back of the sales ₄₄ slip for the coffee they were drinking.

The brother-in-law smiled. He chewed his cigarillo. "The man agrees to ₄₅ take forty-five dollars, saying he has had no other calls. I look at the stove again and see a spot of rust. I say I will give him forty dollars. He agrees to this, on condition that I myself haul it away. I say I will haul it away if he comes down to thirty. You, of course, see where I am going."

The grocer nodded. "The circumstances of his situation, his need to get rid ₄₆ of the stove quickly, placed him in a position where he has little room to bargain?"

47   "Yes," Thomas answered. "So? Is it ethical, Harry?"

48   Harold Green frowned. He had never liked his brother-in-law, and now he thought the insurance agent was being crafty. "But," he answered, "this man does not *have* to sell! It is his choice whether to wait for other calls. It is not the fault of the buyer that the seller is in a hurry. It is the right of the buyer to get what he wants at the lowest price possible. That is the rule. That has *always* been the rule. And the reverse of it applies to the seller as well."

49   "Yes," Thomas said, sipping coffee from the Styrofoam cup. "But suppose that in addition to his hurry to sell, the owner was also of a weak soul. There are, after all, many such people." He smiled. "Suppose he placed no value on the money?"

50   "Then," Green answered, "your example is academic. Here we are not talking about real life. One man lives by the code, one man does not. Who is there free enough to make a judgment?" He laughed. "Now you see," he told his brother-in-law. "Much more than a few dollars are at stake. If this one buyer is to be condemned, then so are most people in the history of the world. An examination of history provides the only answer to your question. This code will be here tomorrow, long after the ones who do not honor it are not."

51   They argued fiercely late into the afternoon, the brother-in-law leaning heavily on his readings. When they parted, a little before 5:00 P.M., nothing had been resolved.

52   Neither was much resolved during the meeting between Green and Nelson Reed. Reached at home by the grocer in the early evening, the leader of the group spoke coldly at first, but consented finally to meet his adversary at a nearby drugstore for coffee and a talk. They met at the lunch counter, shook hands awkwardly, and sat for a few minutes discussing the weather. Then the grocer pulled two gray ledgers from his briefcase. "You have for years come into my place," he told the man. "In my memory I have always treated you well. Now our relationship has come to this." He slid the books along the counter until they touched Nelson Reed's arm.

53   Reed opened the top book and flipped the thick green pages with his thumb. He did not examine the figures. "All I know," he said, "is over at your place a can of soup cost me fifty-five cents, and two miles away at your other store for white folks you chargin' thirty-nine cents." He said this with the calm authority of an outraged soul. A quality of condescension tinged with pity crept into his gaze.

54   The grocer drummed his fingers on the counter top. He twisted his head and looked away, toward shelves containing cosmetics, laxatives, toothpaste. His eyes lingered on a poster of a woman's apple red lips and milk white teeth. The rest of the face was missing.

55   "Ain't no use to hide," Nelson Reed said, as to a child. "*I* know you wrong, *you* know you wrong, and before I finish, *everybody in this city* g'on know you wrong. God don't *like* ugly." He closed his eyes and gripped the cup of coffee. Then he swung his head suddenly and faced the grocer again. "Man, why you want to *do* people that way?" he asked. "We human, same as you."

"Before *God!*" Green exclaimed, looking squarely into the face of Nelson 56 Reed. "Before God!" he said again. *"I am not an evil man!"* These last words sounded more like a moan as he tightened the muscles in his throat to lower the sound of his voice. He tossed his left shoulder as if adjusting the sleeve of his coat, or as if throwing off some unwanted weight. Then he peered along the countertop. No one was watching. At the end of the counter the waitress was scrubbing the coffee urn. "Look at these figures, please," he said to Reed.

The man did not drop his gaze. His eyes remained fixed on the grocer's 57 face.

"All right," Green said. "Don't look. I'll tell you what is in these books, 58 believe me if you want. I work twelve hours a day, one day off per week, running my business in three stores. I am not a wealthy person. In one place, in the area you call white, I get by barely by smiling lustily at old ladies, stocking gourmet stuff on the chance I will build a reputation as a quality store. The two clerks there cheat me: there is nothing I can do. In this business you must be friendly with everybody. The second place is on the other side of town, in a neighborhood as poor as this one. I get out there seldom. The profits are not worth the gas. I use the loss there as a write-off against some other properties." He paused. "Do you understand write-off?" he asked Nelson Reed.

"Naw," the man said. 59

Harold Green laughed. "What does it matter?" he said in a tone of voice 60 intended for himself alone. "In this area I will admit I make a profit, but it is not so much as you think. But I do not make a profit here because the people are black. I make a profit because a profit is here to be made. I invest more here in window bars, theft losses, insurance, spoilage; I deserve to make more here than at the other places." He looked, almost imploringly, at the man seated next to him. "You don't accept this as the right of a man in business?"

Reed grunted. "Did the bear shit in the woods?" he said. 61

Again Green laughed. He gulped his coffee awkwardly, as if eager to go. 62 Yet his motions slowed once he had set the coffee cup down on the blue plastic saucer. "Place yourself in *my* situation," he said, his voice high and tentative. "If *you* were running my store in this neighborhood, what would be *your* position? Say on a profit scale of fifteen to forty percent, at what point in between would you draw the line?"

Nelson Reed thought. He sipped his coffee and seemed to chew the liq- 63 uid. "Fifteen to forty?" he repeated.

"Yes." 64

"I'm a churchgoin' man," he said. "Closer to fifteen than to forty." 65

"How close?" 66

Nelson Reed thought. "In church you tithe ten percent." 67

"In restaurants you tip fifteen," the grocer said quickly. 68

"All right," Reed said, "Over fifteen." 69

"How much over?" 70

Nelson Reed thought. 71

72   "Twenty, thirty, thirty-five?" Green chanted, leaning closer to Reed. Still the man thought.

73   "Forty? Maybe even forty-five or fifty?" the grocer breathed in Reed's ear. "In the supermarkets, you know, they have more subtle ways of accomplishing such feats."

74   Reed slapped his coffee cup with the back of his right hand. The brown liquid swirled across the counter top, wetting the books. *"Damn this!"* he shouted.

75   Startled, Green rose from his stool.

76   Nelson Reed was trembling. "I ain't *you,*" he said in a deep baritone. "I ain't the *supermarket* neither. All I is is a poor man that works *too* hard to see his pay slip through his fingers like rainwater. All I know is you done *cheat* me, you done *cheat* everybody in the neighborhood, and we organized now to get some of it *back!*" Then he stood and faced the grocer. "My daddy sharecropped down in Mississippi and bought in the company store. He owed them twenty-three years when he died. I paid off five of them years and then run away to up here. Now, I'm a deacon in the Baptist church. I raised my kids the way my daddy raise me and don't bother nobody. Now come to find out, after all my runnin', they done lift that *same company store* up out of Mississippi and slip it down on us here! Well, my daddy was a *fighter,* and if he hadn't owed all them years he would of raise him some hell. Me, I'm steady my daddy's child, plus I got seniority in my union. I'm a free man. Buddy, don't you know *I'm gonna raise me some hell!*"

77   Harold Green reached for a paper napkin to sop the coffee soaking into his books.

78   Nelson Reed threw a dollar on top of the books and walked away.

79   "I *will not* do it!" Harold Green said to his wife that same evening. They were in the bathroom of their home. Bending over the face bowl, she was washing her hair with a towel draped around her neck. The grocer stood by the door, looking in at her. "I will not bankrupt myself tomorrow," he said.

80   "I've been thinking about it, too," Ruth Green said, shaking her wet hair. "You'll do it, Harry."

81   "Why should I?" he asked. "You won't leave. You know it was a bluff. I've waited this long for you to calm down. Tomorrow is Saturday. This week has been a hard one. Tonight let's be realistic."

82   "Of course you'll do it," Ruth Green said. She said it the way she would say "Have some toast." She said, "You'll do it because you want to see your children grow up."

83   "And for what other reason?" he asked.

84   She pulled the towel tighter around her neck. "Because you are at heart a moral man."

85   He grinned painfully. "If I am, why should I have to prove it to *them?*"

86   "Not them," Ruth Green said, freezing her movements and looking in the mirror. "Certainly not them. By no means them. They have absolutely nothing to do with this."

"Who, then?" he asked, moving from the door into the room. "Who else 87 should I prove something to?"

His wife was crying. But her entire face was wet. The tears moved secretly 88 down her face.

"Who else?" Harold Green asked. 89

It was almost 11:00 P.M. and the children were in bed. They had also cried 90 when they came home from school. Ruth Green said, "For yourself, Harry. For the love that lives inside your heart."

All night the grocer thought about this. 91

Nelson Reed also slept little that Friday night. When he returned home 92 from the drugstore, he reported to his wife as much of the conversation as he could remember. At first he had joked about the exchange between himself and the grocer, but as more details returned to his conscious mind he grew solemn and then bitter. "He ask me to put myself in *his* place," Reed told his wife. "Can you imagine that kind of gumption? I never cheated nobody in my life. All my life I have lived on Bible principles. I am a deacon in the church. I have work all my life for other folks and I don't even own the house I live in." He paced up and down the kitchen, his big arms flapping loosely at his sides. Betty Reed sat at the table, watching. "This here's a low-down, ass-kicking world," he said. "I swear to God it is! All my life I have lived on principle and I ain't got a dime in the bank. Betty," he turned suddenly toward her, "don't you think I'm a fool?"

"Mr. Reed," she said. "Let's go on to bed." 93

But he would not go to bed. Instead, he took the fifth of bourbon from the 94 cabinet under the sink and poured himself a shot. His wife refused to join him. Reed drained the glass of whiskey, and then another, while he resumed pacing the kitchen floor. He slapped his hands against his sides. "I think I'm a fool," he said. "Ain't got a dime in the bank, ain't got a pot to *pee* in or a wall to pitch it over, and that there *cheat* ask me to put myself inside *his* shoes. Hell, I can't even *afford* the kind of shoes he wears." He stopped pacing and looked at his wife.

"Mr. Reed," she whispered, "tomorrow ain't a work day. Let's go to bed." 95

Nelson Reed laughed, the bitterness in his voice rattling his wife. "The *hell* 96 I will!" he said.

He strode to the yellow telephone on the wall beside the sink and began 97 to dial. The first call was to Lloyd Dukes, a neighbor two blocks away and a lieutenant in the organization. Dukes was not at home. The second call was to McElroy's Bar on the corner of 6th and Carroll, where Stanley Harper, another of the lieutenants, worked as a bartender. It was Harper who spread the word, among those men at the bar, that the organization would picket the grocer's store the following morning. And all through the night, in the bedroom of their house, Betty Reed was awakened by telephone calls coming from Lester Jones, Nat Lucas, Mrs. Tyrone Brown, the widow-woman named Murphy, all coordinating the time when they would march in a group against the store owned by Harold Green. Betty Reed's heart beat loudly beneath the covers as she listened to the bitterness and rage in her husband's voice. On several occasions, hearing him declare himself a fool, she pressed the pillow against her eyes and cried.

98   The grocer opened later than usual this Saturday morning, but still it was early enough to make him one of the first walkers in the neighborhood. He parked his car one block from the store and strolled to work. There were no birds singing. The sky in this area was not blue. It was smog-smutted and gray, seeming on the verge of a light rain. The street, as always, was littered with cans, papers, bits of broken glass. As always the garbage cans overflowed. The morning breeze plastered a sheet of newspaper playfully around the sides of a rusted garbage can. For some reason, using his right foot, he loosened the paper and stood watching it slide into the street and down the block. The movement made him feel good. He whistled while unlocking the bars shielding the windows and door of his store. When he had unlocked the main door he stepped in quickly and threw a switch to the right of the jamb, before the shrill sound of the alarm could shatter his mood. Then he switched on the lights. Everything was as it had been the night before. He had already telephoned his two employees and given them the day off. He busied himself doing the usual things—hauling milk and vegetables from the cooler, putting cash in the till—not thinking about the silence of his wife, or the look in her eyes, only an hour before when he left home. He had determined, at some point while driving through the city, that today it would be business as usual. But he expected very few customers.

99   The first customer of the day was Mrs. Nelson Reed. She came in around 9:00 A.M. and wandered about the store. He watched her from the checkout counter. She seemed uncertain of what she wanted to buy. She kept glancing at him down the center aisle. His suspicions aroused, he said finally. "Yes, may I help you, Mrs. Reed?" His words caused her to jerk, as if some devious thought had been perceived going through her mind. She reached over quickly and lifted a loaf of whole wheat bread from the rack and walked with it to the counter. She looked at him and smiled. The smile was a broad, shy one, that rare kind of smile one sees on virgin girls when they first confess love to themselves. Betty Reed was a woman of about forty-five. For some reason he could not comprehend, this gesture touched him. When she pulled a dollar from her purse and laid it on the counter, an impulse, from no place he could locate with his mind, seized control of his tongue. "Free," he told Betty Reed. She paused, then pushed the dollar toward him with a firm and determined thrust of her arm. "Free," he heard himself saying strongly, his right palm spread and meeting her thrust with absolute force. She clutched the loaf of bread and walked out of his store.

100   The next customer, a little girl, arriving well after 10:30 A.M., selected a candy bar from the rack beside the counter. "Free," Green said cheerfully. The little girl left the candy on the counter and ran out of the store.

101   At 11:15 A.M. a wino came in looking desperate enough to sell his soul. The grocer watched him only for an instant. Then he went to the wine counter and selected a half-gallon of medium-grade red wine. He shoved the jug into

the belly of the wino, the man's sour breath bathing his face. "Free," the grocer said. "But you must not drink it in here."

He felt good about the entire world, watching the wino through the window gulping the wine and looking guiltily around. 102

At 11:25 A.M. the pickets arrived. 103

Two dozen people, men and women, young and old, crowded the pavement in front of his store. Their signs, placards, and voices denounced him as a parasite. The grocer laughed inside himself. He felt lighthearted and wild, like a man drugged. He rushed to the meat counter and pulled a long roll of brown wrapping paper from the rack, tearing it neatly with a quick shift of his body resembling a dance step practiced fervently in his youth. He laid the paper on the chopping block and with the black-inked, felt-tipped marker scrawled, in giant letters, the word Free. This he took to the window and pasted in place with many strands of Scotch tape. He was laughing wildly. "Free!" he shouted from behind the brown paper. "Free! Free! Free! Free! Free! Free!" He rushed to the door, pushed his head out, and screamed to the confused crowd, *"Free!"* Then he ran back to the counter and stood behind it, like a soldier at attention. 104

They came in slowly. 105

Nelson Reed entered first, working his right foot across the dirty tile as if tracking a squiggling worm. The others followed: Lloyd Dukes dragging a placard, Mr. and Mrs. Tyrone Brown, Stanley Harper walking with his fists clenched, Lester Jones with three of his children, Nat Lucas looking sheepish and detached, a clutch of winos, several bashful nuns, ironic-smiling teenagers and a few students. Bringing up the rear was a bearded social scientist holding a tape recorder to his chest. "Free!" the grocer screamed. He threw up his arms in a gesture that embraced, or dismissed, the entire store. *"All free!"* he shouted. He was grinning with the grace of a madman. 106

The winos began grabbing first. They stripped the shelf of wine in a matter of seconds. Then they fled, dropping bottles on the tile in their wake. The others, stepping quickly through this liquid, soon congealed it into a sticky, blood-like consistency. The young men went for the cigarettes and luncheon meats and beer. One of them had the prescience to grab a sack from the counter, while the others loaded their arms swiftly, hugging cartons and packages of cold cuts like long-lost friends. The students joined them, less for greed than for the thrill of the experience. The two nuns backed toward the door. As for the older people, men and women, they stood at first as if stuck to the wine-smeared floor. Then Stanley Harper, the bartender, shouted, "The man said *free,* y'all heard him." He paused. "Didn't you say *free* now?" he called to the grocer. 107

"I said free," Harold Green answered, his temples pounding. 108

A cheer went up. The older people began grabbing, as if the secret lusts of a lifetime had suddenly seized command of their arms and eyes. They grabbed toilet tissue, cold cuts, pickles, sardines, boxes of raisins, boxes of starch, cans of soup, tins of tuna fish and salmon, bottles of spices, cans of boned chicken, slippery cans of olive oil. Here a man, Lester Jones, burdened 109 himself with several heads of lettuce, while his wife, in another aisle, shouted for him to drop those small items and concentrate on the gourmet section. She herself took imported sardines, wheat crackers, bottles of candied pickles, herring, anchovies, imported olives, French wafers, an ancient, half-rusted can of paté, stocked, by mistake, from the inventory of another store. Others packed their arms with detergents, hams, chocolate-coated cereal, whole chickens with hanging asses, wedges of bologna and salami like squashed footballs, chunks of cheeses, yellow and white, shriveled onions, and green peppers. Mrs. Tyrone Brown hung a curve of pepperoni around her neck and seemed to take on instant dignity, much like a person of noble birth in possession now of a long sought-after gem. Another woman, the widow Murphy, stuffed tomatoes into her bosom, holding a half-chewed lemon in her mouth. The more enterprising fought desperately over the three rusted shopping carts, and the victors wheeled these along the narrow aisles, sweeping into them bulk items— beer in six-packs, sacks of sugar, flour, glass bottles of syrup, toilet cleanser, sugar cookies, prune, apple and tomato juices—while others endeavored to snatch the carts from them. There were several fistfights and much cursing. The grocer, standing behind the counter, hummed and rang his cash register like a madman.

110   Nelson Reed, the first into the store, followed the nuns out, empty-handed.

111   In less than half an hour the others had stripped the store and vanished in many directions up and down the block. But still more people came, those late in hearing the news. And when they saw the shelves were bare, they cursed soberly and chased those few stragglers still bearing away goods. Soon only the grocer and the social scientist remained, the latter stationed at the door with his tape recorder sucking in leftover sounds. Then he too slipped away up the block.

112   By 12:10 P.M. the grocer was leaning against the counter, trying to make his mind slow down. Not a man given to drink during work hours, he nonetheless took a swallow from a bottle of wine, a dusty bottle from beneath the wine shelf, somehow overlooked by the winos. Somewhat recovered, he was preparing to remember what he should do next when he glanced toward a figure at the door. Nelson Reed was standing there, watching him.

113   "All gone," Harold Green said. "My friend, Mr. Reed, there is no more." Still the man stood in the doorway, peering into the store.

114   The grocer waved his arms about the empty room. Not a display case had a single item standing. "All gone," he said again, as if addressing a stupid child. "There is nothing left to get. You, my friend, have come back too late for a second load. I am cleaned out."

115   Nelson Reed stepped into the store and strode toward the counter. He moved through wine-stained flour, lettuce leaves, red, green, and blue labels, bits and pieces of broken glass. He walked toward the counter.

116   "All day," the grocer laughed, not quite hysterically now, "all day long I have not made a single cent of profit. The entire day was a loss. This store, like the others, is *bleeding* me." He waved his arms about the room in a mag-

nificent gesture of uncaring loss. "Now do you understand?" he said. "Now will you put yourself in my shoes? I have nothing here. Come, now, Mr. Reed, would it not be so bad a thing to walk in my shoes?"

"Mr. Green," Nelson Reed said coldly. "My wife bought a loaf of bread in 117 here this mornin'. She forgot to pay you. I, myself, have come here to pay you your money."

"Oh," the grocer said.   118

"I think it was brown bread. Don't that cost more than white?" 119

The two men looked away from each other, but not at anything in the 120 store.

"In my store, yes," Harold Green said. He rang the register with the most 121 casual movement of his finger. The register read fifty-five cents.

Nelson Reed held out a dollar.   122

"And two cents tax," the grocer said.   123

The man held out the dollar.   124

"After all," Harold Green said. "We are all, after all, Mr. Reed, in debt to 125 the government."

He rang the register again. It read fifty-seven cents.   126

Nelson Reed held out a dollar.   127

Questions for Discussion

1. What does Mr. Green's store represent to the community? What does he stand for? What tone is established in the beginning of the story?
2. How does the author establish the character of Mr. Green? Mrs. Green? Mr. Reed? Mrs. Reed? What are their respective concerns and values?
3. How does Nelson Reed define justice? How does that definition conflict with Mr. Green's views? What do you think the author's attitudes are toward racism, justice, and poverty?
4. Discuss the community audience described in paragraph 23. Has the author captured a realistic cross section of a community?
5. Do you agree with Ruth Green that her husband is "at heart a moral man"? Discuss.
6. What does "free" mean to Mr. Green? In what sense is he freed along with his groceries? Has Mr. Green been changed by his experience?
7. What is your view about who is right in the struggle represented in this story? How did you reach that conclusion? How does it relate to your own ethics?

Ideas for Writing

1. Compare and contrast this story's social commentary with that of the poems in this chapter. In view of your comparison, discuss the role of literature in examining, reflecting, and perhaps changing society.
2. Write an essay discussing the use of symbolism in "A Loaf of Bread." Relate your discussion of the symbols to the story's theme.
3. Examine the conclusion of the story. What do you foresee as a result of final meeting between Mr. Green and Mr. Reed?

What Is Poverty?

Jo Goodwin Parker

The following selection was published in *America's Other Children: Public Schools Outside Suburbs*, by George Henderson in 1971 by the University of Oklahoma Press. The author has requested that no biographical information about her be distributed. The essay is a personal account, addressed directly to the reader, about living in poverty.

Journal

Discuss an image or experience that you witnessed that presented the humiliating, degrading, or dehumanizing aspects of poverty.

You ask me what is poverty? Listen to me. Here I am, dirty, smelly, and with no "proper" underwear on and with the stench of my rotting teeth near you. I will tell you. Listen to me. Listen without pity. I cannot use your pity. Listen with understanding. Put yourself in my dirty, worn out, ill-fitting shoes, and hear me.

2 Poverty is getting up every morning from a dirt- and illness-stained mattress. The sheets have long since been used for diapers. Poverty is living in a smell that never leaves. This is a smell of urine, sour milk, and spoiling food sometimes joined with the strong smell of long-cooked onions. Onions are cheap. If you have smelled this smell, you did not know how it came. It is the smell of the outdoor privy. It is the smell of young children who cannot walk the long dark way in the night. It is the smell of the mattresses where years of "accidents" have happened. It is the smell of the milk which has gone sour because the refrigerator long has not worked, and it costs money to get it fixed. It is the smell of rotting garbage. I could bury it, but where is the shovel? Shovels cost money.

3 Poverty is being tired. I have always been tired. They told me at the hospital when the last baby came that I had chronic anemia caused from poor diet, a bad case of worms, and that I needed a corrective operation. I listened politely—the poor are always polite. The poor always listen. They don't say that there is no money for iron pills, or better food, or worm medicine. The idea of an operation is frightening and costs so much that, if I had dared, I would have laughed. Who takes care of my children? Recovery from an operation takes a long time. I have three children. When I left them with "Granny" the last time I had a job, I came home to find the baby covered with fly specks, and a diaper that had not been changed since I left. When the dried diaper came off, bits of my baby's flesh came with it. My other child was playing with a sharp bit of broken glass, and my oldest was playing alone at the edge of a lake. I made twenty-two dollars a week, and a good nursery school costs twenty dollars a week for three children. I quit my job.

Poverty is dirt. You can say in your clean clothes coming from your clean 4 house, "Anybody can be clean." Let me explain about housekeeping with no money. For breakfast I give my children grits with no oleo or cornbread without eggs and oleo. This does not use up many dishes. What dishes there are, I wash in cold water and with no soap. Even the cheapest soap has to be saved for the baby's diapers. Look at my hands, so cracked and red. Once I saved for two months to buy a jar of Vaseline for my hands and the baby's diaper rash. When I had saved enough, I went to buy it and the price had gone up two cents. The baby and I suffered on. I have to decide every day if I can bear to put my cracked sore hands into the cold water and strong soap. But you ask, why not hot water? Fuel costs money. If you have a wood fire it costs money. If you burn electricity, it costs money. Hot water is a luxury. I do not have luxuries. I know you will be surprised when I tell you how young I am. I look so much older. My back has been bent over the wash tubs every day for so long, I cannot remember when I ever did anything else. Every night I wash every stitch my school age child has on and just hope her clothes will be dry by morning.

Poverty is staying up all night on cold nights to watch the fire knowing 5 one spark on the newspaper covering the walls means your sleeping child dies in flames. In summer poverty is watching gnats and flies devour your baby's tears when he cries. The screens are torn and you pay so little rent you know they will never be fixed. Poverty means insects in your food, in your nose, in your eyes, and crawling over you when you sleep. Poverty is hoping it never rains because diapers won't dry when it rains and soon you are using newspapers. Poverty is seeing your children forever with runny noses. Paper handkerchiefs cost money and all your rags you need for other things. Even more costly are antihistamines. Poverty is cooking without food and cleaning without soap.

Poverty is asking for help. Have you ever had to ask for help, knowing 6 your children will suffer unless you get it? Think about asking for a loan from a relative, if this is the only way you can imagine asking for help. I will tell you how it feels. You find out where the office is that you are supposed to visit. You circle that block four or five times. Thinking of your children, you go in. Everyone is very busy. Finally, someone comes out and you tell her that you need help. That never is the person you need to see. You go see another person, and after spilling the whole shame of your poverty all over the desk between you, you find that this isn't the right office after all—you must repeat the whole process, and it never is any easier at the next place.

You have asked for help, and after all it has a cost. You are again told to 7 wait. You are told why, but you don't really hear because of the red cloud of shame and the rising cloud of despair.

Poverty is remembering. It is remembering quitting school in junior high 8 because "nice" children had been so cruel about my clothes and my smell. The attendance officer came. My mother told him I was pregnant. I wasn't, but she thought that I could get a job and help out. I had jobs off and on, but never long enough to learn anything. Mostly I remember being married. I was so young then. I am still young. For a time, we had all the things you have. There was a little house in another town, with hot water and everything. Then my husband lost his job. There was unemployment insurance for a while and what few jobs I could get. Soon, all our nice things were repossessed and we moved back here. I was pregnant then. This house didn't look so bad when we first moved in. Every week it gets worse. Nothing is ever fixed. We now had no money. There were a few odd jobs for my husband, but everything went for food then, as it does now. I don't know how we lived through three years and three babies, but we did. I'll tell you something, after the last baby I destroyed my marriage. It had been a good one, but could you keep on bringing children in this dirt? Did you ever think how much it costs for any kind of birth control? I knew my husband was leaving the day he left, but there were no goodbys between us. I hope he has been able to climb out of this mess somewhere. He never could hope with us to drag him down.

9   That's when I asked for help. When I got it, you know how much it was? It was, and is, seventy-eight dollars a month for the four of us; that is all I ever can get. Now you know why there is no soap, no needles and thread, no hot water, no aspirin, no worm medicine, no hand cream, no shampoo. None of these things forever and ever and ever. So that you can see clearly, I pay twenty dollars a month rent, and most of the rest goes for food. For grits and cornmeal, and rice and milk and beans. I try my best to use only the minimum electricity. If I use more, there is that much less for food.

10   Poverty is looking into a black future. Your children won't play with my boys. They will turn to other boys who steal to get what they want. I can already see them behind the bars of their prison instead of behind the bars of my poverty. Or they will turn to the freedom of alcohol or drugs, and find themselves enslaved. And my daughter? At best, there is for her a life like mine.

11   But you say to me, there are schools. Yes, there are schools. My children have no extra books, no magazines, no extra pencils, or crayons, or paper and most important of all, they do not have health. They have worms, they have infections, they have pink-eye all summer. They do not sleep well on the floor, or with me in my one bed. They do not suffer from hunger, my seventy-eight dollars keeps us alive, but they do suffer from malnutrition. Oh yes, I do remember what I was taught about health in school. It doesn't do much good. In some places there is a surplus commodities program. Not here. The country said it cost too much. There is a school lunch program. But I have two children who will already be damaged by the time they get to school.

12   But, you say to me, there are health clinics. Yes, there are health clinics and they are in the towns. I live out here eight miles from town. I can walk that far (even if it is sixteen miles both ways), but can my little children? My neighbor will take me when he goes; but he expects to get paid, *one way or another*. I bet you know my neighbor. He is that large man who spends his time at the gas station, the barbershop, and the corner store complaining about the government spending money on the immoral mothers of illegitimate children.

Poverty is an acid that drips on pride until all pride is worn away. Poverty 13
is a chisel that chips on honor until honor is worn away. Some of you say that
you would do *something* in my situation, and maybe you would, for the first
week or the first month, but for year after year after year?

Even the poor can dream. A dream of a time when there is money. Money 14
for the right kinds of food, for worm medicine, for iron pills, for toothbrushes,
for hand cream, for a hammer and nails and a bit of screening, for a shovel,
for a bit of paint, for some sheeting, for needles and thread. Money to pay *in
money* for a trip to town. And, oh, money for hot water and money for soap.
A dream of when asking for help does not eat away the last bit of pride. When
the office you visit is as nice as the offices of other governmental agencies,
when there are enough workers to help you quickly, when workers do not quit
in defeat and despair. When you have to tell your story to only one person,
and that person can send you for other help and you don't have to prove your
poverty over and over and over again.

I have come out of my despair to tell you this. Remember I did not come 15
from another place or another time. Others like me are all around you. Look
at us with an angry heart, anger that will help you help me. Anger that will
let you tell of me. The poor are always silent. Can you be silent too?

Questions for Discussion

1. Readers aren't often addressed directly in personal essays. What impact has this
   point of view had on you? Why might using a second-person point of view be risky?
   Is this strategy effective in this essay?
2. How is the essay organized? In what ways does it anticipate reader objections to the
   argument?
3. The essay is full of vivid detail. What images do you find most effective? As you
   read, do you feel that an authentic voice is representing real experience?
4. The essay makes its points not only through imagery, but through anecdotes, or
   short narratives within the essay. Select one, and discuss its effectiveness.
5. What is your personal reaction to the essay? Does it affect your perceptions and
   understanding of the lives of the poor? Do you think that these insights will affect
   how you respond to poverty issues?

Ideas for Writing

1. The author's extended definition of poverty is also an argument. Analyze this argument. Compare the impact of experience as evidence to that of statistics or other
   forms of evidence. What kind of response can be made to Parker's argument?
2. Write an argumentative essay, perhaps in the form of a letter to the editor, arguing
   for increasing aid to poor families. You could research some specific aspect of such
   aid, such as current levels of support for families with dependent children as compared to costs of living in your area. Alternatively, you could argue for some of the
   support for working poor parents that is evidently lacking, such as cost-effective
   child care or job training assistance. Consider that you need to address the problem
   of paying for such aid, probably through some sort of tax or reallocation of
   resources.

Helping and Hating the Homeless: The Struggle at the Margins of America

Peter Marin

Peter Marin has written on a number of social issues, including recent work on homelessness. He has also coauthored *Understanding Drug Use: An Adult's Guide to Drugs and the Young* (1971) and *The Limits of Schooling* (1975). He is a contributing editor of *Harper's Magazine*, where the following essay was published in 1987. This essay discusses historical roots of homelessness as well as contemporary issues.

Journal

Who are the homeless? What images does the word "homeless" suggest to you? What do you think causes people to be homeless?

When I was a child, I had a recurring vision of how I would end as an old man: alone, in a sparsely furnished second-story room I could picture quite precisely, in a walk-up on Fourth Avenue in New York, where the secondhand bookstores then were. It was not a picture which frightened me. I liked it. The idea of anonymity and solitude and marginality must have seemed to me, back then, for reasons I do not care to remember, both inviting and inevitable. Later, out of college, I took to the road, hitchhiking and traveling on freights, doing odd jobs here and there, crisscrossing the country. I liked that too: the anonymity and the absence of constraint and the rough community I sometimes found. I felt at home on the road, perhaps because I felt at home nowhere else, and periodically, for years, I would return to that world, always with a sense of relief and release.

2   I have been thinking a lot about that these days, now that transience and homelessness have made their way into the national consciousness, and especially since the town I live in, Santa Barbara, has become well known because of the recent successful campaign to do away with the meanest aspects of its "sleeping ordinances"—a set of foolish laws making it illegal for the homeless to sleep at night in public places. During that campaign I got to know many of the homeless men and women in Santa Barbara, who tend to gather, night and day, in a small park at the lower end of town, not far from the tracks and the harbor, under the rooflike, overarching branches of a gigantic fig tree, said to be the oldest on the continent. There one enters much the same world I thought, as a child, I would die in, and the one in which I traveled as a young man: a "marginal" world inhabited by all those unable to find a place in "our" world. Sometimes, standing on the tracks close to the park, you can sense in the wind, or in the smell of tar and ties, the presence and age of that marginal

world: the way it stretches backward and inevitably forward in time, parallel to our own world, always present, always close, and yet separated from us— at least in the mind—by a gulf few of us are interested in crossing.

Late last summer, at a city council meeting here in Santa Barbara, I saw, close up, the consequences of that strange combination of proximity and distance. The council was meeting to vote on the repeal of the sleeping ordinances, though not out of any sudden sense of compassion or justice. Council members had been pressured into it by the threat of massive demonstrations— "The Selma of the Eighties" was the slogan one heard among the homeless. But this threat that frightened the council enraged the town's citizens. Hundreds of them turned out for the meeting. One by one they filed to the microphone to curse the council and castigate the homeless. Drinking, doping, loitering, panhandling, defecating, urinating, molesting, stealing—the litany went on and on, was repeated over and over, accompanied by fantasies of disaster: the barbarian hordes at the gates, civilization ended.

What astonished me about the meeting was not what was said; one could have predicted that. It was the power and depth of the emotion revealed: the mindlessness of the fear, the vengefulness of the fury. Also, almost none of what was said had anything to do with the homeless people I know—not the ones I once traveled with, not the ones in town. They, the actual homeless men and women, might not have existed at all.

If I write about Santa Barbara, it is not because I think the attitudes at work here are unique. They are not. You find them everywhere in America. In the last few months I have visited several cities around the country, and in each of them I have found the same thing: more and more people in the streets, more and more suffering. (There are at least 350,000 homeless people in the country, perhaps as many as 3 million.) And, in talking to the good citizens of these cities, I found, almost always, the same thing: confusion and ignorance, or simple indifference, but anger too, and fear.

What follows here is an attempt to explain at least some of that anger and fear, to clear up some of the confusion, to chip away at the indifference. It is not meant to be definitive; how could it be? The point is to try to illuminate some of the darker corners of homelessness, those we ordinarily ignore, and those in which the keys to much that is now going on may be hidden.

The trouble begins with the word "homeless." It has become such an abstraction, and is applied to so many different kinds of people, with so many different histories and problems, that it is almost meaningless.

Homelessness, in itself, is nothing more than a condition visited upon men and women (and, increasingly, children) as the final stage of a variety of problems about which the word "homelessness" tells us almost nothing. Or, to put it another way, it is a catch basin into which pour all of the people disenfranchised or marginalized or scared off by processes beyond their control, those which lie close to the heart of American life. Here are the groups packed into the single category of "the homeless":

- Veterans, mainly from the war in Vietnam. In many American cities, vets make up close to 50 percent of all homeless males.
- The mentally ill. In some parts of the country, roughly a quarter of the homeless would, a couple of decades ago, have been institutionalized.
- The physically disabled or chronically ill, who do not receive any benefits or whose benefits do not enable them to afford permanent shelter.
- The elderly on fixed incomes whose funds are no longer sufficient for their needs.
- Men, women, and whole families pauperized by the loss of a job.
- Single parents, usually women, without the resources or skills to establish new lives.
- Runaway children, many of whom have been abused.
- Alcoholics and those in trouble with drugs (whose troubles often begin with one of the other conditions listed here).
- Immigrants, both legal and illegal, who often are not counted among the homeless because they constitute a "problem" in their own right.
- Traditional tramps, hobos, and transients, who have taken to the road or the streets for a variety of reasons and who prefer to be there.

9   You can quickly learn two things about the homeless from this list. First, you can learn that many of the homeless, before they were homeless, were people more or less like ourselves: members of the working or middle class. And you can learn that the world of the homeless has its roots in various policies, events, and ways of life for which some of us are responsible and from which some of us actually prosper.

10   We decide, as a people, to go to war, we ask our children to kill and to die, and the result, years later, is grown men homeless on the street.

11   We change, with the best intentions, the laws pertaining to the mentally ill, and then, without intention, neglect to provide them with services; and the result, in our streets, drives some of us crazy with rage.

12   We cut taxes and prune budgets, we modernize industry and shift the balance of trade, and the result of all these actions and errors can be read, sleeping form by sleeping form, on our city streets.

13   The liberals cannot blame the conservatives. The conservatives cannot blame the liberals. Homelessness is the *sum total* of our dreams, policies, intentions, errors, omissions, cruelties, kindnesses, all of it recorded, in flesh, in the life of the streets.

14   You can also learn from this list one of the most important things there is to know about the homeless—that they can be roughly divided into two groups: those who have had homelessness forced upon them and want nothing more than to escape it; and those who have at least in part chosen it for themselves, and now accept, or in some cases, embrace it.

15   I understand how dangerous it is to introduce the idea of choice into a discussion of homelessness. It can all too easily be used to justify indifference or brutality toward the homeless, or to argue that they are only getting what they "deserve." And yet it seems to me that it is only by taking choice into account,

in all of the intricacies of its various forms and expressions, that one can really understand certain kinds of homelessness.

The fact is, many of the homeless are not only hapless victims but volun- 16
tary exiles, "domestic refugees," people who have turned not against life itself but against *us*, our life, American life. Look for a moment at the vets. The price of returning to America was to forget what they had seen or learned in Vietnam, to "put it behind them." But some could not do that, and the stress of trying showed up as alcoholism, broken marriages, drug addiction, crime. And it showed up too as life on the street, which was for some vets a desperate choice made in the name of life—the best they could manage. It was a way of avoiding what might have occurred had they stayed where they were: suicide, or violence done to others.

We must learn to accept that there may indeed be people, and not only 17
vets, who have seen so much of our world, or seen it so clearly, that to live in it becomes impossible. Here, for example, is the story of Alice, a homeless middle-aged woman in Los Angeles, where there are, perhaps, 50,000 homeless people. It was set down a few months ago by one of my students at the University of California, Santa Barbara, where I taught for a semester. I had encouraged them to go find the homeless and listen to their stories. And so, one day, when this student saw Alice foraging in a dumpster outside a McDonald's, he stopped and talked to her:

> She told me she had led a pretty normal life as she grew up and eventually 18
> went to college. From there she went on to Chicago to teach school. She was single and lived in a small apartment.
>
> One night, after she got off the train after school, a man began to follow 19
> her to her apartment building. When she got to her door she saw a knife and the man hovering behind her. She had no choice but to let him in. The man raped her.
>
> After that, things got steadily worse. She had a nervous breakdown. She 20
> went to a mental institution for three months, and when she went back to her apartment she found her belongings gone. The landlord had sold them to cover the rent she hadn't paid.
>
> She had no place to go and no job because the school had terminated her 21
> employment. She slipped into depression. She lived with friends until she could muster enough money for a ticket to Los Angeles. She said she no longer wanted to burden her friends, and that if she had to live outside, at least Los Angeles was warmer than Chicago.
>
> It is as if she began back then to take on the mentality of a street person. 22
> She resolved herself to homelessness. She's been out West since 1980, without a home or job. She seems happy, with her best friend being her cat. But the scars of memories still haunt her, and she is running from them, or should I say *him*.

This is, in essence, the same story one hears over and over again on the 23
street. You begin with an ordinary life; then an event occurs—traumatic, catastrophic; smaller events follow, each one deepening the original wound; finally, homelessness becomes inevitable, or begins to *seem* inevitable to the

person involved—the only way out of an intolerable situation. You are struck continually, hearing these stories, by something seemingly unique in American life, the absolute isolation involved. In what other culture would there be such an absence or failure of support from familial, social, or institutional sources? Even more disturbing is the fact that it is often our supposed sources of support—family, friends, government organizations—that have caused the problem in the first place.

24   Everything that happened to Alice—the rape, the loss of job and apartment, the breakdown—was part and parcel of a world gone radically wrong, a world, for Alice, no longer to be counted on, no longer worth living in. Her homelessness can be seen as flight, as failure of will or nerve, even, perhaps, as *disease.* But it can also be seen as a mute, furious refusal, a self-imposed exile far less appealing to the rest of us than ordinary life, but *better,* in Alice's terms.

25   We like to think, in America, that everything is redeemable, that everything broken can be magically made whole again, and that what has been "dirtied" can be cleansed. Recently I saw on television that one of the soaps had introduced the character of a homeless old woman. A woman in her thirties discovers that her long-lost mother has appeared in town, on the streets. After much searching the mother is located and identified and embraced; and then she is scrubbed and dressed in style, restored in a matter of days to her former upper-class habits and role.

26   A triumph—but one more likely to occur on television than in real life. Yes, many of those on the streets could be transformed, rehabilitated. But there are others whose lives have been irrevocably changed, damaged beyond repair, and who no longer want help, who no longer recognize the *need* for help, and whose experience in our world has made them want only to be left alone. How, for instance, would one restore Alice's life, or reshape it in a way that would satisfy *our* notion of what a life should be? What would it take to return her to the fold? How to erase the four years of homelessness, which have become as familiar to her, and as much a home, as her "normal" life once was? Whatever we think of the way in which she has resolved her difficulties, it constitutes a sad peace made with the world. Intruding ourselves upon it in the name of redemption is by no means as simple a task—or as justifiable a task—as one might think.

27   It is important to understand too that however disorderly and dirty and unmanageable the world of homeless men and women like Alice appears to us, it is not without its significance, and its rules and rituals. The homeless in our cities mark out for themselves particular neighborhoods, blocks, buildings, doorways. They impose on themselves often obsessively strict routines. They reduce their world to a small area, and thereby protect themselves from a world that might otherwise be too much to bear.

28   Pavlov, the Russian psychologist, once theorized that the two most fundamental reflexes in all animals, including humans, are those involving freedom and orientation. Grab any animal, he said, and it will immediately struggle to accomplish two things: to break free and to orient itself. And this is what one sees in so many of the homeless. Having been stripped of all other forms of connection, and of most kinds of social identity, they are left only with this:

the raw stuff of nature, something encoded in the cells—the desire to be free, the need for familiar space. Perhaps this is why so many of them struggle so vehemently against us when we offer them aid. They are clinging to their freedom and their space, and they do not believe that this is what we, with our programs and our shelters, mean to allow them.

Years ago, when I first came to California, bumming my way west, the marginal world, and the lives of those in it, were very different from what they are now. In those days I spent much of my time in hobo jungles or on the skid rows of various cities, and just as it was easier back then to "get by" in the easygoing beach towns on the California coast, or in the bohemian and artistic worlds in San Francisco or Los Angeles or New York, it was also far easier than it is now to survive in the marginal world. 29

It is important to remember this—important to recognize the immensity of the changes that have occurred in the marginal world in the past twenty years. Whole sections of many cities—the Bowery in New York, the Tenderloin in San Francisco—were once ceded to the transient. In every skid-row area in America you could find what you needed to survive: hash houses, saloons offering free lunches, pawnshops, surplus-clothing stores, and, most important of all, cheap hotels and flophouses and two-bit employment agencies specializing in the kinds of labor (seasonal, shape-up) transients have always done. 30

It was by no means a wonderful world. But it *was* a world. Its rituals were spelled out in ways most of the participants understood. In hobo jungles up and down the tracks, whatever there was to eat went into a common pot and was divided equally. Late at night, in empties crisscrossing the country, men would speak with a certain anonymous openness, as if the shared condition of transience created among them a kind of civility. 31

What most people in that world wanted was simply to be left alone. Some of them had been on the road for years, itinerant workers. Others were recuperating from wounds they could never quite explain. There were young men and a few women with nothing better to do, and older men who had no families or had lost their jobs or wives, or for whom the rigor and pressure of life had proved too demanding. The marginal world offered them a respite from the other world, a world grown too much for them. 32

But things have changed. There began to pour into the marginal world— slowly in the sixties, a bit faster in the seventies, and then faster still in the eighties—more and more people who neither belonged nor knew how to survive there. The sixties brought the counterculture and drugs; the streets filled with young dropouts. Changes in the law loosed upon the streets mentally ill men and women. Inflation took its toll, then recession. Working-class and even middle-class men and women—entire families—began to fall into a world they did not understand. 33

At the same time the transient world was being inundated by new inhabitants, its landscape, its economy, was shrinking radically. Jobs became harder to find. Modernization had something to do with it; machines took the place of men and women. And the influx of workers from Mexico and points farther south created a class of semipermanent workers who took the place of 34 casual transient labor. More important, perhaps, was the fact that the forgotten parts of many cities began to attract attention. Downtown areas were redeveloped, reclaimed. The skid-row sections of smaller cities were turned into "old townes." The old hotels that once catered to transients were upgraded or torn down or became warehouses for welfare families—an arrangement far more profitable to the owners. The price of housing increased; evictions increased. The mentally ill, who once could afford to house themselves in cheap rooms, the alcoholics, who once would drink themselves to sleep at night in their cheap hotels, were out on the street—exposed to the weather and to danger, and also in plain and public view: "problems" to be dealt with.

35   Nor was it only cheap shelter that disappeared. It was also those "open" spaces that had once been available to those without other shelter . . . property rose in value, the nooks and crannies in which the homeless had been able to hide became more visible. Doorways, alleys, abandoned buildings, vacant lots—these "holes" in the cityscape, these gaps in public consciousness, became *real estate*. The homeless, who had been there all the time, were overtaken by economic progress, and they became intruders.

36   You cannot help thinking, as you watch this process, of what happened in parts of Europe in the eighteenth and nineteenth centuries: the effects of the enclosure laws, which eliminated the "commons" in the countryside and drove the rural poor, now homeless, into the cities. The centuries-old tradition of common access and usage was swept away by the beginnings of industrialism; land became *privatized*, a commodity. At the same time something occurred in the cultural psyche. The world itself, space itself, was subtly altered. It was no longer merely to be lived in; it was now to be owned. What was enclosed was not only the land. It was also *the flesh itself* it was cut off from, denied access to, the physical world.

37   And one thinks too, when thinking of the homeless, of the America past, the settlement of the "new" world which occurred at precisely the same time that the commons disappeared. The dream of freedom and equality that brought men and women here had something to do with *space,* as if the wilderness itself conferred upon those arriving here a new beginning: the Eden that had been lost. Once God had sent Christ to redeem men; now he provided a new world. Men discovered, or believed that this world, and perhaps time itself, had no edge, no limit. Space was a sign of God's magnanimity. It was a kind of grace.

38   Somehow, it is all this that is folded into the sad shapes of the homeless. In their mute presence one can sense, however faintly, the dreams of a world gone aglimmering, and the presence of our failed hopes. A kind of claim is made, silently, an ethic is proffered, or, if you will, a whole cosmology, one older than our own ideas of privilege and property. It is as if flesh itself were seeking, this one last time, the home in the world it has been denied.

39 Daily the city eddies around the homeless. The crowds flowing past leave a few feet, a gap. We do not touch the homeless world. Perhaps we cannot touch it. It remains separate even as the city surrounds it.

The homeless, simply because they are homeless, are strangers, alien—and 40 therefore a threat. Their presence, in itself, comes to constitute a kind of violence; it deprives us of our sense of safety. Let me use myself as an example. I know, and respect, many of those now homeless on the streets of Santa Barbara. Twenty years ago, some of them would have been my companions and friends. And yet, these days, if I walk through the park near my home and see strangers bedding down for the night, my first reaction, if not fear, is a sense of annoyance and intrusion, of worry and alarm. I think of my teenage daughter, who often walks through the park, and then of my house, a hundred yards away, and I am tempted—only tempted, but tempted, still—to call the "proper" authorities to have the strangers moved on. Out of sight, out of mind.

Notice: I do not bring them food. I do not offer them shelter or a shower 41 in the morning. I do not even stop to talk. Instead, I think: my daughter, my house, my privacy. What moves me is not the threat of *danger*—nothing as animal as that. Instead there pops up inside of me, neatly in a row, a set of anxieties, ones you might arrange in a dollhouse living room and label: Family of bourgeois fears. The point is this: our response to the homeless is fed by a complex set of cultural attitudes, habits of thought, and fantasies and fears so familiar to us, so common, that they have become *second* nature and might as well be instinctive, for all the control we have over them. And it is by no means easy to untangle this snarl of responses. What does seem clear is that the homeless embody all that bourgeois culture has for centuries tried to eradicate and destroy.

If you look to the history of Europe you find that homelessness first 42 appears (or is first acknowledged) at the very same moment that bourgeois culture begins to appear. The same processes produced them both: the breakup of feudalism, the rise of commerce and cities, the combined triumphs of capitalism, industrialism, and individualism. The historian Fernand Braudel, in *The Wheels of Commerce*, describes, for instance, the armies of impoverished men and women who began to haunt Europe as far back as the eleventh century. And the makeup of these masses? Essentially the same then as it is now: the unfortunates, the throwaways, the misfits, the deviants.

> In the eighteenth century, all sorts and conditions were to be found in this 43
> human dross . . . widows, orphans, cripples . . . journeymen who had broken
> their contracts, out-of-work labourers, homeless priests with no living, old
> men, fire victims . . . war victims, deserters, discharged soldiers, would-be ven-
> dors of useless articles, vagrant preachers with or without licenses, "pregnant
> servant-girls and unmarried mothers driven from home," children sent out "to
> find bread or to maraud."

Then, as now, distinctions were made between the "homeless" and the 44 supposedly "deserving" poor, those who knew their place and willingly sustained, with their labors, the emergent bourgeois world.

> The good paupers were accepted, lined up and registered on the official list; 45
> they had a right to public charity and were sometimes allowed to solicit it out-

side churches in prosperous districts, when the congregation came out, or in market places. . . .

When it comes to beggars and vagrants, it is a very different story, and different pictures meet the eye: crowds, mobs, processions, sometimes mass emigrations, "along the country highways or the streets of the Towns and Villages," by beggars "whom hunger and nakedness has driven from home." . . . The towns dreaded these alarming visitors and drove them out as soon as they appeared on the horizon.

46   And just as the distinctions made about these masses were the same then as they are now, so too was the way society saw them. They seemed to bourgeois eyes (as they still do) the one segment of society that remained resistant to progress, unassimilable and incorrigible, inimical to all order.

47   It is in the nineteenth century, in the Victorian era, that you can find the beginnings of our modern strategies for dealing with the homeless: the notion that they should be controlled and perhaps eliminated through "help." With the Victorians we begin to see the entangling of self-protection with social obligation, the strategy of masking self-interest and the urge to control as *moral duty*. Michel Foucault has spelled this out in his books on madness and punishment: the zeal with which the overseers of early bourgeois culture tried to purge, improve, and purify all of urban civilization—whether through schools and prisons, or quite literally, with public baths and massive new water and sewage systems. Order, ordure—this is, in essence, the tension at the heart of bourgeois culture, and it was the singular genius of the Victorians to make it the main component of their medical, aesthetic, *and* moral systems. It was not a sense of justice or even empathy which called for charity or new attitudes toward the poor; it was *hygiene*. The very same attitudes appear in nineteenth-century America. Charles Loring Brace, in an essay on homeless and vagrant children written in 1876, described the treatment of delinquents in this way: "Many of their vices drop from them like the old and verminous clothing they left behind. . . . The entire change of circumstances seems to cleanse them of bad habits." Here you have it all: *vices, verminous clothing, cleansing them of bad habits*—the triple association of poverty with vice with dirt, an equation in which each term comes to stand for all of them.

48   These attitudes are with us still; that is the point. In our own century the person who has written most revealingly about such things is George Orwell, who tried to analyze his own middle-class attitudes toward the poor. In 1933, in *Down and Out in Paris and London*, he wrote about tramps:

49   In childhood we are taught that tramps are blackguards . . . a repulsive, rather dangerous creature, who would rather die than work or wash, and wants nothing but to beg, drink or rob hen-houses. The tramp monster is no truer to life than the sinister Chinaman of the magazines, but he is very hard to get rid of. The very word "tramp" evokes his image.

50   All of this is still true in America, though now it is not the word "tramp" but the word "homeless" that evokes the images we fear. It is the homeless who smell. Here, for instance, is part of a paper a student of mine wrote about her first visit to a Rescue Mission on skid row.

The sermon began. The room was stuffy and smelly. The mixture of body   51
odors and cooking was nauseating. I remember thinking: how can these people share this facility? They must be repulsed by each other. They had strange
habits and dispositions. They were a group of dirty, dishonored, weird people to me.
   When it was over I ran to my car, went home, and took a shower. I felt
extremely dirty. Through the day I would get flashes of that disgusting smell.

To put it as bluntly as I can, for many of us the homeless are *shit*. And our   52
policies toward them, our spontaneous sense of disgust and horror, our wish
to be rid of them—all of this has hidden in it, close to its heart, our feelings
about excrement. Even Marx, that most bourgeois of revolutionaries, described
the deviant *lumpen* in *The Eighteenth Brumaire of Louis Bonaparte* as "scum, offal,
refuse of all classes." These days, in puritanical Marxist nations, they are called
"parasites"—a word, perhaps not incidentally, one also associates with human
waste.
   What I am getting at here is the *nature* of the desire to help the homeless—   53
what is hidden behind it and why it so often does harm. Every government
program, almost every private project, is geared as much to the needs of those
giving help as it is to the needs of the homeless. Go to any government agency,
or, for that matter, to most private charities, and you will find yourself
enmeshed, at once, in a bureaucracy so tangled and oppressive, or confronted
with so much moral arrogance and contempt, that you will be driven back out
into the streets for relief.
   Santa Barbara, where I live, is as good an example as any. There are three   54
main shelters in the city—all of them private. Between them they provide
fewer than a hundred beds a night for the homeless. Two of the three shelters
are religious in nature: the Rescue Mission and the Salvation Army. In the
mission, as in most places in the country, there are elaborate and stringent
rules. Beds go first to those who have not been there for two months, and you
can stay for only two nights in any two-month period. No shelter is given
to those who are not sober. Even if you go to the mission only for a meal,
you are required to listen to sermons and participate in prayer, and you are
regularly proselytized—sometimes overtly, sometimes subtly. There are oblig-
atory, regimented showers. You go to bed precisely at ten: lights out, no reading, no talking. After the lights go out you will find fifteen men in a room with
double-decker bunks. As the night progresses the room grows stuffier and hot-
ter. Men toss, turn, cough, and moan. In the morning you are awakened precisely at five forty-five. Then breakfast. At seven-thirty you are back on the
street.
   The town's newest shelter was opened almost a year ago by a consortium   55
of local churches. Families and those who are employed have first call on the
beds—a policy which excludes the congenitally homeless. Alcohol is not simply forbidden in the shelter; those with a history of alcoholism must sign a
"contract" pledging to remain sober and chemical-free. Finally, in a paroxysm
of therapeutic bullying, the shelter has added a new wrinkle: if you stay more
than two days you are required to fill out and then discuss with a social worker
a complex form listing what you perceive as your personal failings, goals, and

strategies—all of this for men and women who simply want a place to lie down out of the rain!

56   It is these attitudes, in various forms and permutations, that you find repeated endlessly in America. We are moved either to "redeem" the homeless or to punish them. Perhaps there is nothing consciously hostile about it. Perhaps it is simply that as the machinery of bureaucracy cranks itself up to deal with these problems, attitudes assert themselves automatically. But whatever the case, the fact remains that almost every one of our strategies for helping the homeless is simply an attempt to rearrange the world *cosmetically*, in terms of how it looks and smells to *us*. Compassion is little more than the passion for control.

57 The central question emerging from all this is, What does a society owe to its members in trouble, and *how* is that debt to be paid? It is a question which must be answered in two parts: first, in relation to the men and women who have been marginalized against their will, and then, in a slightly different way, in relation to those who have chosen (or accept or even prize) their marginality.

58   As for those who have been marginalized against their wills, I think the general answer is obvious: A society owes its members whatever it takes for them to regain their places in the social order. And when it comes to specific remedies, one need only read backward the various processes which have created homelessness and then figure out where help is likely to do the most good. But the real point here is not the specific remedies required—affordable housing, say—but the basis upon which they must be offered, the necessary underlying ethical notion we seem in this nation unable to grasp: that those who are the inevitable casualties of modern industrial capitalism and the free-market system are entitled, *by right*, and by the simple virtue of their participation in that system, to whatever help they need. They are entitled to help to find and hold their places in the society whose social contract they have, in effect, signed and observed.

59   Look at that for just a moment: the notion of a contract. The majority of homeless Americans have kept, insofar as they could, to the terms of that contract. In any shelter these days you can find men and women who have worked ten, twenty, forty years, and whose lives have nonetheless come to nothing. These are people who cannot afford a place in the world they helped create. And in return? Is it life on the street they have earned? Or the cruel charity we so grudgingly grant them?

60   But those marginalized against their will are only half the problem. There remains, still, the question of whether we owe anything to those who are voluntarily marginal. What about them: the street people, the rebels, and the recalcitrants, those who have torn up their social contracts or returned them unsigned?

61   I was in Las Vegas last fall, and I went out to the Rescue Mission at the lower end of town, on the edge of the black ghetto, where I first stayed years ago on my way west. It was twilight, still hot; in the vacant lot next-door to

the mission 200 men were lining up for supper. A warm wind blew along the street lined with small houses and salvage yards, and in the distance I could see the desert's edge and the smudge of low hills in the fading light. There were elderly alcoholics in line, and derelicts, but mainly the men were the same sort I had seen here years ago: youngish, out of work, restless and talkative, the drifters and wanderers for whom the word "wanderlust" was invented.

At supper—long communal tables, thin gruel, stale sweet rolls, ice water— 62 a huge black man in his twenties, fierce and muscular, sat across from me. "I'm from the Coast, man," he said. "Never been away from home before. Ain't sure I like it. Sure don't like *this* place. But I lost my job back home a couple of weeks ago and figured, why wait around for another. I thought I'd come out here, see me something of the world."

After supper, a squat Portuguese man in his mid-thirties, hunkered down 63 against the mission wall, offered me a smoke and told me: "Been sleeping in my car, up the street, for a week. Had my own business back in Omaha. But I got bored, man. Sold everything, got a little dough, came out here. Thought I'd work construction. Let me tell you, this is one tough town."

In a world better than ours, I suppose, men (or women) like this might not 64 exist. Conservatives seem to have no trouble imagining a society so well disciplined and moral that deviance of this kind would disappear. And leftists envision a world so just, so generous, that deviance would vanish along with inequity. But I suspect that there will always be something at work in some men and women to make them restless with the systems others devise for them, and to move them outward toward the edges of the world, where life is always riskier, less organized, and easier going.

Do we owe anything to these men and women, who reject our company 65 and what we offer and yet nonetheless seem to demand *something* from us?

We owe them, I think, at least a place to exist, a way to exist. That may 66 not be a *moral* obligation, in the sense that our obligation to the involuntarily marginal is clearly a moral one, but it is an obligation nevertheless, one you might call an existential obligation.

Of course, it may be that I think we owe these men something because I 67 have liked men like them, and because I want their world to be there always, as a place to hide or rest. But there is more to it than that. I think we as a society need men like these. A society needs its margins as much as it needs art and literature. It needs holes and gaps, *breathing spaces,* let us say, into which men and women can escape and live, when necessary, in ways otherwise denied them. Margins guarantee to society a flexibility, an elasticity, and allow it to accommodate itself to the natures and needs of its members. When margins vanish, society becomes too rigid, too oppressive by far, and therefore inimical to life.

It is for such reasons that, in cultures like our own, marginal men and 68 women take on a special significance. They are all we have left to remind us of the narrowness of the received truths we take for granted. "Beyond the pale," they somehow redefine the pale, or remind us, at least, that *something* is still out there, beyond the pale. They preserve, perhaps unconsciously, a dream that would otherwise cease to exist, the dream of having a place in the world, and of being *left alone.*

69   Quixotic? Infantile? Perhaps. But remember Pavlov and his reflexes coded in the flesh: animal, and therefore as if given by God. What we are talking about here is *freedom,* and with it, perhaps, an echo of the dream men brought, long ago, to wilderness America. I use the word "freedom" gingerly, in relation to lives like these: skewed, crippled, emptied of everything we associate with a full, or realized, freedom. But perhaps this is the condition into which freedom has fallen among us. Art has been "appreciated" out of existence; literature has become an extension of the university, replete with tenure and pensions; and as for politics, the ideologies which ring us round seem too silly or shrill by far to speak for life. What is left, then, is this mute and intransigent independence, this "waste" of life which refuses even interpretation, and which cannot be assimilated to any ideology, and which therefore can be put to no one's use. In its crippled innocence and the perfection of its superfluity it amounts, almost, to a rebellion against history, and that is no small thing.

70   Let me put it as simply as I can: what we see on the streets of our cities are two dramas, both of which cut to the troubled heart of the culture and demand from us a response we may not be able to make. There is the drama of those struggling to survive by regaining their place in the social order. And there is the drama of those struggling to survive outside of it.

71   The resolution of both struggles depends on a third drama occurring at the heart of the culture: the tension and contention between the magnanimity we owe to life and the darker tending of the human psyche: our fear of strangeness, our hatred of deviance, our love of order and control. How we mediate by default or design between those contrary forces will determine not only the destinies of the homeless but also something crucial about the nation, and perhaps—let me say it—about our own souls.

Questions for Discussion

1. Summarize some of the factors that cause homelessness and list the groups who make up "the homeless." What common problems among the groups do you see? What kinds of diversity? Do you find any of this information surprising?
2. What does the author suggest as one of the reasons why homeless persons might reject our "shelters and programs"? Does Marin's reasoning make sense to you?
3. How, according to the author, has a marginal, homeless/hobo existence changed over the past few decades? What roles has the faltering economy played? In what ways have the homeless become more "public"?
4. Why was open space essential to America's appeal for early European settlers in the New World?
5. How might the difference between owning land and using land prompt a more tolerant view of transient individuals?
6. According to the author, why are the homeless so threatening? What makes other people fear them? What do we "owe" those who choose a marginal existence?

Ideas for Writing

1. Do you agree that how we deal with the tensions and fears about the homeless can tell us about ourselves and our society? Explain.
2. Research the hobo/tramp cultures of earlier generations. Do your findings support Marin's observations about drastic changes from the free-spirited travelers of the road to the endangered and vulnerable homeless today?
3. What are the roots of modern day organizations that "help" the homeless? How do these roots still influence the organizations and their approaches to social concerns? Write an essay discussing your findings. Perhaps you could focus on one specific organization: the Salvation Army, for example, or a local program in your community.

Politics . . . maybe

Julian Castro

Julian Castro (b. 1974) was born and raised in San Antonio, Texas. His family, especially his mother, was very involved in grassroots politics for the Hispanic community when he was growing up, and Julian plans to continue on in the family tradition. He would like to start a law firm with his identical twin brother. Julian is majoring in communications and will attend law school. He hopes to write professionally and is planning to take classes in creative writing. Julian enjoys working on writing projects with his twin brother. The following essay was written for his first-year college composition course.

Journal

Do people ever make assumptions about what you'll do after college? How do you feel when they do?

How many of these "functions" have I been to in my lifetime? They all seem the same to me now—the same speeches and speakers, the same cheese and ham sandwiches, the same people, ones whom I see only at these political gatherings, "functions" my mother calls them, and, of course, the same expectations of me. "So, what are you going to do after you finish school?" my mother's friend asks me. "Uhh. . . ." Can he see my eyes float along the carpet?

I am told that when I was three years old I was involved in my first political 2 campaign: I handed out flyers. Not of my own volition, but because my mother took part in the hustle and bustle of politics. Today, the very idea of politics makes many people's stomach turn. Conventional wisdom (if we may call it that) is cynical about the motives of politicians and skeptical about the power of the political process to effect change. However, it was never like that for my mother. She sees political activism as an opportunity to change people's lives for the better. Perhaps that is because of her outspoken nature or because Chicanos in the early 1970s (and, of course, for many years before) had no other option. To make themselves heard Chicanos needed the opportunity that the political system provided. In any event, my mother's fervor for activism affected the first years of my life, as it touches it today.

3   I remember buttons and pens, posters, stickers, and pictures: "Viva La Raza!" "Black and Brown United!" "Accept me for who I am—Chicano." These and many other powerful slogans rang in my ears like war cries. And I remember my mother during that time. She worked for what seemed like an infinite number of nonprofit organizations. She sat on this committee and that board. There was the YWCA, Leadership 2000, and others that drift in and out of my memory. She got involved in the PTA at my school because she was the first to show up at a first-of-the-year meeting. Her list of things to do was miles long I thought. At seven or eight years old, I did not understand why my mother worked so diligently for these nonprofit organizations and political causes. I did not see what profit she gained from her work, and I wondered why she would give so much of herself. The slogans and discussions of this and that "-ism" meant nothing either.

4   As a twelve-year-old I liked to disagree with her about her politics. I questioned this stance and that remark. And I asked what in the world she was getting out of speaking up. Even as I continued to visit headquarters and polls, I didn't think of it all as worthwhile. I have seen others of her generation go on to become successful, and I asked her why we did not have the nice house or good car that I saw others with. "Where are the benefits of what you have done?" I demanded.

5   Patiently, over several years, my mother explained to me why she and many others, she said, were trying to better the lives of all Chicanos—the typical, hardworking adult who is relegated by society to a low-income status, the impoverished mothers who, with numerous children to feed and not a single voice, wear badges of tribulation that are their faces. There weren't always Chicanos at this college or attending that major university, she explained. We used to be only farm workers, cooks or, if we were lucky, teachers. My grandmother was a maid, she reminded me.

6   These words my mother spoke again and again. She insisted that things were changing because of political activism, participation in the system. Maria del Rosario Castro has never held a political office. Her name is seldom mentioned in a San Antonio newspaper. However, today, years later, I read the newspapers, and I see that more Valdezes are sitting on school boards, that a greater number of Garcias are now doctors, lawyers, engineers and, of course, teachers. And I look around me and see a few other brown faces in the crowd at this university. I also see in me a product of my mother's diligence and of her friends' hard work. Twenty years ago I would not have been here.

7   Community service isn't always done in a soup kitchen or library, tutoring an adult to read. My opportunities are not a gift of the majority; they are

the result of a lifetime of struggle and commitment endured by a *determined* minority. My mother is one of those persons. And each year I realize more and more how much easier my life has been made by the toil of past generations. I wonder what form *my* service will take, since I am expected by those who know my mother to continue the family tradition. As far back as I can remember, I vowed never to become involved in politics. My young dreams of a fancy car and a nice house would fade as I contemplated a life of grass roots organizing and committee meetings until all hours of the night. "I don't want to be poor!" I would tell my mom.

But profits don't have to be measured in bills. In fact, if we're lucky, they 8 are measured in happiness.

My eyes wander back onto his face and rest as they catch his. "Maybe pol- 9 itics," I answer with a straight smile. His eyes reflect damp brown fields turning into callused hands. The hands have in them pencils, the pencils, power. He laughs back at me.

Questions for Discussion

1. Do you agree with Castro that many people are cynical about politics? Why do you think his mother's attitude was different?
2. Compare the Castros' beliefs about community involvement with Marian Wright Edelman's (Chapter 1). What common themes do you find? What differences?
3. In view of Morris's essay (Chapter 2) and Edelman's (Chapter 1), discuss Mrs. Castro's struggle as a legacy for Julian.
4. Reread the introduction and conclusion. How effective is the narrative frame around the essay?

Ideas for Writing

1. Reflect on your family's or friends' attitudes toward politics and civic duty. In what ways have they influenced you? Discuss, perhaps focusing on one or two specific beliefs or incidents.
2. Do library research on upward mobility among different ethnic groups in America. You could concentrate on one specific ethnic group or do a comparative study. Be sure to consult magazine and newspaper indexes, academic journals, and perhaps general interest literature to find recent information.

Letter from Birmingham Jail

Martin Luther King, Jr.

Martin Luther King, Jr. (1929–1968), minister, civil rights leader, and writer, was born in Atlanta, the son and grandson of Baptist preachers. King graduated from Morehouse College in 1951 and received his Ph.D. from Boston University in 1955. Influenced by Gandhi and by his own religious background, King preached nonviolent resistance as a means to bring about social change and equal rights for black Americans; he organized and lead the Southern Christian Leadership Conference (SCLC), which sponsored numerous boycotts throughout the South. His speech at the march on Washington in 1963, popularly known as the "I Have a Dream" speech, is one of the most famous speeches of this century. His "Letter from Birmingham Jail," below, also written in 1963, was his response to eight clergymen who had criticized his nonviolent protest. In the letter, King discusses the connections between diverse members of American society and explains why their fates are intertwined.

Journal

Do you believe it is ever permissible to break a law?

My Dear Fellow Clergymen[1]:

While confined here in the Birmingham city jail, I came across your recent statement calling my present activities "unwise and untimely." Seldom do I pause to answer criticism of my work and ideas. If I sought to answer all the criticisms that cross my desk, my secretaries would have little time for anything other than such correspondence in the course of the day, and I would have no time for constructive work. But since I feel that you are men of genuine good will and that your criticisms are sincerely set forth, I want to try to answer your statement in what I hope will be patient and reasonable terms.

2   I think I should indicate why I am here in Birmingham, since you have been influenced by the view which argues against "outsiders coming in." I have the honor of serving as president of the Southern Christian Leadership Conference, an organization operating in every southern state, with headquarters in Atlanta, Georgia. We have some eighty-five affiliated organizations across the South, and one of them is the Alabama Christian Movement for Human Rights. Frequently we share staff, educational, and financial resources with our affiliates. Several months ago the affiliate here in Birmingham asked us to be on call to engage in a nonviolent direct-action program if such were deemed necessary. We readily consented, and when the hour came we lived up to our promise. So I, along with several members of my staff, am here because I was invited here. I am here because I have organizational ties here.

3   But more basically, I am in Birmingham because injustice is here. Just as the prophets of the eighth century B.C. left their villages and carried their "thus saith the Lord" far beyond the boundaries of their home towns, and just as the Apostle Paul left his village of Tarsus and carried the gospel of Jesus Christ to

[1]This response to a published statement by eight fellow clergymen from Alabama (Bishop C. C. J. Carpenter, Bishop Joseph A. Durick, Rabbi Milton L. Grafman, Bishop Paul Hardin, Bishop Holan B. Harmon, the Reverend George M. Murray, the Reverend Edward V. Ramage and the Reverend Earl Stallings) was composed under somewhat constricting circumstances. Begun on the margins of the newspaper in which the statement appeared while I was in jail, the letter was continued on scraps of writing paper supplied by a friendly Negro trusty, and concluded on a pad my attorneys were eventually permitted to leave me. Although the text remains in substance unaltered, I have indulged in the author's prerogative of polishing it for publication [King's note].

the far corners of the Greco-Roman world, so am I compelled to carry the gospel of freedom beyond my own home town. Like Paul, I must constantly respond to the Macedonian call for aid.

Moreover, I am cognizant of the interrelatedness of all communities and 4 states. I cannot sit idly by in Atlanta and not be concerned about what happens in Birmingham. Injustice anywhere is a threat to justice everywhere. We are caught in an inescapable network of mutuality, tied in a single garment of destiny. Whatever affects one directly, affects all indirectly. Never again can we afford to live with the narrow, provincial "outside agitator" idea. Anyone who lives inside the United States can never be considered an outsider anywhere within its bounds.

You deplore the demonstrations taking place in Birmingham. But your 5 statement, I am sorry to say, fails to express a similar concern for the conditions that brought about the demonstrations. I am sure that none of you would want to rest content with the superficial kind of social analysis that deals merely with effects and does not grapple with underlying causes. It is unfortunate that demonstrations are taking place in Birmingham, but it is even more unfortunate that the city's white power structure left the Negro community with no alternative.

In any nonviolent campaign there are four basic steps: collection of the 6 facts to determine whether injustices exist; negotiation; self-purification; and direct action. We have gone through all these steps in Birmingham. There can be no gainsaying the fact that racial injustice engulfs this community. Birmingham is probably the most thoroughly segregated city in the United States. Its ugly record of brutality is widely known. Negroes have experienced grossly unjust treatment in the courts. There have been more unsolved bombings of Negro homes and churches in Birmingham than in any other city in the nation. These are the hard, brutal facts of the case. On the basis of these conditions, Negro leaders sought to negotiate with the city fathers. But the latter consistently refused to engage in good-faith negotiation.

Then, last September, came the opportunity to talk with leaders of Birm- 7 ingham's economic community. In the course of the negotiations, certain promises were made by the merchants—for example, to remove the stores' humiliating racial signs. On the basis of these promises, the Reverend Fred Shuttlesworth and the leaders of the Alabama Christian Movement for Human Rights agreed to a moratorium on all demonstrations. As the weeks and months went by, we realized that we were the victims of a broken promise. A few signs, briefly removed, returned; the others remained.

As in so many past experiences, our hopes had been blasted, and the 8 shadow of deep disappointment settled upon us. We had no alternative except to prepare for direct action, whereby we would present our very bodies as a means of laying our case before the conscience of the local and the national community. Mindful of the difficulties involved, we decided to undertake a process of self-purification. We began a series of workshops on nonviolence, and we repeatedly asked ourselves: "Are you able to accept blows without retaliating?" "Are you able to endure the ordeal of jail?" We decided to schedule our direct-action program for the Easter season, realizing that except for Christmas, this is the main shopping period of the year. Knowing that a strong economic-withdrawal program would be the by-product of direct action, we felt that this would be the best time to bring pressure to bear on the merchants for the needed change.

9   Then it occurred to us that Birmingham's mayoral election was coming up in March, and we speedily decided to postpone action until after election day. When we discovered that the Commissioner of Public Safety, Eugene "Bull" Connor, had piled up enough votes to be in the run-off, we decided again to postpone action until the day after the run-off so that the demonstrations could not be used to cloud the issues. Like many others, we wanted to see Mr. Connor defeated, and to this end we endured postponement after postponement. Having aided in this community need, we felt that our direct-action program could be delayed no longer.

10   You may well ask, "Why direct action? Why sit-ins, marches, and so forth? Isn't negotiation a better path?" You are quite right in calling for negotiation. Indeed, this is the very purpose of direct action. Nonviolent direct action seeks to create such a crisis and foster such a tension that a community which has constantly refused to negotiate is forced to confront the issue. It seeks so to dramatize the issue that it can no longer be ignored. My citing the creation of tension as part of the work of the nonviolent-resister may sound rather shocking. But I must confess that I am not afraid of the word "tension." I have earnestly opposed violent tension, but there is a type of constructive, nonviolent tension which is necessary for growth. Just as Socrates felt that it was necessary to create a tension in the mind so that individuals could rise from the bondage of myths and half-truths to the unfettered realm of creative analysis and objective appraisal, so must we see the need for nonviolent gadflies to create the kind of tension in society that will help men rise from the dark depths of prejudice and racism to the majestic heights of understanding and brotherhood.

11   The purpose of our direct-action program is to create a situation so crisis-packed that it will inevitably open the door to negotiation. I therefore concur with you in your call for negotiation. Too long has our beloved Southland been bogged down in a tragic effort to live in monologue rather than dialogue.

12   One of the basic points in your statement is that the action that I and my associates have taken in Birmingham is untimely. Some have asked: "Why didn't you give the new city administration time to act?" The only answer that I can give to this query is that the new Birmingham administration must be prodded about as much as the outgoing one, before it will act. We are sadly mistaken if we feel that the election of Albert Boutwell as mayor will bring the millennium to Birmingham. While Mr. Boutwell is a much more gentle person than Mr. Connor, they are both segregationists, dedicated to maintenance of the status quo. I have hoped that Mr. Boutwell will be reasonable enough to see the futility of massive resistance to desegregation. But he will not see this without pressure from devotees of civil rights. My friends, I must say to you that we have not made a single gain in civil rights without determined

legal and nonviolent pressure. Lamentably, it is an historical fact that privileged groups seldom give up their privileges voluntarily. Individuals may see the moral light and voluntarily give up their unjust posture; but, as Reinhold Niebuhr has reminded us, groups tend to be more immoral than individuals.

We know through painful experience that freedom is never voluntarily 13 given by the oppressor; it must be demanded by the oppressed. Frankly, I have yet to engage in a direct-action campaign that was "well timed" in the view of those who have not suffered unduly from the disease of segregation. For years now I have heard the word "Wait!" It rings in the ear of every Negro with piercing familiarity. This "Wait" has almost always meant "Never." We must come to see, with one of our distinguished jurists, that "justice too long delayed is justice denied."

We have waited for more than 340 years for our constitutional and God- 14 given rights. The nations of Asia and Africa are moving with jetlike speed toward gaining political independence, but we still creep at horse-and-buggy pace toward gaining a cup of coffee at a lunch counter. Perhaps it is easy for those who have never felt the stinging darts of segregation to say, "Wait." But when you have seen vicious mobs lynch your mothers and fathers at will and drown your sisters and brothers at whim; when you have seen hate-filled policemen curse, kick, and even kill your black brothers and sisters; when you see the vast majority of your twenty million Negro brothers smothering in an airtight cage of poverty in the midst of an affluent society; when you suddenly find your tongue twisted and your speech stammering as you seek to explain to your six-year-old daughter why she can't go to the public amusement park that has just been advertised on television, and see tears welling up in her eyes when she is told that Funtown is closed to colored children, and see ominous clouds of inferiority beginning to form in her little mental sky, and see her beginning to distort her personality by developing an unconscious bitterness toward white people; when you have to concoct an answer for a five-year-old son who is asking, "Daddy, why do white people treat colored people so mean?"; when you take a cross-country drive and find it necessary to sleep night after night in the uncomfortable corners of your automobile because no motel will accept you; when you are humiliated day in and day out by nagging signs reading "white" and "colored"; when your first name becomes "nigger," your middle name becomes "boy" (however old you are) and your last name becomes "John," and your wife and mother are never given the respected title "Mrs."; when you are harried by day and haunted by night by the fact that you are a Negro, living constantly at tiptoe stance, never quite knowing what to expect next, and are plagued with inner fears and outer resentments; when you are forever fighting a degenerating sense of "nobodiness"—then you will understand why we find it difficult to wait. There comes a time when the cup of endurance runs over, and men are no longer willing to be plunged into the abyss of despair. I hope, sirs, you can understand our legitimate and unavoidable impatience.

You express a great deal of anxiety over our willingness to break laws. 15 This is certainly a legitimate concern. Since we so diligently urge people to obey the Supreme Court's decision of 1954 outlawing segregation in the public schools, at first glance it may seem rather paradoxical for us consciously to break laws. One may well ask: "How can you advocate breaking some laws and obeying others?" The answer lies in the fact that there are two types of laws: just and unjust. I would be the first to advocate obeying just laws. One has not only a legal but a moral responsibility to obey just laws. Conversely, one has a moral responsibility to disobey unjust laws. I would agree with St. Augustine that "an unjust law is no law at all."

16   Now, what is the difference between the two? How does one determine whether a law is just or unjust? A just law is a man-made code that squares with the moral law or the law of God. An unjust law is a code that is out of harmony with the moral law. To put it in the terms of St. Thomas Aquinas: An unjust law is a human law that is not rooted in eternal law and natural law. Any law that uplifts human personality is just. Any law that degrades human personality is unjust. All segregation statutes are unjust because segregation distorts the soul and damages the personality. It gives the segregator a false sense of superiority and the segregated a false sense of inferiority. Segregation, to use the terminology of the Jewish philosopher Martin Buber, substitutes an "I-it" relationship for an "I-thou" relationship and ends up relegating persons to the status of things. Hence segregation is not only politically, economically, and sociologically unsound, it is morally wrong and sinful. Paul Tillich has said that sin is separation. Is not segregation an existential expression of man's tragic separation, his awful estrangement, his terrible sinfulness? Thus it is that I can urge men to obey the 1954 decision of the Supreme Court, for it is morally right; and I can urge them to disobey segregation ordinances, for they are morally wrong.

17   Let us consider a more concrete example of just and unjust laws. An unjust law is a code that a numerical or power majority group compels a minority group to obey but does not make binding on itself. This is *difference* made legal. By the same token, a just law is a code that a majority compels a minority to follow and that it is willing to follow itself. This is *sameness* made legal.

18   Let me give another explanation. A law is unjust if it is inflicted on a minority that, as a result of being denied the right to vote, had no part in enacting or devising the law. Who can say that the legislature of Alabama which set up that state's segregation laws was democratically elected? Throughout Alabama all sorts of devious methods are used to prevent Negroes from becoming registered voters, and there are some counties in which, even though Negroes constitute a majority of the population, not a single Negro is registered. Can any law enacted under such circumstances be considered democratically structured?

19   Sometimes a law is just on its face and unjust in its application. For instance, I have been arrested on a charge of parading without a permit. Now, there is nothing wrong in having an ordinance which requires a permit for a parade. But such an ordinance becomes unjust when it is used to maintain segregation and to deny citizens the First-Amendment privilege of peaceful assembly and protest.

I hope you are able to see the distinction I am trying to point out. In no 20 sense do I advocate evading or defying the law, as would the rabid segregationist. That would lead to anarchy. One who breaks an unjust law must do so openly, lovingly, and with a willingness to accept the penalty. I submit that an individual who breaks a law that conscience tells him is unjust, and who willingly accepts the penalty of imprisonment in order to arouse the conscience of the community over its injustice, is in reality expressing the highest respect for law.

Of course, there is nothing new about this kind of civil disobedience. It 21 was evidenced sublimely in the refusal of Shadrach, Meshach, and Abednego to obey the laws of Nebuchadnezzar, on the ground that a higher moral law was at stake. It was practiced superbly by the early Christians, who were willing to face hungry lions and the excruciating pain of chopping blocks rather than submit to certain unjust laws of the Roman Empire. To a degree, academic freedom is a reality today because Socrates practiced civil disobedience.[2] In our own nation, the Boston Tea Party represented a massive act of civil disobedience.

We should never forget that everything Adolf Hitler did in Germany was 22 "legal" and everything the Hungarian freedom fighters[3] did in Hungary was "illegal." It was "illegal" to aid and comfort a Jew in Hitler's Germany. Even so, I am sure that, had I lived in Germany at the time, I would have aided and comforted my Jewish brothers. If today I lived in a Communist country where certain principles dear to the Christian faith are suppressed, I would openly advocate disobeying that country's anti-religious laws.

I must make two honest confessions to you, my Christian and Jewish 23 brothers. First, I must confess that over the past few years I have been gravely disappointed with the white moderate. I have almost reached the regrettable conclusion that the Negro's great stumbling block in his stride toward freedom is not the White Citizen's Counciler or the Ku Klux Klanner, but the white moderate, who is more devoted to "order" than to justice; who prefers a negative peace which is the absence of tension to a positive peace which is the presence of justice; who constantly says, "I agree with you in the goal you seek, but I cannot agree with your methods of direct action"; who paternalistically believes he can set the timetable for another man's freedom; who lives by a mythical concept of time and who constantly advises the Negro to wait for a "more convenient season." Shallow understanding from people of good will is more frustrating than absolute misunderstanding from people of ill will. Lukewarm acceptance is much more bewildering than outright rejection.

I had hoped that the white moderate would understand that law and order 24 exist for the purpose of establishing justice and that when they fail in this purpose they become the dangerously structured dams that block the flow of

[2]The ancient Greek philosopher Socrates was tried by the Athenians for corrupting their youth through his skeptical, questioning manner of teaching. He refused to change his ways, and was condemned to death.
[3]In the anti-Communist revolution of 1956, which was quickly put down by the Russian army.

social progress. I had hoped that the white moderate would understand that the present tension in the South is a necessary phase of the transition from an obnoxious negative peace, in which the Negro passively accepted his unjust plight, to a substantive and positive peace, in which all men will respect the dignity and worth of human personality. Actually, we who engage in nonviolent direct action are not the creators of tension. We merely bring to the surface the hidden tension that is already alive. We bring it out in the open, where it can be seen and dealt with. Like a boil that can never be cured so long as it is covered up but must be opened with all its ugliness to the natural medicines of air and light, injustice must be exposed, with all the tension its exposure creates, to the light of human conscience and the air of national opinion, before it can be cured.

25   In your statement you assert that our actions, even though peaceful, must be condemned because they precipitate violence. But is this a logical assertion? Isn't this like condemning a robbed man because his possession of money precipitated the evil act of robbery? Isn't this like condemning Socrates because his unswerving commitment to truth and his philosophical inquiries precipitated the act by the misguided populace in which they made him drink hemlock? Isn't this like condemning Jesus because his unique God-consciousness and never-ceasing devotion to God's will precipitated the evil act of crucifixion? We must come to see that, as the federal courts have consistently affirmed, it is wrong to urge an individual to cease his efforts to gain his basic constitutional rights because the quest may precipitate violence. Society must protect the robbed and punish the robber.

26   I had also hoped that the white moderate would reject the myth concerning time in relation to the struggle for freedom. I have just received a letter from a white brother in Texas. He writes: "All Christians know that the colored people will receive equal rights eventually, but it is possible that you are in too great a religious hurry. It has taken Christianity almost two thousand years to accomplish what it has. The teachings of Christ take time to come to earth." Such an attitude stems from a tragic misconception of time, from the strangely irrational notion that there is something in the very flow of time that will inevitably cure all ills. Actually, time itself is neutral; it can be used either destructively or constructively. More and more I feel that the people of ill will have used time much more effectively than have the people of good will. We will have to repent in this generation not merely for the hateful words and actions of the bad people, but for the appalling silence of the good people. Human progress never rolls in on wheels of inevitability; it comes through the tireless efforts of men willing to be co-workers with God, and without this hard work, time itself becomes an ally of the forces of social stagnation. We must use time creatively, in the knowledge that the time is always ripe to do right. Now is the time to make real the promise of democracy and transform our pending national elegy into a creative psalm of brotherhood. Now is the time to lift our national policy from the quicksand of racial injustice to the solid rock of human dignity.

27   You speak of our activity in Birmingham as extreme. At first I was rather

disappointed that fellow clergymen would see my nonviolent efforts as those of an extremist. I began thinking about the fact that I stand in the middle of two opposing forces in the Negro community. One is a force of complacency, made up in part of Negroes who, as a result of long years of oppression, are so drained of self-respect and a sense of "somebodiness" that they have adjusted to segregation; and in part of a few middle-class Negroes who, because of a degree of academic and economic security and because in some ways they profit by segregation, have become insensitive to the problems of the masses. The other force is one of bitterness and hatred, and it comes perilously close to advocating violence. It is expressed in the various black nationalist groups that are springing up across the nation, the largest and best-known being Elijah Muhammad's Muslim movement. Nourished by the Negro's frustration over the continued existence of racial discrimination, this movement is made up of people who have lost faith in America, who have absolutely repudiated Christianity, and who have concluded that the white man is an incorrigible "devil."

I have tried to stand between these two forces, saying that we need emulate neither the "do-nothingism" of the complacent nor the hatred and despair of the black nationalist. For there is the more excellent way of love and nonviolent protest. I am grateful to God that, through the influence of the Negro church, the way of nonviolence became an integral part of our struggle. 28

If this philosophy had not emerged, by now many streets of the South would, I am convinced, be flowing with blood. And I am further convinced that if our white brothers dismiss as "rabblerousers" and "outside agitators" those of us who employ nonviolent direct action, and if they refuse to support our nonviolent efforts, millions of Negroes will, out of frustration and despair, seek solace and security in black-nationalist ideologies—a development that would inevitably lead to a frightening racial nightmare. 29

Oppressed people cannot remain oppressed forever. The yearning for freedom eventually manifests itself, and that is what has happened to the American Negro. Something within has reminded him of his birthright of freedom, and something without has reminded him that it can be gained. Consciously or unconsciously, he has been caught up by the *Zeitgeist*,[4] and with his black brothers of Africa and his brown and yellow brothers of Asia, South America, and the Caribbean, the United States Negro is moving with a sense of great urgency toward the promised land of racial justice. If one recognizes this vital urge that has engulfed the Negro community, one should readily understand why public demonstrations are taking place. The Negro has many pent-up resentments and latent frustrations, and he must release them. So let him march; let him make prayer pilgrimages to the city hall; let him go on freedom rides—and try to understand why he must do so. If his repressed emotions are not released in nonviolent ways, they will seek expression through violence; this is not a threat but a fact of history. So I have not said to my people, "Get rid of your discontent." Rather, I have tried to say that this normal 30

---

[4]The spirit of the times.

and healthy discontent can be channeled into the creative outlet of nonviolent direct action. And now this approach is being termed extremist.

31   But though I was initially disappointed at being categorized as an extremist, as I continued to think about the matter I gradually gained a measure of satisfaction from the label. Was not Jesus an extremist for love: "Love your enemies, bless them that curse you, do good to them that hate you, and pray for them which despitefully use you, and persecute you." Was not Amos an extremist for justice: "Let justice roll down like waters and righteousness like an ever-flowing stream." Was not Paul an extremist for the Christian gospel: "I bear in my body the marks of the Lord Jesus." Was not Martin Luther an extremist: "Here I stand; I cannot do otherwise, so help me God." And John Bunyan: "I will stay in jail to the end of my days before I make a butchery of my conscience." And Abraham Lincoln: "This nation cannot survive half slave and half free." And Thomas Jefferson: "We hold these truths to be self-evident, that all men are created equal. . . ." So the question is not whether we will be extremists, but what kind of extremists we will be. Will we be extremists for hate or for love? Will we be extremists for the preservation of injustice or for the extension of justice? In that dramatic scene on Calvary's hill three men were crucified. We must never forget that all three were crucified for the same crime—the crime of extremism. Two were extremists for immorality, and thus fell below their environment. The other, Jesus Christ, was an extremist for love, truth, and goodness, and thereby rose above his environment. Perhaps the South, the nation, and the world are in dire need of creative extremists.

32   I had hoped that the white moderate would see this need. Perhaps I was too optimistic; perhaps I expected too much. I suppose I should have realized that few members of the oppressor race can understand the deep groans and passionate yearnings of the oppressed race, and still fewer have the vision to see that injustice must be rooted out by strong, persistent, and determined action. I am thankful, however, that some of our white brothers in the South have grasped the meaning of this social revolution and committed themselves to it. They are still all too few in quantity, but they are big in quality. Some— such as Ralph McGill, Lillian Smith, Harry Golden, James McBridge Dabbs, Ann Braden, and Sarah Patton Boyle—have written about our struggle in eloquent and prophetic terms. Others have marched with us down nameless streets of the South. They have languished in filthy, roach-infested jails, suffering the abuse and brutality of policemen who view them as "dirty nigger-lovers." Unlike so many of their moderate brothers and sisters, they have recognized the urgency of the moment and sensed the need for powerful "action" antidotes to combat the disease of segregation.

33   Let me take note of my other major disappointment. I have been so greatly disappointed with the white church and its leadership. Of course, there are some notable exceptions. I am not unmindful of the fact that each of you has taken some significant stands on this issue. I commend you, Reverend Stallings, for your Christian stand on this past Sunday, in welcoming Negroes to your worship service on a nonsegregated basis. I commend the Catholic leaders of this state for integrating Spring Hill College several years ago.

But despite these notable exceptions, I must honestly reiterate that I have 34 been disappointed with the church. I do not say this as one of those negative critics who can always find something wrong with the church. I say this as a minister of the gospel, who loves the church; who was nurtured in its bosom; who has been sustained by its spiritual blessings and who will remain true to it as long as the cord of life shall lengthen.

When I was suddenly catapulted into the leadership of the bus protest in 35 Montgomery, Alabama, a few years ago, I felt we would be supported by the white church. I felt that the white ministers, priests, and rabbis of the South would be among our strongest allies. Instead, some have been outright opponents, refusing to understand the freedom movement and misrepresenting its leaders; all too many others have been more cautious than courageous and have remained silent behind the anesthetizing security of stainedglass windows.

In spite of my shattered dreams, I came to Birmingham with the hope that 36 the white religious leadership of this community would see the justice of our cause and, with deep moral concern, would serve as the channel through which our just grievances could reach the power structure. I had hoped that each of you would understand. But again I have been disappointed.

I have heard numerous southern religious leaders admonish their wor- 37 shipers to comply with a desegregation decision because it is the law, but I have longed to hear white ministers declare: "Follow this decree because integration is morally right and because the Negro is your brother." In the midst of blatant injustices inflicted upon the Negro, I have watched white churchmen stand on the sideline and mouth pious irrelevancies and sanctimonious trivialities. In the midst of a mighty struggle to rid our nation of racial and economic injustice, I have heard many ministers say: "Those are social issues, with which the gospel has no real concern." And I have watched many churches commit themselves to a completely other worldly religion which makes a strange, un-Biblical distinction between body and soul, between the sacred and the secular.

I have traveled the length and breadth of Alabama, Mississippi, and all 38 the other southern states. On sweltering summer days and crisp autumn mornings I have looked at the South's beautiful churches with their lofty spires pointing heavenward. I have beheld the impressive outlines of her massive religious-education buildings. Over and over I have found myself asking: "What kind of people worship here? Who is their God? Where were their voices when the lips of Governor Barnett dripped with words of interposition and nullification? Where were they when Governor Wallace gave a clarion call for defiance and hatred? Where were their voices of support when bruised and weary Negro men and women decided to rise from the dark dungeons of complacency to the bright hills of creative protest?"

Yes, these questions are still in my mind. In deep disappointment I have 39 wept over the laxity of the church. But be assured that my tears have been tears of love. There can be no deep disappointment where there is not deep love. Yes, I love the church. How could I do otherwise? I am in the rather unique position of being the son, the grandson, and the great-grandson of preachers. Yes, I see the church as the body of Christ. But, oh! How we have blemished and scarred that body through social neglect and through fear of being nonconformists.

40   There was a time when the church was very powerful—in the time when the early Christians rejoiced at being deemed worthy to suffer for what they believed. In those days the church was not merely a thermometer that recorded the ideas and principles of popular opinion; it was a thermostat that transformed the mores of society. Whenever the early Christians entered a town, the people in power became disturbed and immediately sought to convict the Christians for being "disturbers of the peace" and "outside agitators." But the Christians pressed on, in the conviction that they were "a colony of heaven," called to obey God rather than man. Small in number, they were big in commitment. They were too God-intoxicated to be "astronomically intimidated." By their effort and example they brought an end to such ancient evils as infanticide and gladiatorial contests.

41   Things are different now. So often the contemporary church is a weak, ineffectual voice with an uncertain sound. So often it is an arch-defender of the status quo. Far from being disturbed by the presence of the church, the power structure of the average community is consoled by the church's silent—and often even vocal—sanction of things as they are.

42   But the judgment of God is upon the church as never before. If today's church does not recapture the sacrificial spirit of the early church, it will lose its authenticity, forfeit the loyalty of millions, and be dismissed as an irrelevant social club with no meaning for the twentieth century. Every day I meet young people whose disappointment with the church has turned into outright disgust.

43   Perhaps I have once again been too optimistic. Is organized religion too inextricably bound to the status quo to save our nation and the world? Perhaps I must turn my faith to the inner spiritual church, the church within the church, as the true *ekklesia*[5] and the hope of the world. But again I am thankful to God that some noble souls from the ranks of organized religion have broken loose from the paralyzing chains of conformity and joined us as active partners in the struggle for freedom. They have left their secure congregations and walked the streets of Albany, Georgia, with us. They have gone down the highways of the South on tortuous rides for freedom. Yes, they have gone to jail with us. Some have been dismissed from their churches, have lost the support of their bishops and fellow ministers. But they have acted in the faith that right defeated is stronger than evil triumphant. Their witness has been the spiritual salt that has preserved the true meaning of the gospel in these troubled times. They have carved a tunnel of hope through the dark mountain of disappointment.

44   I hope the church as a whole will meet the challenge of this decisive hour. But even if the church does not come to the aid of justice, I have no despair

---

[5]The Greek New Testament word for the early Christian church.

about the future. I have no fear about the outcome of our struggle in Birmingham, even if our motives are at present misunderstood. We will reach the goal of freedom in Birmingham and all over the nation, because the goal of America is freedom. Abused and scorned though we may be, our destiny is tied up with America's destiny. Before the pilgrims landed at Plymouth, we were here. Before the pen of Jefferson etched the majestic words of the Declaration of Independence across the pages of history, we were here. For more than two centuries our forebears labored in this country without wages; they made cotton king; they built the homes of their masters while suffering gross injustice and shameful humiliation—and yet out of a bottomless vitality they continued to thrive and develop. If the inexpressible cruelties of slavery could not stop us, the opposition we now face will surely fail. We will win our freedom because the sacred heritage of our nation and the eternal will of God are embodied in our echoing demands.

Before closing I feel impelled to mention one other point in your statement 45 that has troubled me profoundly. You warmly commended the Birmingham police force for keeping "order" and "preventing violence." I doubt that you would have so warmly commended the police force if you had seen its dogs sinking their teeth into unarmed, nonviolent Negroes. I doubt that you would so quickly commend the policemen if you were to observe their ugly and inhumane treatment of Negroes here in the city jail; if you were to watch them push and curse old Negro women and young Negro girls; if you were to see them slap and kick old Negro men and young boys; if you were to observe them, as they did on two occasions, refuse to give us food because we wanted to sing our grace together. I cannot join you in your praise of the Birmingham police department.

It is true that the police have exercised a degree of discipline in handling 46 the demonstrators. In this sense they have conducted themselves rather "nonviolently" in public. But for what purpose? To preserve the evil system of segregation. Over the past few years I have consistently preached that nonviolence demands that the means we use must be as pure as the ends we seek. I have tried to make clear that it is wrong to use immoral means to attain moral ends. But now I must affirm that it is just as wrong, or perhaps even more so, to use moral means to preserve immoral ends. Perhaps Mr. Connor and his policemen have been rather nonviolent in public, as was Chief Pritchett in Albany, Georgia, but they have used the moral means of nonviolence to maintain the immoral end of racial injustice. As T. S. Eliot has said, "The last temptation is the greatest treason: To do the right deed for the wrong reason."

I wish you had commended the Negro sit-inners and demonstrators of 47 Birmingham for their sublime courage, their willingness to suffer, and their amazing discipline in the midst of great provocation. One day the South will recognize its real heroes. They will be the James Merediths,[6] with the noble sense of purpose that enables them to face jeering and hostile mobs, and with the agonizing loneliness that characterizes the life of the pioneer. They will be

---

[6]Meredith was the first black to enroll at the University of Mississippi.

old, oppressed, battered Negro women, symbolized in a seventy-two-year-old woman in Montgomery, Alabama, who rose up with a sense of dignity and with her people decided not to ride segregated buses, and who responded with ungrammatical profundity to one who inquired about her weariness: "My feets is tired, but my soul is at rest." They will be the young high school and college students, the young ministers of the gospel and a host of their elders, courageously and nonviolently sitting in at lunch counters and willingly going to jail for conscience' sake. One day the South will know that when these disinherited children of God sat down at lunch counters, they were in reality standing up for what is best in the American dream and for the most sacred values in our Judaeo-Christian heritage, thereby bringing our nation back to those great wells of democracy which were dug deep by the founding fathers in their formulation of the Constitution and the Declaration of Independence.

48   Never before have I written so long a letter. I'm afraid it is much too long to take your precious time. I can assure you that it would have been much shorter if I had been writing from a comfortable desk, but what else can one do when he is alone in a narrow jail cell, other than write long letters, think long thoughts, and pray long prayers?

49   If I have said anything in this letter that overstates the truth and indicates an unreasonable impatience, I beg you to forgive me. If I have said anything that understates the truth and indicates my having a patience that allows me to settle for anything less than brotherhood, I beg God to forgive me.

50   I hope this letter finds you strong in the faith. I also hope that circumstances will soon make it possible for me to meet each of you, not as an integrationist or a civil-rights leader but as a fellow clergyman and a Christian brother. Let us all hope that the dark clouds of racial prejudice will soon pass away and the deep fog of misunderstanding will be lifted from our fear-drenched communities, and in some not too distant tomorrow the radiant stars of love and brotherhood will shine over our great nation with all their scintillating beauty.

> Yours for the cause of Peace and Brotherhood,
> Martin Luther King, Jr.

Questions for Discussion

1. In one of King's initial metaphors in this letter, he says, "We are caught in an inescapable network of mutuality, tied in a single garment of destiny." Examine and interpret this metaphor. Study and interpret other metaphors included in this essay that develop images of community.
2. What examples of civil disobedience does King present? How do these particular examples develop his thesis?
3. How does King define just and unjust laws? Do you find his arguments persuasive? Would Nelson Reed (in McPherson's story "A Loaf of Bread") agree? Discuss.
4. In laying the foundation of his argument against the racist policies in Birmingham, why does King make the point that "groups tend to be more immoral than individuals"? Do you agree with his view?

5. Why does King compare himself to the prophet Paul? How does this comparison help to establish his authority, his wisdom, and his purpose?

6. How does King refute the white moderate's assertion that King and his group's actions, "even though peaceful, must be condemned because they precipitate violence"? Do you agree or disagree with King? On the whole, do you think King's letter would be convincing to such an audience?

Ideas for Writing

1. Write an essay in which you agree or disagree with King's views on the need for immediate action on the issues of civil rights. Do you agree that social change needs to be accelerated through protest movements, or do you favor a calmer, more gradual approach?

2. If King were alive, what do you think his reaction would be to the initial Rodney King verdict in Los Angeles? Do you believe that Martin Luther King, Jr.'s nonviolent approach can be effective in today's struggles for civil rights?

Community Service Writing Student Project: "Urban Ministry"

Tamara Watt

The following informational brochure was produced by Tamara Watt for Urban Ministry, an organization providing services to homeless people and others in need. Such student writing not only frees up resources for social service groups to use for other needs, it also teaches students about real-world writing concerns and audience awareness. As you read the brochure, think about the rhetorical strategies used in developing this type of writing.

VOLUNTEER OPPORTUNITIES

Helping Homeless & Low Income People

URBAN MINISTRY OF PALO ALTO relies on 300 local volunteers—& many more are needed! **Call the number listed below.**

Walking Together: Volunteer Case Management Work in an intensive, on-going relationship with a mentally or physically disabled adult to help them secure income and housing. **2–10 hrs/mo. Flexible.**

Day Care Center for Homeless Families Provide day care for children whose families are living in a homeless shelter. **2 hrs/wk. 9–1 pm Tues & Thurs.**

Evening Babysitting Provide child care to children whose parents are attending parenting workshops while staying in homeless shelter. **2 hrs/wk 7–9 pm Thurs.**

Tenant Advocacy List & contact willing apartment and rental landlords on behalf of the shelter for its guests. **Flexible.**

Playcamp Play with children living in a homeless shelter. Groups are ideal. **Flexible.**

Children's Activities Compile list of free things to do for kids living in homeless shelter.

Shelter Clothes Closet Sort and distribute donated clothing in homeless shelter. **3 hrs/wk. Afternoon.**

Food Closet 6 volunteers needed to unpack and organize donated food. **2 hrs/wk.**

Breaking Bread: Meal Program Prepare and serve meal to guests of homeless shelter. **3–4 hrs/mo.**

Driver Give guests of homeless shelter rides to bus stop on regular basis. **Mornings.**

Leftovers Organize a one-time or regular donation to our food and meal programs with a local restaurant or business.

Rolling Estates: Drop-In Center Assist UMPA staff with variety of tasks. **4 hrs/wk.**

Hotel de Zink: Shelter Program Visit shelter guests, assist staff, bring snacks, launder sheets & towels. **Early am's & late pm's.**

Beyond Shelter Host office community room; provide coffee, referrals and conversation. **2 hrs/wk. Afternoon.**

Medical Clinic Provide refreshments and assist medical volunteers. **Sundays 11–2pm.**

Donations of bedding and furniture, children's toys & furniture, children & adult clothes in excellent condition. Also sleeping bags, toiletries, & food always needed.

Money enables **Urban Ministry** to operate consistently and professionally. Most comes from individual and church donations; you can help! Send to: P.O. Box 213 Palo Alto, CA 94302. For **Menlo Park Family Shelter,** send to: **430 Sherman, Palo Alto, CA 94306.**

Questions for Discussion

1. What is the writing situation for this assignment: who is the audience? What is the purpose? How do audience and purpose affect style, organization, and emphasis?
2. How does dividing up the information by subject and into small paragraphs help improve readability—and the likelihood of the brochure reaching its audience?

Ideas for Writing

1. Identify a local club, groups, or organization whose philosophy and interests are consistent with your own or a group about whom you would like to learn more. Meet with the organization's director or other workers, and individually or with peers, research and write up a brochure or flyer about the organization or the services it offers. Be careful to identify the appropriate audience for the brochure and to write and revise with that audience or with those audiences in mind.

CHAPTER WRITING PROJECTS

1. Write an essay analyzing concepts of social justice discussed in this chapter's readings. You could examine the lives of workers and the poor; you could study Martin Luther King's concept of just and unjust laws; you could examine equal rights and opportunities in view of race, gender, and class issues.
2. Interview workers from at least three different occupations. Write some questions for the interview designed to elicit their feelings and attitudes about work and about their contributions to society, Write up your findings in a narrative or dialogue form. What can you infer about work, work ethics, and society from your interviews?
3. What experiences have you had in the work place? Do they support or refute Takaki's or Faludi's assessments? Is your experience in any way parallel to Mike LeFevre's? In an essay that refers to your readings, discuss your experience and observations.
4. Research facilities, laws and statutes, or programs for homeless individuals in your community. You could talk with local government agencies, churches, nonprofit organizations. Summarize your findings in the form of an annotated list; share the list with interested agencies. You might do this as a collaborative project in pairs or groups from your class.
5. Visit your local courthouse, whether municipal, traffic, county, or other. Stop by a case in progress and listen to the testimony of witnesses. To what extent does the testimony rest on narrative? Does everyone tell his or her story in the same way? What factors seems to be involved in different witnesses' credibility? Are all testimonies given equal weight? You could consider the relative advantages or disadvantages given to native or nonnative speakers of English, to ethnicity or language style, to those with and without power in the courtroom. Analyze and discuss your findings in an essay and summarize your results for your class.
6. Do some field research of your own, individually or in a group, finding out the least expensive places to shop, bank, and find gas or clothing in the area. Share your findings with interested shelters or local programs.
7. Compare and contrast two or more expository, fictional, and poetic accounts of struggles in this chapter, selecting a particular theme as your

focus. Which approach or genre do you find most informative and compelling?

8. Investigate local community organizations that support workers, whether mainstream industrial workers, child care workers, newcomer/immigrants, or other groups. Write an essay analyzing your findings in view of this chapter's readings on social and economic struggles.

9. As a class or in small groups, rent or go see one of the following films; afterward, discuss the film in view of your readings and your own observations and experience: *Ironweed, Milagro Beanfield War, Country, American Dream, In the Line of Fire, Norma Rae, Matewan, Roger and Me, Working Girl.*

CHAPTER 5

Health and Community

So the real philosophy here is to take health care—not just medicine, but comprehensive health care—back to the community. . . . We also need to deliver health care in nontraditional settings. We should be providing services in laundromats, in schools, in churches.
——David Smith, "Healing and the Community"

She hadn't allowed herself to mourn until then. She cried for the friend of a friend who'd just died. And she cried for all the people she'd never shed tears for. "All these people who died with me."
——Carol Pogash, from "The Way It's Supposed to Be"

Just as today's educational values and goals are more directly linked to the community, so too are the values and goals of healing and health care. The growing importance of community in health care management reflects the developing emphasis on the role that a patient's family, friends, community, mind, and spirit play in the healing process. The increasing importance of nurses and health care professionals at hospitals and outreach clinics also reflects fundamental changes in health care policies. In addition, individuals in the process of recovering from substance addiction or from the loss of family members or friends are helped in community support groups.

In the past two decades scientific and technological advances have been transforming the practice of medicine. These advances have created situations that ask us to reexamine the importance of the quality of human life. While doctors can prolong their patients' lives, with these scientific advances come painful and paradoxical consequences. Many people who have survived because of the miracles of medical science and technology must accept severe limitations in their life-styles; some live knowing that they are fundamentally at the mercy of an incurable disease. In other cases people can only stay alive on life support systems. What are the costs of these life support systems—the human costs and the financial costs to the individual and to the community? Quality of life as opposed to survival has become an ethical issue that doctors, health care providers, patients, their families, our hospitals, and our government must face.

The chapter's opening selection, "Healing and the Community," is an interview with David Smith M.D., Commissioner of the Texas Department of Health, which first appeared in Bill Moyers' new book *Healing and The Mind*. Smith provides sound reasons for decentralizing community health care needs: working class people at the community clinics benefit from the advice of nutritionists, counselors, and outreach workers because they are able to get more immediate attention and to know the people who are caring for them. In the next selection, "Are Women Doctors Changing the Medical Community?", pediatrician Perri Klass provides evidence that suggests women have different approaches to practicing medicine that will change the way medicine is practiced in clinics and at hospitals.

The importance of looking inward, of considering the feelings and spirits of those who are physically ill while encouraging them to talk about their problems and feelings in supportive communities, provides a thematic focus in the next three selections. In "The Healing Brain," Robert Ornstein and David Sobel assert "there is mounting evidence that 'real' organic diseases are linked to changing beliefs about oneself, to the nature of one's relationships with others and to one's position in the social world." People can help each other; this is also the conclusion of the speaker in Kenneth Fields' poem "The Break." When first we meet the speaker, he has "shuffled along the corridors for days/shaking against the walls." Through listening to and sharing the stories of another alcoholic's pain and determination, "her getting on with it," the speaker begins to see an avenue of hope for himself, begins to feel the courage to go beyond the suffering of his own alcoholism. Journalist Elizabeth Marek writes about her experiences with a support group for teenage mothers in "The Lives of Teenage Mothers." Marek attends the support group's meetings to understand why teenagers chose to keep their babies and comes to understand how important the group support is for these teenage mothers who desperately need to build new lives that can be functional and fulfilling for themselves and for their children.

The social and political realities of our society influence individuals' decisions about abortion, a fact addressed in the next two selections. In her editorial "At the Clinics, April 5, 1992," Pulitzer Prize winning journalist Anna Quindlen reminds her readers that citizens must act at a local level if they want their beliefs about abortion to be translated into the legislation that governs what types of procedures doctors can and cannot perform.

Social pressures within the community are having a growing impact on many individuals' self-esteem and health. In "The Wizard of Prozac," Tracy Thompson, a staff writer for the *Washington Post*, discusses the new drug

Prozac, which "more than ten million people around the world" who are suffering from low self-esteem and depression will take this year to help them to cope with the social pressures they face daily. Self-esteem and happiness are also linked to the social pressure to live up to a cultural standard of beauty. In the past twenty years more and more young women have developed eating disorders and have risked their health as they try to conform to unrealistic ideals of beauty. Student writer Amanda Morgan analyzes this growing health issue in "When Beauty Is the Beast."

In this chapter's final professional selection, "The Way It's Supposed to Be," excerpted from *As Real As It Gets: The Life at a Hospital at the Center of the AIDS Epidemic*, Carol Pogash describes an AIDS ward for terminal patients, a ward where nurses make the final decisions, a ward where definitions of family, of caring, and of community develop new meanings.

The Community Service Writing Student Project was completed for the Cancer Patient Resource Center at the Stanford Hospital. We have included two submissions written for the Center's *Surviving Newsletter*, which is distributed to patients, doctors, nurses, and health care professionals. Melinda Lorensen's "Two Poems" speaks of her despair upon learning about her grandmother's illness and of her hope as she affirms the legacy of courage her grandmother has given her. In "Scenes from the Life of a Cancer Patient" student Jenson Wong tries to imagine how he would feel if he were diagnosed with cancer. In both cases the students have tried to understand their audience; they are writing with authentic concern for people who are facing serious or terminal illnesses.

As John Donne told us many centuries ago, "No man is an *island* unto *himself*. Any Man's *death* diminishes *me*, because I am involved in *Mankind*; And therefore never send to know for whom the *bell* tolls; It tolls for *thee*." Healing and health are life long concerns that we face as individuals and as members of our communities.

Healing and the Community

David Smith and Bill Moyers

Commissioner of the Texas Department of Health and former Senior Vice President of Parkland Memorial Hospital in Dallas, David Smith, M.D., is currently the Chief Executive Officer and Medical Director of the Community-Oriented Primary Care Program of Parkland Memorial Hospital. Dr. Smith also works as a pediatrician and as a consulting faculty member at the University of Texas Southwest Medical Center in Dallas. In the interview with Bill Moyers that follows, taken from Moyers' book *Healing and the Mind* (1993), Smith makes a forceful argument for the decentralization of health care; he believes that people can be treated more successfully if doctors and health care workers use local community resources and facilities.

Journal

Discuss medical experiences that you have had at community health clinics.

MOYERS: You call your clinic a "Community Oriented Primary Care Clinic"—what kind of community is this?

2 SMITH: Well, it's a diverse community, primarily African American, but with pockets of Hispanics as well. But the people no longer own this community—they lease it. For the most part, it's a working community, with many people just trying to make it so they can go somewhere else.

3 MOYERS: What common illnesses do these people experience?

4 SMITH: Of course, the common illnesses vary by age and by ethnicity. But we see a lot of diabetes, and we see a lot of strokes that could have been prevented through dealing earlier with high blood pressure. We see a lot of children who haven't been immunized because the system has failed them, so they get diseases like measles. And we see individuals with large ulcers and sores that should have been taken care of much earlier. Also, we're seeing more and more asthma.

5 MOYERS: These illnesses seem so physical in nature that I wonder if mind/body medicine has anything to do with a community like this?

6 SMITH: Every aspect of those illnesses has a component that relates to mind. The healing process, the motivation to seek help, the understanding of how they got into that state in the first place—all these involve the mind. We know that in the healing process of anything from an ulcer in diabetes to asthma, the mind is very intricately involved with whether the patient gets better or worse. You can actually make yourself more ill. We know there are many different chemical aspects of the body that are controlled by the mind. In fact, you can put patients in a position where they'll actually get worse, even despite the best "medicine."

7 MOYERS: The popular cliché of mind/body medicine is that it's a luxury for affluent people who can afford it. How can you bring it into the lives of

these people, who don't have the resources of the middle or upper middle class? Can you teach it to them?

SMITH: I don't think you teach it. You allow them to learn it. To teach it to 8 them is not going to work. We have to allow them to develop the skills by using more culturally relevant models. We've got to bring in African Americans and Hispanics to work with these families. We've got to be part of the community. For chronic diseases particularly, we've got to find ways to encourage the patients to follow through. Follow-up loses priority for these people because they have so many other things to deal with. We've got to use outreach people who are knowledgeable about the community, and we've got to allow the families to be more involved as part of the treatment team, and we've got to encourage individuals to take more responsibility for their own care.

MOYERS: What does culture have to do with one's attitude toward mind/body 9 medicine, using the mind for dealing with or preventing illness?

SMITH: Well, take religion, for example. It's a very powerful force in this com- 10 munity. So the church is a very appropriate place to begin mind/body medicine. And in fact, we frequently use church leadership and church congregations. For example, when we have terminal patients, and the quality of life becomes an issue, or in the rehabilitation of people with an injury or a chronic disease, we often turn to the church, which becomes part of the therapeutic process.

MOYERS: Some skeptics think of mind/body medicine as a set of fringe 11 practices, like acupuncture, herbal prescriptions, massage—all of those relatively esoteric things. But that's not what you seem to mean by it here.

SMITH: No, it's really very basic. It's bringing a whole body together to pre- 12 vent disease or to help the healing process.

MOYERS: But do you come to this community and say, "You're responsible for 13 your healing, so you've got to use your mind to influence your body"? How do you do it?

SMITH: First you inform. Patients generally aren't even aware of what is going 14 wrong. They aren't told why they're sick, and so they can't be as effective a part of the healing relationship with the doctor. Perhaps as doctors we aren't comfortable developing the kind of relationship with people that would help them heal themselves. Mind/body in many ways is a relationship between the person who's providing care—not necessarily a doctor—and the patient, and then between the patient and the part that needs to be healed.

MOYERS: Are you just talking about the old-fashioned bedside manner of a 15 doctor who comes around and visits you when you need him?

SMITH: That's part of it. But you also need to feel that you have some control 16 in relation to your own body and your illness.

MOYERS: So if you're not talking about acupuncture, or herbs, or massage, or 17 meditation when you talk to these people about their minds and healing, what are you talking about?

18 SMITH: They have a right to be able to deal with their own disease, to be able to take care of themselves, and to understand what's going on.

19 MOYERS: What do you mean?

20 SMITH: We've traditionally not informed people well enough for them to be aware of what's going on. We've not empowered them so that they can help us take care of them. For example, we bring people who are wheezing with asthma into the emergency room, and we give them some wonderful medicines. We say, "Take these pills, and go home, and I'll see you back in two weeks." We don't talk to them about the fact that emotions can affect asthma, or that mold, and the pollens coming off trees, and other environmental factors can affect it. We don't talk to them about the screens that aren't on their houses and that should be. We don't take into account the fact that landlords don't put filters in the furnaces or change them frequently, or that the electrical outlets aren't working, and so they can't use their breathing machine. We simply give them the pills and tell them to come back in two weeks.

21 MOYERS: And if they can't afford the pills, they don't get them.

22 SMITH: That's correct. We're talking about a prevention partnership in which the patient is empowered to be a partner with you in the healing process. And if that doesn't happen, you're going to fail, particularly in a community like this, because there are so many variables that can make that person ill.

23 MOYERS: Stress, financial worries . . .

24 SMITH: Yes, or even the failure of the transport system to get them where they need to go. There's a lot of stress in the community.

25 MOYERS: So you and your colleagues don't tell them, "Well, let's talk about mind/body medicine. You need a little course in meditation, or some herbs."

26 SMITH: No, they'd probably throw us out of the exam room if we did that. We talk to them about the healing process—and it's not just the physician who talks to them. We have other health people who work with us: social workers, for example, and nurses who come out to their homes to work with them. When I see a patient in the emergency room, I initiate a mind/body process in which the patient is the most critical player. In fact, most disease processes that we see get worse if we don't allow the mind to be part of the healing process. For example, if we don't try to decrease the stresses in a patient's life, we'll have a tough time controlling that patient's blood pressure.

27 MOYERS: People who can afford it use biofeedback to learn how to control stress.

28 SMITH: In this community, people use their religious faith to get outside of their stressful world. These folks don't have time to suffer burnout, and they can't afford burnout. That's a middle-class term. To find relief from stress, these people turn to family, friends, and religion. We need to foster these because the people in this community have tremendous stress.

People get blown away in front of their own houses. Crack deals are going down out in front of their houses. Cats and rats and dogs are running through their houses. The water flows through their homes because they have poor drainage. They're chronically worried about where the next dollar's coming from, or where the next meal's coming from, not to mention how to pay for health care, which is way down on their list. Their stress is incredible, and they don't have the opportunity to get away from it. We need to be aware of that stress, because a pill will not make the difference in the disease processes we're seeing.

MOYERS: So you start where people are. You don't try to take them to some 29 spa or retreat.

SMITH: No, it's done in the home. We return to the home and the community. 30 Community is the key word, because a lot of the resources for these families are within this community.

MOYERS: Where do these people go for primary health care, or do they even 31 get primary health care?

SMITH: They really have not been getting good primary health care. For one 32 thing, since most of them work, it's difficult for them to use the services available in the traditional nine-to-five setting. We force them to choose between ignoring health care, or losing a day's wages to go get it. Children have to leave school to get health care, which sends a message that school is not that important. But, of course, those are the traditional messages we've put in our medical system.

MOYERS: Do most of these people see a doctor on a regular basis?   33

SMITH: No. Because it's so difficult for them to get health care, they often put 34 things off. Then, when they really feel sick, they go to the emergency room at Parkland Hospital. Up until recently, that was really the only thing they could do.

MOYERS: But isn't it difficult for a public hospital to provide the care these 35 people need?

SMITH: In fact, we don't. We end up putting band-aids on things. We take care 36 of the acute problem, but we can never deal with the more complicated things, like prevention. A lot of the people who come to us with medical ailments are suffering from much deeper psychosocial problems.

MOYERS: By psychosocial you mean . . .   37

SMITH: By that I mean that they've got problems in their environment, either 38 physically or emotionally. They can't put food on the table. They can't keep a roof over their heads. They're suffering from abuse or neglect.

MOYERS: How do you explain the phenomenon that medical care is not avail- 39 able in communities like these?

SMITH: I think part of the reason is that the incentives are all wrong. The incen- 40 tives right now are for keeping health care in a centralized area. We offer health care in a wonderful medical center in the middle of the city and force everyone to come to us. We make it convenient for the providers of care, for the doctors and nurses, but not for the patients. We think that's great. Perhaps there's even a feeling of omnipotence because of it. But we should be reversing that trend and taking health care back out to the community.

41 MOYERS: So in centralizing medical care in a big place like Parkland, we're in effect denying people like these regular access to medical care.

42 SMITH: Yes, and we create other barriers as well. We talk about the financial barriers all the time in medicine, but what about the other barriers? In fact, we make these people crawl over each other to get health care. It gets so crowded in the clinics and emergency rooms that patients usually have to wait for hours.

43   The other day a child complaining of an earache was brought to the emergency room at Parkland. About eight hours into the wait, he felt better, and the mother said, "I might as well go home." What had happened is that the eardrum had burst, and the fluid had started to drain out of it, releasing the pressure. The problem hadn't been solved. The child now has a hole in his eardrum and is certainly at risk for not being able to hear as well, and to do as well in school, and could have chronic hearing problems for the rest of his life.

44 MOYERS: What finally brings people to a place like Parkland?

45 SMITH: Well, the condition just gets unbearable—often to the family more than to the individual with the condition. People continue to put off seeking help, and stoically bear the pain and suffering, until eventually the family or neighbors will bring them into the emergency room.

46 MOYERS: So they wait until there's a crisis before they reach out for the kind of medical care they truly need.

47 SMITH: Absolutely. And this is one of the reasons we began setting up these community health clinics. Parkland was overwhelmed by people coming in who needed help. There would be something acutely wrong, and all we were doing was just patching them up and giving them band-aids and pills. We were seeing more and more people who were sicker and sicker. We couldn't get to the front end of the problem and try to decrease the number of people coming in by offering preventive services.

48   So the real philosophy here is to take health care—not just medicine, but comprehensive health care—back to the community, and to try to eliminate some of the barriers that we see. When patients try to get access to health care in a centralized health campus or medical complex, they face barriers such as transportation, child care, school, loss of wages, or the fact that they have to wait eight to twelve hours for care.

49 MOYERS: So one of your goals was to bring health care back to the neighborhood.

50 SMITH: Yes, but not just by setting up our main campus in the neighborhood. We also need to deliver health care in nontraditional settings. We should be providing services in laundromats, in schools, in churches—and we are, even in places that are within walking distance of this facility. At first that might seem rather absurd. Why would you build a nice facility and then take your staff two blocks down the street to the high school? Because

that's where the kids are. Why should I pull them out of school? Why can't I be there for them? Why can't I deal with the PTA that meets there every third Tuesday and take care of the parents and the other children?

So, yes, one of our goals was to bring health care back to the neigh- 51 borhood. But another goal was for us to bring a different array of talent to health care—for example, outreach people, the old-fashioned public health nurse, translators.

MOYERS: Translating from English to Spanish, and Spanish to English. 52

SMITH: And in some of our sites, translating Vietnamese, Laotian, and Cam- 53 bodian. If patients call at night, there's a bilingual answering service. If around forty percent of your patients are monolingual Spanish, it's no good having an English answering service. You see, we had to bring a different team to this community if we were going to make any difference. If we just put another hospital out here, where we were waiting for people to come to us, but we couldn't provide outreach and some culturally relevant skills, like translation, we were going to be in trouble, and no better off than we were before.

MOYERS: There's something rather old-fashioned about this. You're talking 54 about the kind of care I got as a kid over in East Texas, when Dr. Tenney and others would pay house calls—their presence was . . . healing.

SMITH: That's right. It is very old-fashioned. We've become technocrats and 55 turned away from this kind of health care, but we really need to come back to it.

MOYERS: Why did we turn away from it? 56

SMITH: Because the incentives are all wrong right now. We pay for the high 57 tech, catastrophic side of health care.

MOYERS: All the gadgets. 58

SMITH: All the gadgets. You create a gadget, we'll pay for it tomorrow. 59

MOYERS: Yes, but I have to tell you, I like some of those gadgets. I've been 60 helped by them.

SMITH: Oh, no question that we need those gadgets, too, because they do won- 61 derful things. But there's not a good balance. We're investing in new technology, but at the same time, we're not investing in prevention or in understanding what makes people tick or why they got sick in the home that's across the street here. We don't know that. And then we don't go back out to see if we can change some of the things that may have precipitated the sickness. These things are very fundamental and basic. But the incentives aren't there.

First of all, we're not even taught how to function in that environment. 62 We're taught in a centralized, mechanized, medical model, not a health model. We don't look at the entire spectrum of health care approaches, including prevention and rehabilitation. We say, "We can cure you," and we give you something to make you better—but then we throw you back out in the environment, which we don't understand very well, and you get sick all over again. The incentives for a health model rather than a medical model just aren't there.

63 MOYERS: And is reimbursement one of the incentives? Medicare and Medic-
    aid and insurance companies will reimburse you if you put one of these
    people in the hospital with the big gadgets, but they won't reimburse you
    for coming out here and talking about prevention, the environment, stress,
    and taking responsibility.

64 SMITH: No, they won't. We are perverse in the way we look at incentives. The
    incentives are back-loaded. Pay me now, or pay more later. In this society
    we take care of our cars at the front end by changing the oil filter and
    doing other preventive maintenance. But our health care system offers no
    incentives for the preventive things, or for getting you to understand how
    you can avoid coming to our emergency room. We don't reimburse for
    prevention, and we also don't train people to do it. We don't use the right
    setting. We don't train out here, for instance, we train in the large, cen-
    tralized medical center, away from the patients, and we make them come
    to us. It's artificial.

65 MOYERS: So by the time people come to you, it's almost too late to help them.

66 SMITH: The statistics show that's what's happening. There are rising rates of
    asthma deaths in communities like this. When we can't even deliver a sim-
    ple vaccine that can prevent measles, then we've got a problem in the sys-
    tem.

67 MOYERS: These people don't have family doctors?

68 SMITH: No, they don't. What we're really trying to set up here, as much as
    anything else, is not a clinic, but an expanded practice. People can see the
    same person every time they come in. They also become attached to some
    of those different talents that we have here. They may be attached very
    closely to an outreach person, or to a VISTA volunteer, or to a social
    worker. It's even a little better than the family doc, because we bring a
    broad array of skills and services to bear on their problems.

69 MOYERS: And do they find it helpful to have the same doctor every time they
    come in?

70 SMITH: Oh, absolutely. They're amazed: "You mean I get to see the same doc-
    tor? You mean you aren't going to have somebody else every time I'm
    here?" Because that's what they get in a training setting—residents in
    training, rotating every month.

71 MOYERS: Will Medicare, Medicaid, and third-party providers reimburse you
    for these "marginal" folks like nutritionists and social workers and trans-
    lators?

72 SMITH: Marginal?

73 MOYERS: I was using that facetiously.

74 SMITH: My profession wouldn't like to hear this, but these people are proba-
    bly as important or more important than the physicians in this scheme of
    things. If they weren't here, we wouldn't be as effective. So we absolutely
    need them. The problem, traditionally, has been the one you've just cited.
    No, they're not covered by Blue Cross–Blue Shield, Medicare, or Medic-
    aid. We're seeing some improvement, but not enough to pay for what I
    call "nonreimbursable staff." But we can't afford not to have them. And
    we do need health care reform that will allow us to keep them. Who pays

for this now? The taxpayers of Dallas. The fact that we have support through that process and the fact that we write over thirty grants a year is how we keep these people.

MOYERS: But an overburdened taxpayer might ask, "Why should we pay for other people to do what they ought to do anyway—take care of themselves?"   75

SMITH: You can look at it two ways. One involves doing what's right. But if you want to take another, self-serving approach, you could say, "If I don't get those kids measles shots, measles will cross over into the middle class section of town"—which it did. So we want kids in this community to be protected against measles so that everyone is. Another example: if we can prevent a stroke that's going to come to $100,000 in intensive care costs, doesn't it make sense to invest $200 a year in health maintenance? One way or the other, you're going to pay.   76

MOYERS: How do you compare the cost of treating people here as opposed to the cost in a traditional hospital?   77

SMITH: We've actually looked at that and found that at Parkland, if you go in for an acute problem, say a sore throat, it will cost you $120 to $125 to be seen by a doctor. If you go to one of Parkland's seven community-center sites, it will cost somewhere around forty-seven dollars by the time you walk out with your prescription. In the meantime you may also have seen a social worker, a health educator, and maybe even stuck your head into the dental department. But forty-seven dollars. It could even be less if we didn't have the overhead associated with keeping our funding sources intact. I've got to keep grant writers, for example. And each of the funding sources insists on using its own forms. But still, the cost savings for coming here rather than to Parkland is immense. And that's not even measuring the potential impact of preventing a really bad outcome, like a stroke in a patient with high blood pressure.   78

So the approach here is not only cheaper, it's more comprehensive. If you want to use the car analogy, what we do here is not only take care of the noise or vibration in the car, we'll go ahead and change your oil and deal with the fact that the radiator needs to be flushed. We don't wait until we have to deal with you in a catastrophic or resurrection mode.   79

MOYERS: Resurrection mode?   80

SMITH: We want to save you. We want to feel like we're in *M*A*S*H*, and we've just done something that's going to bring you off the table, and you'll look at us and say, "Oh, Doctor, you've saved me." We don't feel as wonderful about doing prevention, even though it's cheaper. What happens in the resurrection mode is that we end up paying more later, and the patient is worse off because the condition has gotten more serious in the meantime.   81

MOYERS: But then why doesn't the health care system recognize the need for the kind of preventive care offered by people like nutritionists, psychologists, social workers, and translators?   82

SMITH: I wish I had an answer to that question. I don't know, because prevention is just common sense. It's just common sense to embrace strate-   83 gies that save money and save lives and help people be more functional and enjoy life. One of the things we know is that seventy-five percent of these people work. Who is going to be our labor force in the year 2015? It's going to be predominantly brown and black. And if we don't start investing in these folks, we're going to have to do one of two things—export jobs or import labor. So it's in our best interest to have some solutions to the health care crisis in communities like this.

84 MOYERS: When did you know that you were doing something right here?

85 SMITH: I think we first knew we were doing something right when patients began to come to us who had a choice, but who had heard through word of mouth, which is the most wonderful way to get things across in these communities, that something different was happening here, and that they could get the kind of care they needed.

86 MOYERS: They chose you.

87 SMITH: Yes. Another incident happened just recently at Parkland Hospital that made us think we might be doing something right. We had a patient in from one of our health centers, and the residents were all clustered around her, and the attending doctor was about to pontificate over the case. He leaned over her bed and said, "Mrs. Jones, who's your doctor?"—expecting her to say that one of the residents was her doctor. But she said, "My doctor's Dr. Irvine."

88 "Who's that?" asked the attending physician.

89 "Well, that's my doctor out in east Dallas at the community clinic. He takes care of me. In fact, he was just in here to visit me."

90 The doctor chuckled and gestured to the residents and said, "Well, who are these folks, then?"

91 She said, "Well, I just don't know who these folks are. I think they're in training, and they're trying to learn to be like Dr. Irvine."

92 MOYERS: Or any one of your "family" doctors.

93 SMITH: Because that's what the people really value. They've got somebody that's consistently there for them, not a doctor who is simply walking in and out of their lives.

94 MOYERS: But why is it important to these people to have a family doctor?

95 SMITH: Most of them want consistency and somebody who will listen. They don't want someone moving in and out all the time, who isn't available for them. They also want someone who's in their community. If I establish my practice in their community, I'm not making a value judgment against the place. If I make people go to a different side of town to see me, I'm communicating that I really don't want to have my office over where they live. They appreciate our being in their community.

96 The other thing I think they appreciate is that the rest of the staff is also there to listen. It seems as if they're getting special attention. People like that.

97 MOYERS: Is that just a personal preference? Or is it really a factor in health and healing?

98 SMITH: It's really both. For many patients it is a personal preference, but then you can use that relationship to help in healing the individual.

MOYERS: But what difference does it make if I know the doctor, or the doctor 99
knows me, as long as he or she actually helps me?

SMITH: It gets back to the trust issue, and it also gets back to the issue of mind 100
and body. There's a comfort level when someone is willing to listen and
when you have a relationship with that person. One of the stresses we
don't talk about much is the stress of seeing a doctor. When a doctor does-
n't care, is cold, doesn't have time to talk, and runs in and out of the office,
and if the staff is too busy filling out forms to pay any attention to you,
there's stress. You've come in already stressed, and the situation is more
stressful. And what happens then? You aren't comfortable, and the treatment will not be as effective.

Questions for Discussion

1. How does Smith define mind/body healing? Why does Smith believe that the practice of mind/body healing can be effective at a clinic for working class people?
2. Why are the home, the church, and the community important to the healing of the
patients at the clinic where Smith works? How is Smith's approach at his clinic different from the way medicine has been traditionally practiced at clinics?
3. How does Smith define and differentiate between a "health model" and a "medical
model"?
4. Why does Smith believe that health care should be relocated in the community
instead of being centralized in a large medical center as it typically is now? Do you
agree or disagree with Smith? Explain your point of view.
5. Why does Smith argue that it is cost-effective and ethical to treat patients in their
own communities and to rely on the help of social workers, outreach persons, and
nutritionists as well as doctors? Do you agree or disagree with Smith's point of view?
6. Why does Smith feel that a "family doctor" or a familiar doctor with whom a patient
has built a sense of trust is an essential part of the healing process? Explain why you
agree or disagree.
7. Did reading this interview change your ideas about the relationships between doctors and their patients? About the need for more community health care? How?

Ideas for Writing

1. Describe the type of health care you and your family have, and then discuss the reasons why you are satisfied with it as well as the objections you have to the health
care that is available to you.
2. Do library research on health policies that promote community health models similar to those that Smith advocates. Or visit a community health clinic and speak with
social workers, nurses, and doctors to find out where they offer health care at community centers. Write an essay for your class that synthesizes what you have learned
from your library research and/or your personal interviews.

Are Women Doctors Changing the Medical Community?

Perri Klass

Perri Klass (b. 1958) graduated from Harvard Medical School in 1986 and is practicing as a pediatrician in Boston. She lives with her husband Larry Wolf, a writer and history professor, and their two children. Her point of view about changes in the medical profession became public when her nonfiction reports about going to medical school were published in *The New York Times*, and later as a book, *A Not Entirely Benign Procedure*. In the following selection, which is excerpted from *Baby Doctor: A Pediatrician's Training* (1992), Klass discusses ways in which the practice of medicine is being changed by the increasing numbers of women doctors.

Journal

If you have been cared for by both male and female doctors, do you think that male doctors treat their patients differently than the way that female doctors do? Explain your response. If you have only seen male doctors, do you imagine that a female doctor would treat her patients differently from the way a male doctor would treat them?

I told a friend—a fellow resident—that I was writing about women doctors. "What are you going to say?" she wanted to know. "Are you going to say they're better? Are you going to come right out and say it?" Now, if I read an article saying that men make better doctors than women for certain reasons, I would probably be offended, even hurt. The best I might hope for would be to laugh it off as so much antediluvian their-egos-are-threatened prejudice. Now, I have known superb, brilliant, sensitive male doctors, residents my own age, teachers and attending physicians. Lots of them. The doctor who delivered my son, the pediatrician who takes care of him are men—and yet, I feel I am protesting too much, that these statements have a some-of-my-best-friends air about them. Okay, then, some of my best friends are male doctors.

2   When I interviewed women doctors, I came always to the point where I asked, are women doctors different? And with only a couple of exceptions, I got versions of the same response from the doctors I interviewed, young or old, avowedly feminist or not. First you get that disclaimer, the one I just offered; I've known some wonderful male doctors, I've known some awful female doctors, generalizations are impossible. And then, hesitantly, even apologetically, or else frankly and with a smile, comes the generalization. Yes, women are different as doctors: they're better.

3   Kansas City announces proudly in the courtesy magazine found in fancy hotel rooms: "When Procter & Gamble wants to know if people like its tooth-

paste, it turns to Kansas City. Market researchers call Kansas City a 'typically American' market. The label fits: Kansas Citians thrive on family, hard work, and tradition." In Kansas City, I interviewed a wide range of female doctors—residents, women just out of residency starting up private practices, academic physicians, specialists, older women, and recent graduates. I was surprised by how tight the network of women physicians was. I was immediately referred from doctor to doctor; in specialties where there were fewer women, their names were mentioned again and again by their colleagues. I was able to interview female physicians who stood on both sides of two classic relationships: a mentor and her student protégée, a doctor and her patient—who was also a doctor.

Linda Dorzab started medical school at the University of Missouri, Kansas 4
City, when she was thirty-three years old. She had spent eleven years as a teacher, working with emotionally disturbed children. In June 1987, she finished her internal medicine residency, and is now beginning a private practice as an internist, affiliated with Menorah Medical Center. For the first month or so there were few patients, maybe only one a day, but by February it was up as high as nine a day, mostly new patients coming for their first appointments with her. Dr. Dorzab is proud to make a visitor welcome in her newly arranged office; an ebullient, friendly, informal woman, completely delighted to be starting up a new solo private practice. Ever since she started medical school, she says, she has dreamed of an office where she could make her patients comfortable, where there would be an atmosphere that would make her look forward to coming to work in the morning. Her office is a welcoming, plant-filled place, with gleaming mahogany furniture, including both a large desk and a small table designed for less threatening, more comfortable doctor-patient conversations. I, in the middle of my residency, find myself asking how she figured out the details of starting a practice—what supplies to order, how to find patients. Dr. Dorzab laughs, remembering how she sat down and made a list—"Cotton pads, tongue depressors—I ordered too many syringes and needles. And my proudest possession is my sigmoidoscope" (a device inserted up through the patient's rectum to give the doctor a good look at the lining of the colon). Given her background in working with disturbed children, Dr. Dorzab had originally considered going into psychiatry, "but they gave me a stethoscope and it was all so interesting. You can't get more interesting than medicine." She was older than most of the other students, and had a comparatively weak science background, but the art of medicine, she thinks, came more easily to her than to some of the younger students. Still, she had trouble performing on rounds, the high-pressure on-the-spot situations which can often be the traditional hazing occasions for medical students. "I still have the same personality as when I was a teacher, I tend to show my vulnerability—which is okay with my patients. But with colleagues the smile dims, I can turn on a more businesslike manner."

I asked her about role models, mentors, teachers from medical school who 5
meant a lot to her. She names two women, saying of both of them that "they maintained femininity and class, and always looked confident." One of those

women was Dr. Marjorie Sirridge, who is a dean at Dr. Dorzab's alma mater, UMKC. Marjorie Sirridge graduated from medical school in 1944. There were very few women in her class, but she never felt what she considers overt discrimination. To be sure, her academic advisers told her she'd never get to medical school—but that only made her more determined to go. "I was first in my class from grade one through high school—that gives confidence." Sure enough, she graduated from medical school first in that class too. But during residency she got pregnant and was informed that "pregnant residents were not acceptable." She dropped out of medicine for several years, then found her way back in by working for no pay and no training credit, went into private practice as a hematologist, pursued research on her own, and eventually found her way to academic medicine. Dr. Sirridge's office is decorated with pictures of her children and a poster of Marie Curie. Her white hair is bound up in a knot. She is extremely cordial, but she speaks with the authority of someone who is accustomed to giving out her opinions publicly. It is clear that she feels protective about the medical students she watches over, and that she is proud of Dr. Dorzab, who is striking out on her own, off into solo practice.

6   Dr. Sirridge worries that female medical students do not seem to take leadership roles as readily as their male colleagues. On the other hand, she thinks women do much better when it comes to human relationships. "For the women, relationships with patients are very important, a very positive thing. Many men also have this quality, but men in positions of power in medical education and government by and large do not."

7   The craving for female role models, female mentors, is very strong in medicine. You learn science in medical school—biochemistry, physiology, pathology; you learn these subjects in traditional classroom settings. Then you serve a kind of apprenticeship in the hospital for the second two years of medical school, consolidating the science you learned in the lecture hall, learning hospital logic and medical routine, and also learning how to be a doctor. How will you explain to a patient that he has to undergo a painful diagnostic procedure, how will you tell parents their child is dying, how will you help someone overcome bad habits that are crippling his health, how will you take command when someone is critically ill? Some medical schools are trying, more and more, to teach these skills, or at least to get students thinking and talking about them, instead of just piecing their styles together as they go along. But basically, since there is no single consensus on the best manner of doctoring, you pick up your style by trying to emulate the doctors you admire. And if you're female, it can be very instructive (and very inspiring) to watch women doctors, to learn your style from them. Many of the techniques used traditionally by male doctors tend not to work for women; and many female doctors have found themselves evolving new ways of interacting with patients, with nurses, with fellow doctors. So it isn't just vague inspiration that we're talking about here, it's who you're thinking of as you get ready to walk into that room and tell those parents about their baby dying. Who do you know who could do that as well as it could be done, offer comfort to the parents, inspire trust that their baby's last moments will be made as comfortable and

easy as possible—how do you acknowledge their grief, the failure of medicine to help, even take part in their grief, and yet retain the authority you need as the doctor? And how much authority *do* you need as the doctor, anyway? Medicine is full of these situations, and you model yourself on the people who seem to handle them best.

Nevada Mitchell, MD, practices internal medicine. Her subspecialty is geri- 8 atrics. She was born in Kansas City, went to college at Vassar, then came back to KC, got married, started teaching—she had thought about medical school, but didn't feel she had what it would take to go. But reading in the Vassar alumnae magazine about classmates who had gone to medical school, she decided she wanted to try for it, and five years later she was in medical school. Dr. Mitchell has no doubt at all about the difference between male and female doctors. "There's a world of difference. The women I come into contact with are less aggressive, more likely to have one-on-one-type relationships with patients than men, less likely to go for high volume of patients—but also less likely to be out here in private practice." Dr. Mitchell returned several times to the issue of being "out here," explaining that many women take jobs with HMOs, which offer regular salaries and limited working hours. "You need a certain aggressiveness to choose private practice," she said, with some satisfaction.

Dr. Mitchell feels that older patients are often more receptive to women 9 doctors, since they are looking for more than medical therapy. Her original decision to go into geriatrics was related to watching her younger colleagues in medical school trying to deal with the many elderly patients, and feeling those patients were often neglected or taken for granted. Her medical practice now includes many older patients, but she also does general internal medicine. With a smile, she ticked off the various groups on her fingers: older people are fine, younger and middle-aged women usually have no problem with a female doctor, younger men are initially hesitant, feel self-conscious about the complete physical examination.

Dr. Mitchell cannot think of a female doctor she wanted to be like. "I 10 didn't have that many examples. I developed my own style and image." She did, however, tell me that I ought to talk to the doctor who had operated on her when she needed some gynecological surgery. She felt that when she had discussed the medical issues with a male doctor, he had placed less of a priority on maintaining the option of future pregnancy. Dr. Mitchell, who is thirty-nine and has a sixteen-year-old daughter, wanted to keep her options open, and felt that a female doctor, Marilyn Richardson, had been more willing to take this seriously.

Ironically, Dr. Richardson herself thinks that's nonsense. An obstetrician- 11 gynecologist specializing in reproductive endocrinology, she was a pianist for years before she went to medical school. She is highly professional, authoritative, and decided in her opinions. Patients who come looking for a female gynecologist, she says, are "erroneous—it's a patient's misconception that has evolved with consumer awareness, an erroneous belief that women doctors are more compassionate, more understanding. Well, I don't have menstrual cramps, I didn't have severe pain in labor. Women who come asking for a female doctor are looking for a buddy, and they're not going to find that in me."

12 I repeat to her what Dr. Mitchell said, and she laughs and says with affection, "Nevada Mitchell played the violin in my first piano recital." And then continues to deny that being female has anything to do with her mode of doctoring. "It was a male mentor who taught me sensitivity toward the preservation of fertility." Her style, she says, is a composite of this mentor and of her father, also in OB-GYN—and of techniques of doctoring she has developed for herself.

13 I mention to Dr. Richardson that one of the places I always felt a very sharp difference between male and female doctors was in the operating room. I ask whether she believes this is also erroneous. No, she agrees, the way that women run an OR is different. "Women manage more efficiently if they can strike a balance of authoritativeness and humaneness. Men are often arbitrary, demanding, and disrespectful, and the level of efficiency suffers. Women don't usually command quite as fiercely, will *ask* for an instrument . . . you get camaraderie with the other staff members."

14 Dr. Susan Love agrees. One of the first two female surgical residents at a major Boston teaching hospital, Dr. Love finished her training in 1980. She went into private practice in general surgery, though she initially had trouble getting a position on the staff of the hospital where she had just been chief surgical resident. In her practice, she found she was seeing many patients with breast disease, who preferred to go to a woman doctor, and she eventually decided to specialize in this field. She now has a partner, another woman surgeon, and they have as many patients as they can handle. Dr. Love feels strongly that she had to suppress many of her basic values in order to get through her surgical residency: "Most women have problems—unless they can block out their previous socialization. Surgeons don't really like having women, don't make it comfortable for them. Things that women like, talking to patients, aren't important, it's how many operations you've done, how many hours you've been up, how many notches on your belt. If you get through your five or six years of training, you can regain your values, but it's a real if. Most men never get them back."

15 Dr. Love runs an operating room, she says, by "treating the nurses like intelligent people, talking to them, teaching them. I'm not the big ruler." Are men always so different? "Surgery is a lot of ritual and a little science. The boys need high mass, incense, and altar boys, they need more boosting up. The women are much lower church." A concrete example of something she does differently, something no one taught her: before the patient is put to sleep, she makes it a practice to hold the patient's hand. "I'm usually the only person in the room they really know, and it's the scariest time. The boys scrub, come in when the patient's asleep. I got razzed for it, but they're used to it now."

Unlike Dr. Richardson, Dr. Love does think that women doctors behave 16 differently with their patients. "I spend more time in empathy, talking, explaining, teaching, and it's a much more equal power relationship." And then there's not taking people for granted—she tells the story of a recent patient, an eighty-four-year-old woman with breast cancer who was asked by a male surgeon, "Are you vain?" Embarrassed, the woman said she wasn't. The surgeon advised her, in that case, to have a mastectomy, rather than a more limited procedure—"But then her niece pointed out, but you bought a new bra to come to the doctor, but you combed your hair over your hearing aid." The doctor had simply assumed that an elderly woman would have no particular desire to keep her breast, no vanity left to speak of. Dr. Love's anecdotes are often sharp—she describes a male surgeon who explained that a particular implant used in breast reconstruction felt just like a normal breast; he meant, of course, that to someone touching the breast, the texture was close to natural, not that the woman actually had normal feeling in the implant.

I heard over and over that women are better at talking to people, better at 17 listening. Dr. Carol Lindsley, a rheumatologist at the University of Kansas, says the female medical students are "more sensitive to patient and family needs, more patient, pay more attention to detail." Dr. Marilyn Rymer, a Kansas City neurologist, says that many of her female patients come looking for a woman doctor, some because they feel they can talk to a woman more easily, others because "they find that women listen better, are more empathic, care about explaining things, dealing with the family." Dr. Dorzab agrees: "My patients say women listen better, are better at acknowledging when something is bothering the patient." On the other hand, Dr. Debbie Stanford, a resident in internal medicine at the University of Alabama in Birmingham, feels that there is no difference at all between the male and female interns she supervises: "Capabilities, compassion, endurance—no difference." And Dr. Michelle Harrison, who wrote *A Woman in Residence* in 1982 about her experiences doing an OB-GYN residency, comments, "I think women sometimes *feel* different because they are not totally accepted; as outsiders, we experience ourselves as different, but are we all that different in how we see patients? I don't see any major revolution."

Then there is the question of how women get along with their cowork- 18 ers—with other doctors and with nurses. The assumption has traditionally been that nurses resent female doctors, respond to them with a why-should-I-take-orders-from-*her* attitude, and then there are prurient little remarks about how women doctors resent nurses because of all the romantic attention the nurses supposedly receive from the male doctors.

Women doctors, of course, are often mistaken for nurses; many patients 19 assume that a woman with a stethoscope is by definition a nurse. Some doctors mind this, others take it in stride. "You have to have a sense of humor," said Dr. Lois J. McKinley, an internist in Kansas City. "I took care of one patient for weeks, and when he was getting ready to leave, he was still saying, 'Oh, nurse, would you prop up my pillows.' Nursing people are good people; being mistaken for a nurse is not the worst thing that could happen." Dr. Mitchell agrees: "If I walk into a room and someone asks me for a bedpan, I just go ahead and put 'em on it!" She is laughing. "But when they call my office and assume I'm the nurse and ask, Dr. Mitchell, when will he be in, I tell them, '*He will never be in!*' "

20   It is generally agreed, among women doctors, that we have to be more polite and more careful with nurses than our male colleagues; a fairer way of putting this would probably be to say that nurses have had to take a lot of rudeness and bad behavior from doctors over the years, and that while they make some of the traditional female allowances for traditional male patterns, they are unwilling to accept these same behaviors from women. Or, to quote Dr. Richardson again, "When you make a big mess in the operating room, there's something different in your mind when you walk out and leave it for another woman to clean up." I have found in my own training that nurses generally expect me to clean up after myself (i.e., to gather up all the little alcohol pads and pieces of gauze left on the bed after I draw blood from a baby), to do a fair amount of my own secretarial work, and not to take too high-and-mighty a tone. What would be taken as normal behavior in a male (especially a male surgeon; they have the most traditional doctor-nurse power structure) is considered aggressive and obnoxious in a female. Dr. Lore Nelson, who will be chief resident in pediatrics at the University of Kansas next year, complained, half seriously, "A male surgeon can walk in to do some procedure and everything will be all ready, but if I go to draw blood, nothing's set up for me and I have to go ask a nurse, 'Can you please help me. . . .' " Dr. Sirridge agrees: "The women aren't successful at doing the things men do without criticism—it's easier if they ask politely."

21   This does not seem to be a bad thing—the traditional doctor-nurse relationship, like the traditional male-female relationship that it parodies (the man as authority figure, making decisions, issuing edicts, bearing ultimate responsibility on his broad shoulders; the woman as caretaker, tending to immediate needs and cleaning up messes, but without any real power) left a lot to be desired. Surely a good doctor is part caretaker; surely a good nurse's observations should be part of any decisions being made. I suspect that the more polite, more politic behavior that is demanded of female doctors may be closer to good manners and good medicine than the supposed norm—the license that we sometimes envy our male colleagues.

22   "Cleaning up messes," a number of doctors told me, is something women do well. "Women are better at dealing with the nitty-gritty," says Dr. Sirridge, because they have been taught to clean up, "to do the dishes at home. They tolerate tedious nitty-gritty-type things better." Medicine is full of messes, both palpable (the patient is dirty, the patient is vomiting, the patient is having bloody stools) and impalpable (the patient is ready to be discharged but has no home to go to, the child is medically healthy but will not eat). Some doctors do hold themselves aloof from these messes, seeing their role as some-

thing exclusively medical and dignified ("I didn't go to medical school to learn to clean up vomit"). And women do tend to be better at dealing with messes; it is more often what they have been raised to do, less likely to compromise their dignity, less likely to jar their image of themselves.

Medical training and medical practice are stressful for everyone, male and female. Women often face additional pressures; the issue of combining family and career comes up constantly when you try to write about women in medicine. Why are there discrepancies in status? For example, one study looked at medical school faculty (those with MDs only, excluding those with PhDs or other degrees) given their first appointments in 1976. By 1987, 17 percent of the men were tenured, but only 12 percent of the women. Twelve percent of the men had attained the rank of full professor, but only 3 percent of the women. And 15 percent of the men were not on a tenure track at all, as compared with 22 percent of the women. So either women are meeting prejudice and resistance as they try to make their way in the world of academic medicine and research, or else, as is often suggested, they are diluting their ambition, going more slowly on their climb, usually in order to give time to family. Dr. Harrison, now a family physician and psychiatrist, feels that there are different standards for men and women. "Personality factors enter into the promotion of women, while arrogant and obnoxious men are promoted without that being an issue." But she also thinks that women "have tremendous problems around leadership, issues of power. We aren't raised with the skills to even make it up to the glass ceiling." And finally, she adds, "there's the problem of how to combine a family with a medical career, which tends to relegate women to salaried positions with less possibility for advancement." 23

I had my baby in the second year of medical school; it was not an extremely common thing to do, but neither was it unheard of. Certainly, I didn't feel any pressure to drop out, to take time off, to get my belly out of sight. I didn't feel it would be held against me, or against women in medicine, for me to have a baby along the way, and for that I suppose my medical school and the changing times deserve a lot of credit. Dr. Sirridge got pregnant during her internal medicine residency in the nineteen forties and had to drop out—"Pregnant residents were not acceptable." In my residency program there are several pregnant residents; the program is not particularly designed to accommodate them, but it seems to have been stretching. On the other hand, that's pediatrics again, a field with lots of women, a field where even the biggest guns have to be committed to the idea that babies are important. 24

Residents work nights and come home rarely and in poor condition. Many programs don't have much coverage available in case of sickness; there's a macho ideology that gives points for working when you're sick. So taking days off to stay home with a sick child is really against the rules, and ends up loading more work on your already overloaded fellow residents, which in turn creates animosity toward people with children. Nevada Mitchell's daughter was three years old when her mother started medical school, seven when she 25 started residency. A single mother, she chose her residency program because she could live in the same building as her brother and sister-in-law, requested Friday night call because she didn't have to get up and bring her daughter to school the next day. When her daughter got sick and she decided to stay home, the attending physician commented, "Interns don't stay home unless they're hospitalized or dead." Dr. Mitchell stayed home for that one day only, then sent her daughter, who had mononucleosis, off to stay with relatives. "One Halloween we spent in the CT scanner," Dr. Mitchell recalls. "I brought her candy and her trick-or-treat bag."

26   Most annoying of all, perhaps, for parents, is that being a doctor makes you in a certain sense unreliable. Emergencies come up, unexpected calls come in, and you're home hours later than you promised; you can't keep the promise you made about a family outing. "She knows she can't depend on me to be where I say I'm going to be at any particular time or be home when I say I'm going to be. She has to catch me when I'm there." When Dr. Mitchell opened her practice, her daughter would come by the office after school and they would go home together. Her daughter, who is now sixteen, wants to be a veterinarian.

27   These difficulties are not, of course, unique to the women. Males also have to cope with the hours, with not being there when their children need them, with promises made and broken. They are somewhat more likely to have spouses who delay their own careers. Still, I have heard complaints about male colleagues of mine who are too eager to leave the hospital and get home to their families; some men may even be much less self-conscious about this precisely because they bear no if-I-make-a-fuss-about-my-kid-they'll-think-women-shouldn't-be-doctors burden. No one, after all, is likely to say that fatherhood and medicine don't mix. The fact is, though, that certain intensities of career are essentially incompatible with any kind of parenthood. You don't have very much to do with your child if your ideal is to spend every waking moment in the hospital, whether you are the father or the mother. The influx of women into medicine, we can hope, will help us design medical careers for both men and women that will enable doctors to follow some of their own recommendations (reduce stress, eat a healthy diet, keep regular hours, spend time with your family—we pediatricians, for example, are always telling parents how important it is that they pay lots of attention to their children). Dr. Nelson is married to another doctor, who is doing his residency in internal medicine. She had a baby in her second year of residency, and felt that her fellow residents were very helpful and supportive. She and her husband had been in the habit of taking call on the same nights, so they would be home on the same nights; since the baby, they take call on alternate nights. Her husband, she thinks, has had much more trouble with his colleagues than she did: "The times he had to stay home when the baby was sick the men he worked with said, your wife should stay home."

28   After residency, many doctors continue to work long hours, to cover night call. One way to keep your hours regular is to work for an HMO. Another solution for doctors who want protected time for their families is a part-time

practice. Anne Regier, MD, and Perry Ginder, MD, are rheumatologists in practice together in Kansas City. Each works three days a week and they split night coverage. Dr. Regier is married to an orthopedic surgeon. "We do a lot of juggling," she says. "I'll bring the kids to the hospital and drop them off with you so you can do your consult—or who will round first on the weekend."

Women are a presence in American medicine today in such numbers that 29 in many fields they are no longer curiosities. Not being a curiosity gives you a certain amount of freedom; you don't have to be better than the men, you don't have to pretend that you actually are a man in disguise. But questions remain. Will women move ahead into positions of leadership? Are there subtle prejudices that will allow us the MD degrees, but then shunt us into the less prestigious career paths within medicine? Will the remaining all-male fields ever integrate? Janet Bickel, senior staff associate and director for women's studies at the AAMC, wonders whether we will in fact end up with a medical establishment in which certain jobs (less well paid, less well regarded) will be filled largely by women. And to what extent does this depend on the choices made by the women themselves? It is very difficult to make predictions; the makeup of the medical profession has changed so rapidly from this point of view that there is really no way to say what will happen next.

Many women doctors believe that women do medicine differently, that 30 there are advantages to the way they approach their patients. Almost no doctor I talked to believes that women have simply been transformed by their medical education into cookie-cutter doctors with all the mannerisms and techniques of the male prototype. If this is in fact true, and not just a convenient prejudice on our part (and one I still blush to acknowledge in print), then the effect of women on the medical profession may be larger and more far-reaching than we have yet imagined.

Recently I told my four-year-old son that he was due for a checkup with 31 his pediatrician. He looked distinctly nervous (rumors about shots had obviously been making their way around the day-care center), and asked me anxiously, "Is she a nice doctor?" I thought about the doctors my son knows—me, my close friends, mostly female. I picked my words carefully; it was clearly one of those critical moments when all of a mother's wisdom and tact is required. "Benjamin," I said, "I have to tell you something. Boys can be doctors too, if they want to. If they go to school and learn how, boys can be very good doctors, really."

Questions for Discussion

1. Why does Klass begin her interviews with women doctors in Kansas City? Why do the women doctors whom Klass interviews value learning about being a doctor from female role models? What do their role models or mentors provide them with that medical school doesn't?
2. According to the women doctors interviewed, in what ways are male surgeons different than female surgeons? Klass shares a number of examples stated by female

doctors to illustrate other differences in the ways male and female doctors approach their patients. Which example was most interesting and convincing to you?

3. What struggles do women training to be doctors and attaining positions of leadership find more challenging than male doctors?

4. As she set out to compare and contrast male and female doctors, Klass qualified her remarks by the disclaimer, "generalizations are impossible," yet her interviews and inquiries did lead her to some conclusions. Which of her contrasts and insights did you find most interesting and persuasive?

5. How does Klass answer her question: "How do women [doctors] get along with their coworkers—with other doctors and with nurses"? Were you surprised by the conclusions she develops?

6. Do you think Klass's presentation and conclusions reflect a female bias? Do you think a male doctor would have asked different questions to determine the differences between male and female doctors? What questions do you think a male doctor would have asked?

Ideas for Writing

1. Develop your journal or discussion question 6 into an essay.

2. From reading Klass's piece, in what most significant ways do you think the medical profession is being changed by woman doctors? Do some library research or conduct interviews with women doctors. Write an essay that integrates the interviews or research with your own experiences and knowledge as well as Klass's evidence to discuss the ways in which medical treatment will change over the next ten years as more women become doctors. Consider several of the following issues: How will doctoring styles change? Will there be more or less health care available to people in clinic settings? Will holistic and non-Western treatments become more or less popular? Will more women doctors become surgeons and cardiologists and other specialties traditionally practiced by men? Will more male doctors decide to become pediatricians? How will the role and status of nurses be affected?

The Healing Brain

Robert Ornstein and David Sobel

Robert Ornstein is the President of the Institute for Human Knowledge. He teaches at the University of California Medical Center in San Francisco and at Stanford University. Ornstein is well known for his extensive research on the human brain and is the author of more than twenty books. His most recent books are *Evolution of Consciousness: The Way We Think* (1991) and *The Roots of Self* (1993). **David Sobel** is a medical doctor and the Director of Preventive Medicine for Kaiser Permanente in northern California. The following selection, excerpted from *The Healing Brain* (1987), presents evidence that supports the important role of positive social interaction for the mental and physical health of the individual.

Journal

Discuss a time when you felt that the psychological stress of your life affected your physical well-being.

Every day hundreds upon hundreds of people receive the phone call they 1 dreaded ever receiving: A disembodied voice informs them that a loved one has died. The circumstances might be violent and shocking or the death may have been expected for some time, but in any case the survivors suffer greatly while grieving their losses during the months that follow.

Since the mid 1970s, R. W. Bartrop and his colleagues in New South Wales, 2 Australia, have been systematically studying the effects of bereavement, not only the emotional consequences but the effects on physical health as well— specifically, the body's ability to fight off disease. They followed the lives of surviving spouses, charting the transient changes in immune function during mourning, and in one 1977 study they reported that the immune systems of grieving spouses were indeed weakened. Specifically, they had lower activity levels of what are called "T cells"—one of the blood cells that attack foreign invaders.

That study was the first to show, in human beings, a measurable weak- 3 ening of the body's defense system following severe psychological stress in a real-life setting. It precipitated a number of investigations into the larger question of how mind, brain, body and society are intertwined. At first glance it may seem that changes in one's social world, and in related emotional and mental states, have little to do with disease. But there is mounting evidence that "real" organic diseases are linked to changing beliefs about oneself, to the nature of one's relationships with others and to one's position in the social world. Such links only seem impossible—or at least irrelevant—from the early and simplistic medical view of the body as automaton. Our lungs, hearts and stomachs are hardly independent, autonomous organs. While they certainly have autonomous functions, they are all in communication with and regulated by the brain.

While there is much we still don't know about the relationship of brain, 4 mind, body and society, evidence from many areas of research is beginning to make some of the connections clear. The heart cannot decide that a loved one's death in a train wreck is too much to bear; the liver does not feel the shame of embarrassment; the immune system does not know whether its client is employed or not, divorced or happily married. It is the brain that knows and feels. Indeed a primary function of the brain, perhaps as important as rational thought or language, is health maintenance. The brain has evolved complex "bodyguards," designed to ward off disease, and it may even be that our human tendency toward social connectedness may help keep us well.

There have been many studies since the original Australian investigation. 5 A study at the Mount Sinai School of Medicine confirmed and went beyond those findings. Men who were married to women with terminal breast cancer showed a similar drop in responsiveness of the lymphocytes (another of the blood cells specialized for defense) immediately after their wives' deaths, a drop that continued for two months. But between 4 and 14 months after the death, the husbands' immune functioning had recovered, a change that occurred as their bereavement diminished.

6   But how can grief and bereavement "get into" the immune system? Is it something the bereaved do differently than others? Changes in nutrition, exercise and general activity do affect the workings of the immune system, but the people in this study had maintained their normal habits. What appears more likely is that the numerous connections between the nervous system and the immune system allow the mind to influence resistance or susceptibility to disease. For example, extensive networks of nerve endings have been found in the thymus gland, an organ that plays an essential role in the maturation of certain cells in the immune system. Similarly, the spleen, bone marrow and lymph nodes are richly supplied with nerves supporting a brain-immune system link.

7   In addition, the cells of the immune system appear equipped to respond to chemical signals from the central nervous system. Receptors for a variety of chemical messengers—catecholamines, prostaglandins, growth hormone, thyroid hormone, sex hormones, serotonin and endorphins—have been found on the surfaces of lymphocytes. These neuroendocrines, neurotransmitters and neuropeptides may somehow stimulate the differentiation, migration and activity of the lymphocytes.

8   Given the links between the nervous system and the immune system, the idea that instability in the social world can affect immunity becomes less far-fetched. Research shows that physical and psychological upsets release several powerful neurohormones, including catecholamines, corticosteroids and endorphins. These, in turn, alter immune function. For example, corticosteroids exert such powerful immunosuppressive effects that steroids are widely used as drugs to suppress immunity in allergic conditions like asthma and hay fever and autoimmune disorders like rheumatoid arthritis and to suppress rejection of transplanted organs.

9   During certain types of stress the brain also releases endorphins, the brain's own morphine-like chemicals, which block pain sensation. Psychologist John Liebeskind and colleagues were able to stimulate the release of endorphins by delivering brief, mild electrical shocks to rats, and psychologist Yehuda Shavit later reported a corresponding decrease in tumor-fighting ability in natural killer cells, yet another fighter in the body's immune response.

10   To test whether this immune suppression was mediated by the release of endorphins, the researchers injected the rats with an endorphin antagonist—a drug that blocks the effects of endorphins. They found that the activity of the natural killer cells had been restored, supporting the idea that the immune suppression was caused by endorphins. This explanation was reinforced by the additional finding that natural killer cell potency was also suppressed when the animals were actually given a dose of morphine.

11   Other animal research links stress and the development of disease. The

late Vernon Riley and his colleagues performed scores of experiments on a strain of mice that are genetically predisposed to develop breast cancer. In one series of experiments the mice were subjected to what was called "rotational stress"—that is, they were spun on a record turntable at various speeds (ranging from 16 RPM to 78 RPM). They found that the faster the rotation, the larger the growth in tumors.

Other studies suggest that tumors grow more rapidly in animals exposed [12] to uncontrollable stress than in those exposed to stress they could control. Rats were implanted with tumor cells and the next day experienced either no electrical shock, escapable shock or inescapable shock. Fifty-four percent of the first group rejected the tumor; 63 percent of the rats receiving escapable shock and only 27 percent of the rats receiving inescapable shock rejected the tumors.

These findings are supported by changes in immune function. Steven [13] Maier, Mark Laudenslager and coworkers at the University of Colorado studied how exposing animals to controllable or uncontrollable electric shocks affected immunity. One group of rats was taught that they could terminate a mild electric shock by turning a wheel in their cages. Another group of rats received a shock every time the first group did, but nothing they could do would control the shock. Immune function was assessed by the ability of the T-cells to multiply in response to stimulation. The results showed decreased immune function only in the rats receiving the uncontrollable shocks.

Generalizing from rats to humans is always difficult, but scores of studies [14] on humans show that various types of social instability and the lack of resources to regain stability are associated with subsequent illness. For example, psychologist Stanislav Kasl and his colleagues at Yale University followed the development of infectious mononucleosis among West Point cadets in a study published in 1979. All the entering cadets were given blood tests over a four-year period to screen for the presence of antibodies to Epstein-Barr virus, the agent that causes mononucleosis. In addition the investigators reviewed interview data, which included information about the cadets' expectations and family backgrounds.

Each year about one in five of the susceptible cadets were infected, but [15] only about one-quarter of those infected actually developed symptoms of mono. Cadets who had fathers who were described as "overachievers" and who themselves strongly wanted success in a career but were doing poorly academically were most likely to get sick. The combination of high expectation and poor performance was reflected in increased susceptibility to infectious disease.

More recent studies link the onset and course of virus infections with [16] stress-altered immune function. For example, approximately one person in four suffers from recurrent infections of oral herpes simplex. In a recent study, 18 people between 20 and 43 years old with a history of three to four recurrent episodes of oral herpes per year completed a stress questionnaire twice: once within three days of the first appearance of a lesion marking the recurrence of herpes and another time when they had no active lesions.

17   In the week prior to a recurrence of infection, the group reported increased stressful life events, daily "hassles" and anxiety, indicating that such stressful circumstances are associated with an increased likelihood of recurrent herpes lesions. Later studies suggest that it probably is not the actual stress that brings on the herpes but the person's emotional reaction to the disease. If someone is continually depressed about having herpes, this reaction itself keeps bringing it back.

18   Psychologist Janice Kiecolt-Glaser, virologist Ronald Glaser and colleagues at Ohio State University College of Medicine have shown that even mild upsets—milder, that is, than the loss of a spouse—can affect the immune system. In this study, medical students reported on the number of their "life change events" in the previous months as well as their loneliness. Both loneliness and the mild life stress were associated with decreased immune cell activity.

19   During a situation where there are conflicting signals or a sudden unexplained threat or a threat that is beyond the organism's ability to handle easily, the sympathetic nervous system is activated. This increases the level of circulating hormones that suppress immune function.

20   Most of the research on the relationship of psychological states and immunity has focused on stress-induced immune suppression. But the question of whether positive states of mind enhance immunity is the subject of a growing amount of research. There have been many extravagant claims made for the effects of "positive attitude" and "imagery" on subsequent diseases, but there is little hard evidence that attitude alone can cure serious disease. There is, however, some real evidence that people can voluntarily improve their own immune function and thus prevent disease.

21   In one study, psychologist Howard Hall of Pennsylvania State University and colleagues gave 20 healthy people ages 22 to 85 blood tests before hypnosis, one hour after and one week later in order to measure the response of the lymphocytes to hypnotic suggestion. When they were hypnotized they were told to visualize their white blood cells as powerful "sharks" swimming through the bloodstream attacking weak, confused germs (this is not too far from the truth about lymphocytes). They were told to practice the visualization. The people did self-hypnosis two times a day for a week, each time telling themselves the shark story.

22   Not everyone showed changes in immune function; the older people were less likely to. But enough did show improvement to suggest a link between the separate worlds of the "soft" mental images and the "harder" phenomena of lymphocytes. The younger people showed a small but real increase in the responsiveness of their immune systems following the hypnosis and visualization. In addition, those people who were easily hypnotized showed increased numbers of lymphocytes after their hypnotic sessions.

23   These changes in immune functioning were small, but so was the experimental "treatment"—just two hypnotic sessions and self-hypnosis for a week. But if such a minor series of events can lead to real changes in immune func-

tioning, what might the possibilities be for increasing our ability to control our own immunity?

Kiecolt-Glaser and colleagues have found that relaxation training can also 24 enhance cellular immune function. Forty-five geriatric residents of an independent-living facility were taught progressive relaxation and guided imagery techniques three times a week for one month. Relaxation was presented to these residents as a way to gain some control over their world. By the end of the training period the group showed a significant increase in natural killer cell activity compared to a control group and a group that merely had "social contact" visits from a college student. The relaxation group also showed significant decreases in antibodies to herpes simplex virus, possibly because the herpes virus was being controlled better by the immune system. These relaxation-induced improvements in immune function were accompanied by self-reports of less psychological distress.

A series of interesting and still controversial studies by Boston University 25 psychologist David McClelland and colleagues suggests that the need to exercise power over others is related to differences in immune function and susceptibility to disease. In McClelland's view, some people have a greater need for power—the desire for prestige or influence over others—than they do for affiliation—the desire to form close affectionate relationships. When people who need power are for some reason unable to exercise it, there seem to be changes in their immune function.

McClelland and colleagues have found that college students who were 26 high in power-related life stresses—a major personal achievement, for example, or the threat of physical attack—reported more frequent and more severe illnesses than other individuals. They also showed elevated levels of epinephrine and depressed levels of salivary immunoglobulin A (S-IgA)—considered a factor in resistance to respiratory infections. As expected, lower levels of S-IgA correlated with reports of more frequent illness. McClelland interpreted the findings as indicating that if a strong need for power is inhibited, there is chronic overactivity of the sympathetic nervous system, which suppresses the immune system.

Similar results were obtained in a 1982 study of first-year dental students. 27 Psychologists John Jemmott and colleagues found that students with an inhibited high need for power reported greater incidence of upper respiratory infections following periods of high academic stress than after periods of low stress. However, variations in stress did not appear to correlate significantly with reported illness in students who were below average in their need for power.

Other studies show how feelings, expressed or not, are associated with 28 immune function and disease. In a 1979 study that compared long-term survivors of breast cancer with those who did not survive, psychologist Leonard Derogatis and colleagues at Johns Hopkins University School of Medicine found that long-term survivors expressed much higher levels of anxiety, hostility, alienation and other negative moods and were perceived as having negative attitudes toward their illness.

29   We take a somewhat controversial approach to interpreting many psychological effects on the immune system, looking not only at the individual's attitudes, moods and thoughts but at his or her relationship to the larger social environment. The well-known increase in mortality rates among bereaved spouses cannot be fully understood as individual reactions alone. There seem to be some mechanisms in animals and in human beings that respond to social needs. When the Sika deer suffer from overcrowding, many of the herd die more quickly, even though they have adequate food. Maybe the same phenomenon occurs in humans; the immune system may cut down resistance to disease when a person is grieving or is no longer part of a viable social unit, as in widowhood. It may be an accident of the close neural connection of the systems, or it may well have resulted from some evolutionary selection pressures. But in any case there are relationships between health and the social world that might well be considered from this simple perspective.

30   And conversely, a solid and stable connection to a larger social group, or to humanity in general, may have the opposite result: improved resistance because the person is probably more valuable as a member of a group. From our speculative viewpoint this may be one reason why almost all societies have developed conventions emphasizing the same virtues and why there is such an emphasis in most religions upon caring for others, being generous to others and serving them. Perhaps one of the many reasons is that doing so is not only helpful to the entire community but also to the health of the donor.

31   Consider a final study. When college students were shown a film of Mother Teresa, winner of the Nobel Peace Prize, tending to the sick and dying of Calcutta, their immune functioning (as measured by S-IgA concentrations) immediately increased. So even watching a person engaged in a selfless act of service to others may have important functions for the health of the community. McClelland noted in an interview that this immune effect occurred even in people who said they disliked Mother Teresa: "The results," he suggests, "mean that she was contacting these consciously disapproving people in a part of their brains that they were unaware of and that was still responding to the strength of her tender loving care."

32   We wouldn't necessarily describe it that way and in fact think that McClelland has gone beyond what the data support; but even so, looking outside of the dominant self-system seems to be important. Even attending to a pet or a plant seems to have health benefits. We don't mean to be absurdly reductionist and imply that all social norms exist for health purposes, but one aim of social and religious communities over the millennia has been to keep their adherents alive and well, to encourage health through specific diets and prohibitions, through cleansing rituals and other means.

33   Could attention to the larger group, away from our biologically primary but primitive focus upon ourselves, and away from the hostile reactions to others, be something we are also organized to resound to? All this is very speculative, but we may well have to think differently about how closely we are related to others in order to understand ourselves, our organs, even our white blood cells.

Questions for Discussion

1. Ornstein and Sobel assert that "there is mounting evidence that 'real' organic dis-eases are linked to changing beliefs about oneself, to the nature of one's relation-ships with others and to one's position in the social world." What evidence do they present? Is it convincing?
2. Are you persuaded by the argument that Ornstein and Sobel make about the rela-tionship between the health of the mind and the body being dependent on caring connections with one's social world? Explain your point of view.
3. How do the authors describe the relationships between the nervous system and the immune system? Does their evidence based on the testing of rats under stress seem convincing to you?
4. Ornstein and Sobel suggest that relaxation and relationship training can improve the immune system's ability to fight off disease. Does their assertion make sense to you in the context of the evidence that they present and in light of your own experi-ences?
5. How effective are the studies that Ornstein and Sobel present in this selection?
6. Has your position on the importance of nurturing social relationships and emotional well being for a healthy and functioning body changed through reading this essay and reflecting on their evidence as well as your life experiences?

Ideas for Writing

1. Discuss the impact that your immediate community has on your sense of well being. Do they cause you to experience excessive stress or do they provide support? Con-sider your college dorm, the friends with whom you live, or your family. When appropriate refer to the essay to support your point of view.
2. Ornstein and Sobel argue that "the immune system may cut down resistance to dis-ease when a person is grieving or is no longer part of a viable social unit." Visit a health clinic in your community to see if its policies support the importance of a "viable social unit." Write a discussion of your findings that also includes several descriptions of these policies and how they function for your class and/or a local paper.
3. Write a satire of life on your campus or life in your family that comments on the destructive power of stress.

The Break

Kenneth Fields

Kenneth Fields (b. 1939) is a professor of English and creative writing at Stan-ford University where he directs the program in Composition and Critical Thinking. His books of poetry include *The Other Walker* (1971), *Sunbelly* (1973), *Smoke* (1973), and *The Odysseus Manuscripts* (1981). "The Break" comes from his recently completed book *Classic Rough News*, a collection of poems that deals with many aspects of alcoholism.

Journal

Make a list of what you think are some inaccurate stereotypes about alcoholism. Then make a list of more accurate symptoms or conditions. Try to speculate about which of these conditions might respond more favorably to group rather than individual therapy.

> He shuffled along the corridors for days,
> shaking against the walls, shutting his eyes
> when he passed a doorway or met another patient,
> as if a look could burn him to the quick.
> 5 He could feel violence in the filtered air.
> Mostly the smilers frightened him. At the thought
> *these people want to love you,* Billy fled
> backward and inward down that silent well
> from which had arisen his last cry *you don't need this*
> 10 until the waters poured into his mouth,
> went still over his head, what blessedness!
> The only one to reach him was Yvonne,
> Next-to-the-last cast with After-the-first,
> he might have been Yvonne, she didn't ask
> 15 anything of him, she just told him stories,
> her stories of burning up, drinking away
> her life so palpable within him that
> one day he laughed out loud at some disaster
> diminished by her getting on with it.

Questions for Discussion

1. What images in the poem describe Billy's emotional state in the early stages of his treatment? Does the poem provide enough information for you to speculate about the causes of these emotions?
2. Why do you think the love that the "smilers" offer frightens Billy?
3. What does the silent well represent?
4. Who is Yvonne? Why and how does she "reach" the speaker? How does their relationship open the possibility of recovery through group therapy?
5. What is the relationship of the title to the body of the poem? A "break" often implies separation. Does the poem offer other connotations for the word "break"?
6. Try to flesh out Billy's condition and speculate about what will would facilitate his recovery. Will group therapy help him? What else could support Billy on his path to recovery?

Ideas for Writing

1. The poem suggests that laughter is an important part of the healing process. Many psychologists, doctors, writers, and spiritual leaders agree that laughter can be an important part of a patient's recovery. Write a paper on the topic of laughter and healing that shares your feelings, observations, and experiences.
2. Develop an essay that shares some of your personal experiences or close observa-

tions of peers or family members who have had drinking problems. Focus your essay on a thesis that discusses what you have learned from being exposed to the destructive results of alcoholism and the possibilities of recovery.

3. Research the current theories about why people become alcoholics and how they can be helped. Consider developing a survey and/or conducting interviews to test the validity of the theories that you find most convincing. Write a paper that shares what you have learned. You might want to conclude by discussing how your feelings about alcoholics have changed as a result of your research, writing, and reflection.

The Lives of Teenage Mothers

Elizabeth Marek

Elizabeth Marek (b. 1961) graduated from Harvard College in 1984. Her first book, *The Children at Santa Clara* (1987) is about her work experiences at a home for emotionally disturbed adolescents in New York City. "The Lives of Teenage Mothers" was first published in *Harper's Magazine* (1989). As you read the selection you will be reminded of the many reasons why community support is essential for teenage mothers.

Journal

Discuss the reasons why you think a teenager might choose to have a child instead of having a legal abortion or having her baby and giving it up for adoption.

At two-thirty on a Thursday afternoon in June, when most teenagers, done with school for the day, are hanging out with their friends, the girls I have come to meet are seated in a small office, reaching for cookies with one hand as they settle their babies on their laps with the other. We are at the Kingsbridge Heights Community Center in the Bronx. The center sits at the crossroads of several worlds. The spacious homes of Riverdale dot the rolling green hills to the west; to the south rise the housing projects that cast their shadow on the lower-middle-class single-family homes and the shops which line the blocks closest to the center. The Teen Parenting Program, which provides counseling, education, and health care to teenage parents and soon-to-be parents throughout the Bronx, was started in 1986 with a group of girls from the projects. Once a week the girls in the program, along with their babies and sometimes their boyfriends, crowd into a simply furnished room to drink Coke, munch on snacks, and talk about the difficulties of being a teenage parent.

On this particular Thursday, I have come too. For years I've read about 2 the "problem of teenage parenthood"—children having children. In New York City, teen pregnancies make up 15 percent of all pregnancies and account for more than thirteen thousand births each year. Sociologists and psychologists speculate about social pressures and individual motivation. President George Bush, in his inaugural address, spoke of the need to help young women "who are about to become mothers of children they can't care for and might not love."

3   But despite the concern voiced by others, we've heard very little from the young women themselves. Are they ignorant about birth control, or are they choosing to get pregnant? What are the conditions of loneliness, poverty, and hopelessness in which having a baby might make sense? What happens to these girls and their babies? How does having a baby affect their lives? Where do the fathers fit in?

4   I've come to Kingsbridge because I want to get to know the mothers, most of whom are not much younger than I am. Sophie-Louise, the social worker in charge of the group, introduces me, and the room falls silent. "Well," she laughs, "here we are. Ask away." Looking at the girls, as they tug at a baby's diaper or straighten a barrette, I am not sure where to begin.

5   "Tell me what it's like, having a baby at your age," I ask at last. As if on cue, all heads turn toward Janelle,[1] a heavyset black girl with short, blown-straight hair, who sits in an overstuffed chair with her three-month-old son, Marc, draped across her lap. The baby, dressed in a pale green sleeper embroidered with a blue bunny, is drooling onto her stylish black skirt. She is eating a chocolate cookie and begins to talk about the logistical problems involved in getting to and from high school with an infant. She has just started summer school to make up credits from the classes she missed during her pregnancy. She is seventeen.

6   "Let's see," she begins. "I get myself up and get the baby up and get myself dressed and get the baby dressed, get my books, get the baby's bag, get the stroller. . . ." She laughs. "Do you know how hard it is to get a stroller on the bus? That first day of school, I thought I wasn't going to make it."

7   Newspaper accounts of teen pregnancy tend to dwell on girls from welfare families. Janelle, however, is the daughter of a retired postal-service clerk and grew up in a small, one-family house in a lower-middle-class neighborhood in the North Bronx. Her childhood was relatively secure: her parents were together and could afford to send her to a Catholic school, where she made friends, got good grades, and dreamed about what she would be when she grew up. "I was gonna finish high school," she says. "Gonna go on to college, like my cousins did. I wanted to get married and have a baby someday, but, really, not now. All through high school I never cut classes, hardly was sick even. . . ."

8   The turning point came when Janelle was fifteen and her parents divorced. "When my parents split, my family just fell apart. My mother only wanted my little sister, so she took her, and then my older sister, she left, too, so it was just me and my father all alone in the house." Feeling unwanted and unloved,

---

[1]The names of the young women and their boyfriends and some identifying details have been changed. [Au.]

Janelle moved into a room in the basement, and her father took over the upstairs. Sometimes they met at breakfast, but other times Janelle went for days without seeing him. "So I started hanging out with a bad bunch of kids," she says, "and cutting classes—I went through an entire year and only got three credits. And then I got pregnant and dropped out." She laughs bitterly. "One thing they don't teach you in high school is how to get a stroller on the bus."

Lynda, at twenty the mother of a three-year-old girl, nods sympathetically. 9 She is a pretty, young Hispanic woman with long hair pulled away from her face in a ponytail. Three weeks earlier she had graduated from high school, having gone to classes in the evening and worked during the day as a cashier in a small store in Manhattan. Her daughter, Danielle, a small child with blonde hair and a dirty face, walks unsmiling around the edge of the room. There is little interaction between mother and daughter. They neither look at nor speak to each other.

Lynda's family, like Janelle's, could be classified as lower middle class. 10 Unlike Janelle's, Lynda's parents are strict Roman Catholics. On the day Lynda told her father that she was pregnant, he left home. "I guess it was either that or throw me out," she says. A few months later he moved back, but even now, although he allows her to live at home, she feels that he has not forgiven her. Lynda believes that her father, having worked hard to provide the best for her and her siblings, took her pregnancy as a slap in the face.

Leaning back in the circle of her boyfriend's arms, Lynda's large black eyes 11 are ringed with dark circles. "My mother still talked to me, like, at the table, pass the salt and stuff. I think my father blamed her—if you had brought her up right, this wouldn't have happened."

Janelle nods. "My father blamed my mother, too. I don't understand that, 12 though, because he didn't even know that I was pregnant. Now he thinks it's my fault that he didn't know, and I think it's his fault. He was always telling me to stay downstairs, and we never talked. We never did anything. Now all he does is compare me to his sister's children, who are much older. They got jobs, finished college, and he says you make me look so bad, having babies, dropping out of school. But he didn't want to come back to my mother, he didn't want to try to help me. It was all just, 'Don't make me look bad. Don't make me look bad.' "

"So what did he do when he found out you were pregnant?" asks Lynda. 13

"He never found out! Not until I came home from the hospital. He found 14 out when the baby was a week old."

Lynda's boyfriend, Tony, a construction worker in his early thirties, joins 15 the discussion. "Maybe it's more that he didn't want to know. He wanted to keep it from himself." Tony is not Danielle's father, although he too was a teenage parent and has two boys of his own. He and Lynda have been going out for almost a year. "You know the parents, they blame themselves," he says. "Like maybe they did something wrong with your upbringing."

Janelle lets out her breath in a snort. "Yeah, well now he tells all his friends, 16 'She's so sneaky.' But I think that if he was really interested, he would have known. I mean, the last day, the day that I gave birth, he went out to the store and said, 'I'll be right back.' And I said, 'Fine, but I won't be here.' But he didn't hear me."

17   Later, riding home on the subway, I wonder whether, in part, Janelle got pregnant to get her father's attention. Or, perhaps, as one social worker I spoke with earlier suggested, part of the motivation for teenage girls to have babies is a wish to be reborn themselves, to re-create themselves as children, so they can get the love and attention they feel they were denied.

18   Nine girls, their babies, and a few of their boyfriends are officially enrolled in Sophie-Louise's group, but since the school year ended, only Janelle and Lynda have been coming regularly. The others, Sophie-Louise explains, have drifted away—to the beach, to parties—or are staying home, too overwhelmed by their lives as mothers to make the trip to the center. Janelle and Lynda represent what Sophie-Louise calls the "cream of the crop": the only ones able to structure their lives sufficiently to attend a regular weekly meeting. The others fade in and out.

19   At the next meeting, I notice that Lynda's boyfriend is missing. Sophie-Louise explains to me privately that Tony and Lynda have been having problems lately. Two new people are present, however: Janelle's boyfriend, Eron, and a new girl, April, a sad-looking black teenager, who brings her five-month-old daughter. April is thin, her ribs jut out below the orange halter top she wears. In contrast to the Calvin Klein jeans Lynda wears, April's jeans are frayed and stained. She sits with her shoulders hunched, as though shielding herself from the vagaries of life. Glancing up, she notices my tape recorder on the table, and she stares at me for a moment before busying herself with the baby on her lap. The baby's dark eyes flicker across her mother's face, but neither of them registers a smile. Sophie-Louise has told me a few facts about April's life: she is the oldest child and lives with her mother, her two siblings, and her baby in a two-room apartment in a housing project in the East Bronx. Seemingly the least equipped to care for an infant, April appears to have been the most determined to have a baby: Kisha was the result of her third pregnancy, the other two having ended in abortions.

20   As the meeting starts, Janelle reaches across the table with one hand to grab some potato chips, while her other hand effortlessly settles baby Marc in a sitting position on her leg. April, sitting alone at the far end of the couch, shakes off Sophie-Louise's offer of a Coke and, grabbing a handful of Cheez Doodles, drapes a towel over her shoulder so that Kisha can nurse quietly at her breast. April seems to hover on the periphery of the discussion, offering tangential comments or staring fixedly at a spot on the wall. Sophie-Louise finds some rubber cows for Danielle to play with, but the little girl is more interested in building towers of checkers in the corner and knocking them down with excited squeals. Over the din, I ask the girls whether they had planned their pregnancies, and how they felt when they discovered they were pregnant.

21   As usual, Janelle begins. "At first, you know, I was real scared. I didn't

want to have the baby," she says, smoothing her hand over Marc's diaper. "I was dead set against it. 'Cause you know, I'm just seventeen, and I didn't want to have a baby. I wanted to still go out and have fun with my friends and stuff. But now, you know, it's been three months, and I'm used to it." She pauses. "Of course, I haven't had too much time to myself. Just twice, in three months. I counted it. Twice. The father's family took care of him for a whole day. I couldn't believe it. I was outside and everything was so much fun. But I like being a mom now. I can handle it. All my friends keep telling me, 'Janelle, you're in a closet!' But I'm not in no closet. And if I am, well, they should leave me alone. It's fun in this closet now that I know what I'm doing and everything."

Lynda's mother takes care of Danielle during the day, when she is at work, and again in the evenings, when she attends classes. But Lynda also complains about a lack of freedom. "My mom says, 'Now you are a mother, you have responsibilities.' She will babysit when I go to work or to school, but otherwise, anywhere I go, Danielle goes." 22

"Did either of you ever think about having an abortion?" I ask. 23

"Abortion," muses Janelle. "Well, by the time I knew I was pregnant, I was already six months pregnant." 24

I wonder whether she has misspoken. Surely she can't mean that she had a baby growing inside of her for six months before she was aware of its presence. But, shaking her head, she assures me that it was six months. 25

"Before that, I had no idea," she says. 26

Lynda backs her up. "By the time I knew I was pregnant, I was five months." 27

"Maybe," Sophie-Louise says, "it goes back to what we talked about before. Not knowing because you really didn't want to know." 28

Lynda is adamant. "No. There was no way I could know. I still had my regular monthly period until I was five months, and that's when I found out. And by then I didn't have much choice because they told me they only did abortions until twelve weeks, and I was way past that. And besides, I don't believe in doing abortions at five months. They say that at three months the baby is still not really formed into a baby, but after that the baby starts forming, and then I feel that it's killing. . . ." 29

April reaches down to straighten Kisha's dress. She speaks for the first time, her voice so soft and low that the rest of us have to strain to hear her. "I didn't know I was pregnant until I was three months. I jumped in a pool and felt something move inside me, and that's when I knew." She pulls her daughter to a sitting position on her lap, pushing a Cheez Doodle into the baby's flaccid mouth. 30

Janelle pauses and then says quietly, "I don't think I knew, but then I wonder. Maybe somewhere in me I knew, but it was like I was saying, no, I'm not pregnant. I'm not pregnant . . . I was living day-to-day, one day at a time. I would just get up in the morning and do what I needed to do, and not think about it." 31

As the girls speak, their words reflect their sense of powerlessness. Even 32 their bodies rebel, growing alien creatures without their knowledge, the awareness of their pregnancy dawning only after the possibility for abortion has passed. Does this reflect a yearning for a child? Or is it only a child's way of coping with something too terrifying to acknowledge?

33   Lynda glances at Danielle, who is still amusing herself with the checkers. She brings the group back to the abortion question. "I think that the girl should just make up her own mind, and then that's it," she says. "Because even if you don't let your boyfriend go, you are still going to get left."

34   "What do you mean?" Sophie-Louise asks. Like many working mothers, Lynda has an air of perpetual exhaustion. "Sometimes, if you're in love with a guy, and 'I love you' comes up, that's the one thing that always makes you weak. You say, 'Oh, I love you too.' But then it's time for you both to sit down and talk about the situation, you know, after you say, 'Well, I'm pregnant,' and he says, 'Oh, you are?' and he gets happy and everything. This happened to me. And I said, 'I want an abortion.' Then the brainwash would begin, the 'I love you and it's our baby and I'll give you support.' It was like, if I had an abortion, then I didn't love him. I feel that the woman should just make up her own mind, and make her own decision. But he said, 'Oh, I love you, and I'll do this for you, I'll do that for you, and our baby will have this, and our baby will have that.' Now she's two and a half years old, and all he ever got her was a big box of Pampers and socks and T-shirts and twenty dollars and that was it." Suddenly, the resentment in her voice changes to wistfulness. "She's two and a half. And he was going to buy her a baby crib and a bassinet and clothes. Everything. . . ."

35   I have heard stories like this from other girls I talked with and from social workers as well. One fifteen-year-old mother told me that her boyfriend said that if she really loved him, she would have his baby. Despite her mother's urging, she decided against having an abortion. But by the time the baby was born, she and her boyfriend had broken up, and he was expecting another child by another girl in her school. As Sophie-Louise puts it, the guys like to have three or four "pots on different stoves" at the same time—visible proof of their virility.

36   Sophie-Louise turns to Eron, Janelle's boyfriend. He is seventeen and works two jobs, one in a garage and the other as an attendant at Rye Playland. She asks him how he felt when he found out that Janelle was pregnant. He laughs. "I was scared."

37   "More scared than me!" Janelle adds. "I mean, you were chicken!" "Well my life was changing, too," says Eron. "I mean, I know guys who just say, oh no, a baby, and then walk off, but I'm not that type of person. My father was never there for me when I was little, so, you know, I don't want that to happen to my son. I don't want him to grow up and hate me and all that. I want to have somebody to love me. Even if me and Janelle don't end up together, I got him to remind me of her."

38   It interests me that Eron wants the baby as someone to love him. When I ask the girls what they think of this, April rejoins the discussion. Without rais-

ing her eyes from her baby, she says, "When my boyfriend found out I was pregnant, he just played it off. He would always play at my stomach, sort of punch me in the stomach.

"Now I don't even let him see her anymore. All he wants to do is play 39 with her, and then give her back when it's time for changing."

"That's tough," Sophie-Louise says. "It takes two to make a baby, but then 40 one of the two doesn't want any of the responsibility. Do you think you can talk to him about it?"

"I don't want to," April says. "I don't even want him to see her. Ever since 41 I was pregnant, he kept saying that he was going to get me some stuff. He lied to his mother, saying that he was going to get me a carriage for the baby, but he didn't get me nothing. I had to do it all. And then I found out that he had some kind of drug addict, some girl in his house, some Puerto Rican girl, and his mother went on vacation and she came back and seen all these suitcases in her room, and she seen this Puerto Rican girl in the house with him. They just did it, right there."

As she clutches Kisha to her breast, I see how absorbed they are in each 42 other. With no job, no boyfriend, nothing to fill her days, the baby is her life. Yet both mother and daughter seem drained.

Janelle looks concerned. "But aren't you worried that she might grow up 43 without having a relationship with her father?"

"Well, I don't even want to see her father anymore," April says. "Her 44 father is crazy! He busted my window one time. I tell you about that? He wanted to see the baby so bad and he was drunk one night, four-thirty in the morning, and he came banging on my door, saying, 'I'm not going nowhere until I see my baby.' So then I brought the baby into my mother's room, because he had cracked the window with a rock and he was making a lot of noise. And then he just left. . . . Besides, I don't want him taking her to his house, 'cause his mother is a crackhead."

April falls silent. Sophie-Louise asks her whether her role in her own fam- 45 ily has changed since she got pregnant.

"Oh yeah," April says. "Now, my mother thinks that I have to do every- 46 thing. You know, when I was pregnant, she tried to make me do more than I was supposed to, more than I did before I was pregnant. Now she says, 'You're no more teenager. You're an adult.' But before that, before I had the baby, I wasn't classified as no adult. So what makes us having a baby be an adult?"

During the next session, the last before the August recess, there is a small 47 "graduation" party for Eron. He feels confident about passing his summer-school course, and when he does, he will officially become a high-school grad-uate. After the cake is cut and the group settles down, the talk turns to peer pressure. Sophie-Louise has been telling the story of a fourteen-year-old girl she counseled at a local high school. Although the girl had been taught about birth control and abortion and warned about the difficulties facing teen moth-ers, she became pregnant midway through eighth grade. Speaking with the girl later, Sophie-Louise asked her why, after all they had talked about, had she let this happen. "I don't know," she said. "All my friends have babies. I was beginning to wonder what was wrong with me that I didn't have one too."

48 The girls in the group laugh at the story. "I don't know about her," Janelle says, "but I knew that seventeen was too young to have a baby. None of my friends have babies. My sister, she just had a baby . . . but it wasn't like I wanted to get pregnant."

49 "Were you using birth control?" I ask.

50 Janelle's cheeks flush.

51 "I gotta tell you," she says. "I never used birth control. I mean, now I do, but before, well, I just never thought I would get pregnant. I was like, that can't happen to me. I thought that only happened to the bad girls across town. Who do drugs and stuff. But I didn't do none of that, so I thought I was safe. You know, like when you think it just can't happen to you. To other people *yes*, but not to you."

52 "I can believe that," Lynda says. "Like, I used to think that if the guy didn't come in you, then you couldn't get pregnant."

53 "Well," says Janelle, "my friend told me once that if you took a bath afterward, then you were safe."

54 "Or if you do it standing up!"

55 I could add to the list. A social worker I spoke with said that most of the girls use the chance method. And each month that they don't get pregnant reinforces their belief that they are safe.

56 The existence of these myths may reflect denial rather than ignorance. As the girls talk, I begin to see why the idea of having a baby might be compelling. There is a sense of loneliness eased, of purpose granted, of a glimmering of hope.

57 Janelle smiles. "But now that I am a mother, I do enjoy it. I mean, he keeps me company all the time, so I never have to be bored or lonely. He's my friend, this little guy. He keeps me so busy that I never have time to get into trouble. And before, I never really had a reason to get up in the morning, to go to school, whatever. But now, because of him, I do."

58 In Janelle's words, I hear the unspoken wish that, through the baby, the mothers may get a second chance at childhood, that in loving their babies they may almost be loving themselves.

59 Sophie-Louise asks whether, perhaps, Janelle had some of those thoughts before getting pregnant, whether on some level part of the reason that she did not use birth control was because somewhere inside her she wished for a baby.

60 Janelle pauses to consider the question. "Well, I don't know. Maybe. You know, I was lonely. My parents had split, and I really didn't have anyone, just me and my father together in the house."

61 Sophie-Louise turns to April. Despite the fact that Kisha was the result of her third pregnancy, April is unwilling to admit that she had wanted the baby. "It was an accident," she insists. "I mean, I said that this isn't going to happen to me. I was using all kinds of protection. Most times I even had him use protection."

Sophie-Louise seems surprised. "You were using protection?" she asks. 62
"What kind?"

Indignantly, April answers, "Well, I was taking the Pill. I mean, I wasn't 63
taking it all the time, but I was taking it. But I missed a couple of days, I guess.
I think I took it on the day before my birthday, but not on my birthday, I don't
think. . . ."

"So for you it really was an accident," I say. I am surprised when she con- 64
tradicts me.

"No. I wouldn't really say it was an accident. See, all the other times I got 65
pregnant, my mother made me get rid of it. So I guess part of it was revenge
against my mother, like I was gonna get pregnant but not let her know until
she couldn't do nothing."

"Not with me," says Lynda. "With me it was just a pure accident. Just a 66
pure accident. I wanted to get an abortion. I said that I was going to have one.
But my boyfriend and my parents, my father especially . . . they wanted me
to have it. That's when the brainwash began."

It occurs to me that I've been looking for a motivation, a reason why these 67
girls, and others like them, might *choose* to become pregnant. But the more I
listen, the more I wonder whether the question of choice is relevant. In all their
stories, I hear again and again how little volition these girls feel they have,
how little control over the events of their lives. The deadline for school admission passes and April shrugs. Sophie-Louise makes an appointment for Lynda
with a job counselor, but Lynda forgets to go. Janelle knows about birth control but doesn't believe "it" will happen to her. Sophie-Louise told me once
that these girls exert no more control over their lives than a "leaf falling from
a tree." Perhaps having a baby is less a question of ignorance or choice than
one of inevitability. Once a girl is sexually active, it is not *having* a baby that
requires choice and conscious action, but *not* having one.

Eron shifts in his chair. "You know, all this talk about we didn't want to 68
have the baby, or it was an accident, or whatever . . . I just think it's a waste
of time. I mean, now we have the baby. The question is, what are we going to
do now?"

Sophie-Louise asks him what he means, and he explains that the cycle of 69
babies having babies, single parents raising single parents, has haunted him
as it has haunted most of the teens in the room, and that he feels it can end
with them, but only if they are willing to face the realities of their situation.
"My father was never there when I was little," he says, "but I don't want him
to grow up and hate me and all that. . . . That's why I'm going to finish school
and do whatever I need to do."

His eyes shine as he speaks of his ambition, but he looks down shyly, as 70
if afraid that someone will mock him. Janelle, however, backs him up with
pride and speaks of her own ambition to become a social worker. "It's so easy
to go on welfare," she says. "You just sit home and cash a check. But I'm not
going to get on welfare, 'cause it makes you lazy. It's addictive."

"I couldn't do that," Eron says. "I'm the kind of person who needs to 71
work." But then the realities of fatherhood seem to descend upon him. "I don't

know, though. See, 'cause with a baby, it takes all the money that you don't even have. . . ."

72   At the end of the session, the discussion shifts back to the problems that the girls will encounter when they return to school in the fall. Janelle is telling April that summer school really wasn't so bad. "It was hard leaving him at first," she says, "but I tried not to think about it. And I didn't think about it, because the classes were hard. And I was usually really tired. But I was happy. I just thought about the work, and the time flew by, and I was picking up the baby before I knew it."

73   Sophie-Louise presses April to consider how she will feel when she is separated from her daughter for the first time. "Have you thought at all about what it's going to be like?" Sophie-Louise asks. "How it's going to feel, emotionally, to be separated?"

74   April ignores her at first, and then shakes her head no. Sophie-Louise encourages her, suggesting she might feel relief or worry or sadness, but April clearly does not want to pursue the issue. Finally, in frustration, April says, "Look, I haven't thought about it yet. I haven't thought about it because it hasn't happened."

75   With that, the session ends. Having missed the deadline for entrance to summer school, April stays behind to talk to Sophie-Louise about starting a diploma-geared class in the fall. Danielle tugs at Lynda's arm, asking whether they can finally go to the zoo as she promised. I hear Eron and Janelle bickering about whose turn it is to buy diapers. And I head down the steep hill to the subway that will take me back downtown.

Questions for Discussion

1. Why was the Teen Parenting Program at the Kingsbridge Heights Community Center in the Bronx established? Do you know of similar types of teen parenting programs in your community? Before reading this article, what kinds of issues did you think would be discussed in a teen parenting group? Were the issues and feelings explored in the article different than you expected?

2. Marek states that 15 percent of the pregnancies in New York City are teen mothers. What is the percentage in your community? Why isn't Marek satisfied with the information that the statistics reveal? What new types of insights does Marek hope to gain from visiting the teen parenting group?

3. Can you understand why Marek may feel uncomfortable beginning to talk with the group of teen mothers? How would you feel if you were in Marek's position? If you were one of the teen mothers?

4. Which of Marek's assumptions and/or stereotypes about teen mothers are changed because of the on-going conversations she has with them?

5. From reading Marek's account of her discussions with Janelle, Lynda, and April, what did you learn about the reasons why these young girls got pregnant and gave birth to their babies? Explain why you agree or disagree with Marek's conclusion: "Perhaps having a baby is less a question of ignorance or choice than one of inevitability."

6. Why do the teen mothers need the sense of community provided by the group? What types of support does the group provide?

Ideas for Writing

1. Develop your journal into an essay that presents a point of view about teenage pregnancies. Begin by doing library research on the issue, or interview counselors or social workers who work with teenage mothers—or interview teenage mothers. Write an essay that incorporates your interviews and explores the ways that communities can provide support for teenage mothers and their children.

2. Write an essay that presents a critical perspective on the cultural stereotypes of teenage mothers. Refer to popular films, books for teenagers, or television programs to determine the major stereotypes. Then think critically about these attitudes. Consider the article you have just read and any young women you have known who have had children as teenagers.

At the Clinics, April 5, 1992

Anna Quindlen

Anna Quindlen (b. 1935) graduated from Barnard College in 1974 and worked at *The New York Times* as a reporter and editor from 1977 to 1985. Since 1986 she has written a syndicated column for *The New York Times.* Her first book, *Living Out Loud* (1988), was composed of pieces from her column "Life in the 30's." She has been awarded many prizes for her journalism; in 1992 she received the Pulitzer Prize for commentary. The following selection, "At the Clinics, April 5, 1992," is taken from her most recent essay collection *Thinking Out Loud* (1993). Quindlen has also written a best-selling novel, *Object Lessons* (1991), and a children's book, *The Tree that Came to Stay.* She lives with her husband and three children in northern New Jersey.

Journal

Do you think abortion should continue to be legal? Discuss your point of view on this issue.

Last fall a thirty-year-old woman named Eileen Moran pulled into the parking lot of the Aware Woman clinic in the space coast town of Melbourne, Florida. Ms. Moran was not surprised to see demonstrators; that is commonplace. The surprise came the next day, in a manila envelope full of color photographs of bloody fetuses, anti-abortion tracts, and a letter warning her about procedures performed at the clinic.

"I felt very violated," says Ms. Moran, who is now five months pregnant 2 and had gone to the clinic only for a checkup. "The idea that they could trace my name and address through my license plate and have something in the mail that day was pretty terrifying."

At Aware Woman, it is pretty ordinary. Ms. Moran got off easier than the 3 teenager whose envelope was sent to her parents. And her experience pales in comparison to that of doctors who receive middle-of-the-night hang-up calls on their unlisted lines and whose homes are picketed constantly. Opponents of the Melbourne clinic have issued WANTED posters, offering a $1,000 reward for information leading to "the arrest or conviction" of one doctor who works there.

4   The poster, which describes him as "a hired assassin in that he kills unborn babies for a fee," includes his photograph, his home phone number and that of his mother, and the license-plate number of his car. The poster was taped to the office doors of other gynecologists in central Florida; written at the bottom was "You Are Next."

5   Today in Washington, D.C., there will be a rally for abortion rights, for constitutional protections and federal legislation. But while we have been looking at the big picture we have forgotten something important. What if they gave us abortion and nobody came—no doctors, no clinic administrators, no nurses?

6   The people who run abortion clinics are a tightly knit group, as folks who are under fire tend to be. Their carpenters have been persuaded not to make repairs, their medical labs to turn away their business. Their children have been accosted and told that they are the spawn of murderers. I couldn't blame any of them if they decided that they'd had enough of being the real people behind the legal arguments.

7   You can find the place where the founder of the Melbourne clinic lives because there is a groove in the grass out front, where every morning a woman walks back and forth with a sign that says PAT WINDLE, STOP KILLING GOD'S BABIES.

8   Few new doctors are learning to perform abortions, and those who do, concerned that publicity like the WANTED posters will ruin their practices, often return to the happier task of delivering babies. The big medical organizations, which can lobby like nobody's business when they want to, have been uncommonly low-key. They were more fired up about our right to choose breast implants than they have ever been about our right to choose abortion.

9   Ms. Windle says that a reporter scoffed when she described this as a civil war. But it is a war, and there is battle fatigue. There has sprung up a thirst for some middle ground. Sometimes the talk is of promoting contraception, sometimes of curtailing the period of pregnancy during which abortion is permissible, sometimes of merely allowing abortion while making clear that it is not desirable.

10   But this battle is not being driven by those with a will to compromise. The people who are harassing doctors, patients, and clinics consider any means permissible in their quest to prove that they know what's better for you than you do. The ordinary American standards of personal privacy and personal property don't apply. "God's law is higher than man's law," says Randall Terry, the leader of Operation Rescue, who said in Buffalo that he would be using investigators to dig up dirt on doctors who perform abortions, a part of God's law that I missed in my study of the Bible.

And so it is important today to remember a T-shirt slogan: Think Glob- 11
ally, Act Locally. Many of us who speak out in favor of legal abortion have
had little to do with the day-to-day happenings at the clinics, perhaps because
we were focused on sweeping safeguards, perhaps because it is easier to see
abortion as a crusade than as a business. The truth is it must be both. Freedom
of the press is only as meaningful as the willingness of one person to publish
a newspaper. The right to choose abortion is empty if the people who provide
it are harassed out of existence.

Questions for Discussion

1. Quindlen presents examples of the tactics of "pro-lifers" in the first four paragraphs
   of this short commentary. What is the effect of the placement of these examples prior
   to her thesis?
2. What is Quindlen's purpose? Who is her audience?
3. Why is Quindlen critical of Randall Terry's interpretation of the Bible?
4. What warning does Quindlen present to those who are pro-choice?
5. Why does Quindlen think that the right to have an abortion is as much of a business as a crusade? Do you agree with her? Provide examples to support your point
   of view.
6. Why did you think Quindlen entitled her essay "At the Clinics"? In what other ways
   does Quindlen emphasize that abortion is the responsibility of every community in
   this country?

Ideas for Writing

1. Do some library research into the reasons that pro-choice and anti-abortion activists
   present to support their point of view on abortion. Interview some of your friends
   about their position on the issue. Then write an argumentative essay that presents
   your point of view on the abortion issue. Provide relevant examples and information from your research and your experiences to support your position.
2. Write a paper that traces the changing climate of opinion about abortion since the
   Roe v. Wade decision; and predicts how you think abortion laws will be changed in
   the near future. How do you think communities and clinics will work together to
   solve problems such as those described in the first four paragraphs of this essay?

The Wizard of Prozac

Tracy Thompson

Tracy Thompson (b. 1961) earned an A.B. in political science at Davidson College in 1983 and a M.S. in journalism at Boston University in 1989. She is a staff
writer for the *Washington Post.* "The Wizard of Prozac" appeared in the *Washington Post National Weekly* in December of 1993.

Journal

What responsibility does the community and/or the health care system have to people who are seriously depressed?

> *"I'd rather be myself," he said. "Myself and nasty. Not somebody else, however jolly."*
>
> —Bernard Marx, in Aldous Huxley's *Brave New World*

In my palm is a green and white capsule, slightly larger than a Tic Tac. Inside is a white powder containing 39 quintillion molecules of something called fluoxetine hydrochloride. When reduced to a diagram on paper, the chemical structure of each molecule resembles a pair of aviator goggles with a broken nosepiece.

2   Once they are in my body, those molecules will migrate to my brain, where they will attach to sites on the ends of nerve cells and prevent them from absorbing a chemical called serotonin. Serotonin is a neurotransmitter, the bicycle courier of the brain, shuttling electrical impulses from one nerve to another. With less serotonin being absorbed, more of it will be pedaling around up there, delivering tiny jolts of electricity from nerve to nerve. You could say this little green and white capsule is about to ratchet up the voltage in my head. And, in some way—no one knows precisely how—this will help me feel better. Happier. Without nameless anxiety, able to take pleasure in ordinary things. Sane.

3   And there lies one of the more intriguing medical controversies of our time.

4   The drug is called Prozac, and since it came on the market in 1988 it has proved to be a startlingly effective treatment for a common but potentially deadly mental illness known as depression. This year, more than 10 million people around the world will take it, or one of several copycat drugs it has spawned. For Eli Lilly and Co., its manufacturer, Prozac brought in more than $1 billion in sales in 1992, testimony to its broad medical acceptance.

5   Yet something about it seems scary. Almost from the start, Lilly has been dogged by lawsuits claiming that for some vulnerable patients, Prozac triggered homicidal or suicidal impulses. The evidence has yet to convince any court of law, and the medical debate has largely yielded to a disquieting philosophical one.

6   Prozac is not a sedative or a euphoriant; it is different from anything that has come before, because it fundamentally and selectively alters personality without altering perception. And that gives abstract questions some disturbing reality. By using Prozac, are we fiddling with the human soul? Does its effectiveness mean that we don't have a soul—that the mind is merely a globe of tissue in which electrical and chemical events occur? Should we indulge in what psychiatrist Peter Kramer, author of the bestseller *Listening to Prozac*, calls "cosmetic psychopharmacology"—tinkering with personalities the way a mechanic fine-tunes a car?

7   It comes down to this: Who am I? Am I my un-chemical self, no matter

how unhappy that may make me? Or should I swallow this pill, achieve tranquility and risk obliterating some essential part of me?

Some consider this a paralyzing moral dilemma. I don't. For anyone who 8 has ever lived through an episode of major depression, this is a no-brainer. If there is a pill that will make you well, or make it less likely you will get sick, you take it. My feeling on that point is so strong that I keep taking this pill long after my doctor has said it is okay to quit. If it hasn't saved my life, it has profoundly changed it.

I pour myself a glass of water, and down it goes.   9

But still—there are times when I have the uneasy sense that I am ceding 10 a big part of my autonomy to the pharmaceutical industry. There is the "Brave New World" specter of "soma," the all-purpose psychic pepper-upper that enabled Huxley's futuristic government to create a society of compliant pleasure-seekers. Sometimes I wonder who I would be if I weren't taking Prozac. Maybe I would be a tortured genius, like Byron. Or maybe I would be just me, and nasty. With periods of dank despondency.

So I'm left to ponder: Did the person who made this pill have any idea 11 what he was doing? Did he realize that the promise of surcease from pain would lure millions of people like me into donating their brains to science? What does he think about what he's done?

Then one day, I decided to find this wizard, whoever he was, and ask him. 12

My search took me to Indianapolis, via ancient Greece.   13

The Greeks knew about depression; it was for them a well-known array 14 of symptoms, and their name for it can be poetically translated into modern English as "crazy fear." It's an apt thumbnail description of a complex illness whose symptoms range from anxiety attacks, inability to concentrate on everyday tasks, irritability, weight loss and insomnia to its best-known sign: a deep, chronic sense of emptiness and despair.

The Romans Latinized the Greek word into "melancholia," which in 15 Anglo-Saxon English got translated as "black bile," one of the four "humors" that made up the medieval concept of the human body. Illness, it was thought, resulted from an imbalance in those humors, and melancholy was due to too much black bile. The French spoke of the masque—the blank, soul-dead look of a person caught in the thrall of major depression.

For most of recorded medical history, doctors considered depression an 16 illness of the body, and they treated it with purges, blood-letting and special diets. But it also was seen as an illness of the soul. Though some tried exorcism to drive the demons out, Robert Burton's *Anatomy of Melancholy*, published in 1621, counseled sufferers to seek the comforts of "true religion."

With Sigmund Freud came the classic psychoanalytic theories of depres- 17 sion: that it was anger turned inward, the lingering effects of unresolved trauma. For a while, the long shadow of Freud nearly obliterated any idea that this might be a physical abnormality. When that idea reemerged, it came about as scientific breakthroughs often do: by accident.

In the 1950s, researchers noticed that an antihistamine new on the market in 18

France, chlorpromazine, helped tame the hallucinations and rages of severely psychotic patients, and also helped people suffering from an agitated form of depression. In 1957, American doctors made a related discovery: A tuberculosis drug, iproniazid, also seemed to help perpetually morose patients recover their old vitality.

19   The observations were noted with interest by drug companies, who sensed a market and leapt into the void. Within a few years, a handful of new antidepressants were on the market. The drugs did work for many people, but the side effects were sometimes debilitating. The antidepressants derived from the tuberculosis drug produced jaundice and high blood pressure; those derived from the antihistamine made patients groggy and dry-mouthed. Some severely depressed people, demoralized by the side effects and tired of waiting for results, opted to use the pills to end their pain another way—by downing the whole bottle in one big gulp, with, say, a bottle of vodka.

20   This idea—that an "imaginary" pain of the mind could drive someone to end his life—is a hard one for normal people to grasp. After all, everyone knows what sadness is. And there is grief, a close cousin of depression and a normal part of the human condition.

21   Describing depression is one of the most difficult tasks of language. Like all mental illness, depression exiles people into a foreign territory of the mind, from where they may or may not be able to send back bulletins. Like dreamers, the mentally ill often find that their return to clarity invokes an automatic amnesia; those who find their way home from its exile often forget what they saw in that strange land.

22   As for me, I not only made repeat trips, I kept a travel diary.

MOCKINGBIRD, SINGING IN THE DEAD OF NIGHT

23 Sometimes, in the South, mockingbirds get crazed. They sing all night. This one did, anyway, right outside my window. After a while, I was sure he was mocking me—flaunting his music in the sticky-warm night air, reminding me that it was 4 A.M. and that I had not slept for hours, that soon I would have to get up and face another day of deadening duties and crushing sadness. Exhausted but wide awake, I lay in the sweat-damp bedsheets, unable for the life of me to remember why I was sad. I was 20 years old.

24   I was in college then and keeping my journal, the same one I had begun six years before. By then, it filled up dozens of spiral-bound notebooks, as well as an immense leather-bound ledger I had found in my mother's basement. The journal was my way of trying to make sense of the times when The Beast, as I came to call it, came calling.

25   The Beast was a familiar visitor, though I don't recall precisely when it first arrived. I can remember as a child—memory places it at around fourth grade—crouching behind a toilet in the girls' lavatory, unable to explain why I was there and just wordlessly sad. Depression is a disorder that tends to recur

and to get worse if left untreated, and mine was a classic case: As I went through my teens and twenties, I suffered roughly a half-dozen episodes, lasting from a few months to a year and a half, and each was worse than the one before. The Beast prompted me to start my journal the winter I was 14.

I have it before me now, that first ledger—a green, flip-top stenographer's notebook, filled with my loopy adolescent script. 26

"It sounds horrible, and it is," I wrote on Page 2, "but several times lately I have thought about how nice it would be to kill myself!!!" 27

In that mockingbird spring of my 20th year, The Beast came for its first extended visit. It sat on my chest at night, it rode my back during the day. A half-dozen spiral notebooks later, I would write in my journal: 28

"My face is wet. My hands are icy—I notice these things one at a time, gradually, like an infant. I am cold. Inside, I am a battlefield—Waterloo after Napoleon, Vicksburg after the siege. Always a war; always fighting one emotion or another." 29

And later: "There is a deep, gnawing sadness at the core of everything, everything, and on afternoons like this I feel it most. I am empty inside. There is something in the future which is coming. I am afraid that it will suck out my core and I will be completely empty and anguished." 30

And: "I have to find ways to get myself through it, people I love who will help me. I have to because the alternative is simply existing, crawling in a corner to die. Or going over the edge into madness." 31

Throughout that spring and the year that followed, I felt myself leaving the people I loved. They stood on the shore, growing smaller and indistinct, as I drifted away on a reluctant journey. I felt trapped in an invisible, airless chamber, my frantic gestures ignored or misunderstood. I would sit alone in my dorm room, listening for hours to the violin counter-melody, so full of longing and wordless grief, in the second movement of Beethoven's Seventh Symphony. To others, I merely seemed remote and angry. 32

After many months, the episode ended as imperceptibly as it had begun. But there would be others. In college I found a psychotherapist, and eventually I tried antidepressants. But I didn't know what they were, and my doctors didn't seem to either, since they prescribed them only at my request, and at first in doses too small to do me any good. Not surprisingly, the relief I got from them was fleeting. And there were months, even years, when The Beast stayed away. 33

It was not until 1990 that I tried Prozac. I had been on vacation with friends on Cape Cod. It was August, six months after I had been hospitalized for the most severe episode of depression yet, and I still wasn't well. After a week at the beach, a sudden panic at the approach of my 35th birthday made me bolt; to the bafflement of my friends, I rented a car and drove to Woods Hole, where I checked into a motel and spent one of the worst nights of my life, staring at my bottle of imipramine—a favorite drug among depressives who kill themselves—and wondering if The Beast had won after all, if the moment had come to negotiate a surrender. 34

In the morning, taking the urgent advice of my psychiatrist and a friend, 35

I caught a plane to Washington. A prescription for Prozac was waiting for me at my neighborhood drugstore.

36   Two days later, I was at home when I had a moment of what I can only call clearheadedness. The suffocating anxiety was gone, momentarily, and I felt a deep relief, a sense of sudden calm after eons of warfare inside my head. I had gotten so used to the noise that the quiet was unfamiliar. It was as if the evil person who had been holding my head under water, trying to drown me, had suddenly let go. I picked up the phone and called a friend.

37   "I don't know if I'm imagining this," I said, "but I think I'm starting to feel better."

38   My recovery was not that dramatic, of course; there were several weeks in which I still found it hard to concentrate or sleep, and in which the daily weight of sadness seemed too much to drag around with me. But by October, I definitely knew: I was better. I have been taking Prozac ever since. I am, you might say, chemically altered.

39   Exactly what form this alteration has taken, I will never know. In the bad old days, I didn't always know I was depressed until somebody told me, the way people with leprosy sometimes didn't notice their deterioration until they scalded their hand and it didn't hurt. I can no more describe how that has changed than I can examine the back of my own neck. I don't feel sedated, or jittery, or drugged. I simply feel normal. As if I had been driving a car all these years with the parking brake on, and now it is off. I feel as if the real me has returned—perhaps all the way from childhood, where she lived before The Beast arrived. Sometimes I sense that I have lost something. An intensity of feeling, maybe—a way of noticing the world with wonder. It is a perspective I now find hard to summon. Those instants are Kodachromed in my mind, like one moment from that mockingbird year when I saw a poplar tree in the rain, its yellow leaves falling on the wet pavement, and glimpsed an indescribable sad beauty. I don't have those moments much anymore; they have mostly all gone, along with most of those moments of lacerating despair. I have greedily swapped them for ordinary life. That may sound dull, but I tell you it is sweet. It is not caviar I crave, but clean sheets and hot soup.

40   At some point, the thought came to me that few people have affected my life quite as profoundly as the person who invented this drug. And I decided to tell him that, whoever and wherever he was. Which is how I came to be in Indiana in October, to find the Wizard of Prozac. He might have no idea of what he'd done, I thought, but I imagined he would like to hear from me.

41   I fear I have always tended to romanticize things.

42   The pale pink marble of Eli Lilly's corporate headquarters rises Ozlike out of the flat Indiana farmland. Inside, the atmosphere is something between a temple and a theme park. Three-story ceilings loom over a silver and marble lobby and the comings and goings of people who—as it seems to me—stride past with a sense of high purpose.

43   Through one of the huge lobby windows, I glimpse an immaculate green field with flowers that look so perfect they must be plastic, except they aren't.

Inside is a 90-acre complex of offices and laboratories. Walking through one of the labs, I stumble on a disconcerting sight—a row of live pigeons used in brain experiments, stored headfirst in plastic juice pitchers, tailfeathers sticking up like paper umbrellas in a row of mai tais.

The Lilly public relations department has scheduled an exhaustive tour, the highlight of which is to be my meeting with the Prozac scientists.

The wizard I seek, as it turns out, is not one person, but three: Ray Fuller, David Wong and Bryan Molloy. They are the men collecting awards these days—but even that is an arbitrarily short list. I am informed that hundreds of people at Lilly worked on the Prozac project over a span of 18 years. The era of solitary Pasteurs puttering up miracles in their basement is as dead as the Model T. Because pharmaceutical industry profits often hinge on who gets there first, when a goal seems within reach, vast teams are thrown at projects.

Fuller and Wong seem much alike, even though Fuller is a farm boy from southern Illinois and Wong is a native of Hong Kong. Both are unassuming middle-aged men who convey a genial, pastoral demeanor—a bit like Sunday school teachers, or small-town family doctors.

Molloy is different: Quirky, irascible, he keeps to himself in offices clear on the other side of the Lilly complex. He has a gaunt, angular face and a discernible trace of Scotland in his speech, and he seems intense, at home between his own two ears and impatient with social niceties.

Lining the walls of his office is a series of world maps, growing smaller in scope and more detailed until, on the far wall, there is a sewer commission map of Molloy's native village in Scotland. It even shows alleys and car parks.

Molloy gives me an abbreviated version of how Prozac was developed, a story that sounds self-evident in hindsight, as major discoveries often do.

The idea was simple: Instead of examining existing drugs to discover which ones had antidepressant side effects, Molloy decided to start with the side effect and build a drug that would trigger it. It was the scientific method in reverse—as if Molloy had decided to write a mystery novel with the ending in the first chapter. The mystery became not whodunit it, but how they did it and why.

Molloy started in 1971 with a trip to Lilly's chemical library, the vast catalogue of compounds the company kept in its vaults for research. Antihistamines had yielded the first major antidepressant drugs, so Molloy started with compounds whose chemical structures resembled antihistamines. He began carting books listing compounds over to his office by the wheelbarrow-load.

He knew which neurotransmitters he wanted to leave alone—the ones that produced the grogginess and dry-mouth effects, among others—but he was not sure which ones he wanted to target. Several years before, he and Fuller had collaborated on research involving serotonin, and Fuller was by this point convinced that serotonin was the key to understanding the faulty brain chemistry that results in severe depression.

It was Wong who supplied the last, crucial link in the developmental chain, by creating a precise test for measuring the effect of serotonin in living brain cells, using ground-up brain cells of rats.

55   The initial research went quickly; less than two years after Molloy started, Wong's tests confirmed that one compound Molloy and Fuller had created, known as LY949439, had a potent and selective effect on serotonin, and serotonin only. This was Prozac.

56   "Dr. Fuller and I were reminiscing one day," says Wong, "and we both decided that if we had not become scientists we might have wound up in the seminary."

57   It is an incongruous thought. If your work is based on the certainty that mind and body are indistinguishable, where does a spiritual view of the universe fit in? Isn't there some sort of a logical inconsistency?

58   "People talk about depression as if it's either/or," Fuller says. It is not as simple, he says, as mind or body. "I don't think that distinction has any meaning. The mind, like the rest of the body, functions through molecular changes."

59   He is talking in his office, which is a modest room lined with looseleaf notebooks of clinical data. At times, he gets up to illustrate some point with a diagram of a neuron, pointing to it with a pencil as if he were lecturing in a classroom. A few weeks after Prozac went on the market in 1988, he was in Boston at a scientific conference, riding an escalator in a hotel, when he overheard two women behind him talking. "I'm on Prozac now, and I'm doing much better," one woman said to the other. Telling the story makes him smile, which makes him look very much like a Presbyterian minister.

60   Except that in his theology, the soul is a collection of cells, if a dauntingly complex one. ("If the human brain were simple enough for us to understand, we would be too simple to understand it," another Lilly pharmacologist said in *Listening to Prozac*.) Fuller quotes one of his scientific predecessors, neuroscientist Ralph Gerard: "Behind every crooked thought there lies a crooked molecule." So, I ask, are we just fooling ourselves, to think that we are able to reason our way out of despair? Is there a chemical for every sadness?

61   No, he says: But every sadness is chemical. There was an experiment in which damselfish were kept in a tank with only a transparent wall between them and some big predator fish. The damselfish had every reason to think they were about to be eaten. After a while, the serotonin levels in their brains showed a marked decrease. It's illustrative, in a crude way, he says. Loss, anxiety, repeated rejection—"things we experience do cause neurochemical changes in the brain."

62   And so it is that the pharmacological effects of fluoxetine hydrochloride, properly administered, modify the chemistry of the neuronal synapse to cause the following physical occurrence every Sunday at a certain church in Indianapolis: A woman who used to be clinically depressed walks up to Ray Fuller and hugs his neck.

63 The most important question, the question I had come here to ask, I put to Molloy. After all, it was Molloy who started everything, 20 years ago.

64   How does it make you feel, I ask, to know that what you have done has helped people? To know that this molecule you invented has allowed me to live my life in a way I never thought possible?

There is an awkward pause.   65

"I am not a touchy-feely person," Molloy says uncomfortably, almost 66
sourly. We are sitting in his office, and he has turned his face slightly away
from me.

"I'm happy for you, okay?" He clearly wishes I was not there, asking this 67
sentimental, unscientific question.

"This puts me in a somewhat embarrassing position," Molloy says. He 68
glances at the public relations person for Eli Lilly who has accompanied me
to this interview. What comes out, finally, is so stunningly honest that I do not
know what to say, and so I say nothing.

"The company puts itself in the position of saying it's here to help people, 69
and I'm here saying I didn't do it for that. I just wanted to do it for the intellectual high.

"It looked," he says, "like scientific fun."   70

Reality is rarely what we imagine. Demons do not inhabit our bodies; the heart 71
is not the seat of human emotion; black bile does not make us sad. Great and
noble things do not always happen for great and noble reasons.

I can live with that. Happily ever after.   72

Questions for Discussion

1. How does Prozac affect the brain differently than previous antidepressants? Why
   does Prozac help to relieve people of depression?
2. According to the article, what are some of the social and ethical objections to using
   Prozac? How does Thompson respond to these objections to Prozac that have been
   raised?
3. How was the discovery of Prozac made? How do the scientists who developed the
   drug feel about its success? Why do you think Thompson entitled her article "The
   Wizard of Prozac"?
4. Why does the writer include an account of her struggles against depression? Why
   does she continue to use Prozac even after the doctors think that she no longer needs
   to use the drug? What is your opinion of her decision?
5. Do you think that it is ethical to help people to live happier and saner lives by altering the chemistry of their brains? Has this article encouraged you to think differently about the use of psychopharmacology? Why? In what ways?
6. How do you feel about the use of Prozac? What do you think will be the long-term
   impact of Prozac and similar types of medication on our public health care policy,
   on the mental health profession, and on our communities?

Ideas for Writing

1. Interview several counselors or psychologists in your college community about how
   frequently Prozac is prescribed for college students, and what kinds of problems it
   treats most effectively. Also discuss the negative effects of Prozac. Write a report of
   your findings for your class and/or for your campus paper.
2. Thompson acknowledges that she is afraid at times of giving up her "autonomy to
   the pharmaceutical industry," and sometimes fears Huxley's prediction in *Brave New
   World* where the people are cheered up by the government so that they can be controlled. Do you have objections to the use of Prozac because of its power to control

the mind along with the degree of subjectivity that is involved in prescribing it? Or do you think that Thompson makes a persuasive case for the continued use of Prozac?

3. Develop discussion question 6 into an essay.

When Beauty Is the Beast

Amanda Morgan

Amanda Morgan (b. 1975), a native Texan, remembers writing her first poem, "School Days," when she was four; writing is still the best way for her to develop self-understanding. Morgan is considering a double major in social science and creative writing, She realizes that her interest in writing about the beauty myth is rooted in her experiences as a child training for the ballet; even then being thin was a prerequisite to success that was enforced by competition. At college Morgan sees the destructive impact of the mass fitness and dieting hysteria on many women's self-esteem. In researching and writing this paper, Morgan hoped to create a source of information to "loosen the ties that paralyze women in a contemporary corset: the ideal of thinness."

Journal

Statistics suggest that more and more adolescents and college women are suffering from eating disorders. What do you think are the causes of this health problem? To what extent is the problem a community issue?

Headlines blare "Thin is in," and impossibly lean yet curvaceous models haunt commercials. They smile as if to say, "Go on a strict carrot diet, take 3 aerobics classes a day, and when you look like me . . . you'll be happy!" Unfortunately, most women will never be able to achieve the exclusive ideal that defines beauty in our society. Vegetables and stair master will only go so far; in the end, one's shape is more dependent upon genetics than self-control. Cultural standards of beauty promote body image ideals that are unachievable for most women, and thus detrimental to women's physical and psychological health.

2   All of the ways that a woman views her body, as beautiful, ugly, too fat, or too thin, combine to form her body image, which represents her perception of her physical appearance. Body image is an integral part of a woman's self-concept. The role of body image in the construction of self-confidence has significant implications, considering the importance of self-confidence in determining how people interact with others. Twenty-five to thirty-three percent of a person's sense of confidence is dependent upon body image (Lang 68). Since self-confidence often affects one's ability to communicate, express, and assert oneself, body image impacts all aspects of life from social relationships to occu-

pational success. The significance of body image extends far beyond what a woman eats and wears.

Another cause of eating disorders in women is the social assumption that a woman's unhappiness is trivial compared to other modern social problems. A woman who worries about her appearance is considered vain; in fact, many believe that a woman who diets has a personality flaw. I've long suspected that many men don't hold much respect for dieting, or women who are obsessed with their weight. My suspicions were confirmed once on a dinner date. Usually, I drink diet coke, and have for so long that regular sodas taste much too sweet. However, as I was ordering my dinner, some inner urge compelled me to order a regular coke. After we ordered, my date made a big deal about my drink choice. Explaining that he didn't like to see women drink "those horrible tasting" diet sodas, he offered his approval of what he perceived to be my lack of concern over my weight. My date's focus on what I decided to eat is reflective of a double standard in society that constantly feeds women messages to change their body, often through weight loss, while at the same time being unwilling to witness their struggle to maintain a slender body image or to even acknowledge the legitimacy of their struggle.

While one's appearance may not be crucial in the grand scheme of life, feelings that arise from a negative body image can have serious long-term consequences. Besides low self-esteem, low levels of confidence, and depression, negative body image takes its physical tolls. Feelings of fatness often result in what the American Psychiatric Association refers to as "pathological eating behavior" or disordered eating (Strauman 946). In extreme cases of dieting, women can become anorexic, an eating disorder characterized by self-starvation, or bulimic, an eating disorder characterized by frequent and compulsive binge eating followed by purging (Rodin, *Body Traps* 36). These syndromes aren't always treated with the same seriousness given to other public health threats, despite the prevalence of fatalities. However, eating disorders are real problems and must be recognized as such, for real people die because of them. Statistics suggest that more American women die of anorexia in a period of twelve months than the total number of people who died from AIDS, from the beginning of the epidemic to 1988 (Wolfe 182).

While most women don't suffer to the extreme of becoming anorexic or bulimic, chronic dieting to lose weight has become an unfortunate societal norm. Despite wide-range acceptance of dieting as the solution to body dissatisfaction, dieting has been shown to be ineffective in permanent weight reduction, for all but 1% of women. Kelly Brownell, a psychologist and weight loss expert at Yale University, points out that "if one defines successful [dieting] as reaching ideal body weight and maintaining it for five years, a person is more likely to recover from almost any form of cancer than from obesity" (Rodin, *Body Traps* 167). For the 72% of American women who diet and the ever increasing numbers of men, the quest to mold a better body, while not ending in anorexia or bulimia, often leads to increased unhappiness and increased obesity (Rodin, *Body Traps* 166). Besides being ineffectual, dieting has serious physiological effects, including a suppressed metabolic rate, broken-down muscle tissue (which further decreases the body's calorie burning capacity), increased ability to store food as fat, and increased desire for high-fat foods. Dieting upsets the body's natural chemistry, thus supporting the weight problem it is supposed to remedy (Brainin-Rodriguez 1).

6   Since diets are often hard to maintain, many women end up in a cycle of alternating periods of dieting and nondieting. This inconsistent way of eating further confuses the body's chemistry, increasing the ease of weight gain (through more efficient use of food) and decreasing the body's ability to lose weight. This "yo-yo" dieting and subsequent weight fluctuation has also been correlated with an increased risk for heart disease (Rodin, *Body Traps* 187). If a person desperately desires to lose weight, the most long-term and healthy solution lies in a change of life-styles, a permanent commitment to health, consisting of a balanced but not restrictive low-fat diet and moderate exercise. However, a person must overcome a negative body image and learn to love himself/herself at any weight. Due to widespread failure of dieting efforts and the associated health risks, alleviating body dissatisfaction might be more successful through an emphasis on changing one's attitude rather than changing one's body.

7   In our culture, the decision to diet arises more often in response to a negative body image than a desire to improve health (Myers and Biocca 112). Women diet to lose this weight that doesn't conform to the current beauty ideal, which praises a slim lower body. Most women store fat on their thighs, buttocks, and hips, areas which generally don't pose the risk of later health complications. In fact, this extra fatty tissue is natural and necessary for women's bodies to function properly. Fat is essential for menstruation, childbearing, nursing, and the production and storage of estrogen after menopause (Tavris 34). Many women diet to lose fat, when the fat itself doesn't put them at a medical risk.

8   Not only is dieting often the result of the psychological conflict that occurs when a person's actual body image doesn't compare favorably to her ideal body image, but is compounded with additional negative psychological effects as well, including stress, preoccupation with food, and depression (Tavris 35). Dieting is also seen by society as an indication or sign of an individual's self-control and will power. By correlating dieting with self-control, dieting takes on additional importance in a woman's identity, which can result in intense feelings of worthlessness and personal failure if the diet is broken. Women's "obsession" and dissatisfaction with their physiques have serious physical and psychological implications.

9   The fact that there are so many women afflicted by body dissatisfaction in America indicates that it is not just an individual, personal problem, but a societal issue derived from values in American or Western culture. Society must begin to recognize negative body image as a harmful disorder that deserves and requires treatment, rather than trivialize its significance by confusing it with vanity. Women are judging themselves against unrealistic standards of beauty presented through the media. "Every day women are flooded with por-

trayals of flawless models and actresses. Their beauty seems real and attainable and becomes the standard for attractiveness" (Lang 68). The standards of "beauty" that women strive to emulate are distorted and misleading. Magazine pictures, for example, have a hidden agenda; they manipulate women into believing that it is easy to look like the models when in fact models spend many hours with professional make-up artists and hair stylists before a shoot. Hundreds of pictures are taken from every angle, for each picture printed. Then the photo is airbrushed and sometimes literally cut with scissors to eliminate every minute flaw (Wolfe 83). The resulting faces and bodies that confront women are impossibly perfect; they only serve to lower women's self-esteem.

Fashion magazines play an intimate role in the lives of many women. I 10 read *Seventeen* magazine from the time I was eleven years old to the middle of my high school career. From the time I spent pouring over the images and articles, I learned the secrets of womanhood, such as what a woman should look like, how a woman should dress, and how a woman must look, dress, and behave if she wishes to be competitive in the Great Boyfriend Quest. While deeply engrossed in a magazine, I experienced a feeling comparable to identifying with the heroine of a novel. For a brief period of time I could mentally become that model, imagining what it must feel like to be so beautiful—a method of vicariously feeling desirable. Then, of course, the advertisements and articles unveiled the secrets to the models' beauty, providing hope to transform that beautiful, confident feeling from a fantasy to reality. I've since learned that you can't buy happiness in a mascara bottle. However, I have discovered that it is possible to purchase misery in the form of women's fashion magazines. Once I realized that they made me feel insufficient and undesirable, I quit reading them.

Not only are women comparing themselves to unrealistic ideals, they are 11 judging themselves through fun house mirrors, focusing on imagined and magnified imperfections. "A recent study showed that 95 percent of women think they are heavier than they really are—by an average of 25 percent" (Rodin, "The New Meaning of Thin" 226). Women's resulting body images are thus as hopelessly distorted as the images presented to them in the media. The media not only emphasize to a woman the differences between her body and the "ideal," but serve to broaden the gap in her mind, as she distorts her *actual* figure into perceived ugliness. A study measuring the effect of television advertising and programming on body image distortions in young women found that a woman's perception of her body shape can be altered by watching even 30 minutes of TV broadcasting (Myers and Biocca 108).

The media's gender bias in the promotion of thinness is well documented, 12 from television shows and their characters to magazine advertisements and articles, and might explain why women seem to be more vulnerable to body dissatisfaction than men. For example, 69.1% of female TV characters were rated thin compared to 17.5% of male characters, while only 5% of women characters were rated as heavy, compared to 25.5% of male characters (Tavris

32). While the media may not be the original or only promoters of this exaggerated standard of thinness for women, it is one of the most influential due to the popularity of television, movies, and magazines (Myers and Biocca 110).

13   Advertisers take advantage of women's need to appear beautiful. They specifically target and exploit women's feelings about their body image, successfully promoting a $33-billion-a-year diet industry, a $20-billion-a-year cosmetics industry, and a $300-million-a-year cosmetic surgery industry (Wolfe, 17). "Ads aimed at women work by lowering their self-esteem" (Wolfe 276). Ads make women feel like they must alter some aspect of themselves in order to be beautiful, and then present the magical remedy in the form of the advertised product. If ads didn't make women feel incomplete, women wouldn't have a need for the promoted product. Day in and day out, women are manipulated in ways that are ultimately disempowering and destructive, all in the name of money.

14   Media images become even more powerful as thinness comes to reflect more than mere aesthetic ideal; in today's culture thinness is a social virtue that reflects acceptable personality, behavioral, and life-style patterns. "For many, weight is a quick and concrete barometer by which to measure how well they are doing as women" (Rodin "The New Meaning of Thin," 224). Thinness has become a metaphor for success, and a status symbol associated with "the good life" (Myers and Biocca 111). Due to the perceived correlation between achievement and thinness, women in professions and higher education are especially vulnerable to the obsession with body weight and to eating disorders, which can arise from a negative body image (Tavris 32). For example, I met a young woman the summer before her freshman year at University of Michigan who has struggled against bulimia since junior high school. In her environment, bulimia seemed to be as communicable as the bubonic plague. She reported that the administrators of her New York City college preparatory school were forced to lock all women's bathrooms during the lunch hour to prevent women from vomiting their lunches.

15   The shape of a woman's body is perceived as a visible statement to the world of her success, assuming that a "good body" represents personality characteristics such as discipline and willpower that would lead to success in other areas of her life as well. By allowing thinness and weight control to represent self-control, we are assuming that body shape is more malleable than it actually is. There is a tendency to disregard the medical fact that the female body is genetically programmed to store fat (Rodin "The New Meaning of Thin" 224). The fat that is necessary for the proper functioning of a woman's body has become a symbol of an unwillingness to strive toward self-improvement. "Americans become convinced that weight reveals something desperately true about the person beneath the pounds" (Schwartz 5).

16   The female body is often seen as a symbol whose meaning evolves with the changing social standards. The beauty ideal by which we judge women is constantly in flux, from Twiggy's straight boyish figure, to the voluptuous curves of Marilyn Monroe. For any culture, at any specific time, beauty requires a definition. This unstable definition is written in response to the his-

torical and socio-economic realities of the era. During the years in which motherhood and domesticity are promoted, the beauty ideal leans toward voluptuous, full-breasted women. Conversely, during ages in which women have entered the work force or pursued educational opportunities, slender, strong, "boyish" figures are esteemed (Tavris 30). The current "hybrid" ideal, valuing full breasts, narrow hips, and a slim lower body, is a reflection of society's uncertainty with regard to the woman's role within society, requiring women to be both career- and family-oriented (Tavris 33).

America's willingness to "judge the book by the cover" and assume a correlation between personality characteristics and body shape is irrational, for the beauty ideal is neither timeless or universal. Images of ideal beauty are "wholly socially constructed" (Ussher 38). However, there does seem to be a recurring trend of a beauty ideal which rejects women's natural bodies, requiring barbaric, painful and often deforming and debilitating alterations. For example, wealthy Chinese women succumbed to "footbinding," which stunted foot growth, producing 3-inch stubs for feet. Unable to walk without assistance, women achieved this feminine ideal at the expense of excruciating pain and handicap (Ussher 33). Female circumcision is another example of an ideal that promotes the mutilation of women's bodies to fit into a standard of feminine and sexual attractiveness (Ussher 33). [17]

This barbarism in the name of beauty is also prevalent in Western culture and history. For instance, Victorian women wore corsets that forced their bodies into exaggerated hourglass shapes, sometimes crushing and damaging internal organs. Despite popular belief, modern day "liberated" women are not much better off than their Victorian sisters. Though the corset has been abandoned, women are still "forcing their bodies into exaggeratedly slim shapes, or increasingly, into exaggeratedly voluptuous shapes" to fit societal ideals of beauty and fashion (Tavris 36). Women diet, exercise excessively, and even seek a surgeon's knife to conform to modern, Western ideals of sexual appeal. All these varied cultural practices "share the violent subjugation of women in the name of feminine beauty and enhancement of sexual desirability, permissible because of the ideology which defines a woman's worth through her attractiveness to men" (Ussher 33). [18]

In the quest to overcome a negative body image, there are other aspects of one's life that are more malleable to permanent change than the actual flesh of one's physique. For instance a change in attitude may go a long way in contributing to the creation of a healthy body image. The body should be regarded in a respectful manner, and treated with equal respect by nourishing it with healthy food, moderate exercise, relaxation, and pleasure (Rodin, *Body Traps* 249). Developing strategies to avoid situations and people who contribute to feelings of personal negativism is also helpful. For example, if working out is painful and leaves one with feelings of inferiority because the "workout buddy" looks like spandex was created especially to display every perfect curve of her body, then one should find another activity to share with Ms. Spandex Queen (and another workout buddy!). [19]

In the struggle to forge a positive body image, it is also important to guard [20] against the careless acceptance of society's ideals as one's own. As long as women accept the external, narrow standards of beauty dictated by society, they will be subjected to feelings of failure and low self-esteem. Actress Rosanne Barr Arnold is a good example of a person who has chosen to accept her body, rather than strive to conform to external socially constructed standards that for her may be genetically unreachable. Arnold is not only a role model in terms of her positive individual decisions, but in her attempt to change society's narrowly defined ideals by publicly challenging widespread, common attitudes toward the stereotypes associated with obesity and the importance placed upon thinness.

21   Individuals need to recognize that a person's human value is in no way correlated with external, socially constructed concepts of "beauty." Women must learn to be content with their own unique and innate beauty, and abandon the endless struggle to be beautiful according to the culturally prescribed definition. Once women learn to find beauty by looking inward instead of out, they will be more likely to find confidence and success.

Works Cited

Brainin-Rodriguez, Laura. "Dieting and You." Joint Nutrition Education Program by Stanford University Food Service and Cowell's Health Promotion Program Information Sheet.

Lang, Susan. "Shape Up Your Body Image." *New Woman* March 1993: 68–70.

Myers, Philip, and Frank Biocca. "The Elastic Body Image: The Effect of Television Advertising and Programming on Body Image Distortions in Young Women." *Journal of Communication,* 42.3 (1992): 108–33.

Rodin, Dr. Judith. *Body Traps.* New York: William Morrow Company, 1992.

———. "The New Meaning of Thin." *Glamour Magazine* May 1992: 224–227.

Schwartz, Hillel. *Never Satisfied.* New York: The Free Press, 1986.

Strauman, Timothy J. "Self-Discrepancies and Vulnerability to Body Dissatisfaction and Disordered Eating." *Journal of Personality and Social Psychology* 61 (1991): 946–956.

Tavris, Carol. *The Mismeasure of Women.* New York: Simon & Schuster, 1992.

Ussher, Jane M. *The Psychology of the Female Body.* New York: Routledge, 1989.

Wolfe, Naomi. *The Beauty Myth.* New York: Anchor Books, Doubleday, 1991.

Questions for Discussion

1. State Morgan's thesis in your own words.
2. List several examples of media images that perpetuate the myth that beautiful women are more desirable. Do these beauty myths affect you?
3. According to Morgan, in what ways do cultural standards of beauty affect a society and individuals within a society? Could you develop Morgan's argument? Explain why you agree or disagree with her point of view.
4. How much power do you think the media have in influencing individuals and social trends? For example, how powerful is the beauty myth? Develop your responses with evidence from your own experiences or observations.
5. How has the media's portrayal of women's social roles changed in the twentieth century? What new types of media portrayals would you like to see developed?
6. Was the essay convincing? Do you have any suggestions for ways to strengthen the argument?

Ideas for Writing

1. Write a proposal that suggests methods that will help to release women from the trap of the beauty myth.
2. Write a short story or an essay that portrays an intelligent species (possibly on a different planet); consider the following: What is its standard of beauty? Through what standards is the concept of beauty spread in the species' society, and how does it affect the relationships between specific individuals in this community? Create characters and use your imagination.

The Way It's Supposed to Be

Carol Pogash

Carol Pogash, who began her career as a radio journalist for San Francisco's Public Broadcasting station, worked for many years as a reporter, columnist, and magazine writer for the *San Francisco Examiner.* Her articles have appeared in a number of publications that include *The New York Times,* the *Washington Post,* and *Working Woman.* She lives with her husband, food and wine writer Jim Wood, and their two children in the San Francisco Bay Area. Pogash's most recent book, *As Real As It Gets: The Life at a Hospital at the Center of the AIDS Epidemic* (1992), presents thirty-five portraits about life at San Francisco General Hospital, which is located in the center of the AIDS crisis in America. For over ten years the entire range of medical, social, ethical, and political issues raised by the epidemic have been worked through at this hospital. The selection that follows captures the political and human struggles that went on as dedicated nurses and a hospital administrator fought to establish a place for the patients dying of AIDS to live out the last days of their lives.

Journal

In what ways has your family and community of friends been affected by AIDS? Or if you have a friend who has AIDS or who has died from AIDS, write about how that experience affected you.

I'll be in room ten for a while," the nurse told the desk. She shut the door, put some soft music on the radio and did what she felt was needed.

This is where men in their prime and those not yet in it came to heal temporarily, and this was where they came to die. For Nurse Sue Kiely, the deaths of young men had become as ordinary as the morning paper. She never knew what her patients did, who their mothers were or where they grew up. Here, they were stripped of life's accoutrements.

In earlier visits, the patient in Room 10 had insisted on meticulous cleanliness. After a night of spiking fever, he'd asked to wash off the sweat, shampoo his hair and use deodorant, even though he was receiving oxygen.

4   Now he was dying. But for his moans, he showed no expression. He'd lost consciousness two days before. He seemed to drift in and out; mostly out.

5   Having seen so many men in this condition, Nurse Kiely knew how frightened her patients were of pain and of death. Sometimes she rubbed their chests, in the place below the neck where her own chest tightened when she was frightened. Sometimes she just wiped a brow and listened. She thought she knew what might soothe this patient.

6   "I really think you would like to be clean right now," she said, approaching the hospital bed. He did not respond. Filling an umber bucket with warm water, she swirled in some Keri bath oil, purchased from the special AIDS fund to which the public frequently donated. With a washcloth in her right hand she grasped the patient's thumb, then his index finger, washing each finger as if he were her only patient. From the bony fingers, she moved to his whole hand and his wrist and then his forearm and elbow with the warm, silky water. As she went, she massaged his muscles and she spoke softly to him. When she finished one limb, she patted it dry, covered it and moved on to another. And when she completed a side, she stuffed pillows up against the bed rail, rolled the patient on his side and tucked in clean sheets.

7   Here at the AIDS inpatient unit known as 5A (the ward is on the fifth floor of the imposing main hospital building) Dr. Day's views were all but irrelevant. All of the patients were HIV positive and some of the staff was as well. Yet Kiely occasionally sympathized with a portion of what Day said and she recognized the risk of performing orthopedic surgery was greater than that of most other jobs at the hospital. She knew that as an AIDS nurse she, too, was taking some risk. She'd kept her fears under wraps until Jane Doe stuck herself. After that, Kiely could no longer ignore the risks.

8   She wasn't sure if she gave the bed bath for herself or for her patient. But doing it suited her and the unit. "You feel like a little kid when you're sick. You want your momma. You want someone to hold your head. That's how people feel when they're sick. I wouldn't imagine it's any different when you're sick with AIDS or when you're dying."

9   When the national media arrived in San Francisco to do AIDS stories, they came to the inpatient AIDS unit at the General to illustrate how it was supposed to be. Although it had only twenty private rooms and sometimes only enough nurses to serve sixteen of them, the AIDS unit came to be known as the ultimate example of AIDS care in the world. The floor plan, the nursing station and the rooms looked no different from any other ward at the hospital. But the place seemed airy, with butter-yellow and white walls; it appeared lighter. Large windows looked out over the hills of Twin Peaks and the city's Mission District. The walls were decorated with patients' artwork. On one wall hung photographs of the nursing staff taken at the annual gay parade. And the unit's lounge had more amenities than others. Named the Elizabeth Taylor Lounge, after the star who has visited several times (insisting that there be no publicity), the lounge contained the piano she donated (on top of which sat a group photo of Taylor's wedding party), a ficus tree Taylor gave one year, other plants, a big-screen TV and a VCR.

Created in 1983 by Nurse Cliff Morrison, the AIDS unit was designed to 10
give humane care to patients who'd been denied it elsewhere in the hospital.
Ironically, Morrison had strongly opposed isolating AIDS patients. Appointed
AIDS coordinator that same year, he felt one of his duties was to prevent the
hospital from designating an AIDS ward. He figured he had enough influence
to halt it and if he couldn't, as a gay man, he could galvanize the gay community to stop it. When the director of nursing broached the subject of opening a separate unit, Morrison balked but agreed to consider it.

Each day, as he visited AIDS patients throughout the hospital, he was 11
appalled by the treatment they received. He found trays of dried and rotting
food piled in corners, floors unwashed and unswept and wastebaskets brim-
ming over. Feverish young men with nightsweats were unable to find nurses
to change their soaked sheets or to bring them Tylenol. When bed linens were
removed, they were thrown out. Frightened staff were posting signs on
patients' doors—CONTAMINATED AREA. Many nurses wore gloves whenever
they entered the room. One patient confided, "You don't know what it's like
to only be touched by rubber."

The first member of his large, poor, Catholic family to finish high school 12
and graduate from college, Morrison was raised by his mother, who worked
in a hospital laundry. While openly gay, Morrison maintained close ties to his
church.

One day, the deaf mother of a dying AIDS patient signed to one of the 13
nurses that she wanted her son to have his last rites. The hospital priest
arrived, observed the gowns, masks and gloves stationed outside the patient's
room, and remarked, "He's got that gay disease, doesn't he?

"I'm sorry. I can't give him last rites," the priest said. "He brought it on 14
himself."

The patient's nurse, Morrison and other Catholic nurses, who happened 15
to be nearby, performed the last rites.

Perhaps more than any other, that incident led Morrison to believe that 16
AIDS patients might need their own unit and their own staff.

He was not alone in his views. One of Volberding's patients with Kaposi's 17
sarcoma shared a room with one of the doctor's cancer patients, an older, black
southerner, suffering from dementia. As if the KS patient weren't suffering
enough, the older patient lectured him, saying he had sinned, that he had it
coming, that he was suffering the curse of Job with pustules on the skin. The
diatribe convinced Volberding that separating AIDS patients from the rest of
the hospital population could be helpful.

When he discussed the plan with AIDS doctors in New York City that 18
spring, they thought the concept was crazy. Nurses wouldn't want to work
there. The house staff would try to avoid it. They warned him that he would
be creating a unit for lepers.

Nurse Morrison, who teamed up with Volberding on the idea, went to the 19
Shanti Project and to South of Market leather bars in search of patrons to sup-
port the idea. Morrison, like Volberding, had natural political instincts. Yet
Morrison had no ambition—which worked to his advantage. He knew that a

lot of men in the gay community opposed the idea of an AIDS ward, which sounded a lot like quarantine. He also knew that some of the hospital administrators, department heads and his peers were skeptical of it.

20 Creating an AIDS ward would violate nearly every nursing concept Morrison had been taught in school. He knew what he was doing was a risk. He also knew it was right. At thirty, he didn't really care who opposed the concept or what they thought. If it didn't work, he'd be unemployed and could always start over again.

21 It seemed surprising that a hospital, especially a teaching hospital, would give the authority to create such a controversial ward to a nurse. Morrison thought he understood why. Enough people agreed with him that something had to be done, but no one wanted to take the responsibility for it. They were willing to let him do it, he said, "mainly because they thought we wouldn't be able to accomplish anything."

22 Every day for three months, he rounded up the AIDS patients well enough to leave their beds, gingerly lowering them into wheelchairs, and pushed them to an empty ward on the fifth floor of the main hospital that would become the inpatient AIDS unit. Together, the dying men and the gay nurse designed the new facility.

23 When Morrison inquired, "What bothers you most about us?" the AIDS patients invariably responded, "Your arrogance. Your egos. You don't listen to us. You never approach us as humans."

24 Morrison determined that AIDS patients staying at the hospital would be taught about their disease and would make many of their own medical decisions, just as was being done in Ward 86, the AIDS outpatient unit. Everything in Morrison's unit was designed with the patients' needs, not that of the staff, in mind. Visitors were allowed to come any time. Patients were encouraged to bring things from home, to add warmth to institutional rooms. When early patients brought in crystal, wine, china, linen and an occasional candelabra, the AIDS unit earned an unfair reputation for snobbery. But what Morrison was doing helped turn the entire General around. Both destitute and well-off AIDS patients wanted to come to the county hospital.

25 One AIDS patient, unable to speak because he was on a ventilator, was visited by his mother, whom he hadn't had contact with in years. She stood in the doorway, arms outstretched with palms wrapped around either door molding and announced, "I'm in control here." To her son's lover she declared, "I don't want you in this room. That's how he got it. I don't want any of those homosexual doctors or nurses in this room. I am legally in charge of him. I will decide who comes into this room!"

26 After that, Morrison widened the definition of family. If he took his policy through committee, he suspected it would have been debated for months, maybe even years. He simply declared that henceforth AIDS patients would determine who their families were. Once the new family policy was publicized and praised, Morrison knew that the hospital administration wouldn't be likely to change it.

Another time, Morrison asked an AIDS patient, "Is there anything I can 27 do for you?"

"What I want you to do you won't be able to do," the patient responded. 28 "I want you to get in bed and hold me."

Morrison did.   29

The patient's regular nurse walked in, saw the AIDS nurse in bed, hug- 30 ging the patient, and in shock, walked out. Various nurses complained about Morrison's unprofessional behavior. But his supervising nurse never objected. (Morrison had a protective shield with his powerful ally, San Francisco health director Dr. Mervyn Silverman. Silverman told the hospital to give Morrison anything he needed and he told Morrison that if he had any difficulty, just call. Morrison used the threat of calling Silverman sparingly. But many people went along with the nurse, knowing of his closely held clout.)

Many of the early patients were without family or a steady lover, and 31 many died longing for human contact. When he formed the unit, Morrison worked against the nursing philosophy of distancing oneself from patients. He told his nurses to hold their patients' hands, to sit on their beds. He didn't expect them to lie down with everyone, but he wanted the nurses to know they had permission to do it and to hug a dying man if he needed to be hugged. He encouraged the nurses to cry. Tears, he said, were a sign of their strength and humanity.

Only nurses who volunteered for the unit were considered. It turned out 32 that about half of the nurses were gay. Almost all, Morrison said with pride, were "troublemakers." Giving the nurses autonomy many of them hadn't sought, Morrison refused to name himself head nurse, preferring to be the coordinator. He insisted they work out their own schedules and settle problems among themselves. He served less as an authority figure and more as a role model. Because his AIDS unit was seen as such a risky concept, no one in the hospital was hovering over him. The unit was without a medical director for its first few years.

In many ways, AIDS is a nursing disease. Doctors couldn't cure AIDS 33 patients, although they could control one opportunistic infection after another. In short order, the AIDS nurses became far more knowledgeable about the disease's many manifestations than were the medical students, interns and residents rotating through. An AIDS nurse might be seeing his seven-hundredth case of PCP while for a medical student, it might be his first.

San Franciscans regularly delivered gifts to the unit, which was known 34 citywide as 5A. The San Francisco Tavern Guild, an organization of gay bar owners, contributed goody bags of toothbrush, toothpaste, body lotion, hairbrush, fleece-lined slippers and teddy bear to each AIDS patient. A refrigerator and VCRs were also donated. Smiling, camp Rita Rockett—cheerleader, chef, cancan and tap dancer and full-time altruist—cooked Sunday-night dinners, delivering them in her racy, mini black-and-white waitress uniform. Once a week "the cookie man" dropped by with shortbread cookies and pumpkin bread. "Some day," he told the nurses, "I may come down with AIDS. I want you to remember me." Just Desserts, a San Francisco-based baking company that uses only natural ingredients, brought cakes and other sweets daily. And Mrs. Fields sent over so many leftovers that it was rumored the bakers were purposely turning out dozens of extra chocolate-chip cookies every day.

35 In the early months there had been so much food that Morrison often invited other units to the daily buffet. As homophobic as some of the nurses and doctors were, as terrified of AIDS as they might have been, they nevertheless enjoyed the fruit salads, turkeys and cookies in the AIDS unit. Seizing on the opportunity, Morrison used the food to entertain and ensnare people from whom he sought cooperation. In the beginning, nobody at the hospital was offering much more than skepticism. Morrison begged, bartered, coerced and outsmarted administrators. When he sought the help of Dr. Sande, director of medicine at the hospital, Morrison knew he could make Sande's life easier, and that if the inpatient AIDS unit worked, he could make Sande look good. "I let him take the credit," Morrison said. "It was a good bargain."

36 When Morrison wanted workers from the Shanti Project, where he was a volunteer, to help patients with their emotions or with physical problems, he called and suggested that Shanti propose it to the hospital administration. If the suggestion had come from him, Morrison felt certain it would have been vetoed. Following his suggestion, Shanti's leadership proposed placing its volunteers in the AIDS unit. When hospital officials consulted Morrison, he endorsed the Shanti proposal. Shanti workers became an integral part of AIDS care at the hospital. When housekeeping refused to mop up the unit, Morrison found money to offer the department two new job slots specifically for the AIDS inpatient unit. When dietary workers objected to bringing food to AIDS patients, Morrison, along with others, taught them what little was known about the disease, a course that had to be repeated over and over again as new employees were hired.

37 Morrison never sensed he was developing a model that would be replicated wherever good AIDS care is given. He wasn't even sure what the public reaction would be to the first AIDS unit anywhere until the media began coming by to do stories. The favorable pieces overcame any criticism of the unit. Morrison was impressed with how fast doubting administrators and politicians changed their minds, all making publicized pilgrimages to the AIDS unit to have their pictures taken there.

38 At times Morrison felt a nagging sense of guilt. He wondered how he could feel good when all around him there was so much sadness and death. Knowing he was making patients' lives better, seeing them live longer, he felt a sense of accomplishment.

39 The leper colony many feared constructing, never materialized. The unit came to be seen worldwide as the model of care. Morrison eventually was promoted to director of medical nursing, a position he thought he was given because he'd become too powerful in AIDS work. Nevertheless, he retained his position as AIDS coordinator. Weary of fighting for every little concession, assured the unit would survive, he left the General in 1986.

40 Over the years, doctors, nurses, politicians and celebrities have continued

to flock to 5A. When she was still mayor, the tidy Dianne Feinstein was escorted to the new unit by Volberding. The two passed through the underground tunnels of the hospital, where they bumped into the hospital administrator and city health director Silverman. Just then, Feinstein spotted a pile of dust-covered vomit on the floor of the tunnel. She was told it would be cleaned up immediately. When she boarded the elevator, Feinstein winced at the graffiti on its walls. That, too, she was assured, would be taken care of pronto. Just as she reached the nursing station of the AIDS unit a wall behind her burst and a blast of steaming hot water shot across the floor like water from a hydrant on a hot summer's day. A pipe had broken. With sheets grabbed from the linen closet, janitors scurried around the mayor, soaking up the flood. Since then, celebrity visits have been smoother. Not long ago, Mother Teresa came at the request of former Mayor Agnos. She had showed up at his home one night—while he was out buying milk for his kids—to ask the mayor for an unused fire station for her soup kitchen. She took him to see the property and, in exchange, he took her to 5A to see the patients. After his advance people called to arrange for a minority patient to meet with him, Jesse Jackson came through the unit. Neither of the black patients on the unit had wanted to welcome him, but a Central American man, who'd not been out of bed in days, happily rose to greet Jackson.

The outpouring of love mingled with death. In a bathroom on 5A, some- 41 one had written DENIAL IS TERROR MANAGEMENT. And among the racks of information that line the front wall of the unit are brochures about funerals and cremations.

Like other nurses on 5A, Kiely grew used to sickness and death. It satu- 42 rated her work and it was there when she went home to the Castro district, where delivery trucks dropped off tanks of oxygen and ambulances regularly raced to the neighborhood. Surviving meant that sometimes Kiely went numb. "You can't get a patient's IV line in," she said, "when you're sobbing all the time."

Struggling to maintain her idealism, sometimes, just sometimes, her fer- 43 vor wavered. "I haven't cured anybody yet," she said, "and that's tough."

Sometimes she felt like a stand-up comic. She couldn't be on all the time. 44 She couldn't perform to her fullest twelve hours of every working day without letup. On those days when she couldn't stand the suffering, instead of being Kiely, the loving nurse, she was just a good nurse.

In the early years, the unit experienced almost no turnover of its nursing 45 staff. Back then, many patients came for therapy while complaining of boredom. Night nurses played checkers with their patients. But recent AIDS therapies allow patients to stay at home longer. Today, 5A patients are closer to death, and the nurses who care for them sometimes try to help them fall asleep when they're afraid they may not wake. Frequently nurses have to place bodies in zippered shrouds before having their morning coffee.

Before coming to 5A, one young nurse had worked in Calcutta for a cou- 46 ple of months, assisting Mother Teresa. She thought she understood death. "But I really didn't understand the scope of the AIDS virus: how young they were, how much they hurt, how little can be done for them, how short their life spans were, how quickly it came on, how devastating it was."

47 She sometimes found it analogous to the shock of war, and she thought most people didn't experience the bundle of emotions she felt until they reached old age.

48 The hardest part was that "people are suffering and they want to live," she said. "They're full of life and they're dying." Helplessly she watched as an artist lost his sight, a musician his hearing or someone who was independent his ability to walk. She might work hard to help a patient walk out of 5A, only to see him return six months later to die.

49 Like the other nurses on the unit, she tried to allow her patients to die with dignity, which meant without a lot of futile medical intervention. She just wanted to help the patient reconcile his life and die in peace. She did it by listening, and sometimes by calling in a Shanti worker to help, and sometimes just by holding on. In her melodic voice she said, "All a person needs sometimes is a touch or a word or a look. It's probably what they were looking for their whole lives anyway."

50 AIDS hadn't crushed her philosophy. She still believed that for every problem there must be a solution. She failed to understand why curing AIDS should take so long. She understood the medical reasons. Still, she said, "I want these people to get cured. I don't care why they're dying. I just don't want them to die anymore."

51 Although nursing at 5A is considered the pinnacle of the profession, some nurses have begun to leave. Some have gone back to school, had babies or decided to work elsewhere. A few gay nurses have become ill with AIDS. The pressure, already there, has increased, as nurses are caring for fewer middle-class gay patients.

52 "People are on this ward to take care of AIDS patients," said one of the unit's supernurses. "But really, we're here to take care of gay AIDS patients." (Many other 5A nurses didn't feel the way she did. Nurse Alise Martinez, for example, came not because the patients were gay but because theirs was a new disease and because she wanted to care for people others were afraid to care for.) She was drawn to 5A because she knew she was needed there. Patients appreciated her.

53 As AIDS spread into the drug-using population, the 5A nurses found themselves caring for patients whose last home was a sidewalk. Some were angry at everyone, including the selfless nurses. When she described the two groups, generalizing to make her point, the supernurse thought about the appreciative, well-informed gay patients and the extreme IV drug-using ones who sometimes told her, "Fuck you. I'm not going to do anything you tell me to do, bitch." Some of them have tried to stuff their hands down narrow-necked Sharps boxes to retrieve used needles. Others have demanded more pain medications. Nurses were having to call hospital security more often.

54 Once, when the supernurse went to care for a drug addict AIDS patient, his sixteen-year-old-daughter confronted her: " 'What the fuck are you doing for my father?' " Times like that, she had to remind herself why she was there.

She told the daughter she understood how frightening it must be for her to see her father so ill.

Despite the loving dispositions of the AIDS nurses, with some of the IV 55 drug-using population, they found they could no longer be unconditionally caring. Having grown used to patients they could have fun with and whose psychic pain they could lessen, they sometimes felt uncomfortable with some of the new population. They wanted it to be the way it had been.

As chronic rescuers, they felt guilty disliking some of these difficult 56 patients. Many of the IV drug-using patients were good patients. But when the cantankerous, sometimes treacherous ones were hostile or threatening, the nurses wanted to retreat. "We do what we need to do," a nurse said, "but it isn't sitting on the bed holding a hand."

Being a nurse at 5A was Tony Lobb's way of being there for his commu- 57 nity. He'd grown up in rural Kentucky with an inborn sense of patriotism. If there'd been a war, Tony would have enlisted. But when he got to 5A, "it wasn't my community or what I perceived to be my community." Sometimes the IV drug-using population resented Lobb's Truman Capote-esque manner-isms, his calling patients "honey." While most patients assigned to 5A and their friends were pleased to get a room there, some drug-using patients didn't want to be associated with the unit. One screaming man, clutching his fake Luis Vuitton purse as he was being wheeled on a gurney into 5A at 1:30 A.M., pulled himself up long enough to holler in his falsetto voice: "I be's a bisex-ual! I be's a bisexual!"—presumably, a cut above a gay.

Nurse Lobb longed for what he thought of as the stereotypical AIDS 58 patient: sweet, handsome, knowledgeable and appreciative. Sometimes even when he did care for such patients, he found the work upsetting. Too often, they were tangled in tubes with no hope of living very long and believed they were at the hospital for the big fix. In time, Lobb came to feel he was presid-ing over death.

Having been tested for HIV, he knew he was negative. He felt survivor's 59 guilt and he felt as if he were being left behind. That he could do so little gnawed at him. "What do I say to these people when they're reaching out, wanting hope and wanting a cure? And I know I can get them through part of it. I can't do anything in the long run. It's so hard. It's so hard to go in every day."

In some ways, working at 5A was anathema to nursing. "The things I do 60 as a nurse are to keep people alive," he said.

For Nurse Kiely, 5A was nursing the way it was supposed to be. But she 61 knew that if she weren't watchful, her profession could bleed her dry. More and more, she found herself working her three-day, twelve-hour shifts, going home, pouring herself into a hot bath and healing for four days so she could return to work. Days off she had to close up the psychic wounds of patients who'd affected her. At a café, she'd sip coffee but not talk to other people. The longer Kiely worked at 5A, the weaker were her defenses.

She used to call her patients her "babies." Men who might have been 62 friends outside the hospital became her friends in the ward. Their deaths hurt her more than those of the others. Over two months, a cluster of her favorite patients died, leaving Kiely feeling like a raw nerve rubbed up against a wire brush.

63   Hating funerals, Kiely rarely went to one. But one Sunday, when she tagged along with a friend visiting a dying man with AIDS, the sick man died. As were his wishes, his friends gathered around his body to reminisce. She hadn't allowed herself to mourn until then. She cried for the friend of a friend who'd just died. And she cried for all the people she'd never shed tears for. "All these people who died with me."

Questions for Discussion

1. The inpatient AIDS unit at the San Francisco General Hospital is known "as the ultimate example of AIDS care in the world." Why is it such an exemplary unit? How were the patients dying of AIDS treated at the hospital before the unit was established?

2. Pogash gives family history and background information on Cliff Morrison, who was the key figure in getting the AIDS unit established at the hospital. How does this information help you to understand his motivation and courage to fight in the struggle to establish the unit? What examples in the article reflect that Morrison is a shrewd politician and a competent administrator?

3. What do the AIDS patients dislike most about the treatment they are given? How does Morrison create an atmosphere in the ward that makes the patients as comfortable as possible? Why and how does Morrison widen the definition of family?

4. How did Morrison select nurses for the unit? In what ways does his philosophy of nursing and the nurses who worked on this unit reflect a rebellion against traditional nursing conduct? Pogash claims, "AIDS is a nursing disease." Does this article and your knowledge of the treatment for AIDS patients support her claim? Explain your answer.

5. How does the increase in drug users in unit 5A make the job of the nurses even more difficult? The essay begins with a portrait of Nurse Kiely, who is totally devoted to her patients, and ends with her at the funeral of an AIDS patient. How has Nurse Kiely changed over the years that she has worked in the AIDS unit?

Ideas for Writing

1. Write an essay that explores the insights you developed through reading and reflecting on this selection about the nursing profession and the treatment of AIDS patients. Were any of your preconceptions or assumptions about nurses and AIDS patients changed?

2. Write an essay that explores and reflects on your feelings about AIDS. You can do some more reading on the subject to clarify your position on a particular issue related to AIDS—for example, the national funding for AIDS research, the effects of AIDS on the dying person's family, the effects of AIDS on health care policy planning, health care workers' safety rights, or education about AIDS in the schools and the community.

3. If you are interested, volunteer to work at a nonprofit agency in your community that helps people with AIDS and their families. Write for the agency or write a reflection on your volunteer experience.

Community Service Writing Student Project: *Surviving Newsletter*

Melinda Lorensen and Jenson Wong

The *Surviving Newsletter* is produced by the Patient Resource Center at the Stanford University Hospital. The publication is written and produced by cancer patients as part of their recovery process. This organization has provided students with a range of learning and writing experiences. Students have been responsible for helping to select materials from the *Surviving Newsletter* that will be included in a book, have written for the newsletter, and have attended newsletter meetings and group sessions for cancer survivors. The two pieces that follow were published in the *Surviving Newsletter*. The first, by Melinda Lorensen, is a poem that presents two points of view about her grandmother's death. Jenson Wong's article is speculative as he tries to imagine how he would feel if he were diagnosed with cancer.

Journal

Write about your feelings when you learned that someone you knew had a chronic or terminal illness.

TWO POEMS BY MELINDA LORENSON

Last year, my grandmother died of a cancer that had started in her colon. I have a poem that I wrote at that time and one that I wrote recently. I hope readers who have lost friends or relatives to cancer will recognize that others have experienced such a loss. I also hope that readers with cancer will see that their cancer can cause relatives to learn just a little bit more about their relationships, and a lot more about their lives from your example.

Granddad is here
Not
grandmother and granddad
not Ruth and Al
5 just
granddad

When dad said
she's gone
I was fine:
10 Cancer
we were all
prepared.

For today
and tomorrow too,
I have more than
mere
5 memories
of my grandmother.

I remember our
sunny
healthy
10 days on our sailboat
before
cancer.

Michele called
suddenly
15 preparation pointless
I cried:
she was
gone.

Tuesday night
20 picking out cello pieces
Playing each song through
judging
what was pleasant enough to play
at a funeral.

25 The family gathered for the funeral.

My cousin's young eyes
vibrant
But her tears only
streamed sorrow for
30 her grandmother's
death.

I was shunted to a balcony
transcending
the church
35 me and my cello
to remember
my grandmother.

But
I learn from
15 frigid
emotional
hospital days:
she was the one who smiled

While the cancer
20 controlled
and stole
her body
her soul will always be
her own.

25 She did not really leave.

Her sturdy sailboat
sailed
beyond
our horizon:
30 Indeed
she still watches over me.

Now
I sail
onward
35 forward
toward
my own horizon.

"SCENES FROM THE LIFE OF A CANCER PATIENT" BY JENSON WONG

"Aaaaaaa!! Why me?!!" I screamed into my pillow. My life, my experiences, all filed through my head like postcards blown into the whirlwinds of time. What am I supposed to do now? Where do I go? The questions ended abruptly . . . with no answers. They gave way to tears—not of sadness or anger, but confusion and frustration.

2   Face down in a pillow, my thoughts drifted towards my doctor's office. . . . I tried turning myself around, but instead of pushing off the mattress, all I could grasp was air. Suddenly, I realized that I was standing right next to the receptionist's desk in my doctor's office. Certainly I wasn't caught inside of a memory; it was today's date, the 17th of April, (it said so on the desk calendar). I knew immediately something strange was about to happen. I was so disoriented by my apparent teleportation that I really didn't feel confident that I could walk the three blocks back to the hospital and into my room. Besides, I was still wearing my hospital gown!

Looking puzzledly at the nurse at her desk, I asked tentatively, "Miss, how ₃ did I get here?" I was speaking to her directly. She couldn't have been more than five feet away. She didn't look up from her desk. "Hello? Nurse?" I scratched my head, and suddenly, I noticed a doddering old gentleman standing next to me.

"She can't hear you, you know," he said somewhat matter-of-factly. He ₄ had something of a grandfatherly look to him. He wore a brown suit, complete with vest and bow-tie, and topped off his costume with a derby and cane. His hair was mostly covered by the derby, but what stuck out had the color of chalk. The creases of his old age crisscrossed his face, which sagged with the wisdom that emanated from within. Out of this nest of wrinkles came two beady eyes, in which I noticed the fire of his ticking mind. The bushy mustache that lazily cloaked his upper lip completed the picture. Evidently, this guy heard me just fine. "The name's Jules. I understand that you are somewhat confused about why you are here."

At the time, the whole scene reminded me of Dickens, although I wasn't ₅ sure why. I opened my mouth to ask a question, but he interrupted before I could utter the first word.

"Yes, I know, you're supposed to be in your room in bed. You are . . . but ₆ you're here with me too," he explained.

I puzzled over that for a moment, and decided that it still wasn't an ade- ₇ quate explanation. "Am I . . . dead?" I ventured.

"No, not yet anyway," said Jules, calmly. He had anticipated all the rest ₈ of my questions, and began answering them one by one. As we watched patient after patient enter and leave the waiting area, he explained that he was a messenger, though he could not explain from where. We were here to observe the goings on in the world, from outside my body. The doctor's office was only the beginning.

After we talked for a while, he got up from the chair, and seemed to glide ₉ effortlessly to the nurse's desk. I wondered what the purpose of the cane was. My question was answered when he waved the cane, and out of the filing cabinet behind her desk, my file came out and laid itself open on the desk. He turned the pages with another wave of the cane, and revealed the doctor's notes from my visit last week. My eyes seemed to jump from line to line of his notes. "Symptoms: Swollen lymph nodes, general discomfort. . . . Tests: Abnormal WBC count." The word "Leukemia" stood out above the rest of the doctor's handwriting in bold letters.

"Why are we doing this? Why did you pull my file?" I looked on him with ₁₀ anguish.

"This is the truth—the cold hard facts. The doctor has written down what ₁₁ he knows is wrong with you. It's not the time to give up on your life. It is a time to reflect on your life and those around you. It's a question of priorities."

His last words seemed to fade, and moments later my vision failed me. As ₁₂ if I were moving the rabbit ears to tune my TV into a distant station, the picture came back. I was back home. My mother and sister were preparing dinner. There was an air of melancholy and they seemed tired. I noticed Jules standing next to me. They called father to the table and sat down to eat at the table with one place missing. The usual lively conversation was absent from dinner. They ate slowly, periodically looking up, perhaps expecting to see me there eating with them. My sister picked at her food; it all looked unappetizing.

13   I felt bad watching them suffer like that.

14   "Your family suffers with you greatly. Your leukemia is not just your disease, it's theirs too. They love you. I'm sure you are aware of that. Your fight for survival is the same as theirs. Your family needs you as much as you need them. Look to them for support, but you need to have your own strength to defeat the disease in you."

15   "I want to tell them how much I miss them," I said. Tears seemed to melt the scene into a patchwork of color.

16   "There's no time for any of that" he declared, and the scene faded back into the waiting area in front of the records desk. My best friend Alex was there, sitting in one of the seats. He was waiting for Gloria and Irene to come visit me—I guess he had called me earlier that day. He was looking around at the paintings that lined the walls. Apparently, he didn't want to be there at all.

17   "Look at how he's just sitting there! He looks like he wants to leave. I'm definitely not trying to hold him here. Geez!!"

18   "He's thinking about you. He's thinking about how it must be to stay in the hospital and undergo chemotherapy. It's not that he doesn't want to be here. He wants for you not to be here."

19   I looked down at my toes. I felt ashamed of the feelings I experienced just moments ago. The emotions were just too much for me. I didn't know what to feel at all. I was numb to it all. It brought me back to where I started. Why me?

20   "It's not up to you to give reasons for everything that happens to you. That's up to the Top Banana. You are an example to those you love. What you *can* control is your will to fight this scourge. It's all up to you. If you give up, all your friends and family can do is hope. If you fight, you have their strength behind you."

21   Jules' words trailed off into the distance just as they had before, but this time when the room faded, I opened my eyes. The nurse was standing next to my bed.

22   "Your friends are here to see you. . . ."

Questions for Discussion

1. Melinda and Jenson wrote their articles for patients and families of patients who had cancer. How do you think this audience affected their writing process and their attitude toward their topic?
2. Why do you think Melinda wrote poems instead of an essay?
3. Why do you think Jenson wrote a story instead of an essay?
4. What evidence do you see in the texts that the students were aware of their audience?

Ideas for Writing

1. Develop your journal into a poem or story.
2. Volunteer to write an article for a health support group on your campus. Or inform yourself about a health or fitness issue that is of interest to you. Write an essay for your class that shares what you have learned.

CHAPTER WRITING PROJECTS

1. Write an essay that explores the concept of community health as it is introduced by David Smith and Bill Moyers in the opening selection of this chapter. You will need to do library research to develop your understanding of this concept.
2. A number of the writers in this chapter have discussed nontraditional medicine. Write a paper that is focused on a definition of nontraditional medicine. Consider the historical and cultural precedents for this approach to medicine that is currently growing more popular and respectable.
3. New national health policies have been passed since the production of this text. Do some research into recent legislation and its effects on health policy. As you compose your paper, explore the ways that this health policy helps to serve and protect a wide range of people in your community.
4. Write a research paper on the community resources available for people in your neighborhood who have a particular health concern that interests you. It could be an issue presented in this chapter or one that was not covered but is of social concern, such as exercise to combat job-related stress, nutritional standards, fertility issues, or mental health and poverty.
5. Write a paper that includes library and/or field research on the causes and effects of one of the health issues explored in this chapter, such as teen pregnancies, AIDS, abortion, nontraditional medicine, alcoholism, aid for the disabled, helping the terminally ill and their families. Consider the causes and effects through the perspective of the individual as a member of a health community.
6. As this chapter suggests, a group that is focused on a particular health issue can help individuals to heal. Write an essay that discusses what you have learned from the readings in this chapter about how groups help people to recover and lead stable and productive lives. Refer to particular essays as you develop your point of view. What do these groups or mini communities have in common? You can do some library research or interviews to support your point of view.
7. Write a review of a recent book or film about a health issue. For film choices we suggest *Awakenings, Passion Fish, And the Band Played On, Whose Life Is This Anyway?, Lorenzo's Oil,* or *Philadelphia.* Present the review to your class. Consider rewriting the review for a local or campus paper or a health library.

8. Attend a group for teenage mothers to learn more about the struggles and conflicts that these young women face trying to finish high school, work, and raise a child. Write an essay based on your experience with the group. Propose solutions to the problems these young mothers and their children must overcome. Point out positive ways that the community can provide support for these young mothers.

9. Choose an addictive form of behavior that you would like to understand better. After doing some research in the library on your topic, consider visiting a local treatment clinic that helps people to get over their addictive form of behavior to speak with some of the health professionals or their clients. Write an essay that discusses what you have learned from your library and field research.

10. Do some library research into the relationship between stress and illness. Also try to visit a health clinic in your community. Interview some of the social workers and doctors at the clinic to gather more information on the relationship between stress and illness. Then write an essay for your class giving them advice on ways to become more healthy and less "stressed out."

11. Interview individuals in your community who have experienced the grieving process of many families through their work—perhaps a gerontologist, a hospice nurse, a priest, a rabbi, or a doctor. Before doing your interview, do some research into the backgrounds of those you will be interviewing and into the issues that concern you. Ask about ways that a community can be a crucial support for families facing loss. Then write a paper based on your research and interviews; share it with your class. After discussing your paper with your class, rewrite it for a local or campus paper or for an organization in your community that helps families who are facing the terminal illness of one of their members.

12. Write an essay on the policy issues that you consider to be the most significant in the debate over the medical ethics of life support and/or euthanasia.

CHAPTER 6

Nature and Community

To look upon that landscape in the early morning, with the sun at your back, is to lose the sense of proportion. Your imagination comes to life, and this, you think, is where Creation began.
—N. Scott Momaday, "The Way to Rainy Mountain"

As long as civilization as a whole, with its vast technological power, continues to follow a pattern of thinking that encourages the domination and exploitation of the natural world for short term gains, this juggernaut will continue to devastate the earth no matter what any of us does.
—Al Gore, *Earth in the Balance*

How often do you take time away from your busy schedule to spend a few hours, a day, or even longer, alone with nature? When do you feel closest to the natural world? We can be reminded of who we are through staying in touch with nature's cycles; the natural world can nurture and heal us. In fact, we can think of the natural world as being an extension of our human community. For centuries, philosophers and naturalists have pointed to the relationships between the laws that govern our social order and the natural rhythms of animals, plants, the movement of the stars, and the ecological balance of the earth.

We share the earth. The land, the rivers, the oceans, the mountains, and the skies: all are our guides. Nature helps to shape our destinies with its creative and sometimes destructive powers that can be beyond the control of our human intelligence. While we cannot predict or subdue all of the natural forces of creation and destruction, we can try to respect and channel the powers of nature that provide energy and sustenance for our lives. Each of the writers included in this chapter suggests a unique perspective on the ways that individuals can respect our natural community.

Annie Dillard captures the frightening, mysterious, and intensely compelling power of the natural world in the chapter's first selection, "Total Eclipse." Dillard takes her readers back to the place where she witnessed a total eclipse, hoping to discern more about what she learned about the meaning of human existence when the sun disappeared: "There was no world. We were the world's dead people rotating and orbiting around and around, embedded in the planet's crust, while the earth rolled down. Our minds were light-years distant, forgetful of almost everything."

Nature is also represented as an eternal and creative force in the next selection, N. Scott Momaday's "The Way to Rainy Mountain." Momaday's journey to his grandmother's grave on Rainy Mountain helps him to remember his connection with his ancestors, his culture, his own creativity, and his spiritual connection to the creation of the world: "To look upon that landscape in the early morning, with the sun at your back, is to lose the sense of proportion. Your imagination comes to life, and this, you think, is where Creation was begun." Alice Walker's feelings and imagination come to life in her essay "Am I Blue?" Walker explains how she came to understand herself as she reflects on her identification with and love for a horse that, as a child, she grew up with, tasting the bitterness of life, of slavery and humiliation, that can make both humans and animals into beasts.

Knowing that nature feeds our bodies, imaginations, and spirits, how should we protect our natural world from the ravages of human exploitation? What are our responsibilities as citizens to help maintain the ecological balance of the earth? This chapter's fourth selection, "A New Common Purpose," excerpted from Al Gore's 1993 national bestseller, *Earth in the Balance*, questions our current environmental policies that exploit the earth: "As long as civilization as a whole, with its vast technological power, continues to follow a pattern of thinking that encourages the domination and exploitation of the natural world for short-term gains, this juggernaut will continue to devastate the earth no matter what any of us does."

Each of the next four writers discusses a different approach to showing respect for our natural environment. The first two focus on struggles within communities while the third and fourth highlight how individuals in a community can work together. Cynthia Hamilton presents her struggle to protect the increasingly polluted environment adjacent to downtown Los Angeles for the community's children in "Women, Home, and Community: The Struggle in an Urban Environment." In "Owls Are Not Threatened, Jobs Are," Randy Fitzgerald argues for a compromise: "The hardships visited on logging families by the spotted-owl controversy will eventually touch all Americans through higher prices for wood products. But these problems could have been avoided—and still can be—if environmentalists, timber owners and federal officials would compromise."

The next two selections provide examples of how individuals have worked together to preserve their community's natural resources and to better the quality of life in their communities. In "On Water" Gretel Erhlich traces the periodic floods and droughts in Wyoming that have shaped the lives of sheep and cattle ranchers. While Erhlich emphasizes how the ranchers needed to develop strategies to survive the floods and droughts that can be harsh and inhospitable, at the same time she sees water as a vessel that symbolizes the natural rhythm of the mind's creative spirit: "Everything in nature invites us constantly to be what we are. We are often like rivers: careless and forceful, timid and dangerous, lucid and muddied, eddying, gleaming, still." In "Winter" from *A Country Year*, Sue Hubbell discusses what she learns about her neighbors' values as they meet to formulate a strategy to stop the city's plans for creating an artificial lake that would destroy their community's natural landscape. Hubbell's essay demonstrates that even when individuals have differing cultural values, they can work together to preserve the natural resources in their community.

As Gretel Erhlich's image of the river's path suggests, practical struggles to preserve the natural resources and ecological balance of a community are illuminated and shadowed by a fundamental source of creativity: the power of the wilderness. In the next selection, "Coda: Wilderness Letter," Wallace Stegner writes the Wildland Research Center's Agricultural Experiment Station to remind them to value and preserve the wilderness because its spirit is larger than ours, because its spirit nourishes ours.

The next-to-last selection in the chapter is an excerpt from Ernest Callenbach's utopian novel *Ecotopia* (1975), which was an immediate success upon its publication and continues to be widely read. In the excerpted section, "A Future Community Tomorrow: Ecotopia," we are invited to visit a community with an alternative life style; Ecotopians commute on transit systems from one small decentralized community to another, own factories and farms in common, keep their unemployment under control, and respect their natural resources. The chapter concludes with a community service writing project completed by a group of four students who helped to compile Natural Histories for the San Francisco Zoo.

As humans we are limited by the boundaries of our understanding, the current reach of scientific discovery, and our own mortality. Observing, living with, and reflecting upon the rhythms and the changes of the natural world may bring us inner peace, self-acceptance, and happiness; then, too, these activities may help us create socially responsible laws that will allow us to protect our natural world.

Total Eclipse

Annie Dillard

Annie Dillard (b. 1945) was born in Pittsburgh, Pennsylvania. She is one of our most highly respected nature writers, uncompromising in her method of revealing the mysteries of the natural world. Dillard attended Hollins College in rural Virginia, where she began working on the manuscript that later became *Pilgrim at Tinker Creek.* Her first work of nonfiction was awarded the Pulitzer Prize in 1974. Other works by Dillard include *Living by Fiction* (1982), *An American Childhood* (1987), *The Writing Life* (1989), and most recently her first novel, *The Farm* (1992). "Total Eclipse," one of Dillard's most intense and imaginative essays, was written in 1981 and is the first essay in her collection *Teaching a Stone to Talk* (1982).

Journal

Write about an inspiring natural event, such as a beautiful sunset or a very low tide at the beach, that you witnessed with other people in your community.

1

It had been like dying, that sliding down the mountain pass. It had been like the death of someone, irrational, that sliding down the mountain pass and into the region of dread. It was like slipping into fever, or falling down that hole in sleep from which you wake yourself whimpering. We had crossed the mountains that day, and now we were in a strange place—a hotel in central Washington, in a town near Yakima. The eclipse we had traveled here to see would occur early the next morning.

2   I lay in bed. My husband, Gary, was reading beside me. I lay in bed and looked at the painting on the hotel room wall. It was a print of a detailed and lifelike painting of a smiling clown's head, made out of vegetables. It was a painting of the sort which you do not intend to look at, and which, alas, you never forget. Some tasteless fate presses it upon you; it becomes part of the complex interior junk you carry with you wherever you go. Two years have passed since the total eclipse of which I write. During those years I have forgotten, I assume, a great many things I wanted to remember—but I have not forgotten that clown painting or its lunatic setting in the old hotel.

3   The clown was bald. Actually, he wore a clown's tight rubber wig, painted white; this stretched over the top of his skull, which was a cabbage. His hair was bunches of baby carrots. Inset in his white clown makeup, and in his cabbage skull, were his small and laughing human eyes. The clown's glance was like the glance of Rembrandt in some of the self-portraits: lively, knowing, deep, and loving. The crinkled shadows around his eyes were string beans. His eyebrows were parsley. Each of his ears was a broad bean. His thin, joy-

ful lips were red chili peppers; between his lips were wet rows of human teeth and a suggestion of a real tongue. The clown print was framed in gilt and glassed.

To put ourselves in the path of the total eclipse, that day we had driven 4 five hours inland from the Washington coast, where we lived. When we tried to cross the Cascades range, an avalanche had blocked the pass.

A slope's worth of snow blocked the road; traffic backed up. Had the 5 avalanche buried any cars that morning? We could not learn. This highway was the only winter road over the mountains. We waited as highway crews bulldozed a passage through the avalanche. With two-by-fours and walls of plyboard, they erected a one-way, roofed tunnel through the avalanche. We drove through the avalanche tunnel, crossed the pass, and descended several thousand feet into central Washington and the broad Yakima valley, about which we knew only that it was orchard country. As we lost altitude, the snows disappeared, our ears popped; the trees changed, and in the trees were strange birds. I watched the landscape innocently, like a fool, like a diver in the rapture of the deep who plays on the bottom while his air runs out.

The hotel lobby was a dark, derelict room, narrow as a corridor, and seem- 6 ingly without air. We waited on a couch while the manager vanished upstairs to do something unknown to our room. Beside us on an overstuffed chair, absolutely motionless, was a platinum-blond woman in her forties wearing a black silk dress and a strand of pearls. Her long legs were crossed; she sup- ported her head on her fist. At the dim far end of the room, their backs toward us, sat six bald old men in their shirtsleeves, around a loud television. Two of them seemed asleep. They were drunks. "Number six!" cried the man on tele- vision, "Number six!"

On the broad lobby desk, lighted and bubbling, was a ten-gallon aquar- 7 ium containing one large fish; the fish tilted up and down in its water. Against the long opposite wall sang a live canary in its cage. Beneath the cage, among spilled millet seeds on the carpet, were a decorated child's sand bucket and matching sand shovel.

Now the alarm was set for six. I lay awake remembering an article I had 8 read downstairs in the lobby, in an engineering magazine. The article was about gold mining.

In South Africa, in India, and in South Dakota, the gold mines extend so 9 deeply into the earth's crust that they are hot. The rock walls burn the min- ers' hands. The companies have to air-condition the mines; if the air condi- tioners break, the miners die. The elevators in the mine shafts run very slowly, down, and up, so the miners' ears will not pop in their skulls. When the min- ers return to the surface, their faces are deathly pale.

Early the next morning we checked out. It was February 26, 1979, a Mon- 10 day morning. We would drive out of town, find a hilltop, watch the eclipse, and then drive back over the mountains and home to the coast. How familiar things are here; how adept we are; how smoothly and professionally we check out! I had forgotten the clown's smiling head and the hotel lobby as if they had never existed. Gary put the car in gear and off we went, as off we have gone to a hundred other adventures.

11   It was before dawn when we found a highway out of town and drove into the unfamiliar countryside. By the growing light we could see a band of cirrostratus clouds in the sky. Later the rising sun would clear these clouds before the eclipse began. We drove at random until we came to a range of unfenced hills. We pulled off the highway, bundled up, and climbed one of these hills.

2

12 The hill was five hundred feet high. Long winter-killed grass covered it, as high as our knees. We climbed and rested, sweating in the cold; we passed clumps of bundled people on the hillside who were setting up telescopes and fiddling with cameras. The top of the hill stuck up in the middle of the sky. We tightened our scarves and looked around.

13   East of us rose another hill like ours. Between the hills, far below, was the highway which threaded south into the valley. This was the Yakima valley; I had never seen it before. It is justly famous for its beauty, like every planted valley. It extended south into the horizon, a distant dream of a valley, a Shangri-la. All its hundreds of low, golden slopes bore orchards. Among the orchards were towns, and roads, and plowed and fallow fields. Through the valley wandered a thin, shining river; from the river extended fine, frozen irrigation ditches. Distance blurred and blued the sight, so that the whole valley looked like a thickness or sediment at the bottom of the sky. Directly behind us was more sky, and empty lowlands blued by distance, and Mount Adams. Mount Adams was an enormous, snow-covered volcanic cone rising flat, like so much scenery.

14   Now the sun was up. We could not see it; but the sky behind the band of clouds was yellow, and, far down the valley, some hillside orchards had lighted up. More people were parking near the highway and climbing the hills. It was the West. All of us rugged individualists were wearing knit caps and blue nylon parkas. People were climbing the nearby hills and setting up shop in clumps among the dead grasses. It looked as though we had all gathered on hilltops to pray for the world on its last day. It looked as though we had all crawled out of spaceships and were preparing to assault the valley below. It looked as though we were scattered on hilltops at dawn to sacrifice virgins, make rain, set stone stelae in a ring. There was no place out of the wind. The straw grasses banged our legs.

15   Up in the sky where we stood the air was lusterless yellow. To the west the sky was blue. Now the sun cleared the clouds. We cast rough shadows on the blowing grass; freezing, we waved our arms. Near the sun, the sky was bright and colorless. There was nothing to see.

It began with no ado. It was odd that such a well-advertised public event 16 should have no starting gun, no overture, no introductory speaker. I should have known right then that I was out of my depth. Without pause or preamble, silent as orbits, a piece of the sun went away. We looked at it through welders' goggles. A piece of the sun was missing; in its place we saw empty sky.

I had seen a partial eclipse in 1970. A partial eclipse is very interesting. It 17 bears almost no relation to a total eclipse. Seeing a partial eclipse bears the same relation to seeing a total eclipse as kissing a man does to marrying him, or as flying in an airplane does to falling out of an airplane. Although the one experience precedes the other, it in no way prepares you for it. During a partial eclipse the sky does not darken—not even when 94 percent of the sun is hidden. Nor does the sun, seen colorless through protective devices, seem terribly strange. We have all seen a sliver of light in the sky; we have all seen the crescent moon by day. However, during a partial eclipse the air does indeed get cold, precisely as if someone were standing between you and the fire. And blackbirds do fly back to their roosts. I had seen a partial eclipse before, and here was another.

What you see in an eclipse is entirely different from what you know. It is 18 especially different for those of us whose grasp of astronomy is so frail that, given a flashlight, a grapefruit, two oranges, and fifteen years, we still could not figure out which way to set the clocks for Daylight Saving Time. Usually it is a bit of a trick to keep your knowledge from blinding you. But during an eclipse it is easy. What you see is much more convincing than any wild-eyed theory you may know.

You may read that the moon has something to do with eclipses. I have 19 never seen the moon yet. You do not see the moon. So near the sun, it is as completely invisible as the stars are by day. What you see before your eyes is the sun going through phases. It gets narrower and narrower, as the waning moon does, and, like the ordinary moon, it travels alone in the simple sky. The sky is of course background. It does not appear to eat the sun; it is far behind the sun. The sun simply shaves away; gradually, you see less sun and more sky.

The sky's blue was deepening, but there was no darkness. The sun was a 20 wide crescent, like a segment of tangerine. The wind freshened and blew steadily over the hill. The eastern hill across the highway grew dusky and sharp. The towns and orchards in the valley to the south were dissolving into the blue light. Only the thin river held a trickle of sun.

Now the sky to the west deepened to indigo, a color never seen. A dark 21 sky usually loses color. This was a saturated, deep indigo, up in the air. Stuck up into that unworldly sky was the cone of Mount Adams, and the alpenglow was upon it. The alpenglow is that red light of sunset which holds out on snowy mountaintops long after the valleys and tablelands are dimmed. "Look at Mount Adams," I said, and that was the last sane moment I remember.

22   I turned back to the sun. It was going. The sun was going, and the world was wrong. The grasses were wrong; they were platinum. Their every detail of stem, head, and blade shone lightless and artificially distinct as an art photographer's platinum print. This color has never been seen on earth. The hues were metallic; their finish was matte. The hillside was a nineteenth-century tinted photograph from which the tints had faded. All the people you see in the photograph, distinct and detailed as their faces look, are now dead. The sky was navy blue. My hands were silver. All the distant hills' grasses were finespun metal which the wind laid down. I was watching a faded color print of a movie filmed in the Middle Ages; I was standing in it, by some mistake. I was standing in a movie of hillside grasses filmed in the Middle Ages. I missed my own century, the people I knew, and the real light of day.

23   I looked at Gary. He was in the film. Everything was lost. He was a platinum print, a dead artist's version of life. I saw on his skull the darkness of night mixed with the colors of day. My mind was going out; my eyes were receding the way galaxies recede to the rim of space. Gary was light-years away, gesturing inside a circle of darkness, down the wrong end of a telescope. He smiled as if he saw me; the stringy crinkles around his eyes moved. The sight of him, familiar and wrong, was something I was remembering from centuries hence, from the other side of death: yes, *that* is the way he used to look, when we were living. When it was our generation's turn to be alive. I could not hear him; the wind was too loud. Behind him the sun was going. We had all started down a chute of time. At first it was pleasant; now there was no stopping it. Gary was chuting away across space, moving and talking and catching my eye, chuting down the long corridor of separation. The skin on his face moved like thin bronze plating that would peel.

24   The grass at our feet was wild barley. It was the wild einkorn wheat which grew on the hilly flanks of the Zagros Mountains, above the Euphrates valley, above the valley of the river we called *River*. We harvested the grass with stone sickles, I remember. We found the grasses on the hillsides; we built our shelter beside them and cut them down. That is how he used to look then, that one, moving and living and catching my eye, with the sky so dark behind him, and the wind blowing. God save our life.

25   From all the hills came screams. A piece of sky beside the crescent sun was detaching. It was a loosened circle of evening sky, suddenly lighted from the back. It was an abrupt black body out of nowhere; it was a flat disk; it was almost over the sun. That is when there were screams. At once this disk of sky slid over the sun like a lid. The sky snapped over the sun like a lens cover. The hatch in the brain slammed. Abruptly it was dark night, on the land and in the sky. In the night sky was a tiny ring of light. The hole where the sun belongs is very small. A thin ring of light marked its place. There was no sound. The eyes dried, the arteries drained, the lungs hushed. There was no world. We were the world's dead people rotating and orbiting around and around, embedded in the planet's crust, while the earth rolled down. Our minds were light-years distant, forgetful of almost everything. Only an extra-

ordinary act of will could recall to us our former, living selves and our contexts in matter and time. We had, it seems, loved the planet and loved our lives, but could no longer remember the way of them. We got the light wrong. In the sky was something that should not be there. In the black sky was a ring of light. It was a thin ring, an old, thin silver wedding band, an old, worn ring. It was an old wedding band in the sky, or a morsel of bone. There were stars. It was all over.

3

It is now that the temptation is strongest to leave these regions. We have seen 26 enough; let's go. Why burn our hands any more than we have to? But two years have passed; the price of gold has risen. I return to the same buried alluvial beds and pick through the strata again.

I saw, early in the morning, the sun diminish against a backdrop of sky. I 27 saw a circular piece of that sky appear, suddenly detached, blackened, and backlighted; from nowhere it came and overlapped the sun. It did not look like the moon. It was enormous and black. If I had not read that it was the moon, I could have seen the sight a hundred times and never thought of the moon once. (If, however, I had not read that it was the moon—if, like most of the world's people throughout time, I had simply glanced up and seen this thing—then I doubtless would not have speculated much, but would have, like Emperor Louis of Bavaria in 840, simply died of fright on the spot.) It did not look like a dragon, although it looked more like a dragon than the moon. It looked like a lens cover, or the lid of a pot. It materialized out of thin air— black, and flat, and sliding, outlined in flame.

Seeing this black body was like seeing a mushroom cloud. The heart 28 screeched. The meaning of the sight overwhelmed its fascination. It obliterated meaning itself. If you were to glance out one day and see a row of mushroom clouds rising on the horizon, you would know at once that what you were seeing, remarkable as it was, was intrinsically not worth remarking. No use running to tell anyone. Significant as it was, it did not matter a whit. For what is significance? It is significance for people. No people, no significance. This is all I have to tell you.

In the deeps are the violence and terror of which psychology has warned 29 us. But if you ride these monsters deeper down, if you drop with them farther over the world's rim, you find what our sciences cannot locate or name, the substrate, the ocean or matrix or ether which buoys the rest, which gives goodness its power for good, and evil its power for evil, the unified field: our complex and inexplicable caring for each other, and for our life together here. This is given. It is not learned.

The world which lay under darkness and stillness following the closing of 30 the lid was not the world we know. The event was over. Its devastation lay round about us. The clamoring mind and heart stilled, almost indifferent, certainly disembodied, frail, and exhausted. The hills were hushed, obliterated. Up in the sky, like a crater from some distant cataclysm, was a hollow ring.

31   You have seen photographs of the sun taken during a total eclipse. The corona fills the print. All of those photographs were taken through telescopes. The lenses of telescopes and cameras can no more cover the breadth and scale of the visual array than language can cover the breadth and simultaneity of internal experience. Lenses enlarge the sight, omit its context, and make of it a pretty and sensible picture, like something on a Christmas card. I assure you, if you send any shepherds a Christmas card on which is printed a three-by-three photograph of the angel of the Lord, the glory of the Lord, and a multitude of the heavenly host, they will not be sore afraid. More fearsome things can come in envelopes. More moving photographs than those of the sun's corona can appear in magazines. But I pray you will never see anything more awful in the sky.

32   You see the wide world swaddled in darkness; you see a vast breadth of hilly land, and an enormous, distant, blackened valley; you see towns' lights, a river's path, and blurred portions of your hat and scarf; you see your husband's face looking like an early black-and-white film; and you see a sprawl of black sky and blue sky together, with unfamiliar stars in it, some barely visible bands of cloud, and over there, a small white ring. The ring is as small as one goose in a flock of migrating geese—if you happen to notice a flock of migrating geese. It is one 360th part of the visible sky. The sun we see is less than half the diameter of a dime held at arm's length.

33   The Crab Nebula, in the constellation Taurus, looks, through binoculars, like a smoke ring. It is a star in the process of exploding. Light from its explosion first reached the earth in 1054; it was a supernova then, and so bright it shone in the daytime. Now it is not so bright, but it is still exploding. It expands at the rate of seventy million miles a day. It is interesting to look through binoculars at something expanding seventy million miles a day. It does not budge. Its apparent size does not increase. Photographs of the Crab Nebula taken fifteen years ago seem identical to photographs of it taken yesterday. Some lichens are similar. Botanists have measured some ordinary lichens twice, at fifty-year intervals, without detecting any growth at all. And yet their cells divide; they live.

34   The small ring of light was like these things—like a ridiculous lichen up in the sky, like a perfectly still explosion 4,200 light-years away: it was interesting, and lovely, and in witless motion, and it had nothing to do with anything.

35   It had nothing to do with anything. The sun was too small, and too cold, and too far away, to keep the world alive. The white ring was not enough. It was feeble and worthless. It was as useless as a memory; it was as off kilter and hollow and wretched as a memory.

36   When you try your hardest to recall someone's face, or the look of a place, you see in your mind's eye some vague and terrible sight such as this. It is dark; it is insubstantial; it is all wrong.

The white ring and the saturated darkness made the earth and the sky look 37 as they must look in the memories of the careless dead. What I saw, what I seemed to be standing in, was all the wrecked light that the memories of the dead could shed upon the living world. We had all died in our boots on the hilltops of Yakima, and were alone in eternity. Empty space stoppered our eyes and mouths; we cared for nothing. We remembered our living days wrong. With great effort we had remembered some sort of circular light in the sky—but only the outline. Oh, and then the orchard trees withered, the ground froze, the glaciers slid down the valleys and overlapped the towns. If there had ever been people on earth, nobody knew it. The dead had forgotten those they had loved. The dead were parted one from the other and could no longer remember the faces and lands they had loved in the light. They seemed to stand on darkened hilltops, looking down.

4

We teach our children one thing only, as we were taught: to wake up. We teach 38 our children to look alive there, to join by words and activities the life of human culture on the planet's crust. As adults we are almost all adept at waking up. We have so mastered the transition we have forgotten we ever learned it. Yet it is a transition we make a hundred times a day, as, like so many will-less dolphins, we plunge and surface, lapse and emerge. We live half our waking lives and all of our sleeping lives in some private, useless, and insensible waters we never mention or recall. Useless, I say. Valueless, I might add—until someone hauls their wealth up to the surface and into the wide-awake city, in a form that people can use.

I do not know how we got to the restaurant. Like Roethke, "I take my wak- 39 ing slow." Gradually I seemed more or less alive, and already forgetful. It was now almost nine in the morning. It was the day of a solar eclipse in central Washington, and a fine adventure for everyone. The sky was clear; there was a fresh breeze out of the north.

The restaurant was a roadside place with tables and booths. The other 40 eclipse-watchers were there. From our booth we could see their cars' California license plates, their University of Washington parking stickers. Inside the restaurant we were all eating eggs or waffles; people were fairly shouting and exchanging enthusiasms, like fans after a World Series game. Did you see . . . ? Did you see . . . ? Then somebody said something which knocked me for a loop.

A college student, a boy in a blue parka who carried a Hasselblad, said to 41 us, "Did you see that little white ring? It looked like a Life Saver. It looked like a Life Saver up in the sky."

And so it did. The boy spoke well. He was a walking alarm clock. I my- 42 self had at that time no access to such a word. He could write a sentence, and I could not. I grabbed that Life Saver and rode it to the surface. And

I had to laugh. I had been dumbstruck on the Euphrates River, I had been dead and gone and grieving, all over the sight of something which, if you could claw your way up to that level, you would grant looked very much like a Life Saver. It was good to be back among people so clever; it was good to have all the world's words at the mind's disposal, so the mind could begin its task. All those things for which we have no words are lost. The mind—the culture—has two little tools, grammar and lexicon: a decorated sand bucket and a matching shovel. With these we bluster about the continents and do all the world's work. With these we try to save our very lives.

43   There are a few more things to tell from this level, the level of the restaurant. One is the old joke about breakfast. "It can never be satisfied, the mind, never." Wallace Stevens[1] wrote that, and in the long run he was right. The mind wants to live forever, or to learn a very good reason why not. The mind wants the world to return its love, or its awareness; the mind wants to know all the world, and all eternity, and God. The mind's sidekick, however, will settle for two eggs over easy.

44   The dear, stupid body is as easily satisfied as a spaniel. And, incredibly, the simple spaniel can lure the brawling mind to its dish. It is everlastingly funny that the proud, metaphysically ambitious, clamoring mind will hush if you give it an egg.

45   Further: while the mind reels in deep space, while the mind grieves or fears or exults, the workaday senses, in ignorance or idiocy, like so many computer terminals printing out market prices while the world blows up, still transcribe their little data and transmit them to the warehouse in the skull. Later, under the tranquilizing influence of fried eggs, the mind can sort through this data. The restaurant was a halfway house, a decompression chamber. There I remembered a few things more.

46   The deepest, and most terrifying, was this: I have said that I heard screams. (I have since read that screaming, with hysteria, is a common reaction even to expected total eclipses.) People on all the hillsides, including, I think, myself, screamed when the black body of the moon detached from the sky and rolled over the sun. But something else was happening at that same instant, and it was this, I believe, which made us scream.

47   The second before the sun went out we saw a wall of dark shadow come speeding at us. We no sooner saw it than it was upon us, like thunder. It roared up the valley. It slammed our hill and knocked us out. It was the monstrous swift shadow cone of the moon. I have since read that this wave of shadow moves 1,800 miles an hour. Language can give no sense of this sort of speed—1,800 miles an hour. It was 195 miles wide. No end was in sight—you saw

---

[1]*Wallace Stevens* (1879–1955): Prominent American poet whose work often deals with our perception of nature; quoted above is another distinguished American poet, Theodore Roethke (1908–1963).

only the edge. It rolled at you across the land at 1,800 miles an hour, hauling darkness like plague behind it. Seeing it, and knowing it was coming straight for you, was like feeling a slug of anesthetic shoot up your arm. If you think very fast, you may have time to think, "Soon it will hit my brain." You can feel the deadness race up your arm; you can feel the appalling, inhuman speed of your own blood. We saw the wall of shadow coming, and screamed before it hit.

This was the universe about which we have read so much and never before 48 felt: the universe as a clockwork of loose spheres flung at stupefying, unauthorized speeds. How could anything moving so fast not crash, not veer from its orbit amok like a car out of control on a turn?

Less than two minutes later, when the sun emerged, the trailing edge of 49 the shadow cone sped away. It coursed down our hill and raced eastward over the plain, faster than the eye could believe; it swept over the plain and dropped over the planet's rim in a twinkling. It had clobbered us, and now it roared away. We blinked in the light. It was as though an enormous, loping god in the sky had reached down and slapped the earth's face.

Something else, something more ordinary, came back to me along about 50 the third cup of coffee. During the moments of totality, it was so dark that drivers on the highway below turned on their cars' headlights. We could see the highway's route as a strand of lights. It was bumper-to-bumper down there. It was eight-fifteen in the morning, Monday morning, and people were driving into Yakima to work. That it was as dark as night, and eerie as hell, an hour after dawn, apparently meant that in order to *see* to drive to work, people had to use their headlights. Four or five cars pulled off the road. The rest, in a line at least five miles long, drove to town. The highway ran between hills; the people could not have seen any of the eclipsed sun at all. Yakima will have another total eclipse in 2086. Perhaps, in 2086, businesses will give their employees an hour off.

From the restaurant we drove back to the coast. The highway crossing the 51 Cascades range was open. We drove over the mountain like old pros. We joined our places on the planet's thin crust; it held. For the time being, we were home free.

Early that morning at six, when we had checked out, the six bald men were 52 sitting on folding chairs in the dim hotel lobby. The television was on. Most of them were awake. You might drown in your own spittle, God knows, at any time; you might wake up dead in a small hotel, a cabbage head watching TV while snows pile up in the passes, watching TV while the chili peppers smile and the moon passes over the sun and nothing changes and nothing is learned because you have lost your bucket and shovel and no longer care. What if you regain the surface and open your sack and find, instead of treasure, a beast which jumps at you? Or you may not come back at all. The winches may jam, the scaffolding buckle, the air conditioning collapse. You may glance up one day and see by your headlamp the canary keeled over in its cage. You may reach into a cranny for pearls and touch a moray eel. You yank on your rope; it is too late.

53   Apparently people share a sense of these hazards, for when the total eclipse ended, an odd thing happened.

54   When the sun appeared as a blinding bead on the ring's side, the eclipse was over. The black lens cover appeared again, backlighted, and slid away. At once the yellow light made the sky blue again; the black lid dissolved and vanished. The real world began there. I remember now: we all hurried away. We were born and bored at a stroke. We rushed down the hill. We found our car; we saw the other people streaming down the hillsides; we joined the highway traffic and drove away.

55   We never looked back. It was a general vamoose, and an odd one, for when we left the hill, the sun was still partially eclipsed—a sight rare enough, and one which, in itself, we would probably have driven five hours to see. But enough is enough. One turns at last even from glory itself with a sigh of relief. From the depths of mystery, and even from the heights of splendor, we bounce back and hurry for the latitudes of home.

Questions for Discussion

1. Dillard describes in careful detail the "lifelike painting of a smiling clown's head, made out of vegetables." Why do you think that she has not forgotten the picture of the clown while she has forgotten many other minor details of her trip? Why does she open her essay with this image?
2. Dillard suggests that in the case of the total eclipse, "What you see is much more convincing than any wild-eyed theory you may know." Can you apply this insight of Dillard's to other types of experiences you have had in the natural world?
3. What insights into the relationships between humans and the natural world do you get from reading this account of the total eclipse?
4. How does Dillard's comment that she "was standing in a movie of hillside grasses filmed in the Middle Ages" help to capture her particular sense of dislocation during the eclipse? How do you interpret the meaning of this image?
5. Why are the people who are witnessing the eclipse screaming? What do these screams signify for Dillard? What is most frightening to you about the eclipse as Dillard describes it?
6. As the eclipse ends, Dillard contrasts the emerging ring of light around the sun to an old silver wedding band or a morsel of bone. What meaning is implied by each image? What is the impact of these sharply contrasting images at the end of the eclipse?
7. Does this natural event have a religious meaning for Dillard? Discuss.

Ideas for Writing

1. Write about an inspiring natural event, such as a total eclipse, that you witnessed with other people. Discuss the psychological and spiritual effect that the event had on you as an individual and on your community.
2. Write an essay that explores the ways that the natural world can embody a religious

or mystical power. When relevant refer to selections in this chapter that illustrate the idea that the power of natural events can put human aspirations and goals into perspective.

The Way to Rainy Mountain

N. Scott Momaday

N. Scott Momaday (b. 1934) came from different Native American tribes; his father was Kiowa and his mother was part Cherokee. Momaday was educated on his family's reservation in Oklahoma, and then at public and parochial schools off the reservation. He earned a B.A. from the University of New Mexico in 1958 and a Ph.D. in English at Stanford University in 1963. Momaday taught at a number of universities, including the University of California at Santa Barbara and at Berkeley, as well as at Stanford. Since 1982 he has been a professor of English at the University of Arizona. His first novel *House Made of Dawn* (1968) was awarded the Pulitzer Prize for fiction. In the selection from *The Way to Rainy Mountain* (1969) that follows, Momaday develops a compelling symbol of his tribe's historical and spiritual community through the image of the mountain where his grandmother was buried.

Journal

Describe your favorite natural place. Does this place symbolize the legacy of your community or family?

A single knoll rises out of the plain in Oklahoma, north and west of the Wichita Range. For my people, the Kiowas, it is an old landmark, and they gave it the name Rainy Mountain. The hardest weather in the world is there. Winter brings blizzards, hot tornadic winds arise in the spring, and in summer the prairie is an anvil's edge. The grass turns brittle and brown, and it cracks beneath your feet. There are green belts along the rivers and creeks, linear groves of hickory and pecan, willow and witch hazel. At a distance in July or August the steaming foliage seems almost to writhe in fire. Great green and yellow grasshoppers are everywhere in the tall grass, popping up like corn to sting the flesh, and tortoises crawl about on the red earth, going nowhere in the plenty of time. Loneliness is an aspect of the land. All things in the plain are isolate; there is no confusion of objects in the eye, but *one* hill or *one* tree or *one* man. To look upon that landscape in the early morning, with the sun at your back, is to lose the sense of proportion. Your imagination comes to life, and this, you think, is where Creation was begun.

I returned to Rainy Mountain in July. My grandmother had died in the 2 spring, and I wanted to be at her grave. She had lived to be very old and at last infirm. Her only living daughter was with her when she died, and I was told that in death her face was that of a child.

3   I like to think of her as a child. When she was born, the Kiowas were living the last great moment of their history. For more than a hundred years they had controlled the open range from the Smoky Hill River to the Red, from the headwaters of the Canadian to the fork of the Arkansas and Cimarron. In alliance with the Comanches, they had ruled the whole of the southern Plains. War was their sacred business, and they were among the finest horsemen the world has ever known. But warfare for the Kiowas was preeminently a matter of disposition rather than of survival, and they never understood the grim, unrelenting advance of the U.S. Cavalry. When at last, divided and ill-provisioned, they were driven onto the Staked Plains in the cold rains of autumn, they fell into panic. In Palo Duro Canyon they abandoned their crucial stores to pillage and had nothing then but their lives. In order to save themselves, they surrendered to the soldiers at Fort Sill and were imprisoned in the old stone corral that now stands as a military museum. My grandmother was spared the humiliation of those high gray walls by eight or ten years, but she must have known from birth the affliction of defeat, the dark brooding of old warriors.

4   Her name was Aho, and she belonged to the last culture to evolve in North America. Her forebears came down from the high country in western Montana nearly three centuries ago. They were a mountain people, a mysterious tribe of hunters whose language has never been positively classified in any major group. In the late seventeenth century they began a long migration to the south and east. It was a journey toward the dawn, and it led to a golden age. Along the way the Kiowas were befriended by the Crows, who gave them the culture and religion of the Plains. They acquired horses, and their ancient nomadic spirit was suddenly free of the ground. They acquired Tai-me, the sacred Sun Dance doll, from that moment the object and symbol of their worship, and so shared in the divinity of the sun. Not least, they acquired the sense of destiny, therefore courage and pride. When they entered upon the southern Plains they had been transformed. No longer were they slaves to the simple necessity of survival; they were a lordly and dangerous society of fighters and thieves, hunters and priests of the sun. According to their origin myth, they entered the world through a hollow log. From one point of view, their migration was the fruit of an old prophecy, for indeed they emerged from a sunless world.

5   Although my grandmother lived out her long life in the shadow of Rainy Mountain, the immense landscape of the continental interior lay like memory in her blood. She could tell of the Crows, whom she had never seen, and of the Black Hills, where she had never been. I wanted to see in reality what she had seen more perfectly in the mind's eye, and traveled fifteen hundred miles to begin my pilgrimage.

6   Yellowstone, it seemed to me, was the top of the world, a region of deep lakes and dark timber, canyons and waterfalls. But, beautiful as it is, one might have the sense of confinement there. The skyline in all directions is close at hand, the high wall of the woods and deep cleavages of shade. There is a perfect freedom in the mountains, but it belongs to the eagle and the elk, the bad-

ger and the bear. The Kiowas reckoned their stature by the distance they could see, and they were bent and blind in the wilderness.

Descending eastward, the highland meadows are a stairway to the plain. 7 In July the inland slope of the Rockies is luxuriant with flax and buckwheat, stonecrop and larkspur. The earth unfolds and the limit of the land recedes. Clusters of trees, and animals grazing far in the distance, cause the vision to reach away and wonder to build upon the mind. The sun follows a longer course in the day, and the sky is immense beyond all comparison. The great billowing clouds that sail upon it are the shadows that move upon the grain like water, dividing light. Farther down, in the land of the Crows and Black-feet, the plain is yellow. Sweet clover takes hold of the hills and bends upon itself to cover and seal the soil. There the Kiowas paused on their way; they had come to the place where they must change their lives. The sun is at home on the plains. Precisely there does it have the certain character of a god. When the Kiowas came to the land of the Crows, they could see the dark lees of the hills at dawn across the Bighorn River, the profusion of light on the grain shelves, the oldest deity ranging after the solstices. Not yet would they veer southward to the caldron of the land that lay below; they must wean their blood from the northern winter and hold the mountains a while longer in their view. They bore Tai-me in procession to the east.

A dark mist lay over the Black Hills, and the land was like iron. At the top 8 of a ridge I caught sight of Devil's Tower upthrust against the gray sky as if in the birth of time the core of the earth had broken through its crust and the motion of the world was begun. There are things in nature that engender an awful quiet in the heart of man; Devil's Tower is one of them. Two centuries ago, because they could not do otherwise, the Kiowas made a legend at the base of the rock. My grandmother said:

> Eight children were there at play, seven sisters and their brother. Suddenly 9 the boy was struck dumb; he trembled and began to run upon his hands and feet. His fingers became claws, and his body was covered with fur. Directly there was a bear where the boy had been. The sisters were terrified; they ran, and the bear after them. They came to the stump of a great tree, and the tree spoke to them. It bade them climb upon it, and as they did so it began to rise into the air. The bear came to kill them, but they were just beyond its reach. It reared against the tree and scored the bark all around with its claws. The seven sisters were borne into the sky, and they became the stars of the Big Dipper.

From that moment, and so long as the legend lives, the Kiowas have kinsmen 10 in the night sky. Whatever they were in the mountains, they could be no more. However tenuous their well-being, however much they had suffered and would suffer again, they had found a way out of the wilderness.

My grandmother had a reverence for the sun, a holy regard that now is 11 all but gone out of mankind. There was a wariness in her, and an ancient awe. She was a Christian in her later years, but she had come a long way about, and she never forgot her birthright. As a child she had been to the Sun Dances;

she had taken part in those annual rites, and by them she had learned the restoration of her people in the presence of Tai-me. She was about seven when the last Kiowa Sun Dance was held in 1887 on the Washita River above Rainy Mountain Creek. The buffalo were gone. In order to consummate the ancient sacrifice—to impale the head of a buffalo bull upon the medicine tree—a delegation of old men journeyed into Texas, there to beg and barter for an animal from the Goodnight herd. She was ten when the Kiowas came together for the last time as a living Sun Dance culture. They could find no buffalo; they had to hang an old hide from the sacred tree. Before the dance could begin, a company of soldiers rode out from Fort Sill under orders to disperse the tribe. Forbidden without cause the essential act of their faith, having seen the wild herds slaughtered and left to rot upon the ground, the Kiowas backed away forever from the medicine tree. That was July 20, 1890, at the great bend of the Washita. My grandmother was there. Without bitterness, and for as long as she lived, she bore a vision of deicide.

12   Now that I can have her only in memory, I see my grandmother in the several postures that were peculiar to her: standing at the wood stove on a winter morning and turning meat in a great iron skillet; sitting at the south window, bent above her beadwork, and afterwards, when her vision failed, looking down for a long time into the fold of her hands; going out upon a cane, very slowly as she did when the weight of age came upon her; praying. I remember her most often at prayer. She made long, rambling prayers out of suffering and hope, having seen many things. I was never sure that I had the right to hear, so exclusive where they of all mere custom and company. The last time I saw her she prayed standing by the side of her bed at night, naked to the waist, the light of a kerosene lamp moving upon her dark skin. Her long, black hair, always drawn and braided in the day, lay upon her shoulders and against her breasts like a shawl. I do not speak Kiowa, and I never understood her prayers, but there was something inherently sad in the sound, some merest hesitation upon the syllables of sorrow. She began in a high and descending pitch, exhausting her breath to silence; then again and again—and always the same intensity of effort, of something that is, and is not, like urgency in the human voice. Transported so in the dancing light among the shadows of her room, she seemed beyond the reach of time. But that was illusion; I think I knew then that I should not see her again.

13   Houses are like sentinels in the plain, old keepers of the weather watch. There, in a very little while, wood takes on the appearance of great age. All colors wear soon away in the wind and rain, and then the wood is burned gray and the grain appears and the nails turn red with rust. The windowpanes are black and opaque; you imagine there is nothing within, and indeed there are many ghosts, bones given up to the land. They stand here and there against the sky, and you approach them for a longer time than you expect. They belong in the distance; it is their domain.

14   Once there was a lot of sound in my grandmother's house, a lot of coming and going, feasting and talk. The summers there were full of excitement and reunion. The Kiowas are a summer people; they abide the cold and keep

to themselves, but when the season turns and the land becomes warm and vital they cannot hold still; an old love of going returns upon them. The aged visitors who came to my grandmother's house when I was a child were made of lean and leather, and they bore themselves upright. They wore great black hats and bright ample shirts that shook in the wind. They rubbed fat upon their hair and wound their braids with strips of colored cloth. Some of them painted their faces and carried the scars of old and cherished enmities. They were an old council of warlords, come to remind and be reminded of who they were. Their wives and daughters served them well. The women might indulge themselves; gossip was at once the mark and compensation of their servitude. They made loud and elaborate talk among themselves, full of jest and gesture, fright and false alarm. They went abroad in fringed and flowered shawls, bright beadwork and German silver. They were at home in the kitchen, and they prepared meals that were banquets.

There were frequent prayer meetings, and great nocturnal feasts. When I 15 was a child I played with my cousins outside, where the lamplight fell upon the ground and the singing of the old people rose up around us and carried away into the darkness. There were a lot of good things to eat, a lot of laughter and surprise. And afterwards, when the quiet returned, I lay down with my grandmother and could hear the frogs away by the river and feel the motion of the air.

Now there is a funeral silence in the rooms, the endless wake of some final 16 word. The walls have closed in upon my grandmother's house. When I returned to it in mourning, I saw for the first time in my life how small it was. It was late at night, and there was a white moon, nearly full. I sat for a long time on the stone steps by the kitchen door. From there I could see out across the land; I could see the long row of trees by the creek, the low light upon the rolling plains, and the stars of the Big Dipper. Once I looked at the moon and caught sight of a strange thing. A cricket had perched upon the handrail, only a few inches away from me. My line of vision was such that the creature filled the moon like a fossil. It had gone there, I thought, to live and die, for there, of all places, was its small definition made whole and eternal. A warm wind rose up and purled like the longing within me.

The next morning I awoke at dawn and went out on the dirt road to Rainy 17 Mountain. It was already hot, and the grasshoppers began to fill the air. Still, it was early in the morning, and the birds sang out of the shadows. The long yellow grass on the mountain shone in the bright light, and a scissortail hied above the land. There, where it ought to be, at the end of a long and legendary way, was my grandmother's grave. Here and there on the dark stones were ancestral names. Looking back once, I saw the mountain and came away.

Questions for Discussion

1. Discuss several of the metaphors or similes in the first paragraph that you think are especially vivid. What is the effect of Momaday's beginning with the description of

Rainy Mountain before letting his readers know that he is going there to visit his grandmother's grave?

2. How do the land and its creatures give the Kiowas a legacy of spiritual power, community, and destiny? What are the most important landmarks in their territory?

3. How does the legend of Devil's Tower protect the Kiowas from the unpredictable wrath of the wilderness?

4. What meaning did the last Kiowa Sun Dance, which took place in 1887, hold for Momaday's grandmother, for Momaday, for you? Why are the Kiowas a summer people?

5. How do Momaday's final memories of his grandmother help you to understand what she meant to him?

6. How does Momaday recreate the legacy of the Kiowa tribe through the portrait of his grandmother's life? How are the natural world, the Native American community, and immortality linked through the symbol of Rainy Mountain?

Ideas for Writing

1. Like Momaday, write about a journey to the grave site of a relative or ancestor. After narrating the journey, discuss what you learned on your trip about your heritage, your relative or ancestor, the importance of the landscape to your community, and yourself. Or write about a natural setting that has come to symbolize the legacy of your community or cultural's values and immortality.

2. Write about a natural place in your community that has the power to inspire and heal you. Submit your essay to a local paper to encourage others to visit and share your appreciation and respect for this natural setting.

Am I Blue?

Alice Walker

Alice Walker (b. 1944) was born in Eatonton, Georgia. She graduated from Sarah Lawrence in 1967 and has taught at a number of colleges, including Wellesley and Yale. She now lives in San Francisco and teaches at the University of California at Berkeley. Walker is one of the most widely read contemporary writers. Her work has had a powerful impact on the creation of a history and identity for the black family and the black artist. Walker won the Pulitzer Prize for *The Color Purple* in 1983. Her latest best-selling novel is *Possessing the Secret of Joy* (1992). Her most recent nonfiction work, *Warrior Marks* (1993), was written with Pratibha Parmar. The selection that follows is taken from a collection of short writings, *Living by the Word: Selected Writings from 1973–1987* (1989).

Journal

Write about an animal that you treated like a person and a friend. Why do you think you attributed human qualities to this animal? What did you learn from your relationship?

Ain't these tears in these eyes tellin' you? *

For about three years my companion and I rented a small house in the country that stood on the edge of a large meadow that appeared to run from the end of our deck straight into the mountains. The mountains, however, were quite far away, and between us and them there was, in fact, a town. It was one of the many pleasant aspects of the house that you never really were aware of this.

It was a house of many windows, low, wide, nearly floor to ceiling in the 2 living room, which faced the meadow, and it was from one of these that I first saw our closest neighbor, a large white horse, cropping grass, flipping its mane, and ambling about—not over the entire meadow, which stretched well out of sight of the house, but over the five or so fenced-in acres that were next to the twenty-odd that we had rented. I soon learned that the horse, whose name was Blue, belonged to a man who lived in another town, but was boarded by our neighbors next door. Occasionally, one of the children, usually a stocky teenager, but sometimes a much younger girl or boy, could be seen riding Blue. They would appear in the meadow, climb up on his back, ride furiously for ten or fifteen minutes, then get off, slap Blue on the flanks, and not be seen again for a month or more.

There were many apple trees in our yard, and one by the fence that Blue 3 could almost reach. We were soon in the habit of feeding him apples, which he relished, especially because by the middle of summer the meadow grasses—so green and succulent since January—had dried out from lack of rain, and Blue stumbled about munching the dried stalks half-heartedly. Sometimes he would stand very still just by the apple tree, and when one of us came out he would whinny, snort loudly, or stamp the ground. This meant, of course: I want an apple.

It was quite wonderful to pick a few apples, or collect those that had fallen 4 to the ground overnight, and patiently hold them, one by one, up to his large, toothy mouth. I remained as thrilled as a child by his flexible dark lips; huge, cubelike teeth that crunched the apples, core and all, with such finality; and high, broad-breasted *enormity* beside which I felt small indeed. When I was a child, I used to ride horses, and was especially friendly with one named Nan until the day I was riding and my brother deliberately spooked her and I was thrown, head first, against the trunk of a tree. When I came to, I was in bed and my mother was bending worriedly over me; we silently agreed that perhaps horseback riding was not the safest sport for me. Since then I have walked, and prefer walking to horseback riding—but I had forgotten the depth of feeling one could see in horses' eyes.

I was therefore unprepared for the expression in Blue's. Blue was lonely. 5 Blue was horribly lonely and bored. I was not shocked that this should be the case; five acres to tramp by yourself, endlessly, even in the most beautiful of meadows—and his was—cannot provide many interesting events, and once rainy season turned to dry that was about it. No, I was shocked that I had forgotten that human animals and nonhuman animals can communicate quite well; if we are brought up around animals as children we take this for granted. By the time we are adults we no longer remember. However, the animals have not changed. They are in fact *completed* creations (at least they seem to be, so much more than we) who are not likely *to* change; it is their nature to express themselves. What else are they going to express? And they do. And, generally speaking, they are ignored.

6   After giving Blue the apples, I would wander back to the house, aware that he was observing me. Were more apples not forthcoming then? Was that to be his sole entertainment for the day? My partner's small son had decided he wanted to learn how to piece a quilt; we worked in silence on our respective squares as I thought. . . .

7   Well, about slavery: about white children, who were raised by black people, who knew their first all-accepting love from black women, and then, when they were twelve or so, were told they must "forget" the deep levels of communication between themselves and the "mammy" that they knew. Later they would be able to relate quite calmly. "My old mammy was sold to another good family." "My old mammy was——." Fill in the blank. Many more years later a white woman would say: "I can't understand these Negroes, these blacks. What do they want? They're so different from us."

8   And about the Indians, considered to be "like animals" by the "settlers" (a very benign euphemism for what they actually were), who did not understand their description as a compliment.

9   And about the thousands of American men who marry Japanese, Korean, Filipino, and other non-English-speaking women and of how happy they report they are, *"blissfully,"* until their brides learn to speak English, at which point the marriages tend to fall apart. What then did the men see, when they looked into the eyes of the women they married, before they could speak English? Apparently only their own reflections.

10   I thought of society's impatience with the young. "Why are they playing the music so loud?" Perhaps the children have listened to much of the music of oppressed people their parents danced to before they were born, with its passionate but soft cries for acceptance and love, and they have wondered why their parents failed to hear.

11   I do not know how long Blue had inhabited his five beautiful, boring acres before we moved into our house; a year after we had arrived—and had also traveled to other valleys, other cities, other worlds—he was still there.

12   But then, in our second year at the house, something happened in Blue's life. One morning, looking out the window at the fog that lay like a ribbon over the meadow, I saw another horse, a brown one, at the other end of Blue's field. Blue appeared to be afraid of it, and for several days made no attempt to go near. We went away for a week. When we returned, Blue had decided to make friends and the two horses ambled or galloped along together, and Blue did not come nearly as often to the fence underneath the apple tree.

When he did, bringing his new friend with him, there was a different look 13
in his eyes. A look of independence, of self-possession, of inalienable *horse*ness.
His friend eventually became pregnant. For months and months there was, it
seemed to me, a mutual feeling between me and the horses of justice, of peace.
I fed apples to them both. The look in Blue's eyes was one of unabashed "this
is *it*ness."

It did not, however, last forever. One day, after a visit to the city, I went 14
out to give Blue some apples. He stood waiting, or so I thought, though not
beneath the tree. When I shook the tree and jumped back from the shower of
apples, he made no move. I carried some over to him. He managed to half-
crunch one. The rest he let fall to the ground. I dreaded looking into his eyes—
because I had of course noticed that Brown, his partner, had gone—but I did
look. If I had been born into slavery, and my partner had been sold or killed,
my eyes would have looked like that. The children next door explained that
Blue's partner had been "put with him" (the same expression that old people
used, I had noticed, when speaking of an ancestor during slavery who had
been impregnated by her owner) so that they could mate and she conceive.
Since that was accomplished, she had been taken back by her owner, who lived
somewhere else.

Will she be back? I asked. 15

They didn't know. 16

Blue was like a crazed person. Blue *was*, to me, a crazed person. He gal- 17
loped furiously, as if he were being ridden, around and around his five beautiful acres. He whinnied until he couldn't. He tore at the ground with his
hooves. He butted himself against his single shade tree. He looked always and
always toward the road down which his partner had gone. And then, occasionally, when he came up for apples, or I took apples to him, he looked at
me. It was a look so piercing, so full of grief, a look so *human*, I almost laughed
(I felt too sad to cry) to think there are people who do not know that animals
suffer. People like me who have forgotten, and daily forget, all that animals
try to tell us. "Everything you do to us will happen to you; we are your teachers, as you are ours. We are one lesson" is essentially it, I think. There are those
who never once have even considered animals' rights: those who have been
taught that animals actually want to be used and abused by us, as small children "love" to be frightened, or women "love" to be mutilated and raped. . . .
They are the great-grandchildren of those who honestly thought, because
someone taught them this: "Women can't think," and "niggers can't faint." But
most disturbing of all, in Blue's large brown eyes was a new look, more painful
than the look of despair: the look of disgust with human beings, with life; the
look of hatred. And it was odd what the look of hatred did. It gave him, for
the first time, the look of a beast. And what that meant was that he had put
up a barrier within to protect himself from further violence; all the apples in
the world wouldn't change that fact.

And so Blue remained, a beautiful part of our landscape, very peaceful to 18
look at from the window, white against the grass. Once a friend came to visit
and said, looking out on the soothing view: "And it *would* have to be a *white*

horse; the very image of freedom." And I thought, yes, the animals are forced to become for us merely "images" of what they once so beautifully expressed. And we are used to drinking milk from containers showing "contented" cows, whose real lives we want to hear nothing about, eating eggs and drumsticks from "happy" hens, and munching hamburgers advertised by bulls of integrity who seem to command their fate.

19   As we talked of freedom and justice one day for all, we sat down to steaks. I am eating misery, I thought, as I took the first bite. And spit it out.

Questions for Discussion

1. How does Walker include you as the reader into Blue's world and into the web of feelings that she has for Blue and shares with him? Do you identify with Blue or with Walker?
2. When you are first introduced to Blue, why do you think his name is fitting to his personality and role? As the essay closes, how have the symbolic meanings of Blue's name and social role deepened?
3. How does Walker develop the idea that a horse's eyes can hold a depth of meaning? How does the meaning that Blue's eyes hold change as the essay develops?
4. Why does Walker believe that animals and humans can communicate? Do you agree with her? Explain your point of view through reference to personal examples.
5. How does Walker establish a parallel between the lives and feelings of slaves and of non-English-speaking women married to American men, and the lives and feelings of animals as exemplified by Blue?
6. What brings Blue a sense of independence? What kills his spirit? How do Blue's eyes change?
7. How does Walker define the meaning of "beast" in this essay?

Ideas For Writing

1. Write an essay that explains what Walker thinks we can learn about ourselves and our relationships to our social and natural community through thinking about our relationship with animals. Explain why you agree or disagree with Walker's perspective.
2. Walker's essay explores the meaning that one can see in the eyes of another person or animal. She begins with the quote: "Ain't these tears in these eyes tellin' you?" Write an essay that discusses how you have come to believe in a particular value through studying and knowing the eyes of loved ones, or of strangers, in your community.

A New Common Purpose

Al Gore

Vice-President **Al Gore (b. 1948)** was born and raised in Tennessee. Gore earned his B.A. at Harvard and then enlisted in the army during the Vietnam War, where he served as an army reporter. When he returned from the war, he worked as a reporter in his home state. Gore, who is a devout Baptist, enrolled in Vanderbilt Graduate School of Religion to study spiritual issues. He also studied law at Vanderbilt for two years. In 1976 Gore was elected to the Tennessee House of Representatives, and in 1984 he was elected to the Tennessee Senate. Gore has always been interested in health and environmental issues and disarmament. In his book, *Earth in the Balance* (1993), Gore argues that only a radical rethinking of our relationship with nature can save the earth's ecology for future generations. The following selection "A New Common Purpose," excerpted from Gore's book, warns us to change our policies that sanction exploitation of the natural resources in Third World countries.

Journal

Write about an environmental project that was successful in your community. Why was the project important and successful? What problems did the group undertaking it have to overcome in order to achieve success?

Modern industrial civilization, as presently organized, is colliding violently with our planet's ecological system. The ferocity of its assault on the earth is breathtaking, and the horrific consequences are occurring so quickly as to defy our capacity to recognize them, comprehend their global implications, and organize an appropriate and timely response. Isolated pockets of resistance fighters who have experienced this juggernaut at first hand have begun to fight back in inspiring but, in the final analysis, woefully inadequate ways. It is not that they lack courage, imagination, or skill; it is simply that what they are up against is nothing less than the current logic of world civilization. As long as civilization as a whole, with its vast technological power, continues to follow a pattern of thinking that encourages the domination and exploitation of the natural world for short-term gains, this juggernaut will continue to devastate the earth no matter what any of us does.

I have come to believe that we must take bold and unequivocal action: we 2 must make the rescue of the environment the central organizing principle for civilization. Whether we realize it or not, we are now engaged in an epic battle to right the balance of our earth, and the tide of this battle will turn only when the majority of people in the world become sufficiently aroused by a shared sense of urgent danger to join an all-out effort. It is time to come to terms with exactly how this can be accomplished. Having attempted in earlier chapters to understand the crisis from the perspectives offered by the earth sciences, economics, sociology, history, information theory, psychology, philosophy, and religion, I now want to examine, from my vantage point as a politician, what I think can be done about it.

Politics, broadly defined, is the means by which we make collective deci- 3 sions and choices. We now confront a set of choices as difficult as any in human history. The art of politics must be brought to bear in defining these choices, raising public awareness of the imminent danger facing us, and catalyzing decisions in favor of a collective course of action that has a reasonable chance of success.

4   There is no doubt that with sufficient agreement on our goals, we can achieve the victory we are seeking. Although very difficult changes in established patterns of thought and action will be required, the task of restoring the natural balance of the earth's ecological system is both within our capacity and desirable for other reasons—including our interest in social justice, democratic government, and free market economics. Ultimately, a commitment to healing the environment represents a renewed dedication to what Jefferson believed were not merely American but universal inalienable rights: life, liberty, and the pursuit of happiness.

5   The hard part, of course, will be securing a sufficient measure of agreement that difficult comprehensive changes are needed. Fortunately, however, there are ample precedents for the kinds of pervasive institutional changes and shared effort that will be necessary. Though it has never yet been accomplished on a global scale, the establishment of a single shared goal as the central organizing principle for every institution in society has been realized by free nations several times in modern history. Most recently, a coalition of free nations committed to democracy and free markets demonstrated a remarkable capacity to persevere for nearly half a century in their effort to prevent the spread of communism by military, political, or economic means. To the surprise of many, this coalition secured a resounding victory for the idea of freedom in the philosophical war that lasted from the time of the Russian Revolution until the jailers of Eastern Europe released their "enemies of the people"—who were then freely elected as democratic leaders of, by, and for the people. And the political earthquake that accompanied that victory has continued to topple statues of Lenin for several years, from Nicaragua to Angola to Ethiopia, until it brought down the former Soviet Union itself.

6   What made this dramatic victory possible was a conscious and shared decision by men and women in the nations of the "free world" to make the defeat of the communist system the central organizing principle of not only their governments' policies but of society itself. That is not to say that this goal dominated every waking thought or guided every policy decision, but opposition to communism was the principle underlying almost all of the geopolitical strategies and social policies designed by the West after World War II. The Marshall Plan, for example, was conceived primarily as a means of strengthening Western Europe's ability to withstand the spread of the communist idea. Similarly, MacArthur's blueprint for reconstituting Japan's society and economy and Truman's decision in 1947 to extend massive aid to Greece and Turkey were principally motivated by the same objective. NATO and the other military alliances organized under U.S. leadership also grew out of the same central principle. U.S. advocacy of free trade and the granting of foreign aid to underdeveloped nations were in part altruistic but mainly motivated by the struggle against communism. Of course, some of the policies were painful, costly, and controversial. Wars in Korea and Vietnam, the nuclear arms race, arms sales to dictators who disagreed with every American principle save opposition to Soviet communism—these and virtually every other foreign policy and national security decision were made because they served the same

central principle, albeit in ways that sometimes reflected poor judgment. Though mistakes were made, the basic soundness of the underlying principle continued to motivate the citizens and governments of the free world, and the idea of democracy slowly began to win the battle.

The multiple expressions of anticommunism took some unexpected forms. 7 Here in the United States, when we built the interstate highway system, the Defense Interstate Highway Bill authorized the money, and the legislation was approved by a majority partly because it would serve our overriding objective, the defeat of communism. When the Soviet Union demonstrated its technological prowess by sending Sputnik into orbit in 1957, the United States implemented the first federal aid-to-education policy—not because the president and a majority in Congress finally recognized the importance of improving education for its own sake, but because of the new importance of training scientists and engineers in service of our struggle with the communist system. We simultaneously launched the American space program, not because a majority in Congress was suddenly motivated by a desire to explore the universe, but because the program became tied to our desire to defeat the communist idea.

Many of these programs made sense on their own merits; many of their 8 proponents pushed them mainly because of those merits. But they gained sufficient support from society as a whole because they served the central organizing principle to which we were wholeheartedly committed. Commitment sometimes led to terrible excesses: the McCarthyist smear campaigns and the exposure of human guinea pigs to the effects of nuclear radiation are only two examples of how overzealousness can have tragic results. But the point is that virtually every policy and program was analyzed and either supported or rejected primarily according to whether it served our basic organizing principle. Even such widely disparate policies as the green revolution to expand food production in Third World countries and the CIA's encouragement of trade unions in Europe were conceived because they were effective in helping us achieve our main objective.

The long struggle between democracy and communism is in many ways 9 the clearest example of how free societies can sustain a shared commitment to a single overarching goal over a long period of time and in the face of daunting obstacles. But it is hardly the only such example. Before the Cold War, there was an even more consuming central organizing principle behind the policies of the United States and other free nations: the defeat of Nazi Germany and imperial Japan. Industry, commerce, agriculture, transportation— all were mobilized for war. Extremely effective recycling programs were widespread during World War II, not for environmental reasons, but because they helped to win the war. Our resources, our people, our art, and even our gardens played a role in the struggle to save civilization as we knew it.

It is worth remembering how long we waited before finally facing the chal- 10 lenge posed by Nazi totalitarianism and Hitler. Many were reluctant to acknowledge that an effort on the scale of what became World War II was actually necessary, and most wanted to believe that the threat could be wished away with trivial sacrifices. For several years before the awful truth was accepted, one Western leader spoke out forcefully and eloquently about the gathering storm. Winston Churchill was uncompromising in his insistence that every effort be immediately bent to the task of ensuring Hitler's defeat. After Neville Chamberlain concluded the Munich Pact of 1938, which gave Czechoslovakia to Hitler in return for his pledge not to take over still more territory, most Britons were happy and supported the policy that later was condemned as appeasement. Churchill, however, grasped the essence of what had occurred and of the unavoidable conflict that lay ahead: "I do not begrudge our loyal, brave people . . . the natural, spontaneous outburst of joy and relief when they learned that the hard ordeal would no longer be required of them at the moment; but they should know the truth . . . this is only the beginning of the reckoning. This is only the first sip, the first foretaste of a bitter cup which will be proffered to us year by year unless by a supreme recovery of moral health and martial vigor we arise again and take our stand for freedom."

11   Thus do we meekly acquiesce in the loss of the world's rain forests and their living species, the loss of the Everglades, the Aral Sea, the old-growth forests of the Pacific Northwest, the topsoil of the Midwest, the vegetation and soils of the Himalayas, Lake Baikal, the Sahel, the unnecessary deaths of 37,000 children every day, the thinning of the stratospheric ozone layer, the disruption of the climate balance we have known since the dawn of the human species. Bitter cups all—but only "the beginning of the reckoning," only the first of a steady stream of progressively more serious ecological catastrophes that will be repeatedly proffered to us and will, sooner or later, arouse us to action and convince us to fight back.

12   What does it mean to make the effort to save the global environment the central organizing principle of our civilization? For one thing, it means securing widespread agreement that it *should* be the organizing principle, and the way such a consensus is formed is especially important because this is when priorities are established and goals are set. Historically, such a consensus has usually been secured only with the emergence of a life-or-death threat to the existence of society itself; this time, however, the crisis could well be irreversible by the time its consequences become sufficiently clear to congeal public opinion—if not panic. This time, the crisis has a long fuse: the natural processes do not immediately display the full extent of the damage we are inflicting. Once set in motion, however, some of the changes we are imposing will be very difficult to reverse. It is essential, therefore, that we refuse to wait for the obvious signs of impending catastrophe, that we begin immediately to catalyze a consensus for this new organizing principle.

13   Adopting a central organizing principle—one agreed to voluntarily— means embarking on an all-out effort to use every policy and program, every law and institution, every treaty and alliance, every tactic and strategy, every plan and course of action—to use, in short, every means to halt the destruction of the environment and to preserve and nurture our ecological system. Minor shifts in policy, marginal adjustments in ongoing programs, moderate improvements in laws and regulations, rhetoric offered in lieu of genuine

change—these are all forms of appeasement, designed to satisfy the public's desire to believe that sacrifice, struggle, and a wrenching transformation of society will not be necessary. The Chamberlains of this crisis carry not umbrellas but "floppy hats and sunglasses"—the palliative allegedly suggested by a former secretary of the interior as an appropriate response to the increased ultraviolet radiation caused by the thinning of the ozone layer.

Some are willing to assume that we can easily adapt to the effects of our 14 assault on the environment—and indeed, some adaptation will be necessary because of the changes that have already been set irrevocably in motion. But those who propose adaptation as our principal response are really advocating just another form of appeasement. And of course the soothing message of reassurance they bring—that all is well and nothing need be done—is almost always welcome and even flattering to those who believe their complacency is justified.

But there are terrible moral consequences to the current policy of delay, 15 just as there were when we tried to postpone World War II. Then, as now, the real enemy was a dysfunctional way of thinking. In Nazi Germany, dysfunctional thinking was institutionalized in the totalitarian state, its dogma, and its war machine. Today, a different dysfunction takes the form of ravenous, insatiable consumption, its dogma, and the mechanisms by which ever more resources are obtained. Totalitarianism and consumptionism have led to crises peculiar to advanced industrial civilization: both are examples of alienation and technology run amok. Just as totalitarianism collapses individuals into "the state," the new ideology of consumption collapses individuals into the desire for what they consume, even as it fosters the assumption that we are separate from the earth. It is this strange and destructive way of thinking about our relationship to the physical world that is our real enemy.

The struggle to save the global environment is in one way much more dif- 16 ficult than the struggle to vanquish Hitler, for this time the war is with ourselves. We are the enemy, just as we have only ourselves as allies. In a war such as this, then, what is victory and how will we recognize it?

It is not merely in the service of analogy that I have referred so often to 17 the struggles against Nazi and communist totalitarianism, because I believe that the emerging effort to save the environment is a continuation of these struggles, a crucial new phase of the long battle for true freedom and human dignity. My reasoning here is simple: free men and women who feel individual responsibility for a particular part of the earth are, by and large, its most effective protectors, defenders, and stewards. Wherever this sense of responsibility is diluted or compromised by competing imperatives, the likelihood of stewardship and care for the environment diminishes. For example, when a farmer with a short-term lease is under financial pressure to maximize profits, the land is vulnerable to exploitation. When the officers of a timber company are given annual bonuses based on the size of its quarterly profits, they are likely to cut more trees at a younger age and plant fewer seedlings for harvest in future decades—and care less about the soil erosion that often results. When the voters in a democracy are not prepared by knowledge or conviction to hold their politicians accountable for the polluting of public air and water resources by private parties, then the politicians will be loath to assert the people's right to freely enjoy public property.

18   The fact that these abuses occur in free countries does not in any sense support the argument that the principles of private ownership, capitalism, or democracy are to blame—any more than the existence of slavery during the first seventy-four years of the American republic could be blamed on representative democracy. As we now understand, the genius of the American founders in conceiving liberty and devising the means for guaranteeing it lies not in the eternal perfection of the laws and institutions they crafted in the late eighteenth century but in the truths they enshrined as guiding principles. Referring to those truths, subsequent generations could and did reinterpret the meaning of freedom for themselves in the context of new knowledge, changed circumstances, and accumulated experience.

19   Most, though not all, of the generation that wrote the Constitution were partially blind when it came to the inalienable rights of the African Americans held as slaves. They felt themselves separate from people of a different color, so they failed to understand that the rights they so passionately defended for themselves and all others to whom they felt connected by "common destiny" were rights held in common by all. Similarly, most were blind when it came to the right of women to vote. But this blindness did not prevent subsequent generations from developing a fuller understanding of the truths embodied in the Constitution, even if they were not fully visible to those who first had the courage to use them as the foundation stones for democratic government.

20   Today, most—though not all—are partially blind when it comes to our connection with the natural world. The philosophy of life we have inherited, which tells us we are separate from the earth, obscures our understanding of our common destiny and renders us vulnerable to an ecological catastrophe, just as our forebears' assumption that they were morally and spiritually connected to their slaves led to the catastrophe of the Civil War. What we need now is an expanded understanding of what these freedoms involve and how they can be extended once more.

21   The largest promise of the democratic idea is that, given the right to govern themselves, free men and women will prove to be the best stewards of their own destiny. It is a promise that has been redeemed against the challenge of every competing idea. The assertion that we might be half slave and half free, that only men should vote, that the common resolve of free nations would wither against the singular will of totalitarianism—all these ideas have fallen while ours remains. But now a new challenge—the threat to the global environment—may wrest control of our destiny away from us. Our response to this challenge must become our new central organizing principle.

22   The service of this principle is consistent in every way with democracy and free markets. But just as the abolition of slavery required a fuller understanding of the nature of both democracy and private property—and the relationship between the two, so this new struggle will require a still larger conception of how democracy and free markets enhance each other. Just as the

extension of civil rights to women and African Americans required a deeper insight into the meaning of democratic government and a broader definition of what all human beings have in common, this global challenge will require a fuller understanding of our connection to all people today and our obligations to future generations.

Let there be no doubt: Unless we can grow in these understandings, we will lose our ability to redeem the promise of freedom. 23

Empowered by a new way of thinking, we can without question succeed in an all-out effort to save the environment. But this effort will require an even deeper respect on the part of governments for the political and economic freedom of individuals; it will also require dramatic measures to ensure that individuals are given both the information to comprehend the enormity of the challenge and adequate political and economic power to be true stewards of the places where they live and work. By themselves, well-motivated individuals cannot hope to win this struggle, but as soon as enough people agree to make it our central organizing principle, success will come within our grasp and we can begin to make rapid progress. 24

But in those countries that already consider themselves free, there is another political prerequisite as well. The emphasis on the rights of the individual must be accompanied by a deeper understanding of the responsibilities to the community that every individual must accept if the community is to have an organizing principle at all. 25

This notion is itself an ecological question, in the sense that it involves a balance between rights and responsibilities. In fact, what many feel is a deep philosophical crisis in the West has occurred in part because this balance has been disrupted: we have tilted so far toward individual rights and so far away from any sense of obligation that it is now difficult to muster an adequate defense of any rights vested in the community at large or in the nation—much less rights properly vested in all humankind or in posterity. Today, about the only way to mobilize public opinion sufficiently to stop transgressions of what may be called ecological rights is to spotlight individuals who have been victimized by this or that environmentally unsound practice. The harm done to the community, to the world at large, or to future generations, is then treated as incidental to the harm done to these individuals; their rights are sufficiently similar to our own individual rights that we are willing to defend them, since, after all, we might thereby build desirable protections for ourselves. 26

This separation from community is clearly related to the assumption that we are separate from the earth. It has not only the same philosophical cause—the overriding faith in the power of the individual intellect—but also the same solution: a more balanced way of thinking about our relationship to the world, including our communities. This reaffirmation of our connection to others involves an obligation to join *with others* in adequately defending and protecting those of our rights—such as the right to breathe clean air and drink clean water—that are naturally among the individual rights belonging to others as well as to us, and are vested in the community—or nation, or world—as a whole. 27

28   Another threat to this new organizing principle is the pervasiveness of corruption in both the underdeveloped and developed worlds. This too, in a sense, is an ecological problem. Corruption pollutes the healthy patterns of accountability on which democratic government—and our ability to share stewardship of the environment—depend. Indeed, in almost every case of environmental devastation, corruption has played a significant role in deadening the ability of the political system to respond to the early signals of degradation brought to its attention.

29   But since corruption affects the system, many feel sufficiently detached to acquiesce in the general lethargy and inertia that allow it to continue. In order for this new central organizing principle to be effectively established, however, the political pollution of corruption must be confronted as an evil that is, in essence, similar to that embodied in the physical pollution of the air and water.

30   Likewise, the continued tolerance of widespread social injustice has the same corrosive effect on our ability to contemplate vigorous and sustained mutual initiatives. The promotion of justice and the protection of the environment must go hand in hand in any society, whether in the context of a nation's domestic policies or in the design of "North-South" agreements between the industrial nations and the Third World. Without such commitments, the world cannot contemplate the all-out effort urgently needed. Already, the dialogue between poor and wealthy nations is poisoned by Third World cynicism about the industrial nations' motives. But recently it has also been enriched by proposals such as "debt for nature swaps," in which debts are canceled in return for cooperation in protecting endangered parts of the environment.

31   Rapid economic improvements represent a life-or-death imperative throughout the Third World. Its people will not be denied that hope, no matter the environmental costs. As a result, that choice must not be forced upon them. And from their point of view, why should they accept what we, manifestly, will not accept for ourselves? Who is so bold as to say that any developed nation is prepared to abandon industrial and economic growth? Who will proclaim that any wealthy nation will accept serious compromises in comfort levels for the sake of environmental balance?

32   The industrial world must understand that the Third World does not have a choice of whether to develop economically. And one hopes it will do so according to a more rational pattern than has thus far been urged upon it. If it does not, then poverty, hunger, and disease will consume entire populations. Long before that, whole societies will experience revolutionary political disorder, and it is not inconceivable that some of the resulting wars could be fought with crude nuclear weapons, because nuclear proliferation continues to reflect our general failure to manage technology wisely. Indeed, some of those wars could be fought over natural resources themselves, like fresh water.

33   Finally, we must come to a deeper understanding of what is meant by development. Many people of good will recognized early on the need to bring some coherence to the efforts of rich and poor nations to build a more just world civilization; what came to be called development is now the chief means by which wealthy nations—often working through multilateral institutions

like the World Bank and the regional development banks—can help underdeveloped nations accelerate their transition into modernity. Unfortunately, the international development programs have often been catastrophic for the countries on the receiving end, because so many of the large projects involved have tried to jump-start industrial growth even if it put the environment at risk. The problems so common in international development programs have been ecologically dangerous in another sense too: there has rarely been much balance between the projects financed by the industrial world and the true needs of the Third World. As a result, too many projects have ended up doing more harm than good, disrupting both ecological balance and societal stability. Part of the price paid is in discouragement, cynicism, and a simplistic conclusion by some that development itself is inherently undesirable. A sad example is the aftermath of the flooding in 1991 of large areas in Bangladesh and the enormous loss of life from drowning, disease, and starvation. The mild response of the industrial world seemed to reflect a fatalistic surrender to the idea that such suffering is certainly tragic but essentially unavoidable. Moreover, serious analysts argued that almost any kind of help from the West was unwise because by facilitating the resettlement of low-lying areas vulnerable to flooding and by increasing the population through the feeding of many who would otherwise starve, Western aid would only sow the seeds of even worse tragedies at the time of the next floods.

Unless the industrial world refines its understanding of how it can help 34 effectively and what kind of development is appropriate, there will be a great many more such political and moral surrenders in the face of horrendous tragedy. We in the rich nations will lie to ourselves and pretend that since development didn't work and often made the problems much worse, the best course of action is to do nothing—to become a silent partner with mass death in the cynical culling of the human species.

Questions for Discussion

1. Gore asserts that "restoring the natural balance of the earth's ecological system . . . represents a renewed dedication" to Jefferson's belief in our inalienable rights. Explain why you agree or disagree with Gore.
2. Do you agree with Gore when he claims that privileging of rights of the individual more than the responsibility to the community reflects our disregard and lack of respect for the earth's well-being? Explain your response through references to specific examples.
3. State your understanding of Gore's definition of the word "community." Compare and contrast his definition with yours.
4. Explain why you agree or disagree with Gore's assertion that the struggle to save the global environment will be more difficult than the struggle to defeat Hitler.
5. Like Gore, do you think that adaptation to environmental crises is appeasement and that saving the global environment needs to be a central organizing principle of the world's nations? Explain your point of view through references to specific situations.
6. Do you think the rich nations will help the Third World nations to develop rationally in order to avoid environmental crises and the exploitation of their natural

resources for immediate profit? Explain your response through references to specific examples.

Ideas for Writing

1. Write an argument that supports or refutes Gore's position. Also refer to specific environmental situations to support your point of view.
2. Do some research in the library to learn more about the legislation in your city or state that is designed to improve the environment in your community, region, or state. Try contacting several environmental agencies in your community or on your campus to learn more about the issues and legislation. Write an essay that discusses the environmental problem and solutions to it for your class and for a community paper.
3. Write about an environmental struggle in a Third World country.

Women, Home, and Community: The Struggle in an Urban Environment

Cynthia Hamilton

Cynthia Hamilton studied political science at Stanford University, where she earned her B.A.; she completed her Ph.D. at Boston University. Currently she is a professor in the Pan American Studies Department at California State University, Los Angeles. A political activist as well as a scholar, Hamilton fought against the construction of a solid waste incinerator in Los Angeles, which is the topic of the following essay that is anthologized in *Reweaving the World: The Emergence of Ecofeminism* (1990).

Journal

Discuss a polluted area in your community that you would like to see cleaned up. How do you think your community should approach solving the problem?

In 1956, women in South Africa began an organized protest against the pass laws. As they stood in front of the office of the prime minister, they began a new freedom song with the refrain "now you have touched the women, you have struck a rock." This refrain provides a description of the personal commitment and intensity women bring to social change. Women's actions have been characterized as "spontaneous and dramatic," women in action portrayed as "intractable and uncompromising."[1] Society has summarily dismissed these

---

[1]See Cynthia Cockburn, "When Women Get Involved in Community Action," in Marjorie Mayo (ed.), *Women in the Community* (London: Routledge & Kegan Paul, 1977).

as negative attributes. When in 1986 the City Council of Los Angeles decided that a 13-acre incinerator called LANCER (for Los Angeles City Energy Recovery Project), burning 2,000 tons a day of municipal waste, should be built in a poor residential, black, and Hispanic community, the women there said "No." Officials had indeed dislodged a boulder of opposition. According to Charlotte Bullock, one of the protestors, "I noticed when we first started fighting the issue how the men would laugh at the women . . . they would say, 'Don't pay no attention to them, that's only one or two women . . . they won't make a difference.' But now since we've been fighting for about a year the smiles have gone."[2]

Minority communities shoulder a disproportionately high share of the by-   2 products of industrial development: waste, abandoned factories and warehouses, leftover chemicals and debris. These communities are also asked to house the waste and pollution no longer acceptable in white communities, such as hazardous landfills or dump sites. In 1987, the Commission for Racial Justice of the United Church of Christ published *Toxic Wastes and Race*. The commission concluded that race is a major factor related to the presence of hazardous wastes in residential communities throughout the United States. Three out of every five black and Hispanic Americans live in communities with uncontrolled toxic sites; 75 percent of the residents in rural areas in the Southwest, mainly Hispanics, are drinking pesticide-contaminated water; more than 2 million tons of uranium tailings are dumped on Native-American reservations each year, resulting in Navajo teenagers having seventeen times the national average of organ cancers; more than 700,000 inner city children, 50 percent of them black, are said to be suffering from lead poisoning, resulting in learning disorders. Working-class minority women are therefore motivated to organize around very pragmatic environmental issues, rather than those associated with more middle-class organizations. According to Charlotte Bullock, "I did not come to the fight against environmental problems as an intellectual but rather as a concerned mother. . . . People say, 'But you're not a scientist, how do you know it's not safe?' I have common sense. I know if dioxin and mercury are going to come out of an incinerator stack, somebody's going to be affected."

When Concerned Citizens of South Central Los Angeles came together in   3 1986 to oppose the solid waste incinerator planned for the community, no one thought much about environmentalism or feminism. These were just words in a community with a 78 percent unemployment rate, an average income ($8,158) less than half that of the general Los Angeles population, and a residential density more than twice that of the whole city. In the first stages of organization, what motivated and directed individual actions was the need to protect home and children; for the group this individual orientation emerged as a community-centered battle. What was left in this deteriorating district on the periphery of the central business and commercial district had to be defended—a "garbage dump" was the final insult after years of neglect, watch-

[2]All of the quotes from Charlotte Bullock and Robin Cannon are personal communications, 1986.

ing downtown flourish while residents were prevented from borrowing enough to even build a new roof.

4   The organization was never gender restricted but it became apparent after a while that women were the majority. The particular kind of organization the group assumed, the actions engaged in, even the content of what was said, were all a product not only of the issue itself, the waste incinerator, but also a function of the particular nature of women's oppression and what happens as the process of consciousness begins.

5   Women often play a primary part in community action because it is about things they know best. Minority women in several urban areas have found themselves part of a new radical core as the new wave of environmental action, precipitated by the irrationalities of capital-intensive growth, has catapulted them forward. These individuals are responding not to "nature" in the abstract but to the threat to their homes and to the health of their children. Robin Cannon, another activist in the fight against the Los Angeles incinerator, says, "I have asthma, my children have asthma, my brothers and sisters have asthma, there are a lot of health problems that people living around an incinerator might be subjected to and I said, 'They can't do this to me and my family.' "

6   Women are more likely than men to take on these issues precisely because the home has been defined and prescribed as a woman's domain. According to British sociologist Cynthia Cockburn, "In a housing situation that is a health hazard, the woman is more likely to act than the man because she lives there all day and because she is impelled by fear for her children. Community action of this kind is a significant phase of class struggle, but it is also an element of women's liberation."[3]

7   This phenomenon was most apparent in the battle over the Los Angeles incinerator. Women who had had no history of organizing responded as protectors of their children. Many were single parents, others were older women who had raised families. While the experts were convinced that their smug dismissal of the validity of the health concerns these women raised would send them away, their smugness only reinforced the women's determination. According to Charlotte Bullock:

8   People's jobs were threatened, ministers were threatened . . . but I said, "I'm not going to be intimidated." My child's health comes first, . . . that's more important than my job.

9   In the 1950s the city banned small incinerators in the yard and yet they want to build a big incinerator . . . the Council is going to build something in my community which might kill my child. . . . I don't need a scientist to tell me that's wrong.

10 None of the officials were prepared for the intensity of concern or the consistency of agitation. In fact, the consultants they hired had concluded that these women did not fit the prototype of opposition. The consultants had concluded:

[3]Cockburn, "When Women," p. 62.

Certain types of people are likely to participate in politics, either by virtue of   11
their issue awareness or their financial resources, or both. Members of middle
or higher socioeconomic strata (a composite index of level of education, occu-
pational prestige, and income) are more likely to organize into effective groups
to express their political interests and views. All socioeconomic groupings
tend to resent the nearby siting of major facilities, but the middle and upper
socioeconomic strata possess better resources to effectuate their opposition.
Middle and higher socioeconomic strata neighborhoods should not fall at least
within the one mile and five mile radii of the proposed site.

. . . although environmental concerns cut across all subgroups, people   12
with a college education, young or middle aged, and liberal in philosophy are
most likely to organize opposition to the siting of a major facility. Older people, with a high school education or less, and those who adhere to a free market orientation are least likely to oppose a facility.[4]

The organizers against the incinerator in South Central Los Angeles are   13
the antithesis of the prototype: they are high school educated or less, above
middle age and young, nonprofessionals and unemployed and low-income,
without previous political experience. The consultants and politicians thus
found it easy to believe that opposition from this group could not be serious.

The intransigence of the City Council intensified the agitation, and the   14
women became less willing to compromise as time passed. Each passing
month gave them greater strength, knowledge, and perseverance. The council
and its consultants had a more formidable enemy than they had expected, and
in the end they have had to compromise. The politicians have backed away
from their previous embrace of incineration as a solution to the trash crisis,
and they have backed away from this particular site in a poor, black and Hispanic, residential area. While the issues are far from resolved, it is important
that the willingness to compromise has become the official position of the city
as a result of the determination of "a few women."

The women in South Central Los Angeles were not alone in their battle.   15
They were joined by women from across the city, White, middle-class, and
professional women. As Robin Cannon puts it, "I didn't know we all had so
many things in common . . . millions of people in the city had something in
common with us—the environment." These two groups of women, together,
have created something previously unknown in Los Angeles—unity of purpose across neighborhood and racial lines. According to Charlotte Bullock,
"We are making a difference . . . when we come together as a whole and stick
with it, we can win because we are right."

This unity has been accomplished by informality, respect, tolerance of   16
spontaneity, and decentralization. All of the activities that we have been told
destroy organizations have instead worked to sustain this movement. For
example, for a year and a half the group functioned without a formal leadership structure. The unconscious acceptance of equality and democratic process
resulted practically in rotating the chair's position at meetings. Newspeople

[4]Cerrell Associates, *Political Difficulties Facing Waste to Energy Conversion Plant Siting* (Los Angeles:
California Waste Management Board, 1984), pp. 42–43.

were disoriented when they asked for the spokesperson and the group responded that everyone could speak for the neighborhood.

17   It may be the case that women, unlike men, are less conditioned to see the value of small advances.[5] These women were all guided by their vision of the possible: that it *was* possible to completely stop the construction of the incinerator, that it is possible in a city like Los Angeles to have reasonable growth, that it is possible to humanize community structures and services. As Robin Cannon says, "My neighbors said, 'You can't fight City Hall . . . and besides, you work there.' I told them I would fight anyway."

18   None of these women was convinced by the consultants and their traditional justifications for capital-intensive growth: that it increases property values by intensifying land use, that it draws new businesses and investment to the area, that it removes blight and deterioration—and the key argument used to persuade the working class—that growth creates jobs. Again, to quote Robin Cannon, "They're not bringing real development to our community. . . . They're going to bring this incinerator to us, and then say 'We're going to *give* you fifty jobs when you get this plant.' Meanwhile they're going to shut down another factory [in Riverside] and eliminate two hundred jobs to buy more pollution rights. . . . They may close more shops."

19   Ironically, the consultants' advice backfired. They had suggested that emphasizing employment and a gift to the community (of $2 million for a community development fund for park improvement) would persuade the opponents. But promises of heated swimming pools, air-conditioned basketball courts and fifty jobs at the facility were more insulting than encouraging. Similarly, at a public hearing, an expert witness's assurance that health risks associated with dioxin exposure were less than those associated with "eating peanut butter" unleashed a flurry of derision.

20   The experts' insistence on referring to congenital deformities and cancers as "acceptable risks" cut to the hearts of women who rose to speak of a child's asthma, or a parent's influenza, or the high rate of cancer, heart disease, and pneumonia in this poverty-stricken community. The callous disregard of human concerns brought the women closer together. They came to rely on each other as they were subjected to the sarcastic rebuffs of men who referred to their concerns as "irrational, uninformed, and disruptive." The contempt of the male experts was directed at professionals and the unemployed, at Whites and Blacks—all the women were castigated as irrational and uncompromising. As a result, new levels of consciousness were sparked in these women.

21   The reactions of the men backing the incinerator provided a very serious learning experience for the women, both professionals and nonprofessionals, who came to the movement without a critique of patriarchy. They developed their critique in practice. In confronting the need for equality, these women forced the men to a new level of recognition—that working-class women's concerns cannot be simply dismissed.

[5]See Cockburn, "When Women," p. 63.

Individual transformations accompanied the group process. As the strug- 22
gle against the incinerator proceeded to take on some elements of class struggle, individual consciousness matured and developed. Women began to recognize something of their own oppression as women. This led to new forms
of action not only against institutions but to the transformation of social relations in the home as well. As Robin Cannon explains:

> My husband didn't take me seriously at first either. . . . He just saw a whole   23
> lot of women meeting and assumed we wouldn't get anything done. . . . I had
> to split my time . . . I'm the one who usually comes home from work, cooks,
> helps the kids with their homework, then I watch a little TV and go to bed to
> get ready for the next morning. Now I would rush home, cook, read my mate-
> rials on LANCER . . . now the kids were on their own . . . I had my own home-
> work. . . . My husband still wasn't taking me seriously. . . . After about 6
> months everyone finally took me seriously. My husband had to learn to allo-
> cate more time for baby sitting. Now on Saturdays, if they went to the show
> or to the park, I couldn't attend . . . in the evening there were hearings . . . I
> was using my vacation time to go to hearings during the workday.

As parents, particularly single parents, time in the home was strained for these 24
women. Children and husbands complained that meetings and public hearings had taken priority over the family and relations in the home. According
to Charlotte Bullock, "My children understand, but then they don't want to
understand. . . . They say, 'You're not spending time with me.' " Ironically, it
was the concern for family, their love of their families, that had catapulted
these women into action to begin with. But, in a pragmatic sense, the home
did have to come second in order for health and safety to be preserved. These
were hard learning experiences. But meetings in individual homes ultimately
involved children and spouses alike—everyone worked and everyone listened.
The transformation of relations continued as women spoke up at hearings and
demonstrations and husbands transported children, made signs, and looked
on with pride and support at public forums.

The critical perspective of women in the battle against LANCER went far 25
beyond what the women themselves had intended. For these women, the political issues were personal and in that sense they became feminist issues. These
women, in the end, were fighting for what they felt was "right" rather than
what men argued might be reasonable. The coincidence of the principles of
feminism and ecology that Carolyn Merchant explains in *The Death of Nature*
(San Francisco: Harper & Row, 1981) found expression and developed in the
consciousness of these women: the concern for Earth as a home, the recognition that all parts of a system have equal value, the acknowledgment of
process, and, finally, that capitalist growth has social costs. As Robin Cannon
says, "This fight has really turned me around, things are intertwined in ways
I hadn't realized. . . . All these social issues as well as political and economic
issues are really intertwined. Before, I was concerned only about health and
then I began to get into the politics, decision making, and so many things."

26   In two years, what started as the outrage of a small group of mothers has transformed the political climate of a major metropolitan area. What these women have aimed for is a greater level of democracy, a greater level of involvement, not only in their organization but in the development process of the city generally. They have demanded accountability regarding land use and ownership, very subversive concerns in a capitalist society. In their organizing, the group process, collectivism, was of primary importance. It allowed the women to see their own power and potential and therefore allowed them to consolidate effective opposition. The movement underscored the role of principles. In fact, we citizens have lived so long with an unquestioning acceptance of profit and expediency that sometimes we forget that our objective is to do "what's right." Women are beginning to raise moral concerns in a very forthright manner, emphasizing that experts have left us no other choice but to follow our own moral convictions rather than accept neutrality and capitulate in the face of crisis.

27   The environmental crisis will escalate in this decade and women are sure to play pivotal roles in the struggle to save our planet. If women are able to sustain for longer periods some of the qualities and behavioral forms they have displayed in crisis situations (such as direct participatory democracy and the critique of patriarchal bureaucracy), they may be able to reintroduce equality and democracy into progressive action. They may also reintroduce the value of being moved by principle and morality. Pragmatism has come to dominate all forms of political behavior and the results have often been disastrous. If women resist the "normal" organizational thrust to barter, bargain, and fragment ideas and issues, they may help set new standards for action in the new environment movement.

Questions for Discussion

1. How do the women of the community react to the LANCER project? How do the men in the community respond to the political goals of the women?
2. This environmental struggle over the solid waste incinerator is led by women of color. According to Hamilton, why are they taking more risks than middle-class or professional women? Why are they successful? How do they reach out to their "sisters" from all classes throughout the country?
3. Why is this particular example of the LANCER project especially appropriate support for the larger generalizations that Hamilton makes about women's commitment to saving the environment for their children? How does the metaphor of the incinerator as garbage dump for the rebuilt and elegant downtown area reinforce her argument?
4. Why are the women in Hamilton's project successful in spite of the fact that they have no political experience and limited scientific evidence?
5. Hamilton argues that women may be about to "reintroduce the value of being moved by principle and morality." Do you agree or disagree with Hamilton's assertion that women have the potential to act more ethically toward the environment because of their roles as caretakers of the home and of their children?

6. Discuss an environmental problem that affects the health of the children in your community.

Ideas for Writing

1. Develop discussion question 6 into an essay that describes an environmental problem that is detrimental to the health of the children in your community; then propose a solution to this problem. You may need to do library research to understand the problem better. Also contact some local environmental agencies to see what information they may have and what work has been done to date.

2. Interview several men and several women about environmental issues in your community. Try to determine if men and women take different positions on environmental issues and/or organize different types of political strategies for change. Write an essay that discusses what you have learned.

Owls Are Not Threatened, Jobs Are

Randy Fitzgerald

Randall Fitzgerald (b. 1950) was born in Texas and earned his B.S. at the University of Texas at Austin in 1974. He went on to attend journalism school in Washington, DC, and has worked as a reporter, syndicated columnist, and a freelance writer. The piece that follows originally appeared in the November 1992 issue of the *Readers Digest*.

Journal

Decisions to protect a particular species or natural resource can have economic consequences for industry and workers. Discuss an example of such a conflict among environmentalists, industry, and workers in your community or region.

One afternoon last November, Donald Walker, Jr., got a four-page letter from an attorney for an environmental group calling itself the Forest Conservation Council. The organization threatened to sue, seeking heavy fines and imprisonment, if Walker cut down a single tree on his 200 acres of Oregon timberland.

Walker, his wife Kay and two daughters live in central Oregon on land 2 that has been in the family for three generations. Since being laid off from his lumber-mill job in 1989, Walker had cut a few trees each year for income to help support the family.

Barely able to control his mounting anger, Walker called his 77-year-old 3 father, who lives nearby. He had received a similar letter. Then Walker talked to a neighbor, a retired log-truck driver, who cut timber on his land just to pay his property taxes every year. The same threat had been mailed to him.

4   Kay Walker reacted with disbelief. "Here we are caught up in this owl mess again," she fumed.

5   The "mess" had begun when environmentalists challenged the Interior Department's decision not to list the northern spotted owl as a threatened or endangered species under the Endangered Species Act. The act permits anyone to sue to enforce provisions protecting a species in peril and its suspected habitat.

6   As a result of this and related court action, most timber sales on federal forest land in the Pacific Northwest have been halted, throwing thousands of loggers and mill employees out of work.

7   Now the act is being used against private landowners. Besides the Walkers, about 190 other landowners in Oregon have received legal threats from the same environmental group. Most are small private landowners or modest local logging companies. "We can't afford to fight this in court," Walker says. "I'm out of work, and last year our property taxes nearly doubled. Our tree farm is the last hope we have to survive."

8   The hardships visited on logging families by the spotted-owl controversy will eventually touch all Americans through higher prices for wood products. But these problems could have been avoided—and still can be—if environmentalists, timber owners and federal officials would compromise.

9   **The Real Agenda**   In 1987, a Massachusetts group called Greenworld petitioned the U.S. Fish and Wildlife Service to list the northern spotted owl as an endangered species. After a review, the FWS ruled that the owl was not in danger of extinction. In retaliation, 22 environmental groups—ranging from the Seattle Audubon Society to the Sierra Club—sued to reverse the decision.

10   A number of these groups had another agenda—to outlaw logging in old-growth forests throughout much of the Northwest—and were using the owl as a tool. "The northern spotted owl is the wildlife species of choice to act as a surrogate for old-growth forest protection," explained Andy Stahl, staff forester for the Sierra Club Legal Defense Fund, at a 1988 law clinic for other environmentalists. "Thank goodness the spotted owl evolved in the Pacific Northwest," he joked, "for if it hadn't, we'd have to genetically engineer it."

11   Old-growth forests are often defined as stands of trees at least 200 years of age that have never been exposed to cutting. There are nine million acres of old-growth forest on federal lands in Oregon, California and Washington. Of this, some six million acres—enough to form a three-mile-wide band of trees from New York to Seattle—are already off-limits to logging, preserved mostly in national parks and federal wilderness areas.

12   So the fight came down to the remaining three million acres, which were being cut at the rate of some 60,000 acres a year. By time this old growth was harvested, foresters for the Northwest Forestry Association argued, a like

amount of acreage in other forests would have matured into old growth. Environmental groups countered that the spotted owl would be extinct by then because it can't survive in sufficient numbers in younger forests.

Responding to the environmentalists' petition, U.S. District Judge Thomas 13 Zilly ordered the FWS to take a second look. Then, U.S. District Judge William Dwyer stopped most Pacific Northwest timber sales on U.S. Forest Service land. And last June, U.S. District Judge Helen Frye banned old-growth timber sales on most of the Bureau of Land Management's Pacific Northwest land.

In June 1990, the FWS reversed course and listed the owl as threatened, 14 after a committee representing four federal agencies concluded that the owl population was declining. The estimated 2000 owl pairs still alive, the committee decided, were dependent primarily on the old-growth timberland. The FWS has since proposed a critical spotted-owl habitat in the three states, with suggested sizes ranging from 11.6 million to 6.9 million acres.

Later academic studies have challenged the government's conclusions. A 15 timber-industry group, the American Forest Resource Alliance, summarized 15 studies by forest experts at major universities and discovered that, as more land is surveyed, the known owl population continues to increase. Even the FWS's current projections show 3500 known pairs, nearly twice the number federal bureaucrats first estimated.

Furthermore, the Alliance contends that the owls do not require old- 16 growth forest; they can adapt to younger forests. Northern spotted owls thrive in Boise Cascade's 50,000-acre forest near Yakima, Wash., which has been harvested and regrown repeatedly. The same situation exists on 70,000 acres of Weyerhaeuser timberland near Eugene, Ore.

Despite the evidence, the wheels of government and the federal courts 17 have been set in motion to protect the owl. The result has been havoc for people.

"Alaska Windows"   Nestled in a picturesque river valley at the foot of Ore- 18 gon's Cascade Mountains, the town of Oakridge calls itself the tree-planting capital of the world. Its 3400 residents are surrounded by the Willamette National Forest, which teems with elk and deer, bear and cougar.

After timber-sale restrictions began to take effect, logging companies 19 started laying off workers, and truckers who had hauled the wood were idled. Mill workers who had been making as much as $17 an hour found that the few jobs available were sacking groceries or pumping gas at minimum wage, and even those soon disappeared.

Local unemployment shot up to 25 percent. For-sale signs sprouted like 20 mushrooms. Businesses began to go bankrupt—first the variety store and the animal-feed store, then three gas stations, two clothing stores, several restaurants and the town's only movie theater.

To survive financially, several dozen Oakridge men sought employment 21 in the only section of the West Coast still hiring loggers—Alaska. Separated from their families ten months at a time, they live on rafts in a region accessible only by floatplane or boat. Left behind in Oakridge are the wives, who call themselves Alaska Widows.

22   Cheryl Osborne, who has three children, rises each morning at 5:30 to cook breakfast in the restaurant she and her husband opened in the building next to their house. The house is up for sale, and the restaurant is barely making it. In the afternoons Osborne works as a bookkeeper for a small logging company that's just making ends meet.

23   Linda Cutsforth hasn't been able to find full-time work since she lost her mill job after 25 years of employment. She has seen the strain take its toll on timber families. "Loggers look like whipped dogs," she says. "My husband feels like he's sentenced to prison in Alaska."

24   Jill Silvey works at the local elementary school, where she has seen the economic casualties up close. One fourth-grade boy lived in a tent on the river with his family after they lost their home. Several children from another family live in a camp-ground and arrive hungry at school each day.

25   In timber towns across the pacific Northwest, families and entire communities that had once been close-knit are disintegrating. Loggers in towns with names like Happy Camp and Sweet Home, who had taken pride in their self-sufficiency and hard work, now feel abandoned and betrayed.

26 **Adding Up Costs**   "Environmentalists predicted in 1990 that only 2300 jobs would be affected in the three states," remembers Chris West, vice president of the Northwest Forestry Association.

27   Earlier this year, the FWS projected the loss of 32,100 jobs. As compiled by timber-industry groups and labor unions, the ultimate figure, taking privately owned woodlands into account, may exceed 100,000.

28   Ripple effects have begun to reach consumers nationwide. Pacific Northwest states supply more than one-third of all the softwood lumber and plywood produced in America. In 1991 the volume of wood withdrawn from harvest because of owl restrictions was enough to construct 270,000 new homes. The scarcity drove up lumber prices at least 30 percent, adding more than $3000 to the cost of building a $150,000 home.

29   If the restrictions on cutting continue, most economists expect a further sharp rise in timber prices. For every 20-percent increase in wood costs, up to 65,000 American families are priced out of houses they could have afforded previously. Prices will also rise on paper products and furniture.

30   Short-term relief would be available if the Forest Service could salvage wood presently rotting on the ground. Major storms, for example, have blown down 195 million board feet of timber in Oregon's spotted-owl habitat, enough to keep more than 1300 people employed for up to a year and provide enough timber to construct some 16,000 American homes.

31   But environmental groups have blocked the Forest Service from salvaging the wood—this despite the government and industry contention that not all of the blow-downs are essential to the owl's habitat.

32 **Striking a Balance**   "There have certainly been forest abuses," admits Cheryl

Osborne, herself a former member of the Audubon Society. Clear-cutting, for example, leaves large, ugly bald spots sprinkled with the charred remains of stumps and debris. Congress, too, is to blame, having directed the overcutting of trees in the national forests to increase federal revenues. "But you can't wipe out the livelihoods of tens of thousands of people just to accommodate the spotted owl," declares Osborne. "Why can't there be a balance?"

There can be, if loggers use a range of techniques known as New Forestry. 33 At Collins Pine Company's 91,500-acre forest in northeastern California, no clear-cutting is permitted. Old-growth-forest trees such as ponderosa pine are mingled with other species of new growth. Most trees killed by insects, burned or blown down are weeded out, but vigorous ones are left to help replenish the forest with seed.

At Collins, more trees are always growing than are being cut. The result 34 is a thriving wildlife population, including bald eagles, ospreys and California spotted owls.

"We should be able to manage forests for spotted owls," says wildlife biol- 35 ogist Larry Irwin. "We know of hundreds of cases where owl habitat was created by accident as a result of management practices. Surely, then, we can do it by design."

Most environmental groups are skeptical of New Forestry: it still means 36 cutting trees. Many timber companies resist it, claiming it is a less efficient way to harvest fewer trees. A growing number of foresters and wildlife biologists, however, are accepting New Forestry as a bridge to cross the deep chasm that separates most environmental groups from most timber growers.

Spotted owls and logging are not incompatible—and Congress must take 37 this controversy away from the courts and carve out a compromise that serves the national interest. "The reign of terror against private landowners must end," says Donald Walker, Jr. "Loggers need their jobs back, the Alaska Widows need their husbands, and the nation needs the renewable resource that this group of hard-working Americans provides."

Questions for Discussion

1. State Fitzgerald's thesis in your own words.
2. How does Fitzgerald encourage the reader to feel sympathetic to the loggers' position?
3. Fitzgerald claims that "The northern spotted owl is the wildlife species of choice to act as a surrogate for old-growth forest protection." Why is Fitzgerald critical of the environmentalist's point of view?
4. What are the consequences of the court-mandated ban on logging for the community of Oakridge? Why does Fitzgerald predict that the decision will affect the nation?
5. What compromise does Fitzgerald propose? Explain why you agree or disagree with his conclusions.
6. Has this essay changed your position on the spotted owl controversy? On the role that environmentalist can play in a legal battle? On the extent to which we should protect our environment? How can thinking about this particular issue help you to

make better decisions about preserving our natural environment while not eliminating jobs?

Ideas for Writing

1. Write a letter to Randy Fitzgerald explaining your position on his article.
2. Research a controversial environmental issue in your community. Present the situation and your point of view. After sharing the essay with your class, consider submitting it to a campus or local paper.

On Water

Gretel Erhlich

Gretel Erhlich (b. 1946) was born and raised in California. She attended Bennington College, the UCLA film school, and the New School for Social Research in New York. Erhlich began her career in film and relocated in Wyoming in 1976 after doing a documentary on sheep herders. Erhlich has a particular vision as she writes: "The truest art I would strive for in any work would be to give the page the same qualities as earth: weather would land on it harshly; light would elucidate the most difficult truths; wind would sweep away obtuse padding." After the death of her fiancé, Erhlich wrote *The Solace of Open Spaces* (1985) to recount and capture the intensity of her experience of moving to Wyoming permanently. In "On Water," Erhlich shows how nature has a practical, unpredictable, and spiritual influence on the life of the people in her community.

Journal

Write about an experience that helped you to understand the economic and psychological impact of the weather on your community. What was the effect of either too much or too little water or of some other natural resource?

Frank Hinckley, a neighboring rancher in his seventies, would rather irrigate than ride a horse. He started spreading water on his father's hay- and grain-fields when he was nine, and his long-term enthusiasm for what's thought of disdainfully by cowboys as "farmers' work" is an example of how a discipline—a daily chore—can grow into a fidelity. When I saw Frank in May he was standing in a dry irrigation ditch looking toward the mountains. The orange tarp dams, hung like curtains from ten-foot-long poles, fluttered in the wind like prayer flags. In Wyoming we are supplicants, waiting all spring for the water to come down, for the snow pack to melt and fill the creeks from which we irrigate. Fall and spring rains amount to less than eight inches a year, while above our ranches, the mountains hold their snows like a secret: no one knows when they will melt or how fast. When the water does come, it floods through the state as if the peaks were silver pitchers tipped forward by mistake. When I looked in, the ditch water had begun dripping over Frank's feet. Then we heard a sound that might have been wind in a steep patch of pines.

"Jumpin' Jesus, here it comes," he said, as a head of water, brown and foamy as beer, snaked toward us. He set five dams, digging the bright edges of plastic into silt. Water filled them the way wind fattens a sail, and from three notches cut in the ditch above each dam, water coursed out over a hundred acres of hayfield. When he finished, and the beadwork wetness had spread through the grass, he lowered himself to the ditch and rubbed his face with water.

A season of irrigating here lasts four months. Twenty, thirty, or as many 2 as two hundred dams are changed every twelve hours, ditches are repaired and head gates adjusted to match the inconsistencies of water flow. By September it's over: all but the major Wyoming rivers dry up. Running water is so seasonal it's thought of as a mark on the calendar—a vague wet spot— rather than a geographical site. In May, June, July, and August, water is the sacristy at which we kneel; it equates time going by too fast.

Waiting for water is just one of the ways Wyoming ranchers find them- 3 selves at the mercy of weather. The hay they irrigate, for example, has to be cut when it's dry but baled with a little dew on it to preserve the leaf. Three days after Frank's water came down, a storm dumped three feet of snow on his alfalfa and the creeks froze up again. His wife, "Mike," who grew up in the arid Powder River country, and I rode to the headwaters of our creeks. The elk we startled had been licking ice in a draw. A snow squall rose up from behind a bare ridge and engulfed us. We built a twig fire behind a rock to warm ourselves, then rode home. The creeks didn't thaw completely until June.

Despite the freak snow, April was the second driest in a century; in the 4 lower elevations there had been no precipitation at all. Brisk winds forwarded thunderclouds into local skies—commuters from other states—but the streamers of rain they let down evaporated before touching us. All month farmers and ranchers burned their irrigation ditches to clear them of obstacles and weeds—optimistic that water would soon come. Shell Valley resembled a battlefield: lines of blue smoke banded every horizon and the cottonwoods that had caught fire by mistake, their outstretched branches blazing, looked human. April, the cruelest month, the month of dry storms.

Six years ago, when I lived on a large sheep ranch, a drought threatened. 5 Every water hole on 100,000 acres of grazing land went dry. We hauled water in clumsy beet-harvest trucks forty miles to spring range, and when we emptied them into a circle of stock tanks, the sheep ran toward us. They pushed to get at the water, trampling lambs in the process, then drank it all in one collective gulp. Other Aprils have brought too much moisture in the form of deadly storms. When a ground blizzard hit one friend's herd in the flatter, eastern part of the state, he knew he had to keep his cattle drifting. If they hit a fence line and had to face the storm, snow would blow into their noses and they'd drown. "We cut wire all the way to Nebraska," he told me. During the same storm another cowboy found his cattle too late: they were buried in a draw under a fifteen-foot drift.

High water comes in June when the runoff peaks, and it's another buga- 6 boo for the ranchers. The otherwise amiable thirty-foot-wide creeks swell and change courses so that when we cross them with livestock, the water is belly-deep or more. Cowboys in the 1800s who rode with the trail herds from Texas often worked in the big rivers on horseback for a week just to cross a thousand head of longhorn steers, losing half of them in the process. On a less-grand scale we have drownings and near drownings here each spring. When we crossed a creek this year the swift current toppled a horse and carried the rider under a log. A cowboy who happened to look back saw her head go under, dove in from horseback, and saved her. At Trapper Creek, where Owen Wister spent several summers in the 1920s and entertained Mr. Hemingway, a cloudburst slapped down on us like a black eye. Scraps of rainbow moved in vertical sweeps of rain that broke apart and disappeared behind a ridge. The creek flooded, taking out a house and a field of corn. We saw one resident walking in a flattened alfalfa field where the river had flowed briefly. "Want to go fishing?" he yelled to us as we rode by. The fish he was throwing into a white bucket were trout that had been "beached" by the flood.

7   Westerners are ambivalent about water because they've never seen what it can create except havoc and mud. They've never walked through a forest of wild orchids or witnessed the unfurling of five-foot-high ferns. "The only way I like my water is if there's whiskey in it," one rancher told me as we weaned calves in a driving rainstorm. That day we spent twelve hours on horseback in the rain. Despite protective layers of clothing: wool union suits, chaps, ankle-length yellow slickers, neck scarves and hats, we were drenched. Water drips off hat brims into your crotch; boots and gloves soak through. But to stay home out of the storm is deemed by some as a worse fate: "Hell, my wife had me cannin' beans for a week," one cowboy complained. "I'd rather drown like a muskrat out there."

8   Dryness is the common denominator in Wyoming. We're drenched more often in dust than in water; it is the scalpel and the suit of armor that make westerners what they are. Dry air presses a stockman's insides outward. The secret, inner self is worn not on the sleeve but in the skin. It's an unlubricated condition: there's not enough moisture in the air to keep the whole emotional machinery oiled and working. "What you see is what you get, but you have to learn to look to see all that's there," one young rancher told me. He was physically reckless when coming to see me or leaving. That was his way of saying he had and would miss me, and in the clean, broad sweeps of passion between us, there was no heaviness, no muddy residue. Cowboys have learned not to waste words from not having wasted water, as if verbosity would create a thirst too extreme to bear. If voices are raspy, it's because vocal cords are coated with dust. When I helped ship seven thousand head of steers one fall, the dust in the big, roomy sorting corrals churned as deeply and sensually as water. We wore scarves over our noses and mouths; the rest of our faces blackened with dirt so we looked like raccoons or coal miners. The westerner's face is stiff and dark red as jerky. It gives no clues beyond the discerning look that says, "You've been observed." Perhaps the too-early lines of aging that pull across these ranchers' necks are really cracks in a wall through which we might see the contradictory signs of their character: a complacency, a restlessness, a shy, boyish pride.

I knew a sheepherder who had the words "hard luck" tattooed across his 9 knuckles. "That's for all the times I've been dry," he explained. "And when you've been as thirsty as I've been, you don't forget how something tastes." That's how he mapped out the big ranch he worked for: from thirst to thirst, whiskey to whiskey. To follow the water courses in Wyoming—seven rivers and a network of good-sized creeks—is to trace the history of settlement here. After a few bad winters the early ranchers quickly discovered the necessity of raising feed for livestock. Long strips of land on both sides of the creeks and rivers were grabbed up in the 1870s and '80s before Wyoming was a state. Land was cheap and relatively easy to accumulate, but control of water was crucial. The early ranches such as the Swan Land & Cattle Company, the Budd Ranch, the M-L, the Bug Ranch, and the Pitchfork took up land along the Chugwater, Green, Greybull, Big Horn, and Shoshone rivers. It was not long before feuds over water began. The old law of "full and undiminished flow" to those who owned land along a creek was changed to one that adjudicated and allocated water by the acre foot to specified pieces of land. By 1890 residents had to file claims for the right to use the water that flowed through their ranches. These rights were, and still are, awarded according to the date a ranch was established regardless of ownership changes. This solved the increasing problem of upstream-downstream disputes, enabling the first ranch established on a creek to maintain the first water right, regardless of how many newer settlements occurred upstream.

Land through which no water flowed posed another problem. Frank's 10 father was one of the Mormon colonists sent by Brigham Young to settle and put under cultivation the arid Big Horn Basin. The twenty thousand acres they claimed were barren and waterless. To remedy this problem they dug a canal thirty-seven miles long, twenty-seven feet across, and sixteen feet deep by hand. The project took four years to complete. Along the way a huge boulder gave the canal diggers trouble: it couldn't be moved. As a last resort the Mormon men held hands around the rock and prayed. The next morning the boulder rolled out of the way.

Piousness was not always the rule. Feuds over water became venomous 11 as the population of the state grew. Ditch riders—so called because they monitored on horseback the flow and use of water—often found themselves on the wrong end of an irrigating shovel. Frank remembers when the ditch rider in his district was hit over the head so hard by the rancher whose water he was turning off that he fell unconscious into the canal, floating on his back until he bumped into the next head gate.

With the completion of the canal, the Mormons built churches, schools, 12 and houses communally, working in unison as if taking their cue from the water that snaked by them. "It was a socialistic sonofabitch from the beginning," Frank recalls, "a beautiful damned thing. These 'western individualists' forget how things got done around here and not so damned many years ago at that."

Frank is the opposite of the strapping, conservative western man. Sturdy, 13 but small-boned, he has an awkward, knock-kneed gait that adds to his chronic amiability. Though he's made his life close to home, he has a natural, panoramic vision as if he had upped-periscope through the Basin's dust clouds and had a good look around. Frank's generosity runs like water: it follows the path of least resistance and, tumbling downhill, takes on a fullness so replete and indiscriminate as to sometimes appear absurd. "You can't cheat an honest man," he'll tell you and laugh at the paradox implied. His wide face and forehead indicate the breadth of his unruly fair-mindedness—one that includes not just local affections but the whole human community.

14   When Frank started irrigating there were no tarp dams. "We plugged up those ditches with any old thing we had—rags, bones, car parts, sod." Though he could afford to hire an irrigator now he prefers to do the work himself, and when I'm away he turns my water as well, then mows my lawn. "Irrigating is a contemptible damned job. I've been fighting water all my life. Mother Nature is a bitter old bitch, isn't she? But we have to have that challenge. We crave it and I'll be goddamned if I know why. I feel sorry for these damned rich ranchers with their pumps and sprinkler systems and gated pipe because they're missing out on something. When I go to change my water at dawn and just before dark, it's peaceful out there, away from everybody. I love the fragrances—grass growing, wild rose on the ditch bank—and hearing the damned old birds twittering away. How can we live without that?"

15   Two thousand years before the Sidon Canal was built in Wyoming, the Hohokam, a people who lived in what became Arizona, used digging sticks to channel water from the Salt and Gila rivers to dry land. Theirs was the most extensive irrigation system in aboriginal North America. Water was brought thirty miles to spread over fields of corn, beans, and pumpkins—crops inherited from tribes in South and Central America. "It's a primitive damned thing," Frank said about the business of using water. "The change from a digging stick to a shovel isn't much of an evolution. Playing with water is something all kids have done, whether it's in creeks or in front of fire hydrants. Maybe that's how agriculture got started in the first place."

16   Romans applied their insoluble cement to waterways as if it could arrest the flux and impermanence they knew water to signify. Of the fourteen aqueducts that brought water from mountains and lakes to Rome, several are still in use today. On a Roman latifundium—their equivalent of a ranch—they grew alfalfa, a hot-weather crop introduced by way of Persia and Greece around the fifth century B.C., and fed it to their horses as we do here. Feuds over water were common: Nero was reprimanded for bathing in the canal that carried the city's drinking water, the brothels tapped aqueducts on the sly until once the whole city went dry. The Empire's staying power began to collapse when the waterways fell into disrepair. Crops dried up and the water that had carried life to the great cities stagnated and became breeding grounds for mosquitoes until malaria, not water, flowed into the heart of Rome.

17   There is nothing in nature that can't be taken as a sign of both mortality and invigoration. Cascading water equates loss followed by loss, a momentum of things falling in the direction of death, then life. In Conrad's *Heart of Darkness*, the river is a redundancy flowing through rain forest, a channel of solitude, a solid thing, a trap. Hemingway's Big Two-Hearted River is the opposite:

it's an accepting, restorative place. Water can stand for what is unconscious, instinctive, and sexual in us, for the creative swill in which we fish for ideas. It carries, weightlessly, the imponderable things in our lives: death and creation. We can drown in it or else stay buoyant, quench our thirst, stay alive.

In Navajo mythology, rain is the sun's sperm coming down. A Crow 18 woman I met on a plane told me that. She wore a flowered dress, a man's wool jacket with a package of Vantages stuck in one pocket, and calf-high moccasins held together with two paper clips. "Traditional Crow think water is medicinal," she said as we flew over the Yellowstone River which runs through the tribal land where she lives. "The old tribal crier used to call out every morning for our people to drink all they could, to make water touch their bodies. 'Water is your body,' they used to say." Looking down on the seared landscape below, it wasn't difficult to understand the real and imagined potency of water. "All that would be a big death yard," she said with a sweep of her arm. That's how the drought would come: one sweep and all moisture would be banished. Bluebunch and June grass would wither. Elk and deer would trample sidehills into sand. Draws would fill up with dead horses and cows. Tucked under ledges of shale, dens of rattlesnakes would grow into city-states of snakes. The roots of trees would rise to the surface and flail through dust in search of water.

Everything in nature invites us constantly to be what we are. We are often like 19 rivers: careless and forceful, timid and dangerous, lucid and muddied, eddying, gleaming, still. Lovers, farmers, and artists have one thing in common, at least—a fear of "dry spells," dormant periods in which we do no blooming, internal droughts only the waters of imagination and psychic release can civilize. All such matters are delicate of course. But a good irrigator knows this: too little water brings on the weeds while too much degrades the soil the way too much easy money can trivialize a person's initiative. In his journal Thoreau wrote, "A man's life should be as fresh as a river. It should be the same channel but a new water every instant."

This morning I walked the length of a narrow, dry wash. Slabs of stone, bro- 20 ken off in great squares, lay propped against the banks like blank mirrors. A sagebrush had drilled a hole through one of these rocks. The roots fanned out and down like hooked noses. Farther up, a quarry of red rock bore the fossilized marks of rippling water. Just yesterday, a cloudburst sent a skinny stream beneath these frozen undulations. Its passage carved the same kind of watery ridges into the sand at my feet. Even in this dry country, where internal and external droughts always threaten, water is self-registering no matter how ancient, recent, or brief.

Questions for Discussion

1. Erhlich uses many images and comparisons in the first paragraph of her essay. How do these figures of speech, such as "mountains hold their snows like a secret," "tarp

dams . . . fluttered in the wind like prayer flags" help to establish a tone or mood for the essay and also provide support for her main ideas?

2. What examples does Ehrlich use to support her assertion that "Wyoming ranchers find themselves at the mercy of weather"? Are her examples effective?

3. What conditions and problems related to weather do the Wyoming ranchers have to confront during the different seasons of the year? What point is Erhlich making through exploring the ranchers' ambivalence? How do the ranchers work together to solve their problems? Is their sense of community strengthened through their struggle?

4. How does Erhlich create a causal relationship between the ranchers' personalities, their physical appearance, and the weather that is often their adversary? Are her images and examples, such as her extended portrait of the rancher Frank Hinckley, effective?

5. How does Ehrlich's brief historical account of water use in Roman times, among the Hohokam, and in the frontier days of the American West, help you to better understand the importance of water for today's ranchers?

6. Ehrlich's last four paragraphs create an extended conclusion for her essay. According to Erhlich, why is water crucial to the survival of the human community?

Ideas for Writing

1. Write an essay that explores the ways that nature and natural resources make your community unique. Show how nature or natural events have helped to shape rituals and special events in your community. Share your essay with your class and/or a community publication.

2. Write about a natural resource, such as the forests or the rivers, that is crucial to the survival of your community. Do library research into the importance and treatment of this resource; also try contacting local environmental agencies for information. Write an essay in which you explain how the resource is being supported or abused.

3. Write an essay or a letter to the editor of a local paper exploring the devastation brought to your community by nature. What continuing impact has this natural disaster had on your community?

Winter

Sue Hubbell

Sue Hubbell (b. 1935) was raised in Michigan and worked for a time as a librarian on the East Coast. In 1973 she moved to the Ozark Mountains in southern Missouri. Her widely acclaimed book of essays, *A Country Year: Living the Questions* (1986), explores her reflections on that life. Describing her life in the Ozarks, Hubbell writes, "Wild things and wild places pull me more strongly than they did a few years ago, and domesticity, dusting and cookery interest me not at all." Reading the following selection, which is excerpted from "Winter," an essay in *A Coun-*

try Year, will help you to understand why Hubbell feels a great responsibility to the natural world—the land and the animals—in her community.

Journal

Discuss an organization that worked to preserve a natural resource in your neighborhood or community.

A group of people concerned about a proposal to dam the river came over to my place last evening to talk. The first to arrive was my nearest neighbor. He burst excitedly into the cabin, asking me to bring a flashlight and come back to his pickup; he had something to show me. I followed him to his truck, where he took the flashlight and switched it on to reveal a newly killed bobcat stretched out in the bed of his truck. The bobcat was a small one, probably a female. Her broad face was set off by longer hair behind her jaws, and her pointed ears ended in short tufts of fur. Her tawny winter coat, heavy and full, was spotted with black, and her short stubby tail had black bars. Her body was beginning to stiffen in death, and I noticed a small trickle of blood from her nostrils.

"They pay thirty-five dollars a pelt now over at the county seat," my neigh- 2 bor explained. "That's groceries for next week," he said proudly. None of us back here on the river has much money, and an opportunity to make next week's grocery money was fortunate for him, I knew. "And I guess you'll thank me because that's surely the varmint that's been getting your chickens," he added, for I had said nothing yet.

But I wasn't grateful. I was shocked and sad in a way that my neighbor 3 would not have understood.

I had not heard a shot and didn't see the gun that he usually carries in the 4 rack in his pickup, so I asked him how he had killed her.

"It was just standing there in the headlights when I turned the corner 5 before your place," he said, "so I rammed it with the pickup bumper and knocked it out, and then I got out and finished it off with the tire iron."

His method of killing sounds more savage than it probably was. Animals 6 in slaughterhouses are stunned before they are killed. Once stunned, the important thing was to kill the bobcat quickly, and I am sure my neighbor did so, for he is a practiced hunter.

Others began to arrive at the meeting and took note of the kill. One of 7 them, a trapper, said that the going price of $35 a pelt was a good one. Not many years ago, the pelt price was under $2. Demand for the fur, formerly scorned for its poor quality, was created by a ban on imported cat fur and a continuing market for fur coats and trim.

My neighbor and the trapper are both third-generation Ozarkers. They 8 could have gone away from here after high school, as did many of their classmates, and made easy money in the cities, but they stayed because they love the land. This brings us together in our opposition to damming the river to create a recreational lake, but our sensibilities are different, the product of different personalities and backgrounds. They come from families who have lived off the land from necessity; they have a deep practical knowledge of it and better skills than I have for living here with very little money. The land, the woods and the rivers, and all that are in and on them are resources to be used for those who have the knowledge and skills. They can cut and sell timber, clear the land for pasture, sell the gravel from the river. Ozarkers pick up wild black walnuts and sell them to the food-processing companies that bring hulling machines to town in October. There are fur buyers, too, so they trap animals and sell the pelts. These Ozarkers do not question the happy fact that they are at the top of the food chain, but kill to eat what swims in the river and walks in the woods, and accept as a matter of course that it takes life to maintain life. In this they are more responsible than I am; I buy my meat in neat sanitized packages from the grocery store.

9   Troubled by this a few years back, I raised a dozen chickens as meat birds, then killed and dressed the lot, but found that killing chicken Number Twelve was no easier than killing chicken Number One. I didn't like taking responsibility for killing my own meat, and went back to buying it at the grocery store. I concluded sourly that righteousness and consistency are not my strong points, since it bothered me not at all to pull a carrot from the garden, an act quite as life-ending as shooting a deer.

10   I love this land, too, and I was grateful that we could all come together to stop it from being destroyed by an artificial lake. But my aesthetic is a different one, and comes from having lived in places where beauty, plants and animals are gone, so I place a different value on what remains than do my Ozark friends and neighbors. Others at the meeting last night had lived at one time in cities, and shared my prejudices. In our arrogance, we sometimes tell one another that we are taking a longer view. But in the very long run I'm not so sure, and as in most lofty matters, like my failed meat project, I suspect that all our opinions are simply an expression of a personal sense of what is fitting and proper.

11   Certainly my reaction to seeing the dead bobcat was personal. I knew that bobcat, and she probably knew me somewhat better, for she would have been a more careful observer than I.

12   Four or five years ago, a man from town told me he had seen a mountain lion on Pigeon Hawk Bluff, the cliffs above the river just to the west of my place. There is a rocky outcropping there, and he had left his car on the road and walked out to it to look at the river two hundred and fifty feet below. He could see a dead turkey lying on a rock shelf, and climbed down to take a closer look. As he reached out to pick up the bird, he was attacked by a mountain lion who came out of a small cave he had not been able to see from above. He showed me the marks along his forearm—scars, he claimed, where the mountain lion had raked him before he could scramble away. There were marks on his arm, to be sure, but I don't know that a mountain lion or any other animal put them there. I suspect that the story was an Ozark stretcher, for the teller, who logs in many hours with the good old boys at the café in town, is a heavy and slow-moving man; it is hard to imagine him climbing

nimbly up or down a steep rock face. Nor would I trust his identification of a mountain lion, an animal more talked of at the café than ever seen in this country.

Mountain lions are large, slender, brownish cats with long tails and small 13 rounded ears. This area used to be part of their range, but as men moved in to cut timber and hunt deer, the cats' chief prey, their habitat was destroyed and they retreated to the west and south. Today they are seen regularly in Arkansas, but now and again there are reports of mountain lions in this part of the Ozarks. With the deer population growing, as it has in recent years under the Department of Conservation's supervision, wildlife biologists say that mountain lions will return to rocky and remote places to feed on them.

After the man told me his story, I watched around Pigeon Hawk Bluff on 14 the outside chance that he might really have seen a mountain lion but in the years since I have never spotted one. I did, however, see a bobcat one evening, near the rock outcropping. This part of the Ozarks is still considered a normal part of bobcat range, but they are threatened by the same destruction of habitat that pushed the mountain lion back to wilder places, and they are uncommon.

Bobcats also kill and feed on deer, but for the most part they eat smaller 15 animals: mice, squirrels, opossums, turkey, quail and perhaps some of my chickens. They are night hunters, and seek out caves or other suitable shelters during the day. In breeding season, the females often chose a rocky cliff cave as a den. I never saw the bobcat's den, but it may have been the cave below the lookout point on the road, although that seems a trifle public for a bobcat's taste. The cliff is studded with other caves of many sizes, and most are inaccessible to all but the most sure-footed. I saw the bobcat several times after that, walking silently along the cliff's edge at dusk. Sometimes in the evening I heard the piercing scream of a bobcat from that direction, and once, coming home late at night, I caught her in the road in the pickup's headlight beam. She stood there, blinded, until I switched off the headlights. Then she padded away into the shadows.

That stretch of land along the river, with its thickets, rocky cliffs and no 16 human houses, would make as good a home ground as any for a bobcat. Females are more particular about their five miles or so of territory than are males, who sometimes intrude upon one another's bigger personal ranges, but bobcats all mark their territories and have little contact with other adults during their ten years or so of life.

I don't know for sure that the bobcat I have seen and heard over the past 17 several years was always the same one, but it probably was, and last night probably I saw her dead in the back of my neighbor's pickup truck.

Questions for Discussion

1. What is the effect of the first paragraph, especially the contrast Hubbell develops between the group's intention to keep the river flowing freely through their community and her neighbor's excitement about killing the bobcat? Why does Hubbell describe the bobcat in such careful detail? How does the community's point of view on the river and the bobcat influence Hubbell?

2. Explain the differences in Hubbell's and her neighbor's points of view about the value of the bobcat. Whose position do you favor? Why?

3. Hubbell develops several examples to clarify the different economic, cultural, and aesthetic assumptions between the third-generation Ozark residents and herself. Why are her examples effective?

4. How does Hubbell develop her identification with the bobcat? What does the bobcat come to symbolize in this selection? Do you think that Hubbell's identification with the bobcat implies that men and women value the natural world for different reasons? Discuss your response.

5. Hubbell concludes her analysis of the two different cultural points of view on how to treat nature: "Certainly my reaction to seeing the dead bobcat was personal." Why is she not critical of the Ozarkers' treatment of the land and the bobcat? Do you agree with Hubbell's point of view? Why or why not?

6. After reading this selection and thinking about the issues it explores, do you think that an individual's personal relationship to the natural world can be separated from the attitudes of those in his or her community? Explain your response.

Ideas for Writing

1. Write about an experience that you had in nature which you shared with a close friend. Analyze your different responses to the event and how they reflect both your own and your friend's unique economic and cultural assumptions about an individual's responsibility to respect nature. What did you learn from your experience?

2. Organize a group meeting or a series of meetings on your campus or in your community to discuss an environmental policy that needs to be changed. As a group write up an explanation of the problem, the serious impact of the problem, and a proposal for change. Try to get your paper published in a campus or local paper.

Coda: Wilderness Letter

Wallace Stegner

Wallace Stegner (1909–1993) was born in Iowa, but lived in 21 different houses between the ages of 12 and 21. Of his early life Stegner wrote, "I grew up without history in a place where human occupation had left fewer traces than the passage of buffalo and antelope herds. I early acquired the desire to find some history in which I myself belonged." The American West became the subject of Stegner's fiction and nonfiction. Throughout his life Stegner demonstrated his belief in the value of the natural world; not only did he write about nature, but he also advocated legislation that would encourage people in his community to preserve their environment. Stegner taught at the Universities of Utah, Wisconsin, and Harvard before becoming a member of Stanford's Creative Writing Program, which he directed from 1946 to 1971. Stegner published over forty books. In 1972 he won the Pulitzer Prize for his novel *Angle of Repose*. Wallace Stegner died at 84 in April of 1993.

The selection that follows reflects Stegner's intense concern for the preservation of the wilderness with its spiritual power.

Journal

Do you believe that the wilderness has spiritual or mystical power? Explain your response.

Los Altos, Calif. Dec. 3, 1960

David E. Pesonen
Wildland Research Center
Agricultural Experiment Station
243 Mulford Hall
University of California
Berkeley 4, Calif.

Dear Mr. Pesonen:

I believe that you are working on the wilderness portion of the Outdoor Recreation Resources Review Commission's report. If I may, I should like to urge some arguments for wilderness preservation that involve recreation, as it is ordinarily conceived, hardly at all. Hunting, fishing, hiking, mountain-climbing, camping, photography, and the enjoyment of natural scenery will all, surely, figure in your report. So will the wilderness as a genetic reserve, a scientific yardstick by which we may measure the world in its natural balance against the world in its man-made imbalance. What I want to speak for is not so much the wilderness uses, valuable as those are, but the wilderness *idea,* which is a resource in itself. Being an intangible and spiritual resource, it will seem mystical to the practical-minded—but then anything that cannot be moved by a bulldozer is likely to seem mystical to them.

I want to speak for the wilderness idea as something that has helped form 2 our character and that has certainly shaped our history as a people. It has no more to do with recreation than churches have to do with recreation, or than the strenuousness and optimism and expansiveness of what historians call the "American Dream" have to do with recreation. Nevertheless, since it is only in this recreation survey that the values of wilderness are being compiled, I hope you will permit me to insert this idea between the leaves, as it were, of the recreation report.

Something will have gone out of us as a people if we ever let the remain- 3 ing wilderness be destroyed; if we permit the last virgin forests to be turned into comic books and plastic cigarette cases; if we drive the few remaining members of the wild species into zoos or to extinction; if we pollute the last clear air and dirty the last clean streams and push our paved roads through the last of the silence, so that never again will Americans be free in their own country from the noise, the exhausts, the stinks of human and automotive waste. And so that never again can we have the chance to see ourselves single, separate, vertical and individual in the world, part of the environment of trees and rocks and soil, brother to the other animals, part of the natural world and competent to belong in it. Without any remaining wilderness we are committed wholly, without chance for even momentary reflection and rest, to a headlong drive into our technological termite-life, the Brave New World of a completely man-controlled environment. We need wilderness preserved—as much of it as is still left, and as many kinds—because it was the challenge against which our character as a people was formed. The reminder and the reassurance that it is still there is good for our spiritual health even if we never once in ten years set foot in it. It is good for us when we are young, because of the incomparable sanity it can bring briefly, as vacation and rest, into our insane lives. It is important to us when we are old simply because it is there—important, that is, simply as idea.

4　　　We are a wild species, as Darwin pointed out. Nobody ever tamed or domesticated or scientifically bred us. But for at least three millennia we have been engaged in a cumulative and ambitious race to modify and gain control of our environment, and in the process we have come close to domesticating ourselves. Not many people are likely, any more, to look upon what we call "progress" as an unmixed blessing. Just as surely as it has brought us increased comfort and more material goods, it has brought us spiritual losses, and it threatens now to become the Frankenstein that will destroy us. One means of sanity is to retain a hold on the natural world, to remain, insofar as we can, good animals. Americans still have that chance, more than many peoples; for while we were demonstrating ourselves the most efficient and ruthless environment-busters in history, and slashing and burning and cutting our way through a wilderness continent, the wilderness was working on us. It remains in us as surely as Indian names remain on the land. If the abstract dream of human liberty and human dignity became, in America, something more than an abstract dream, mark it down at least partially to the fact that we were in subtle ways subdued by what we conquered.

5　　　The Connecticut Yankee, sending likely candidates from King Arthur's unjust kingdom to his Man Factory for rehabilitation, was over optimistic, as he later admitted. These things cannot be forced, they have to grow. To make such a man, such a democrat, such a believer in human individual dignity, as Mark Twain himself, the frontier was necessary, Hannibal and the Mississippi and Virginia City, and reaching out from those the wilderness; the wilderness as opportunity and as idea, the thing that has helped to make an American different from and, until we forget it in the roar of our industrial cities, more fortunate than other men. For an American, insofar as he is new and different at all, is a civilized man who has renewed himself in the wild. The American experience has been the confrontation by old peoples and cultures of a world as new as if it had just risen from the sea. That gave us our hope and our excitement, and the hope and excitement can be passed on to newer Americans, Americans who never saw any phase of the frontier. But only so long as we keep the remainder of our wild as a reserve and a promise—a sort of wilderness bank.

As a novelist, I may perhaps be forgiven for taking literature as a reflection, indirect but profoundly true, of our national consciousness. And our literature, as perhaps you are aware, is sick, embittered, losing its mind, losing its faith. Our novelists are the declared enemies of their society. There has hardly been a serious or important novel in this century that did not repudiate in part or in whole American technological culture for its commercialism, its vulgarity, and the way in which it has dirtied a clean continent and a clean dream. I do not expect that the preservation of our remaining wilderness is going to cure this condition. But the mere example that we can as a nation apply some other criteria than commercial and exploitative considerations would be heartening to many Americans, novelists or otherwise. We need to demonstrate our acceptance of the natural world, including ourselves; we need the spiritual refreshment that being natural can produce. And one of the best places for us to get that is in the wilderness where the fun houses, the bulldozers, and the pavements of our civilization are shut out. 6

Sherwood Anderson, in a letter to Waldo Frank in the 1920's, said it better than I can. "Is it not likely that when the country was new and men were often alone in the fields and the forest they got a sense of bigness outside themselves that has now in some way been lost. . . . Mystery whispered in the grass, played in the branches of trees overhead, was caught up and blown across the American line in clouds of dust at evening on the prairies. . . . I am old enough to remember tales that strengthen my belief in a deep semi-religious influence that was formerly at work among our people. The flavor of it hangs over the best work of Mark Twain. . . . I can remember old fellows in my home town speaking feelingly of an evening spent on the big empty plains. It had taken the shrillness out of them. They had learned the trick of quiet. . . ." 7

We could learn it too, even yet; even our children and grandchildren could learn it. But only if we save, for just such absolutely non-recreational, impractical, and mystical uses as this, all the wild that still remains to us. 8

It seems to me significant that the distinct downturn in our literature from hope to bitterness took place almost at the precise time when the frontier officially came to an end, in 1890, and when the American way of life had begun to turn strongly urban and industrial. The more urban it has become, and the more frantic with technological change, the sicker and more embittered our literature, and I believe our people, have become. For myself, I grew up on the empty plains of Saskatchewan and Montana and in the mountains of Utah, and I put a very high valuation on what those places gave me. And if I had not been able periodically to renew myself in the mountains and deserts of western America I would be very nearly bughouse. Even when I can't get to the back country, the thought of the colored deserts of southern Utah, or the reassurance that there are still stretches of prairie where the world can be instantaneously perceived as disk and bowl, and where the little but intensely important human being is exposed to the five directions and the thirty-six 9 winds, is a positive consolation. The idea alone can sustain me. But as the wilderness areas are progressively exploited or "improved," as the jeeps and bulldozers of uranium prospectors scar up the deserts and the roads are cut into the alpine timberlands, and as the remnants of the unspoiled and natural world are progressively eroded, every such loss is a little death in me. In us.

10   I am not moved by the argument that those wilderness areas which have already been exposed to grazing or mining are already deflowered, and so might as well be "harvested." For mining I cannot say much good except that its operations are generally short-lived. The extractable wealth is taken and the shafts, the tailings, and the ruins left, and in a dry country such as the American West the wounds men make in the earth do not quickly heal. Still, they are only wounds; they aren't absolutely mortal. Better a wounded wilderness than none at all. And as for grazing, if it is strictly controlled so that it does not destroy the ground cover, damage the ecology, or compete with the wildlife it is in itself nothing that need conflict with the wilderness feeling or the validity of the wilderness experience. I have known enough range cattle to recognize them as wild animals; and the people who herd them have, in the wilderness context, the dignity of rareness; they belong on the frontier, moreover, and have a look of rightness. The invasion they make on the virgin country is a sort of invasion that is as old as Neolithic man, and they can, in moderation, even emphasize a man's feeling of belonging to the natural world. Under surveillance, they can belong; under control, they need not deface or mar. I do not believe that in wilderness areas where grazing has never been permitted, it should be permitted; but I do not believe either that an otherwise untouched wilderness should be eliminated from the preservation plan because of limited existing uses such as grazing which are in consonance with the frontier condition and image.

11   Let me say something on the subject of the kinds of wilderness worth preserving. Most of those areas contemplated are in the national forests and in high mountain country. For all the usual recreational purposes, the alpine and forest wilderness are obviously the most important, both as genetic banks and as beauty spots. But for the spiritual renewal, the recognition of identity, the birth of awe, other kinds will serve every bit as well. Perhaps, because they are less friendly to life, more abstractly non-human, they will serve even better. On our Saskatchewan prairie, the nearest neighbor was four miles away, and at night we saw only two lights on all the dark rounding earth. The earth was full of animals—field mice, ground squirrels, weasels, ferrets, badgers, coyotes, burrowing owls, snakes. I knew them as my little brothers, as fellow creatures, and I have never been able to look upon animals in any other way since. The sky in that country came clear down to the ground on every side, and it was full of great weathers, and clouds, and winds, and hawks. I hope I learned something from knowing intimately the creatures of the earth; I hope I learned something from looking a long way, from looking up, from being much alone. A prairie like that, one big enough to carry the eye clear to the sinking, rounding horizon, can be as lonely and grand and simple in its forms as the sea. It is as good a place as any for the wilderness experience to hap-

pen; the vanishing prairie is as worth preserving for the wilderness idea as the alpine forests.

So are great reaches of our western deserts, scarred somewhat by prospec- 12 tors but otherwise open, beautiful, waiting, close to whatever God you want to see in them. Just as a sample, let me suggest the Robbers' Roost country in Wayne County, Utah, near the Capitol Reef National Monument. In that desert climate the dozer and jeep tracks will not soon melt back into the earth, but the country has a way of making the scars insignificant. It is a lovely and terrible wilderness, such a wilderness as Christ and the prophets went out into; harshly and beautifully colored, broken and worn until its bones are exposed, its great sky without a smudge or taint from Technocracy, and in hidden corners and pockets under its cliffs the sudden poetry of springs. Save a piece of country like that intact, and it does not matter in the slightest that only a few people every year will go into it. That is precisely its value. Roads would be a desecration, crowds would ruin it. But those who haven't the strength or youth to go into it and live can simply sit and look. They can look two hundred miles, clear into Colorado; and looking down over the cliffs and canyons of the San Rafael Swell and the Robbers' Roost they can also look as deeply into themselves as anywhere I know. And if they can't even get to the places on the Aquarius Plateau where the present roads will carry them, they can simply contemplate the *idea*, take pleasure in the fact that such a timeless and uncontrolled part of earth is still there.

These are some of the things wilderness can do for us. That is the reason 13 we need to put into effect, for its preservation, some other principle than the principles of exploitation or "usefulness" or even recreation. We simply need that wild country available to us, even if we never do more than drive to its edge and look in. For it can be a means of reassuring ourselves of our sanity as creatures, a part of the geography of hope.

Very sincerely yours,

Wallace Stegner

Questions For Discussion

1. What is Stegner's purpose in writing this letter to the Wildland Research Center? What image does he use to clarify the uniqueness of his point of view about the wilderness?
2. What writing strategies, specific examples, and tone does Stegner develop to reflect his awareness of his audience, a scientific research agency? How does Stegner develop the metaphorical and reflective qualities of his statement, even though it is a letter to a scientific audience? Would his letter serve as a model if you were writing a persuasive letter to an institution? Why or why not?
3. Why is Stegner particularly afraid of "a headlong drive into our technological termite-life, the Brave New World of a completely man-controlled environment"? Do his fears seem justified?
4. Explain how Stegner presents the relationship between the wilderness and the for-

mation of the American character. Discuss why you agree or disagree with Stegner's analysis.

5. What relationship does Stegner find between the disenchantment and increasing bitterness of writers toward society and the settling of the frontier? According to Stegner, in what ways are literature, the wilderness, and the spirit connected?

6. Why does Stegner think that the scars of nature are a testimony to the spiritual power of the wilderness? How do you interpret Stegner's claim that these scars are "a part of the geography of hope"?

Ideas for Writing

1. Write a letter to an organization or publication in your community to protest the exploitation of one of your community's natural resources.

2. Write an essay about a specific experience that you had in the wilderness which helped you to understand its healing and spiritual powers. What continuing impact has this experience in the wilderness had on you?

A Future Community Tomorrow: Ecotopia

Ernest Callenbach

Ernest Callenbach (b. 1929) was born in Williamsport, Pennsylvania, and earned his M.A. (1953) at the University of Chicago. Callenbach began working as an editor at the University of California at Berkeley Press, where he founded the critical journal *Film Quarterly* in 1958. After his utopian environmental novel *Ecotopia* was rejected by 25 publishers, Callenbach started the Banyan Tree Books Press to publish it. Ecotopia was an immediate success in America and has been translated into six different languages. The excerpt we have included, "A Future Community Tomorrow: Ecotopia," presents a decentralized community that values its natural resources.

Journal

Develop a description of an ecotopia.

San Francisco, May 7. Under the new regime, the established cities of Ecotopia have to some extent been broken up into neighborhoods or communities, but they are still considered to be somewhat outside the ideal long-term line of development of Ecotopian living patterns. I have just had the opportunity to visit one of the strange new minicities that are arising to carry out the more extreme urban vision of this decentralized society. Once a sleepy village, it is called Alviso, and is located on the southern shores of San Francisco Bay. You get there on the interurban train, which drops you off in the basement of a large complex of buildings. The main structure, it turns out, is not the city hall or courthouse, but a factory. It produces the electric traction units—they hardly qualify as cars or trucks in our terms—that are used for transporting people and goods in Ecotopian cities and for general transportation in the country-side. (Individually owned vehicles were prohibited in "car-free" zones soon after Independence. These zones at first covered only downtown areas where pollution and congestion were most severe. As minibus service was extended, these zones expanded, and now cover all densely settled city areas.)

Around the factory, where we would have a huge parking lot, Alviso has 2 a cluttered collection of buildings, with trees everywhere. There are restau-rants, a library, bakeries, a "core store" selling groceries and clothes, small shops, even factories and workshops—all jumbled amid apartment buildings. These are generally of three or four stories, arranged around a central court-yard of the type that used to be common in Paris. They are built almost entirely of wood, which has become the predominant building material in Ecotopia, due to the reforestation program. Though these structures are old-fashioned looking, they have pleasant small balconies, roof gardens, and verandas—often covered with plants, or even small trees. The apartments themselves are very large by our standards—with 10 or 15 rooms, to accommodate their commu-nal living groups.

Alviso streets are named, not numbered, and they are almost as narrow 3 and winding as those of medieval cities—not easy for a stranger to get around in. They are hardly wide enough for two cars to pass; but then of course there *are* no cars, so that is no problem. Pedestrians and bicyclists meander along. Once in a while you see a delivery truck hauling a piece of furniture or some other large object, but the Ecotopians bring their groceries home in string bags or large bicycle baskets. Supplies for the shops, like most goods in Ecotopia, are moved in containers. These are much smaller than our cargo containers, and proportioned to fit into Ecotopian freight cars and onto their electric trucks. Farm produce, for instance, is loaded into such containers either at the farms or at the container terminal located on the edge of each minicity. From the terminal an underground conveyor belt system connects to all the shops and factories in the minicity, each of which has a kind of siding where the con-tainers are shunted off. This idea was probably lifted from our automated warehouses, but turned backwards. It seems to work very well, though there must be a terrible mess if there is some kind of jam-up underground.

My guides on this expedition were two young students who have just fin- 4 ished an apprenticeship year in the factory. They're full of information and observations. It seems that the entire population of Alviso, about 9,000 people, lives within a radius of a half mile from the transit station. But even this den-sity allows for many small park-like places: sometimes merely widenings of the streets, sometimes planted gardens. Trees are everywhere—there are no large paved areas exposed to the sun. Around the edges of town are the schools and various recreation grounds. At the northeast corner of town you meet the marshes and sloughs and slatflats of the Bay. A harbor has been dredged for small craft; this opens onto the ship channel through which a freighter can move right up to the factory dock. My informants admitted rather uncomfortably that there is a modest export trade in electric vehicles—the Eco-topians allow themselves to import just enough metal to replace what is used in the exported electric motors and other metal parts.

5   Kids fish off the factory dock; the water is clear. Ecotopians love the water, and the boats in the harbor are a beautiful collection of both traditional and highly unorthodox designs. From this harbor, my enthusiastic guides tell me, they often sail up the Bay and into the Delta, and even out to sea through the Golden Gate, then down the coast to Monterey. Their boat is a lovely though heavy-looking craft, and they proudly offered to take me out on it if I have time.

6   We toured the factory, which is a confusing place. Like other Ecotopian workplaces, I am told, it is not organized on the assembly-line principles gen-erally thought essential to really efficient mass production. Certain aspects are automated: the production of the electric motors, suspension frames, and other major elements. However, the assembly of these items is done by groups of workers who actually fasten the parts together one by one, taking them from supply bins kept full by the automated machines. The plant is quiet and pleas-ant compared to the crashing racket of a Detroit plant, and the workers do not seem to be under Detroit's high output pressures. Of course the extreme sim-plification of Ecotopian vehicles must make the manufacturing process much easier to plan and manage—indeed there seems little reason why it could not be automated entirely.

7   Also, I discovered, much of the factory's output does not consist of fin-ished vehicles at all. Following the mania for "doing it yourself" which is such a basic part of Ecotopian life, this plant chiefly turns out "front ends," "rear ends," and battery units. Individuals and organizations then connect these to bodies of their own design.

8   The battery units, which seem to be smaller and lighter than even our best Japanese imports, are designed for use in vehicles of various configurations. Each comes with a long reel-in extension cord to plug into recharging outlets.

9   The factory does produce several types of standard bodies, to which the propulsion units can be attached with only four bolts at each end. (They are always removed for repair.) The smallest and commonest body is a shrunken version of our pick-up truck. It has a tiny cab that seats only two people, and a low, square, open box in back. The rear of the cab can be swung upward to make a roof, and sometimes canvas sides are rigged to close in the box entirely.

10   A taxi-type body is still manufactured in small numbers. Many of these were used in the cities after Independence as a stop-gap measure while minibus and transit systems were developing. These bodies are molded from heavy plastic in one huge mold.

11   These primitive and underpowered vehicles obviously cannot satisfy the urge for speed and freedom which has been so well met by the American auto industry and our aggressive highway program. My guides and I got into a hot debate on this question, in which I must admit they proved uncomfortably knowledgeable about the conditions that sometimes prevail on our urban

throughways—where movement at *any* speed can become impossible. When I asked, however, why Ecotopia did not build speedy cars for its thousands of miles of rural highways—which are now totally uncongested even if their rights of way have partly been taken over for trains—they were left speechless. I attempted to sow a few seeds of doubt in their minds: no one can be utterly insensitive to the pleasures of the open road, I told them, and I related how it feels to roll along in one of our powerful, comfortable cars, a girl's hair blowing in the wind. . . .

We had lunch in one of the restaurants near the factory, amid a cheery, 12 noisy crowd of citizens and workers. I noticed that they drank a fair amount of the excellent local wine with their soups and sandwiches. Afterward we visited the town hall, a modest wood structure indistinguishable from the apartment buildings. There I was shown a map on which adjacent new towns are drawn, each centered on its own rapid-transit stop. It appears that a ring of such new towns is being built to surround the Bay, each one a self-contained community, but linked to its neighbors by train so that the entire necklace of towns will constitute one city. It is promised that you can, for instance, walk five minutes to your transit station, take a train within five minutes to a town ten stops away, and then walk another five minutes to your destination. My informants are convinced that this represents a halving of the time we would spend on a similar trip, not to mention problems of parking, traffic, and of course the pollution.

What will be the fate of the existing cities as these new mini-cities come 13 into existence? They will gradually be razed, although a few districts will be preserved as living museum displays (of "our barbarian past," as the boys jokingly phrased it). The land will be returned to grassland, forest, orchards, or gardens—often, it appears, groups from the city own plots of land outside in the country, where they probably have a small shack and perhaps grow vegetables, or just go for a change of scene.

After leaving Alviso we took the train to Redwood City, where the rever- 14 sion process can be seen in action. Three new towns have sprung up there along the Bay, separated by a half mile or so of open country, and two more are under construction as part of another string several miles back from the Bay, in the foothills. In between, part of the former suburban residential area has already been turned into alternating woods and grassland. The scene reminded me a little of my boyhood country summers in Pennsylvania. Wooded strips follow the winding lines of creeks. Hawks circle lazily. Boys out hunting with bows and arrows wave to the train as it zips by. The signs of a once busy civilization—streets, cars, service stations, supermarkets—have been entirely obliterated, as if they never existed. The scene was sobering, and made one wonder what a Carthaginian might have felt after ancient Carthage was destroyed and plowed under by the conquering Romans.

Gilroy Hot Springs, June 22. The more I have discovered about Ecotopian work 15 habits, the more amazed I am that their system functions at all. It is not only that they have adopted a 20-hour week; you can't even tell when an Ecotopian is working, and when he is at leisure. During an important discussion in a government office, suddenly everybody will decide to go to the sauna bath. It is true they have worked out informal arrangements whereby, as their phrase has it, they "cover" for each other—somebody stays behind to answer phones and handle visitors. And it is also true that even in the sauna our discussion continued, on a more personal level, which turned out to be quite delightful. But Ecotopian society offers so many opportunities for pleasures and distractions that it is hard to see how people maintain even their present levels of efficiency.

16   Things happen in their factories, warehouses, and stores which would be quite incredible to our managers and supervisors. I have seen a whole section close down without notice; somebody will bring out beer or marijuana, and a party will ensue, right there amid the crates and machines. Workers in Ecotopian enterprises do not have a normal worker's attitude at all. Perhaps because of their part ownership of them, they seem to regard the plants as home, or at least as their own terrain. They must be intolerable to supervise: the slightest change in work plans is the occasion for a group discussion in which the supervisors (who are elected and thus in a weak position anyway) are given a good deal of sarcastic questioning, and in which their original plans are seldom accepted without change. The supervisors try to take this with good grace, of course, even claiming that the workers often come up with better ideas than they do; and they believe that Ecotopian output per person hour is remarkably high. It may be.

17   Incidentally, many rather intellectual people seem to be members of the ordinary factory and farm work force. Partly this seems to be due to the relative lack of opportunity for class differentiation in Ecotopia; partly it is due to a deliberate policy which requires students to alternate a year of work with each year of study. This is perhaps one of the most startling arrangements in the whole Ecotopian economy—for not only is the students' education prolonged, but their ideological influence is responsible for many of the new policies that prevail in Ecotopian enterprises. (I was told, for example, that it was students who were originally behind the whole movement toward workers' control.)

18   Ecotopians are adept at turning practically any situation toward pleasure, amusement, and often intimacy. At first I was surprised by the ease with which they strike up very personal conversations with casual strangers. I have now gotten used to this, indeed I usually enjoy it, especially where the lovely Ecotopian women are concerned. But I am still disconcerted when, after speaking with someone on the street in a loose and utterly unpressured way for perhaps ten minutes, he mentions that he is working and trots off. The distinction between work and non-work seems to be eroding away in Ecotopia, along with our whole concept of jobs as something separate from "real life." Ecotopians, incredibly enough, *enjoy* their work.

19   Unemployment does not seem to worry Ecotopians in the slightest. There

were many unemployed just before Independence, but the switch to a 20-hour week almost doubled the number of jobs—although some were eliminated because of ecological shutdowns and simplifications, and of course the average real income of most families dropped somewhat. Apparently in the transition period when an entirely new concept of living standards was evolving, the country's money policy had to be managed with great flexibility to balance sudden inflationary or deflationary tendencies. But the result now seems to be that, while enterprises are not seriously short of member-workers, there is also no significant number of people involuntarily unemployed. In any case, because of the minimal-guaranteed income system and the core stores, periods of unemployment are not considered disasters or threats by individuals; they are usually put to use, and sometimes deliberately extended, for some kind of creative, educational or recreational purposes. Thus in Ecotopia friends who are unemployed (usually through the collapse of their previous enterprise) often band together and undertake studies that lead them into another enterprise of their own.

If it is sometimes hard to tell whether Ecotopians are working or playing, 20 they are surprisingly generous with their time. I was told, for instance, that many workers in factories put in extra hours to fix machines that have broken down. They evidently regard the 20-hour week quota as applying to productive time only, and take the repair of machinery almost as a sideline responsibility. Or perhaps it is just that they enjoy tinkering: despite the de-emphasis of goods in Ecotopia, people seem to love fixing things. If a bicycle loses a chain or has a flat tire, its rider is soon surrounded by five people volunteering to help fix it. . . .

Questions For Discussion

1. Describe the new minicity, Alviso. In what ways is it a response to the problems of urban life? How do these changes reflect ecological values and respect for nature?
2. Why is the decentralization of authority and services as well as the construction of small communities priorities in Ecotopia? How are these priorities realized in Alviso? Why is there a mania for "doing it yourself" in Ecotopia?
3. Does the plan for transportation between minicommunities in Ecotopia seem like a good solution to the urban congestion and gridlock experienced in today's urban areas? Could you imagine a similar type of plan working in the county in which you live?
4. How are the attitudes toward work different in Ecotopia than in our society? Which "work ethic" is more like your own? Is one work ethic preferable? Why?
5. Why are students in Ecotopia required to alternate a year of study and a year of work? How does this policy affect the work force and the students' learning in college? Do you think our society would benefit from an educational policy similar to the one in Ecotopia? Why or why not?
6. How have problems of unemployment been solved in Ecotopia? How are the attitudes about standard of living different in Ecotopia than in our society? What would be the benefits of having our society promote a standard of living that is more similar to the one described in Ecotopia? What would be the drawbacks?

Ideas for Writing

1. Write an argument in support of the ideas implemented in Ecotopia or write an argument to prove that the innovations in Ecotopia are unrealistic, impossible dreams, given what you see as the limitations of human nature.
2. Write up your own version of Ecotopia.

Community Service Writing Student Project: "Natural Histories for the San Francisco Zoo"

Jane Harris, Albert Chong, Sarah Tubessing, and David Leung

Students **Jane Harris, Albert Chong, Sarah Tubessing,** and **David Leung** worked for the San Francisco Zoo's Animal Resource Center. Their task was to research, synthesize, and write up informational sheets for training materials used by zoo volunteers to teach the public about animals at the center. The students were required to use at least five sources; their information had to be accurate and up to date. Since some of the resources were specialized, such as zoological journals, they were only available at the Animal Resource Center, but the students were able to use the college library system as well. The students followed a specific format consistent with the other zoo training materials that included scientific terminology. Their prose had to be concise yet comprehensible to a range of general audiences with differing educational levels and a primary age group of eight to fifteen. The bibliographies that the students developed were used by the zoo volunteers and workers for reference when additional information was necessary. Two of the histories are included below.

Journal

Discuss the reasons why you do or do not enjoy visiting the zoo.

	Savanna Monitor		
REPTILIA	Squamata	Varanidae	*Varanus exanthematicus*

GEOGRAPHIC RANGE: Africa south of the Sahara, absent only in the W African rain forests.

2 *HABITAT:* Young live in trees, but adults live solely on land.

3 *NICHE:* Carnivorous, diurnal—active in the daytime and sleep at night (like humans).

DIET: Mollusks or snails. Adults will eat large snails, crabs, and meat, even carrion. 4

DESCRIPTION: Short, wide, tapered head. Long, slitted tongue like a snake. Covered with small scales that don't overlap. Instead, they fit together like tiles in a granular pattern. Bodies are low, wide and slightly flattened. Brown-gray in color, with dark edged yellow spots. 5

WEIGHT: 10 ft monitors can weigh from 102 kg to 250 kg, so with extrapolation Savanna monitors should weigh up to 80 kg 6

TOTAL LENGTH: up to 6 ft 7

HABITAT AND ADAPTATIONS: Usually dormant during the cold season. Will fight if frightened, but if suddenly grabbed, will pretend to be dead (like an opossum). 8

DENTITION: As they become adults and their diet changes, the crowns of their teeth become thick, blunt, and barrel-shaped for cracking their prey. 9

REPRODUCTIVE INFORMATION: Fills burrows with leaves, rubbish, sometimes even manure. Then female lays the eggs (30–40 at a time) inside burrow and covers it with sand or vegetable material to act as an incubator. Differs from other species of monitors in that the Savanna monitor's eggs clump together. 10

LIFE SPAN: monitors as a whole average 10 yrs 11

MISCELLANEOUS: Also called Bosc's monitor or Veld monitor. The name "monitor" comes from an error in translation. The Arabian word for these animals, "waran," was translated into German as "warnen," meaning warning. Thus, these reptiles became known as "warning lizards." In earlier times, "to monitor" meant "to give somebody warning." Belongs to same genus as Komodo dragon. 12

Bibliography

Auffenberg, Walter. *The Komodo Monitor.* Gainesville: University Presses of Florida, 1981. 24–25, 155.

The Concise Oxford Dictionary of Zoology. New York: Oxford University Press, 1991. 492.

Grzimek's Animal Life Encyclopedia, Volume 6. Ed. by Dr. H. C. Bernard Grzimek. Cincinnati: Van Nostrand Reinhold Company, 1975. 317, 321, 323–332.

Inger, Robert F., and Karl P. Schmidt. *Living Reptiles of the World.* New York: Hanover House, 1957, 170.

International Wildlife Encyclopedia. Volume 11. New York: Marshall Cavendish Corporation, 1969. 1493–1495.

Lanwarn, R.A. *The Book of Reptiles.* New York: The Hamlyn Publishing Group Limited, 1972. 26, 35, 40.

Larousse Encyclopedia of Animal Life. New York: McGraw-Hill Book Company, 1967. 310.

MacLachlan, G.R. *South Africa Red Data Book—Reptiles & Amphibians.* Council for Scientific and Industrial Research, 1978. 23.

World Encyclopedia of Animals. Ed. by Maurice Burton. New York: World Publishing, 1972. 251–252.

SWAINSON'S HAWK

AVES	Falconiformes	Accipitridae	*Buteo Swainsoni*

GEOGRAPHIC RANGE: The Western half of North America from part of Canada down to the Northern part of Mexico. Travels in the winter to South America in the Argentina region.

2 *HABITAT:* Open country such as plains, deserts, and ranges with few trees or bushes. Nests in solitary trees or bushes that are close to a stream. They tend to return to their old nesting area each spring.

3 *NICHE:* Carnivorous—meat eating.

4 *DIET:* Swainson's hawks usually feed on crickets and grasshoppers but also eat small animals such as mice, squirrels, gophers, and young rabbits.

5 *DESCRIPTION:* Swainson's Hawks are between 19–22 inches long. Their wing span is between 48–56 inches wide. There are two different phases, or types, of coloring. In the dark phase, the hawks are all dark brown except for a white area in the chin and forehead areas plus a grey tail that has thin, dark, horizontal bands, the thickest one being at the end. In the light phase, the hawks are basically the same except their bellys are white, leaving a dark area on their upper chest, and the front part of their wings are white with large dark flight feathers.

6 *WEIGHT:* male: 760–980 grams
            female: 870–1090 grams

7 *TOTAL LENGTH:* male: 48–51 cm
                 female: 51–56 cm

8 *HABITS AND ADAPTIONS:* Migrate in huge flocks called "kettles" that number in the thousands. They travel for 11 to 17 thousand miles from North America to South America. Swainson's Hawk population is decreasing in California because the areas that they live in are disappearing and because their nests are easy to reach and destroy. Hawk population has increased in Canada, however. Hawks have been known to fly behind tractors, waiting for them to dig up small rodents.

9 *DENTITION:* The normal hooked beak of predatory birds—birds of prey.

10 *REPRODUCTIVE INFORMATION:* Begin to breed when they are 2 years old. Usually lay eggs between mid-April and mid-June. The normal number of eggs is either 2 or 3; usually 2. The eggs are about 6 cm long and are at first a grainy pale blue or green, but later become a dull white, usually lightly spotted with some brown. The eggs usually hatch about 5 weeks (34–35 days) after being layed. While there are chicks, the family eats more meat for energy. Fledglings start flying about 6 weeks (42–44 days) after hatching but stay with their parents until migration. Young Swainson's Hawks look different from the adults. The normally white chest has stripes on it.

LIFE SPAN: Although one was recorded to have lived for 16 years, most 11 Swainson's Hawks live 8–9 years.

MISCELLANEOUS: Because they have delicate feet, they cannot lift very 12 heavy prey, so the largest things they eat are young rabbits. They hunt in many ways. In the air, they grab their food with their talons peck at it with their beak. On the ground, they usually chase their prey on foot, running with their wings spread. They are also known to simply perch on a post near animal mounds and wait, ready to snatch up anything that comes out.

Bibliography

1. Aikenhead, Donna Ikenberry. "The Swainson's Hawk." *Outdoor California.* July–August 1986. 6–10.
2. Brunn, Bertel, Chandler S. Robbins, and Herbert S. Zim. "Swainson's Hawk." *A Guide to Field Identification: Birds of North America.* New York: Golden Press, 1983. 74–75.
3. Bull, Edith, and John Bull. "Swainson's Hawk." *Birds of North America: Western Region.* New York: Collier Books, 1989. 70–71.
4. Dobkin, David S., Paul R. Ehrlich, and Darryl Wheye. "Swainson's Hawk." *The Birder's Handbook: A Field Guide to the Natural History of North American Birds.* New York: Simon & Schuster Inc., 1986.
5. Dunning, John B., Jr., Ed., *CRC Handbook of Avian Body Masses.* London: CRC Press, 1993. 35.
6. Farrand, John, Jr., "Swainson's Hawk." *Western Birds.* New York: McGraw-Hill Book Company, 1988. 216.
7. Palmer, Ralph S. "Swainson's Hawk." *Handbook of North American Birds: vol 5.* New Haven: Yale University Press, 1988, 48–73.
8. Peterson, Roger Tony. "Swainson's Hawk." *A Field Guide to Western Birds.* Boston: Houghton Mifflin Company, 1990. 174, 192–193.
9. Ryser, Fred A. Jr. "Swainson's Hawk." *Birds of the Great Basin.* Reno: University of Nevada Press, 1985. 229–231.
10. Terres, John K. "Hawk, Swainson's." *The Audubon Society Encyclopedia of North American Birds,* First Edition. New York: Alfred A. Knopf, Inc., 1980. 538.
11. Udvardy, Miklos D. F. "Swainson's Hawk." *The Audubon Society Field Guide to North American Birds: Western Region.* New York: Alfred A. Knopf, 1977.

Questions for Discussion

1. What do you think would be the challenges of writing technical descriptions of animals as these students have done?
2. Select one of the animals profiled; then write several expository paragraphs based on the information provided in the technical description. You might need to refer to other sources to complete the paragraphs.
3. Working with other students in your class who have written paragraphs on one of the animals whose technical description you did not rewrite, compare and contrast your experiences revising the technical descriptions.
4. As a class discuss the educational materials that you think a zoo should provide for its visitors.

5. Take the list of educational materials that you think a zoo should provide to your local zoo to compare and evaluate the materials that the zoo actually gives to visitors. Discuss what you have learned from this experience with your class.

6. Develop a proposal that profiles what you think are the ideal educational materials for visitors to a zoo. Consider the range of ages of the visitors.

Ideas for Writing

1. If you haven't been to your local zoo recently, visit it. Then write a paper that includes personal observations and research about the role that zoos play in the lives of their communities. In doing your research, you might discover that some zoos provide better homes for their creatures than others. You might want to discuss particular zoos that serve as role models.

2. Contact a local zoo to find out if they can use student writers to help them prepare educational materials. Working with your peers or individually, develop the materials.

CHAPTER WRITING PROJECTS

1. Discuss how your understanding of the natural world as an extension of our human community has developed through reading and reflecting upon the selections in this chapter.

2. The writers in this chapter disagree about the extent of the threat of technology to the natural world. What is your perspective on this delicate and dangerous balance? Refer to selections in the chapter to support what you think humans should do to channel and preserve the energy of the natural world.

3. Many of the writers in this chapter suggest that individuals need to change their attitudes toward and treatment of the natural world. Develop a plan either in defense of the status quo or for altering your life-style to help preserve your community's natural resources and well-being. To provide evidence for your plan, consider referring to selections in this chapter, to your own experiences, to literature, or to popular culture that helped you to come to your conclusions.

4. With a group of students in your class discuss a policy in your community that needs to be changed to reflect greater respect for your environment. The group could set up a research project divided into parts to find out more about the topic. You might also want to refer to writers in this chapter. As a group write up an explanation of how you understand the problem and why the problem is a serious one; propose ways to improve the situation.

5. What relationships do you see between the laws that govern our social order and the rhythms that you observe or learn about through the study of animals, plants, and ecology? Refer to the writers in this chapter to help

you explain how the natural world can be seen as an extension of your human community.

6. As a small group project, or as a class, see a movie that explores the relationships between nature and community. You might consider such films as *Gorillas in the Mist, Out of Africa, Emerald Forest, At Play in the Fields of the Lord, Mosquito Coast.* As a group or individually, write an essay that evaluates the film's perspective on the relationship between nature and the human community. Refer to writers in this chapter when relevant to develop your interpretation and critique of the film. In what ways does the film add new insights into the relationships between nature and the human community that are presented by the variety of writers in this chapter?

7. Write a story that reflects your concern for your community and its natural environment; for example, you might want to develop the earth as a metaphor for your community.

8. Nature can provide sanctuary and heal people's spirits. Research this topic and develop a paper that discusses and illustrates this concept. Refer to writers in this chapter when relevant.

9. Volunteer to work at a local environmental agency. Write a paper for your class that discusses the goals of the agency, how you are helping the agency to meet its goals, and what you are learning from your experience. Also consider offering to do writing or research for this environmental group if you support its goals.

10. Dillard, Norris, Stegner, and Momaday allude to the spiritual power and qualities of nature that encourage people to experience a sense of community with their neighbors. Through careful textual analysis illustrate the ideas of two or three of these writers and discuss the meaning that these ideas hold for you.

Acknowledgments

Alexander, P. W., "Christmas at Home." Reprinted by permission of the author.

Anaya, Rudolfo A. From *Bless Me, Ultima* by Rudolfo A. Anaya. Copyright © 1975 Rudolfo A. Anaya. Reprinted by permission of the author.

Angelou, Maya, "Graduation." From *I Know Why the Caged Bird Sings* by Maya Angelou. Copyright © 1969 by Maya Angelou. Reprinted by permission of Random House, Inc.

Bambara, Toni Cade, "My Man Bovanne." From *Gorilla, My Love* by Toni Cade Bambara. Copyright © 1971 by Toni Cade Bambara. Reprinted by permission of Random House, Inc.

Barber, Benjamin. From *An Aristocracy of Everyone* by Benjamin Barber. Copyright © 1990 by Benjamin Barber. Reprinted by permission of Ballantine Books, a Division of Random House, Inc.

Buckley, William F., "A Call to Arms." From *Gratitude* by William F. Buckley. Copyright © 1990 by William F. Buckley, Jr. Reprinted by permission of Random House, Inc.

Cain, Nora, "A Treasury of Quilts." Reprinted by permission of Nora Cain.

Callenbach, Ernest, "A Future Community Tomorrow: Ecotopia." From *Ecotopia* by Ernest Callenbach. Copyright © 1975 by Ernest Callenbach. Used by permission of Bantam Books, a division of Bantam Doubleday Dell Publishing Group, Inc.

Cervantes, Lorna Dee, "Cannery Town in August" is reprinted from *Emplumada*, by Lorna Dee Cervantes, by permission of the University of Pittsburgh Press. Copyright © 1981 by Lorna Dee Cervantes.

Coles, Robert, "Problem Child." From *Children of Crisis*, Vol. 5, by Robert Coles. Copyright © 1977 by Robert Coles. By permission of Little, Brown and Company.

Dillard, Annie, "Total Eclipse" from *Teaching a Stone to Talk* by Annie Dillard. Copyright © 1982 by Annie Dillard. Reprinted by permission of HarperCollins Publishers, Inc.

Edelman, Marian Wright, "A Family Legacy." From *The Measure of Our Success* by Marian Wright Edelman. Copyright © 1992 by Marian Wright Edelman. Reprinted by permission of Beacon Press.

Ehrlich, Gretel, "On Water," from *The Solace of Open Spaces* by Gretel Ehrlich. Copyright © 1985 by Gretel Ehrlich. Used by

Paley, Grace, "The Loudest Voice," from *The Little Disturbances of Man* by Grace Paley. Copyright © 1956, 1957, 1958, 1959 by Grace Paley. Used by permission of Viking Penguin, a division of Penguin Books USA Inc.

Parker, Jo Goodwin, "What Is Poverty?" from *America's Other Children: Public Schools Outside Suburbia,* edited by George Henderson. Copyright © 1971 by The University of Oklahoma Press.

Pogash, Carol. From *As Real as It Gets* by Carol Pogash. Copyright © 1992 by Carol Pogash. Published by arrangement with Carol Publishing Group. A Birch Lane Press Book.

Quindlen, Anna. From *Thinking Out Loud* by Anna Quindlen. Copyright © 1993 by Anna Quindlen. Reprinted by permission of Random House, Inc.

Rose, Mike, "I Just Wanna Be Average." Reprinted with the permission of The Free Press, Macmillan Publishing, from *Lives on the Boundary: The Struggles and Achievements of America's Underprepared* by Mike Rose. Copyright © 1989 by Mike Rose.

Rouse, Jacqueline Anne. From "The New First Lady" in *Lugenia Burns Hope: Black Southern Reformer.* Copyright © 1989 by The University of Georgia Press. Reprinted by permission.

Stegner, Wallace, "Coda: Wilderness Letter." From *The Sound of Mountain Water* by Wallace Stegner. Copyright © 1969 by Wallace Stegner. Used by permission of Doubleday, a division of Bantam Doubleday Dell Publishing Group, Inc.

Stein, Benjamin J. Excerpt from "The Cheerful Ignorance of the Young in L.A." by Benjamin J. Stein, *The Washington Post,* October 3, 1983. Copyright © 1983 by Benjamin J. Stein. Used by permission of The Wallace Literary Agency, Inc.

Takaki, Ronald, "Breaking Silences." From *Strangers from a Different Shore* by Ronald Takaki. Copyright © 1989 by Ronald Takaki. By permission of Little, Brown and Company.

Tan, Amy, "Mother Tongue." Copyright © 1989 by Amy Tan. As first appeared in "Threepenny Review." Reprinted by permission of the author and the Sandra Dijkstra Literary Agency.

Terkel, Studs. From *Working* by Studs Terkel. Copyright © 1972, 1974 by Studs Terkel. Reprinted by permission of Pantheon Books, a division of Random House, Inc.

Thompson, Tracy, "The Wizard of Prozac." From *The Washington Post National Weekly,* December 6–12, 1993. Copyright © 1994 The Washington Post. Reprinted with permission.

Walker, Alice. "Am I Blue?" from *Living by the Word: Selected Writings 1973–1987,* copyright © 1986 by Alice Walker, reprinted by permission of Harcourt Brace & Company. "Am I Blue" (Harry Akst, Grant Clarke) © 1929 (Renewed) Warner Bros. Inc. All Rights Reserved. Used by permission.

Wilson, James Q., "The Family-Values Debate." Reprinted from *Commentary,* April 1993, by permission of Commentary and James Q. Wilson; all rights reserved.

Woo, Merle, "Poem for the Creative Writing Class." Reprinted by permission of Merle Woo.

Index